macroeconomics
in context

Neva Goodwin
Julie A. Nelson
Jonathan Harris

with contributions by
Brian Roach and James Devine

M.E.Sharpe
Armonk, New York
London, England

Library of Congress Cataloging-in-Publication Data

Goodwin, Neva R.
Macro economics in context / Neva Goodwin, Julie A. Nelson, and Jonathan
Harris.
    p. cm.
ISBN 978-0-7656-2297-6 (pbk. : alk. paper)
1. Macroeconomics. I. Nelson, Julie A., 1956- II. Harris, Jonathan, 1948-
III. Title. IV. Title: Macroeconomics in context.
HB172.5.G663 2008
339—dc22   2008004397

Printed in the United States of America

The paper used in this publication meets the minimum requirements of
American National Standard for Information Sciences
Permanence of Paper for Printed Library Materials,
ANSI Z 39.48-1984.

∞

BM (p)   10   9   8   7   6   5   4   3

Brief Table of Contents

Contents

Preface

Macroeconomics in Context provides a thorough introduction to the principles of macroeconomics for students taking an introductory macroeconomics course. It introduces students both to the standard topics and tools taught in most introductory courses and to a broader and richer set of topics and tools that offer a fresh understanding of the economic realities of the twenty-first century. Too often, introductory macroeconomics textbooks, in attempting to simplify the complexities of the real world to a comprehensible level, present material that not only abstracts from reality, but sometimes directly contradicts it. In this respect it is more difficult to provide an introductory description of the macroeconomy than it is to introduce economic behavior on the microeconomic level. *Macroeconomics in Context* addresses this challenge by keeping the theoretic exposition close to experience. The authors believe that students will achieve a deeper and more memorable understanding of economic theory if they can relate it to contemporary issues of interest and importance.

This book encourages engaged and critical thinking about topics in economics. Whether students take this class simply to gain some understanding of how economics can be useful to them, or go on to study economics or business in depth, this comprehensive and up-to-date book will help equip them with the standard tools *and* the critical knowledge they need to succeed.

While this book attempts to open up students' minds about the uses of economic theory, it also aims to provide a variety of viewpoints. Instructors who are largely satisfied with standard treatments, and instructors tightly confined by the requirements of the larger curriculum, can be assured that the materials typically treated in Introduction to Macroeconomics courses—including the classical, Keynesian, monetarist, classical-Keynesian synthesis, and new classical approaches—are presented in full. Economics instructors who are frustrated by the lack of attention to history, institutions, ecology, gender, social divisions, ethics, or poverty in other textbooks will find much to be enthusiastic about in our treatment, as these topics are integrated throughout the book. Even some instructors who prefer approaches based on full-employment equilibrium or GDP growth will appreciate this text for the way in which its discussion of historical, institutional, political, and social factors encourages students to engage with the subject matter.

Macroeconomics in Context is the companion textbook to *Microeconomics in Context 2nd Edition,* also published by M.E. Sharpe.

Content and Organization

Some of the innovative features of this text are apparent in even a quick scan of the table of contents, the sample course outlines on pp. xxi–xxiv, or Chapter 1. Although this textbook takes a broader and more contextual approach to economic activities, it fits these within a familiar overall organizational strategy:

- Part One, "The Context for Economic Analysis," presents the themes of the book and the major actors in the economy. Students are introduced to a range of macroeconomic questions and goals, to basic empirical and theoretical tools, and to the basic activities and institutions of a modern economy. This section concludes with an overview of supply-and-demand analysis, as is now customary in macroeconomic textbooks.
- Part Two, "Macroeconomic Basics," introduces the usual basic macroeconomic definitions (GDP, inflation, unemployment, and so on) and accounting methods. These are supplemented with a discussion of how new accounts are being developed to measure the economic contributions of the natural environment, unpaid household labor, and other previously uncounted factors, and by a description of the structure of the U.S. macroeconomy.
- Part Three, "Macroeconomic Theory and Policy," explores the issue of macroeconomic fluctuations. The first chapters clearly present Keynesian and classical theories of aggregate demand determination and the effects of fiscal and monetary policies. The last chapter in this section presents an "ADE/ASR" (Aggregate Demand Equilibrium/Aggregate Supply Response) model of output and inflation.
- Part Four, "Macroeconomic Issues and Applications," explores issues of economic growth, global economic relationships, and development. Important social and cultural aspects of growth and development, environmental sustainability, the quality of working life, distribution and poverty, and controversies over globalization are integrated into these discussions. At the instructor's discretion, growth theory (in Chapter 14) could, alternatively, be introduced earlier in the course. The instructor would need to give only a modest amount of explanation to assure continuity.

In order to make room for "contextual" discussions, we have reduced coverage in two areas. First, instruction in algebraic modeling techniques receives relatively less emphasis here than it does in other texts. Instructors who feel that students going on to intermediate-level classes should master such material will find it available in optional appendices to the chapters. Many students, however, do not go on to take intermediate classes—or they complain, when they do, that they are presented with the same material all over again. Hence, in designing the material for the main flow of the text, we have preferred to err on the side of teaching topics relevant for informed citizenship, rather than on the side of preparing students to understand the lingo of professional mainstream macroeconomists. Second, while this book reviews the basics of supply and demand and includes "new classical" macroeconomics among the theories discussed, it devotes fewer pages to the concept of market efficiency than many books, and certainly less than those recent books that have adopted a strongly new classical slant. In taking this approach, we have followed the lead of those advanced researchers in the profession who convincingly argue that "micro foundations" are of limited usefulness in explaining macroeconomic phenomena. This approach also makes the course less repetitive for students who take both Introduction to Microeconomics and Introduction to Macroeconomics courses.

WHAT MAKES THIS BOOK DIFFERENT FROM OTHER TEXTS?

This text covers the traditional topics included in most macroeconomics texts, but treats them from a broader, more holistic perspective. The following chapter-by-chapter synopsis shows how this book manages both to be "similar enough" to fit into a standard curriculum and "different enough" to respond to commonly expressed needs and dissatisfactions.

Chapter 1, "Economic Activity in Context," presents standard macroeconomic topics such as the macroeconomic goals of growth and stability and a basic roadmap of the most significant events and theories of the last century. We place these subjects into a broader context of concern for well-being. Many texts define economics as the study of choice in the face of scarcity, and focus on economic growth as a (if not *the*) goal of macroeconomic policy. In this chapter, however, we take the view that growth in GDP, while important to understand for the study of macroeconomics, may or may not contribute to the general goal of human well-being. We define the well-being goals of macroeconomics as (1) improvement in living standards, (2) stability and security, and (3) financial, social, and ecological sustainability.

As is the pattern in most contemporary macroeconomics textbooks, a review of microeconomic concepts comes next. This is the case here, as well. Chapters 2, 3, and 4 repeat material from the companion textbook, *Microeconomics in Context*—but with a contextual twist. Chapter 2, "Useful Tools and Concepts," introduces standard concepts of economic modeling, efficiency, scarcity, opportunity cost, the production-possibilities frontier, and the advantages of market systems, and includes a review of graphing techniques. In contrast to most standard texts, however, we place these within a broader context of concern for well-being. We discuss the institutional requirements of markets and introduce the concepts of externalities, public goods, market power, transaction costs, information and expectations, and concern for human needs and equity. The early introduction of these topics allows us to demonstrate why markets, while useful, are not on their own sufficient for organizing economic life in service of well-being.

Chapter 3, "What Economies Do," presents brief discussions of the four essential economic activities. Most textbooks discuss three essential activities—production, distribution, and consumption—but we add the activity of "resource maintenance" in order to draw attention to the importance of maintaining capital stocks, and particularly stocks of natural (environmental) capital. In addition, we incorporate a discussion of the important topic of income and wealth distribution into this early chapter, rather than relegate it to a later chapter, as most textbooks do.

Chapter 4, "Supply and Demand," contains a brief but clear exposition of traditional supply-and-demand curve analysis, including discussions of the slopes of the curves, factors that shift the curves, equilibrium and market adjustment, and a simple discussion of elasticities. Our contextual approach, however, leads to some subtle shifts in presentation. First, the model is explicitly presented as a thought experiment—as a humanly created analytical tool that may help us gain insight—rather than as a set of "laws" about "the way the world works." Second, discussions of price changes that are either too slow (i.e., "sticky") or too volatile (e.g., financial market speculation) lead students to think about how market adjustment in the real world may not be as smooth and welfare-maximizing as the model is often taken to imply.

Chapter 5, "Macroeconomic Measurement: The Current Approach," begins Part Two of the book, "Macroeconomic Basics." It presents a fairly standard introduction to national income accounting, but with a contextual flavor. It emphasizes that the accounts have been created for specific purposes. It notes how the production and investment undertaken in the "household and institutions" and government sectors have historically been deemphasized in national accounting, and how these have been completely ignored in common abstract representations of the macroeconomy.

Chapter 6, "Macroeconomic Measurement: Environmental and Social Dimensions," gives a more thorough introduction to alternative measures of economic performance than can be found in any other introductory economics textbook. In place of the usual economic "circular flow" diagram, which ignores the resource base of production, this chapter introduces an image of economic activity as embedded in social and physical contexts, and relates this approach to issues of macroeconomic concern. The chapter includes discussions of issues in the valuation of environmental and household services, satellite accounts for environmental and household production, the Genuine Progress Indicator, and the Human Development Index.

Chapter 7, "Employment and Unemployment," discusses standard macroeconomic labor topics such the definition of the unemployment rate, the different types of unemployment, and theories of the causes of unemployment. Unlike more classically oriented textbooks, however, more attention is paid to labor market institutions and aggregate demand issues, and the "natural rate of unemployment" concept is presented as hypothesis, not fact. A final section discusses changes in labor force participation rates and questions of labor market "flexibility."

Chapter 8, "The Structure of the United States Economy," is an addition unique to this book. It describes key features of production and employment in the U.S. economy, broken down into its primary, secondary, and tertiary sectors. We include this material for several reasons. First, it makes the text more "real world" to students. Second, it provides basic economic literacy that we believe is sorely lacking among most economics students. Finally, it presents the context to illustrate several economic debates, such as the loss of manufacturing jobs and the rising costs of health care. While this chapter is written with a U.S. focus, its description of sectoral shifts is relevant to many economies around the world.

Part Three of the book, "Macroeconomic Theory and Policy," builds up a basic, but insightful, model of macroeconomic fluctuations. Chapter 9, "Aggregate Demand and Economic Fluctuations," introduces the analysis of business cycles, presents the classical theory of savings-investment balance through the market for loanable funds, and develops Keynesian aggregate demand analysis in the form of the traditional "Keynesian cross" diagram. Our treatment of these topics is fairly standard, although our contextual approach gives more emphasis to the possibility of persistent unemployment than do many other current textbooks.

Chapter 10, "Fiscal Policy," balances formal analysis of fiscal policy with real-world data and examples. Analysis of fiscal policy impacts is presented in fairly simple terms, with an algebraic treatment of more complex multiplier effects in appendices. While the basic analysis presented here follows the Keynesian model, the text also discusses classical or supply-side perspectives. The section on budgets and deficits should give students an understanding of deficits, debt, and how these affect the economy. The difference between automatic stabilizers and discretionary policy is made clear, and recent fiscal policies are discussed. The foreign sector is added to give a complete macroeconomic model including saving, investment, taxes, government spending, exports and imports.

Chapter 11, "Money and Monetary Policy," presents treatments of the banking system and monetary policy that are quite standard, with the exception that the graphical exposition of monetary policy focuses on the market for federal funds. We have chosen this approach because it corresponds closely to the way that students will find the Federal Reserve's actions presented and discussed in the media. However, should an instructor prefer a more traditional approach oriented around money supply and money demand, this—along with other approaches and additional topics that may be treated at the discretion of the instructor—is laid out in an appendix.

Chapter 12, "Aggregate Supply, Aggregate Demand, and Inflation: Putting It All Together," addresses the tricky problem of how to teach the relation between output and inflation to introductory students in a way that is simple yet intellectually defensible. The model presented in this chapter, "Aggregate Supply Response/Aggregate Demand Equilibrium" (or "ASR/ADE"), has many features that will be familiar to instructors. But unlike AS/AD models that put the price level on the vertical axis, this model has the inflation rate on the vertical axis, which makes it more relevant for discussing current events.* Unlike many new classical–influenced textbooks,

---

* Regarding the theoretical underpinnings of our model, our downward-sloped ADE is based on the AD developed by David Romer ("Keynesian Macroeconomics without the LM Curve," *Journal of Economic Perspectives* 14:2, 2000, 149–169), and adopted by other introductory textbooks writers including John B. Taylor (*Principles*

our basic presentation is not centered on a notion of long-run full-employment equilibrium output. We emphasize, instead, how the macroeconomy adjusts dynamically in the short and medium terms to often unpredictable economic events. This also makes relating the model to current events more realistic. (Classical theory is not, however, neglected. It is also discussed within the chapter and the appendix.)

Part Four, "Macroeconomic Issues and Applications," begins with Chapter 13, "The Global Economy." This chapter takes students through the basics of international trade and finance, and introduces them to controversies over globalization. It presents the usual Ricardian gains-from-trade story, but goes considerably deeper than most textbooks into the real-world political economy of international economic relations. Vulnerabilities arising from trade, environmental standards, and actions of the World Trade Organization and the International Monetary Fund are among the topics discussed.

Chapter 14, "How Economies Grow and Develop," presents basic concepts related to economic growth, such as the Solow growth model and the importance of investment in manufactured capital. This standard material is complemented by in-depth discussion of the role of strong institutions, industrial policy, and human capital and describes the global inequality in income. The debate on economic convergence is described, with evidence both supporting and refuting a reduction in global inequities. The chapter concludes that the "one size fits all" approach to economic development emphasizing structural reforms has produced disappointing results, and that different approaches are required in response to the circumstances in each country.

Chapter 15, "Macroeconomic Challenges for the Twenty-First Century," is an unusual chapter for a macro textbook—but a crucially important one, in terms of economic education for intelligent citizenship. It examines two major issues: (1) human development, both in poor and rich countries, and (2) ecological challenges, particularly, but not exclusively, global climate change. While it covers standard theories such as the environmental Kuznets curve, it raises serious challenges to the belief that economic growth and markets will solve this century's social and environmental problems on their own.

SPECIAL FEATURES

Each chapter in this text contains many features designed to enhance student learning.

- *Key terms* are highlighted in boldface type throughout the text, and important ideas and definitions are set off from the main text.
- *Discussion Questions* at the end of each section encourage immediate review of what has been read, and relate the material to the students' own experiences. The frequent appearance of these questions throughout each chapter helps students review manageable portions of material and thus boosts comprehension. The questions can be used for participatory exercises involving the entire class or for small-group discussion.
- *End-of-Chapter Review Questions* are designed to encourage students to create their own summary of concepts. They also serve as helpful guidelines to the importance of various points.

---

of Macroeconomics, Houghton Mifflin, various editions). Our deeply curved ASR is based on the notion of an expectations-augmented Phillips curve, translated into inflation and output space. The idea of a dynamically evolving economy, rather than one always headed toward settling at full employment, is an approach based on Keynes' own (rather than new Keynesian) thought, as explained in the appendix to Chapter 12.

- *End-of-Chapter Exercises* encourage students to work with and apply the material, thereby gaining increased mastery of concepts, models, and investigative techniques.
- Throughout all the chapters *Economics in the Real World* and *News in Context* boxes enliven the material with real-world illustrations drawn from a variety of sources.
- In order to make the chapters as lively and accessible as possible, some formal and technical material (suitable for inclusion in some but not all course designs) is carefully and concisely explained in chapter appendices.

A glossary at the end of the book contains all key terms, their definitions, and the number of the chapter in which each was first used and defined.

SUPPLEMENTS

The supplements package for this book provides a set of teaching tools and resources for instructors using this text. The authors have worked closely with our associate Brian Roach to create a brief *Instructor's Resource Manual* and brief *Test Bank* to accompany *Macroeconomics in Context*. To receive these electronically, send an e-mail to GDAE@tufts.edu that contains sufficient information for us to verify your instructor status.

For each chapter, the *Instructor's Resource Manual* includes an introductory note and answers to all review questions and end-of-chapter exercises. In addition, the "Notes on Discussion Questions" section provides not only suggested answers to these questions but also ideas on how the questions might be used in the classroom. And sections entitled "Web Resources" and "Extensions" provide supplementary material and links to other passages in the book or other materials that can be used to enrich lectures and discussion.

The *Test Bank* includes multiple-choice and true/false questions for each chapter. The correct answer for each question is indicated.

PowerPoint slides of figures and tables from the text, and a *Student Study Guide* prepared by Marjolein van der Veen that provides ample opportunity for students to review and practice the key concepts, are available for free download at http://www.ase.tufts.edu/gdae/publications/textbooks/macroeconomics.html.

HOW TO USE THIS TEXT

The feedback we have received from instructors who reviewed and/or class-tested this text in its preliminary edition has been enthusiastic and gratifying. We've found that this book works in a variety of courses with a variety of approaches, and we'd like to share some of these instructors' suggestions on tailoring this book to meet your own course needs.

First, even if you are among those rare instructors who normally get their class all the way through a macroeconomics principles text in a semester, you may find that, with a text that is quite different from those you have used before, it is harder to anticipate which chapters will require the most time. Many instructors do not expect to cover all of the material in the textbook. In either case, it is wise to anticipate that the semester may end with some chapters not covered in class—and to plan in advance how to deal with this possibility.

On pages xxi to xxiv you'll find several possible course plans based on different emphases (such as neoclassical, ecological, social, and public policy). We hope this will help you plan the course that will best suit your and your students' needs.

Acknowledgments

Macroeconomics in Context was written under the auspices of the Global Development And Environment Institute (GDAE), a research institute at Tufts University. In addition to the main authorship team, considerable research and editing efforts were put into this textbook by Brian Roach of GDAE. James Devine of Loyola Marymount University, Los Angeles contributed many ideas for the modeling chapters.

We would also like to thank a number of instructors who were exceptionally generous in giving us detailed comments on the preliminary edition. These include Alison Butler, Willamette University; Gary Flomenhoft, University of Vermont; Robin King, Georgetown University; Valerie Luzadis, SUNY-ESF, Syracuse; Chiara Piovani, University of Utah; Saranna Thornton, Hampden-Sydney College; and Marjolein van der Veen, Bellevue Community College. We also thank Thomas White and his students at Assumption College for their comments. A number of anonymous reviewers also provided extremely helpful suggestions. Participants at the GDAE-sponsored conferences "Rethinking Macroeconomics" in 2002 and "Growth vs. Sustainability? Economic Responses to Ecological Challenges" in 2006 (both generously supported by the Rockefeller Brothers Fund) provided stimulating input on many topics.

We also thank the staff of M.E. Sharpe publishing, particularly Lynn Taylor, Katie Corasaniti, Nicole Cirino, and Angela Piliouras for their enthusiasm and work in getting this book to press.

All contributors of written materials were paid through grants raised by the Global Development And Environment Institute. By agreement with the authors, all royalties from sales of the book will go to support the work of the institute. We are extremely appreciative of the financial support we have received from a number of foundations including the O'Neill Foundation, the Barnsley Foundation, the RGR Fund, the Rockefeller Brothers Fund, and the G. G. Monks Foundation.

Sample Course Outlines

The span of a term imposes severe constraints on what an instructor can teach. We believe that *Macroeconomics in Context* can be used as the basis for a variety of approaches, depending on how much flexibility you have and how much time you choose to devote to topics and approaches that may be of particular interest to you and your students.

To help you identify the chapter assignments that make the most sense for your class, we have put together some ideas for course outlines. These appear below. Arranged in terms of broad selections and more specific emphases, they are designed to help you choose among chapters when you find that there is not enough time to cover everything that appears in this textbook.

We understand that one primary objective of the introductory course in most departments is teaching in some detail "how (neoclassical) economists think." For those instructors who either must or choose to focus exclusively on neoclassical content, the most traditional combination of the selections described below—the Base Chapters, combined with some or all of the Basic Macroeconomics Selection and the Macro-Modeling Emphasis—will provide what you need. This combination of chapters does not come close to exploiting fully the richness of *Macroeconomics in Context*, but the contextual discussions (a hallmark of this text) that are interwoven into the standard material will broaden the students' understanding of macroeconomic theory and provide some critical thinking tools.

Many instructors have somewhat more leeway and can combine coverage of traditional neoclassical ideas with other material. Addressing such users of *Macroeconomics in Context,* we suggest that you make use of the special structure of the book, which enables you to introduce traditional concepts in your introductory course while still reserving class time for other areas of interest. Ecological sustainability, for example, is an issue of increasing importance, and deeply linked to the functioning of the macroeconomy. If you are an instructor with some flexibility, you might choose the Base Chapters Selection and most of the Basic Macroeconomics Selection, combining these with one or more of the emphases described below.

Some of you may have even more flexibility, perhaps because you teach primarily nonmajors or teach outside of an economics department, such as in a public policy school, environmental sciences department, or interdisciplinary social studies department. If you are in this category, you can set aside altogether those portions of the traditional neoclassical curriculum that you find less relevant and teach a course that is even richer in its variety of topics and intellectual scope. Such a course might include the Base Chapters Selection, some material from the Basic Macroeconomics Selection, and much more material from the topical emphases.

We also suggest that, in any course, you might have your students reread Chapter 1, Section 3, "Macroeconomics in Context" after finishing Part Three, the section of the book that models economic fluctuations and policy responses. While the initial overview of controversies laid out

---

Summary of Possible Course Options When Not All of the Text Can be Taught

Curriculum Focus	Likely Selections (see descriptions below)
Traditional macroeconomics	Base Chapters
	Basic Macroeconomics
	Modeling Emphasis
Strong focus on traditional macroeconomics, with other themes woven in	Base Chapters
	Basic Macroeconomics
	Choose from other Emphases
Coverage of basic traditional concepts within course tailored to instructor and student interests	Base Chapters
	Choose selections from Basic Macroeconomics
	Choose from other Emphases

---

in Chapter 1 is important to set the stage, it will probably be much better understood after the students have more exposure to macroeconomics.

BASE CHAPTERS SELECTION

- Chapter 1, "Economic Activity in Context"
- Chapter 2, "Useful Tools and Concepts"
- Chapter 3, Section 1, "Introducing the Four Essential Economic Activities"
- Chapter 4, "Supply and Demand." (If microeconomics is a prerequisite, you may wish to assign only Section 5, "Macroeconomics and the Dynamics of Real World Markets.")

BASIC MACROECONOMICS SELECTION

- Chapter 5, "Macroeconomic Measurement: The Current Approach"
- Chapter 7, "Employment and Unemployment," Sections 1–3
- Chapter 9, "Aggregate Demand and Economic Fluctuations"
- Chapter 10, "Fiscal Policy," Sections 1 and 2
- Chapter 11, "Money and Monetary Policy," Sections 1, 4, and 5
- Chapter 12, "Aggregate Supply, Aggregate Demand, and Inflation: Putting It All Together," Sections 1–3
- Chapter 14, "How Economies Grow and Develop," Sections 1–3

ECOLOGICAL EMPHASIS

- Chapter 3, Section 2, "Resource Maintenance: Attending to the Asset Base of the Macroeconomy"
- Chapter 6, Section 2, "Accounting for the Environment"
- Chapter 8, Section 1, "The Three Major Productive Sectors in an Economy," and Section 2, "Natural Resources; the Primary Sector"
- Chapter 12, Section 5, "Are Stabilization and Sustainability in Conflict?"
- Chapter 15, Section 3, "Macroeconomics and Ecological Sustainability"

GLOBAL EMPHASIS

- Chapter 10, Section 3, "The International Sector"
- Chapter 13, "The Global Economy"
- Chapter 14, "How Economies Grow and Develop"
- Chapter 15, "Macroeconomic Challenges for the Twenty-First Century"

HUMAN DEVELOPMENT EMPHASIS

- Chapter 6, Section 3, "Measuring Household Production," and Section 4, "Measuring Economic Well-Being"
- Chapter 12, Section 5, "Are Stabilization and Sustainability in Conflict?"
- Chapter 14, "How Economies Grow and Develop," Sections 2–4
- Chapter 15, Section 2, "Macroeconomics and Human Development"

STRUCTURAL EMPHASIS

- Chapter 8, "The Structure of the United States Economy"

KEYNESIAN/POST-KEYNESIAN/INSTITUTIONALIST EMPHASIS

- Chapter 2, Section 3, "The Role of Markets"
- Chapter 4, Section 5, "Macroeconomics and the Dynamics of Real World Markets"
- Chapter 12, Appendix A3, "Post-Keynesian Macroeconomics"

MACRO-MODELING EMPHASIS

- Chapter 9, Appendix, "An Algebraic Approach to the Multiplier"
- Chapter 10, Appendix, "More Algebraic Approaches to the Multiplier"
- Chapter 11, Appendix, "More Models and Issues of Monetary Policy"
- Chapter 12, Appendix "More Schools of Macroeconomics"
- Chapter 13, Section 4, "International Finance"
- Chapter 14, Section 1, "The Standard Theory of Economic Growth"

MONEY AND FINANCE EMPHASIS

- Chapter 11, "Money and Monetary Policy," Sections 2 and 3 and Appendix
- Chapter 13, Section 4, "International Finance"

POVERTY/INEQUALITY/SOCIAL JUSTICE EMPHASIS

- Chapter 3, Section 3, "Distribution: Who Gets What, and How?"
- Chapter 6, Section 3, "Measuring Household Production," and Section 4, "Measuring Economic Well-Being"
- Chapter 7, Section 4, "Employment, Unemployment, and Well-Being"
- Chapter 12, Section 5, "Are Stabilization and Sustainability in Conflict"?
- Chapter 15, Section 2.3, "Human Development When There Is Already 'Enough'"

CONTRASTING SCHOOLS OF THOUGHT EMPHASIS

- Have students reread Chapter 1, Section 3, "Macroeconomics in Context," after finishing Part Three
- Chapter 12, Section 4, "Competing Theories," and Appendix, "More Schools of Macroeconomics"
- See also the companion volume, *Microeconomics in Context,* Chapter 19, "Market Systems and Normative Claims"

Part One
The Context for Economic Analysis

1 Economic Activity in Context

What do you expect—and what do you want—from the macroeconomic system in which you live? Life, liberty, and the pursuit of happiness? Justice, peace, national security, and general welfare? Do you feel that you have a right to access to a job when you need or want one? Is a job essential for general welfare, or the pursuit of happiness? And will you feel satisfied with access to just any job, or do you hope for one that will use your knowledge and talents, will provide you with some minimum level of income, and will earn respect from others? What does the macroeconomy have to do with these questions? And what other questions should we be asking about it?

What are your goals for this course? How do they relate to your larger life goals? How have you imagined your future career—with work as the central element, or friends and family, or vacations and fun, or some combination of these? You, and your goals, are part of what this course is about. As a resident of a nation, your beliefs and expectations, taken together with those of many other people, contribute to the mood of optimism (called "animal spirits" by a famous economist we will encounter later on) or pessimism that helps create economic booms or slumps. Other aspects of your economic behavior may contribute to the country's overall productivity. Goals are not the only determining factor for beliefs and actions, but they are an important element. This book will pay attention to your goals because they are a part of what makes up the macroeconomy.

But there is another, more important reason to ask you, at the outset, about your life goals. Macroeconomics is about how economies work. This is not only interesting as an intellectual puzzle. It matters because when the economy works well people have more opportunities to achieve their goals than when it is working badly. Depending on what your goals are, there are a variety of ways in which you could interpret what it means for an economy to be working "well" or "badly." As you read through this book you will have plenty of opportunities to consider this idea, and to think about how an understanding of basic economic principles can be used to judge, or even to make, economic policies.

1. What Is Macroeconomics About?

Economics is the study of the way people organize themselves to sustain life and enhance its quality. Individuals engage in four essential economic activities: resource maintenance, production of goods and services, distribution of goods and services, and consumption of goods and services. Resource maintenance means tending to, preserving, or improving the natural, produced, human, and social resources that form the basis for the preservation and quality of life. Production is the conversion of some of these resources into usable products. Distribution refers to the sharing of products and resources among people, while consumption refers to their final use.

Economists study how individuals engage in these activities and how their social coordination is achieved. ("Social organization" and "social coordination" are used here in the broad sense to mean "involving a number of people.")

> **economics:** the study of the way people organize themselves to sustain life and enhance its quality
>
> The four essential economic activities are resource maintenance and the production, distribution and consumption of goods and services.

Often, for the convenience of organizing curricula, the study of economics is broken down into two parts: Micro- and macro-economics. This book, *Macroeconomics in Context,* is the companion to another textbook called (not surprisingly) *Microeconomics in Context.* Where **microeconomics** emphasizes the economic activities and interactions of individuals and particular organizations (such as businesses, households, community groups, nonprofits, and government agencies), **macroeconomics** looks at how all of these activities join together to create an overall economic environment at the national—and often the global—level.

> **microeconomics:** the study of the economic activities and interactions of individuals, households, businesses, and other groups at the sub-national level
>
> **macroeconomics:** the study of how economic activities at all levels create a national (and global) economic environment
>
> Economic conditions at the aggregate level, such as rates of unemployment and inflation, create the environment in which individual economic actors make their decisions.

For example, when you seek paid work in your chosen field, your success will depend in part on both micro- and macroeconomic factors. On the microeconomic side, you will need to have prepared yourself for the work—invested in your own "human capital," an economist would say. You will need to find a particular business or other agency that can use your skills—or find direct buyers for your services, if you decide to strike out on your own. You will want to find work that gives you a combination of job satisfaction, income, and benefits that you like.

But will employers in general be hiring? Some graduating classes are unlucky, and flood the job market just as the national economy is "going sour"—that is, entering a recession. No matter how well-prepared you are, finding a job can be tough during a period of high **unemployment**, when many people who seek jobs are not successful in finding one. And if you do find a job, how far will your paycheck go to meet your standard-of-living desires? If you start working during a period of high **inflation**, when the overall level of prices is increasing, the purchasing power of a fixed paycheck will be quickly eroded. Macroeconomic conditions also affect personal debt. If you are like most students these days, you will be paying back loans for a number of years. The higher the prevailing real interest rates in the economy, the more costly this borrowing will be. Your own economic well-being will also be tied to global issues such as trade flows and currency exchange rates—especially if you go to work for a business that does a lot of importing or exporting, or you send money back to relatives in a home country. If you are lucky, all these factors will fall in your favor. If you are not . . . well, then you can join the chorus blaming "the economy" for your troubles.

> **unemployment:** seeking a paying job, but not being able to get one
>
> **inflation:** a rise in the general level of prices

Such macroeconomic issues are considered "short run"—economists refer to them as having to do with macroeconomic "fluctuations." Sometimes unemployment is high and sometimes it is low, and the same goes for inflation, interest rates, trade deficits, and exchange rates.

Other macroeconomic issues have to do with the long run. Can you expect your standard of living fifty years from now, or the standard of living of your children, to be higher or lower than what you enjoy now? Are you living in a society where all people have a chance to develop themselves, or are extremes of wealth and poverty getting more pronounced over time?

Macroeconomics seeks to explain an especially interesting phenomenon: the fact that bad things can often happen on a national or global level even though virtually no individual or microeconomic-level organization *wants* or *intends* them to happen. People generally agree that high unemployment, persistent high inflation, and destruction of the natural environment, for example, are bad things. Yet they occur nonetheless.

Microeconomics and macroeconomics are terms that are applied rather loosely, covering or emphasizing different topics as times and circumstances change. Many issues have both macroeconomic and microeconomic aspects. For example, imposition of a sales tax will affect microeconomic behavior—people may consume less, or shift their patterns of consumption toward untaxed items—but it also affects government revenues, which, as we will see, are an important element of macroeconomic analysis. No one speaks of "the microeconomy" because there are too many sub-national economic systems of varied sizes that are studied in the field of microeconomics. However the term **macroeconomy** is used to refer to a national economic system. People also speak of the **global economy**, meaning the system of economic rules, norms, and interactions by which economic actors and actions in different parts of the world are connected to one another. **Economic actors** (or **economic agents**) include all individuals, groups, and organizations that engage in or influence economic activity. As the global economy has become an increasingly important part of the experience of more and more people, it has become appropriate and important to include its study within introductory economics courses. By default, it falls into the field of macroeconomics. Given contemporary realities, and the importance of global economic issues for most people's lives, perhaps this book would be more appropriately titled "Macro and Global Economics in Context." You may, in any case, expect to find global as well as macroeconomic issues covered in this book.

> **macroeconomy:** an economic system whose boundaries are normally understood to be the boundaries of a nation
>
> **global economy:** the system of economic rules, norms and interactions by which economic actors and actions in different parts of the world are connected to one another
>
> **economic actor (economic agent):** an individual, group, or organization that is involved in economic activities

Discussion Questions

1. You have evidently made a decision to dedicate some of your personal resources of time and money to studying college economics. Why? What do you hope to learn in this course that will be helpful for you in reaching your goals?
2. Are you familiar with the following terms? While you will study them in detail in this course, see how well you can come up with a definition for them just from your previous knowledge. (It does not matter at this point if you do not know them.)

unemployment	recession
inflation	economic boom
economic growth	money
development	fiscal policy
GDP	monetary policy
investment	sustainability

2. MACROECONOMIC GOALS

We have introduced the idea of an economy working "well" or "badly," and have referred to high unemployment, persistent high inflation, and destruction of the natural environment as bad things that virtually no one wants. "Bad" and "good" are value-laden terms. Do they belong in an economic textbook?

Social scientists often make a distinction between **positive questions**, which concern issues of fact, or "what is," and **normative questions**, which have to do with goals and values, or "what should be." For example, "What is the level of production in our country?" is a positive question, requiring descriptive facts as an answer. "What level of production would be most desirable?" is a normative question, requiring analysis of what it is we value and what goals should be set. However, both of these questions require a definition of production; as we will see in Chapters 5 and 6, positive and normative issues are inevitably intertwined in efforts to reach such a definition.

> **positive questions:** questions about how things are

> **normative questions:** questions about how things should be

Much of this textbook will be concerned with positive issues. Using both empirical evidence and various theories, we will describe—using the best available economic research—how an economy functions at the macro level. Yet, although a few people perhaps enjoy studying economic principles for their own sake, the main reason anyone would study macroeconomics is to try to understand how we—as a society, nation, and world—can reach the goals we desire. Thus we cannot avoid the normative question of what goals the macroeconomy *should* achieve.

Not everyone has the same goals, on a personal level, or in their idea of a "good" society. However, agreement becomes easier at a more general level. Therefore, we will start with the term **well-being** as a way of referring to the broad goal of promoting the sustenance and flourishing of life.

> **well-being:** a shorthand term for the broad goal of promoting the sustenance and flourishing of life

In the context of macroeconomics, we can say that three especially important components of well-being are good living standards, stability and security, and sustainability.

> The three major macroeconomic goals are the achievement of good living standards, stability and security, and sustainability.

2.1 LIVING STANDARDS

One macroeconomic goal is to get and keep people's living standards high enough that their lives can be long, healthy, enjoyable, and offer them the opportunity to accomplish the things they believe give their lives meaning.

The most basic living standard issues relate to the quality of people's diets and housing, their access to means of transportation and communication, and the quality of medical attention they receive. Taking a somewhat broader view, we might also include less tangible aspects of life such as the quality of education people receive and the variety of entertainments they can enjoy. In addition, the way in which people participate in producing goods and services—as well as their consumption of them—has important implications for their health and happiness. So, for working-age people, the quality of their working lives is part of their standard of living. On the other hand, for many people who cannot do much work because they are too young, old, ill, or handicapped, the quality of the hands-on care they receive is a major component of living standards. As we will see in Chapter 6, we could add even more categories to broaden our notion of well-being, going beyond economic issues to include things like political freedom and social inclusion. Economics has traditionally, however, taken the goods-and-services or provisioning aspect of life as its central focus, and **living standards growth** has been a top concern.

> **living standards growth:** improvements in people's diet, housing, medical attention, education, working conditions and access to care, transportation, communication, entertainment and the like, that can allow people to have long and enjoyable lives and have the opportunity to accomplish the things that give their lives meaning

How can living standards be maintained or improved? For a long time, "raising living standards" was considered to be nearly synonymous with "achieving economic growth." By **economic growth** we mean growth in the level of production or output. Traditionally, this has been measured within a country by the growth of its gross domestic product (GDP)—a measure you will hear much more about in later chapters.

> **economic growth:** increases in the level of production in a country or region

Global economic growth has been impressive in recent decades. Figure 1.1 plots the sum of GDP for all countries from 1960 to 2006. The data from which this chart has been plotted are far from perfect—different countries have at different times used a variety of methods (some approaching guesswork) to calculate their GDP. The conceptual definition of GDP is also controversial, as we will explore in Chapters 5 and 6. Nevertheless, we can view as a reasonable approximation the conclusion from this picture that global production has increased greatly over the last few decades. By this measure, the value of global production in 2006 was about 5.2 times the value in 1960.

But the growth in economic production has not been equal in all countries, and living standards are still very low in much of the world. This fact has important meaning for people's options and for their enjoyment of life. Poverty can mean that people are crowded together in unsanitary urban slums or isolated in rural huts, have barely enough to eat, receive little or no education, and never see a doctor. Worldwide, extreme poverty is still a major concern. The United Nations estimates that about 1.2 billion people—or about 20 percent of the world's population—live in absolute poverty, subsisting on the equivalent of US $1 per day or less. The production of more and better housing, better roads, more grain, more schooling, and more medical care—*more goods and services*—is necessary to raise living standards in such situations.

It is because of such an underlying concern with living standards that for many decades economists focused very strongly on measures of economic growth, and the question of how it could be maintained and even speeded up. The process of moving from a general situation of poverty and deprivation toward one of increased production and plenty is what has traditionally been referred to as **economic development**. (This topic will be discussed at greater length in Chapter 14.) Generally, economic development has been thought of as a process of increasing agricultural

Figure 1.1   **Global Production, 1960–2006**

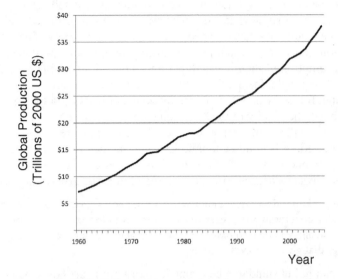

As measured by summing up the GDP of all countries, global production has more than quintupled in the last several decades. (Source: The World Bank Group, World Development Indicators Online)

productivity, investing in machinery and technology, and making changes in the organization of work (from home-based shops to factories, for example), so that **labor productivity** rises. That is, people can produce more in each hour that they work.

> **economic development:** the process of moving from a situation of poverty and deprivation to a situation of increased production and plenty, through investments and changes in the organization of work

> **labor productivity:** the level of output that can be produced per worker

Of course, while increased production is *necessary* in such a situation, it is not *sufficient* on its own to improve living standards for the people living in a poor country. For one thing, the increase in production may not be enough to keep pace with a growing population. Improvement in general living standards can only result if production *per person* (GDP *per capita*) on average rises. Some of the increase in global production shown in Figure 1.1 is simply a result of more people producing goods and services. When we adjust for the growth in the world's population, we see that production per capita, as measured by dividing global production by global population, has also grown over the last several decades, but not by as much. Figure 1.2 shows that global production per capita has increased by about a factor of 2.4 between 1960 and 2006, according to this measure.

If we were to disaggregate from the global figures we would see that changes in economic production over these years vary significantly across different regions and countries. In East Asian countries, GDP per capita has increased by over seven times. In sub-Saharan Africa, however, GDP per capita is actually *lower* now than it was in the 1970s.

Even if GDP *per capita* is rising, other factors are still important in ensuring that economic growth benefits the world's and each country's population as a whole:

Figure 1.2 **Global Production per Capita, 1960–2006**

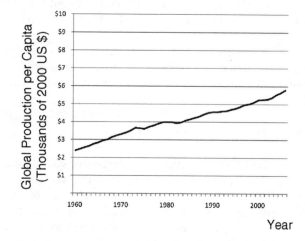

Global production per person has more than doubled in the last several decades. (Source: The World Bank Group, World Development Indicators Online)

- First, it matters *what* is produced. An economy may experience "economic growth" by increasing its production of military hardware or large public monuments, for example, but these kinds of production are much less likely to raise living standards than growth in production of nutritious food, widely available health care, or the quality of basic education.
- Second, it matters *how* it is produced. In some poorer countries today, many workers—including young children—work fourteen- to sixteen-hour days in unsafe, badly ventilated mines and factories; many suffer severe illnesses and early death.
- Third, it matters *for whom* economic growth occurs. How are the increases in production, or incomes arising from production, distributed among the population? Do some regions, or some groups of people as defined by income class, race, ethnicity, gender, or other factors, receive more of the gains from growth than others? If the benefits of economic growth go only to a tiny global or national elite, the bulk of the population may remain desperately poor.

Sometimes these queries about "what, how, and for whom?" are referred to as the "three basic economic questions." Even given the qualifications raised by these questions, you can still see that some economic growth is necessary in regions that are very poor.

In richer regions, the situation may be different. In a country that is already rich, is economic growth still the key to improving living standards and increasing overall well-being? In most highly industrialized countries, populations are growing very slowly—or even declining. When the population isn't growing, and when the majority of families already enjoy decent housing, safe water, plenty of food, easily washed and dried clothing, readily available heating and refrigeration, a car or two (or more), airline travel, TV sets, DVD players and the like, do we really need *more* in general? Some people would say that we do, but others believe that we should instead switch our national priorities into making sure that production is designed to increase well-being. In countries that already have a high level of production, *living standards growth* may be achievable even in the absence of *economic growth,* by improving cultural, educational, and environmental conditions, raising the quality of work-life, and promoting an equitable allocation of the economic rewards of production among workers, non-workers, managers, and owners. Another possible shift in priorities would be to put less emphasis on economic growth, and more emphasis on other elements of well-being, such as long-term environmental and social sustainability (discussed below).

We will return to these questions—and to the critical issue of the relationships among economic growth, job creation, and well-being—in later chapters. In Chapter 15, the relationship between economic development and a very important broader concept of development—*human development*—will be explored.

2.2 STABILITY AND SECURITY

While closely linked to living standards goals, the goal of stability and security brings in a temporal dimension that we have not yet discussed. Imagine that you are an old person, and looking back over your life you can say that *on average,* you enjoyed a good standard of living. This might arise from two quite different scenarios. In one scenario, you enjoy a fairly steady, or gently rising, living standard and are always able to plan confidently for your financial future.

In the other scenario, you are quite successful at some points in your life, but also periodically have to face the real possibility of "losing it all." You do well and buy a very nice house, but then you become unemployed and your house is foreclosed on because you are not able to make the payments. Then you start to do well again, and believe you are on a solid path to a pleasant retirement, but steeply rising price levels or a jumpy stock market wipe out the value of your savings and pensions. Even if, after the fact and "over the long run," you can say that *on average* you have done OK in terms of your living standards, the uncertainty and anxiety of living with economic fluctuations in the second scenario would take a toll on your overall well-being, relative to the more stable case.

High rates of unemployment are associated with many indicators of individual and social stress, such as suicide, domestic violence, and stress-related illnesses among those affected, and crime. Unpredictable fluctuations in employment levels and rates of inflation, as well as asset prices, interest rates, and foreign exchange rates, make it difficult—and in the worst cases, impossible—for individuals and organizations to make productive and economically sensible plans for the future.

One common pattern is for fluctuations in the level of production to occur as a cycle in which recessions (or "contractions" or "slumps") and their attendant problem of high unemployment alternate with booms (also called "expansions" or "recoveries"), which often bring with them the problem of more rapidly rising prices. This is called the **business cycle** or **trade cycle**. Even if these problems are "short-run" and do not last long—people eventually find jobs or inflation slows down—fluctuations cause considerable "ill-being" while they last. So creating a stable, secure economic environment is a separate important macroeconomic goal.

> **business (trade) cycle:** recurrent fluctuations in the level of national production, with alternating periods of recession and boom

Figure 1.3 shows GDP for the United States going back all the way to 1800. You can see that while the general trend is upward, the curve on the graph does not indicate *steady* growth. The curve is somewhat wavy. There are periods in which GDP fell as the country experienced economic contractions, and other periods of rapid expansion during which GDP rose very steeply. (As in all other graphs of production in this chapter, GDP numbers in Figure 1.3 are expressed in "real" terms. Without this adjustment, inflation would make the growth in economic activity appear larger than it actually was. This issue will be discussed in Chapter 5.)

Figure 1.3   **GDP in the United States, 1800–2006**

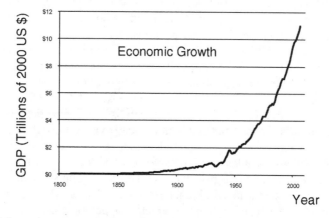

GDP in the United States has grown over time, but it has not grown steadily. The economy has experienced alternating periods of expansion and contraction. (Source: Louis D. Johnston and Samuel H. Williamson, "The Annual Real and Nominal GDP for the United States, 1790–Present." Economic History Services, http://www. eh.net/hmit/gdp/)

A widely accepted macroeconomic goal is the achievement of sufficient economic stability to enable individuals and families to enjoy economic security and to be able to make reasonable predictions about their future. In the light of new knowledge about our dependence on the natural world, which is undergoing radical alterations due to human economic activity, the goal of security now must also include a much longer time horizon, recognizing a serious responsibility to future generations. This leads us to our third goal: sustainability.

2.3 SUSTAINABILITY

We want good living standards and stability not only for ourselves right now, but also for ourselves later in our lives, and for our children, grandchildren, and other generations to come. That is, we would like a macroeconomic environment that is not only good now, but sustainable into the future. In particular, the goal of sustainability requires that we address the questions:

- Are economic activities *financially* sustainable into the future? Or is a nation incurring a high amount of debt that may create a heavy burden on its future workers?
- Are economic activities *socially* sustainable into the future? Are disparities between the "haves" and the "have nots" accelerating or diminishing? Are they based on justifiable causes or unequal power relations? Is the next generation receiving the upbringing and education required to enable them to contribute to a healthy economy and society? Or is the current structure of economic activity setting the stage for future social disruption and political strife?
- Are economic activities *ecologically* sustainable into the future? Is the natural environment that supports life being treated in a way that will sustain its quality into the future? Or is it becoming depleted or degraded?

Financial, social, and ecological sustainability are important macroeconomic goals.

For many generations, it seemed that technological progress and economic growth were magical keys that unlocked the door to unlimited improvements in the standard of living. In 1970, for example, real output per person in the United States was about ten times what it had been in 1840. "Developed" countries in North America, Western Europe, and elsewhere experienced long-run rising standards of living through industrialization, improvements in agricultural technology, and the development of service industries.

Some observers believe that this process can continue forever, and that any sustainability problems can be remedied by *more* GDP growth. For example, the issue of financial sustainability includes both concerns about the level of government debt (which accumulates whenever governments spend more than they take in) and external debt (what all people and organizations in a country owe to foreigners). Too much debt is a problem since it means that a large proportion of a country's income may in the future need to go to into servicing the debt rather than into other, more socially beneficial, uses. Indebtedness, however, is usually considered manageable as long as GDP grows at least as fast as the level of debt. Regarding social sustainability, some people believe that economic growth is also the way to relieve social ills and political strife. They reason that the bigger the pie, the bigger everyone's share can be, and that rising personal incomes will naturally lead to a peaceful and productive population. Concerning ecological issues, some economists think that any current negative effects of economic growth on the environment can be remedied by additional economic growth, since higher incomes give countries the wherewithal to invest in new exploration for resources and new pollution-controlling technologies. So, to the most growth-oriented economists, "sustainable growth" simply means making sure that the growth rate of GDP stays high well into the future.

As against those who continue to believe that economic growth and development, as traditionally defined, hold out the best answers to financial, social, and environmental problems, by the end of the twentieth century many other economists had started asking whether these might instead *contribute to* these problems.

> Financial, social, and environmental concerns have many people worried that the traditional macroeconomic emphasis on economic growth and development might actually be *contributing to* the creation of severe problems for the future of human society, rather than helping to solve them.

To the extent that a country's economic prosperity depends on short-sighted or unrealistic financial planning, prosperity may be unsustainable. For decades, for example, many poorer countries were encouraged to borrow heavily from richer countries in order to progress in economic development. However, many of them did not achieve the high rate of economic growth that was supposed to result from the borrowing, and a severe "debt crisis" has resulted. Some very poor countries currently send more funds *out* of their countries simply to pay the interest on their debt than they pay for health care for their own populations; many also pay more in interest than they currently receive in grants and loans.

Meanwhile, in some industrialized countries, including the United States, governments have recently cut taxes in order to "spur economic growth." But this means that governments instead borrow heavily to fund their activities. Many fear that such borrowing may already have become so excessive that dramatically higher taxes will be required in the future in order to pay interest on the debt. Those called on to pay these higher taxes—and hence suffer lower living standards—would be future workers like you. Setting good priorities about how we borrow is important to long-run sustainability.

Turning to social sustainability, many economists and other observers have come to question whether "development" as traditionally defined will solve the problem of global disparities in living standards. Some economists suggest that historical factors such as the legacy of colonization, and political factors such as rich countries' protection of their own industries within the system of global trade, mean that it is impossible to expect poorer countries to "develop" in the same way as countries that industrialized earlier. Analysts have also estimated that giving everyone in the world a U.S. lifestyle, including a meat-rich diet, multiple cars per family, etc., would require an extra two to four planets to supply resources and absorb waste.

Traditional goals of unlimited material affluence have also been called into question within richer countries, to the extent that social scientists have noticed that consumerist and more-is-better values may actually contribute to personal and social discontent and the weakening of social norms of trust and reciprocity. Societies that suffer bitter divisions between "haves" and "have nots," or a general sense that everybody is just out for him- or herself, are more likely to suffer social and political breakdown—perhaps to the point of violence—than societies where people enjoy a greater sense of social cohesion.

Regarding environmental issues, increased urban concentration and certain agricultural practices have caused extinction of some species and notable decreases in genetic diversity in others. Contemporary "developed" economies are presently heavily dependent on the consumption of fossil fuels. Yet these fuels are not in unlimited supply, and high-level scientific panels concur in believing that their burning contributes to global climate change.

Because of these and other problems, ecologists emphasize the complexity of natural systems and our relative ignorance about long-term, irreversible, or potentially catastrophic effects of economic behavior on the natural systems that support us. They suggest that, instead of placing blind faith in technological progress and economic growth, society should adopt a **precautionary principle**. This principle says that we should err on the cautious side, preferring to cooperate with natural systems rather than assuming we can safely replace them. Or, as stated by one group of experts, "When an activity raises threats of harm to the environment or human health, precautionary measures should be taken even if some cause and effect relationships are not fully established scientifically."[1] Such attention to environmental sustainability need not preclude also giving attention to the goals of living standards improvement and stability, but it does clearly call into question the idea that economic growth, in itself, is always the only, or the best goal.

> **precautionary principle:** the principle that we should err on the cautious side when dealing with natural systems or human health, especially when major health or environmental damage could result

Traditionally, many economists did not recognize a separate goal of sustainability, since they believed that achieving economic growth would naturally contribute to the achievement of any other goals that we might choose. In this textbook, we will present both this view and the view that suggests that environmental, social, and financial sustainability need to be considered as goals in their own right, perhaps requiring a dramatic shift in how we think about economic growth.

Discussion Questions

1. Which of the macroeconomic goals just discussed do you think should have the highest priority? Why? Are there other major goals you think are missing from the above discussion?
2. No one would argue that the goal of macroeconomics is to make people *worse* off! Yet the above outline of macroeconomic goals suggests that trying too hard to achieve some narrowly defined goals may lead to such a result. Why do you think some economists would view economic growth as the major goal, while others view it as potentially in conflict with other goals such as sustainability?

3. Macroeconomics in Context

Macroeconomics, as a field of study, is not a set of principles that is set in stone. Rather, the field has developed and changed over time as new empirical and theoretical techniques have been invented and as historical events have raised new questions for which people have urgently desired answers. To give you an idea about how the various principles in this book fit into social and historical context, we end this chapter with a short overview of the major historical developments in macroeconomics. This is not just dusty history; you will see as you progress through this textbook that many themes keep arising in just slightly new forms, while other challenges are unique to our twenty-first-century world.

3.1 The Classical Period

Centuries ago, most people in Europe were involved in agriculture or in home production, such as when a family would work together to card, spin, and weave raw wool into cloth. Merchants were a minority, and industrial production and large-scale trade were unknown. All this changed with the coming of the Industrial Revolution, which began in England in the mid-eighteenth century. In many countries technological progress led to new methods of production, and more productive economies both increased and diversified their output. Necessities like food and clothing used up a decreasing proportion of the average family income, while a growing fraction of the population was able to acquire more comforts and luxuries—better bedding, plumbing, housing, and transportation, to name just a few of the improvements to living standards. Academic thinkers started to try to understand and explain how these changes came about—and **classical economics** was born.

> **classical economics:** the school of economics, originating in the eighteenth century, that stressed issues of growth and distribution, based on an image of smoothly-functioning markets

During this period macroeconomic study focused on economic growth and distribution. The most famous classical economist was Scottish philosopher Adam Smith (1723–90) whose 1776 book *An Inquiry into the Nature and Causes of the Wealth of Nations* set the terms of discussion for centuries to come. Smith attributed the growing "wealth of nations" to various factors. One was changes in the organization of work, particularly the **division of labor** that assigned workers to **specialized**, narrowly defined tasks. Whereas in family-based production each individual had usually performed a variety of tasks, in industrial production a person would repeat one very specific task over and over, presumably becoming more proficient with increased practice. Another factor was technological progress, such as the invention of new machines powered by burning coal. The third was the accumulation of funds to invest in plants and machinery ("capital accumulation"). Classical economists were also particularly concerned with theorizing about how the funds generated by selling output would come to be distributed between the people who worked in factories and the capitalists who owned the factories.

> **division of labor:** an approach to production in which a process is broken down into smaller tasks, with each worker assigned only one or a few tasks
>
> **specialization:** in production, a system of organization in which each worker performs only one type of task
>
> Classical economists, from Adam Smith through Karl Marx, were interested in several questions that are still among the most important issues for macroeconomics: How is the total wealth generated by a society divided between those who own the means of production and those who

work for them? Is the existing division optimal? What are the forces that determine how society's wealth will be divided?

Smith is particularly known for promulgating the idea that market systems could coordinate the self-interested actions of individuals so that they would ultimately serve the social good. While Smith himself supported a number of government interventions and discussed the moral basis for social and economic behavior at length in others of his works, the school of classical economics has been popularly identified with the idea that individual self-interest is a positive force and that governments should let markets function without interference—that economies should be **laissez-faire**.

laissez-faire economy: an economy with little government regulation

The classical economists did not much address the problem of economic fluctuations. A smoothly functioning market system, a number of them thought, should be entirely self-regulating. At the macroeconomic level, full employment should generally prevail. This view was summarized in **Say's Law**, named after French classical economist Jean-Baptiste Say (1767–1832), which was said to prove that "supply creates its own demand." The example Say gave was of a tradesman, for example a shoemaker, who sold $100 worth of shoes. Say argued that the shoemaker would naturally want to spend the $100 on other goods, thereby creating a level of demand that was exactly equal in monetary value to the supply of shoes he had provided. If this example is extended to the whole economy, it suggests that the quantities demanded and quantities supplied of goods will exactly balance, meaning that employment—producing shoes or something else—will be available for anyone willing to work. Classical economists discussed issues related to a country's monetary system, but tended to assume that monetary issues affected only the price levels, and not the level of production, in a country.

Say's Law: the classical belief that "supply creates its own demand"

3.2 THE GREAT DEPRESSION, KEYNES, AND MONETARISM

Yet economies did not seem to be working so smoothly, in practice. Some periods, like 1904–06 and the 1920s in the United States, were boom years where everyone seemed eager to invest and spend. People with extra funds would buy stocks (ownership shares in companies) or deposit their funds in banks (to be lent to others) with great confidence and optimism. On the other hand, these booms seemed to frequently end in painful recessions. Suddenly the tide would turn and everyone would want to sell—not buy—and stock prices would plummet. A lack of confidence in banks would lead to "bank runs" or "banking panics," such as occurred in 1907 and 1930–33 in the United States, when many people tried to pull out their deposits all at once. With financial markets in tatters, businesses and individuals would be unable or unwilling to maintain or expand their activities. With people cutting back on spending, produced goods would go unsold. Industries would cut back on production. People would become unemployed.

A great many people in the United States (and much of the rest of the industrialized world) suffered considerable hardship during the Great Depression that followed the 1929 stock market crash. Production dropped by about 30 percent between 1929 and 1933. At its worst, the unemployment rate during the Great Depression topped 25 percent—one in four workers could not find a job. High unemployment persisted throughout the 1930s, and classical economic theory did not seem to be of much help in either explaining or correcting the situation.

The publication of British economist John Maynard Keynes' *The General Theory of Employment, Interest, and Money* in 1936 was a watershed event. In this book, Keynes (pronounced "canes") argued that Say's Law was wrong. It *is* possible for an economy to have a level of demand for goods that is insufficient to meet the supply from production, he said. In such a case, producers, unable to sell their goods, will cut back on production, laying off workers, and thus creating economic slumps. The key to getting out of such a slump, Keynes argued, is to increase **aggregate demand**—the total demand for goods and services in the national economy as a whole.

> **aggregate demand:** the total demand for all goods and services in a national economy

Keynes suggested a number of ways to achieve this. People could be encouraged to consume more, the government could buy more goods and services, or businesses could be encouraged to spend more. Some economists thought that the best way to encourage business spending was to keep interest rates low, so that businesses could borrow easily to invest in their enterprises. But, while Keynes believed that increasing investment spending would be the key to getting out of a depression, he thought that low interest rates alone would be insufficient to tempt discouraged and uncertain business leaders to start investing again. He wrote in *The General Theory* that the solution to business cycles lay in the government taking more direct control of the level of national investment. In his view capitalist economies were inherently unstable, and only a more socially oriented direction of investment could cure this instability.* This policy, however, was not generally adopted and the Great Depression continued for the remainder of the 1930s.

In actuality, it was the high government spending associated with national mobilization for World War II that finally brought the Great Depression to an end. Perhaps this is one reason why the followers of what came to be known as **Keynesian economics** did not follow Keynes on all points. While they retained his emphasis on deficiencies in aggregate demand, they tended to emphasize the use of fiscal policy to keep employment rates up. **Fiscal policy** is the manipulation of levels of government spending and taxation to raise or lower the level of aggregate demand.

> **Keynesian economics:** the school of thought, named after John Maynard Keynes, that argued for the active use of fiscal policy to keep aggregate demand high and employment rates up
>
> **fiscal policy:** the manipulation of levels of government spending and taxation to raise or lower the level of aggregate demand

Other economists in these post-WWII years—most notably University of Chicago economist Milton Friedman—took a different tack. While the Keynesians argued that active government fiscal policies were the way to get *out* of a recession, the **monetarists** argued that bad government **monetary policies** were how economies tend to get *into* bad situations in the first place. It was primarily the United States government's poor use of its monetary policy tools, such as banking regulations and the issuance of currency (most often understood as "printing money"), that led to the Great Depression, they said. They blamed government policies encouraging overly "loose" money (that is, easy credit, low interest rates, and high levels of money supply) for the overspending of the late 1920s. Then, they claimed, "tight" money policies (tight credit, higher-than-optimal interest rates, and low money supply) during the early 1930s turned what could have been a more minor slump into a major depression. They argued that governments should focus on keeping the money supply steady, and not try to take an active role in directing the economy, even when unemployment is high. Like the classical economists, they believed that the economy should best be left to adjust on its own.

---

* "It is the return of confidence, so to speak in ordinary language, which is so insusceptible to control in an economy of individualistic capitalism . . . I conclude that the duty of ordering the current volume of investment cannot safely be left in private hands" *The General Theory* (NY: Harcourt Brace Jovanovich, [1936] 1964), p. 317, 320.

> **monetarist economics:** the school that focused on the effects of monetary policy, and argued that governments should aim for steadiness in the money supply rather than play an active role
>
> **monetary policy:** the use of tools controlled by the government, such as banking regulations and the issuance of currency, to try to affect the levels of money supply, interest rates, and credit

As time went on, the Keynesian approach was expanded to include a role for monetary policy. This approach had a strong influence on macroeconomic policymaking in the United States and many other countries up through the 1960s. The idea became popular that the government might even be able to "fine tune" the economy, counteracting any tendencies to slump with expansionary (high spending and/or loose money) policies, and any excessive expansion with contractionary (low spending and/or tight money) policies, thereby largely eliminating business cycles. A related idea was that the government could choose to "trade off" unemployment and inflation—letting the economy suffer a little more inflation to get the unemployment rate down, or vice versa.

3.3 SYNTHESIZING CLASSICAL AND KEYNESIAN ECONOMICS

In the early 1970s this rosy picture was shattered, however, as many industrialized countries began to experience rising unemployment *without* a decrease in inflation. To explain this, many macroeconomists began combining elements of both classical and Keynesian economics, making a distinction between the long-run and the short-run as follows:

- Classical theories assert, first, that economies should naturally settle at full-employment levels of output and, second, that the primary outcome of changes in money supply are changes in the price level or rate of inflation. In an idealized smoothly functioning market system—as we will see in detail in a later chapter—any unemployment (that is, surplus of labor) should be corrected by a drop in the (equilibrium) wage. In the emerging synthesis, full employment and purely inflationary effects came to be thought of as *long-run* outcomes, which occur only after all markets have had sufficient time to adjust.
- Keynesian economists after World War II had come to accept the idea that their theories should be explainable in terms of market models, but explained unemployment as being due to the fact that markets for labor do not adjust quite as quickly as classical theory implies. Keynesian economists argued that wages are "sticky" in real-world markets and will not fall fast enough during a slump for full employment to be quickly restored. Fiscal and monetary policies were thought, in this emerging synthesis, to be effective mechanisms for coping with this *short-run* phenomenon.

Thus the dominant macroeconomic theory that emerged argued that in the short run—a period of some months or years—we are in a primarily Keynesian world where fiscal and monetary policies can be effective. In the long run, however—after such a period of time that even "sticky" markets are able to adjust—we are in a classical world, where markets adjustments assure full employment and money only affects prices.

Economists thus explained the inflation that occurred in the first few years of the 1970s (in spite of the simultaneous presence of unemployment) as the long-run outcome of expansionary monetary policies of the previous years. It appeared that short run active (Keynesian) government policies could have unintended negative long-term (classical) consequences.

While many economists have come to agree on this general theoretical picture, debates have continued, now centered around the question of whether the short-run benefits of active government policies are worth their long-run, presumably mostly negative, consequences.

Macroeconomists at the more classical end of the spectrum tend to emphasize market efficiency and a small role for government. They are suspicious about the use of monetary policy because of the possible negative effects we just discussed. They are suspicious about the use of fiscal policy, as well, arguing that increases in government spending or taxation primarily lead to a larger government. Large governments, they believe, discourage private sector activities and economic growth.

Economists on the more Keynesian end of the spectrum, meanwhile, tend to emphasize the way in which unemployment can cause severe human suffering and be very persistent. They argue for a more active role for government. Waiting for markets to adjust on their own, they believe, may mean waiting too long. And, as Keynes himself put in, "In the long run, we are all dead."

While it might seem that many economists have finally come to at least a general agreement about how the macroeconomy works, real-world developments have brought still new issues to public attention.

3.4 SUBSEQUENT CHALLENGES

In 1973–74 the macroeconomic environment of the United States and most other industrialized economies took a sharp hit when countries belonging to the Organization of Petroleum Exporting Countries (OPEC) cut production, drastically increased the price at which they would sell crude oil, and even for several months completely stopped shipping oil to certain nations. The price of oil, a key input to many production and consumption activities, suddenly quadrupled. Stock markets fell, inflation rose, and unemployment shot up as people struggled to adjust. People waited in long lines at gas stations, or were even limited to buying gas only on certain days. The price of crude oil continued to rise until at its peak in 1979 a barrel of crude oil in the United States cost over ten times as much as it had in 1973.

This crisis brought increased attention to two areas. First, the oil price shock made it clear how closely national economies are tied to each other. While many previous theories had neglected to take into account international linkages, the implications of globalization now became more prominent in macroeconomic thinking. Second, while Keynes had led the field into paying attention to aggregate *demand,* this "supply shock" encouraged economists to think more about the *supply* side of the economy—the resources and technology that allow production to occur. In later chapters of this book, you will study some of the theories economists have created to try to explain these phenomena.

3.5 MACROECONOMICS FOR THE TWENTY-FIRST CENTURY

While issues of economic growth and the business cycle preoccupied macroeconomic thinking for generations, once again, in the twenty-first century, new developments are demanding new ways of looking at the economic world.

First, the environmental impact of long-term, fossil-fuel-based economic growth is becoming increasingly a topic of economic, social, and political concern. Most previous theories assumed that resources and the capacity of the environment to absorb the by-products of economic growth were essentially unlimited—or at least that continued developments in technology would keep problems of depletion and pollution at bay. This is increasingly questioned as the scale of human economic activity grows larger.

The graphs of economic growth, seen earlier in this chapter, illustrate an impressive human ability to increase production. The growth in global atmospheric carbon dioxide illustrated in Figure 1.4 is equally impressive, but more sobering, as it shows the human ability to affect our

Figure 1.4 **Growth in Atmospheric Carbon Dioxide, 1800–2004**

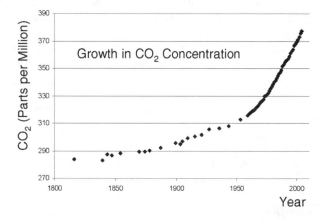

As fossil-fuel based industrialization and deforestation have increased, so has the atmospheric concentration of the gases involved in global warming. (Source: Carbon Dioxide Information Analysis Center, http://cdiac. ornl.gov/ftp/trends/co2/siple2.013 and http://cdiac.ornl.gov/trends/co2/sio-mlo.htm)

environment significantly—sometimes in dangerous ways. Carbon dioxide is released in fossil-fuel-burning industrial production, transportation, and heating, and more is released the more such production takes place. Deforestation also contributes to increases in atmospheric CO_2. Carbon dioxide is the main gas involved in global climate change, a problem that scientists say is already starting to cause floods, droughts, and irreversible disturbances to ecosystems.

Unless slowed or reversed, within the next twenty years we can expect to see increasingly dramatic disturbances to agriculture, disruptions in water supply, and an expansion of the reach of tropical diseases. How national and international economic environments can be made ecologically sustainable, while keeping employment and standards of living high, is rising in prominence as a macroeconomic issue. New thinking about the relation between production and living standards, and about the quality of our working lives, will likely be central to these discussions.

Second, the persistence of substantial global poverty, as mentioned in the earlier discussion of social sustainability, has called into question the appropriateness of traditional ideas about economic development. Questions of *what, how* and *for whom*—rather than just "how much"—are becoming increasingly important in evaluating the effect of economic activity on human well-being. The lopsided global distribution of resources, disparities in power, war and peace, and global institutions of trade and finance will become increasingly important issues as economists continue to participate in the humanitarian attempt to increase human well-being on a global scale.

Discussion Questions

1. What were some of the major historical events that influenced the development of macroeconomics as a field of study? In addition to the problems listed in the text, do you think there are other current problems that macroeconomics should be addressing?

2. It might be confusing to you to realize that there are a number of alternative "schools" of macroeconomic thought, and that the field continues to develop. It may help to think about, or discuss in a group, how economics compares to other subjects you or your classmates have studied. Do you think that physics or biology are the same now as they were a hundred years ago? Have you found that all psychologists, sociologists, and political scientists have settled on explaining things the same way? Or are there disagreements and new developments in those fields as well?

REVIEW QUESTIONS

1. What is economics?
2. How does macroeconomics differ from microeconomics?
3. What is the difference between positive and normative questions?
4. What is meant by "living standards growth"? Is this the same as "economic growth"?
5. What is economic development? What factors are important in ensuring that economic growth benefits a country's population as a whole?
6. Why are macroeconomic fluctuations a cause for concern?
7. What global developments have caused financial, social, and ecological sustainability to become increasingly prominent as macroeconomic concerns?
8. What is the "precautionary principle"?
9. What historical developments and concerns motivated—and what beliefs characterized—the classical economists? The work of John Maynard Keynes? The school of Keynesian economics? The work of the monetarists? The synthesis of Keynesian and classical thought?
10. What historical development took place in 1973–74, and what ongoing macroeconomic issues did it bring into focus?
11. What are two recent developments that will likely shape the development of macroeconomics in the twenty-first century?

EXERCISES

1. The more you pay attention to what is going on in the macroeconomy around you, the more meaningful this class will be to you. Find an article in a newspaper or newsmagazine (hard copy or on-line) that deals with a macroeconomic topic. Make a list of terms, concepts, people, organizations, or historical events mentioned in the article that are also mentioned in this chapter.
2. Classify each of the following as to whether it is an example of a positive question or a normative question.
   a. "What is the level of U.S. foreign debt?"
   b. "How low should the unemployment rate be?"
   c. "What policies can lower the unemployment rate?"
   d. "What kinds of production should be counted in measuring gross domestic product?"
   e. "Is it better to have low unemployment or low inflation?"
3. State whether the following statements are true or false. If false, also write a corrected statement.

a. Macroeconomics is about the activities of governmental agencies.
b. Economic growth always leads to living standards growth.
c. The three areas to consider in thinking about sustainability are financial, monetary, and ecological.
d. About 20 percent of the world's population lives in absolute poverty.
e. Poor countries were offered many foreign loans for economic development over the last several decades; now all of them are paying back the loans easily.

4. State whether the following statements are true or false. If false, also write a corrected statement.
   a. Fiscal policy refers to government influences on credit and interest rates.
   b. Specialization and the division of labor are characteristics of industrial production.
   c. Classical economists believe that the Great Depression was caused by aggregate demand being too low.
   d. During "bank runs" and stock market crashes, people lose confidence in the financial system and tend to cut back on their spending.
   e. Keynesian economists believe that an economy that experiences a high rate of unemployment will quickly self-correct.

5. Match each concept in Column A with a definition or example in Column B.

Column A	Column B
a. Keynesian economics	1. Lowering the tax rate on corporations
b. Classical economics	2. Studies how economics applies at the national and global level
c. Monetary policy	3. "It is not possible, at a national level, for there to be more goods and services supplied than people want to buy."
d. Fiscal policy	4. GDP rises as a heavily polluting factory begins production
e. Living standards growth	5. A school that focuses on aggregate demand and encourages government action
f. Business cycle	6. Government encouragement of easy credit
g. Monetarism	7. The short-run fluctuations of a national economy
h. Macroeconomics	8. The school of economic thought originally associated with the idea of laissez-faire economics
i. Say's law	9. More of the population gets access to basic health care
j. Microeconomics	10. Studies how economics applies at the level of households, businesses, and other organizations
k. Economic growth	11. A school that argues that active government monetary policies usually make economic fluctuations worse

NOTE

1. This well-known formulation of the precautionary principle, sometimes called "the Wingspread statement," was spelled out in a January 1998 meeting of scientists, lawyers, policymakers, and environmentalists at Wingspread, the headquarters of the Johnson Foundation in Racine, Wisconsin.

2 Useful Tools and Concepts

Economists have developed a number of basic concepts that are useful when we want to describe how an economy works, and to think about how we, in our private roles and through government action, might make it work better. This chapter will present some of the most important concepts in economics, including how to approach trade-offs (when we have to choose among different things we might want); what markets really are (hint: they aren't just one thing); and the importance, in economics, of such abstract things as trust and money. (You didn't think money was abstract? Wait and see!) Before we get into these concepts, however, we'll review economists' basic tools of investigation. The concepts and methods we discuss in this chapter will reappear throughout the book and help us better understand modern macroeconomic debates.

1. OUR TOOLS FOR UNDERSTANDING

Explaining macroeconomic phenomena, we will see, involves using three main modes of investigation: empirical, theoretical, and historical.

> Three main modes of investigation are empirical, theoretical, and historical

1.1 EMPIRICAL INVESTIGATION

Empirical investigation is observation and recording of specific happenings in the world. It is convenient when the happenings of interest can be adequately described in terms of numerical data. However, useful empirical investigation of a specific item of interest may also be represented in words or images.

> **empirical investigation:** observation and recording of the specific phenomena of concern

When the observations take the form of showing how a numerical economic variable changes over time, we call them **time series data**. We saw important examples of time series data in Chapter 1, in graphs that showed how production and atmospheric carbon dioxide levels have grown over time.

> **time series data:** observations of how a numerical variable changes over time

We will be seeing many such graphs in this book—for price levels, employment, exchange rates, and other economic variables. The accompanying Math Review box will help you refresh your skills in working with data and graphs.

It is tempting to think that if two economic variables have an empirical relationship with each other, that there must be some kind of *underlying* relation between the two—or, in particular,

Math Review: Graphing Empirical Data

To help you review your math skills, we will recreate a famous macroeconomic graph. The Phillips curve, originally derived by economist A.W. Phillips using British data, played a very important role in U.S. economic theorizing and policymaking, especially during the 1960s.

First, we can present the data in terms of a table. Table 2.1 presents data for the years 1963–69, showing the average unemployment rate for the United States and the year-to-year inflation rate (i.e., the rate at which prices rose from one year to the next).

We can interpret this data in visual form, using graphs. Figure 2.1 plots the evolution of the unemployment rate as a time series, with the year on the horizontal or X axis, and the unemployment rate on the vertical or Y axis. For example, the third point from the left in Figure 2.1 represents the fact that, in the year 1965, the unemployment rate was 4.5 percent. What does the point labeled with a question mark represent? Figure 2.1 presents a visual picture of the fact that unemployment fell fairly steadily throughout this period. Figure 2.2, also a time-series graph, reveals that inflation steadily rose over this same time period. You can create graphs such as these by carefully plotting the axes and data points on graph paper, or entering the data into a computer spreadsheet or presentation program and then generating a chart.

We might also be interested in how the two measures empirically relate *to each other* over time. For this, we can make a scatter plot graph, as shown in Figure 2.3. For example, the dot to the far right in this graph indicates that when the unemployment rate was 5.7 percent, inflation was 1.1 percent. The label on the point tells us that the year when this occurred was 1963. Interpret another point on the graph, with reference to Table 2.1, for practice.

When high values for one variable are associated with low values for the other (and low with high), we say the two variables have a **negative or inverse relationship**. On a scatter plot graph, such data points look as if could be grouped around an (imagined) downward-sloping line. Conversely, when high values for one variable are associated with high values for another, and low with low, we say the two variables have a **positive or direct relationship**. On a graph, such a pattern of points suggests a upward-sloping line. Sometimes in empirical data such relationships, one way or the other, are very apparent. Other times, the data points may seem to be randomly scattered across a graph (or lie on perfectly horizontal or vertical lines), and so neither type of empirical relationship is apparent. If you study statistics and econometrics, you will learn how to describe empirical economic relationships (or the lack thereof) in a more formal and detailed way.

In the case of inflation and unemployment rates over this period in the 1960s, the data points seem to form a very clear pattern. We have added a smooth line to Figure 2.3 that comes very close to going through every data point. Anyone looking at this graph would conclude that inflation and unemployment are *negatively or inversely* related in these data. It seems that *low* unemployment is associated with *high* inflation. The smooth line drawn in Figure 2.3 is the famous Phillips curve.

> **negative (or inverse) relationship:** the relationship between two variables if an increase in one is associated with a decrease in the other
>
> **positive (or direct) relationship:** the relationship between two variables when an increase in one is associated with an increase in the other

Table 2.1   **Unemployment and Inflation, 1963-69**

Year	Unemployment Rate (percent)	Inflation Rate (percent per year)
1963	5.7	1.1
1964	5.2	1.5
1965	4.5	1.8
1966	3.8	2.8
1967	3.8	3.1
1968	3.6	4.3
1969	3.5	5.0

Source: Economic Report of the President.

Figure 2.1   **The U.S. Unemployment Rate, 1963–69**

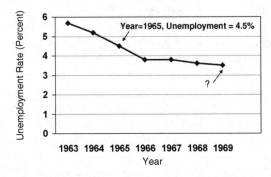

During this period in the 1960s, the unemployment rate was generally falling.

Figure 2.2   **The U.S. Inflation Rate, 1963–69**

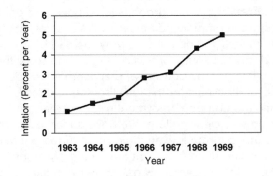

During this period in the 1960s, the inflation rate rose from year to year.

Figure 2.3 **The Empirical Relation between Unemployment and Inflation in the United States, 1963–69**

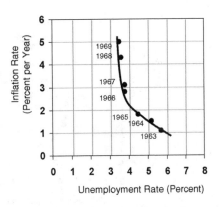

The smooth line that can be fitted to data points such as these became known as the Phillips curve.

that changes in one variable must be *causing* changes in the other. Sometimes this is true. In the case of the upward trends over time that we saw for both global production and carbon dioxide levels, as shown in Chapter 1, there *is* causality: Growing industrial production has led, over time, to increasing accumulations of CO_2. There are good scientific reasons to believe that the rise in accumulated carbon dioxide we observed in Figure 1.4 is a direct result of years of fossil-fuels-intensive economic growth, as we observed in Figures 1.1 and 1.3.

But two variables may be related empirically (or be "correlated" with each other, to use the statistical term) *without* there being a well-defined causal relationship between them. In the case of unemployment rates and inflation, graphed in the Math Review box, the two economic variables display a very strong empirical inverse relation for the period 1963–69. As we mentioned in Chapter 1, many economists during this period came to believe that this association was based on an underlying causal relationship. They thought that the government could "trade off" inflation and unemployment, suffering a little more inflation in order to get more people working. That is, it was thought that the government could make unemployment rates fall by allowing some additional inflation.

> The existence of an observable relationship between two economic variables does not imply that changes in one variable *cause* changes in the other. An important warning to keep in mind in all empirical work is that "correlation does not imply causality."

We can see why this sort of thinking had to be modified when we add data points for later years. In 1970 inflation continued to rise slightly, to 5.3 percent, while the unemployment rate unexpectedly also *rose,* to 4.9 percent. As you can see in Figure 2.4, the idea that there was a clear, causal relationship between these two variables became far less plausible as the nation moved into the 1970s and 1980s!

Empirical investigation creates the foundation for relevant macroeconomic analysis. Looking at the puzzle presented by the data on unemployment and inflation, we can see, however, that more tools are clearly needed if economists are to try to *explain,* rather than simply describe, macroeconomic phenomena.

Figure 2.4   **The Empirical Relation between Unemployment and Inflation in the United States, 1963–83**

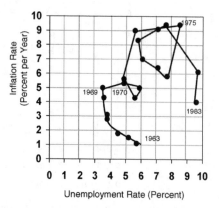

The inverse relationship suggested by the Phillips curve during the 1960s disappeared as the nation moved into the 1970s and 1980s.

1.2 THEORETICAL INVESTIGATION

The adjective "empirical" is usually contrasted with "theoretical," where the latter refers to statements made on the basis of mental constructs and processes, such as assumptions and logical deductions. This book will introduce, at length, the economists' **theories** of macroeconomics.

As you will see, the theories we introduce are often based on "thought experiments." Rarely having access to controlled laboratory experiments, as in the physical sciences, economists create theories based on assumptions about economic agents and institutions, from which, with careful reasoning, they draw out potential implications for economic behavior.

> **theoretical investigation:** analysis based in abstract thought

In the mid-1960s, for example, economists created theories that plausibly (that is, believably) explained how the downward-sloping Phillips curve might have come about. They made assumptions about how workers and investors would respond to monetary and fiscal policies and other economic conditions. They created plausible stories about a chain of events that would connect higher inflation to more people wanting to offer or accept jobs.

In order to make it possible to build a theory, it is sometimes useful temporarily to isolate certain aspects of economic behavior from their larger historical and environmental context, in order to examine more closely the complex elements involved. A **model** is an analytical tool that highlights some aspects of reality while ignoring others. It can take the form of a simplified story, an image, a figure, a graph, or a set of equations, and it always involves simplifying assumptions. We'll take a look at a couple of examples of economic models later in this chapter when we examine the production-possibility frontier and the basic neoclassical model. Other models will appear as examples throughout this course.

> **model:** an analytical tool that highlights some aspects of reality while ignoring others

An important part of many models is the **ceteris paribus** assumption. This Latin phrase means "other things equal" or "all else constant." In the models built around the Phillips curve relation in the mid-1960s, for example, one of the things "held constant" was people's expectations about future inflation. The models assumed that even though inflation was rising steadily, people essentially wouldn't notice. This assumption seemed to hold reasonably well for the period 1963–69. Most economists now believe, however, that one of the main reasons for the jump in unemployment in 1970 was that people started to *expect* inflation, and to build inflation adjustments (such as cost-of-living raises) into the contracts they made for employment. The theory built around the Phillips curve assumed that something (expectations) would stay constant, and the theory provided a plausible description of reality only as long as this ceteris paribus assumption held. When it ceased to hold, new theories—now including an additional factor of *expectations*—were created.

> **ceteris paribus:** a Latin phrase meaning "other things equal" or "all else constant"

Theorizing takes place in economists' heads—hence the term "thought experiment." "Is the resulting theory true?" you may rightly wonder. Generally, that is not a question that can be strictly answered "yes" or "no," since our theories reflect only some selected aspects of the real world. Better questions to ask about economic theories include "Is the theory helpful in giving insight?" "Does it focus on things that we consider important?" Models can be useful—even though they require temporarily setting aside many complications and much of the larger context—when they are understood simply as tools to understanding, and when they remain open to revision as history evolves and new evidence is acquired.

1.3 HISTORICAL INVESTIGATION

Throughout the book, we will include a crucial third mode: knowledge of **historical** events—observations of happenings in the near or distant past, within the context of what went before and what came after, that are broader than the more narrowly focused empirical investigation. The Great Depression of the 1930s, any major war, the Bretton Woods monetary agreement of 1947, the oil crisis of 1973, the invention of computers, the entry of women into market work, and the growing concern about environmental issues—all are examples of historical events that have had significant macroeconomic impact.

> **historical investigation:** study of past events

Economists have become increasingly aware that, while gathering and analyzing data and thinking theoretically about what *could* be true are valid and important tasks, a knowledge of the real-world evolution of political, economic, and social life is indispensable to understanding macroeconomics.

Discussion Questions

1. Consider the following examples of investigation. For each one, indicate which mode of investigation it most closely represents—empirical, theoretical, or historical.
   a. A biologist tries to determine the number of different species of plants found on a plot of rainforest
   b. Albert Einstein develops his theory of relativity
   c. An economist measures how GDP varies across countries
   d. The political unrest in the United States during the 1960s and 1970s is explained primarily as a result of the Vietnam War
   e. An economist states that a rise in inflation will lead to a fall in unemployment

2. Model building is sometimes compared to map making. If someone asks you how to get to your house, what will you put on the map you draw for them? On the other hand, what if the question asked has to do with the location of the highest point in town, or the town's political boundaries, or how your dwelling links up to the local sewer system? Is it possible for a single, readable map to answer every possible question? Does the goal you have in mind for the map affect what you put on it?

2. ECONOMIC TRADEOFFS

As individuals, and as members of a larger society, people make choices about *what* should be produced, *how* it should be produced, and *for whom* it should be produced.

2.1 ABUNDANCE AND SCARCITY

When you think of all the abundant natural resources in our world, all the human time and intelligence that exist, all the investments that have been made in organizing human societies, and the massive stock of machinery and other productive resources now accumulated, you realize that the world is wealthy indeed. Although the distribution of resources is far from even, across countries or among people within countries, contemporary human society as a whole still has a rich resource base on which to build. No wonder that many world religions and ethical teachings encourage an attitude of gratefulness on the part of their adherents toward the sources of life's **abundance**.

> **abundance:** resources are abundant to the extent that they exist in plentiful supply for meeting various goals

It may seem odd, then, that many economists emphasize the notion of **scarcity**—that is, the notion that there is too little to go around—when discussing society's choices concerning *what, how* and for *whom*. What this really means is that even with all the available resources, and even with a steady eye on the goal of well-being, not everything that is socially desirable can be accomplished, at least not all at once.* The current capacity of a particular hospital, for example, may allow it to increase the number of heart transplants it performs *or* increase the amount of care it can provide for the severely mentally ill, but not both. A given resource, such as an hour of your time, when dedicated to one beneficial activity (such as studying) will be unavailable for certain other beneficial activities (such as relaxing with your friends). Choices have to be made.

> **scarcity:** resources are scarce to the extent that they are not sufficient to allow all goals to be accomplished at once

Macroeconomics is centrally concerned with how an overall economic environment emerges from the choices made by individuals and organizations, and to what extent choices made by governments can make this economic environment better or worse.

---

* An alternative definition of scarcity, dating to the 1930s, defined resources as scarce relative to presumably unlimited human *wants,* without any question of whether these wants promoted well-being or not.

2.2 SOCIETY'S PRODUCTION-POSSIBILITIES FRONTIER

Economists use the notion of a societal production-possibilities frontier to illustrate concepts of scarcity, tradeoffs, and efficiency. To make matters very simple, let's assume that society is considering only two possible flows of output over the coming year, which are to be made from a given stock of currently available resources, using the current state of technology. (The question of how much of the total resource stock of a society should be considered "currently available" will be taken up in the next section.) The classic example is to take guns as one output and butter as the other. In more general terms, the guns-and-butter tradeoff can refer to any society's more general, and real-world, choice between becoming a more militarized society (guns) and becoming a more civilian- or consumer-oriented society (butter).

Figure 2.5 shows a **production-possibilities frontier** (PPF) for this case. In this graph, the quantity of butter produced over a year is measured on the horizontal axis. The quantity of guns is measured on the vertical axis. The points on the PPF curve illustrate the maximum quantities of guns and butter that the society could produce. For example, point A, where the curve intersects the horizontal axis, shows that this society can produce 120 units of butter if it does not produce any guns. Moving up and to the left, point B illustrates production, over the year, of 60 units of butter and 8 units of guns. (At this level of abstraction, it is not necessary to be specific about what is meant by "units." You may imagine these as kilos of butter and numbers of guns, if you like.) If the society produces no butter, how many guns can it produce? While it may seem odd to think about a society that only produces two goods, the PPF figure is nevertheless helpful for illustrating several important economic concepts.

> **production-possibilities frontier (PPF):** a curve showing the maximum amounts of two outputs that society could produce from given resources, over a given time period

Scarcity. Point C in Figure 2.5 represents a production combination that is not attainable, given existing resources. To produce at that point would take more resources than society has. The PPF is specifically defined so that only those points on or inside it represent outputs that can actually be produced.

Tradeoffs. Points that lie on the PPF illustrate the important notion that scarcity creates a need for tradeoffs. Along the frontier, one can get more of one output only by "trading off" some of the other. Figure 2.5 illustrates the important concept of **opportunity cost**. Opportunity cost is the value of the best alternative to the choice one actually makes. Looking at the PPF, we see that the cost of increasing gun production is less butter. For example, suppose the economy is at Point A, producing 120 units of butter and no guns, but then decides that it needs to produce eight guns. Point B illustrates that after some resources have been moved from butter production into producing the eight guns, the maximum amount of butter that can be produced is 60 units. The gain of eight guns comes at a "cost" to the economy of a loss of 60 units of butter. Likewise, starting from a point where the economy is producing some guns, the "cost" of producing more butter would be fewer guns.

> **opportunity cost:** the value of the best alternative that is foregone when a choice is made

Efficiency. An **efficient** process is one that uses the *minimum value of resources* to achieve the desired result. Put another way, efficiency is achieved when the *maximum value of output* is produced from a given set of inputs. Points that lie *on* the PPF illustrate the maximum combinations that a society can produce. But what about points *inside* the frontier, such as point D? At point D, the economy is not producing as much as it could. It is producing 40 units of butter and 4 guns, even though it *could* produce more of one or the other, or both. Some resources

Figure 2.5   **Society's Production-Possibilities Frontier**

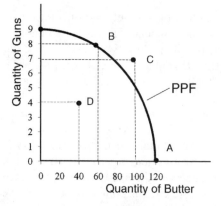

The PPF diagram illustrates the concept of scarcity, since combinations of goods that lie outside the frontier (such as C) are not attainable. A comparison of points that lie on the curve (such as A and B) illustrates the concept of trade-offs, since with efficient production the quantity of butter must fall if the quantity of guns produced rises. Inefficient use of resources is illustrated by points (such as D) that are inside the curve.

are apparently being wasted. There are at least three reasons why this could occur. First, the resources may be wasted because they are being left idle. For example, workers may be left unemployed, or cows could be left unmilked. Second, even if resources are fully employed, the technology and social organization being applied to the resources may be less than the best. For example, suppose the gun factory is poorly designed, so that a lot of the workers' time is wasted carting parts from one area to another. In this case, a better, more efficient organization of the work flow could increase production, with no increase in resources. Third, the allocation of resources between the two production activities (that is, guns and butter) might not be optimal. For example, if gun factories are built on the best pasture land when they could just as well be built on poorer land, the ability of the economy to graze cows and produce butter would be hampered. When an economy is imagined to be *on* the PPF, and thus producing efficiently, the only way to produce more of one good is to produce less of the other. If an economy is *inside* the PPF, on the other hand, it is producing inefficiently, and improvements in the employment of resources, the application of available technology and social organization, or allocation of resources among production activities could allow it to move toward the frontier (that is, to produce more of both goods).

> **efficiency:** the use of resources in a way that does not waste any inputs. Inputs are used in such a way that they yield the highest possible value of output, or a given output is produced using the lowest possible value of inputs.

The bowed-out shape of the curve comes from the fact that some resources are likely to be more suited for production of one good than for the other. We can see, for example, that the society only has to give up 60 units of butter production to get the first eight guns. Workers, for example, can be pulled out of butter production and set to work on relatively plentiful supplies of the materials most suited for guns, such as easily tapped veins of iron ore and minerals for gunpowder. Gun manufacturing plants can—if allocation decisions are made wisely—be built on land unsuitable for pasture. The last single gun, on the other hand, gained by moving from point B up to where the PPF hits the vertical axis, comes at the cost of 60 units of butter! Pulling the remaining workers and land out of butter production, and directing the workers toward increasingly less accessible veins of mineral ores, or to the now-crowded gun assembly lines, dramatically decreases butter production while adding little to the production of guns.

Of course, we could put on the axis many other pairs of outputs, besides guns and butter, and still illustrate these concepts. We could look at Coke and pizza, cars and bicycles, or health care and highways. This classic example, however, is a good one. In the real world, such guns/butter or militarization/peacetime tradeoffs can be crucially important. (See the accompanying Economics in the Real World box.)

What precise combination of outputs, such as guns and butter, or health care and highways, should society choose to produce? The PPF does *not* answer this question. The curve shows the range of efficient possibilities, but does not tell us which one of these combinations of outputs is best. To determine this, we would have to know more about a society's requirements and priorities. Is civilian satisfaction a high priority? Then the society would lean toward production of butter. Does the society fear attack by a foreign power? Perhaps then it would choose a point more toward the guns axis. For good social decision making, this production question would have to be considered right alongside questions of resource maintenance, distribution, and consumption, since all have effects on well-being. In a society with free speech and democratic discussion, there is wide room for disagreement about what the best mix of goods might be. The PPF provides a mental image for thinking about scarcity, tradeoffs, and efficiency but does not, itself, tell us how to choose among the possibilities it illustrates.

2.3 TRADEOFFS OVER TIME

We have said that a PPF reflects possible production combinations given the stock of currently available resources, and using the current state of technology. These ideas deserve more investigation. If we remember that achieving well-being involves questions of *how* and *for whom,* then the question becomes complex. For example, we generally want to conserve resources so that we can produce goods not only right now but later in our lives. And we have an obligation to future generations to include them in our considerations of *for whom.*

Some production activities are also resource-maintenance activities, of course, and the flow of output from these adds to the stock of resources available for the future. Investments in plant and equipment can provide productive capacity not just for a few months, but often for years. Production of goods and services that protect the environment, or that encourage the formation of new forms of knowledge and social organization, also lead to an improved resource base. **Technological progress** can lead to long-run improvements in productive capacity. New technologies can create new, more efficient methods for converting resources into outputs—or even create kinds of products never before imagined. To the extent that production is of this sort, production can *add* to the production possibilities for the future. The PPF may expand over time, out and to the right, making previously unobtainable points obtainable, as shown in Figure 2.6.

> **technological progress:** the development of new products and new, more efficient, methods of production

Some productive activities contribute an ongoing flow of outputs without drawing down the stock of capital resources. Sustainable production activities, such as some agricultural and forestry processes when they are suitably planned and carried out, may not add to the resource base, but neither do they deplete it.

But many other productive activities lead to resource depletion or degradation. The intensive use of fossil fuels is now depleting petroleum reserves, degrading air quality, and contributing

Economics in the Real World:
The Opportunity Cost of Military Expenditures

What do military buildups and wars really cost? One way to look at this is to consider what else could have been bought with the money spent on armaments.

World military expenditures in 2006 totaled $1,204 billion, or 2.5 percent of world GDP. This represents a 37 percent increase, in real terms, over the previous ten years. The United States is by far the biggest spender, accounting on its own for 46 percent of the global total. The United Kingdom, France, China, and Japan are the next biggest military spenders. Smaller and poorer countries spend less, but some of the poorest countries—including Eritrea and Burundi—spend more on the military than they do on public services such as health and education. Where do such countries get their weapons? The United States and Russia are the leading suppliers of military goods to international markets.

Meanwhile, about ten million children every year—over 27,000 every day—die before they reach the age of five, most of them from malnutrition and poverty. The Millenium Development Goals set out by the United Nations aspire to cutting the rates of extreme poverty in half, and improving health, literacy, gender equity, and environmental sustainability in the poorest areas of the world. All this comes at a cost, of course. The amount of money that would be needed to achieve these goals has been estimated to be between $121 and $189 billion per year, from now until 2015—that is, about 10–15 percent of what is currently spent on arms. This amount of funding has not been forthcoming, however, and indications are that a number of the goals will not be met. (See Chapter 15.)

As former U.S. president Dwight D. Eisenhower said back in 1953, "Every gun that is made, every warship launched, every rocket fired, signifies in the final sense a theft from those who hunger and are not fed, those who are cold and are not clothed."

Sources: Stockholm International Peace Research Institute, *SIPRI Yearbook 2007* (Stockholm, 2007); United Nations Development Project, *Human Development Report 2007/2008* (New York, 2007); The Millennium Project, *Investing in Development: A Practical Plan to Achieve the Millennium Development Goals* (New York, 2005).

to global climate change. Production processes that destroy important watersheds and wildlife habitats are also resource-depleting. Mind-numbing drudgery, or work in dangerous circumstances, can degrade human resources by leaving people exhausted or in bad mental or physical health. These kinds of productive activities are at odds with resource maintenance.

Taking a longer-term view, then, it is clear that getting the absolute most production, right now, out of the available resources is not an intelligent social goal. Decisions such as guns vs. butter need to be accompanied by another decision about now vs. later. What needs to be currently produced, what needs to be maintained, and what investments are needed to increase future productivity?

Figure 2.7 shows a production/maintenance frontier, which illustrates the tradeoff between resource-depleting kinds of production and resource-maintenance activities (the latter including

Figure 2.6   **An Expanded Production-Possibilities Frontier**

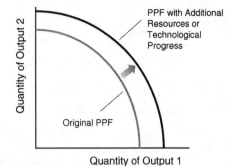

When the PPF moves "out" (away from the origin) our choices are still constrained, but, overall, it becomes possible to get more of both things, as compared to the "lower" PPF.

both conservation and investment). Point A illustrates a societal decision to engage in considerable resource-depleting production in the present year, while putting little emphasis on maintenance for the future. Point B illustrates a decision to engage in a higher level of maintenance this year and in a lower level of resource-depleting production.

The consequences of choosing between points A and B are illustrated in Figure 2.8, where once again we portray a two-output (such as guns-vs.-butter) PPF. Now, however, the depiction is of some time in the future, following the current choice between A and B. As Figure 2.8 shows, a decision to maintain more for the future, by choosing point B in Figure 2.7, leads to a larger set of production possibilities in future years. A decision to engage in considerable resource deple-tion, by choosing point A in Figure 2.7, leads to the smaller future PPF shown in Figure 2.8.

Of course, some will argue that advances in technology (which we have included as a re-source-maintaining type of production) will always push out the PPF (as in Figure 2.6) more than resource depletion will pull it in (as in Figure 2.8). But this is no more than an assertion of belief. If this belief turns out not to be warranted, then acting on the basis of it may lead to large-scale, unfortunate, and irreversible consequences.

Discussion Questions

    1. Suppose that your study time can be allocated either to studying for this course or to studying for another course. Your two "outputs" are your grades in each course. Draw a production possibilities curve for these two outputs. Would the curve be shaped like the PPF in Figure 2.5? Discuss.

    2. Consider the following activities. Which ones do you think would expand society's PPF in the future? Which ones would shrink it? (There may be room for disagree-ment on some.)

       a. Increasing education spending

       b. Increasing the production of sport utility vehicles

       c. Building a nuclear power plant

       d. Restoring wetlands

       e. Building a new interstate highway

       f. Expanding Internet capacity

Figure 2.7   **Society's Production/Maintenance Frontier**

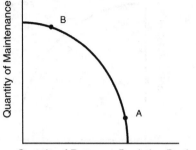

We choose not only what to produce, but how to produce it; some production methods are more resource-depleting than others.

Figure 2.8   **Possible Future PPFs**

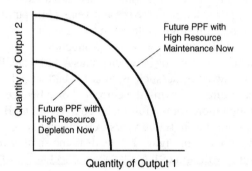

Present-day decisions about how to produce will affect future possibilities concerning what can be produced.

3. THE ROLE OF MARKETS

As we saw in Chapter 1, one of the major areas of interest—and dispute—among economists concerns how markets function. Those who develop theories along the lines of classical economics believe that market systems function fairly smoothly and are largely self-regulating. Those who lean more toward the Keynesian side believe that market economies need some help from government policy to serve goals of human well-being. But what do economists mean by "markets"?

3.1 THE MEANING OF MARKETS

When people talk about markets, they may be referring to a number of different meanings of the word, from very concrete to very abstract. In the language of economics there are at least three different uses of the word "market," and the appropriate meaning must be judged from the context in which it appears. We will start with the most concrete and move toward the more abstract definitions.

The most concrete and commonsense definition of a market is the idea that a **market** is a *location*—that is, a *place* where people go to buy and sell things. This is historically appropriate: Markets such as the Grand Bazaar in Istanbul, or African village produce stands, have flourished for ages as meeting places for people who wish to make exchange transactions. The same criterion applies today, even when the "market" has become a shopping center or mall, with many retail stores sharing one huge building, or a stock or commodity exchange, where brokers stand on a crowded floor and wave signals to each other. A market, as suggested by these examples, can be defined as a physical place where there is a reasonable expectation of finding both buyers and sellers for the same product or service.

> **market** (first meaning): a physical place where there is a reasonable expectation of finding both buyers and sellers for the same product or service

However not all markets are physical places where buyers and sellers interact. We can think of markets in more general terms as *institutions* that bring buyers and sellers together.

Institutions are ways of structuring the interactions between individuals and groups. Like markets, institutions can also be thought of in concrete or abstract terms. A hospital can be considered an institution that structures the interactions between doctors and patients. A university is an institution that structures the interactions between professors and students. But institutions can also be embodied in the customs and laws of a society. For example, marriage is an institution that places some structure on family relationships. Laws, courts, and police forces are institutions that structure the acceptable and unacceptable ways that individuals and groups interact.

> **institutions:** ways of structuring interactions between individuals and groups, including both formally constituted establishments and the generally recognized patterns of organization embodied in customs, habits, and laws

When we think of markets as institutions, we see that a market does not need to be a physical location. Internet auctions, such as eBay, are market institutions that bring buyers and sellers together. The New York Stock Exchange can be considered both a physical location—a building on Wall Street where brokers buy and sell stocks—and an institution where investors all over the world interact indirectly according to a set of established rules and structures.

> **market** (second meaning): an institution that brings buyers and sellers into communication with each other, structuring and coordinating their actions

Thinking of markets as institutions, rather than concrete places, leads to various ways of discussing *particular* markets. Many economists spend much of their time investigating one or more such specific institutional markets. They may track the trades made at various prices over time for a specific good, such as heating oil or AT&T bonds, try to forecast what might happen in the future, or advise on the specifics of market structures. When such an economist speaks of a market, he or she most often means the institutional market for such a specific good.

In this sense, several different markets may operate under one roof, within the same organization. For example, in the United States the Chicago Board of Trade operates many markets for a variety of farm products, including wheat, corn, and soybeans, among many others. Indeed, even a term such as "wheat" may be too general to define a market for some purposes, given the existence of such distinct varieties as "No. 2 dark winter wheat" and "No. 1 dark northern spring wheat." Or such an institutional market might cover a number of different physical locations, such as when an economist speaks of a market in regional terms. The "New England market for home heating oil," for example, may involve transactions by a number of different companies at a number of different physical locations.

In the most abstract terms, people sometimes talk of **"the market"** as a situation of idealized unencumbered exchange. Without reference to either physical places or social institutions, buyers and sellers are imagined to come to instantaneous, costless agreements. This definition of the market may refer to all market relationships at a national or even global level. When economists speak of the merits (or limitations) of "free markets," they are referring to the concept at this level of abstraction. Often what people have in mind in this case is not so much specific, institutional markets as a particular model of how markets *could* behave, in an ideal case. Economists who have a "pro-market" view believe that markets should generally be left to function with very little government intervention in order to maximize economic prosperity. They may claim, for example, that problems of environmental protection can and should be solved by "the market." Others recognize the effectiveness of markets but believe that problems such as poverty, inequality, environmental degradation, and declining social ethics may be caused or exacerbated by unchecked and unregulated markets.

> **"the market"** (third meaning): a phrase that people often use to mean an abstract situation of pure exchange or a global system of exchange relationships

3.2 THE BASIC NEOCLASSICAL MODEL

The **basic neoclassical model**, traditionally taught in detail in most *micro*economics courses at the introductory level, is a model of market exchange that—while abstracting away from many real-world factors, some of which are discussed below—portrays in a simple and elegant way some important aspects of markets. Neoclassical economics arose during the late nineteenth and early twentieth centuries. It took the eighteenth-century classical idea that economies can be thought of as systems of smoothly-functioning markets, and expressed this idea in terms of formalized assumptions, equations and graphs. (The prefix "neo-" means "new.")

In this model, the world is simplified to two kinds of economic actors. Households are assumed to consume and to maximize their utility (or satisfaction). Firms are assumed to produce and to maximize profits. Households are considered to be the ultimate owners of all resources of land, labor, and capital. They rent the services of these to firms on "factor markets," receiving monetary payments in return. Firms produce goods and services, which they sell to households on "product markets" in return for monetary payments. This model can be portrayed in the circular flow diagram in Figure 2.9. The model further assumes that there are so many firms and households involved in the market for any good or service that a situation of "perfect competition" reigns, in which prices are determined purely by forces of supply and demand.

> **basic neoclassical (traditional microeconomic) model:** a simple, mechanical model that portrays the economy as a collection of profit-maximizing firms and utility-maximizing households interacting through perfectly competitive markets

In this idealized world, goods and services are produced, distributed, and consumed in such a way that the market value of production is as high as it can be. The model combines important observations about markets with assumptions about human values and human behavior, as both producers and consumers. In reading through the following statements, see if you can recognize which parts are "positive" observations of facts, and which are assumptions, which may include a "normative" slant, toward "the way things ought to be." Full social and economic efficiency is said to arise because:

- The prices set by the forces of supply and demand in smoothly functioning markets carry signals throughout the economy, coordinating the actions of many individual decision makers in a highly decentralized way

Figure 2.9 **The Circular Flow Diagram for the Basic Neoclassical Model**

Factor Markets
Land, Labor, and Capital Services

Wages, Rents,
Interest, and Profits

Households   Firms

Payments for
Produced Goods
and Services

Produced Goods and Services
Product Markets

The neoclassical circular flow diagram represents a model in which there are only two kinds of economic actors, interacting through markets.

- The profit motive gives perfectly competitive firms an incentive to look for low-cost inputs and convert them into highly valuable outputs. Production decisions are thus made in such a way that resources are put to their most (market) valuable uses
- Consumption decisions made by individuals and households are assumed to maximize the "utility" or satisfaction of consumers
- Maximizing the market value of production is assumed to be a reasonable proxy for maximizing human well-being

Extending the model to include international trade, the story of "comparative advantage," which will be discussed in Chapter 13, similarly demonstrates how specialization and trade may lead to a greater (market) value of production on an international scale, compared to a situation in which each country produces only for itself.

3.3 THE ADVANTAGES OF MARKETS

Economies that rely heavily on markets to coordinate production, distribution, and consumption have certain important advantages over the main recent historical alternative to markets, central planning.

The bureaucratic socialist systems that used to exist in the former Soviet Union and Eastern Europe, for example, were notorious for their inefficiency in resource allocation—both within enterprises and across the whole economy. According to economic historian Alec Nove, Soviet economic planning at its peak spelled out production targets for almost 50,000 commodities, involving a staggering and virtually unmanageable level of detail. Separate production decisions had to be made for the millions of distinguishable commodities in the Soviet Union (e.g., every size for each different style of shoes). A large bureaucracy had to be established to run all this. The economy was steered very much toward the heavy industry and military production that allowed the Soviet Union to become a world power—but consumer goods and agriculture were neglected. Dissatisfaction with the results of this centrally controlled system contributed greatly to its collapse in 1992.

Because information and decision making in a market economy are decentralized, and producers have an incentive to respond to consumer desires, market systems can lead to a more efficient use of resources than entirely centrally planned economic systems. While the workings of real-world markets are more complex, the principle of efficiency highlighted in the basic neoclassical model is of great importance.

The fact that market exchange is *voluntary,* not coerced, is often considered to be an additional advantage of markets. While most people are in some sense forced to offer their labor for pay in order to survive in a market economy, market systems generally offer people some choice about where they work and what they buy. Other market advocates claim that, by offering financial incentives, markets encourage people to be creative and innovate, and to communicate with each other.

However, it is one thing to recognize that markets have advantages, and another to claim that markets are *always* the best way to organize economic activity.

Classically minded macroeconomists tend to emphasize potential efficiency gains from markets, and stay fairly close to the basic neoclassical model in their theories. They tend to believe that most economic decisions should be left to "free markets."

More Keynesian-oriented macroeconomists, on the other hand, tend to emphasize how real-world markets might differ from the smoothly functioning markets that exist in theory. Real-world markets require an impressive set of associated institutions to work well, they point out. And markets on their own are not well-suited to addressing certain kinds of economic problems.

3.4 THE INSTITUTIONAL REQUIREMENTS OF MARKETS

Contemporary large-scale markets do an amazing thing: They allow many, many separate decision makers, acting from decentralized information, to coordinate their behavior, resulting in highly complex patterns of voluntary exchange transactions. They do not, however, operate in a vacuum. Economists have identified a number of even more basic institutions that market institutions require in order to function. We will classify these in four broad groups: individualist institutions related to property and decision making; social institutions of trust; infrastructure for the smooth flow of goods and information; and money as a medium of exchange.

> Markets require individualist institutions related to property and decision making, social institutions of trust, infrastructure for the smooth flow of goods and information, and money as a medium of exchange.

Individualist institutions related to property and decision making

For markets to work, people need to know what belongs to whom. Private property is the ownership of physical or financial assets by nongovernment economic actors. Actors must also be allowed to make their own decisions about how to allocate and exchange resources. Prices, in particular, must not be under the complete control of guilds or central bureaus; generally, they should be set by the interactions of market participants themselves.

> **private property:** ownership of assets by nongovernment economic actors

The institutions of private property and individualist decision making exist both formally, in codes of law, and informally, in social norms. For example, some Western economists expected markets to grow quickly in the countries of the former Soviet Union as soon as communism was dismantled and opportunities for markets opened up. However, many people were accustomed to being told where to work and what to do by the state. Norms of individual initiative and entrepreneurship, it turns out, do not just arise naturally but need to be fostered and developed.

Social institutions of trust

A second critical institutional requirement for markets is that some degree of trust must exist between buyers and sellers. When a buyer puts down her payment, she must trust that the seller will hand over the merchandise and that it will be of good quality. A seller must be able to trust that the payment offered is valid, whether it is in the form of currency, personal check, credit-card charges, or other kinds of promise of future payment. Social institutions must be created to reduce the risk involved.

Again, trust is an institution that exists both in social norms and formal establishments. Cultural norms and ethical or religious codes can help establish and maintain an atmosphere of trustworthiness. One-on-one exchanges between customers and businesses help build trust and make future transactions smoother. Many companies have built up a reputation for making quality products or providing good service. Marketers try to capitalize on the tendency of buyers to depend on reputation by using advertising to link certain expectations about quality and price to a recognizable brand name, thus creating "brand loyalty" among repeat customers.

In modern complex economies, contracts are often needed to define the terms of an exchange. An informal or **implicit contract** exists when the terms of an exchange are defined verbally or through commonly accepted norms and traditions. **Explicit contracts** are formal, usually written, agreements that provide a legally enforceable description of the agreed-upon terms of exchange. For formal contracts to work, there must be laws that define contracts, state the legal obligation to honor contracts, and establish penalties for those who fail to do so. There must also be a system for enforcing those laws.

> **implicit contract:** an informal agreement about the terms of exchange, based on verbal discussions and on common norms, traditions, and expectations
>
> **explicit contract:** a formal, often written, agreement that states the terms of exchange and may be enforceable through a legal system

In highly marketized economies, many other institutions have evolved to deal with the issue of trust. For example, credit bureaus keep track of consumer credit trustworthiness, Better Business Bureaus keep track of complaints against businesses, money-back guarantees give consumers a chance to test the quality of a good before they commit to purchasing, and escrow accounts provide a place where money can be put until goods or services are delivered. Government agencies such as the U.S. Food and Drug Administration and local boards of health are charged with monitoring the quality and purity of many goods that are sold.

However, even in complex transactions among large groups of strangers, social norms are still essential. Detailed formal contracts are costly to write and costly to enforce. It is not practical to police every detail of every contract, and it is impossible to cover every conceivable contingency. The legal system can work smoothly only if most people willingly obey most laws and believe that it is dishonorable to cheat. In effect, relationships, social norms, and the governmentally created apparatus of law are institutions that must exist side by side, reinforcing one another. None of these alone can carry the whole burden of making complex contracts work, and hence make markets possible.

Infrastructure for the smooth flow of goods and information

A third set of basic institutions for market functioning have to do with making possible a smooth flow of goods and information. Most obviously, there needs to be a system of **physical infrastructure** for transportation and storage that provides the basic foundation for moving goods around. Such infrastructure includes roads, ports, railroads, and warehouses in which to store goods awaiting transport or sale. This sort of infrastructure can be most noticeable when it is absent, as in economies ravaged by war.

> **physical infrastructure:** the equipment, buildings, physical communication lines, roads, and other tangible structures that provide the foundation for economic activity

In addition, there needs to be infrastructure in place for the flow of information. Producers and sellers need information on what, and how much, their customers want to buy; in a well-functioning marketized economy, this information indicates what, and how much, should be produced and offered for sale. At the same time, consumers need to know what is available, and how much of something else they will have to give up (i.e., how much they will have to pay) to get the products that are on the market. Ideally, consumers should be able to compare all potential purchases, as a basis for deciding what to acquire and what to do without.

Money as a medium of exchange

The final critical institution required for markets to operate smoothly is a generally accepted form of money. Gold, silver, and other metal coins were the most common type of money for many centuries; more recently, paper currency has become important. Today, financial instruments such as bank account balances play an even larger role. While once backed by precious metals in Fort Knox, the value of a U.S. dollar is now based only on the understanding that other people will take it in exchange. In this sense, money is also a social institution of trust, as well as part of the institutional infrastructure of functioning markets. Money will be discussed at greater length in Chapter 11.

3.5 The Limitations of Markets

Real-world choices are not limited either to a system where a centralized government exerts total control, or to the radically "free market" system described in the basic neoclassical model. Actual market-oriented economies always include a mixture of decentralized private decision making and more public-oriented decision making.

This is not because voters and government officials are not aware of the advantages markets can have in helping an economy run efficiently. Rather, it is because in real world economies there are a number of important, complex factors that are not taken account of in the basic neoclassical model. We will discuss these issues more fully in later chapters; here we briefly define and discuss some of the major factors that are important for macroeconomics. These include public goods, externalities, transaction costs, market power, questions of information and expectations, and concerns for human needs and equity.

> Economic systems cannot rely solely on "free markets" to organize activity because of factors including public goods, externalities, transaction costs, market power, questions of information and expectations, and concerns for human needs and equity.

Public goods

Some goods cannot, or would not, be provided well by private individuals or organizations acting alone. A **public good** (or service) is one where the use of it by one person does not diminish the ability of another person to benefit from it ("nondiminishable"), and where it would be difficult to keep any individuals from enjoying its benefit ("nonexcludable").

> **public goods:** goods for which (1) use by one person does not diminish usefulness to others, and (2) it would be difficult to exclude anyone from benefiting

For example, if a local police force helps make a neighborhood safe, all the residents benefit. Public roads (at least those that are not congested and have no tolls) are also public goods, as is national defense. Education and quality childcare are public goods because everyone benefits from living with a more skilled and socially well-adjusted population. A system of laws and courts provides the basic legal infrastructure on which all business contracting depends. Environmental protection that makes for cleaner air benefits everyone.

Because it is difficult to exclude anyone from benefiting, public goods cannot generally be bought and sold on markets. Even if individual actors would be willing to pay if necessary, they have little incentive to pay because they can't be excluded from the benefit. Economists call people who seek to enjoy a benefit without paying for it **free riders**. Because of the problem of free riders, it often makes sense to provide public goods through government agencies, supported by taxes, so that the cost of the public benefit is also borne by the public at large. The effect of taxation and government spending on the macroeconomic environment will be an important theme in this book.

> **free riders:** people who seek to enjoy the benefit of a public good without paying for it

Externalities

Other activities, while they may involve goods and services that are bought and sold in markets, create **externalities**. Externalities are side effects or unintended consequences of economic activities. They affect persons, or entities such as the environment, that are not among the economic actors directly involved in a particular economic activity. These effects can be positive or negative. Sometimes positive externalities are referred to as "external benefits" and negative externalities are referred to as "external costs." Externalities are one of the primary ways in which the true *social* value of a good or service may differ from its *market* value.

> **externalities:** side effects or unintended consequences, either positive or negative, that affect persons, or entities such as the environment, that are not among the economic actors directly involved in the economic activity that caused the effect.

Examples of negative externalities include a manufacturing firm dumping pollutants in a river, decreasing water quality downstream; or a bar that plays loud music that annoys its neighbors. Examples of positive externalities include the fact that parents who, out of love for their children, raise them to become decent people (rather than violent criminals) also create benefits for society at large; or the way in which people who get vaccinated against a communicable disease to protect themselves also protect those around them from the disease's spread. In both cases, there are social benefits from individual actions. Well-educated, productive citizens are an asset to the community as well as to their own families, and disease control reduces risks to everyone.

Some of the most important externalities have to do with the economic activity of resource maintenance. Relying on markets alone to coordinate economic activities allows many activities to happen that damage or deplete the natural environment, because the damage often does not carry a price tag and because people in future generations are not direct parties to the decision making.

If economic activities affected only the actors directly involved in decision making, we might be able to think about economic activity primarily in terms of individuals making decisions for their own benefit. But we live in a social and ecological world, in which actions, interactions, and consequences are generally both widespread and interknit. If decisions are left purely to individual self-interest, then from a societal point of view too many negative externalities will be created, and too few positive externalities. The streets might be strewn with industrial wastes, while children might be taught to be honest in dealings within their family, but not outside of it. Market values and human or social values do not always coincide.

Transaction costs

Transaction costs are the costs of arranging economic activities. In the basic neoclassical model, transaction costs are assumed to be zero. If a firm wants to hire a worker, for example, it is assumed in that model that the only cost involved is the wage paid. In the real world, however, the activity of getting to a hiring agreement may involve its own set of costs. The firm may need to pay costs related to searching, such as placing an ad or paying for the services of a recruiting company. The prospective worker may need to pay for preparation of a résumé and transportation to an interview. One or both sides might hire lawyers to make sure that the contract's terms reflect their interests. Because of the existence of such costs, some economic interactions that might be lead to greater efficiency, and that would occur in an idealized, transaction-cost-free, frictionless world, may not happen in the real world.

> **transaction costs:** the costs of arranging economic activities

Market power

In the basic neoclassical model, all markets are assumed to be "perfectly competitive," such that no one buyer or seller has the power to influence the prices or other market conditions they face. In the real world, however, we see that many firms have **market power**. For example, when there is only one firm (a monopolist) or a few firms selling a good, they may be able to use their power to increase their prices and their profits, creating inefficient allocations of resources in the process. Workers may also be able to gain a degree of market power by joining together to negotiate as a labor union. A government, too, can have market power, for example when the Department of Defense is the sole purchaser of military equipment from private firms.

> **market power:** the ability to control, or at least affect, the terms and conditions of the exchanges in which one participates

Businesses may also gain power by their sheer size—many corporations now function internationally, and have revenues in the tens of billions of dollars. The decisions of individual large corporations can have substantial effects on the employment levels, economic growth, living standards, and economic stability of regions and countries. Governments may need to factor in the responses of powerful business groups in making their macroeconomic decisions. National leaders may fear, for example, that raising business tax rates or the national minimum wage may cause companies to leave their country and go elsewhere. Corporations frequently also try to influence government policies directly, through lobbying, campaign contributions, and other methods. We will explore the implications of corporate globalization for macroeconomic policy at more length in a later chapter.

Information and expectations

In the basic neoclassical model, in which purely decentralized decisions lead to efficient outcomes, people are assumed to have easy access to all the information they need to make good choices. This analysis is **static**; that is, it deals with an idealized case in a timeless manner. The model doesn't consider the time it might take for a person to make a decision, or the time it might take for a factory to gear up to produce a good. In the real, **dynamic**, world, getting good information may be difficult, and planning for an uncertain future is a big part of anyone's economic decision making.

> **static analysis:** analysis that does not take into account the passage of time
>
> **dynamic analysis:** analysis that takes into account the passage of time

A manufacturing business, for example, might be considering whether or not to borrow funds to build an additional factory. If the company's directors were able to know in advance exactly what demand for its products will be like in the future and what interest rates will be—along with additional information about things such as future wages, energy costs, and returns on alternative investments—the decision would be a simple matter of mathematical calculation.

But the directors will have to guess at most of these things. They will form expectations about the future, but these expectations may turn out to be correct or incorrect. If their expectations are optimistic, they will tend to make the new investment and hire new workers. Often optimism is "contagious," and if a lot of *other* business leaders become optimistic, too, then the economy will boom. If, on the other hand, people share an attitude of pessimism, they may all tend to cut back on spending and hiring.

Since no one business wants to take the risk of jumping the gun by expanding too soon, it can be very difficult to get a decentralized market economy out of a slump. How people get their information, how they time their actions, and how they form their expectations of the future, then, are all important topics in macroeconomics that are not addressed in the basic neoclassical model. Taking these factors into account means that sometimes markets do not work as smoothly as that model suggests.

Human needs and equity

In the basic neoclassical model, the only consumer demands for goods and services that count are those that are backed up by a consumer's ability to pay. This has several implications.

First, there is nothing in the model that assures that resources are distributed in such a way that people can meet their basic human needs. If a few rich people have a lot of money to spend on diamonds, for example, while a great number of poor people lack the money to pay for basic health care, "free markets" will motivate producers to respond to the demand for diamonds, but not to the need for basic health care. More deliberate policies of economic development, government provision, subsidies, or income redistribution—sometimes incorporating, or sometimes replacing, market means—are often enacted to try to ensure that decent living standards become more widespread.

Second, the model does not take into account non-marketed production, such as the care given to children, the sick, and the elderly by family and friends. There is nothing in the basic neoclassical model that assures that these sorts of production will be supplied in adequate quantities and quality.

Lastly, it is also the case that problems such as unemployment and inflation tend to affect some people more than others, so that how a country deals with these problems also has distributional consequences.

Clearly, although market systems have strong advantages in some areas, they cannot solve all economic problems. Economists sometimes use the term **market failure** to refer to a situation in which a market form of organization would lead to inefficient or harmful results. Because of the existence of public goods, externalities, transaction costs, market power, questions of information and expectations, and concerns for human needs and equity, macroeconomic systems cannot rely on "free markets" alone if they are to generate human well-being.

> **market failure:** a situation in which markets yield inefficient or inappropriate outcomes

To some extent *private* non-market institutions may help remedy "market failure." For example, a group of privately owned factories located around a lake may voluntarily decide to restrict their waste emissions, because too much deterioration in water quality hurts them all. Likewise, a widespread custom of private charitable giving may help alleviate poverty. But sometimes the problems are so large or widespread that only governmental, *public* actions at the national or international levels seem to offer a solution. Exactly how much governmental action is required, and exactly what governments should do, however, are much-debated questions within contemporary macroeconomics.

Discussion Questions

1. In what sense is the term "market" being used in each of the following sentences? "Go to the market and get some bananas." "The market is the best invention of humankind." "The labor market for new Ph.D.s is bad this year." "The advance of the market leads to a decline in social morality." "The market performance of IBM stock weakened last month." Can you think of other examples from your own readings or experience?
2. "Indeed it has been said that democracy is the worst form of Government," said British prime minister Winston Churchill (1874–1965), "except all those other forms that have been tried from time to time." Some people make the same claim about more marketized forms of economic systems. What do they mean? Would you agree or disagree?

REVIEW QUESTIONS

1. What are the three main modes of economic investigation? Describe each.
2. What is a model? How does the *ceteris paribus* assumption simplify the creation of a model?
3. How do abundance and scarcity create the possibility of, and the necessity of, economic decision making?
4. What three requirements are met in producing along a production-possibilities frontier?
5. Draw a societal production-possibilities frontier, and use it to explain the concepts of trade-offs (opportunity cost), attainable and unattainable output combinations, and efficiency.
6. What kinds of decisions would make a PPF expand over time? What kinds of decisions would make it shrink over time?

7. What are the three different meanings of the term "markets"?
8. What are some of the assumptions of the basic neoclassical model? Why are markets said to be efficient according to this model?
9. What are the four institutional requirements of markets?
10. What is a public good? Why will private markets generally undersupply public goods?
11. What are negative and positive externalities? Give examples of each.
12. Besides public goods and externalities, describe four real world factors that can cause market outcomes to be less than ideal.

EXERCISES

1. Consider the following data, taken from the *Economic Report of the President* 2004. Perform the graphing exercises below using either pencil and graph paper or a computer spreadsheet or presentation program.

Year	Unemployment Rate (percent)	Inflation (percent per year)
1992	7.5	2.3
1993	6.9	2.3
1994	6.1	2.1
1995	5.6	2
1996	5.4	1.9
1997	4.9	1.7
1998	4.5	1.1
1999	4.2	1.4

   a. Looking at the data listed in the chart, can you detect a trend in the unemployment rate during these years? In the inflation rate? If so, what sort of trends do you see?
   b. Create a time-series graph for the unemployment rate during 1992–99.
   c. Create a scatter-plot graph with the unemployment rate on the horizontal axis and inflation on the vertical axis.
   d. Using your graph in part (c), do the two variables seem to have an empirical relationship during this period, or do the points seem to be randomly scattered? If there appears to be an empirical relationship, is it inverse or direct?
   e. How does the empirical relationship between unemployment and inflation in this period compare to the period 1963–69 (discussed in the chapter)?

2. The notion of "scarcity" reflects the idea that resources cannot be stretched to meet all the goals that people desire. But what makes a particular resource "scarce"? If there seems to be more of it around than is needed, such as desert sand, is it scarce? If it is freely open to the use of many people at once, such as music on the radio waves, is it scarce? What about resources such as social attitudes of trust and respect? Make a list of a few resources that clearly *are* "scarce" in economists' sense. Make another list of a few resources that are not.

3. How is the concept of efficiency related to the concept of scarcity? Consider, for example, your own use of time. When do you feel time to be more, and when less, scarce? Do you think about how to use your time differently during exam week, compared to when you are on vacation?

4. Suppose that society could produce the following combinations of pizzas and books:

Alternative	Quantity of Pizzas	Quantity of Books
A	50	0
B	40	10
C	30	18
D	20	24
E	10	28
F	0	30

a. Using graph paper (or a computer program), draw the production-possibilities frontier (PPF) for pizza and books, being as exact and neat as possible. (Put books on the horizontal axis. Assume that the dots define a complete curve.)

b. Is it possible and/or efficient for this society to produce 25 pizzas and 25 books?

c. Is it possible and/or efficient for this society to produce 42 pizzas and 1 book?

d. If society is currently producing alternative B, then the opportunity cost of moving to alternative A (and getting 10 more pizzas) is _____ books.

e. Is the opportunity cost of producing pizzas higher or lower moving from alternative F to E than moving from alternative B to A? Why is this likely to be so?

f. Suppose that the technologies used in producing both pizzas and books improve. Draw one possible new production-possibilities frontier in the graph above that represents the results of this change. Indicate the direction of the change that occurs with an arrow.

5. Match each concept in Column A with a definition or example in Column B.

Column A	Column B
a. A positive externality	1. An apple pie producer trusts that apple growers will supply the apples they promise to deliver
b. Theoretical investigation	2. The annual harvest of apples in a country from 1970–2000
c. Time-series data	3. Producing a combination along a production-possibilities frontier
d. A public good	4. Apple growers will seek to maximize their profits
e. Opportunity cost of buying an apple	5. You don't get to have an orange
f. Scarcity	6. There is only one apple producer who is able to make very high profits
g. Efficient production	7. Doesn't take into account the passage of time
h. Technological progress	8. An orchard used to grow a full crop of apples cannot also be used to grow a full crop of pears
i. An institutional requirement of markets	9. The apple tree you plant for your own enjoyment also pleases people passing by
j. Market power	10. Can expand a production-possibilities frontier outward over time
k. A negative externality	11. An inspection program for imported apples protects the nation's orchards from a severe tree disease
l. An assumption of the basic neoclassical model	12. Inspired by a falling apple, Isaac Newton proposes the existence of something called "gravity"
m. Static analysis	13. The production of apple pie creates water pollution that harms downstream communities

3 What Economies Do

You cannot build a comfortable, secure house without a good understanding of bricks, pipes, and building techniques. Likewise, to understand how societies might be able to achieve the macroeconomic goals of good living standards, stability, and sustainability, we first need to understand some of the "building blocks" of any economy. While an in-depth analysis of specific parts of the economy is the subject of *micro*economics, not macroeconomics, some familiarity with micro-level activities is a prerequisite for a macroeconomic understanding of how all these activities add up to make a national (and global) economy.

1. INTRODUCING THE FOUR ESSENTIAL ECONOMIC ACTIVITIES

In introducing the subject matter of economics in Chapter 1, we briefly mentioned that the four essential economic activities are resource maintenance, production, distribution, and consumption. Now it is time to look at these more directly.

1.1 RESOURCE MAINTENANCE

Resource maintenance means tending to, preserving, or improving the stocks of resources that form the basis for the preservation and quality of life. A **capital stock** is a quantity of any resource that is valued for its potential economic contributions. Capital stocks are also often referred to as "capital assets."

> **resource maintenance:** the management of capital stocks so that their productivity is sustained

> **capital stock:** a quantity of any resource that is valued for its potential economic contributions

We can identify four types of capital that contribute to an economy's productivity. **Natural capital** refers to physical assets provided by nature, such as land that is suitable for agriculture or other human uses, fresh water sources, and stocks of minerals and crude oil that are still in the ground. **Manufactured capital** means physical assets that are generated by applying human productive activities to natural capital. These include such things as buildings, machinery, stocks of refined oil, transportation infrastructure, and inventories of produced goods that are waiting to be sold or to be used in further production. **Human capital** refers to individual people's capacity for labor, particularly the knowledge and skills each can personally bring to his or her work. **Social capital** means the stock of trust, mutual understanding, shared values, and socially held knowledge that facilitates the social coordination of economic activity.

> **natural capital:** physical assets provided by nature

> **manufactured capital:** physical assets generated by applying human productive activities to natural capital

> **human capital:** people's capacity for labor and their individual knowledge and skills

> **social capital:** the stock of trust, mutual understanding, shared values, and socially held knowledge that facilitates the social coordination of economic activity

Lastly, there is a fifth sort of resource, **financial capital**, which is a fund of purchasing power available to an economic actor. While financial capital doesn't directly help to produce anything, it indirectly contributes to production by making it possible for people to produce goods and services in advance of getting paid for them. It also facilitates the activities of distribution and consumption. Key examples of financial capital would be a bank checking account, filled with funds that have been either saved up by the economic agent who owns it or loaned to the agent by a bank.

> **financial capital:** funds of purchasing power available to facilitate economic activity

Notice that economists' description of "capital" is different from what you might hear in everyday use. In common usage, sometimes people take "capital" to mean *only* financial capital. We hear this in everyday references to "capital markets," "undercapitalized businesses," "venture capital," etc. Economists take a broader view.

Capital stocks may increase or decrease as a consequence of natural forces, as in the case of a natural forest; or they may be deliberately managed by humans, in order to provide needed inputs for the production of desired goods and services. When the quantity or quality of a nonfinancial resource is increased now in order to make benefits possible in the future, this is what economists mean by **investment**. The activity of "resource maintenance" is about making sure that investments are sufficient to provide an economy with good asset base for future years and future generations. You, right now, are investing in your "human capital" by studying economics.

> **investment:** actions taken to increase the quantity or quality of a resource now, in order to make benefits possible in the future

1.2 PRODUCTION

The second of the four basic economic activities is **production**. Production is the conversion of resources into usable products, which may be either goods or services. Goods are tangible objects, like bread or books, whereas services are intangibles, like TV broadcasting, teaching, or haircuts. Manufactured assets, such as machines and buildings, are also the result of human productive activity—that is, some items are produced for investment purposes. Popular bands producing music, recording companies producing CDs, local governments building roads, and individuals producing cooked meals are all engaged in the economic activity of production.

> **production:** the conversion of resources to goods and services

The economic activity of production converts some resources, which we call **inputs**, into new goods and services, which we refer to as **outputs**, as a flow over some period of time. The way in which this production occurs depends on available technologies. Production processes can also lead to undesirable outputs, such as **waste products**. We consider only *useful* outputs to be economic goods and services.

> **inputs:** resources that go into production

outputs: the results of production

waste products: outputs that are not used either for consumption or in a further production process

Inputs include materials that become part of the produced good, supplies that are used up in the production process, and labor time. For example, were we to ask a chef how to prepare one of his specialties, say ginger chicken, we would be given an answer in terms of ingredients (chicken, ginger, oil, etc.) and a method for combining them. The food ingredients become part of the produced good. Other inputs that will be used up in the process probably include the natural gas or electricity that provides heat, and other supplies such as paper towels. The chef's labor time is necessary for the dish to be prepared, and is used up by the process.

But the recipe, the chef's skills, and the stove and cooking implements that will be used neither become part of the produced good nor are "used up," although they are crucial for the production process. We can best think of these as *flows of services* arising out of capital *stocks*. The production process draws on services from social capital, in the form of the social knowledge embodied in a recipe; services of the chef's human capital in the form of the chef's acquired knowledge; and services of manufactured capital in the form of the stove and implements. But unlike materials and supplies, these capital stocks are not themselves transformed or used up in production.

In the case of commercial production, the services of another form of capital—financial capital—are also vitally important. This is because the production process *takes time*. Imagine that the chef and her husband, for example, are also entrepreneurs. They need to be able to buy the ingredients, buy or rent kitchen space, and get to work well *before* they can prepare the meal and sell it. They therefore need to have financial capital available at the start of the process—either financial assets of their own, or loans they can use to pay the bills until their revenues start coming in. If, at the end of the process, they can sell the meal, cover all their expenses, and make a profit, they will end up with more financial capital than before.

This is illustrated in Figure 3.1. The reliance of commercial production on manufactured and financial capital is very important for macroeconomics, as we will see when we study issues of credit and investment. Production by noncommercial organizations such as households, nonprofit organizations, and governments, also begins with resources—including financial resources, if any of the inputs are going to be bought on markets. Generally, however, such production is intended for purposes other than making a financial profit.

1.3 DISTRIBUTION

Distribution is the sharing of products and resources among people. In contemporary economies, distribution activities take two main forms: exchange and transfer.

distribution: the allocation of products and resources among people

When you hand over money in return for goods and services produced by other people, or when you receive a wage for the work you have provided to an employer, you are engaging in **exchange**. As we discussed in the previous chapter, markets are social institutions that facilitate exchange relations. People are generally much better off if they specialize in the production of some limited range of goods and services, and meet at least some of their other needs through exchange, than if they try to produce everything they need themselves. (We will study this in more detail in Chapter 13 of this book.)

exchange: trading one thing for another

Figure 3.1   **The Role of Financial Capital in Commercial Production**

This diagram illustrates how a commercial production process must begin with a stock of financial capital. If profitable, the production and sale of goods yields results in a larger stock of financial capital.

Distribution also takes place through **transfer**. Transfers are payments given with nothing specific expected in return. For example, wealth is transferred from one generation to the next by inheritance. Social Security payments from the federal government to the elderly, to give another example, are transfers.

> **transfer:** the giving of something with nothing specific expected in return

Distribution also takes place through transfers of goods, services, or assets as well as transfers of money. Local public school boards, for example, distribute education services to child and teenage students in their districts, tuition-free. Parents in households transfer food and care to children. These sorts of nonmonetary transfers are called **in-kind transfers**.

> **in-kind transfers:** transfers of goods or services

1.4 CONSUMPTION

Consumption refers to the process by which goods and services are, at last, put to final use by people. In some cases, such as eating a meal or burning gasoline in a car, goods are literally "consumed" in the sense that they are used up and are no longer available for other uses. In other cases, such as enjoying art in a museum, the experience may be "consumed" without excluding others or using up material resources.

> **consumption:** the final use of a good or service to satisfy current wants

The activity of consumption is frequently contrasted, in macroeconomics, to the resource-maintenance activity of *investment*. The two activities are linked by the activity of **saving**, or refraining from consumption today in order to gain benefits in the future.

> **saving:** refraining from consuming in the current period

For example, suppose a subsistence farmer grows a crop of corn. To the extent the farmer eats some of the corn, the farmer *consumes*—the corn is used up in the process of eating, and is not available for future use. To the extent that the farmer sets some of this year's corn crop aside for planting next season, the farmer *saves*. The farmer also *invests*—that is, creates a resource that will aid production in the future. Having an inventory of seeds is what makes growing a crop in the next season possible.

In a modern, financially sophisticated economy, the situation is more complex, but the basic idea is the same. Modern households can save by spending less money on consumption than their income would allow. Governments and nonprofit organizations can save by spending less on consumption goods than their budgets would allow. Businesses save by retaining some of their earnings, instead of paying out to their shareholders (as dividends) all of what they make beyond their (non-investment) expenses. These flows of savings add to the stock of available financial assets. Financial intermediaries such as banks and bond markets allow savers to loan

NEWS IN CONTEXT:
Lawmakers Are Quick to Pledge Infrastructure Overhaul, But the Cost Is Staggering

WASHINGTON—One of Congress' more obscure priorities—the upkeep of the nation's infrastructure—has suddenly gained urgency in the wake of the Minneapolis bridge collapse. But the job of rebuilding it may be easier for engineers than politicians.

On Wednesday, key lawmakers pledged to push for billions of additional dollars to repair America's transportation infrastructure when Congress returns from its summer recess. But they will run into plenty of political obstacles.

For one, the sheer number of structurally deficient or functionally obsolete bridges—more than 150,000 or about one-fourth of the nation's bridges—would require an investment of at least $65 billion. That's more than the Department of Homeland Security expects to spend next fiscal year. . . . "The reality remains that we have outdated and failing structures around the country and the trust fund used to fix them is rapidly going bankrupt," said [the chair of] the Senate transportation appropriations subcommittee.

Source: Richard Simon, *Los Angeles Times*, August 9, 2007

The collapse of a major highway bridge in Minnesota in August 2007 killed thirteen people and injured over one hundred. To which of the four essential economic activities does this story relate?

out the use of their financial capital to households, nonprofits, businesses, and governments that want to borrow. Some of the borrowers will use the funds to pay for the creation of new investment goods, such as buildings, factories, or a college education.

Discussion Questions

1. Think of some common activity you enjoy. For example, perhaps you like to get together with friends and listen to CDs while popping popcorn in the microwave. List the stocks of natural, manufactured, human, and social capital you draw on when engaging in this activity.

2. Classify each of the following according to which economic activity, or activities, it involves. If any seem like they include aspects of more than one activity, name the activities and explain your reasoning.
   a. Planting a forest
   b. Sponsoring a scholarship for a college student
   c. Building an addition onto a factory
   d. Buying a government savings bond
   e. Giving someone a haircut

2. RESOURCE MAINTENANCE: ATTENDING TO THE ASSET BASE OF THE MACROECONOMY

The activity of resource maintenance deserves more attention, because sustainability is an important macroeconomic goal, and is only achievable if care is taken to maintain the asset base of an economy. Several concepts are important in understanding the economics of resource maintenance.

2.1 STOCKS VERSUS FLOWS

When noneconomists use the term "stock," they often mean ownership shares in enterprises that are traded on the "stock market." To an economist, however, the concept of a **stock** refers to something as it is measured at a particular point in time. For example, the amount of water in a bathtub can be measured at one particular instant, and that quantity would be considered a stock. The number of computers in an office at ten o'clock on Tuesday morning is a stock, as is the number of trees in a forest at two o'clock on Saturday afternoon.

On the other hand, **flows** are measured *over* a period of time. For example, the water that goes into a bathtub from a faucet is a flow; its quantity can be measured per minute or per hour. The number of computers purchased by an office over the course of this week or this month is a flow. So is the number of computers sold or junked over a period of time. As trees grow or are cut down or felled by lightning, these flows add to or subtract from forest resources.

> **stock:** something whose quantity can be measured at a point in time
>
> **flow:** something whose quantity can be measured over a period of time

Flows are like a movie; stocks are like a still photograph. Flows can either add to stocks or decrease them. Figure 3.2 is a generalized **stock-flow diagram**, which shows how flows change the level of a stock over time, by either adding to it or taking away from it. For example, the balance in your checking account on January 1 is a stock value.

The deposits and withdrawals you make to your checking account are flows; your bank statement will tell you what the various flows were during a month.

> **stock-flow diagram:** an illustration of how stocks can be changed, over time, by flows

Figure 3.3 gives an alternative representation of the relation of stocks and flows, this time showing a stock at only *one* point in time. Like water running through the tap (additions) and the drain (subtractions) of a bathtub, flows raise or lower the level of the water in the tub (stock).

2.2 INVESTMENT AND DEPRECIATION

Investment, as mentioned earlier, is a primary form of the activity of resource maintenance. When you read the word "investment" in this textbook, the image in your mind should be of someone buying new computers for an office or planting new trees in a forest—*not* of someone playing the stock market or "investing in" corporate bonds. Those sort of financial transactions usually merely shift the ownership of an existing financial asset from one economic actor to another; they don't add to productivity-enhancing capital stocks for the economy at large.

"*Dis*investment," or the running down of capital stocks, can also occur, due to the forces of nature or human activities. When a capital stock is reduced, we say it has undergone **depreciation**. Natural capital depreciates when rivers become fouled by pollution or more trees are

Figure 3.2 **The General Stock-Flow Diagram**

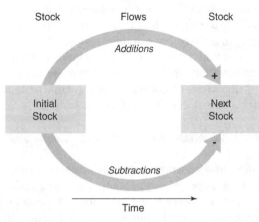

Stock   Flows   Stock

Additions

Initial
Stock

Next
Stock

+

-

Subtractions

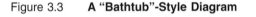

Time

Starting from an initial quantity of a stock, flows into and out of the stock determine how great the quantity is the next time the stock is measured.

Figure 3.3 **A "Bathtub"-Style Diagram**

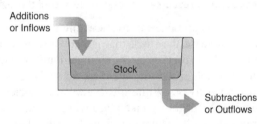

Additions
or Inflows

Stock

Subtractions
or Outflows

Like water flowing into a bathtub, flows that add to a stock will tend to raise its level over time. Like water flowing out of a bathtub, flows that subtract from a stock will tend to lower its level over time.

cut down than are naturally regenerated. Manufactured assets commonly lose their usefulness over time, as computers become obsolete, roads develop potholes, and equipment breaks. (See the earlier News in Context box.) Human capital depreciates if skills are forgotten, or if age or illness renders a person less productive, and social capital can depreciate if norms of trust and peaceable interaction become less widely held.

> **depreciation**: decreases in the quantity or quality of a stock of capital

If we measure **gross investment**, we include all flows into the capital stock over a period of time. **Net investment**, on the other hand, adjusts this measure for the fact that some portion of the capital stock also depreciates over the same period. The capital stock at the end of the period is equal to the capital stock at the beginning of the period plus only *net* investment. If depreciation is rapid, net investment can be negative—if the flow of replenishment is not sufficient to keep up with depreciation, the level of the stock will fall.

> **gross investment:** all flows into the capital stock over a period of time

> **net investment:** gross investment minus an adjustment for depreciation of the capital stock

Resource-maintenance activities help to keep up the quantity and quality of important capital stocks. They include such activities as monitoring the water quality of a lake, repairing machinery, or encouraging people to refresh their knowledge. Sometimes resource maintenance "activity" means *not* engaging in activity. For example, people who make voluntary decisions to minimize their unnecessary gasoline consumption are helping to maintain petroleum resources. While this may look like inactivity, including resource maintenance as an economic activity implies that minimizing some kinds of consumption can contribute to well-being. Issues of resource maintenance will be further explored in Chapter 6.

2.3 Renewable Resources, Nonrenewable Resources, and Sustainability

In recent years, questions concerning the rate of depreciation of many forms of natural capital have come to the fore. Types of natural capital can be classified as either renewable or nonrenewable. A **renewable resource** regenerates itself through biological or other short-term processes, which may be helped out by human activity. The quantity and quality of its stock depend simultaneously on the rate at which the stock maintains its productivity and grows, and on the rate at which it is harvested or polluted. A healthy forest will go on indefinitely producing trees that may be harvested, yielding a flow of lumber that will be used up in production processes such as paper making.

> **renewable resource:** a resource that regenerates itself through short-term processes

Other kinds of natural capital are **nonrenewable resources**. Their supply is fixed, although new discoveries can increase the stock that is known to be available. For example, there is a finite amount of fossil fuel reserves, and a finite amount of each kind of mineral, available on the earth. For nonrenewable resources, there are no self-regenerating flows—at least over time spans relevant to human lives. (While oil reserves or species diversity could in principle be "renewed," the time scale for this to take place would be millions of years.) The stock can only diminish over time as a result of human use and/or natural deterioration.

> **nonrenewable resource:** a resource that cannot be reproduced on a human time-scale, so that its stock diminishes with use over time

How much of its stock of natural resources a society chooses to turn into inputs for current production processes, rather than to preserve for the future, is clearly a very important economic question. Even those natural inputs that are renewable—such as lumber from forests and fish from the seas—may be extinguished if so much of them is destroyed or extracted that they can no longer renew themselves. In addition, there are limits to the ability of nature to absorb polluting by-products of production processes. There are tipping points past which degraded natural capital may dramatically alter in some essential respect.

For example, in the case of climate change, rising global temperature due to human-made emissions from the burning of fossil fuels and the use of other chemicals may bring dramatic changes within this century. Ocean levels could rise by up to a meter, or even more because of melting of the Antarctic ice cap and other factors. This could cause the flooding of many low-lying areas, including New Orleans, south Florida, and Bangladesh. Some island nations are already losing significant land mass. Resource maintenance for natural capital means tracking the size, quality, and changes in natural resources and making wise decisions about their management.

Sometimes, when it is pointed out that processes of production and consumption in the industrialized nations are currently depleting many important natural capital stocks much more rapidly than they can be replenished, the issue of **substitutability** is raised. That is, the depletion of any one resource (such as fossil fuels) is a less serious problem for future well-being, if other resources (such as nuclear or solar energy) can be cheaply and safely substituted for it in production and consumption. The extent of substitutability that can be achieved depends both on the characteristics of the resources and on the speed of technological advance.

> **substitutability**: the possibility of using one resource instead of another

During the late nineteenth and first half of the twentieth centuries, there was a widely felt confidence that human beings could not create any problems to which we could not find adequate and timely solutions. In the late twentieth century, however, this faith began to fade in light of increasing ecological damage. Ecologists emphasize the complexity of natural systems and our relative ignorance about long-term, irreversible, or potentially catastrophic effects of economic behavior on the natural systems that support us. They suggest that instead of placing blind faith in technological progress and economic substitutability, society should adopt a precautionary principle, as was discussed in Chapter 1.

A **sustainable socioeconomic system** creates a flow of whatever is needed (in an economic system, this is goods and services) by using its renewable capital stocks without depleting them. Although some portion of some (especially nonrenewable) capital stocks may be used up in the process of production, the overall quality and quantity of the resource base for sustaining life and well-being are preserved.

> **sustainable socioeconomic system:** a system in which the overall quality and quantity of the resource base required for sustaining life and well-being do not erode

Discussion Questions

1. Linda thinks a rich person is someone who earns a lot of money. Meng thinks a rich person is someone who has a big house and owns lots of corporate shares and bonds. How would the distinction between stocks and flows lend clarity to their discussion?
2. Do you think that a cheap and safe substitute for the use of fossil fuels in cars will ever be found? What about a substitute for the ozone layer, an atmospheric layer that protects the earth from damaging radiation from the sun? Discuss.

3. DISTRIBUTION: WHO GETS WHAT, AND HOW?

The topic of distribution also deserves further discussion, because it is important to distinguish between distribution in the form of exchange, and distribution in the form of transfer—and also to see the importance of each. In particular, macroeconomists are usually particularly interested in who receives the incomes generated by production, and the roles the government plays in economic distribution. This section examines distribution among households residing in a single country, with the United States as the main example. The issue of distribution across countries is taken up in Chapters 14 and 15.

3.1 LABOR AND CAPITAL INCOMES

In exchange relations, as mentioned earlier, two actors come to an agreement to trade with each other on mutually agreed-upon terms. Something is delivered, and something is expected in return, in a *quid pro quo* ("something for something") relation. In product and labor markets, exchanges typically involve a flow of goods or services from seller to buyer, in return for a monetary payment. The monetary payments in turn create flows of labor and capital income. For example, when customers buy shoes from a mall shoe store, the incomes created include the payment of a wage to the shoe salesperson, rent to the owners of the mall, and profits to the owners of the business. **Labor income** is compensation received by workers in the form of wages, salaries, and fringe benefits. **Capital income** includes rents, profits, and interest. ("Rent," as economists use the term, refers not just to rent for housing, but to payments for the use of any asset.)

> **labor income:** payments to workers, including wages, salaries, and fringe benefits
>
> **capital income:** rents, profits, and interest

Economists have, historically, engaged in vigorous debate about whether profits, rents, and interest income are compensation for productive activities. Some economists argue that such capital incomes are payments that are absolutely necessary and justified for the undertaking of production. Interest, they argue, is what gives people the incentive to save and invest, rather than spending all their income on immediate consumption. Rents encourage people to devote their assets to the most productive uses. Profits, these economists claim, represent a return to an entrepreneur's contribution of creative talent and compensation to investors for their willingness to take risks. Such economists take a classical view of markets, and believe that markets always generate the appropriate reward.

When profits, rents, and interest seem excessive, however, they have often become controversial. Most economists believe that there is a legitimate role for fair and reasonable profits and dividends, interest payments, and rents. But many economists also acknowledge that ill-gained or excessive capital incomes do not serve the social good. Persistently high profits may be a sign that a company has market power, indicating that a market is not competitive. Substantial profits might not be a sign of economic health, if the companies who earn them create significant negative social or environmental externalities in the process of getting them. Large capital incomes that arise from practices that violate the human dignity of workers are also socially harmful. When high capital incomes contribute to a concentration of wealth and power, political democracy itself may be threatened. Profits, interest, and rents are legitimate compensation, in this view, only if they are earned and used in ways that serve the common good as well as the good of the individual owner of capital.

3.2 TRANSFERS AND TAXES

While incomes from production are vital to supporting economic life, distribution by means of one-way transfer also has a very significant role to play in explaining distribution in contemporary economies. Transfers are flows of money, goods, or services for which nothing specific is given in return—or at least nothing specific at the current time. Transfers can take place between individuals, or between the government and individuals; macroeconomists are particularly interested in transfers involving government.

Transfers *from* the government are often made in response to people's **dependency needs**. Our individual basic needs during some portions of our lifetimes—as infants and children, or when incapacitated by age or illness—cannot be satisfied through exchange, because we have little or nothing to give at those times. During childhood we have no choice but to rely on others—in our families, communities, and nations—to transfer to us the care, shelter, food, etc. that we need to survive and flourish. We may need such transfers again later in life if we become unemployed or incapacitated by injury, ill-health, or old age. Some government programs deliver specific goods and services directly as in-kind transfers, such as when public schools deliver education services, government programs provide free medical services, or international aid programs deliver food.

> **dependency needs:** the need to have others provide one with care, shelter, food, etc., when one is unable to provide these for oneself

In the United States, the government runs various cash transfer programs designed to help households achieve income security. Economists often distinguish between two major types.

In the case of **social insurance programs**, transfers are designed to help people if certain specific events occur. Since no one can predict how long into old age they will live, or whether unfortunate events will befall them, it is difficult for a worker to know just how much to save for retirement or "for a rainy day." By coming together to create a pool of social insurance, people can be assured of basic provisioning even if their personal needs turn out to exceed their personal savings. Social insurance programs in the United States include the federal Social Security and Medicare programs (mostly for retired persons) and programs at all levels of government that have been designed to help workers and their families should a worker suffer a disability or a period of unemployment. Eligibility for these programs generally depends on a family member having been in the paid labor force for a period of time, but does not depend on the income or wealth of the recipient.

Means-tested programs, on the other hand, are intended to help people who simply have insufficient resources. Unlike most of the social insurance programs, recipients do not need to have established a substantial history of market work in order to qualify for means-tested benefits. Also unlike the social insurance programs, recipients must demonstrate that their other means of support (income and resources) are very low. In recent years, access to means-tested programs in the United States has become increasingly restrictive, with many now limiting assistance to a certain number of months and/or requiring recipients to work a minimum number of hours per week to stay eligible.

> **social insurance programs:** programs designed to transfer income to recipients if and when certain events (like retirement or disability) occur
>
> **means-tested programs:** programs designed to transfer income to those most in need

Other funds flow *toward* the government. The federal income tax collects taxes on both wage income and many forms of capital income. Most states also collect income taxes, and you are probably familiar with state sales taxes from your purchases at retail stores. Many localities collect taxes on real estate, figured as a percentage of the value of the property. A **progressive income tax** system is a system that taxes higher-income households more heavily, in percentage terms, than lower-income households. A progressive tax embodies the principle that those with high incomes should pay more in taxes because of their greater ability to pay without critical sacrifices. While a very poor household, for example, might have to give up eating some meals in order to pay even a small percentage of their income in taxes, a very rich household could pay a substantially larger percentage without much loss in well-being. A **proportional income tax** applies the same percentage tax rate to all income levels. A **regressive income tax** applies a higher tax rate to poorer households.

> **progressive income tax:** a tax which collects a larger share of the income from those most able to pay
>
> **proportional income tax:** a tax which collects the same share of income from households, no matter what their income level

| **regressive income tax:** a tax which collects a larger share of income from poorer households

For example, a 10 percent proportional tax would collect $1,000 from someone with an income of $10,000 per year, and $100,000 from someone with an income of $1,000,000 per year. If, instead, the system collected 10 percent from the poorer person and more than 10 percent from the richer, it would be progressive. If the richer person pays a *smaller* percentage, the tax is regressive. In the United States the federal income tax is a progressive tax, although the rates paid by the highest earners have dropped over time. Sales taxes on basic consumer goods, on the other hand, tend to be regressive, since poorer people spend a larger proportion of their income on such goods.

3.3 THE DISTRIBUTION OF INCOME

In the previous sections we discussed the broad *sources* of household income. But how is income distributed across households? Where do you stand, in terms of outcomes of the distributional process? Is your family in the top, middle, or lower portion of the income distribution?

The U.S. Census Bureau has, for a number of decades, published information on the distribution of incomes in the United States, as shown for 2006 in Table 3.1. The Census Bureau measures incomes by summing up households' incomes from wages and salaries, rent, interest, and profits, and cash transfer payments received from government agencies.

To understand what this table means, imagine dividing up U.S. households into five equal-sized groups (called "quintiles"), with the poorest households all in one group, and then the next poorest in the next group, and so on. The last group to be formed has the richest one-fifth (or 20 percent) of households. The highest-income household in the poorest group would, according to Table 3.1, have an income just short of $20,035. This group, the poorest fifth, received 3.4 percent of all the household income in the country. The richest fifth, those with incomes of $97,032 or more, received 50.5 percent—that is, half—of all the income received in the United States.

Suppose we look at just the top 5 percent of households by income. Households in this very top group have annual incomes above $174,012. In 2006, this group—containing one-twentieth of the total population—received over one-fifth of the total income in the country.

3.4 MEASURING INEQUALITY

Economists frequently use a graph called the **Lorenz curve**—named after the statistician who first developed the technique—to describe the pattern of inequality within an economy. A Lorenz curve for household income in the United States, based on the data in Table 3.1, is shown in Figure 3.4. To construct this curve, you first draw the axes, as shown in the figure. The horizontal axis represents households, lined up from left to right in order of increasing income. The vertical axis measures the cumulative percentage of total income received by households up to a given income level.

| **Lorenz curve:** a line used to portray an income distribution, drawn on a graph with percentiles
| of households on the horizontal axis and the cumulative percentage of income on the vertical axis

In our example, the data shown in Table 3.1 are entered into the Lorenz curve in Figure 3.4 as follows. First, point A represents the fact that the lowest 20 percent of households received 3.4 percent of total income. Point B indicates that the lowest 40 percent of households received 3.4 percent + 8.6 percent = 12.0 percent of total income; point C indicates that the lowest 60 percent of households received 3.4 percent + 8.6 percent + 14.5 percent = 26.5 percent of total income; point D similarly shows the income of the lowest 80 percent, and point E the income of the lowest

Table 3.1   **Distribution of U.S. Household Income in 2006**

Group of Households	Share of Aggregate Income	Lower Limit of Each Fifth
Poorest fifth	3.4%	
Second fifth	8.6%	$20,035
Middle fifth	14.5%	$37,774
Fourth fifth	22.9%	$60,000
Richest fifth	50.5%	$97,032
Richest 5%	22.3%	$174,012

Source: U.S. Census Bureau, Historical Income Tables—Households, Tables H1, H2.

Figure 3.4   **Lorenz Curve for U.S. Household Income, 2006**

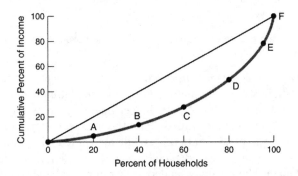

A Lorenz curve is a way of graphically portraying an income distribution. For example, point C indicates that the poorest 60 percent of households received about 27 percent of total household income. If income were perfectly equally distributed, the Lorenz curve would be a straight line from the origin to point F.

95 percent. The Lorenz curve must start at the origin, at the lower left corner of the graph (since 0 percent of households have 0 percent of the total income) and end at point F in the upper right corner (since 100 percent of households have 100 percent of the total income).

If income were distributed equally among all households, the Lorenz curve would be a straight line connecting the origin and point F (the diagonal line in Figure 3.4). This line thus represents a situation of maximum equality. At the other extreme, if one household received all the income, then the Lorenz curve would hug the horizontal axis until all but the very last household was accounted for and then shoot up to point F, creating a vertical line at the right-hand side. Such a line would represent a situation of maximum inequality.

In all real situations, Lorenz curves for distributions of income will fall between these extremes. Graphically, the curve will sag downward to some extent below the diagonal—as in Figure 3.4. The more the curve sags, the greater is the extent of inequality in the income distribution. This observation led an economist by the name of Corrado Gini to introduce a numerical measure of inequality known as the **Gini ratio** (or, as it is sometimes called, the "Gini coefficient"). This is defined as the ratio of the area between the Lorenz curve and the diagonal to the total area under the diagonal line. Referring to areas A and B in Figure 3.5, the Gini ratio is A/(A+B). Clearly, the Gini ratio can vary from 0 for perfect equality to 1 for complete inequality. According to calculations by the U.S. Census Bureau, the Gini ratio for U.S. household income in 2006 was 0.47.

Figure 3.5   **The Gini Ratio, A/(A + B)**

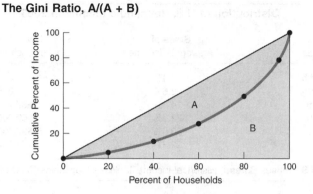

The Gini ratio (or Gini coefficient) sums up the income distribution in a single number: the ratio of the area A to the sum of the areas A and B. If income were perfectly equally distributed, the Gini ratio would be equal to 0.

> **Gini ratio:** a measure of inequality, based on the Lorenz curve, that goes from 0 (perfect equality) up to 1 (complete inequality)

The *Human Development Report 2007/2008* issued by the United Nations Development Program uses a slightly different methodology for calculating the Gini, and comes up with a ratio of 0.41 for the United States. This is higher than the values for all other major industrialized countries, signifying that the United States has a greater degree of income inequality. The Gini for Canada, for example, is about 0.33, while the United Kingdom has a Gini of 0.36, Germany about 0.28, and Japan and Sweden both about 0.25. Countries with more unequal distributions of income than the United States tend to be less industrialized countries, such as Malaysia (0.49) and Brazil (0.57).

Perhaps, you might object, something is wrong with the measure of income we are using. Shouldn't the effect of tax and transfer programs be more fully included? The U.S. Census Bureau has experimented with at least fifteen different definitions of personal income, each of which includes a different way of accounting for income, taxes, and transfers. In one definition, for example, it subtracts the value of government transfers and adds in the value of health insurance fringe benefits paid by businesses for their (often middle-class or higher) employees and the value of net capital gains (discussed later in this chapter, these are usually earned by the relatively wealthy). Under this definition, the Gini ratio, not surprisingly, rises, showing greater inequality. The share of the bottom fifth drops considerably, while the share of the top fifth rises. Another measure adjusts for the effects of the tax system. This causes some change at the top, but little at the bottom. When they further add in the effects of both cash *and non-cash* government transfer programs (such as food stamps), the Gini ratio drops, indicating less inequality.

Government tax and transfer policies—and especially the transfer side—have significant effects on the U.S. household income distribution. Even with the most thorough accounting for transfer aid to low-income households, however, the income of the top fifth of the population is still roughly ten times that of the bottom fifth.

Some important goods and services are obtained, of course, without the use of cash income. Many families prefer to produce at least some services (such as child care and cooking) for themselves. In addition, many of the things we enjoy—such as pleasant parks, safe roads, or clean air—add to our well-being without requiring payments out of our cash income. If we were to look at the distribution of *well-being* rather than just the distribution of income, we would need to take account of these non-income sources of important goods and services. No such comprehensive study has been done. Some of these goods may contribute to lessening inequality—for example, everyone, rich or poor, can enjoy a public park or use a public library. Evidence suggests, however, that at least in some cases the distribution of such non-purchased goods may accentuate, rather than lessen, measures of inequality. Proponents of "environmental justice," for example, point out that polluting industries and toxic waste disposal sites tend to be disproportionately located near poor and minority communities.

3.5 INCOME INEQUALITY OVER TIME

The U.S. household income distribution has been recorded every year since 1967. A similar but not quite identical measure, the family income distribution, has been recorded since 1947. These data show that inequality was gradually decreasing—that is, income was becoming more equally distributed—until 1968. In that year, the Gini ratio for household income was 0.388, the lowest (most equal) on record in the United States. Since 1968 the Gini ratio has increased in almost every year.

Figure 3.6 shows what has happened in recent decades at the very top and the very bottom of the income distribution. The general trend has been for a larger share of income to go to the very richest households (from about 16 percent in 1968 to about 22 percent in 2006), while the share going to the bottom quintile (and, not shown in this figure, the middle quintiles, too) has gradually fallen.

Why has income inequality increased in the United States over this period? One point economists agree on is that some of the increase in inequality has been due to changing demographic characteristics of the U.S. population.

Increases in the proportion of the population that is aged, and increases in single parenthood, have tended to drive down incomes at the low end. People too old to work and people in single-parent households (where paid work and caring activities compete for a limited resource—the adult's time) often lack economic resources. About 18 percent of U.S. children live in poor families. (A household is defined as poor if its income falls below a poverty threshold based on its family size. In 2008, the poverty threshold for a family of four was $21,200.) Meanwhile, the increasing numbers of women entering the labor force have helped boost the incomes of married-couple households at the top. Demographic change, however, is only part of the story and cannot explain the whole pattern of increasing inequality. Economists continue to debate the relative importance of at least three other explanations. (Note that all three explanations propose reasons why the poor have become poorer or more numerous, while the third one also addresses why the rich have gotten richer.)

First, international trade has been increasing. Competition from imports has eliminated many industrial jobs that formerly fell in the middle of the U.S. income distribution. If middle-income industrial jobs are replaced by lower-income service and retail jobs, inequality will increase.

Second, new technologies such as computers and biotechnology have become more important, increasing the incomes of skilled workers who understand and use the new techniques and equipment, while leaving behind the less-skilled workers who remain in low-technology occupations.

Finally, unions have grown weaker and government policy has become markedly less supportive of unions and low-wage workers, while the compensation given to top executives and board members of large corporations has skyrocketed. According to studies done by *Business Week*, in 1980 chief executive officers (CEOs) of large U.S. corporations earned an average of 42 times the amount earned by the average hourly worker. In 1990, they earned 85 times as much. In 2000, they earned 531 times as much.[1]

Figure 3.6   **Income Shares of the Richest and Poorest Households, 1968–2006**

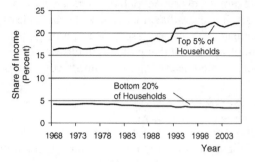

Inequality in the United States has been increasing since 1968. The share of the richest households in aggregate income rose from about 16 percent to about 22 percent, while the share of the poorest 20 percent of the population fell from about 4.2 percent to about 3.4 percent.

In short, along with demographic change, global competition, technology, or changes in government and business policies—or some combination of these factors—may account for the rise in inequality within the United States.

3.6 WEALTH INEQUALITY

The distribution of wealth (what people own in assets—a stock) tends to be much more unequal than the distribution of income (what people receive in the course of a year—a flow). Most people own relatively little wealth, relying mainly on labor income and/or government, nonprofit, or family transfers to support their expenditures. It is possible to have *negative* wealth. This happens when the value of a person's debts (such as for a car, house, or credit cards) is greater than the value of her assets. For people in the middle class, the equity they have in their house is often their most significant asset. On the other hand, those who *do* own substantial physical and financial wealth are generally in a position to put much of it into assets that increase in value over time and/or yield flows of capital income—which can in turn be invested in the acquisition of still more assets.

The distribution of wealth is, however, less frequently and less systematically studied than the distribution of money income. Partly, this is because wealth can be hard to measure. Much wealth is held in the form of unrealized **capital gains**. A household receives a capital gain if it sells an appreciated asset, such as shares in a company, land, or antiques, for more than the price at which it purchased the asset. An asset may appreciate in value for a long time before it is actually sold. No one, however, will know exactly how much such an asset has really gained or lost in value until the owner actually *does* sell it, thus "realizing"—turning into actual dollars—the capital gain. Another reason why it is harder to get information on wealth is that although the government requires people to report their annual *incomes* from wages and many investments for tax purposes, it does not require everyone to regularly and comprehensively report their asset holdings.

  capital gain: an increase in the value of an asset over time

One study estimates that the Gini ratio for the distribution of wealth in the United States was .83 in 2001—indicating much more inequality than is found in the distribution of income.[2] It has been estimated that in 1998 the top 1 percent of U.S. households owned about 38 percent of all household assets, and the top 10 percent owned about 71 percent, while the bottom 40 percent owned only 0.2 percent.[3]

Discussion Questions

1. In your own life so far, how big a role has exchange played in giving you what you need to live? (That is, to what extent have you received assets, goods, or services *because of something specific you have traded in return*?) How big a role has transfer played? Do you expect this to change in coming years?
2. What do you think is the minimal amount of income an individual, or a small family, would need to live in *your* community? (Think about the rent or mortgage on a one- or two-bedroom residence, etc.) What does this probably mean about where the average level of income in your community fits into the U.S. income distribution shown in Table 3.1?

4. THE THREE SPHERES OF ECONOMIC ACTIVITY

Economic activity takes place in three major spheres, which we designate here as the core, public-purpose, and business spheres. Economists often refer to these groups as household, government, and business spheres. In this chapter, however we use the term "core" instead of "households," in order to emphasize the importance of communities, in addition to households, in the "core" activities described below. (Think of the maxim, "It takes a village to raise a child.") Instead of "government," we use the term "public purpose" to include both government and nongovernmental nonprofit organizations whose activities are of growing importance in modern societies. We will explore the roles of the core, public-purpose, and business spheres below.

4.1 THE CORE SPHERE

Long before the invention of money, of organized markets, and of systems of government, human societies organized themselves along lines of kinship and community to undertake the economic activities essential to maintaining and improving the conditions for human life. The **core sphere** is made up of household, family, and community institutions that organize resource management, production, distribution, and consumption, usually on a small scale, and largely without the use of money.

> **core sphere:** households, families, and communities

One distinguishing characteristic of the core sphere is how work activities are rewarded: Instead of extrinsic monetary rewards, work tends to be rewarded directly by what it produces. For example, work in a home garden is rewarded with tomatoes, and the reward of good child care is a happy and healthy child. People may volunteer their services to their community because they recognize that living in a healthy community is important. People play cards, soccer, or music together because they find these activities intrinsically enjoyable. Another distinguishing characteristic is that core sphere activities tend to be organized to respond to immediately perceived needs—rather than, for example, to the ability to pay.

The core economy is the central location of many important economic activities that sustain human life. These include:

Childbearing and child raising. Parents—even when assisted by family-planning services, child care centers, public schools, extended family, and the like—still carry the primary responsibility for fertility decisions and for caring for and nurturing children. Bearing and rearing a child is the ultimate "human capital" activity—populating the society for the future. Younger children need direct feeding, dressing, bathing, holding, and responsive interaction with caring adults. Older children need less hands-on care but still need supervision and help in learning many physical, mental, and emotional skills. Much of the work of childrearing also involves the building up of "social capital"—helping children function in larger communities. Community supports like playgroups and carpools can also assist in the productive activities of childrearing work.

Decisions regarding investing in skills and education. Other human capital decisions are also often made on a household basis. How long children stay in school, or whether an adult goes for further education or training, are often household decisions.

Care of the sick, elderly, or otherwise needy. In countries like the United States, hospitals, nursing homes, mental health clinics, and other institutions exist for people who are acutely ill or incapacitated. However, families, friends, and neighbors remain the first source of support for people with dependency needs. People who are temporarily mildly ill, recovering from surgery, or upset over life events are primarily cared for by friends and family. People with chronic mental or physical health problems may require considerable support services from their families and other people in their communities, perhaps for decades.

The final stage of production of many goods and services. Pasta cannot be eaten until it is cooked. A vacuum cleaner provides no services until someone plugs it in and pushes it around. Grass seed does nothing until someone plants it. Household production activities such as cooking, cleaning, and house and yard maintenance convert many goods and services (often bought on markets) into forms suitable for final use. These production processes generally involve the use of labor time, materials, and the services of household capital goods (such as stoves and lawn mowers). As we will see in Chapters 5 and 6, national accounting frameworks have been slow to recognize the importance of household production.

The organization of savings and investment. Households decide how much of their cash income to allocate to saving. They also decide how to allocate their financial saving—whether to hold them in retirement funds, real estate, money market funds, etc. While households also save through more structured (and less voluntary) channels such as pension plans, the savings decisions of individual households are of much interest to macroeconomists. Family and friends also frequently use savings to make gifts or loans among themselves—for example, to finance food and rent in times of need, or to help a friend or relative to acquire the funds for a house down payment or to start a business.

The allocation of consumption spending. Households are the final decision makers about whether to buy denim pants or DVDs, hybrid cars or SUVs. As we will see, the level and composition of consumption in an economy as a whole plays an important role in determining macroeconomic living standards, stability, and sustainability.

Decisions regarding the supply of labor services. Decisions to work in the labor market, to become self-employed, or to engage in household production are often made not simply by individuals, but by households as part of a joint plan for family support.

The organization of the use of leisure time. Besides putting in work time in core sphere production, people enjoy "play" time with their family, friends, and neighbors as well. Vacations and visits are very often planned on a family basis, and activities of recreation and relaxation are largely organized around core sphere networks of family and community. Having leisure time, and the goods and services to enjoy it with friends and family, is a substantial component of the standard of living.

When the core sphere is working effectively to support the quality of life, important goods and services are provided to many, many people, even if the scale of production in each specific case is quite small. Because most core sphere activities involve face-to-face interaction, the core sphere is the primary location in which the ability to form good social relations is developed.

Of course, core spheres can also work badly or inadequately. For example, responsibilities for children or elderly and ill people may be inequitably assigned between women and men. Such responsibilities may also overwhelm the personal resources of impoverished families and communities. There are limits to what can be accomplished within small-scale, largely informal networks of personal relations. For many economic goals, more formal and larger-scale organizations are also needed.

4.2 THE PUBLIC-PURPOSE SPHERE

Kinship and community were the earliest modes of human organization, but larger organizations soon arose. Communities found advantages to banding together in larger groups for mutual protection, increased social contact, etc.

The **public-purpose sphere** includes governments and their agencies, as well as nonprofit organizations such as charities and professional associations, and international institutions such as the World Bank and the United Nations.

The distinguishing characteristic of these institutions is that they exist for an explicit purpose related to "the public good"—that is, the common good of some group larger than a household or informal community. Their definitions of "the public good," however, may vary widely and may even contradict one another. They are charged with purposes such as defending a country's borders, relieving poverty, providing formal health care and education, protecting the natural environment, and stabilizing global financial markets.

> **public-purpose sphere:** governments and other local, national, and international organizations established for some public purpose beyond individual or family self-interest, and not operating with the goal of making a profit

Organizations in the public-purpose sphere tend to be larger and more formally structured than those in the core sphere, and usually they are more monetized. Work is often motivated by a mixture of pay and volunteerism. Jobs in nonprofit organizations often pay less than jobs of equivalent skill and responsibility in the business sphere. It is sometimes said that government employees are in "public service."

We can break down the economic functions of public-purpose organizations into two general categories: *regulation,* where the public-purpose organization sets rules or standards for the actions of other economic entities, and *direct provision,* where a public-purpose organization itself takes on economic activities.

Regulation. One very basic function of public-purpose organizations is to **regulate** economic activities—that is, to set the standards and "rules of the game" by which other economic actors will "play." Public-purpose organizations that promote, legislate, or enforce property rights, rules about contracts or disclosure of information, laws, or norms of obligation; promulgate standards; and/or perform other coordinating functions create the legal and social infrastructure for economic activity.

Many people think of "regulation" entirely in terms of "government regulation," and it is true that the government sets many rules and standards with which other economic actors are legally obligated to comply. Government regulation of financial and securities markets, for example, plays an important role in macroeconomics. However, many nonprofit groups participate in regulating economic activity, particularly in the area of standard setting. For example, chances are you have taken a standardized exam like the AP, SAT I or II, GRE, GMAT, or TOEFL. These are all developed and administered by the Educational Testing Service, which is a large private nonprofit organization. While we might not commonly think of such privately provided standards as "regulation," the standards implicit in these exams do, in fact, influence what is taught by institutions, if they wish their students to be well prepared for taking them. Public-purpose organizations often provide the legal, social, and informational infrastructure that both support and constrain other actors in their economic activity.

regulation: setting standards or laws to govern behavior

Direct Provision. Public-purpose organizations produce many goods and services, including national defense, physical infrastructure like highways and port facilities, and such services as education and, in many countries, health care. Direct public provision is often used to supply goods that cannot be supplied equitably or efficiently by private provision. Some goods are provided by the public-purpose sphere because, as a society, we believe that everyone should have access to them, regardless of the kind of family or community they were born in and regardless of their ability to pay. Public schooling from kindergarten through high school is a primary example. In large U.S. cities, public hospitals provide necessary emergency medical care to the poor and uninsured. Compared to Canada and most of Europe, the United States puts fewer resources into these activities. For example, Canada and most European countries have more extensive public health systems, which provide widely accessible nonemergency care as well. France and the Canadian province of Quebec provide highly subsidized care and education for prekindergarten children.

Nonprofit organizations also often offer services related to education, health, and welfare. Both governments and private charities often transfer income to people in need. Other goods and services are provided by public-purpose organizations because they are of a type that is called a "public good," as discussed in Chapter 2. Sometimes it is more efficient for a public-purpose organization to provide a good or service because of the presence of significant externalities, transaction costs, market power, or advantages to centralized information (as also discussed in Chapter 2).

Although in some instances public-purpose organizations offer goods and services for sale, much as businesses do, this is generally not their primary focus. Public-purpose organizations usually raise much of the money they need to function by soliciting (or, in the case of governments, requiring) monetary contributions in the form of taxes, donations, or membership fees.

The interplay of governments and nonprofits in providing and regulating services can be quite complex. For example, in the United States the government Securities and Exchange Commission (SEC) regulates the exchange of securities such as stocks and bonds. The SEC accepts what are called Generally Accepted Accounting Principles (GAAP) as the authoritative standard for financial reporting. These principles are actually written, however, by the nonprofit Financial Accounting Standards Board.

The main strength of public-purpose institutions is that (like core institutions) they can provide goods and services of high intrinsic value, but (unlike core institutions) they are big enough to take on jobs that require broader social coordination. Unlike the business sphere, the provision of goods and services itself, and not the financial results of these activities, remains the primary intended focus of public-purpose organizations.

The public-purpose sphere has its weaknesses, of course. Compared to the core sphere, the government, in particular, is often criticized as being cold and impersonal. Compared to the business sphere, institutions in the public-purpose sphere are sometimes accused of being rigid, slow to adapt, and made inefficient by an overgrowth of regulations and a bloated bureaucracy. Organizations can lose sight of the intrinsic, common-good goal of providing "public service" and become more interested in increasing their own organizational budget. Because public-purpose organizations are commonly supported by taxes or donations that are often not tightly linked to the quality of their services, they may not have financial incentives to improve the quality of what they provide. Many current debates about reforms in governments and nonprofits concern how incentives for efficiency can be improved without eroding these organizations' orientation toward providing goods and services of high intrinsic value.

4.3 THE BUSINESS SPHERE

The U.S. government defines businesses as "entities that produce goods and services for sale at a price intended at least to approximate the costs of production."[4] The **business sphere** is made up of such firms. A business firm is expected to look for opportunities to buy and manage resources in such a way that, after the product is sold, the owners of the firm will earn profits.

> **business sphere:** firms that produce goods and services for profitable sale

Whereas the core sphere responds to direct needs, and the public-purpose sphere responds to its constituents, business firms are responsive to demands for goods and services, as expressed through markets by people who can afford to buy the firms' products.

Private for-profit enterprises in the United States and many other countries fall into four main legal forms: proprietorships, partnerships, corporations, and cooperatives. Proprietorships are businesses owned by single individuals or families. Partnerships are owned by a group of two or more individuals. Corporations are business firms that, through a process of becoming chartered by a state or federal government, attain a legal existence separate from the individuals or organizations who own it. Individual owners can come and go, but the corporation remains. If the corporation goes bankrupt and is forced to dissolve, the owners of a corporation cannot lose more than their investment. On the other hand, there is no legal limit to the profit they can make if the corporation is successful. This asymmetry, along with its other legal advantages, makes the corporation the preferred structure for major business activities in most countries.

Corporations that issue stock are governed by shareholders according to the principle of one-share, one-vote. In principle, shareholders elect a board of directors, who in turn hire professional managers to run the day-to-day operations of the corporation. (In fact, shareholders often lack the power to propose directors other than those put forward by the existing board and/or management. There are ongoing struggles about how or whether to increase the investors' control in this respect.) Cooperatives, in contrast to corporations, cannot issue stock and are governed by a different ownership principle. Each member of the cooperative, no matter what his or her position, has one and only one vote. In practice, cooperatives are owned by one of three groups: their workers, their suppliers, or their consumers.

A strength of business organization is that, because businesses have at least one clear goal of making profit, they may operate with superior efficiency. A profit orientation is commonly thought to drive firms to choose the most valuable outputs to produce, and to produce them at the least possible cost. The profit motivation is often thought also to encourage *innovation:* People are more motivated to come up with clever new ideas when they know they may reap financial rewards. We all benefit, in terms of our material standard of living, from business efficiency and innovations that bring us improved products at lower prices.

The relative weakness of the business sphere comes from the fact that business interests may or may not coincide with overall social well-being. Firms *may* act to enhance social well-being—for example, by making decisions that consider the full needs of their customers and their workers and take into account externalities, including those that affect the natural environment. They may be guided in these directions by the goodwill of their owners and managers, by pressure from their customers or workers, or by government regulation. Production for market exchange, however, has no *built-in* correction for market externalities. And sometimes "innovation" can take a perverse form. Enron Corporation, for example, in the late 1990s and early 2000s boosted its reported earnings primarily by inventing unusual and "innovative" accounting practices, which served to hide the extreme weakness of its financial situation from investors. In fields such as health care and education, where it can be difficult to define clear goals, businesses may increase profits by "innovatively" cutting corners on the less measurable and less-often-marketed aspects of quality of life.

4.4 A COMPARATIVE NOTE: LESS INDUSTRIALIZED ECONOMIES

Many less industrialized economies have large **informal spheres** of small market enterprises operating outside of government oversight and regulation. Although this sphere could be classified as "business" because it involves private production for sale, it is also similar to the "core sphere" in that the activities are very small-scale and often depend on family and community connections. Like the core sphere, informal business activities are often ignored in government-compiled accounts.

In the United States, street-level illegal drug trades and housecleaning services provided "off the books" by illegal immigrants would be two examples of the "informal" sphere. In less industrialized counties, however, it is sometimes the case that *most* people are employed in small-scale agriculture, trade, and services that often go uncounted.

> **informal sphere:** made up of businesses operating outside of government oversight and regulation. In less industrialized countries it may constitute the majority of economic activity.

If we were focusing mainly on less developed countries, it would be necessary to pay a great deal more attention to the complicating reality of "informal" economic activity and perhaps to discuss it as a fourth sphere. For industrialized economies, however, we can deal with this issue by simply noting, as we have just done, that it could legitimately be classified as occurring within either the business sphere or the core sphere, leaving open the question as to which of these classifications is more appropriate.

Discussion Questions

1. Education is sometimes provided within the core sphere (at-home preschool activities, and home schooling), often provided by the public-purpose sphere (public and nonprofit schools), and occasionally provided by for-profit firms ("charter schools" or firms offering specific training programs). Can you think of some possible advantages and disadvantages of each type of provision?
2. Make a list of several things that, over the last few days, you have eaten, drunk, been entertained by, been transported by, been sheltered by, or received other services from. (For example, "dinner at Gina's," "my apartment," "the health clinic," etc.) Then, using the definitions above, determine which of the three spheres provided each item.

REVIEW QUESTIONS

1. What are the four essential economic activities?
2. What four types of capital contribute to productivity? Describe them.
3. How does economists' use of the term "capital" differ from common use?
4. What do economists mean by "investment"?
5. Describe the economic activity of production.
6. What are the two main forms that the activity of distribution takes? Describe.
7. Describe the relationship between consumption and saving.
8. Describe the difference between a stock and a flow, giving examples.
9. Explain the difference between gross and net investment.
10. What is the difference between renewable and nonrenewable resources?
11. What is a sustainable socioeconomic system?
12. What are the two major forms of income received in exchange?
13. What is the main reason for transfer programs?
14. What is the difference between means-tested and social insurance programs?
15. Describe progressive, proportional, and regressive taxation.
16. What share of aggregate income does each quintile of households receive?
17. What is a Lorenz curve? What does it measure?
18. What is the Gini ratio? What does a higher value of the ratio signify?
19. Has income inequality decreased or increased over recent decades? What are some of the reasons?
20. Is wealth or more less equally distributed than income? Why?
21. What are the three spheres of economic activity?
22. What are some major characteristics and functions of the core sphere?
23. What are some major characteristics and functions of the public-purpose sphere?
24. What are some major characteristics, and strengths and weaknesses, of the business sphere?

EXERCISES

1. Which of the following are flows? Which are stocks? If a flow, which of the five major kind(s) of capital does it increase or decrease? If a stock, what kind of capital is it?
   a. The fish in a lake
   b. The output of a factory during a year
   c. The income you receive in a month
   d. The reputation of a business among its customers
   e. The assets of a bank
   f. The equipment in a factory
   g. A process of diplomatic negotiations
   h. The discussion in an economics class

2. Which of the following are examples of exchange? Of transfer?
   a. De Beers mining company sells diamonds to wholesalers
   b. De Beers mining company takes diamonds from the mines

c. You pay interest on credit card balances

d. Your bank donates posters for a local community fair

3. Statistics from the government of Thailand describe the household income distribution in that country, for 2000, as follows:

Group of Households	Share of Aggregate Income
Poorest fifth	5.5%
Second fifth	8.8%
Middle fifth	13.2%
Fourth fifth	21.5%
Richest fifth	51.0%

Source: National Statistics Office Thailand, "Household Socio-Economic Survey," Table 9. http://www.nso.go.th/eng/stat/socio/soctab6.htm

a. Create a carefully labeled Lorenz curve describing this distribution. (Be precise about the labels on the vertical axis.)

b. Compare this distribution to the distribution in the United States. Would you expect the Gini ratio for Thailand to be much higher or lower? Why?

4. Match each concept in Column A with a definition or example in Column B.

Column A	Column B
a. An important function of the core sphere	1. Fish in the ocean
b. Social capital	2. Regulation
c. Progressive taxation	3. A very unequal income distribution
d. A nonrenewable natural resource	4. Taxation that collects proportionally more from the poor
e. Capital gain	5. What you are adding in the way of new computers to your office, minus what has become obsolete
f. Quintile	6. A gift of food
g. An important function of the public purpose sphere	7. A house you own increases in value over time
h. Net investment	8. A shared language within a community
i. Regressive taxation	9. A very equal income distribution
j. A Gini ratio close to 1	10. Decisions regarding skills and education
k. A renewable natural resource	11. A group containing 20 percent of the total
l. Manufactured capital	12. Taxation that collects proportionally more from the rich
m. In-kind transfer	13. A factory building
n. A Gini ratio close to 0	14. Iron ore

5. Suppose a tax system is set up as follows: everyone gets to subtract $3,000 from their income, and then pays the government 20 percent of the rest. Is this tax proportional, progressive, or regressive? Show your reasoning. (Hint: calculate what households with incomes of $10,000 per year, $50,000 per year, and $100,000 per year would pay in taxes, and the percent their taxes represent of their total income.)

6. How does inequality vary across countries? Choose two countries not mentioned in the text, and write a paragraph comparing their performance on the Gini ratio and according to income share by quintile. Which country seems to have a more unequal distribution of income? For data, consult the United Nations Development Program's *Human Development Report,* available through its website (www.undp.org). Or, if

your library subscribes, consult the World Development Indicators Online database. Note which data source you used.

NOTES

1. Jennifer Gill, "We're Back to Serfs and Royalty," *Business Week Online,* April 9, 2001.

2. Edward N. Wolff and Ajit Zacharias, "Household Wealth and the Measurement of Economic Well-Being in the United States," The Levy Economics Institute Working Paper No. 447, 2006.

3. Edward N. Wolff, "Recent Trends in Wealth Ownership, 1983–1998." Jerome Levy Economics Institute Working Paper No. 300.

4. U.S. Bureau of Economic Analysis, "A Guide to the NIPAs," p. M–20, http://www.bea.doc.gov/bea/an/nipaguid.pdf (17 February 2002).

4 Supply and Demand

The on-line auction site eBay has more than 248 million users. Every second, $1,812 worth of products—recreational vehicles, high-definition televisions, commemorative coins, T-shirts, condominiums, you name it—are traded. From its beginnings in the United States in 1995, eBay has grown into a global marketing service for individuals and small businesses. Perhaps you have bought or sold something on eBay. If you have, then you have had direct experience with a real-world market very similar, in some ways, to the sort of idealized market that forms the basis for economists' theory of supply and demand.

1. MARKETS AND MACROECONOMICS

As we discussed in Chapter 2, markets are places where individuals, businesses, and other organizations engage in buying and selling. The economic theory of supply and demand is an exceptionally useful example of a "thought experiment" that seeks to describe, in abstract terms, how people make their decisions about buying and selling.

The theory provides an elegant, simple picture of how potential sellers decide how much of a good or service to offer to sell (supply) on a market, and how potential buyers decide how much to purchase (demand). The theory then goes on to show how a market, when it functions in a smooth, idealized way, coordinates these decisions.

The real world sometimes works pretty much as the theory predicts; at other times there are other forces that push decisions, and prices, away from the result predicted in the theory. When the real world is behaving according to the theory, the result is that "the market"—not any particular individual agent or bureaucracy—determines the number of units of a good or service that are actually sold on a market, and the price at which the units sell.

1.1 CLASSICALS AND KEYNESIANS

The direct study of actual markets is more of a *micro*economic topic than a *macro*economic one, as we defined these terms in Chapter 1. One reason we particularly need to introduce (or review, for those of you who have taken microeconomics) the model of supply and demand here is that understanding this model is crucial for understanding the classical approach to macroeconomics. Classical macroeconomists tend to believe that markets generally function smoothly, as portrayed in this model—at least as long as governments don't interfere.

Keynesian economists, on the other hand, tend to believe that market economies need more help from government policies. They agree that the model of supply and demand has an important role to play in economics, but claim that understanding the workings of the macroeconomy requires that one go beyond this model, for two reasons. First, real-world markets may deviate in important ways from the one portrayed in the abstract model. Second, explaining economic phenomena at the national level may require a different set of theoretical tools from those designed for analyzing individual markets for particular goods.

The first four sections of this chapter lay out the basic supply and demand model. In the last section, we return to the question of how this model sometimes may be, and sometimes may not be, helpful in understanding macroeconomics.

1.2 A PARTICULAR KIND OF MARKET

The sort of market imagined in the classical world has three noteworthy characteristics. It is envisioned as:

1. **Perfectly competitive**. In a perfectly competitive market, there many buyers and sellers of a good, all units of the good are identical, anyone can enter or leave the market at will, and everyone has perfect information.

2. **Spot**. A spot market is a market for immediate delivery of a good or service.

3. **Double auction**. An auction market is a market where an item is sold to the highest bidder. In a *double* auction, both buyers and sellers state prices at which they are willing to make transactions.

eBay, for example, is a pretty good real-world example of an auction market in which there are many buyers and sellers. You have experienced other kinds of markets, as well, however. If you want to buy the Microsoft Windows operating system, for example, the sole ultimate supplier is Microsoft. Microsoft's dominance means that the market for computer operating systems is far from perfectly competitive. If you sign a contract for a year's lease on an apartment, you are making a long-term agreement to buy housing services over an extended period of time. Markets for rental housing are examples of markets that are not "spot." Or if you go into a retail clothing store in the United States to buy a shirt, you pay the price on the tag. You will be considered to be acting strangely if you attempt to get the sales assistant to accept a lower bid. Retail stores in the United States do not operate on an auction basis.

> **perfectly competitive market:** a market in which there are many buyers and sellers, all units of the good are identical, and there is free entry and exit and perfect information
>
> **spot market:** a market for immediate delivery
>
> **double-auction market:** a market in which both buyers and sellers state prices at which they are willing to make transactions, and the item is sold to the highest bidder

Many of the controversies in macroeconomics come down to a question of the degree to which real-world markets—and, in particular, real-world labor markets and financial markets—are similar to, or differ in important ways from, the perfectly competitive, spot, double-auction markets assumed in basic market theory.

Discussion Questions

1. Have you ever traded on eBay or a similar Internet auction site? If you have, describe to your classmates how it works.
2. Think about a case recently where you exchanged money for some good or service. Was that market "perfectly competitive"? Was it a "spot" market? Was it a "double-auction" market?

Table 4.1	**A Supply Schedule for Apartments**										
Price ($1000s)	100	99	98	97	96	95	94	93	92	91	90
Quantity of Apartments Supplied	10	9	8	7	6	5	4	3	2	1	0

2. The Theory of Supply

We will start with the following thought experiment. Suppose there is a condominium apartment building where all the apartments are identical, and each apartment has a different owner. Suppose that a number of them might be interested in selling their apartments. For the purposes of this thought experiment, we will assume that they are all well informed and interested primarily in their potential monetary gain.

Each owner has a slightly different idea of what would be an acceptable price. No owner will accept less than $91,000 for his or her apartment. At a price of $91,000, one owner is willing to sell. At a price of $92,000, two owners are willing to sell. In fact, it turns out that each time the price rises by $1,000 there is one more owner willing to sell an apartment. None would be willing to sell at $90,000.

2.1 The Supply Schedule and Curve

The result of this pattern is the schedule that is shown in Table 4.1, which we call a supply schedule. A supply schedule shows us, in the form of a table, the quantity of a good or service that would be offered by the sellers at each possible price.

From the supply schedule, we can graph a **supply curve**, as shown in Figure 4.1, which shows the same information in a different form.* If we ask how many apartments will be offered for sale at a price of $96,000, for example, we can look across from $96,000 on the vertical (price) axis over to the supply curve, and then drop down to the horizontal (quantity) axis to find that the answer is six.

| **supply curve:** a curve indicating the quantities that sellers are willing to supply at various prices

Note that the supply curve in Figure 4.1 slopes upward. This seems reasonable, consistent with an expectation that suppliers of a good or service will tend to offer more for sale, the higher the price they receive. Price and quantity have a positive (or direct) relationship along the supply curve.

We see *movement along a supply curve* when we note, for example, that the quantity of apartments that will be offered for sale rises from six to seven as the price rises from $96,000 to $97,000. This is a case of **change in quantity supplied**. It is important to refer to movement along a supply curve as change in the *quantity* supplied in order to avoid confusion with the topic of the next section.

| **change in quantity supplied:** movement along a supply curve in response to a price change

---

* Unlike the graph we drew in Chapter 2 based on *time-series* data, here our (made-up) "data" are what are called *cross-section* data. That is, the "data" show various values for the variables (price and quantity) all measured at a single point in time. Note that, for ease in presentation, we have started the vertical axis in Figure 4.1 at a number other than zero.

Figure 4.1   **The Supply Curve for Apartments**

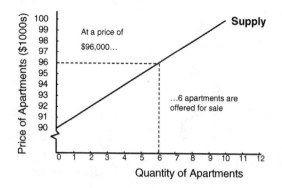

The supply curve shows the same information as the supply schedule. At higher prices, more apartments are offered on the market by people who are in a position to sell.

Check yourself by answering this question with reference to Table 4.1 or Figure 4.1: By how much does the *quantity supplied* change when the price changes from $97,000 to $100,000?*

2.2 CHANGES IN SUPPLY

In contrast to *changes in quantity supplied*, we say there has been a **change in supply** when the whole supply curve shifts.

> **change in supply:** a shift of the supply curve in response to some determinant other than the item's price

Why might the whole curve shift? As we noted in Chapter 2, models make frequent use of *ceteris paribus* ("all else constant") assumptions. The supply curve shown in Figure 4.1 holds, we presume, for a given set of circumstances. But what if circumstances were different? What if there were more sellers at each price? Or what if the same sellers were generally willing to accept lower offers?

Suppose that at each price there were two more potential sellers. The supply curve would shift to the right from S_1 to S_2 as illustrated in Figure 4.2. Now, at a price of $96,000, for example, eight owners are willing to sell, instead of only six. We can describe this increase in supply by saying either that "supply has risen" or that "the supply curve has shifted out." (It may seem confusing that a supply *increase* shifts the supply curve *down*. Remember to start the "story" by reading across horizontally from the price axis. Then you will notice that the shift goes out toward *higher* numbers on the quantity axis.)

We would see the same result if, instead of new sellers entering the market, the existing sellers each became willing to accept $2,000 less. (This might happen, for instance, because increasing flood danger or crime in the area makes them more eager to sell.) In this case as well, eight owners would now be willing to sell at a price of $96,000, whereas before it took a price of $98,000 to get eight owners to want to sell. This would also be termed an "increase in supply," and again the supply curve would shift as illustrated in Figure 4.2.

---

* Answer: The quantity supplied rises by three apartments, from seven apartments up to ten.

Figure 4.2   **An Increase in Supply**

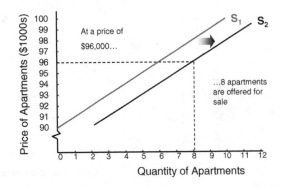

The supply curve shifts outward (to the right) when sellers decide to supply a larger quantity to the market at a given price, or to charge less for a given quantity.

Figure 4.3   **A Decrease in Supply**

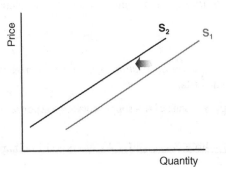

The supply curve shifts backward (to the left) when sellers decide to supply a smaller quantity to the market at a given price, or to charge more for a given quantity.

If instead, the number of sellers goes *down,* or the minimum price each seller is willing to accept *rises,* the supply curve will lie to the *left* of the original one, as shown in Figure 4.3. We say that "supply has decreased," or "supply has fallen," or "the supply curve has shifted back."

Thus the number of sellers and their preferences are among the things that can affect the location of the supply curve. Many other factors affect the location of the supply curve. What exactly these non-price determinants of supply are will generally depend on what, specifically, is being sold in a market. While we've rather arbitrarily chosen a simple real-estate market for our example, the determinants of supply will vary depending on whether the item in question is an asset, produced good, or service, and on particular characteristics of the item. For example, in the market for oil, the determinants of supply will include the success of oil exploration and discovery (a big new discovery will increase supply), while in the market for computers technological innovations that lower chip costs will increase supply. In the market for corn, a bad harvest would reduce supply, but new, more productive varieties of corn would increase it. You can easily think of similar examples for other goods and services.

Discussion Questions

1. Explain in words why the supply curve slopes upward.
2. Verbally explain the difference between a change in *quantity supplied* and a change in *supply.* Considering the supply side of the market for lawn-mowing services, what kind of change (*increase* or *decrease, in quantity supplied* or *supply*) would each of the following events cause?
   a. A rise in the going price for lawn-mowing services
   b. More people decide to offer to mow lawns
   c. Gasoline for lawn movers gets much more expensive (assume the person doing the mowing buys the gas)

3. THE THEORY OF DEMAND

Now let us assume that there a number of potential *buyers* of apartments, and that they are also well informed and interested in purchasing an apartment, to live in or rent out, if they can get one at a good price. However, they have a different point of view. They all regard a price of $100,000 as too high: None of them will purchase an apartment at that price. However, one of them is willing to purchase at $99,000; that individual and another potential buyer are both willing to buy if the price drops to $98,000; and so on.

3.1 THE DEMAND SCHEDULE AND CURVE

In Table 4.2, we show the demand schedule that reflects this case. A demand schedule describes, in the form of a table, the quantity of a good or service that buyers are willing to purchase at each possible price.

From the demand schedule we can graph a **demand curve**, as shown in Figure 4.4. Note that the demand curve in Figure 4.4 slopes downward. It seems reasonable to expect that, generally, the higher the price of a good, the fewer people will want to buy. Price and quantity have a nega-tive (or inverse) relationship along the demand curve.

> **demand curve:** a curve indicating the quantities that buyers are ready to purchase at various prices

A movement *along* a demand curve—for example, if we note that the quantity of apartments that will be purchased falls from four to three as the price rises from $96,000 to $97,000—must always be referred to as a **change in the quantity demanded**.

> **change in quantity demanded:** movement along a demand curve in response to a price change

Check yourself by answering this question with reference to Table 4.2 or Figure 4.4: By how much does the *quantity demanded* change when the price changes from $97,000 to $100,000?*

---

* Answer: The quantity demanded drops by three apartments, from three apartments down to none.

Table 4.2	**A Demand Schedule for Apartments**										
Price ($1000s)	100	99	98	97	96	95	94	93	92	91	90
Quantity of Apartments Demanded		0	1	2	3	4	5	6	7	8	9	10

Figure 4.4   **The Demand Curve for Apartments**

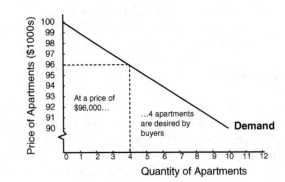

The demand curve shows the same information as the demand schedule. At higher prices, fewer apartments are desired by people looking to buy.

3.2 Changes in Demand

As with supply, we distinguish between *a change in quantity demanded* and a **change in demand**. When there is a change in demand, the whole curve shifts.

> **change in demand:** a shift of the demand curve in response to some determinant other than the item's price

Why might the whole curve shift? Suppose there is a large movement of population into the area around our hypothetical apartment building. Many more people need housing. Or suppose that a number of potential buyers experience an increase in income or inherit money from relatives, becoming able (and willing) to pay more than they formerly could afford. Specifically, suppose that at every price there are now four more willing buyers for apartments in this building. Such a change is illustrated by the shift to the right from D$_1$ to D$_2$ in Figure 4.5. We say that "demand has risen" or "the demand curve has shifted out." (Because of the curve's negative slope, in this case shifting "out" also means shifting "up.")

We would see the same result if, instead of new buyers entering the market, the existing buyers each became willing to pay $4,000 more for an apartment. This could be because prices for similar apartments in other buildings in this city have risen. Other, similar apartments are what economists call **substitutes**. That is, they are items that can be used *in place of* other items.

A classic example of substitute goods is Coke versus Pepsi. An *in*crease in the price of a substitute good tends to *in*crease the demand for the good in question (because people who are unwilling to pay the higher price will shift to the substitute good whose price has not risen). A rise in the price of comparable apartments could lead to an "increase in demand" for apartments in this building. This would also be illustrated by Figure 4.5.

Figure 4.5   **An Increase in Demand**

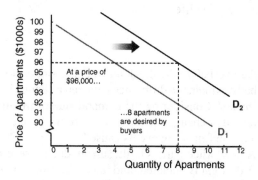

The demand curve shifts outward (to the right) when more buyers want to buy at a given price, or buyers are willing to pay a higher price for a given quantity.

Figure 4.6   **A Decrease in Demand**

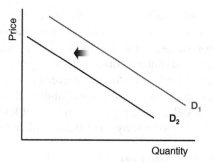

When the demand curve shifts inward (to the left), we say that demand has decreased.

| **substitute good:** a good that can be used in place of another

On the other hand, other things might be **complements** to these apartments. Complements are goods that are used along *with* the good in question. A classic example of complementary goods is hot dogs *and* mustard. Suppose, for example, the apartments are far from the locations in which people work. A rise in the price of gasoline would make these apartments less attractive. Demand for the good in question tends to *de*crease with an *in*crease in the price of a complementary good. This is shown in Figure 4.6.

| **complementary good:** a good that is used along with another good

Thus the number of potential buyers, their ability to pay, and things such as prices of substitutes and complements are among the things that can affect the location of the demand curve. Many other factors affect the location of the demand curves, depending on the specific market in question. For example, in the market for steel, overall economic growth will increase the demand for steel, while the development of substitute materials, such as plastic composites for use in automobiles, will decrease it. Hotter weather will increase demand for ice cream, but will decrease the demand for sweaters—and so forth. We can easily identify many examples of other demand shifts in everyday life.

Discussion Questions

1. Explain verbally why the demand curve slopes downward.
2. Verbally explain the difference between a change in *quantity demanded* and a change in *demand.* Considering the demand side of the market for lawn-mowing services, what kind of change (*increase* or *decrease,* in *quantity demanded* or *demand*) would each of the following events cause?
   a. A new office park is built, surrounded by several acres of lawn
   b. A drought is declared, and lawn watering is banned
   c. The going price for lawn-mowing services rises
   d. A more natural, wild yard becomes the "in" thing, as people become concerned about the effects of fertilizers and pesticides on the environment

4. THE THEORY OF MARKET ADJUSTMENT

Now that we have considered the sellers and the buyers separately, it is time to bring them together. In our thought-experiment world, we assume that the buyers and sellers all meet at once and use a double-auction spot market to make the sales. Of course, in actual real-estate markets, condo apartments are usually sold one at a time, for varying prices—with the sellers, buyers, and their agents spending considerable time haggling over the terms of the sale. But in our convenient, fictional world, every apartment that changes hands will sell at the same price. (Remember, they are identical—why would anyone pay more, or accept less, than the going price?) In this world we are now ready to ask: How many apartments will change hands?

4.1 SURPLUS, SHORTAGE, AND EQUILIBRIUM

Using the original supply and demand curves, reproduced here in Figure 4.7, we can look for the answer by considering possible prices. Suppose we start with a high price of $99,000. At this price, nine owners will be willing to sell, but only one person will be willing to buy. Economists call a situation in which the quantity supplied is greater than the quantity demanded a **surplus**. This is illustrated in the upper part of Figure 4.7.

> **surplus:** a situation in which the quantity that sellers wish to sell at the stated price is greater than the quantity that buyers will buy at that price

Since suppliers who are willing to sell at this price cannot find buyers, what will they do? For a number of sellers, $99,000 is more than they need to persuade them to sell. To find buyers, they will suggest a lower selling price. At $98,000 a surplus still occurs—there are eight willing sellers and only two willing buyers, so there will be further downward pressure on the price. When the price reaches $95,000, all the owners who want to sell at this price will find potential buyers who want to buy at this price. The number of apartments supplied—and demanded—is equal to five. The price for these apartments is $95,000. Economists call this a situation in which the "market clears" and an **equilibrium** is reached. "Equilibrium" describes a situation that has reached a resting point, where there are no forces to acting to change it. (Economists borrowed this term from natural science.) In a market situation, equilibrium is reached when the quantity

Figure 4.7 **Surplus, Shortage, and Equilibrium**

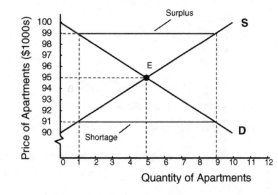

At a price of $99,000 a surplus occurs because the quantity of apartments being offered for sale is larger than the quantity that people want to buy. On the other hand, at a price of $91,000 many people want to buy apartments but few want to sell, so a shortage occurs. Only at market equilibrium (point E) does quantity supplied equal quantity demanded.

supplied is equal to the quantity demanded. The price will stop falling. Figure 4.7 illustrates the **market-clearing equilibrium** point, labeled E.

> **equilibrium:** a situation of rest, in which there are no forces that create change

> **market-clearing equilibrium:** a situation in which quantity supplied equals quantity demanded

What if the price had started out too low, for example at $91,000? In this case a **shortage** occurs, where the quantity supplied is less than the quantity demanded, as illustrated in the lower part of Figure 4.7. Since there are nine willing buyers and only one willing seller at that price, the buyers who are willing to pay more to get an apartment will bid the price up. As the price rises, some prospective buyers drop out of the action, while more prospective sellers enter. At $95,000, just five buyers remain, matched by five sellers.

> **shortage:** a situation in which the quantity that buyers wish to buy at the stated price is greater than the quantity that sellers are willing to sell at that price

The **theory of market adjustment** says that market forces will tend to make price and quantity move toward the equilibrium point. Surpluses will lead to declines in price, and shortages will lead to rises in price. Surplus and shortage are both instances of **market disequilibrium**. Only at equilibrium is there no tendency to change. In this example, the equilibrium price is $95,000, and the equilibrium quantity is five.

> **theory of market adjustment:** the theory that market forces will tend to make shortages and surpluses disappear

> **market disequilibrium:** a situation of either shortage or surplus

4.2 SHIFTS IN SUPPLY AND DEMAND

With the two curves now combined, we can investigate how market forces will cause equilibrium prices and quantities to change in response to changes in the underlying nonprice determinants of supply and demand.

Figure 4.8   **Market Adjustment to an Increase in Supply**

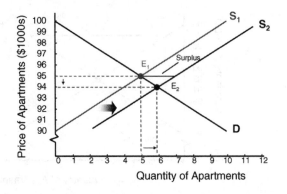

With an increase in the supply of apartments, there now would be a surplus at the original equilibrium price of $95,000. Market adjustment forces should cause the price to fall, until a new equilibrium is established at a price of $94,000. Six apartments will sell at this new equilibrium price. The equilibrium price has fallen and the equilibrium quantity has risen.

In our condo market, let us compare the original case shown in Figure 4.7 to a case in which supply has risen. How would the auction's result now differ, compared to the original case?* In Figure 4.8, the original equilibrium is marked as E_1 with supply curve S_1. When the supply curve shifts to S_2, we see that a surplus results at the original equilibrium price of $95,000. At point E_2, with a price of $94,000, the market clears, with six apartments being traded. As Figure 4.8 illustrates, *an increase in supply will tend to decrease equilibrium price and increase equilibrium quantity.*

Suppose that instead of an increase in supply in this market, we have an increase in demand. In Figure 4.9, we see the effect of that demand increase: At the original equilibrium price of $95,000, a shortage results. The price will be bid up to $97,000, where seven transactions will be made. As Figure 4.9 illustrates, *an increase in demand will tend to increase equilibrium price and increase equilibrium quantity.*

Notice that both supply and demand increases tend to increase the equilibrium quantity transacted. Their price effects, however, go in opposite directions. Increases in supply make the good more plentiful, driving its equilibrium price down. Increases in demand drive up the equilibrium price.

Likewise, decreases in supply and demand both tend to decrease the equilibrium quantity transacted. A decrease in supply will tend to raise the equilibrium price, as the good is harder to get. A decrease in demand will tend to decrease the equilibrium price, as fewer attempts to obtain the good are made. These effects are summarized in Table 4.3.

What if *both* curves shift at the same time? What if, for example, there is an increase in the number of sellers of condos *and* at the same time an increase in the number of buyers? In this case the new equilibrium will be found at the intersection of two new curves, rather than one new curve and one old one. Comparing the new equilibrium with the original one in the case

---

* Conventionally, economists talk about this model as if the economy *is first* at E_1 and then *moves to* E_2. For example, you could think of apartment auctions occurring just once per month, so that the shift shown in Figure 4.8 comes from an increase in potential sellers between one month and the next (*ceteris paribus*). The formal model, however, does not actually represent any passage of time.

Figure 4.9   **Market Adjustment to an Increase in Demand**

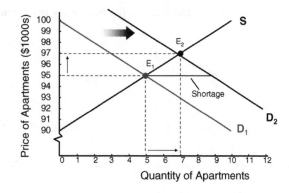

Quantity of Apartments

With an increase in demand, there would be a shortage of apartments at the original equilibrium price of $95,000. Market forces should cause the price to rise, until a new equilibrium is established at $97,000. Seven apartments will sell at this new equilibrium price. The equilibrium price has risen and the equilibrium quantity has risen.

Table 4.3   **Summary of Effects of Supply and Demand Shifts**

	Effect on Equilibrium Price	Effect on Equilibrium Quantity
Increase in Supply	fall	rise
Decrease in Supply	rise	fall
Increase in Demand	rise	rise
Decrease in Demand	fall	fall

in which both supply and demand increase, for example, the equilibrium quantity clearly rises, but the effect on the equilibrium price is ambiguous. That is, the equilibrium price may go up, down, or stay the same depending on how far each of the curves shifts. In other cases, it may be the change in the price that is clear, but the change in equilibrium quantity that is ambiguous. One of the end-of-chapter exercises will consider such a case. For the most part we will examine only changes that affect *one* side of the market, not simultaneous changes in both.

4.3 ELASTICITIES

By *how much* will the equilibrium quantity change, when there is a shift in the market? Economists are often interested in the answer to this question. The **price elasticity of demand** measures the degree to which buyers of a good respond to a change in its price. Mathematically, it is defined as the absolute value of the percentage change in quantity demanded divided by the percentage change in price. The larger is the quantity response, relative to the size of the price change, the "more elastic" demand is said to be. If the response is small, demand is said to be relatively "price inelastic."

> **price elasticity of demand:** a measure of the responsiveness of quantity demanded to changes in price

Figure 4.10 graphs two different demand curves, along with identical supply curve shifts. In Figure 4.10(a), with the relatively flat demand curve, we see that there is a large drop in the

Figure 4.10   **Price Elasticity of Demand**

(a) Relatively price-elastic demand.   **(b) Relatively price-inelastic demand.**

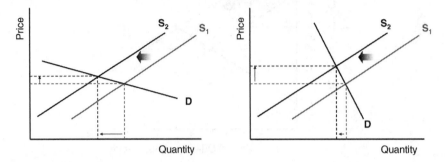

When a small change in price leads buyers to make a large change in the quantity they demand, demand is said to be relatively elastic. If buyers' response is, instead, weak, demand is said to be relatively inelastic.

quantity demanded associated with a small increase in price. In Figure 4.10(b), on the other hand, with a relatively steep demand curve, only a small decrease in quantity demanded is associated with a substantial increase in price. The demand curve shown in (a) is hence *relatively more price elastic* than the demand curve in (b).

Goods for which there are many substitutes, which are merely wanted rather than needed, or which make up a large part of the budget of the buyer tend to have relatively elastic demands. On the other hand, goods for which there are few substitutes, that are badly needed (such as essential medicines), or which make up a small part of the buyer's budget tend to have relatively inelastic demands.

The **price elasticity of supply** measures the same sort of responsiveness, but this time on the part of sellers. Mathematically, it is defined as the percentage change in quantity supplied divided by the percentage change in price. When suppliers respond to a small increase in price by offering a much larger quantity of goods, we say that supply is relatively elastic. If they hardly react at all, supply is relatively inelastic.

> **price elasticity of supply:** a measure of the responsiveness of quantity supplied to changes in price

Discussion Questions

1. Think about the market for high-quality basketballs. In each of the following cases, determine which curve shifts, and in which direction. Also draw a graph and describe, in words, the changes in price and quantity. (Treat each case separately.)
   a. A rise in basketball players' incomes
   b. An increase in wages paid to the workers who make the balls
   c. A decrease in the price of basketball hoops and other basketball gear
   d. The nation becoming obsessed with soccer

2. Have you ever found yourself shut out of a class you wanted to take, because it was already full? Or has this happened to a friend of yours? Analyze this situation in terms of surplus or shortage. Are classes supplied "in a market"? Do you think it would be good if they were?

5. MACROECONOMICS AND THE DYNAMICS OF REAL-WORLD MARKETS

Although supply-and-demand analysis can be a very useful tool, not every market is a perfectly competitive spot market with smoothly functioning double-auction mechanisms. Markets may be characterized by market power (as mentioned in Chapter 2 and with the example of Microsoft), differentiated goods, imperfect information, long-term contracts, or very different approaches to price determination. An issue of particular importance to macroeconomics is the question of the speed at which real-world price adjustments take place.

5.1 WHEN PRICE ADJUSTMENTS ARE SLOW

How long will it take our hypothetical condo traders to reach equilibrium? Minutes? An hour? A day? The theory of supply and demand doesn't tell us. The graphs represent a static model. Recall from Chapter 2 that this means that the model does not take into account the passage of time.

Some markets, such as stock markets in which traders are constantly yelling bids to each other, clear quickly. But what if you don't have everyone in a room, agreeing on trades minute-by-minute? For example, consider the market for shirts. When you go into a clothing store, you see a rack of shirts and, on their tags, a given price. The price probably reflects a mark-up by the retailer over what he or she paid to a distributor to get the shirts. The distributor in turn probably charged a mark-up over the price charged by the manufacturer. Now, if the shirts are overpriced, they won't sell very well. In the terms we introduced, there will be a surplus. If the market worked like the perfect double auction just described, the supplier and demander would quickly be able to fine tune the price and quantity to get it just right, similar to what we saw for our hypothetical apartment market in Figure 4.7. The price would fall, the surplus of shirts would disappear immediately, and equilibrium would be restored.

In a realistic, complicated case such as this one, however, there is actually a *chain* of markets involved—the manufacturer sells to the distributor, the distributor to the retailer, and the retailer to the final buyer. A quick adjustment of prices is unlikely. More commonly, when retailers mark down the prices on the shirts they have in stock in order to clear them out, this drop in the price won't immediately travel back up the supply chain. In the next order the retailers place with their distributors, the retailers may just ask for a smaller quantity of shirts, at the price at which the distributor is offering them—especially if the retailer is small relative to the distributor and has little power to bargain over prices. Any changes in prices or quantities at the manufacturing level will only develop over time, as the manufacturers see the level of their inventories either rise (because the shirts are not selling) or fall (because the distributors order more).

Because of the time it takes for all these things to happen, some economists believe that the most likely first response to a surplus situation is that manufacturers will cut *production*—perhaps laying off workers—rather than reducing their price. In this case, the *quantity* produced adjusts to meet the quantity demanded at a given price, rather than the price adjusting to clear the market. If such **quantity adjustments** happen economy-wide, unemployment could rise.

> **quantity adjustments:** a response by suppliers in which they react to unexpectedly low sales of their good primarily by reducing production levels rather than by reducing the price, and to unexpectedly high sales by increasing production rather than raising the price

Suppliers may also be reluctant rapidly to change the prices they offer due to **menu costs**—literally, the costs of changing the prices listed on such things as order forms and restaurant menus. In real-world markets, we generally expect market forces arising from surpluses and shortages to exert pressure on quantities and/or prices *in the direction of* equilibrium. This is why it is important to be familiar with the model of supply and demand. But we can't be sure that these pressures will be strongly felt, or that an equilibrium will actually be reached. The pure market forces we have examined in our hypothetical perfectly competitive, spot, double-auction market are not the *only* forces in the world, nor do these forces always work smoothly and quickly. In later chapters of this book we will discuss the possible macroeconomic consequences of factors such as union contracts, lengthy production processes, and information problems. These and other factors can slow down adjustment to equilibrium—or mean that a market equilibrium doesn't even exist.

> **menu costs:** the costs to a supplier of changing prices listed on order forms, brochures, menus and the like

5.2 When Prices Swing Too Much

Other markets have adjustment processes in which prices may change rapidly. In highly organized stock markets and certain other auction-like markets, thousands of trades may take place every minute, as buyers and sellers find each other and quickly negotiate a price. Such a market can probably be thought of as in an equilibrium, or moving quickly toward one, nearly all the time.

Very rapid adjustments of prices, however, create their own set of problems. In our hypothetical market for apartments, we assumed that people wanted an apartment because they wanted to live in it, or perhaps because they saw it as long-term investment (desiring the income they might get from owning an apartment and renting it out). But sometimes in markets where prices are expected to move, buyers are not really interested in the *item itself* at all—only its price, and the direction in which it is likely to go. **Speculation** is the buying and selling of assets with the expectation of profiting from appreciation or depreciation in their values, usually over a relatively short period of time. Speculators buy items such as stocks in companies, commodities futures (e.g. contracts to buy or sell items such as pork bellies or copper at a specific price on a future date), foreign exchange, real estate, or other investment vehicles, purely in the hopes that they will be able to sell them in the future for more than they have paid.

> **speculation:** buying and selling assets with the expectation of profiting from appreciation or depreciation in asset values

When many people come to believe that the price of something will rise, a **speculative bubble** can occur, in which people buy the asset because so many other people also believe that that asset's price will continue to rise. In a mass phenomenon often referred to by terms such as "herd mentality" or "bandwagon effect," the price of the asset becomes inflated. People's mutually reinforcing optimism causes asset values to rise far above any price that could be rationalized in terms of "economic fundamentals." In the case of a stock price, for example, the rational economic base for valuation should be the returns that an investor can expect from a firm, while in the case of real estate, the value should be rationally determined by the stream of likely rents, from the present into the future. During a bubble, however, people pay less attention to (or take a biased view of) such fundamental factors. Instead, demand for the asset is largely determined by purchasers' perception that they will be able to find someone to sell the asset to, at a higher price. Eventually, however, people begin to figure out that prices have become unrealistically high, demand drops, the bubble bursts, and prices fall.

> **speculative bubble:** the situation that occurs when mutually reinforcing investor optimism raises the value of an asset far above what could be realistically justified

Figure 4.11 **The Stock Market Bubble of 1999–2000**

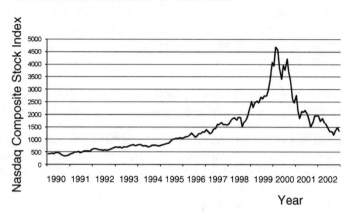

Enthusiasm about new technologies, and Internet e-commerce in particular, temporarily drove the prices of many company's stocks very high. During the bubble, the prices of stocks as determined by supply and demand rose far above the prices that would occur if valuation had been based on the companies' actual performances. (Source: Yahoo! Finance, Monthly data)

One recent U.S. experience with a speculative bubble in stock prices is illustrated in Figure 4.11. The Nasdaq Composite stock index measures the prices of a group of stocks traded in the United States. Investors' enthusiasm about new technologies, particularly the use of the Internet for business purposes, drove technology stocks to a high peak in the late 1990s in what has been called the "dot-com" bubble. In the early months of 2000, a more realistic view started to catch on, and prices soon plummeted. It may be easy, of course, to recognize a bubble after the fact. During the spectacular rise in stock prices, however, many otherwise rational and intelligent people convinced each other—and themselves—that the stock market boom reflected an immense jump in productivity, not a speculative bubble.

From 2004 to early 2007 a similar bubble and crash occurred in the United States market for sub-prime mortgages. Sub-prime mortgages are housing loans given to people whose incomes or credit histories are not good enough to qualify them for regular mortgages. Because these loans are risky, the interest rate charged the borrower is usually higher than on regular mortgages. Many lenders aggressively marketed such loans to prospective homeowners during this period (sometimes using fraudulent techniques), making profits by collecting fees on each loan made. Some of the world's largest banks moved aggressively into this area, bundling and repackaging the mortgages in such a way that their riskiness was not immediately apparent. Eventually, however, softening of housing prices and rising adjustable interest rates caused a steep increase in the number of U.S. home buyers who were defaulting on their loans. Securities based on sub-prime mortgages rapidly lost market value as questions were finally raised about the actual worth of the assets on which they were based. During the sub-prime crisis, many people lost their homes, and many of the largest commercial banks lost billions of dollars.

Situations of speculative bubbles and volatile (that is, rapidly changing) prices have important implications for macroeconomics. It is not merely a coincidence that some months after the "dot-com" bubble burst, the United States economy slipped into a recession. The sub-prime mortgage crisis of 2007 was similarly followed by signs of a weakening economy. An even more famous and dramatic case occurred in 1929, when a sudden and dramatic stock market crash precipitated the onset of the Great Depression in the United States. The bursting of a bubble in real estate and stocks in 1989 similarly led to a period of macroeconomic contraction in Japan. Wild swings in foreign exchange markets, such as swept through Indonesia, South Korea, Thailand, Hong Kong, and other countries during the Asian financial crisis of 1997–98, caused great economic dislocation and threw many people into poverty.

Economists debate the importance of market volatility in creating macroeconomic insecurity. Economists who take a classical point of view tend to downplay such market-related problems, believing that even if market performance seems sometimes counter to human welfare, it is still better than what could be achieved by any sort of regulation or intervention. Other economists, particular some with Keynesian views or those who are particularly concerned with the economics of less industrialized nations, believe that some sort of regulation may be desirable. Some have suggested, for example, that a small tax be levied on currency trades. Proponents of such a tax—called a "Tobin Tax" after economist James Tobin, who first suggested it—argue that this would discourage speculative trades, while still allowing for productive trading. The revenues, they suggest, could be put into an international fund to combat poverty and disease. Several governments, including the government of Canada, have passed legislation agreeing to implement a Tobin Tax if enough other countries agree to participate.

5.3 FROM MICROECONOMICS TO MACROECONOMICS?

How far does the model of supply and demand get us in explaining macroeconomic phenomena? That question can be broken down into two parts. First, are real-world markets similar to the one portrayed in the model? Second, even to the extent that some markets do behave as the model predicts, might explaining national-level economic phenomena require different theoretical tools?

Later chapters of this book will examine more specifically how classical market equilibrium models of markets for labor, finance, and produced goods compare and contrast with more Keynesian explanations of unemployment, savings and investment, and aggregate demand.

Discussion Questions

1. Think of several things you regularly buy. For which of these goods or services do prices seem to change rapidly? For which do they seem to change slowly? Can you explain why?
2. Has there been any talk of "speculative bubbles" in news reports recently? If so, what markets are being discussed? What explanations are given for why prices may be so high?

REVIEW QUESTIONS

1. Describe three characteristics of the type of market featured in classical analysis.
2. Define and sketch a supply curve.
3. Illustrate on a clearly-labeled graph (a) a decrease in quantity supplied, and (b) a decrease in supply.
4. Describe two factors that might cause a supply curve to shift.
5. Define and sketch a demand curve.
6. Illustrate on a clearly-labeled graph (a) a decrease in quantity demanded, and (b) a decrease in demand.
7. Describe two factors that might cause a demand curve to shift.

8. Describe how goods can be "substitutes." Describe how the demand curve for a good may be affected by an increase in the price of a second good that is a substitute for the first.

9. Describe how goods can be "complements." Describe how the demand curve for a good may be affected by an increase in the price of a second good that is a complement to the first.

10. Draw a graph illustrating surplus, shortage, and equilibrium.

11. Describe, using graphs, how an increase in supply affects equilibrium quantity and price. Repeat for a decrease in supply.

12. Describe, using graphs, how an increase in demand affects equilibrium quantity and price. Repeat for a decrease in demand.

13. Describe what is meant by the price elasticity of demand and the price elasticity of supply.

14. Describe how and why sellers of a good might adjust the quantity of what they produce, rather than the price.

15. What are some of the problems that can be created by wild price swings?

EXERCISES

1. Suppose the supply and demand schedules for a local electric utility are as follows.

Price	17	16	15	14	13	12	11
Quantity Supplied	9	7	5	3	1	—	—
Quantity Demanded	3	4	5	6	7	8	9

The price is in cents per kilowatt hour (kWh), and the quantity is millions of kilowatt hours. The utility does not operate at prices less than 13 cents per kWh.

a. Using graph paper and a ruler, or a computer spreadsheet or presentation program, carefully graph and label the supply curve for electricity.

b. On the same graph, draw and label the demand curve for electricity.

c. What is the equilibrium price of electricity? The equilibrium quantity? Label this point on your graph.

d. At a price of 17 cents per kWh, what is the quantity supplied? What is the quantity demanded? What is the relationship between quantity supplied and quantity demanded? What term do economists use to describe this situation?

e. At a price of 14 cents per kWh, what is the relationship between quantity supplied and quantity demanded? What term do economists use to describe this situation?

f. Sometimes cities experience "blackouts," where the demands on the utility get so high relative to its capacity to produce electricity that the system shuts down, leaving everyone in the dark. Using the analysis you have just completed, describe an *economic* factor that would make blackouts more likely to occur.

2. Continuing on from the previous problem, suppose new innovations in energy efficiency reduce people's need for electricity. The supply side of the market does not change, but at each price buyers now demand 3 million kilowatt hours fewer than before. For example, at a price of 11 cents per kWh, buyers now demand only 6 kWh instead of 9 kWh.

a. On a new graph, draw supply and demand curves corresponding to prices of 16 cents per kWh or less, after the innovations in efficiency. Also, for reference, mark the old equilibrium point from the previous exercise, labeling it E_1.

b. If the price were to remain at the old equilibrium level determined in part (c) of question 1 above, what sort of situation would result?

c. What is the new equilibrium price? The new equilibrium quantity? Give this point on your graph the label E_2.

d. Has there been a change in demand? Has a change in the price (relative to the original situation) led to a change in the quantity demanded?

e. Has there been a change in supply? Has a change in the price (relative to the original situation) led to a decrease in the quantity supplied?

3. Using your understanding of the non-price determinants of supply and of demand, analyze each of the following market cases. Draw a graph showing what happens in each situation, indicate what happens to equilibrium price and quantity, and explain why. The first case is done as an example.

Question: Market for gasoline: A hurricane hits the Gulf of Mexico, destroying many refineries that produce gasoline from crude oil.

Answer:
S shifts back.
P rises.
Q falls.
The hurricane reduces the number of producers.

a. Market for bananas: New health reports indicate that eating bananas leads to important health benefits

b. Market for shoes: A new technology for shoe making means that shoes can be made at a lower cost per pair

c. Market for Internet design services: Several thousand new graduates of design schools enter the market, ready to supply their services

d. Market for expensive meals: A booming economy raises the incomes of many households

e. Market for grapes *from California:* A freeze in Chile, usually a major world provider of fresh fruit, raises the price of Chilean grapes

f. Market for salsa dance lessons: The only nightclub in town featuring salsa music triples its entrance fee

g. Market for bottled water: A rumor circulates that the price of bottled water is about to triple. (Think only about the demand side.)

h. Market for Internet design services: Several thousand new graduates of design schools enter the market, ready to supply their services *and,* at the same time, many firms want to create new Internet Web sites.

4. Sketch a supply curve graph illustrating a student's willingness to sell his textbooks from all his classes, right now. Assume the student will receive offers of this sort: "I'll give you [a fixed number of dollars] apiece for all the books you want to sell." Carefully label the vertical and horizontal axes. Suppose that at an original offer of $30 per book, the student will be willing to sell three books, since he knows he can

replace these three for less than $30 each at a local bookstore. Mark this point on your first graph. Assume further that at $40 he would be willing to sell four books, at $50 he would supply five books, etc. Now, on separate graphs labeled (a), (b), and (c), show this line and his offer at $30 and the precise new *point* or an approximate new *curve* that illustrates each of the following contrasts. Consider them separately, returning to the case of no Internet resources in considering (c).

a. He is offered $70 per book instead of $30
b. He discovers that the textbook materials for many of his classes are available free on the Internet
c. The local bookstore raises its prices substantially

5. State whether the following statements are true or false. If false, write a corrected statement.
   a. A fall in the price of a good will cause its supply curve to shift to the left
   b. Increased costs of supplying a good will cause the supply curve to shift to the left
   c. A fall in the price of a substitute good will cause the demand for the good in question to fall
   d. An decrease in supply will have a small effect on the quantity demanded if the demand curve is very elastic

6. Consider the market for diamond rings. For each of the following, draw a graph and describe the likely effects on equilibrium price and quantity (assuming the market functions like the one described in the text.) Explain your reasoning.
   a. Valentines' Day is approaching
   b. Manufacturers discover new industrial uses for diamonds, driving up the prices that jewelers have to pay to obtain the gems
   c. New deposits of diamonds are discovered
   d. The price of cubic zirconium "gems" (high quality fake diamonds) falls
   e. People experience an increase in their wealth

7. Match each concept in Column A with a definition or example in Column B.

Column A	Column B
a. Substitute goods	1. The stock market
b. Shifts the supply curve	2. A tiny drop in the price of a good leads to a big increase in quantity demanded
c. A "bubble"	3. Shoes and shoelaces
d. Complementary goods	4. A shoe manufacturer responds to a decline in shoe sales by cutting back on production and laying off workers
e. Speculation	5. Tea and coffee
f. Market equilibrium	6. Quantity supplied is greater than quantity demanded
g. Auction market	7. Buying an asset largely in hope of selling it later for a higher price
h. Quantity adjustment	8. Quantity supplied is equal to quantity demanded
i. Price elastic demand	9. A change in the number of sellers
j. Surplus	10. When investors' optimism pushes the price of an asset artificially high

8. Suppose a newspaper report indicates that the price of wheat has fallen. Which of the following could be possible explanations? (There may be more than one.) Illustrate *one* case you choose on a supply and demand graph.
   a. A drought has hit wheat-growing areas
   b. An increase in the price of rice
   c. Due to increasing health concerns, tobacco farmers have begun growing other crops
   d. A new science report suggests that wheat is bad for one's health

9. Prices of many financial assets such as stocks and foreign exchange are now readily available on the Internet. Search for a chart such as Figure 4.11 for a stock index or foreign currency of your choosing, and print it out. During the time period covered by the graph you found, does it seem like this market is fairly calm, or is it characterized by periods of volatility? (Caution: because price swings can be made to look relatively large or small simply by changing the scale of the graph, you may want to choose a fairly long time series, or compare the behavior of the asset you've chosen with a similar asset, in answering this question.) Is there any evidence of a speculative bubble?

Part Two
Macroeconomic Basics

5 Macroeconomic Measurement: The Current Approach

As we pointed out in Chapter 3, being able to make wise economic choices depends on having a good sense about the size of the relevant economic stocks and flows. Whether you are deciding how much money to spend in the bookstore, or groups such as households, community organizations, businesses, nonprofits, or governments are deciding how to use their resources, good decision making requires good information.

In macroeconomics, we consider how good economic choices could be made at a *national* level, usually by governments interested in maintaining high employment levels, stable prices, and/or achieving other national goals such as sustainable growth or national security. The amount of information required for such large tasks is daunting! While learning about how data are gathered and organized in order to create measures of macroeconomic performance may seem dry and dull at times, it is crucial for you to understand how common measures of economic performance are put together. What do they include? What do they leave out? Why might they be biased? To what extent might they be useful as measures of human well-being, and to what extent might they be misleading?

1. MEASURING A COUNTRY'S AGGREGATE BEHAVIOR

The idea of creating a system of national accounts to guide U.S. decision makers first took hold during the Great Depression in the 1930s. Presidents Hoover and Roosevelt knew that national production was down, but other than a few numbers representing the volumes of railroad shipments and steel production, they had no information on by *how much* it was down. Likewise, they had little way of knowing whether the policy actions they were trying were actually helping the economy rebound.

The Department of Commerce commissioned economist Simon Kuznets to begin to develop national accounts. The first set of accounts was presented to Congress in 1937. Interest in keeping national accounts increased in the 1940s because of the need for national economic mobilization during World War II.

The national accounts have evolved over the decades for several reasons. The economy itself has evolved, for example moving from being strongly oriented toward agriculture and manufacturing toward a structure in which service and information activities are increasingly important. Improved data collection techniques and new statistical methods have been developed in the decades since the 1930s. Perhaps most importantly, the purposes for which the accounts are intended and the most pressing topics of concern also change over time. Keeping track of environmental degradation, for example, was not a purpose for which the accounts were originally developed, although it is a pressing problem today.

In this chapter we explain how U.S. government agencies construct the major economic indicators used by contemporary macroeconomists. Even though GDP is often referred to as if it measures economic well-being, it is in fact not very well suited for that purpose—although it does a good job of addressing some of the questions for which it was specifically designed. This chapter will demonstrate how GDP, economic growth, measures of price changes, and national saving are commonly measured. In the next chapter, we discuss extensions of the national accounts that are currently being developed in order to update them to reflect better the concerns of the twenty-first century.

Discussion Questions

1. How might the purpose for which accounts are intended affect their design? For example, what sorts of economic activities do you think it would it be most important to track if the purpose were to plan for fighting a war? To look at the level of overall well-being? To help ensure the present and future well-being of people who are children today?
2. What statistics about national economic performance have you seen mentioned in the news? Do you know what these statistics mean?

2. THE NATIONAL ACCOUNTS AND THEIR CONVENTIONS

In the United States, the **Bureau of Economic Analysis (BEA)** publishes statistics concerning production, income, spending, prices and employment in the **National Income and Product Accounts (NIPA)**.

> **Bureau of Economic Analysis (BEA):** the agency in the United States in charge of compiling and publishing the national accounts

> **National Income and Product Accounts (NIPA):** a set of statistics compiled by the BEA concerning production, income, spending, prices, and employment

All systems of accounting make considerable use of "conventions" or assumptions. Accounting conventions are simply habits or agreements, adopted by people in order to try to make accounts as standardized and comparable across different time periods as possible. It is important for you to realize that the conventions do not simply reflect the "world as it is." There are many different ways of describing the world, and each convention chosen reflects just one of many possibilities.

A personal example might help you understand this problem. Perhaps you keep track of your own expenditures. Suppose you buy soft drinks at a grocery store, even though you don't like them yourself, because you want to have a stock of them around to serve your friends when they visit. Suppose you then want to summarize your expenses by grouping them into larger categories such as "groceries" and "entertainment." In which of these categories should you classify your soft-drink purchases? They arguably could be classified as either. To keep your accounts meaningful, you will need to decide on—and consistently apply—a convention that assigns your soft-drink expenditures to one category or the other, or in fixed proportions to each. But, in national accounts, as in this personal case, there is often an element of arbitrariness about conventions. And conventions can change over time, as old ways of doing things become outdated in the face of new developments.

Internationally, the **United Nations System of National Accounts (SNA)** provides guidelines to countries about how to construct systems of accounts, with a view to making national statistics more comparable *across countries* as well as across time periods. In 2003, the United States NIPA underwent a comprehensive revision, one of the objectives of which was greater harmonization with the SNA.

> **United Nations System of National Accounts (SNA):** a set of guidelines for countries about how to construct systems of national accounts

2.1 CONVENTIONS ABOUT SECTORS

The official system of U.S. national accounts uses the following four-way classification of sectors.

Households and institutions sector. The first sector includes both households and nonprofit institutions that serve households. These include organizations such as nonprofit hospitals, universities, museums, trade unions, and charities. The BEA also refers to the **households and institutions sector** as the "personal" sector.

> **households and institutions sector** (BEA definition): the sector consisting of households and nonprofit institutions serving households

Business sector. The BEA **business sector** is somewhat broader than just for-profit businesses. Certain business-serving nonprofit organizations, such as trade associations and chambers of commerce, are included in this category. In addition, government agencies that are like business enterprises in that they produce goods and services for sale—such as the U.S. Postal Service, municipal gas and electric companies, and airports—are also classified as being in the business sector.

> **business sector** (BEA definition): the sector including all entities concerned with producing goods and services for profitable sale. It also includes business-serving nonprofit organizations and government enterprises.

Government sector. The **government sector** includes all federal, state, and local government entities, except for the "business-like" government enterprises mentioned above.

> **government sector** (BEA definition): the sector that includes all federal, state, and local government entities (except for government enterprises).

Foreign sector. The entities in the first three sectors include, for the national accounts, only those that are located within the physical borders of the United States. The **foreign sector** (or "rest of the world") includes all entities—household, nonprofit, business, or government—located outside the borders of the United States. An individual in another country who buys imported U.S. products, for example, or a company located abroad that sells goods or services to the United States, figure into U.S. accounts as part of the foreign sector.

> **foreign sector** (BEA definition): the sector consisting of entities located outside the borders of the United States.

2.2 CONVENTIONS ABOUT CAPITAL STOCKS

While natural, manufactured, human, and social capital are all crucial resources for economic activity, it is largely only *manufactured* capital that is currently included in the accounting of national non-financial assets. This might be due to the national accounts having originally been devised at a time when the relatively recent rise of manufacturing made the accumulation of machinery and factory buildings appear to be the main road to prosperity. In the twenty-first century, the rise in importance of knowledge and ecological concerns suggests that additional accounts should be added—a topic we will take up in the next chapter.

> For the most part, the national accounts currently include only manufactured capital in the accounting of national assets.

The first category of manufactured capital in the national accounts is called **fixed assets**. Fixed assets include equipment owned by businesses and governments, structures such as factories and office buildings, and residences (that is, houses and apartment buildings). In 1999, in partial recognition of the increasingly important role of knowledge and technology in production, computer software was added as an additional type of fixed asset.

> **fixed assets** (BEA definition): equipment owned by businesses and governments; structures; residences; and software

A second—and much smaller—component of the manufactured capital stock is **inventories**. Inventories are stocks of raw materials, such as crude oil awaiting refining, or manufactured goods, such as the shoe inventory of a retail shoe store, that are being held until they can be used or sold. The BEA only counts inventories held by the business sector.

> **inventories:** stocks of raw materials or manufactured goods being held until they can be used or sold

Equipment used by governments and businesses is included in "fixed assets." But what about equipment owned by households, such as cars and stoves, that are used in household production of goods and services? The BEA calls all goods bought by households that are expected to last longer than three years **consumer durable goods**. In 2003, the BEA began including consumer durables in its accounts of assets.

> **consumer durable goods:** consumer purchases that are expected to last longer than three years. These are generally items of equipment, such as vehicles and appliances, used by households to produce goods and services for their own use.

The BEA estimates of the dollar value of the nation's stock of manufactured assets at the end of 2006 are given in Table 5.1. (Numbers may not add up exactly due to rounding.)

2.3 CONVENTIONS ABOUT INVESTMENT

The way the national accounts measure investment spending may seem confusing if one does not keep in mind some basic facts. First, recall from Chapter 3 that economists use the term "investment" to mean additions to stocks of *non*-financial assets. This contrasts with the common on-the-street use of the term "investment" to refer to financial investment, such as the purchase of stocks and bonds. Second, it is important to remember that investment represents a *flow*. A machine added to a factory in 2005, for example, is considered to be part of the national *stock* of nonresidential assets for every year from the time it is installed until the time it is junked. However, the machine was only an *addition* to assets in 2005, and hence its value would only be counted as an *investment* in that one year. Lastly, as was discussed in Chapter 3, *gross* investment includes all measured flows into the capital stock over a period of time while *net* investment adjusts this measure for the fact that some portion of the capital stock wears out, becomes obsolete, or is destroyed—that is, depreciates—over the period.

Table 5.1   **The Estimated Size of U.S. Manufactured Capital Stock, 2006**

Type of Capital	Value in Trillions of Dollars at the End of the Year
Equipment and software	5.9
Structures	17.2
Residences	17.4
Inventories	1.9
Consumer durable goods	3.9
Total Value of Manufactured Capital	46.4

Source: BEA, Standard Fixed Assets Table 1.1 and NIPA Table 5.7.5B, and authors' calculations.

For example, suppose an office complex built in 1965 is torn down this year and replaced by a new, larger office complex. Measured *gross* investment for this year would include the full value of the new office complex. *Net* investment for this year would be calculated as the value of the new office complex *minus* the value of the (thoroughly depreciated) building that was torn down. If the new building has 100,000 square feet of space, while the old one had 60,000 square feet, for example, the economy has a net gain of only 40,000 square feet of office space. Net investment, which measures only the value of the *new* space and any improvements in quality, gives a better idea of the actual addition to productive capacity.

Gross investment in fixed assets is always zero or positive. However, if, over a period of time, the capital stock depreciates faster than it is being replaced, net investment can be negative. This can sometimes happen to manufactured capital stocks when a country is hit by major disasters such as wars or floods.

Inventory investment is a bit different from investment in fixed assets, since the primary reason the volume of inventories may decline is not depreciation, but rather that goods or materials may be taken out of inventory to be used or sold faster than they are being replaced. Measured inventory investment will be negative if the outflows from inventories exceed inflows.

You may have noted that the numbers given for fixed assets in Table 5.1 are quoted as dollar values. Determining a money value for assets is not an easy thing—even when, as in the national accounts, we limit attention only to manufactured capital. If you have ever taken an accounting class, you know that numerous conventions have been invented reflecting different ways of thinking about how to measure such things as depreciation and the value of inventories.

Ideally, productive investments by all sectors would be recognized in the national accounts. But it was not until 1996 that government investment in fixed assets was recognized, and household investment in consumer durables is still, by convention, not considered to be part of investment in the national accounts.

Discussion Questions

1. The BEA definitions of sectors use some conventions that are not obvious. To which sector might the BEA assign each of the following entities? Why?
   a. A local city-government-owned golf course that charges fees similar to local private courses
   b. A large nonprofit hospital

    c. A U.S.-owned movie company whose offices and studio are in Japan

    d. A nonprofit trade association, such as the Chocolate Manufacturers Association

2. Under the BEA definitions, would spending on education be counted as investment? Would buying shares in a company be considered investment? Why?

3. GROSS DOMESTIC PRODUCT: WHAT IT REPRESENTS

Certainly the most talked-about single number that comes out of the national accounts is GDP. A wide range of policymakers and media outlets have traditionally awaited the announcement of newly published figures on GDP with great anticipation. The figures on the growth rate of GDP are often taken to signal the success or failure of macroeconomic policymaking.

3.1 THE DEFINITION OF GROSS DOMESTIC PRODUCT

According to the BEA, **gross domestic product (GDP)** is supposed to measure the total value of final goods and services newly produced in a country over a period of time (usually one year).

> **gross domestic product (GDP)** (BEA definition): a measure of the total value of final goods and services newly produced in a country over a period of time (usually one year)

This definition contains several key phrases. Some of them are easy to understand, while others rely on complicated conventions.

"Final goods and services." A **final good** is one that is ready for use. That is, no further productive activity needs to be applied before the good can be consumed (if it is a good that is used up as it is put to use) or put to work producing other goods and services (for example, if it is a piece of equipment). The reason for limiting measurement to *final* goods and services is to avoid double counting. For example, suppose that during a year, paper is produced by one company and sold to another company that uses it to make books. The books are then sold to their final buyers. Books in this case are the final goods, while the paper used in them is an **intermediate good**. By limiting the accounting to final goods, production is only counted once—the paper is only counted as part of the books.

> **final good:** a good that is ready for use, needing no further processing

> **intermediate good:** a good that will undergo further processing

"Over a period of time." Since GDP measures a flow, it of course must be measured over some time period. Macroeconomists usually work with GDP measured on a yearly basis. Estimates of GDP are released more often than once a year—generally on a quarterly basis (the first quarter covering January through March, the second April through June, and so on). However, even when only a part of the year is being covered, GDP and its growth rates are usually expressed in annual terms.

"Newly produced." Only new goods and services are counted. For example, if you buy a book published in 2005 at a used book shop, the value of the book itself is not included in this year's GDP. Only the retail services provided by the used book shop are "newly produced," and are part of this year's GDP.

"In a country." This means that the goods and services are produced within the physical borders of the country. If a U.S. citizen goes abroad to work, for example, what he or she pro-

duces while away is *not* part of U.S. GDP. On the other hand, the work of a Japanese citizen at a Japanese-owned factory *is* part of U.S. GDP if that factory is located inside the borders of the United States.

How is the "*total value*" measured? This is a complicated topic, coming up next. It is also a controversial one, as we will see in the next chapter.

3.2 THE THREE APPROACHES TO MEASURING GDP: AN INTRODUCTION

The BEA publishes tables showing the components of GDP, as well as many other tables dealing with assets, employment, prices, and other topics in the National Income and Product Accounts. (These are easily accessed at www.bea.gov.) To understand these tabulations, however, you need to understand how aggregate *production, spending,* and *income* are related in an economic system.

Imagine a simple economy with no foreign sector, no depreciation, no inventories, no transfers, no non-market production, and in which all the profits that companies earn end up in the wallets of households. In this case, three quite different measures of counting GDP would in theory all add up to the same number:

Value of Production = Value of Spending = Value of Income

Using a *production approach,* which might seem to be the most natural and direct method, we could sum up the dollar value of all final goods and services produced in each sector—by the household and institutions sector, the business sector, and the government sector.

However, using the *spending approach,* we could look at who *buys* the final goods and services that have been produced. Since we assumed that no goods are carried as inventory in this very simple economy, everything produced must be bought. Totaling up the dollar value of spending on all various kinds of goods and services by all sectors in this imaginary simple economy will give a second way of arriving at the figure for a country's aggregate production.

Lastly, since in this simple economy everyone who is involved in production also receives a monetary payment for their contribution to it, we could, alternatively, take an *income approach.* In this approach, we total up the compensation received by everyone involved in production, including workers, investors, creditors, and owners of land or equipment rented for productive use.

In this very simple economy if, say, $10 million worth of goods and services is produced, then the amount spent on goods and services must also be $10 million and the amount of payment received as income must also be $10 million. Sometimes in dealing with national accounts economists hence use the terms "production," "income," and "expenditure" interchangeably.

Discussion Questions

1. Which of the following would be included in U.S. GDP?
    a. The value of Los Angeles hotel rooms rented to Italian tourists
    b. The value of a Renaissance-era painting sold at an auction in New York
    c. The value of steel production, that is used in making cars during the same year
    d. The value of new military aircraft

2. Can you explain why economists often use the terms "production," "income," and "spending" interchangeably?

4. GROSS DOMESTIC PRODUCT: CALCULATING ITS VALUE

While there is a rough equivalence in theory among the product, spending, and income approaches to calculating GDP, making estimates for an actual economy requires a number of conventions and adjustments.

4.1 THE PRODUCT APPROACH

The BEA measures the "value" of final goods and services primarily—at least in concept—by their *dollar market value.* For example, if the business sector produces 1,000 automobiles of a certain type this year, which are which are then sold to final users for $20,000 each, this adds $20 million to GDP.

Rather than looking at the final sale, however, it is sometimes useful for accounting and analytical purposes to follow an alternative approach. This is to think about how much each *industry* contributes to the value of the final good or service. In the **value-added** approach to GDP accounting, you start with the raw materials—say, iron ore—used in producing a good or service—say, an automobile—and then see how much market value is added at each stage in the production process.

> **value-added:** the value of what a producer sells, less the value of the intermediate inputs it uses. This is equal to the incomes paid out by the producer.

For example:

1. You find the value of iron ore as it is sold from the mining company to the steel manufacturer. Minus the value of any intermediate goods used, this is counted as being the value added to the ore in the ground by the mining company. Conveniently, this value added in production can also be measured as the sum of the incomes paid out by the mining company.

2. Then, the value added by the steel manufacturer is calculated as the value of the steel sold to the auto manufacturer, *minus* the amount the steel maker paid for the iron ore, other material, and energy inputs. (We subtract the value of the intermediate good, iron ore, so we don't count it twice.) This value added by the steel manufacturer can also be measured by looking at the incomes it pays out.

3. The value added by the auto manufacturer is calculated as the value of the automobile it sells, less the value of the intermediate inputs (steel, rubber, etc.) it purchased. This is equivalent to the incomes paid out in the process of auto production.

4. Summing up the value added at each stage of production should lead to the same number we would get by directly assessing the final value of the car—the amount it sells for on the market.

The BEA maintains an extensive set of Input-Output Accounts to keep track of the contributions to GDP by various industries. These tables show outputs of each industrial sector (for example, agriculture, manufacturing, or services) can become inputs (intermediate goods) to production in other sectors. (What about the contribution of natural resources, such as the deposits of iron ore, to the production of the car? The production of the car depletes these resources. The national accounts, as currently structured, however, do not seek to keep track of changes in natural capital.)

The fact that the calculated total value of final goods should add up to be the same number, whichever of the two methods is used—looking only at the markets for final goods, or, alternatively, going through a value-added accounting—serves to provide "checks" on the validity of data the BEA collects from different sources.

While finding the market value of production may seem fairly straightforward for manufacturing industries, in practice the idea of "market value" is often much harder to determine. In practice, the BEA uses **imputation** to estimate the value of many components of GDP. An imputation is a sort of educated guess, usually based on the value of similar outputs or on the value of inputs used in production.

> **imputation:** a procedure in which values are assigned for some category of products, usually using values of related products or inputs

For example, the housing stock of a country produces a flow of services—the services of shelter. For housing units that are rented, the rent paid is the market value of the housing services. But how can we find out the value of the services generated by houses occupied by their owners? For these, the BEA must *impute* a value. They use data from the rental housing market to impute what owner-occupiers might be said to be "paying in rent" to themselves.

In cases where no similar marketed product exists, the BEA often falls back on using a value-added approach, looking exclusively at the value of inputs. We know, for example, that governments purchase many intermediate goods, and then produce their outputs of goods and services using the services of workers they employ and the services of structures and equipment. But rarely are government outputs—new highways, the services of parks, the services of public education, national defense, etc.—actually sold on markets. How, then, is the production of the government to be valued?

In the actual GDP accounts, the value of government production is *imputed* by adding up the amount that governments pay their workers, the amount they pay for intermediate goods and services, and an allowance for depreciation of fixed assets. Likewise, the production of nonprofit institutions is measured in large part by looking at their inputs. For example, data on payroll expenses forms an important part of the information used in estimating the value of the services produced by nonprofit agencies.

> The value of *non-marketed production* by governments and nonprofit institutions is usually imputed by measuring the value of *inputs* used.

Imputations are also used when data are difficult or impossible to obtain. Although it might be tempting to imagine the BEA as an all-knowing agency that can directly observe all market transactions, gathering data is a laborious (and often expensive) process. The BEA relies on a variety of censuses and surveys to obtain information, as well as on regulatory and administrative data such as government budgets and tax records. Market transactions that people take pains *not* to have observed by the government—such as illegal drug deals or work performed "off the books" to avoid taxes—hence are usually not represented in the national statistics. The BEA updates all its estimates periodically, as it receives better data or improves its statistical techniques—hence you may see many slightly varying numbers quoted for, say "U.S. GDP, 2006" depending on when the data were published.

In one significant case, however, the designers of the national accounts decided not even to attempt to impute a value for production. This is the case of the production of goods and services within households for their own use. The official measure of production by households includes the value of services produced by the *house* (that is, the rent or imputed rent) and production within the households to the extent that work is *paid* (that is, done by hired housekeepers, nannies, private gardeners, and so on). But activities such as unpaid child care, cooking, or the cleaning or landscaping of a home done without pay by household members—traditionally, mostly by women—are not counted in GDP. This creates an anomaly in the accounts. For many years, textbooks noted that "if a man marries his housekeeper, GDP falls." That is, marriage would convert the woman's housekeeping work from being paid and counted, to being unpaid and uncounted.

How much of GDP is *produced* by entities within each of the BEA-defined sectors? Not surprisingly, given the conventions and accounting procedures, the BEA attributes a very large share of productive activity to the business sector, as shown in Table 5.2. For the period from January through December of 2006, the business sector was estimated to have produced goods and services worth about $10 trillion, or slightly more than 77 percent of the total GDP of $13 trillion. The household and institutions sector, and the government sector, were each estimated to have contributed about 11 percent. (In Table 5.2, as in later tables, the numbers in the column to the far right, showing contribution by sector, are added up to reach the total at the bottom of the table. The other numerical column gives values for subcategories. Numbers may not add exactly due to rounding.)

We can also summarize the product approach by the equation:

$$GDP = Business\ production$$
$$+ Household\ and\ institutions\ production$$
$$+ Government\ production$$

This sort of equation is called an **identity** or an **accounting identity**. It holds simply because of the way that the various terms have been defined. If we once agree on the definitions of terms, then there remains nothing controversial about an identity. (When we begin to deal with macroeconomic modeling in Chapter 9, we will introduce another kind of equation, called a behavioral equation. A behavioral equation represents an economist's supposition about how some economic actor behaves—and since it may or may not hold well in practice, it can be more controversial.)

> **identity (accounting identity):** an equation where the two sides are equal by definition

The foreign sector does not contribute to the production of GDP. Can you explain why? (Hint: Look back at the definition of GDP.)

4.2 THE SPENDING APPROACH

The spending approach adds up the value of newly produced goods and services bought by the household and institution, business, foreign, and government sectors. The estimated values for these expenditures for 2006 are listed in Table 5.3.

Purchases of goods and services by households and nonprofit institutions serving households are called "personal consumption expenditures" by the BEA. By convention, these are all considered "final" goods and services (even though, as discussed earlier, many of these are used in household and nonprofit production processes).

Business spending on final goods and services is called "gross private domestic investment" by the BEA. This includes business spending on fixed assets including structures, equipment, and software, as well as the value of changes in inventories within that sector.*

---

* Why isn't business spending on wages or on materials such as energy and raw goods counted here? Recall that GDP only accounts for *final* goods and services. The value of such inputs will be reflected in GDP as the products of the businesses are bought by households, institutions, or governments. Including the value of such inputs with business spending as well would result in double counting. Investment goods and inventories, however, stay within the business sector.

Table 5.2   **Gross Domestic Product, Product Approach, 2006**

Sector and Subsector	Production by Subsector (trillions of dollars)	Production by Sector (trillions of dollars)
Households and institutions production		1.50
Private households	.83	
Nonprofit institutions	.67	
Business production		10.19
Government production		1.50
Federal government	.46	
State and local governments	1.04	
Total: Gross domestic product		13.20

Source: BEA, NIPA Table 1.3.5, published 10/31/2007.

Table 5.3   **Gross Domestic Product, Spending Approach, 2006**

Sector and Type of Spending	Spending by Type (trillions of dollars)	Spending by Sector (trillions of dollars)
Household and institutions spending (*personal consumption expenditures*)		9.22
Durable goods	1.05	
Nondurable goods	2.69	
Services	5.49	
Business spending (*gross private domestic investment*)		2.21
Fixed investment	2.16	
Change in private inventories	.05	
Net foreign sector spending (*net exports of goods and services*)		-.76
Exports	1.47	
Less: Imports	2.23	
Government spending (*government consumption expenditures and gross investment*)		2.52
Federal	.93	
State and local	1.59	
Total: Gross domestic product		13.20

Source: BEA, NIPA Table 1.1.5, published 10/31/2007.

The simple economy we discussed when noting how, in concept, "production = spending = income" was a **closed economy**, with no foreign sector. While sometimes countries isolate themselves from world trade (China during 1960s being a prime example), for the most part global economic relations have become increasingly important as advances in transportation and communication have accelerated. Since the United States is an **open economy**, we need to take into account interactions with the foreign sector.

closed economy: an economy with no foreign sector

open economy: an economy with a foreign sector

Some of the goods and services produced inside the United States are bought by entities in the foreign sector. The value of these exported goods must be added to the value of domestic spending in calculating GDP. On the other hand, some of the spending by U.S. residents is for goods and services produced abroad. Such spending is, in fact, already included in the calculation of spending by the various other sectors in Table 5.4. So the value of imported goods and services must be subtracted to arrive at a measure of *domestic* production.

Net exports measures the overall impact of international trade on GDP. It is the difference between exports and imports.

$$Net\ exports = Exports - Imports$$

Net exports may be either positive (if we sell more abroad than we buy) or negative (if we buy more than we sell). In 2006, for example, we can see in Table 5.3 that the United States imported goods and services worth $0.76 trillion (that is, $760 billion) more than the value of the goods and services exported. (In the table, the fact that the value of imports is subtracted rather than added is denoted by putting the number in italic type.) Net exports were hence negative in that year.

> **net exports:** the value of exports less the value of imports

Lastly, we come to the expenditures made by the government sector. The BEA calls these "government consumption expenditures and gross investment" and breaks these down by whether they are made at the federal level or at the state and local level. These figures represent only spending for final goods and services, so they exclude the parts of government budgets that go for transfers (such as Social Security). In 2006, about 67 percent (that is, two-thirds) of federal government spending went for national defense. About 17 percent of total government spending was considered to be investment spending, while the rest was considered consumption.

If we want to highlight the various sectors involved, we can summarize the spending approach with the identity:

GDP = Household and institution spending
+ Business spending
+ Government spending
+ Net foreign sector spending

Or, if we want to highlight the portions that are (by convention) considered to be consumption versus those considered to be investment, we can summarize this approach with the identity:

GDP = Personal consumption
+ Private investment
+ Government consumption + Government investment
+ Net exports

4.3 THE INCOME APPROACH

The production-related incomes (such as from wages, rents, and profits) earned by all people and organizations located inside the United States are summed up in a measure called **national income (NI)**.

> **national income (NI):** a measure of all domestic incomes earned in production

Table 5.4   **Gross Domestic Product, Income Approach, 2006**

Types of Income and Adjustments	Income and Adjustments (trillions of dollars)
National income	11.66
Less: Net income payments from the rest of the world	.06
Plus: Depreciation *(consumption of fixed capital)*	1.62
Less: Statistical discrepancy	.02
Total: Gross domestic product	13.20

Source: BEA, NIPA, Table 1.7.5, published 10/31/2007, and authors' calculations.

If this were a simple economy with no foreign sector and no depreciation, the sum of the incomes from production, NI, would exactly equal GDP. But in our more complex economy, three adjustments are needed to reconcile figures on domestic income and domestic production.

First, we need to note that some domestic incomes reflect *foreign* production. For example, as mentioned above, the profits of a U.S. company may include earnings from overseas plants. Such incomes must be subtracted from NI order to reconcile this measure with the figure for *gross domestic product.* Conversely, the income from some domestic production is received by foreign residents, and so not counted in NI. A German factory located in the United States may send its profits back to its Berlin headquarters, for example. The value of these incomes must be added to NI in order to approximate GDP.* In 2006, income receipts from the rest of the world exceeded income paid out by nearly $60 billion. These "net income payments from the rest of the world" must be subtracted off NI to get a measure closer to GDP, as shown in Table 5.4.

Second, we need to account for the fact that not all of GDP creates income, since some domestic production simply goes into replacing structures, equipment, and software that have worn out or become obsolete. So we must add in depreciation (what the BEA calls "consumption of fixed capital") to get a number closer to GDP. The third adjustment in Table 5.4 is what is called the "statistical discrepancy." It reflects the fact that, no matter how diligently the BEA compiles the accounts, it cannot exactly reconcile the results from the income approach with the results from the product and spending approaches.

We can summarize the meaningful parts of the income approach by the identity:

$$GDP = \text{National income}$$
$$- \text{Net income payments from the foreign sector}$$
$$+ \text{Depreciation}$$

Discussion Questions

1. The previous section explained why a nation's "production" and "income" can be thought of as roughly equal in a conceptual sense. Why, in practice, does the value of domestic production actually differ from the total of domestic incomes?

---

* When net income payments from the rest of the world are added to GDP, the result is a measure called gross national product (GNP). For many years, GNP was used as the primary measure of U.S. production. It measures a country's production in terms of the output produced *by its workers and companies,* no matter where in the world they were located. The BEA switched its emphasis from GNP to GDP in 1991, believing that it is more important, for the purposes for which the accounts are used, to track economic activity *within the borders* of a country.

2. Sometimes you may see GDP defined as "The total *market* value of *all* final goods and services newly produced in a country over a period of time." Given the above discussion, how true is this definition, really? Does GDP really count only goods and services exchanged *in markets?* Does it really account for *all* production?

5. GROWTH, PRICE CHANGES, AND REAL GDP

Economic growth, traditionally defined as a state in which GDP is on the rise, is historically a topic of wide concern to policymakers and the media. Likewise, inflation, or the growth rate of prices, is also closely followed.

5.1 CALCULATING GDP GROWTH RATES

So far, we have concentrated on calculating GDP in only one year. To calculate rates of economic growth, economists must look at how GDP changes over time. The percentage change in GDP from year to year can be calculated using the standard percentage change formula. The standard formula, for something that takes one value in year 1 and another in year 2, is:

$$percentage\ change = \frac{Value_2 - Value_1}{Value_1} \times 100$$

So to compute the growth rate of GDP from, say, 2005 to 2006, we calculate:

$$growth\ rate\ of\ GDP = \frac{GDP_{2006} - GDP_{2005}}{GDP_{2005}} \times 100$$

For example, United States GDP in 2005 was estimated to be \$12.43 trillion, while in 2006 it was estimated to be \$13.20 trillion. Fitting these into the equation, we have

$$growth\ rate\ of\ GDP = \frac{13.20 - 12.43}{12.43} \times 100$$

$$= .062 \times 100$$
$$= 6.2$$

indicating that GDP grew about 6.2 percent between 2005 and 2006.

The BEA and newspapers commonly report the GDP growth rates for quarters, expressed in terms of an "annual growth rate." This measures by how much the economy would grow if it were to continue to expand for the entire year at the speed reported for the three-month period. (See News in Context.)

5.2 NOMINAL VS. REAL GDP

Does the number we just calculated mean that the level of aggregate production in 2006 was 6.2 percent larger than production in 2005? Not necessarily. The measure of GDP used in the previous section is **nominal or current-dollar GDP**, or GDP expressed in terms of the prices of goods and services that were current at the time. The figure for GDP for 2006 that we used, for example, is based on prices as they were in 2006, and the figure for GDP in 2005 is based on prices that prevailed in 2005.

NEWS IN CONTEXT:
Real GDP Grew at a 0.6 Percent Rate in the Fourth Quarter

The U.S. BEA issues regular news releases concerning GDP growth. Here are excerpts from its release of February 28, 2008.

Real gross domestic product—the output of goods and services produced by labor and property located in the United States—increased at an annual rate of 0.6 percent in the fourth quarter of 2007, according to preliminary estimates released by the Bureau of Economic Analysis. In the third quarter, real GDP increased 4.9 percent.

The GDP estimates released today are based on more complete source data than were available for the advance estimates issued last month. . . .

The increase in real GDP in the fourth quarter primarily reflected positive contributions from personal consumption expenditures (PCE), exports, nonresidential structures, state and local government spending, and equipment and software that were largely offset by a negative contributions from private inventory investment and residential fixed investment. Imports, which are a subtraction in the calculation of GDP, decreased . . .

The deceleration in real GDP growth in the fourth quarter primarily reflected a downturn in inventory investment and decelerations in exports, in PCE, and in federal government spending that were partly offset by a downturn in imports.

---

nominal (current dollar) GDP: gross domestic product expressed in terms of current prices

Not only does output change between two years, but generally the *prices at which output is valued* change as well. **Real GDP** is a measure that seeks to reflect the actual value of goods and services produced, by removing the effect of changes in prices.

real GDP: a measure of gross domestic product that seeks to reflect the actual value of production goods and services produced, by removing the effect of changes in prices

For example, suppose a very simple economy produces only two goods, apples and oranges. Columns (1) through (3) of Table 5.5 describe the number of each produced in each of two years, and the market prices in each year. Nominal GDP is just the sum of the dollar values of the goods produced in a year, evaluated at the prices in that same year:

Nominal GDP = Total production valued at current prices

As we can see in Table 5.5, in Year 1 the value of nominal GDP is $200. In Year 2, the value of nominal GDP is $300. The percentage growth of GDP from Year 1 to Year 2 can be calculated as 50 percent, applying the percentage change formula from the previous section.

But if you look carefully, you can see that only part of the change in nominal GDP is due to an increase in production: The quantity of oranges produced rises from 50 pounds to 75 pounds from Year 1 to Year 2. The rest of the year-to-year increase is due an increase in the price of apples, from $1.00 to $1.50.

Table 5.5   **Calculation of Nominal GDP in an "Apples-and-Oranges" Economy**

(1) Description	(2) Price this Year	(3) Quantity this Year	(4) Nominal GDP = *sum of* *[column (2) × column (3)]*
Year 1			
Apples	$1.00	100	$100
Oranges	$2.00	50	$100
			$200
Year 2			
Apples	$1.50	100	$150
Oranges	$2.00	75	$150
			$300

5.3 CALCULATING REAL GDP

Until 1995, the BEA calculated real GDP using the "constant-dollar method." Since the constant-dollar method is relatively easy to understand and contains most of the intuition you need as a beginning economics student, we will cover it in some detail.

The constant-dollar method uses prices from one particular year, called the **base year**, to evaluate the value of production in all years.

> **base year** (in the constant-dollar method of estimating GDP): the year whose prices are chosen for evaluating production in all years. Real and nominal GDP are equal in the base year

Constant-dollar real GDP is calculated by doing the same sort of multiplying and summing exercise as shown in Table 5.6, but using the *same* prices for all years:

Constant-Dollar Real GDP = Total production valued at base year prices

Applying the constant-dollar method to our simple "apples-and-oranges" example, for instance, we might take Year 1 as the base year, and express GDP in both Year 1 and Year 2 in terms of Year 1's prices. Calculations of constant-dollar real GDP for each year are shown in Table 5.6. While the quantities in column (3) are the same as in Table 5.5, the prices in column (2) are *all from Year 1*. GDP in Year 2 expressed in "constant (Year 1) dollars" is the sum of quantities in Year 2 multiplied by prices in Year 1. This comes out to be $250. In the base year, real and nominal GDP are the same.

Using the percentage growth rate formula from the previous section, we can see that constant-dollar *real* GDP has grown by 25 percent. Note that this is less than the 50 percent growth figure for nominal GDP. Some of the growth in nominal GDP is due to price changes, not production changes.

The convention of using "constant dollars," however, has a number of problems. One of the most bothersome is that it makes measured GDP growth calculations depend on which year is chosen as base. For example, what if we chose Year 2 to be the base instead of Year 1? Applying Year 2 prices to both years would yield a measured growth rate of 20 percent, instead of the 25 percent we calculated using Year 1 as base. (You can check this as an exercise.) The method also suffers from various biases, which become more important the more dissimilar relative prices and spending patterns are between the base year and a current year.

Beginning in 1996, the BEA switched to calculating real GDP using the "chained-dollar" method. The concept behind the new measure is still the same—real GDP still is an attempt

Table 5.6   **Calculation of Constant-Dollar Real GDP**

(1) Description	(2) Price in Base Year	(3) Quantity this Year	(4) Real GDP =sum of [column (2) × column (3)]
Year 1 **(Base)**			
Apples	$1.00	100	$100
Oranges	$2.00	50	$100
			$200
Year 2			
Apples	**$1.00**	100	$100
Oranges	**$2.00**	75	$150
			$250

to measure output change free of the influence of changing prices. While there is still one year for which real and nominal GDP are equal, it is now called the "reference year," and real GDP is currently expressed in BEA publications in terms of "chained (2000) dollars." Unlike the constant-dollar method, the chained-dollar method yields a unique estimated growth rate. Unfortunately, while this method has arguably increased the accuracy of GDP growth calculations, one drawback is a steep jump in computational complexity. Because these calculations are much harder than for the constant-dollar method, their explanation has been placed in the Appendix to this chapter.

In Figure 5.1 you can see how measures of real and nominal GDP diverge. Because prices were generally rising over the period 1990–2006, nominal GDP grew faster than real GDP, as shown by the more steeply rising line.

5.4 Price Indexes and Inflation Rates

Price indexes are interesting both for how they relate to calculation of real GDP and on their own because of the policy interest in measuring (and controlling) inflation. An **index number** is a figure that measures the change in size of a magnitude, in this case the price level, as compared to its magnitude in some other period. Generally, the value of the index number in the reference or base year is set to 100, though sometimes other values (such as 1 or 10) are used.

index number: a figure that measures the change in size of a magnitude, such as a quantity or price, as compared to its magnitude in some other period

The price index most often reported in the news is the **consumer price index (CPI)**, calculated by the U.S. Bureau of Labor Statistics (BLS). The CPI measures changes in the prices of goods and services bought by households.

consumer price index (CPI): an index measuring changes in prices of goods and services bought by households

The CPI is calculated using a *weighted average* of the prices of the various goods and services it tracks. The mathematics of this is worth a little explaining. A "weighted average" is an average in which the different numbers being averaged together are "weighted" to indicate their relative importance in the calculation. You are probably already familiar with this, in the calculation of your own Grade Point Average now or in high school. Each grade you receive in a course is "weighted" by the number of credits or hours the course is worth. These weighted grade points

Figure 5.1   **Real versus Nominal GDP, 1990–2006**

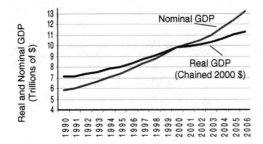

Nominal GDP grows faster than real GDP when prices are rising. (Data source: BEA NIPA Tables 1.1.5 and 1.1.6, published 10/31/2007)

are summed up and then divided by the total number of credits or hours to yield your GPA. An "A" received in a two-credit course thus properly receives less emphasis in the calculation than an "A" received in a four-credit course.

Similarly, in measuring price levels in the economy, we want to give greater emphasis to prices at which many transactions are made, and less emphasis to the prices of relatively minor goods and services. The way to do this is to weight each price by a corresponding quantity of goods produced and sold at that price.

Once again, however, we face choices about what standards to use. Should we use as weights the quantities bought in Year 1, Year 2, or some combination? Until recently, the Bureau of Labor Statistics used a *constant-weight method* to calculate the CPI. Quantities bought during one time period are chosen as "base." These quantities are said to represent a typical "market basket" of goods bought by households. A constant-weight price index is calculated according to the following formula:

$$\text{Constant Weight Price Index} = \frac{\text{sum of current prices weighted by base quantities}}{\text{sum of base prices weighted by base quantities}} \times 100$$

The price-index problem is analogous to the calculation of "constant-dollar" GDP—only now it is a common set of *quantity weights,* rather than prices, from the base period that are applied to every calculation.

Consider, again, our "apples-and-oranges" economy, assuming that the quantities given reflect purchases by consumers. Table 5.7 shows how we would calculate the numerator and denominator for the constant-weight price index formula, considering Year 2 to be the current year and using the Year 1 "market basket" as the base. The sum of current (Year 2) prices weighted by base quantities is $250, while the sum of base prices weighted by base quantities is $200. The CPI for Year 2 is therefore calculated as (250 ÷ 200) × 100 = 125. The price index for the base year (here, Year 1) is always equal to 100.

The growth rate of prices—that is, the inflation rate affecting consumers—is measured by the growth rate of this price index:

$$\text{Inflation rate} = \frac{CPI_2 - CPI_1}{CPI_1} \times 100$$

So, in this case, with the price index rising from 100 to 125, the inflation rate is 25 percent.

Table 5.7   **Calculation of Parts of a Constant-Weight Price Index**

(1)	(2)	(3)	(4)
			Sum of (Prices × Base
	Price	Quantity **in**	Quantities) = *sum of*
Description	this Year	**Base Year**	*[column (2) × column (3)]*
Year 1 **(Base)**			
Apples	$1.00	100	$100
Oranges	$2.00	50	$100
			$200
Year 2			
Apples	$1.50	**100**	$150
Oranges	$2.00	**50**	$100
			$250

Unfortunately, when a price index is based on constant weights, it may tend to overstate inflation for periods after the base year. When the price of a good is rising particularly fast relative to other goods, people tend to look for cheaper substitutes. But a constant-weight index assumes that people are still buying the same quantities of the expensive goods. Various innovations have recently been made in the CPI to attempt to get around this problem. Currently, the "market basket" is updated periodically using data from ongoing household expenditure surveys. The BLS now also publishes "chained" price indexes. The mathematics of these more advanced calculations will not be presented here.

The CPI is not the only price index in use. The producer price index (PPI) measures prices that domestic producers receive for their output, and so tracks many intermediate goods not included in the CPI market basket. Import and export price indexes track prices of goods traded between domestic residents and the foreign sector. Because they track different goods, these indexes—and inflation rates calculated from them—may vary from each other.

The BEA uses the CPI, PPI and other indexes created by the BLS in creating its own national income and product statistics, and also creates a price index of its own. While the other indexes reflect price levels of specific groups of goods and services of interest to consumers and producers, the index published by the BEA reflects changes in all the prices of goods and services included in GDP. Called the **implicit price deflator** (or the **GDP deflator**), it is calculated for any year as:

Implicit Price Deflator = (Nominal GDP/Real GDP) × 100

where real GDP is calculated using the chained-dollar method. Calculations are demonstrated in the Appendix.

> **implicit price deflator (GDP deflator):** a price index derived by dividing nominal GDP by real GDP

5.5 GROWTH AND GROWTH RATES

We have calculated year-to-year growth rates for GDP and prices. But suppose we want to ask how much GDP has grown over the last five years, or twenty years? How do we calculate those numbers? The answer is rather complicated, but fortunately you can use NIPA's published tables to answer such questions.

Economics in the Real World:
How Quantity Weights Can Lose Validity Over Time

Why do economists and statisticians make a fuss about updating the quantity weights used in calculating the Consumer Price Index? Consider how household expenditure patterns have changed over time.

In 1901, nearly half of the budget of a typical urban, working family went towards food, while 15 percent went towards shelter and an equal proportion towards clothing. The family probably spent nothing at all on cars or gasoline—since automobiles were not yet in wide use!

By 1950, the picture had changed considerably. Now only a third of the family's spending went towards food, while only 11 percent went towards shelter and 12 percent towards clothing. On average, families now spent about 12 percent of their budget on expenses related to private vehicles, since by this time automobile ownership was becoming widespread.

In recent data on consumer expenditures, the share devoted to food has dropped even further—to 14 percent. Expenditures on clothing have dropped to less than 5 percent of a household's budget, on average. Meanwhile, families are spending more on shelter (19 percent of their budget) and private vehicle expenses (18 percent of their budget), than they were at mid-century.

Using expenditure patterns from one of these periods to "weight" the CPI in another would clearly result in biased figures. Using the 1901 expenditure pattern nowadays would, for example, mean that auto and gasoline prices would not figure into the CPI at all.

The invention of new goods and services (for example, MP3 players) and quality improvements in existing goods (for example, in products for home entertainment and computing) continue to create special challenges for the economists working on measuring price changes.

Sources: Eva Jacobs and Stephanie Shipp, "How Family Spending Has Changed in the U.S." *Monthly Labor Review* March 1990; U.S. Bureau of Labor Statistics, *Consumer Expenditures in 2002*, Feb 2004; and authors' calculations.

However, a handy way to get a grasp on the relation of annual growth rates to changes over a longer period of time is by using the **rule of 72**. Taking the number 72 and dividing by an annual growth rate will give you approximately the number of years it will take for an amount to double if it grows at that constant rate (as long as the numbers you are using are not extremely high or low). For example, if real GDP grew at a constant 4 percent rate per year, it would double in about eighteen years (since 72/4 = 18).

rule of 72: a shorthand calculation that states that dividing an annual growth rate into the number 72 yields approximately the number of years it will take for an amount to double

Discussion Questions

1. The "constant-dollar" method of estimating real GDP uses prices for one year to calculate measures of GDP for all years. Why is it sometimes important to evaluate GDP in the current year using prices from some other year? Why can't we just always use current prices? Explain.
2. How is the "constant-dollar" method of estimating real GDP similar to the use of "constant weights" in the computation of the price indexes? Explain.

6. SAVINGS, INVESTMENT, AND TRADE

At a personal level, you produce goods and services, earn income, consume, save, and borrow or lend. One of the reasons you keep personal accounts is to try to track your inflows and outflows, so you know whether you are running down your personal assets or building them up. If you can save money from your current income, you are bettering your financial position for the future. On the other hand, if you run down your savings or go into debt merely to finance a high level of consumption, you may find yourself in trouble later on. Running down financial savings or going into debt can be a good choice for your future only if you use the funds to gain some other valuable asset. Students often go into debt in order to finance their education, for example, with the idea that it will later pay off by enabling them to earn higher income.

There are analogous issues at the national level. Besides keeping track of economic growth and inflation, systems of national accounts serve another important purpose. They allow us to look at the savings-and-asset situation of a national economy as a whole (at least as far as *manufactured* assets and financial flows are concerned).

6.1 THE RELATIONSHIP OF SAVINGS, INVESTMENT, AND TRADE

The analogous category at the national level to your personal day-to-day consumption spending is the consumption spending done by the household and institutions and government sectors. This is spending on goods and services that are presumably "used up" right now—they are not expected to help the country over the long term. The analogous category to your income is—at least roughly—GDP.

Recall that the spending approach to GDP says that

> *GDP =*
> *Personal consumption + Private investment*
> *+ Government consumption + Government investment + Net exports*

Rearranging, we can get

> *GDP – Personal consumption – Government consumption =*
> *Private investment + Government investment + Net exports*

Since saving is what is left over from income after spending on consumption,

> *Saving = Investment + Net Exports*

Thinking about these quantities in terms of valuable goods and services, this important identity says, intuitively, that goods and services that are produced in our domestic economy in excess of what we currently use for consumption can be investment goods—additions to our stock of manufactured assets (including replacement of depreciated assets)—or can sold to foreign countries (in excess of the value of what we import from them.)

6.2 FINANCING SPENDING

Another way to look at the relation of saving, investment, and trade is to think of how the various sectors *finance* their purchases of goods and services. In a contemporary economy, goods are rarely traded for goods, but rather money is used as a means of exchange. So corresponding to any flow of goods and services transacted in exchanges there is an equivalent flow of monetary funds.

Consider, for a moment, a closed economy. In this case the last identity would reduce to:

Saving = Investment

This says that, in a closed economy as a whole, the total amounts that the various sectors choose not to spend on consumption goods is available for spending on investment goods. How does financial saving get turned into tangible investments?

In the national accounts, it is primarily businesses and the government who are counted as investing. They finance their investment expenditures either from their own savings or by borrowing someone else's savings. Household savings, in the form of income not spent on consumption, can be made available for investment by the other sectors—as when the funds in a household's bank deposit are lent out to a business, or a household buys a government bond. The "saving = investment" identity tells us that at an aggregate national level in a closed economy, only what the country as a whole saves out of current income can be available to finance investment for the future.

When we consider an open economy, things get more complicated. Now the nation as a whole can also borrow from, or lend to, the foreign sector, and the relevant identity is:

Saving = Investment + Net Exports

If net exports are positive, we sell more goods abroad than we buy. How do people abroad pay for all our goods, if the value of what we sell to them exceeds the value of what they sell to us? They are not earning enough from their sales to pay us! The most important way they can finance their purchases of our goods is by borrowing from us. They would need to borrow the amount by which our exports to them exceed our imports from them. So the identity can be (approximately) rewritten as:*

Saving = Investment + Net foreign lending

That is, if we have extra savings, above and beyond what is being used for domestic investment, we can loan it to foreigners so they can buy our goods.

In recent years, however, the United States has tended to have net exports that are negative—we tend to buy more from foreign countries than we sell. This means that *we* need to borrow from *them*. The following identity means exactly the same thing as the last one, but is easier to use to represent the recent U.S. situation:

---

* Other ways foreigners can get more goods and services from us than they sell to us is by receiving our goods as gifts, paying for them out of transfer income, or selling us their assets, such as land or businesses, in return. So the equation above is only approximate.

$$Saving = Investment - Net\ foreign\ borrowing$$

When we are in a situation of borrowing (that is, when net foreign borrowing is a positive number) then the amount we are really "putting away for the future"—that is, saving—is less than what we would guess if we only looked at what we are investing. While we may be investing domestically, if "net foreign borrowing" is positive we are also putting the country's future financially "in hock" to other countries by borrowing from them.

Should we worry if our country has to borrow from foreigners? As in the case of your personal finances, it makes a difference what the borrowing is *for*. If the borrowing finances the purchase of productive new private or government investment goods, then it may be a way of actually improving the country's outlook for the future. As mentioned in Chapter 1, international authorities encouraged poor countries for many decades to borrow heavily for development projects, using exactly this reasoning. But if the funds borrowed largely go into investments that do not pay off financially, or if the borrowing only finances a high level of consumption, there is reason to worry. A country that borrows a lot may be in trouble when it comes time to pay back its loans. Many poor countries have, in recent years, in fact found themselves unable to pay the *interest* on—much less pay *back*—the enormous foreign debts that they have built up over the years.

6.3 NET DOMESTIC PRODUCTION AND SAVING

The investment concept used in defining *gross* domestic product (GDP) is *gross* investment. To calculate what the level of production is during a year, above and beyond the production that simply replaces worn-out manufactured capital, we need another concept, **net domestic product (NDP)**. NDP is GDP less depreciation (just as net investment, we saw earlier, is gross investment less depreciation):

$$Net\ domestic\ product = GDP - Depreciation$$

> **net domestic product (NDP):** a measure of national production above that needed to replace worn-out manufactured capital, found by subtracting depreciation from GDP

So far we have discussed gross saving, the gross amount a country sets aside from spending. But at the same time that we are saving, some capital goods are wearing out. To really find out what we have "put aside for the future," we need to subtract depreciation from our measures of saving, as well. For example, even if our savings were positive, if they did not finance enough investment to make up for deterioration of the capital stock, we would actually start the next year in a *worse* position. **Net saving** is gross saving minus depreciation.

$$Net\ saving = (Gross)\ Saving - Depreciation$$

Using the equation from the "financing spending" section (above) that relates savings to investment and foreign borrowing, we can rewrite this as:

$$Net\ saving = (Gross)\ Investment - Depreciation - Net\ foreign\ borrowing$$

Net saving is a better measure than gross saving of whether we are "putting aside for the future."

How much has the United States been "putting aside for the future" lately? BEA estimates of gross investment, depreciation, and net foreign borrowing for 2006 are approximately $2.6 trillion, $1.6 trillion, and $0.8 trillion, respectively. Allowing for the fact that some of the statistics used in these calculations may contain errors, the BEA estimates that net saving for that year was only about $250 billion (that is, $0.25 trillion).

Discussion Questions

1. Suppose the country of Atlantis is investing and exporting a great deal, while it imports little. What can you say about its level of national saving? Suppose the country of Olympus invests more than it saves. How can it do this?

2. For many years it was often said that the level of government debt was not much of a problem, no matter how high it was, since we "owe it to ourselves." Taxpayers within the United States would, of course, eventually have to pay back the debt (or at least pay interest on it, as it gets refinanced time after time). But their payments would be going to owners of government bonds who were *also* primarily people within the United States. Over the years, however, many U.S. government bonds have been purchased by foreigners. Does this complicate this picture? Explain.

7. GROSS DOMESTIC PRODUCT IN THE TRADITIONAL MACROECONOMIC MODEL

During the mid-to-late twentieth century, it became popular to teach macroeconomic principles using an especially simple representation of the basic macroeconomic identities. The **traditional macroeconomic model** that will be explored at length in later chapters is based on a representation of national accounts that adds further simplifications to the conventions adopted by the BEA.

> **traditional macroeconomic model:** a simple, mechanical model that portrays the macroeconomy as being made up of businesses that produce and invest, and households and governments that (only) consume.

As in the NIPA, three of the recognized sectors in the traditional model are the business, government, and foreign sectors. Instead of a "household and institutions" sector, however, the model posits only a "household" sector. While in actuality nearly 10 percent of measured Personal Consumption Expenditures comes from nonprofit institutions such as hospitals and universities, nonprofit institutions are ignored in the traditional model. Personal consumption expenditures—shortened to **consumption** and denoted by *C*—are treated as representing only *household* spending.

> **consumption (C)** (traditional macro model): the component of GDP that represents spending by households.

The traditional model follows the NIPA in not accounting for investments in natural, human, and social capital. **Investment** (*I*) is limited to spending on structures, equipment, and inventories. While current BEA practice recognizes that governments undertake investments, investment in the traditional model is assumed to be exclusively an activity of the business sector. In this model, **government spending** (*G*) on goods and services is not generally considered to have an investment component.

> **investment (I)** (traditional macro model): the component of GDP that represents spending on structures, equipment and inventories by business firms
>
> **government spending (G)** (traditional macro model): the component of GDP that represents spending by federal, state and local governments (and which is assumed to be consumption-oriented)

The foreign sector and **net exports (NX)** are treated similarly to the way they are in the national accounts. GDP is often represented by the notation *Y,* and referred to interchangeably

Figure 5.2   **The Traditional Macroeconomic Model "Circular Flow" Diagram**

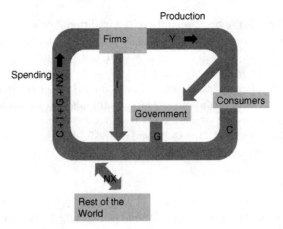

In the traditional macroeconomic model, only business firms are portrayed as producing. Governments and households appear only as actors who buy the firms' products, and non-profit institutions and the environment do not appear at all.

as aggregate "product," "income," or "spending." The basic identity of the model is taken from the spending approach to GDP accounting:

$$Y = C + I + G + NX$$

That is, aggregate spending (or income or product) in the traditional macro model is defined as the sum of consumption spending by households, investment spending by business firms, government spending, and net exports. (Compare this to Table 5.3 above.)

> **net exports (NX)** (traditional macro model): the component of GDP that represents the value of exports less the value of imports
>
> The basic identity of the traditional macro model is $Y = C + I + G + NX$

What might be the most startling assumption of this model, however, is that not only is it assumed that governments and households do not invest, it is *assumed that governments and households do not produce.* Production is assumed to be accomplished only by the business sector. For example, most presentations of this model include a circular flow diagram for production and spending similar to Figure 5.2. (In some cases, the diagrams include financial flows such as taxes, transfers, and savings. These are omitted here for simplicity.) In this diagram, business firms are represented as producing the whole of GDP. The government and "consumers" (households) make use of this production, by buying most of the goods and services provided. Business investment spending also contributes to total spending. The effect of the rest of the world can be to either add to, or subtract from, the flow of spending, depending on whether net exports are positive or negative.

While this simplified model can be useful in some applications, users also need to be aware of how this very simple image of an economy, which leaves out important aspects of real economies, can create distortions in our way of thinking about economic life.

Discussion Questions

1. What is the basic identity of the traditional macro model? Why is the left-hand side of the equation referred to interchangeably as "product," "income," or "spending"? Which approach to counting GDP does the identity reflect?
2. Do you think the National Income and Product Accounts focus attention on the most important characteristics of an economy in the twenty-first century? What about the traditional macro model? Give examples of some important contemporary economic problems for which the national accounts and the traditional model might give useful frameworks for study and analysis, and some examples of some problems where they would not.

REVIEW QUESTIONS

1. For what purpose was national accounting in the United States originally begun?
2. Who compiles the National Income and Product Accounts?
3. What are the four sectors of the economy, according to the BEA? What sorts of entities are included in each?
4. What forms of capital assets are tracked by the BEA?
5. Explain the difference between gross and net investment.
6. Explain four key phrases that appear in the definition of GDP.
7. What are the three approaches to GDP measurement?
8. Explain why, in a simple economy, the three approaches would yield the same figure for the value of total production.
9. Explain why the following two approaches arrive at the same number for the value of a final good: (a) looking at the market price of the good and (b) counting up the value-added at each stage of its production.
10. How are "market values" determined for goods and services that are not exchanged in markets, or when data is not available?
11. Describe the components of GDP according to the product approach.
12. Describe the components of GDP according to the spending approach.
13. What are the major differences between GDP and national income?
14. Describe the reasoning behind the "constant-dollar" approach to calculating real GDP.
15. What are some problems with the "constant-dollar" approach to calculating real GDP? Identify a problem with the "chained-dollar" approach.
16. Describe the reasoning behind the "constant-weight" method traditionally used in estimating the price indexes.
17. Is there only one kind of price index? Explain.
18. Explain how savings, investment, and trade are related in the national accounts.
19. Explain how a country can finance an excess of imports over exports.
20. What additional simplifying assumptions does the traditional macro model impose, beyond those made in the NIPA?

EXERCISES

1. If you look at the government-supplied statistical tables regarding the national accounts, you might find that they often go into considerable detail about "farm" vs.

"non-farm" activities, while it is much harder to dig out good information on, for example, the activities of the finance industry. Can you conjecture how this might relate to the history of the national accounts?

2. In which line (or lines) of Table 5.2 (the product approach) would the value of each of the following be counted? "Not counted in any category" is also an option.
   a. Production of fresh apples, domestically grown for profitable sale
   b. State health inspection services
   c. Education services provided by a private, nonprofit domestic college
   d. Childcare services provided by a child's parents and relatives
   e. Production by a U.S.-owned company at its factory in Singapore

3. In which line (or lines) of Table 5.4 (the income approach) would the value of each of the following be counted? If it is part of "net income flows from the rest of the world" explain whether it reflects domestic (or foreign) production, and whether it reflects domestic (or foreign) income. "Not counted in any category" is also an option.
   a. Wages paid by your local supermarket to its employees
   b. Profits received by a U.S. electronics firm from its factory in Mexico
   c. Business spending to replace worn-out equipment
   d. Wages paid by a U.S. electronics firm to the employees of its factory in Mexico
   e. Profits received by a Japanese automaker from its factory in the United States

4. In which line (or lines) of Table 5.3 (the spending approach) would the value of each of the following be counted? "Not counted in any category" is also an option.
   a. A new refrigerator bought by a family
   b. A book newly produced in Indiana and bought by a store in Mexico
   c. New computers, manufactured in Asia, bought by a U.S. accounting company
   d. Meals produced and served in Virginia to military personnel
   e. New computers, produced in the United States, bought by a U.S. computer retail chain, and not yet sold by the end of the year
   f. A three-year-old couch bought by a used furniture store in Arizona
   g. Cleaning services bought by a nonprofit hospital in New York
   h. The services of volunteers in an environmental action campaign

5. Using the relations among accounting categories demonstrated in the tables and identities in the text, use the following information on values (measured in Neverlandian pesos) from the country of Neverland in 2010

Household and institutions spending = 650	Business spending = 50
Household and institutions production =150	Exports = 225
Net income payments from the rest of the world = 5	Imports = 125
Nonprofit institutions production = 50	Government production = 200
State and local government spending = 30	Statistical discrepancy = 0
Change in private inventories = 2	GDP = 850
Depreciation = 60	

   to find values for the following categories:

   a. Private household production
   b. Business production

      c. Fixed investment spending (by business)

      d. Federal government spending

      e. National income

6. Suppose an extremely simple economy produces only two goods, pillows and rugs. In the first year, 50 pillows are produced, and sold at $5 each; 11 rugs are produced, and sold at $50 each. In the second year, 56 pillows are produced, and sold for $5 each; 12 rugs are produced, and sold at $60 each.

    a. What is nominal GDP in each of the two years?

    b. What is the growth rate of nominal GDP?

    c. What is real GDP in each year, expressed in terms of constant Year 1 dollars?

    d. What is the growth rate of real GDP (in constant Year 1 dollars)?

7. Assume the same simple economy described in the previous question.

    a. Calculate a constant-weight price index for the second year, using the first year as the base.

    b. What is the growth rate of prices (inflation rate) from the first to the second year?

8. Match each concept in Column A with a definition or example in Column B

Column A	Column B
a. A negative (subtracted) item in GDP	1. The year in which real and nominal values are equal
b. A major cause of difference between GDP and NI	2. Purchases of computer software
c. An imputed value	3. Consumption of fixed capital (depreciation)
d. An entity in the government sector	4. Unpaid household production
e. Reflects the prices of all goods and services counted in GDP	5. Implicit price deflator
f. Base year	6. National income
g. An assumption of the traditional macro model	7. Spending on imported cheese
h. Something not counted in by the BEA in calculating GDP	8. A measure that seeks to remove the effects of price changes
i. Real GDP	9. Uses a fixed "market basket"
j. A component of the "income approach" to GDP accounting	10. What homeowners "pay" themselves in rent
k. A constant-weight price index	11. "Governments do not produce"
l. Part of business investment (gross private domestic investment)	12. A state university

9. List the key simplifying assumptions of the traditional macro model concerning:

    a. The forms of capital included in the model

    b. The sectors of the economy

    c. Who in the economy produces and invests

10. Go to the Bureau of Economic Analysis Web site (www.bea.gov). What are the latest figures for real GDP, current dollar GDP, and the growth rate of GDP? What time period do these represent? In what sort of dollars is real GDP expressed?

11. Go to the Bureau of Labor Statistics Web site (www.bls.gov) and locate its information on the Consumer Price Index for All Urban Consumers (called the "CPI-U"). What is its current value? What month is this for? How does its value in this month

compare to its value for the same month a year ago? (That is, by what percentage has the index risen? Use the "seasonally adjusted" number.)

12. (If Appendix is assigned.) The "chained Year 1 dollar" estimate of real GDP in the apples-and-oranges example (see Appendix) is smaller than the "constant Year 1 dollar" estimate of real GDP. Can you explain why? (Hint: Compare the GDP growth rates derived using the two methods.)

APPENDIX: CHAINED-DOLLAR REAL GDP

The key new concept in the "chained-dollar" method is an emphasis on estimating **quantity indexes** for GDP in the current year relative to the year before and relative to the reference year.

> **quantity index:** an index measuring changes in levels of quantities produced

Chained-dollar measures of real GDP and GDP growth are based on the use of index numbers. The ratio of two values of GDP in adjacent years, measured at a common set of prices, can be used as a quantity index to measure production in one year relative to another.

The calculation of chained-dollar real GDP starts with the calculation of a **Fisher quantity index** which measures production in one year relative to an adjacent year by using an *average* of the ratios that would be found by using first one year, and then the other, as the source of prices at which production is valued. The type of average used is a "geometric" average. Instead of adding two numbers and then dividing by two, as you would in calculating the most common type of average (the arithmetic mean), to get a geometric average you *multiply* the two numbers together and then take the *square root*. The formula for this Fisher quantity index is:

Fisher quantity index (for year-to-year comparison)

$$= \sqrt{\left(\frac{Year\ 2\ GDP\ in\ Year\ 1\ prices}{Year\ 1\ GDP\ in\ Year\ 1\ prices}\right) \times \left(\frac{Year\ 2\ GDP\ in\ Year\ 2\ prices}{Year\ 1\ GDP\ in\ Year\ 2\ prices}\right)}$$

This index has a value of 1 in the reference year, which we take to be Year 1.

> **Fisher quantity index:** an index that measures production in one year relative to an adjacent year by using an average of the ratios that would be found by using first one year, and then the other, as the source of prices at which production is valued

The growth rate of real GDP between the reference year and the next year can then be calculated as:

growth rate = (Fisher quantity index − 1) × 100

For example, we have already made many of the necessary calculations for the "apples-and-oranges" economy in Tables 5.5 and 5.6. Plugging these in, we get

Fisher quantity index (for Year 2 compared to Year 1)

$$= \sqrt{\left(\frac{250}{200}\right) \times \left(\frac{300}{250}\right)} = \sqrt{1.25 \times 1.20} = \sqrt{1.5} = 1.225$$

The growth rate of real GDP for the "apples-and-oranges" economy between these two years is

growth rate = (1.225 − 1) × 100 = 22.5 percent

Table 5.8　　**Deriving Real GDP in Chained (Year 1) Dollars**

Type of Measure	Year 1	Year 2
Nominal GDP	$200	$300
Fisher quantity index (current to previous year)	——	1.225
Chain-type quantity index	100	100 ×1.225 = 122.5
Real GDP (chained Year 1 dollars)	= $200	(122.5 × $200)/100 = $245

Notice that this growth rate is *between* the two growth rates (20 percent and 25 percent) we obtained by using the constant-dollar method with various base years. The Fisher quantity index method gives us a unique *average* number for estimated growth.

A quantity index for the current year in terms of a reference year that may be several years in the past is created by "chaining together" year-to-year Fisher quantity indexes to make a **chain-type quantity index** comparing real production relative to the reference year. The chain-type quantity index has a value of 100 in the reference year. In any subsequent year, it is set equal to the chain-type quantity index from the previous year multiplied by the Fisher quantity index calculated for the current year.

> **chain-type quantity index:** an index comparing real production in the current year to the reference year, calculated using a series of year-to-year Fisher quantity indexes

Finally, estimation of real GDP in (chained) dollar terms is made by multiplying the chain-type quantity index for a year times the level of nominal GDP in the reference year, and dividing by 100.

For example, suppose we take our "apples-and-oranges" economy, making Year 1 the reference year. Year 1's chain-type quantity index is thus set equal to 100, and its nominal and real GDP are equal. These are shown in Table 5.8. The chain-type quantity index for Year 2 is the previous year's value (100) times the Fisher quantity index we just calculated (1.225). We multiply this result, the new index number 122.5, times nominal GDP in the base year ($200) and divide by 100 to get real GDP, $245. Whew!

This can be continued for many years into the future—or into the past. (For example, if the Fisher quantity index calculated for Year 3 were to come out to be 1.152, then the chain-type quantity index for Year 3 would be 122.5 × 1.152.) If you want to check to see that this method actually makes some sense, calculate the percentage change in real GDP from Year 1 to Year 2 using the values in the table above. You will find it does, in fact, equal 22.5 percent!

The implicit price deflator can be calculated for Year 2 (using Year 1 as the reference year) as (300/245) × 100 = 122.5, showing a 22.5 percent price increase over Year 1.

The new method has some other drawbacks, as well. The sum of real components of GDP in chained-dollar terms do not generally exactly add up to real GDP. Users of the data are also warned not to make comparisons of chained-dollar amounts for years far away from the reference year. The BEA tries to make the data more usable by providing tables in which, for example, year-to-year growth rates in components of GDP are already calculated for the user.

Macroeconomic Measurement: Environmental and Social Dimensions

6

With the increasing need to recognize issues of ecological and social sustainability, many economists have in recent decades examined the question of how national accounting—and macroeconomic analysis based on such accounts—can be improved. As economist William D. Nordhaus, chair of a blue-ribbon National Research Council panel, put it in a 1999 report to the U.S. Bureau of Economic Analysis:

> Over the last quarter century, we have become increasingly aware of the interactions between human societies and the natural environment in which they thrive and upon which they depend . . . The idea of including environmental assets and services in the national economic accounts is part of a larger movement to develop broader social and environmental indicators. This movement reflects the reality that economic and social welfare does not stop at the market's border, but extends to many nonmarket activities.[1]

1. NEW UNDERSTANDINGS FOR THE TWENTY-FIRST CENTURY

The traditional macroeconomic model introduced at the end of the last chapter portrays a hypothetical economy in which only businesses engage in production, and in which the natural environment plays no role. This was illustrated in the flow diagram, Figure 5.2. Increasingly, however, people have raised questions about whether this gives an adequate picture of the macroeconomy.

People have come to realize that economic activity actually takes place within the context of human social institutions that in turn are inextricably embedded in the natural environment. This embeddedness is illustrated by the outer rings labeled "Social Context" and "Physical Context" in Figure 6.1. In addition, the contributions to production of households and community groups (within the core sphere), and of nonprofit as well as government institutions (within the public-purpose sphere) have recently received more attention, as illustrated in the center of Figure 6.1. Of course, the role of businesses, both foreign and domestic, is recognized in both the traditional and newer approaches.

Many researchers argue that national governments need to start gathering new kinds of data in order to face the challenges of twenty-first-century concerns. Building on these new kinds of information, some researchers are concentrating on developing refined measures of national assets and production, keeping as close as possible to the framework of the National Income and Product Accounts. In this chapter, we discuss the two major areas in which improvements in data gathering and possibly in the design of national accounts seem to be most badly needed: accounting for the environment and accounting for unpaid work in households.

Figure 6.1   **Macroeconomics in Context**

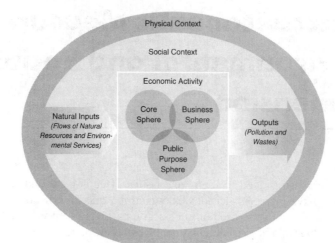

An emerging understanding of macroeconomic performance notes that businesses (both foreign and domestic), households and communities (the core sphere) and public-purpose institutions (governments and nonprofit organizations) are all involved in the productive activities. Economies are, in turn, embedded in a context of larger social institutions and the natural (physical) environment.

Other researchers aim to design indicators that more directly measure social and economic well-being. Rather than seeking to measure the volume of *production,* these researchers seek to develop indicators of the *quality of life* (see last section of this chapter).

Discussion Questions

1. GDP can be characterized as a (rough) measure of the amount of "throughput" going on in an economy—as measuring the level of activity whose purpose it is to turn renewable and non-renewable resources into new products. How does "throughput" relate to sustainable well-being? Is more "throughput" always a good thing?
2. In Chapter 3 we discussed how economies are based on natural, manufactured, social, and human capital. Only the value of manufactured capital (structures and equipment)—and recently, software—is estimated in the current national accounts. Can you think of ways that the stocks of natural, social, and human capital might be measured? What kind of information would be needed?

2. ACCOUNTING FOR THE ENVIRONMENT

The natural environment plays roles that are indispensable to economic life. Environmental economists describe these under the headings of three functions:

1. **Resource functions:** The natural environment provides natural resources that are inputs into human production processes. These include such things as mineral ores, crude petroleum, fish, and forests. Some of these resources, such as fish and forests, are renewable while others, such as minerals and petroleum, are not.

2. **Environmental service functions**: The natural environment provides the basic habitat of clean air, drinkable water, and suitable climate that directly support all forms of life on the planet. Water filtration provided by wetlands and erosion control provided by tree-covered hillsides are other examples of services provided by ecosystems. People enjoy the services of the natural environment directly when they enjoy pleasant scenery or outdoor recreation.

3. **Sink functions**: The natural environment serves as a "sink" which absorbs (up to a point) the pollution and wastes generated by economic activity. Car exhaust dissipates into the atmosphere, for example, while used packaging goes into landfills and fluid industrial wastes end up in rivers and oceans. Some wastes break down relatively quickly into harmless substances. Others are toxic and/or accumulate over time, eventually compromising the quality of the environment.

The way in which the natural environment provides the resources and environmental services that sustain economic activity is illustrated by the arrow on the left in Figure 6.1, showing inflows into economic activity. The way in which economic activity puts waste products into environmental sinks is illustrated by the arrow on the right in Figure 6.1, showing the economy generating flows back into the environment.

> The three main ways in which the environment interacts with the economy are through resource functions, environmental service functions, and sink functions.
>
> **resource functions**: the provision by the natural environment of inputs into human production processes
>
> **environmental service functions**: the provision by the natural environment of the ecosystem services that support and enhance life
>
> **sink functions**: the provision by the natural environment of places to put waste materials

Although these three environmental functions were treated for centuries as though they were provided "free" and in unlimited amounts, more recently the problems of depletion of resources, degradation of environmental services, and overuse of environmental sink functions have become increasingly apparent. (See News in Context.)

2.1 PHYSICAL ACCOUNTS

A first step toward accounting for the environment is simply to attempt to quantify some of the major environmental effects of economic activity in physical terms, such as in terms of proportions of fish stocks lost or tons of coal burned.

Many governments have already committed in principle to creating such accounts for their own nation, at least on one issue of major concern. The burning of fossil fuels and the resulting release of carbon dioxide into the atmosphere has been scientifically linked to global changes in climate that may, if not halted, have catastrophic results within the next few decades. In 1997 the Kyoto Protocol on Greenhouse Gas Emissions was drafted. It aims to reduce climate-change-causing greenhouse gas emissions (such as emissions of carbon dioxide) to 5 to 7 percent below 1990 levels by 2012. Individual goals were set for different countries. By mid-2007, 175 parties, including most industrialized countries such as Canada, the United Kingdom, France, Germany, Italy, Spain, Switzerland, Sweden, Norway, Japan, the Republic of Korea, and New Zealand (as well as many less industrialized countries including China and Mexico) had ratified the agreement.

Of course, for a country to monitor its own efforts in this area, it needs to know how many tons of greenhouse gasses it released into the atmosphere in 1990 and how many tons it is releasing

News in Context:
Commercial Fleets Reduced Big Fish by 90 Percent, Study Says

In just 50 years, the global spread of industrial-scale commercial fishing has cut by 90 percent the oceans' population of large predatory fishes, from majestic giants like blue marlin to staples like cod, a new study has found.

Oceanographers not connected with the study say it provides the best evidence yet that recent fish harvests have been sustained at high levels only because fleets have sought and heavily exploited ever more distant fish populations . . . The study, drawing on decades of data from fishing fleets and research boats, paints a 50-year portrait of fish populations under siege as advances like sonar and satellite positioning systems allowed fleets to home in on pockets of abundance . . . In almost all exploited areas, it generally took just 10 or 15 years for populations to crash. One measure was fish caught per 100 hooks on the Japanese lines. The study said the rate went from 10 fish per 100 hooks to 1 or less in that period.

"This shows that the reason we've had so much tuna and swordfish, the only reason this has been sustained, is because boats kept going farther and farther away," said Dr. Jeremy B. C. Jackson, a professor at the Scripps Institution of Oceanography. Dr. Jackson has conducted other studies showing declines and ecological effects in coastal waters but was not involved in the new work. "The problem now is there's no place left to go," he said. "There are a lot of people out there willing to fish the last fish. But that's just not going to work."

Source: Andrew C. Revkin, *The New York Times*, May 15, 2003

Figure 6.2   **The Decline of Large Predatory Fishes in the Tropical Atlantic Ecosystem**

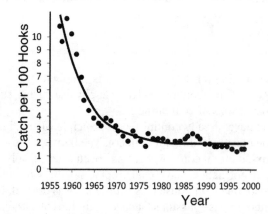

The spread of industrial-scale commercial fishing has seriously depleted the oceans' populations of large fish. (Source: Data taken from "Rapid worldwide depletion of predatory fish communities" by Ransom A. Myers & Boris Worm. *Nature* 423, May 15, 2003, Figure 1)

Which sort of environmental function is discussed in this news article? Why did fish appear to be in "limitless" supply for so long, in spite of the depletion of specific fisheries?

currently. The gathering of scientific and economic information necessary to measure such environmental variables, aggregated to a national level, is thus a new and expanding field.

2.2 NATURAL ASSETS AND THE NATIONAL ACCOUNTS

As we saw in the last chapter, the Bureau of Economic Analysis currently counts only manufactured assets in its tables of national assets, and only investment in manufactured assets in its calculation of investment (and savings). The 1999 National Research Council report pointed out that:

> Natural resources such as petroleum, minerals, clean water, and fertile soils are assets of the economy in much the same way as are computers, homes, and trucks. An important part of the economic picture is therefore missing if natural assets are omitted in creating the national balance sheet. Likewise, consuming stocks of valuable subsoil assets such as fossil fuels or water, or cutting first-growth forests, is just as much a drawdown on the national wealth as is consuming aboveground stocks of wheat, cutting commercially managed forests, or driving a truck.[2]

In principle, then, this panel concluded, the value of a nation's natural resources should be added to the value of its manufactured capital stock in accounting for national assets.

Measures of the natural capital stock of a country should also include the value of assets related to environmental service and sink functions. An old-growth forest, for example, not only provides timber resources, but also environmental services such as water retention, habitat provision, and carbon sequestering, as well as recreational and aesthetic value. Ideally, then, tables in the national accounts that look at a country's assets, such as the one we examined in Table 5.1, should be much expanded.

Asset tables measure *stock* values, as discussed in Chapter 3—the value of assets is measured at a point in time. But more importantly, perhaps, for immediate policy purposes, is the issue of taking into account *changes* in the level of national environmental assets. When, over the course of a year, nonrenewable resources are depleted, or the environment's capacities to provide service flows or function as an effective sink are degraded, the nation's ability to produce in the future is reduced. The natural capital stock has depreciated. This is a *flow* variable, as discussed in Chapter 3—the amount of "disinvestment" that occurs is measured over the course of a year.

In concept, then, whenever the depreciation of manufactured capital is subtracted in the national accounts, *depreciation of natural capital* should be subtracted as well. For example, the 2003 version of the United Nations System of Integrated Environmental and Economic Accounts discusses a measure called **environmentally adjusted net domestic product (eaNDP)**, or GDP less both these kinds of depreciation.

$$eaNDP = GDP$$
$$- \textit{Depreciation of manufactured capital}$$
$$- \textit{Depreciation of natural capital}$$

This measure should more accurately reflect the full picture of production and depreciation in a given year.

> **environmentally adjusted net domestic product (eaNDP):** suggested by the United Nations, this is equal to GDP less depreciation of both manufactured and natural capital

Similarly, the World Bank in 1995 proposed that saving less both kinds of depreciation be called **genuine saving**:

> *Genuine saving   = (Gross) Saving*
> *– Depreciation of manufactured capital*
> *– Depreciation of natural capital*

Under standard measures of net saving, a country only needs to save a little more than the amount it needs to replace its worn-out manufactured capital in order to appear to be saving for the future. The genuine saving measure points out that countries that run down their natural capital may be making things worse for the future, even if their manufactured investment seems to be keeping a healthy pace.

> **genuine saving:** proposed by the World Bank, this is equal to gross saving less depreciation of both manufactured and natural capital

2.3 NATIONAL ACCOUNTS AND WHAT NATURE PRODUCES

The adjustments we just discussed relate to the asset or *stock* value of natural assets, and how the value of these assets can depreciate over time. But, you might have noticed, in calculating eaNDP we started with the traditional measure of the *flow of production* over a year, GDP. Should we also adjust the measures of the flow of national production to account for environmental factors? Should GDP itself be "environmentally adjusted"?

In an ideal accounting system, we might think of the natural environment as yet another productive sphere or sector. The ecosystem, unless severely disturbed, generates over the course of any year such goods and services as new plants in forests and fields, new livestock and fish, clean air and water, spectacular scenery, an amazing diversity of plant and animal species, and services such as protection from solar radiation—often without any effort on the part of humans. Many of these natural processes add to human well-being, and humans could not survive and flourish without them. In theory, then, accounts of production relevant to human well-being should include all the flows of new goods and services that nature generates.

Most economists agree, however, that compiling comprehensive accounts for *all* that nature does for us over the course of a year would be an over-ambitious task. In fact, for productive flows, as for stocks of assets, what we really want to know about for policy purposes are the ways that the *economy and environment interact,* particularly when this interaction leads to undesirable outcomes.

For example, suppose a hillside is stripped of its forest covering, and the wood is sold as pulp for papermaking. The lack of vegetation now means that run-off from rain increases and a town downstream from the hillside suffers flooding and has to repair many buildings. Even if the vegetation should grow back by the end of the year (which is unlikely), something has happened. In the national accounts as currently constructed, the logging activity contributes to GDP in this year (in the form of valuable wood products) *and* the activity of repairing buildings is counted as an economic activity that *also* adds to GDP in this year. It would seem that the more damage we do to the environment, the more "productive" the economy is!

Or consider an alternative scenario, in which the town realizes that flooding is likely, and fills sandbags to line its riverbank. It thereby avoids costly repairs. But, again, both the logging and the sandbag-making are counted as adding to GDP.

What is wrong with this, of course, is that the initial environmental services of the forest in terms of water retention were not counted as part of GDP. If they had been, we would have noticed that the efforts of the town did not reflect new production so much as a *shift* in production from the "nature sector" to the human sector. Had we included the "nature sector" from the beginning, our national accounts would have shown a decrease in the production of that sector (decreased water retention) offsetting the increase in production of the human sector (that is, repairing buildings or constructing sandbag barriers), netting out in something closer to a wash.

Expenditures that are made simply to compensate for or defend against harmful events are called **defensive expenditures**. The town's expenditures on repairs or floodwalls in our example were simply necessary to maintain the status quo.

> **defensive expenditures:** expenditures necessary just to maintain a status quo (that is, necessary to keep well-being from going down in the face of negative developments)

Clearly, including defensive expenditures as positive additions to GDP, while not taking into account the loss of environmental service production that made them necessary, can result in misleading numbers. We will similarly be mislead if our GDP accounts include the rising cost of hospital services to treat asthma attacks made worse by pollution, or the cost of additional fuel required by the fishing industry as boats must travel farther and farther from port to find ever-scarcer fish.

Reductions in "natural-sector production" also often have direct impacts on human well-being without being reflected in measurable defensive expenditures. For example, a person who suffers pain or dies from pollution-aggravated asthma or from contamination of their water by toxic chemicals is harmed by the fall-off in the quality of environmental services, whether or not they "add to GDP" through expenditures on medical treatment.

2.4 THE PROBLEM OF VALUATION

Even if we were able to compile very good information on environmental assets and production in physical terms, there is a very big problem currently standing in the way of directly incorporating environmental accounting into the National Income and Product Accounts. This is the problem of monetary valuation. As you recall from the previous chapter, all assets and flows are counted in *dollar* terms, based on market prices or some imputation that approximates market prices. We cannot add tons of lumber directly to grams of mercury and come up with a meaningful number. Only if all quantities can be converted to a common measure—in the case of NIPA accounts, dollars—can they be added and subtracted to come up with numbers such as "depreciation" or "production."

Putting a dollar value on an asset is tricky even in the simplest case. As discussed in Chapter 5, many conventions have been adopted to try to standardize the accounts, but they are only conventions, not truths. For example, to *really* know the value of a piece of machinery, one would need to know exactly how long it will last and what the availability and prices of all inputs and outputs related to it will be for as long into the future as the piece of machinery is used. Since we never know the future, we can only made educated guesses. The current NIPA accounts rely on many conventions about, for example, how long various types of machinery are expected to be in use and how fast they will depreciate. The resulting estimates may, of course, often be proved wrong as the future unfolds. A computer, for example, may be expected to hold most of its value for two years, but instead, due to the unexpected invention of a new technology, it could be obsolete within two months.

If assigning a monetary value to manufactured assets that are used for only a few years is difficult, think about how much more difficult it is to get a dollar measure for natural assets! Consider, for example, the value of uranium reserves still in the ground. Perhaps uranium will become more valuable a hundred years in the future because countries turn increasingly to nuclear power. Or the price of uranium may fall in the future as countries, concerned about safety and the disposal of wastes, explore other energy sources instead. The discovery of previously unknown mineral deposits, changes in policies, shifts in consumer demand, and new technologies are among the factors that make predicting the future over the long haul very difficult, and thus make it very hard to determine the value of many assets.

Other assets are difficult to value because, although we have a sense that overall ecological balance is important to human as well as other life on the planet, some forms of natural capital have no apparent *market* value. Biologists tell us, for example, that in recent decades there has been a shocking decline in populations of frogs, toads, and salamanders worldwide, and a large increase in deformities in these animals. Clearly degradation of the natural environment is occurring. But since the *market* value of most frog species is zero, there are wide disagreements about how—or even whether—a dollar value could be put on these losses.

Another factor making valuation difficult is the issue of "discounting." A society with a "high time discount rate" tends to put relatively little value on the future, while a society with a "low time discount rate" is willing to set aside some present enjoyment for future rewards. In an environmental context, the future that is relevant includes all generations to come! Yet coming up with a numerical dollar value for assets requires that a decision be made about how much future generations should count in present decision making.

Nevertheless, some agencies have attempted to make at least rough calculations of the value of natural capital or its depreciation. World Bank estimates of genuine saving, for example, yielded negative numbers for some less developed countries, particularly in the Middle East and North Africa. Rather than saving for the future, such countries seem to be financing some of current consumption by running down their natural assets—particularly their petroleum.

Turning from the topic of environmental assets (stocks) and their depreciation to the topic of production (flows) of environmental goods and services, the prospect for accounting is mixed. For some environmental production, a valuation in market prices could be determined relatively straightforwardly. For example, the firewood collected free in forests or the fish caught noncommercially during a year, currently not counted in GDP, could be valued at the price of their market equivalents. But for other cases the problem is more difficult.

Take, for example, the logging and flooding story from the last section. Normally, economists would try to value the production of water retention services by an existing forest by looking at some places in which this value has been translated into dollar terms. Let's imagine towns A, B, and C that are all identical, and identically situated relative to forested hillsides. Near town A, the hillside is logged and the town sustains flood damage. The hillside near town B is also logged, but town B spends on sandbagging and avoids damage. The hillside near town C has not been logged. What, then, is the dollar value of a year's worth of water retention services provided by the forest near town C?

Suppose the cost of repairs in Town A, which did nothing to prevent flooding, was $5 million. If you estimate the value of the water retention services of the hillside forest near town C using the **damage cost approach**, you would say that the services are worth $5 million—the standing forest prevents town C from suffering an estimated $5 million in damage.

> **damage cost approach:** assigning a monetary value to an environmental service that is equal to the actual damage done when the service is withdrawn

What if we use town B as the comparison instead? Suppose it spent $100,000 averting damage by building sandbag barriers. Estimating the value of the forest's services using the equally plausible **maintenance cost approach** you would say that the value of the forest's services is $100,000. (This is sometimes also referred to as the "avoidance cost" or "replacement cost" approach.) Having the forest standing on the hillside near town C provides equivalent services as having a sandbag barrier costing $100,000 (abstracting, of course, from animal habitat damage and other concerns). As you can see, the two approaches may not agree—the value of the forest's services to town C could be estimated at either $5 million or $100,000.

> **maintenance cost approach**: assigning a monetary value to an environmental service that is equal to what it would cost to maintain the same standard of services using an alternative method

Another example would be whether to measure the value of unpolluted air in terms of effects of pollution on human health (damage) or in terms of the cost of pollution-control devices (maintenance). So far, some national and international agencies have adopted one convention and some the other in their experimental environmental accounts.

If the withdrawal of environmental services makes people suffer or die, then you enter the even more controversial area of trying to assign dollar values to human suffering and human lives. And many environmental effects cross national lines. What is the monetary value of a global "public good" such as a stable climate? On whose account should we tally the loss of deep-sea fisheries located in international waters?

The idea of an environmentally adjusted or "greened" GDP appeals to many who are concerned about the problems of a GDP measure that omits important environmental issues. It has proved difficult, however, to arrive at a single estimate of "Green GDP." What may be more useful, at least for the time being, are studies that give ranges of well-reasoned monetary estimates, while making their assumptions and methods clear.

2.5 MAKING CHANGES: SATELLITE ACCOUNTS

As an alternative to defining a "greened" GDP, many nations have chosen to create supplementary or **satellite accounts** that record changes in important environmental and resource sectors in physical rather than monetary terms. Satellite accounts can give a detailed picture of areas such as forest cover, water resources, mineral assets, land quality, pollution emissions, and pollution control measures, without assigning specific money values.

> **satellite accounts**: additional or parallel accounting systems that provide measures of social and environmental factors in physical terms, without necessarily including monetary valuation

Countries whose national incomes are derived in large part from exports of mineral or forestry resources, for example, can assess their stocks of ore and count up their remaining timber acreage. Others, with different concerns, can create input-output accounts to get a better idea of where resources are used, where pollution comes from, and which domestic economic sectors are most reliant on imported resources. The sectors most responsible for carbon dioxide emissions can be identified. These accounts are linked to the existing national accounts: For example, economic production of oil is associated with depletion of petroleum reserves, and physical flows of pollutants are related to the output of pollution-generating industries.

The advantage of using satellite accounts is that an extensive database of environmental information can be created, and related to existing GDP sectors, without having to determine a precise monetary value for each category. Transforming physical into monetary measures is not ruled out, however, and can be done whenever reliable and generally accepted techniques for environmental valuation exist. The United Nations has published a systematic guide to integrated economic and environmental accounting using the satellite approach, and many countries have established such accounts.

Unfortunately for the progress of environmental accounting in the United States, funding for the Commerce Department's Integrated Environmental and Economic Accounts (IEESA) was terminated by Congress in 1994, and was not restored despite the encouragement given by the

National Research Council panel in 1999. The United States has also been the only major industrialized country that has *not* ratified the Kyoto Protocol. In June 2001, President Bush withdrew
U.S. support for the Kyoto Protocol, citing doubt about the scientific evidence on climate change
and unfairness in the application of prescribed cutbacks. He also claimed that compliance with
the prescribed reductions in greenhouse gas emissions would have a "negative impact" on the
U.S. economy. While environmental accounting is moving ahead in many other nations, attention
to environmental issues seems to be lagging behind in the United States.

Discussion Questions

1. In Burgess County, current irrigation methods are leading to rising salt levels in agricultural fields. As a result, the number of bushels of corn that can be harvested per
   acre is declining. If you are a county agricultural economist, what two approaches
   might you consider using to estimate the value of the lost fertility of the soil during
   the current year? What sorts of economic and technological information would you
   need to come up with your estimates?
2. Some people have argued that the monetary valuation of environmental costs and
   benefits is important because "some number is better than no number"—without
   valuation, these factors are omitted entirely from GDP accounts. Others say that it
   is impossible to express environmental factors adequately in dollar terms. What are
   some valid points on each side of this debate? How do you think this debate should
   be resolved?

3. MEASURING HOUSEHOLD PRODUCTION

Another significant omission in the national accounts, as currently constituted, is the value of
much household production. As noted in the previous chapter, only two aspects of household
production are currently counted in GDP: one, the services of the house itself and, two, the
services provided by paid household workers such as housekeepers and gardeners. The household production of goods and services such as childcare, housecleaning, laundry services, meal
preparation, landscaping, and transportation using unpaid labor and household capital goods
(such as automobiles and appliances) is not counted.

Even the most conservative estimates of the total value of household production come up with
numbers equal to about 25–35 percent of standard GDP in the United States, and less conservative estimates put the value as equal to or greater than the value of marketed production. How
did this substantial area of productive activity come to be overlooked, and what is being done
to remedy this omission?

3.1 THE HISTORY OF EXCLUSION

Various reasons have been advanced over the decades for why household activities should not
count in GDP.

"Households are nonproductive"

One reason given was that households were not part of the economy because they did not produce economic goods. This depends on a definition of "economic" in which factories, farms
and office buildings, and the people in them, were taken as defining "the economy." Dating

from Victorian times, households and families were often thought of, conversely, as "non-economic," running along more primitive lines of social development, and as somehow "closer to nature" and naturally self-renewing. There was also a gender aspect to this split: For much of the nineteenth and twentieth centuries, "the economy" was a man's world, while "the home" was assigned to women.

This omission of much household production from the national accounts may contribute to a subtle bias in the perceptions of policymakers who make economic decisions based on them. Since household work is not measured, it may be easy to think that it's not important, or not even an "economic" matter at all. The U.S. Social Security retirement system, for example, gives stipends to people based only on their market wages and years in paid work. Some advocates suggest that people should also get credit for time spent in child raising—for example, up to a year of Social Security credit for time taken off with each child, in recognition of the contribution that such unpaid work makes to social and economic life. Having home production counted in GDP might help keep policymakers more aware of its productive contributions. The foremost advocate of this view is Marilyn Waring, author of the book *If Women Counted*.[3]

"It's too hard to distinguish household production from consumption"

Sometimes an argument has been made on the basis of convenience: it is simply too hard, some commentators have argued, to distinguish production activities from consumption activities within the household. If diapering your baby is considered work, should cuddling be considered work, too? If you enjoy cooking as a hobby, is not that activity more like a form of entertainment than like the work of a paid cook? Should the time you spend playing tennis be considered "productive" and counted in GDP? It's just easier, such commentators argue, to draw the line at the household door than to try to sort out the question of "What parts of the activities are productive?"

Yet the matter of distinguishing production from consumption has been discussed intelligently for decades. A frequently applied rule is what is called the **third-person criterion**: An activity should only be classified as household production if it is in principle replaceable by market or third-person services. Cooking a meal is in this sense "production," since you might alternatively pay someone to cook for you. Playing a game of tennis clearly is not, since paying someone to play on your behalf would be absurd.

> **third-person criterion:** the convention that says that an activity should be considered to be production (rather than leisure) if a person could buy a market replacement or pay someone to do the activity in his or her place

The fact that some household productive activities—like some parts of cooking and child-care—may sometimes be sources of intrinsic pleasure to some of the people doing the work is, arguably, not particularly relevant. If we insisted that only work that is perceived as neutral or unpleasant should count as "work," then substantial portions of time at *paid* jobs should obviously be excluded as well. There is an increasing realization that the definition of "work" should be centered around the idea that it is an activity that produces something valuable—a needed report, an emotionally healthy child—and not around whether the activity is unpleasant (or not) or paid (or not).

"GDP measures market production"

Sometimes it is granted that people do engage in productive activities in their roles as household members. But then you will often hear it said that that GDP aims to only measure production *for the market.* Since household outputs are not sold, this argument goes, it is consistent to exclude them from GDP.

The problem with this argument is that a substantial portion of GDP *already* reflects nonmarket production. Most government production of goods and services is never sold on a market (11 percent of GDP in 2006). Nor do owner-occupiers really pay rent on their houses to themselves (over 6 percent of GDP in 2006). As more market substitutes have developed for formerly home-produced goods and services (day care for home childcare, prepared foods for home cooked, etc.) it has become less and less tenable to draw the line for defining "the economy" at the household door, imputing "market values" for the services of governments and houses, but not for the unpaid work done within homes.

"Including household production would make too big of a change in the accounts."

One might grant that households do, in fact, produce many goods and services, and that estimated monetary values of these flows would be very large. Some statisticians then argue against measuring household production on other grounds: "The inclusion of large non-monetary flows of this kind in the accounts together with monetary flows can obscure what is happening on markets and reduce the analytic usefulness of the data" for addressing topics such as inflation and economic fluctuations.[4]

In reply, some economists argue that current GDP figures are less accurate for having neglected household production. Most obviously, GDP is understated—a substantial area of valuable productive activity has been overlooked. Perhaps more importantly, changes in an economy over time, such as the true growth rate of production, may be misstated. One of the major economic shifts that occurred during the twentieth century was the movement of a large proportion of women from unpaid employment as full-time homemakers into paid employment in market work. In 1870, 40 percent of all U.S. workers (paid and unpaid, male and female) were full-time homemakers; by 2000, the proportion had dropped to 16 percent.[5] This increase in market work, simultaneous with the increase in purchases of substitutes for home production such as paid childcare and prepared foods, were counted as increases in GDP. The value of *lost* household production, however, was not subtracted. This failure to account for reductions in some home-produced goods and services would tend to mean that GDP growth during the period was *overstated.*

The picture is a bit more complex, however, if you also take into account the changes in the *productivity* of household labor time during this period. Homemakers in 1870 had very little in the way of "capital stock" to work with—probably a coal stove that needed daily cleaning (instead of a range), a washtub and clothesline (instead of a washer/dryer), and an icebox (instead of a refrigerator). Productive investments in household technology have, the evidence suggests, led to people now enjoying cleaner clothes and more interesting and varied diets than previously. While the household sector was shrinking relative to other sectors in terms of labor hours devoted to it, the value of its real product, as least in some areas such as cooking and cleaning, was not necessarily falling. This growth in true national product due to changes in household productivity has been entirely missed in standard accounting.

Accounting for household production might also change how we see the cyclical behavior of the economy, since there is reason to believe that the level of household production probably moves **countercyclically**. That is, when the economy is *down*—in recession—people's "do-it-yourself" work probably goes *up*. While the financial and emotional consequences of lack of needed paid employment should not be trivialized, it is likely that many of the unemployed use some of their extra time doing additional childcare and household tasks. When people are in financial straits, they also tend to economize by replacing market purchases with home-produced goods and services.

> **countercyclical movement:** when an indicator moves in the opposite direction from the business cycle. It moves up as the economy goes down (into recession), and down as the economy goes up (into recovery).

Comparisons between countries are also made more difficult by the lack of accounting for household production in GDP. In countries of the global South, where such activities make up a much higher proportion of total production, GDP is even more inadequate as an indicator of national production.

3.2 TIME USE SURVEYS

A first step in determining a value for household production is to find out how much time people spend in unpaid productive activities. In the past, estimates of time use for the United States came from small and sporadic surveys. However, in 2003, following the lead of many other industrialized countries, the U.S. Bureau of Labor Statistics began collecting data for the first national ongoing survey of time use. The American Time Use Study (ATUS), conducted by the U.S. Bureau of Labor Statistics, asks people age sixteen or over in a nationally representative sample to report in detail how they used their time on one particular day.

The results of the survey for 2005 indicate that on average on any given day, 84 percent of women and 65 percent of men spend some time doing household activities including housework, food preparation and cleanup, lawn and garden care, or household management (such as paying bills). When averaged over all responses (including those who had not spent any time on household activities), women spent an average of 2.3 hours per day on these activities, while men spent 1.4 hours. On an average day, 19 percent of men reported doing housework, such as cleaning or doing laundry, compared with 53 percent of women.

Some other highlights are summarized in Table 6.1. These figures are averages for people in all employment categories, and include both weekdays and weekend days.

The largest blocks of time reported were for personal care (including sleeping), leisure and sports (including an average 2.6 hours per day of watching television), and working (for pay) and work-related activities (including commuting time).

Unpaid household production is spread over several categories in Table 6.1. Time spent caring for children or the elderly or ill is included in the category of "caring for and helping people," though these data require closer examination. These tasks may be done as a primary activity, as reported in Table 6.1. Or they may be done as a secondary activity—that is, done while the person is primarily doing something else, such as shopping or watching television. Other tables released by the BLS reveal that in households with children under thirteen, women spend an average of 6.4 hours caring for children as a secondary activity, while men spend an average of 4.2 hours.

The most conservative approach to measuring household production would be to count only primary "household" and "caring and helping" activities as productive, yielding an average figure for household production of 2.59 hours per day, compared to 3.69 for paid work and related activities. Even taking this most conservative approach, household production would then account for 41 percent of total productive time. Less conservative approaches would also include as "productive" at least some of the time spent purchasing (analogous to how working as a "purchaser" in a business is considered productive), in education activities (that is, investing in human capital), and in caring done as a secondary activity. With such approaches, household production could easily be found to account for well over half of total productive time.

Table 6.1   **Average Hours per Day Spent in Primary Activities**

Activity	Total	Men	Women
Personal care	9.34	9.22	9.62
Eating and drinking	1.24	1.30	1.19
Household	1.82	1.35	2.27
Housework	.61	.24	.96
Food preparation and cleanup	.51	.26	.75
Lawn and garden care	.20	.27	.14
Household management	.15	.12	.17
Purchasing goods and services	.80	.63	.96
Caring for and helping people	.77	.55	.97
Working and work-related activities	3.69	4.44	3.00
Educational activities	.45	.47	.43
Organizational, civic, and religious activities	.31	.27	.35
Leisure and sports	5.14	5.50	4.80
Other activities	.35	.28	.41
TOTAL	24.00	24.00	24.00

Source: "American Time Use Survey–2005 Results Announced by BLS" BLS NEWS, July 27, 2006, Table 1.

3.3 METHODS OF VALUING HOUSEHOLD PRODUCTION

Unlike the attempt to incorporate environmental assets and services into the national accounts, which requires considerable development of new techniques of measurement and valuation, the imputation of a value for household production can generally follow a similar procedure to that currently used to impute a value for government production.

Both government production and household production result in goods and services that are generally not sold on markets. Both government production and household production use manufactured capital goods and labor. Hence, as with government production, a quasi-market value for household production could be imputed by summing the values of the labor and capital services devoted to the productive activities.

The major difference is that in the case of household work the labor is *unpaid.* Once time use has been measured in terms of hours spent on various activities, by surveys such as the one just discussed, standard national accounting procedures demand that these hours be assigned a monetary value using some market or quasi-market prices. Economists have developed two main methods of assigning a monetary value to household time use: The replacement cost method and the opportunity cost method.

Replacement cost method. In the **replacement cost method**, hours spent on household labor are valued at what it would cost to pay someone else to do the same job. In the most popular approach—and the one used to generate the most conservative estimates—economists use the wages paid in a general category such as "domestic worker" or "housekeeper" to impute a wage. A variant of this method, which usually results in higher estimates, is to value each type of task separately: childcare time is valued according to the wage of a professional childcare worker, housecleaning by the wages of professional housecleaners, plumbing repair by the wages of a plumber, etc.

> **replacement cost method** (for estimating the value of household production): valuing hours at the amount it would be necessary to pay someone to do the work

Opportunity cost method. The **opportunity cost method** starts from a different view, based on microeconomic "marginal" thinking. Presumably, if someone reduces his or her hours at paid work in order to engage in household production, he or she must (if acting rationally) value the time spent in household production (at the margin) at least at the wage rate that he or she could have been earned by doing paid work for another hour. That is, if you choose to give up $30 you could have earned working overtime in order to spend an hour with your child, you must presumably think that the value of spending that hour with your child is at least $30. This leads to using the wage rate *the household producer would have earned in the market* to value household work time. In this case, estimates of the value of nonmarket production can go quite a bit higher, since some hours would be valued at the wage rates earned by doctors, lawyers, managers, etc.

> **opportunity cost method** (for estimating the value of household production): valuing hours at the amount the unpaid worker could have earned at a paid job

Neither approach to imputing a wage rate is perfect. However, it would be hard to argue that perfection has been achieved in any of the other measurements and imputations involved in creating the national accounts, and many argue that imputing *some* value for household labor time, even using minimal replacement costs, is more accurate than imputing a value of zero.

In addition to valuing the time used in household production, a value must be assigned to the capital services provided by appliances, vehicles, and the like. "Consumer durables" spending by households would need to be renamed "household investment" spending, and included as a subcategory of investment rather than consumption. Adding the flow of services that are yielded by these capital goods to the measurement of GDP would require that new calculations be made. But the techniques for estimating such service flows have already been designed for the case where cars, washing machines, etc., are owned by *businesses*. These same techniques could be extended to household capital goods.

While this section focuses on unpaid household work, similar arguments have also been made concerning unpaid volunteer work in communities and nonprofit organizations—the time people spend coaching children's sports teams, visiting nursing homes, serving on church and school committees, etc. In the ATUS, 13 percent of the people surveyed reported participating in organizational, civic, and religious activities on their surveyed day, a figure that includes organized volunteer activities. Were both these forms of work counted, the proportion of production attributed to the "households and institutions" sector would rise considerably.

3.4 MAKING CHANGES

Perhaps surprisingly, initial estimates of the value of household services for the United States *predate* the design of the NIPA. In 1921 a group of economists at the National Bureau of Economic Research calculated that the value of household services would be about 25 to 30 percent of market national income. Decades later, in 1988, economist Robert Eisner reviewed six major proposed redesigns of the NIPA, all of which included substantial estimated values for household production.[6] Despite numerous demonstrations of its practicality dating back more than 85 years, however, actual inclusion of household production in the U.S. NIPA remains a project for the twenty-first century.

Internationally, there is interest in at least gathering data on household production. Many counties, including Australia, Canada, India, Japan, Mexico, Thailand, and the United Kingdom, have conducted or are conducting national time use surveys to aid their understanding of unpaid productive activities. The United Nations Statistical Commission and Eurostat (the statistical office of the European Union) are encouraging countries to develop satellite accounts that, similar to the satellite accounts for the environment, provide the necessary information to adjust measures of GDP to take household production into account while not changing the definition of official GDP.

Discussion Questions

1. Discuss the reasons why household production has been excluded from national accounting. Do any of the reasons seem convincing to you? What do you think has been the most important reason why household production has been excluded for so long?

2. Think back on at least one household activity you've done in the last couple of days that would be replaceable in principle by market or third-person services. How would that activity be valued by the replacement cost method? By the opportunity cost method? What sorts of manufactured capital goods were important, along with your labor, in the activity?

4. MEASURING ECONOMIC WELL-BEING

Instead of trying to estimate a dollar value for domestic production, some economists insist that instead of—or in addition to—standardized national accounts, more direct indicators of economic well-being are needed. Since the goal of macroeconomics is human well-being, we need to be sure the indicators we pay most attention to are ones that relate to the goal we want to achieve!

4.1 DOES OUTPUT MEASURE WELL-BEING?

Measures of the value of national output (or income) per capita—even improved measures that incorporate environmental concerns and household production—can often be poor indicators of sustainable human well-being. In Chapter 1 we mentioned that neglect of the questions of *what, how* and for *whom* can mean that growth in production per capita may not lead to increased welfare. Now we can go into more detail about the problems that arise from focusing on production alone. These include:

Well-being-reducing products. Some outputs decrease rather than increase human well-being. The production of unhealthy foods and drugs, dangerous equipment, and community-destroying urban developments, for example, may lower, not raise, well-being. Even if it is the case that people are apparently willing to pay for such goods and services, either individually (perhaps influenced by media advertising) or through their governments (perhaps influenced by interest group lobbyists), it may be that such decisions reflect poor information or bad judgment when looked at from a well-being point of view.

Defensive expenditures. As discussed earlier, some outputs merely compensate for, or defend against, harmful events. Environmental defensive expenditures are only one example. Others include armaments necessitated by an increase in international tensions, increased spending on police forces to combat increased crime, increased gun ownership due to fear or societal breakdown, or increased medical spending due to a rise in automotive accidents. These increased expenditures do not reflect an increase in welfare, but only an attempt to maintain a status quo situation.

Loss of leisure. A rise in output might come about because people expend more time and effort at paid—and, in expanded accounts, also in unpaid—work. Only looking at the increase in measured output does not take into account the fact that overwork makes people more tired and stressed, and takes away from time they could use for enjoying other activities.

Loss of human and social capital formation. Measured output is *lower* to the extent that people eliminate or reduce immediately productive activities in order to invest in schooling or training, or participate in community-building activities. Yet if we consider these as investments in the creation of valuable human and social capital, such activities should be seen as *increasing* sustainable well-being.

Well-being-reducing production methods. If people are miserable at their jobs, suffering alienation and unpleasant working conditions, their well-being is compromised. This is even more obvious in cases where their health or survival is threatened by unhealthy or dangerous working conditions, even if their work results in a high volume of marketed goods and services.

Unequal distribution. National income may be very unevenly distributed, making some people very rich but leaving others in extreme poverty (as was discussed in Chapter 3).

For such reasons, and others, some economists argue that other indicators, including direct measures of well-being outcomes, are necessary either instead of—or more often, in addition to—improved official national production accounts.

Some of these base their work on an NIPA-like framework, but they include more qualitative judgments about whether specific kinds of "production" actually add to sustainable well-being or perhaps detract from it instead. Some of the redesigns of national accounting suggested by academic economists have included adjustments for well-being-enhancing, or well-being-damaging, production. In 1989, economist Herman Daly and theologian John Cobb, Jr. suggested an alternative measure to GDP which they called the Index of Sustainable Economic Welfare (ISEW), in a popular book entitled *For the Common Good: Redirecting the Economy Toward Community, the Environment, and a Sustainable Future.* That initiative helped to spawn the design of more such measures, nationally and internationally, generally implemented by nonprofit groups. We will examine one such measure, the Genuine Progress Indicator.

Other academic and nonprofit researchers have moved more directly to the issue of whether the economy is getting better or worse for people by developing indicators of social and economic outcomes enjoyed by the population. We will discuss one such measure, the Human Development Index, developed by a United Nations agency.

4.2 EXAMPLE: THE GENUINE PROGRESS INDICATOR

One measure of well-being expressed in monetary terms is the **Genuine Progress Indicator (GPI)**, calculated for the United States by the nonprofit group Redefining Progress.

> **Genuine Progress Indicator (GPI):** a measure of economic well-being that adds many benefits, and subtracts many costs, that are not included in GDP. This measure is calculated by the nonprofit group Redefining Progress.

The GPI takes as its starting point the Personal Consumption Expenditures (PCE) component of GDP for each year, as calculated by the BLS, on the reasoning that this number approximates the welfare associated with consumption. The adjustments made to Personal Consumption Expenditures in order to arrive at the GPI for a recent year (2004) are described in Table 6.2.

First, the level of PCE is adjusted for increasing income inequality by dividing by a factor that reflects the growth in the Gini ratio since 1968. (Recall from Chapter 3 that a higher Gini ratio indicates greater inequality, and that the ratio was at a low point in the United States in 1968.) Next, some items that increase well-being but are not measured in PCE are added in. Estimates of the value of time spent on household and volunteer work and the value of higher

Table 6.2   **Calculating the 2004 Genuine Progress Indicator**

Category	Value in Billions of 2000 Dollars
The GPI's starting point	
Personal consumption in 2004	7,589
Personal consumption adjusted for income distribution	6,318
Additions of Benefits	
Value of housework and parenting	2,542
Value of higher education	828
Value of volunteer work	131
Services of consumer durables	743
Services of highways and streets	112
Subtractions of Costs	
Social costs	
Cost of crime	-34
Loss of leisure time	-402
Cost of underemployment	-177
Cost of commuting	-523
Costs of automobile accidents	-175
Environmental costs	
Cost of household pollution abatement	-21
Cost of water pollution	-120
Cost of air pollution	-40
Cost of noise pollution	-18
Loss of wetlands	-53
Loss of farmland	-264
Loss of primary forests	-51
Resource depletion	-1,761
Carbon dioxide emissions damage	-1,183
Cost of ozone depletion	-479
Other	
Net capital investment	389
Net foreign borrowing	-254
Cost of consumer durables	-1,090
The Total: The Genuine Progress Indicator	4,419

Source: John Talberth, Clifford Cobb, and Noah Slattery, "The Genuine Progress Indicator 2006: A Tool for Sustainable Development." Oakland: Redefining Progress, 2006.

education are added. A measure of the services of consumer durables is added, reflecting the well-being gained from items such as appliances and cars. While most government spending is excluded from the GPI because is it argued that such spending is defensive, services that come from government spending on highways and streets is added.

Then a number of cost items are subtracted. These include estimates of social costs, such as the costs of crime and lost leisure time, and environmental costs, including water pollution, the loss of wetlands, and carbon dioxide emission damage. A few other adjustments are made. An addition is made for the amount by which the net (manufactured) capital stock grows, on a per-worker basis, on the reasoning that constant or increasing stocks are necessary for sustainability. A measure of net foreign borrowing is subtracted, since consumption financed from foreign borrowing is not economically sustainable. Lastly, the cost of consumer-durable asset purchases is subtracted, to avoid double counting given that a measure of the *services* of consumer durables has already been included.

Figure 6.3   **Real GDP Per Capita and GPI per Capita Compared**

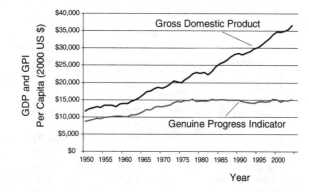

While real GDP per capita has risen substantially since 1950, well-being as measured by per capita GPI has shown less growth. (Source: "The Genuine Progress Indicator 2006: A Tool for Sustainable Development")

Real GPI for the year 2004 was calculated at $4.4 trillion, as can be seen in Table 6.2. This is substantially less than the personal consumption expenditures figure—$7.6 trillion—from which the calculations started. Hence, on net, the subtracted costs—especially environmental costs—are more sizeable than the added benefits. Dividing by the population size, per capita GPI was calculated as $15,035.

Trends in real GDP per capita and real GPI per capita are tracked from 1950 to 2002 in Figure 6.3. Not only is per capita GPI lower than per capita GDP, it has also grown more slowly. That is, environmental and social costs have been increasing faster than the value of the benefits omitted from standard accounting. Looking at the GPI over time, you get a sense of a steady or even falling level of sustainable well-being, which contradicts the trend you see when looking only at measured GDP.

4.3 EXAMPLE: THE HUMAN DEVELOPMENT INDEX

Beginning in 1990, the United Nations Development Program (UNDP), under the direction of Mahbub ul Haq and in consultation with Nobel laureate economist Amartya Sen, began publication of a **Human Development Index (HDI)** designed to compete with GDP as a crude index of human welfare.

> **Human Development Index (HDI):** an index of well-being made by combining measures of health, education, and income. This index is calculated by the United Nations Development Program (UNDP).

The HDI aggregates three indicators of human well-being:

- Life expectancy at birth
- An index reflecting a combination of the adult literacy rate and statistics on enrollments in education
- GDP per capita

That is, not only does the HDI take into account output per capita, but it also takes into account whether national production has been effective in raising well-being outcomes in terms of human longevity and knowledge.

Table 6.3 **Human Development Index**

HDI Rank	Country	Life Expectancy at Birth (years)	Education Index	GDP per Capita[a]	HDI
1	Iceland	81.5	0.98	36,510	0.968
12	United States	77.9	0.97	41,890	0.951
26	Korea, Rep. of	77.9	0.98	22,029	0.921
39	United Arab Emirates	78.3	0.79	25,514	0.868
52	Mexico	75.6	0.86	10,751	0.829
99	Sri Lanka	71.6	0.81	4,595	0.743
125	Namibia	51.6	0.78	7,586	0.650
140	Bangladesh	63.1	0.50	2,053	0.547
162	Angola	44.6	0.54	2,335	0.446
177	Sierra Leone	41.8	0.38	806	0.336

Source: *UNDP Human Development Report 2007/2008.*

[a] Expressed in purchasing power parity U.S. dollars.

The resulting index is a number between zero and one, and is computed by the UNDP for many countries every year. Examples taken from the *Human Development Report 2007/2008* are shown in Table 6.3.

Taking the 177 countries as a whole, there is a rough correspondence between rankings by HDI and rankings you would get by looking at GDP alone. At the top of the rankings by HDI is Iceland, with a life expectancy of 81.5 years, an education index of 0.98, and GDP per capita of $36,510. At the bottom of the rankings is Sierra Leone, with both extremely low GDP per capita and abysmally low indicators for health (life expectancy of only 41.8 years) and education.

Comparisons between HDI and GDP can be revealing about the shortfalls of GDP as an indicator of welfare. For example, the United States ranks forty-second globally in life expectancy, below many lower-income countries as Malta, Chile, and Costa Rica. (See News in Context.) Looking at Table 6.3, you can see that GDP per capita is higher in the United Arab Emirates than the Republic of Korea, but Korea has been more successful in educating its populace (an education index of 0.98 compared to 0.79). Sri Lanka makes a relatively strong showing on the HDI index, in spite of its low levels of GDP per capita ($4,595), compared to, for example, Namibia, which has a substantially higher measured GDP per capita ($7,586). Among even poorer countries, Bangladesh makes a similarly relatively strong showing compared to Angola, which has a higher income per capita but lower health achievements.

HDI and GDP rankings differ for a number of reasons. Countries that score lower on HDI than countries with similar levels of GDP per capita may be plagued by war or by diseases such as AIDS. They often have very unequal income distributions and/or have governments that put a low priority on spending for health and education. Table 6.3 makes it clear that what is important in determining human welfare is not only *how much* is produced, but also *what* is produced (such as armaments vs. clinics) and *how it is distributed.* Countries with good social infrastructure and a lack of extreme gaps between rich and poor tend to score relatively well on HDI, compared to their achievements measured by GDP alone.

The UNDP also gathers a wealth of other statistics that can be used to measure human development in greater detail. These include measures of disparities between males and females in health, literacy, and political and economic participation; measures of poverty and deprivation

NEWS IN CONTEXT:
US Slipping in Life Expectancy Rankings

WASHINGTON—Americans are living longer than ever, but not as long as people in 41 other countries. For decades, the United States has been slipping in international rankings of life expectancy, as other countries improve health care, nutrition and lifestyles. Countries that surpass the U.S. include Japan and most of Europe, as well as Jordan, Guam and the Cayman Islands.

"Something's wrong here when one of the richest countries in the world, the one that spends the most on health care, is not able to keep up with other countries," said Dr. Christopher Murray, head of the Institute for Health Metrics and Evaluation at the University of Washington . . .

The shortest life expectancies were clustered in Sub-Saharan Africa, a region that has been hit hard by an epidemic of HIV and AIDS, as well as famine and civil strife. . . Forty countries, including Cuba, Taiwan and most of Europe had lower infant mortality rates than the U.S. in 2004. The U.S. rate was 6.8 deaths for every 1,000 live births. It was 13.7 for Black Americans, the same as Saudi Arabia.

Source: Stephen Ohlemacher, Washingtonpost.com (The Associated Press), August 12, 2007.

What do you think are some of the reasons for the relatively poor performance of the United States on this indicator? Where might you go to learn more?

(for example, the percent of the population without access to safe water); and statistics on crime and environmental degradation. All of these are important to getting a full picture of human development. They also gather data on topics such as military expenditures, amounts of external debt, and public expenditures on health and education that can help to explain differences in economic and social outcomes.

4.4 THE FUTURE OF MACROECONOMIC INDICATORS

Due to funding cutbacks, progress on improving macroeconomic measurement within the official accounts is currently largely at a standstill within the United States. Many private groups within the United States, however, as well as official statistical agencies in a number of other countries, are making progress in developing better measures to deal with the social and environmental issues of the twenty-first century.

No one—and especially not their creators—would argue that alternative macroeconomic indicators have been perfected. It is quite possible to argue about whether damage cost or replacement cost should be used in evaluating environmental services, for example, or whether more direct measures of poverty should be included in the HDI. Much is still open for discussion. Many of the new measures being developed allow users to see how the results change under different assumptions. Some express their results in terms of well-justified ranges of values, rather than in terms of seemingly precise, but possibly misleading, specific values.

But all indicators have their flaws, whether due to their definitions and classifications, the data they rely on, or the statistical techniques applied. No one intimately involved in the creation of the official NIPA would argue that they are perfect, either! The creation of official statistics has often been compared to sausage making: The closer you are to observing the process, the less attractive the final product appears. Only from a distance—when you can remain naively unaware of all the conventions that their creators have had to impose on messy real-world data and all the imputations they have had to make—do "official" statistics look clean and elegant, just as only from a distance from its processing does sausage look appetizing.

The important contribution of alternative indicators is the way they bring to our attention significant aspects of the economy, such as environmental and social sustainability, that were not taken into account in the design of traditional twentieth-century macroeconomic indicators.

Discussion Questions

1. Does the Genuine Progress Indicator include anything you think should be left out, or fail to account for something that you think should be included? Think hard about what you really think human well-being is about.
2. Which do you think is more useful for judging the progress of an economy—GDP, expanded measures of production, measures of production adjusted for well-being effects, or measures of well-being itself?

REVIEW QUESTIONS

1. What are the three functions through which the natural environment interacts with the human economy?
2. Ideally, how would consideration of the stock of natural assets be included in the national accounts?
3. Ideally, how would consideration of flows of goods and services from the environment be included in the national accounts?
4. List four reasons why it is difficult to put dollar values on environmental assets and the environment's production of goods and services.
5. What is the function of environmental satellite accounts?
6. What reasons have been given for excluding household production from measures of GDP?
7. What difference does it make, to the study of macroeconomic trends and design of policy, that household production has been excluded from the national accounts?
8. What information is gathered in a time-use survey?
9. Describe the two major methods of estimating the value of labor inputs into household production.
10. Is inclusion of household production in the national accounts a new idea?
11. What are some reasons why measuring *output* may be misleading as a guide to *well-being*?
12. What is the Genuine Progress Indicator? What are some of the adjustments it makes relative to GDP?
13. What is the Human Development Indicator? Why do some countries appear to perform more poorly when ranked by HDI than when ranked by GDP per capita?

EXERCISES

1. Which of the following describe a resource function of the natural environment? An environmental service function? A sink function?
   a. A landfill
   b. A copper mine
   c. Carbon dioxide (a byproduct of combustion) entering the atmosphere
   d. Wild blueberries growing in a meadow
   e. A suitable temperature for growing corn
   f. A view of the Grand Canyon

2. In 2003, a massive oil spill caused heavy damage to the fishing and tourist industries on the north coast of Spain. In addition, there were long-term ecological impacts on fish and wildlife. Describe how this might be accounted for in Spain's 2003 national income accounts, if they were environmentally adjusted:
   a. In terms of depreciation of assets
   b. In terms of flows of produced goods and services. (Describe in detail how two approaches to assigning dollar values might be applied.)

3. Consumption of oil, gas, and coal currently fuels the United States economy, but also has other effects. How might the following be accounted for in the United States national accounts, if they were environmentally adjusted?
   a. Depletion of domestic oil, natural gas, and coal reserves
   b. Release of greenhouse gases into the atmosphere
   c. Smoggy air that hides scenery and makes outdoor activity unpleasant

4. How would each of the following activities be classified in the American Time Use Survey? Which ones are productive activities, judged by the third person criterion?
   a. Having lunch
   b. Working as a hospital nurse
   c. Watching TV
   d. Volunteering for a political campaign
   e. Cooking dinner
   f. Grocery shopping with your young child

5. Suppose you buy a bread-making machine, some flour, and other foodstuffs, take them home, and bake bread with a group of young children who are in your care (unpaid). How would these activities be accounted for in current GDP accounting? How might they be accounted for in an expanded account that includes household production?

6. Describe in a short paragraph why measures of *output* do not always measure *well-being*. Include some specific examples beyond those given in the text.

7. In calculating the Genuine Progress Indicator,
   a. Which factors are subtracted off, compared to personal consumption expenditures, because they represent *bad* things?
   b. Which factors are *not* included in GPI, even though they are included in GDP, because they are defensive expenditures or because of differences in accounting methods?

8. Describe the following:
    a. Two ways in which measures of *national assets and output* could be improved
    b. Two attempts to measure *social and economic well-being*

9. Match each concept in Column A with a definition or example in Column B.

Column A	Column B
2 a. Depreciation of natural capital	1. Valuing time at the wage someone gives up
10 b. Satellite accounts	2. Saving less both manufactured and natural depreciation
7 c. An indicator of well-being including health and educational status	3. Costs of cleaning up a toxic waste site
4 (d.) An example of non-marketed production	4. The value of fish killed by toxic waste
1 e. Opportunity cost method	5. Government production
3 f. Genuine saving	6. The effect on copper reserves of copper mining
4 g. Maintenance costs	7. Human Development Index
9 h. Well-being-decreasing production	8. The service performed by a garbage dump
11 i. A way of measuring well-being (not production) using dollar amounts	9. The production of health-damaging foods
3 j. Damage costs	10. Physical measures that can be related to GDP
8 k. Sink function	11. Genuine Progress Indicator

10. The UNDP's Human Development Index, as well as a variety of other indictors of well-being, is published in its *Human Development Report,* which is available through its Web site (www.undp.org). Consult this report, and choose a country that is not included in Table 6.3. Write a paragraph describing this country's performance on the HDI, as well as on four or five other indicators reported in the tables (such as inequality, HIV rates, or undernourishment).

NOTES

1. William D. Nordhaus, "The Future of Environmental and Augmented National Accounts," *Survey of Current Business,* November 1999, p. 45.

2. National Research Council, *Nature's Numbers: Expanding the National Income Accounts to Include the Environment,* 1999, pp. 19–20.

3. Marilyn Waring, *If Women Counted* (Harper & Row, 1988).

4. United Nations, *System of National Accounts 1993,* paragraph I.E.1.21.

5. Nancy Folbre and Julie Nelson. "For Love or Money—Or Both?" *Journal of Economic Perspectives* 14(4), 2000, p. 126.

6. Robert Eisner, "Extended Accounts for National Income and Product," *Journal of Economic Literature* 26(4), December 1988, 1611–1684.

7 Employment and Unemployment

Along with the growth rate of GDP, the rate of unemployment is one of the official measures of macroeconomic performance most discussed in the media, by policymakers, by business leaders, and by economists. Like the other indicators discussed in Chapters 5 and 6, the official unemployment rate is interesting because, in a crude way, it measures something about human well-being—or, in this case, ill-being.

Although some level of unemployment is unavoidable in a changing economy, a high rate of unemployment is a bad thing. Partly this is because high unemployment represents an inefficient utilization of national resources. The economy could be more productive if idle labor resources were put to work.

More dramatically, however, the experience of wanting and needing a job, but not being able to find one, can have a devastating effect on the job seekers themselves and on their families and communities. Besides the obvious strains and difficulties that accompany the loss of income, being unwanted by employers can be a profoundly unsettling experience in a society in which your identity is often tied up with "what you do." Higher rates of suicide, domestic violence, and depression often occur during periods of high and sustained unemployment. Social cohesion can also deteriorate when people feel marginalized from the mainstream of economic life.

How well is this social distress captured in official measures of employment and unemployment? What are some of the causes of unemployment? How has unemployment varied over time? How has the nature of work changed in recent decades, and what will the future hold? These are the questions we will discuss in this chapter.

1. MEASURING EMPLOYMENT AND UNEMPLOYMENT

The U.S. **Bureau of Labor Statistics (BLS),** collects and publishes information on employment and unemployment. Every month, they interview 60,000 households, asking whether individual household members have jobs or are looking for work.*

> **Bureau of Labor Statistics (BLS):** In the United States, the government agency that compiles and publishes employment and unemployment statistics

---

* Actually, the BLS publishes information from *two* surveys. In addition to the household survey, it collects data every month from nearly 400,000 employers. The information from the two surveys can sometimes point in different directions—for example, one survey may suggest a month-to-month gain in employment, while the other indicates a loss. Since employment growth is a politically sensitive topic, there is often debate about which set of numbers should be believed.

1.1 WHO IS "EMPLOYED"?

If you live in a U.S. household, you may someday get a telephone call from a BLS interviewer. After a few preliminaries he or she will ask you the questions shown in Box A of Figure 7.1. If you can answer "no" to *all* of these questions, you are part of the *civilian, noninstitutionalized, age sixteen and over population* about which this survey gathers data, and the interviewer will ask you questions about employment. If you answer any question in Box A "yes," the interviewer will not ask you about employment. Official employment and unemployment statistics do not include you. Trends in employment statistics over time, then, need to be analyzed in the light of considerations such as changes in age demographics, military policy, and rates of disability and incarceration.

If you are part of the surveyed population, you will then be asked the questions in Box B of Figure 7.1, starting with "Last week, did you do any work for pay or profit?"

Anyone who answers "yes" will be classified as **employed**. If you did *any* paid work last week—even if you worked for only an hour or two at a casual job—the interviewer will code you as "employed." If you answer "no," you will then be asked more questions. For example, if you have a paid job but just did not happen to put in any hours last week because you were sick, on vacation, or on certain kinds of leave, you will be coded as working and "employed." Also, if you did *un*paid work in a family-run business, such as a retail store or farm, you will be classified as "employed" as long as you worked in it more than fifteen hours a week.

> **employed person (BLS household survey definition):** a person who did any work for pay or profit during the week before they are surveyed by the BLS or who worked fifteen hours or more in a family business

Note that the "family business" situation is the only case where unpaid work currently counts in the official statistics. If you work fewer hours in your family business, or are, for example, occupied with caring for your children or other family members or doing community volunteer work, you will *not* be considered to be "employed." The BLS is currently seeking to improve its measures of people's productive activities, both paid and unpaid, by instituting a new "time use" survey. This survey gathers data on how much time people spend in activities including paid work, unpaid work taking care of home and family, unpaid volunteer work, and leisure. In the meantime, however, it is important to note that—based on a convention that originated with the first employment statistics collected in the 1940s—terms such as "labor," "work," and "employment" in official statistics generally refer to *paid* work only.

1.2 MEASURING UNEMPLOYMENT

If your answers to the household survey do *not* result in you being classified as "employed," you will be asked the questions about job search and availability shown in Box C of Figure 7.1. Activities such as contacting employers and sending out résumés count as "active" job search. Merely participating in a job training program or reading the want ads do not. The question about whether you could start a job probes to find out if, in fact, you are *available* for work. If, for example, you are a college student searching during April break for a summer job, but you aren't available to start the job until June, you would answer "no" to the availability question. If you can answer "yes" to *both* these questions are you classified as **unemployed**.

> **unemployed person (BLS definition):** a person who is not employed, but who is actively seeking a job and who is immediately available for work

Figure 7.1   **Classifications in the Household Survey**

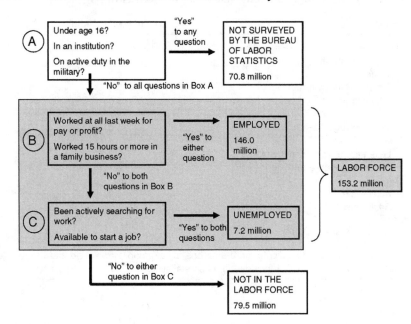

The household survey asks people a series of questions to determine if they are employed, unemployed, or not in the labor force. (Source: BLS *News: The Employment Situation: October 2007;* U.S. Census Bureau Population Clock, November 2007; and authors' calculations)

If you are either employed or unemployed, the BLS classifies you as part of the **labor force.** But what if you are neither "employed" nor "unemployed"? Then you are classified as "**not in the labor force.**" Often people in this category are taking care of a home and family, in school, disabled, or retired.

> **labor force (BLS definition):** made up of people who are employed or unemployed

> **"not in the labor force" (BLS definition):** the classification given to people who are neither "employed" nor "unemployed"

Notice, in Figure 7.1, that the vast majority of U.S. residents who are not "employed" are either "not in the labor force" (about 79.5 million) or are not part of the surveyed population (about 70.8 million). In comparison, about 7.2 million people in this month, October 2007, were formally counted as "unemployed." (Figures are updated monthly at www.bls.gov.)

Every month, having made estimates of the number of employed and unemployed people in the country, the BLS calculates the official **unemployment rate**. This follows the formula:

$$unemployment\ rate = \frac{number\ of\ people\ unemployed}{number\ of\ people\ in\ the\ labor\ force} \times 100$$

For example, in October 2007, looking at Figure 7.1 you can see that the BLS estimated that 146.0 million people were employed and 7.2 million people were unemployed. The unemployment rate was thus calculated as 4.7 percent:

Table 7.1   **Unemployment Rates for Different Groups**

Group	Unemployment rate
All Workers	4.7
Race and ethnicity[a]	
White	4.2
Black or African American	8.5
Hispanic or Latino Ethnicity	5.6
Age	
Teenage (age 16–19)	15.6
Education	
Less than a high school diploma	7.3
Bachelor's degree and higher	2.1
Gender	
Adult Male	4.9
Adult Female	4.5

Source: BLS News: October 2007.

[a] People are allowed to indicate more than one racial group. However, data from people who indicated more than one race are not included in these statistics.

$$unemployment\ rate = \frac{7.2\ million}{146.0\ million + 7.2\ million} \times 100 = 4.7\%$$

The unemployment rate represents the fraction of the officially defined labor force which is made up of people not currently working at paid jobs, but who are currently looking for and available for paid work.

> **unemployment rate:** the percentage of the labor force made up of people who do not have paid jobs, but who are immediately available and actively looking for paid jobs

The unemployment rate reported in the media is often "seasonally adjusted." Over the course of a year, some swings in unemployment are pretty predictable. For example, agriculture and construction tend to employ fewer people in the cold winter months, and each year many students enter the labor force in June. The BLS releases "seasonally adjusted" figures that attempt to reflect only shifts in unemployment that are due to factors *other than* such seasonal patterns.

1.3 HOW PEOPLE ENTER AND EXIT UNEMPLOYMENT

Often, when we think of unemployed people, we think of someone who has lost their job—perhaps a friend or a relative who has been "downsized" from a position. Losing one's job, however, is not the only way of becoming unemployed.

The BLS classifies unemployed people according to four main reasons for unemployment:

- *Job losers* left their last job involuntarily;
- *Job leavers* have voluntarily quit their jobs;
- *Reentrants* are people who were in the labor force at some previous time, and have now joined it again after some period away;
- *Entrants* are people who have just joined the labor force for the first time.

On average, about half of the unemployed are job losers, although the proportions of the unemployed in each group varies over time. During recessions, people are more likely to have

NEWS IN CONTEXT:
New High In U.S. Prison Numbers

More than one in 100 adults in the United States is in jail or prison, an all-time high that is costing state governments nearly $50 billion a year and the federal government $5 billion more, according to a report released yesterday.

With more than 2.3 million people behind bars, the United States leads the world in both the number and percentage of residents it incarcerates, leaving far-more-populous China a distant second, according to a study by the nonpartisan Pew Center on the States.

The growth in prison population is largely because of tougher state and federal sentencing imposed since the mid-1980s. Minorities have been particularly affected...

Five states—Vermont, Michigan, Oregon, Connecticut and Delaware—now spend as much as or more on corrections as on higher education.

Source: N.C. Aizenman, *Washington Post*, February 29, 2008

Do you think, in light of the very high incarceration rate in the United States, that official unemployment statistics are understated, overstated, or about right?

been laid off and less likely to want to voluntarily leave a job (since they are not sure they will find another) than in times of greater prosperity. Sometimes when one family member loses a job, other family members will enter (or reenter) the labor force in order to try to make up for the lost wages.

How do people *get out of* being unemployed? Obviously, one way is by getting a job. However, people can also leave unemployment by leaving the labor force. They may stop actively looking for work because they have decided to go to school or take care of children. Other people leave unemployment when they enlist in the military, go to jail (see News in Context), or die—thus moving out of the surveyed population. Some of these life changes may reflect deliberate, positive decisions. But some unemployed people may simply give up actively searching for work because they have had no success after months of looking.

1.4 DISCOURAGED WORKERS AND UNDEREMPLOYMENT

The fact that some "not in the labor force" people might want jobs but have given up looking for them has troubled employment analysts for some time. To the extent people give up on looking, the official unemployment rate *underestimates* people's need and desire for paid jobs.

In recent years, the BLS has added questions to the survey to try to determine how many people in the "not in the labor force" population may want employment, even if they are not currently searching for work. If someone says that they are available for work, want to work, and have looked for work recently even though they are not looking now, the BLS calls them "marginally attached workers." If they also say that the reason they are no longer looking is that they believe there are no jobs out there for them, they are called **discouraged workers**. They may have become discouraged because they believe their skills don't match available openings, because they have experienced discrimination, or because they have been turned away time after time.

> **discouraged workers:** people who desire and are available for a job, but give discouragement as the reason for no longer looking for a job

But let's take a closer look at the people classified as "employed," too. In the BLS statistics a person is counted as "employed" if they do any paid work *at all* during the reference week, even if only for an hour or two. Some people prefer part-time work, of course, because of the time it leaves them for other activities such as schooling or family care. Some are limited to part-time work for health reasons. But others want and need full-time work, and are only settling for part-time work until they can find something better. The household survey asks people who work part-time about their reasons for doing so. In October 2007, 19.3 million people reported working fewer than thirty-five hours per week for reasons such as health or family responsibilities. In the same month, 4.3 million people reported working part-time for what the BLS calls "economic reasons"—that is, slack business conditions or because part-time work was all they could find.

What indicator, then, should we look at to see if the national employment situation is "bad" or "good"? The BLS now actually publishes various measures of labor underutilization that allow you to see the situation from a variety of different perspectives. For example, adding "marginally attached" workers and people who involuntarily work part-time to the number of unemployed, the rate of labor underutilization in October 2007 was 8.4 percent, as compared to the official unemployment rate of 4.7 percent.

The BLS also counts people as employed even if the kind of work they did does not begin to tap into their skills. Suppose you paint your aunt's living room for cash while you are waiting to hear back on job applications for management or computer positions. The BLS counts you as already employed. People who are working at jobs that underutilize their abilities, as well as those who work fewer hours than they like, can be said to be **underemployed**.

> **underemployment:** working fewer hours than desired, and/or at a job that does not utilize one's skills

If we are concerned about human well-being, underemployment as well as unemployment should be of concern. While underemployment due to an underutilization of skills is certainly of considerable concern for both efficiency and quality-of-life reasons, official surveys do not currently attempt to measure this sort of underemployment.

Discussion Questions

1. How would the BLS classify you, personally, on the basis of your activities last week? Can you think of an example where someone you would think of as *working* would not be considered by the BLS to be officially "employed"? Is it true that people who are *not working* are generally counted as "unemployed"?
2. Do you know anyone who is a "discouraged worker"? How about someone working part time "for economic reasons"?

2. Types of Unemployment

While the BLS statisticians are mainly concerned with calculating the numbers of the unemployed, economists are more concerned with the causes of unemployment. Economists often apply a three-way categorization of types of unemployment, which—while abstract and not tightly related to BLS categories—can be helpful in thinking about some of the major causes of unemployment.

2.1 FRICTIONAL UNEMPLOYMENT

Frictional (or search) **unemployment** merely reflects people's transitions between jobs. The fact that some people are unemployed does not necessarily mean that there are no jobs available. In the fall of 2007, for example, while 7.2 million people were looking for jobs, there were also about 4.1 million job vacancies—that is, jobs looking for people! Even in a well-functioning economy, it may take many weeks for people and suitable jobs to find each other. An unemployment rate of zero percent could only happen if everyone who wants a job always takes one immediately—within a week. Not only is this unlikely, this is also in some ways undesirable. Taking the first job offered is often not the best thing for the person looking for the job, nor for the economy as a whole. Everybody benefits if people take the time to find good job matches—places where their skills and talents can be put to valuable use. Because information about job openings takes time to find, and employers may want to spend time interviewing and testing applicants, making a good job match is not an instantaneous process.

> **frictional unemployment:** unemployment that arises as people are in transition between jobs

For the most part, economists don't worry too much about frictional unemployment, because some amount of frictional unemployment—say, 2 to 3 percent—is inevitable and much of it tends to be short-term. Things such as innovative Web technologies for matching job offers to job seekers may reduce frictional unemployment by reducing search time.

Many job seekers rely on state unemployment insurance programs to ease their income needs while they spend time searching for work. Unemployment compensation benefits are, in many states, set equal to half a worker's earnings or a state-set maximum (whichever is less). Workers who qualify can usually receive benefits for up to twenty-six weeks. Part of the justification for these programs is to allow people the time to make good matches.

2.2 STRUCTURAL UNEMPLOYMENT

Structural unemployment arises in an economy when a mismatch occurs between the kinds of jobs being offered by employers and the skills, experience, education, and/or geographical location of potential employees. One important cause of structural unemployment is sectoral shifts, such as will be described in Chapter 8, where employment in some sectors falls while employment in other sectors rises. The U.S. economy may have a lot of new jobs for financial analysts and nurses' aides in the Southwest, for example. But these won't do you much good if you live in the Northeast and have skills in engine assembly or Web design.

> **structural unemployment:** unemployment that arises because people's skills, experience, education, and/or location do not match what employers need

On the positive side, structural unemployment arises from what economist Joseph Schumpeter (1883–1950) called "creative destruction." Schumpeter thought this was a good and necessary thing for capitalist economies. Technological and entrepreneurial innovations have often contributed to improved living standards, even though they cause some job opportunities to dry up. People skilled in outdated technologies—buggy-whip manufacturing is a classic example—necessarily become unemployed. Society could have tried to prevent unemployment in buggy-whip manufacturing by banning the introduction of the automobile, but the cost in economic growth would have been immense. If we, today, begin to move away from internal combustion engines due to their negative environmental impacts, the conventional auto industry will decline just as the buggy-whip industry declined at the end of the horse-and-buggy era. New technologies, new markets, and new concerns create new opportunities.

On the negative side, shifts in employment patterns by sector and industry are very disruptive, and often very painful, to the people who work in the declining sectors and to their families and communities. People in the declining sectors see the value of their specialized human capital depreciating rapidly. Whole towns and cities may become economically depressed when a major industry closes down, because the unemployed workers spend less at local businesses and property values plummet. Displaced workers *may* be able to train for a new career—especially if they are young and able to move to wherever the new jobs may be. But many displaced workers, particularly older ones, may never find the kind of pay and satisfaction that they had at their earlier occupations. Older displaced workers are more likely than younger ones to stay unemployed for long periods, or exit the labor force.

Governments at all levels have tried various policies to prevent or alleviate structural unemployment. The governments of some countries, notably Germany and Japan in the 1980s and 1990s, have followed industrial policies through which they directly encourage the development and retention of certain key industries through loans, subsidies, and tax credits. During negotiations on international trade (see Chapter 13), one sensitive issue is always the impact that increased trade might have on the employment levels in various industries in each country.

Government policies in the United States that target structural unemployment often focus on attempting to help displaced workers find new employment. For example, the Trade Adjustment Assistance Reform Act of 2002 provides benefits for certain workers displaced as a result of increased imports or the shifting of production to other countries. Workers who qualify for the program can receive retraining along with temporary income support payments and assistance with health insurance. The key feature of these programs is that they are targeted to particular workers, in particular sectors of the economy. There has been some question, however, as to whether they have actually been successful in getting displaced workers into new, good jobs. Business policies at the firm level are also relevant: Firms can help prevent structural unemployment if they make retaining and/or retraining their loyal employees a priority, even while responding to changes in technology and trade.

2.3 CYCLICAL UNEMPLOYMENT

Cyclical unemployment is unemployment due to macroeconomic fluctuations—specifically, unemployment that occurs due to a drop-off in aggregate demand. (As noted in Chapter 1, "aggregate demand" means the total demand for all goods and services in a national economy.) During recessions, unemployment rises as demand for the products of business falls off. During recoveries, this kind of unemployment should decrease.

> **cyclical unemployment:** unemployment caused by a drop in aggregate demand

Traditionally, a **recession** has been defined as a case where GDP falls for two consecutive calendar quarters. Most economists look to the National Bureau of Economic Research (NBER), a nonprofit and nongovernmental economic research organization, to "officially" mark the beginning and end of recessions. The NBER determinations are strongly based on GDP data, though they also look at other indicators such as the levels of industrial production and wholesale-retail sales.

Figure 7.2　**Unemployment Over the Business Cycle, U.S. 1969–2007**

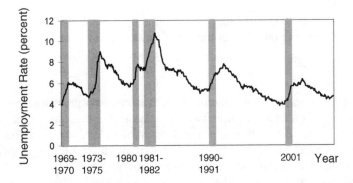

Unemployment rates rise during recessions (shown in grey). During the start of recent "recoveries," they have also continued to climb. (Source: U.S. BLS, Current Population Survey, and NBER)

> **recession:** traditionally defined as occurring when GDP falls for two consecutive calendar quarters, now "officially" marked by the National Bureau of Economic Research

Figure 7.2 shows the monthly unemployment rate in the United States from January 1969 to October 2007. Unemployment was at a low of 3.4 percent in 1969, and at a high of 10.8 percent in 1982. Notice in the figure that since 1982 the U.S. economy has apparently been characterized by less frequent and shorter recessions. However, while earlier recovery periods were characterized by immediate upswings in employment, the recessions that NBER says ended in 1991 and 2001 were followed by continuing job slumps. The continued loss of jobs well into 2003, after the last recession, caused many commentators to call it the "jobless recovery." Apparently, while GDP grew, it grew too slowly to provide jobs for new entrants and keep up with increasing labor productivity. Is an economy really "recovering" if employment is still dropping or stagnating?

Not surprisingly, given that the field of macroeconomics was born out of the problems of the Great Depression, cyclical unemployment is of major concern to macroeconomists. While *structural* unemployment affects only some sectors of the economy and some amount of *frictional* unemployment seems inevitable, cyclical unemployment is spread broadly through the economy and can cause considerable economic hardship. For this reason, it seems that avoiding or minimizing cyclical unemployment should be an important goal of economic policy. Explanations of why macroeconomic fluctuations occur, and what kind of policies might be used to dampen them (and thus reduce cyclical unemployment) are discussed in Part Three of this book.

Discussion Questions

1. Reflecting on the experience of you or someone you know, how long would you say it might normally take for someone to find a job in your area? Comparing your answers in a group, do you find different opinions? What might be some of the factors that make frictional unemployment last a longer or shorter period of time?
2. Do you know of places in your city or region (or nation) that have been particularly hard-hit by unemployment and underemployment, recently or in past decades? Do you know why this hardship occurred? Would you characterize this unemployment as frictional, structural, or cyclical?

3. THEORIES OF UNEMPLOYMENT

Why does unemployment arise, and what can be done about it? Economists favor different theories, depending on whether they take a more classical or a more Keynesian view.

3.1 THE CLASSICAL THEORY OF UNEMPLOYMENT

In classical economic theory, unemployment is seen as a sign that smooth labor market functioning is being obstructed in some way. The classical approach assumes that markets behave as described by the idealized supply-and-demand model presented in Chapter 4: The labor market is seen as though it were a single, static market, characterized by perfect competition, spot transactions, and institutions for double-auction bidding.

Such an abstract labor market is depicted in Figure 7.3. In Chapter 4 we examined markets for assets and produced goods, but in this case "quantity" is not measured as a number of *things* (such as apartments or swimsuits) but rather a quantity of labor *services*. We can think of this quantity as being measured, for example, by the number of workers working full days over a given time period. The "price" of labor is the (real) wage (in this case, per day). Workers supply labor, while employers demand it. We assume that every unit of labor services is the same, and every worker in this market will get exactly the same wage. The equilibrium wage in this example is W_E and the equilibrium quantity of labor supplied is at L_E.

Because the market pictured in Figure 7.3 is free to adjust, there is no involuntary unemployment. Everyone who wants a job at the going wage gets one. There may be many people who would offer their services on this market *if* the wage were higher—as the portion of the supply curve to the right of L_E demonstrates. But, given the currently offered wage rate, these people have made a rational choice not to participate in this labor market.

Within the classical model, the only way true, involuntary unemployment can exist is if something gets in the way of market forces. The presence of a legal minimum wage is commonly pointed to as one such factor. As illustrated in Figure 7.4, if employers are required to pay a minimum wage of W^* ("W-star") that is above the equilibrium wage, this model predicts that they will hire fewer workers. At an artificially high wage W^*, employers want to hire only L_D workers. But at that wage, L_S people want jobs. There is a situation of surplus, as we discussed in Chapter 4. The market is, in this case, prevented from adjusting to equilibrium by legal restrictions on employers. Now there are people who want a job at the going wage, but can't find one. That is, they are unemployed.

The minimum wage only affects a portion of the workforce, however—people who are relatively unskilled, including many teenagers. But unemployment tends to affect people at all wage levels. Classical economists suggest other "market interference" reasons for unemployment, as well. The economy might provide less than the optimal number of jobs, they believe, because:

- Regulations on businesses reduce their growth, restricting growth in the demand for labor
- Labor-related regulations (such as safety regulations, mandated benefits, or restrictions on layoffs and firings) and labor union activities increase the cost of labor to businesses, causing them to turn toward labor-saving technologies and thus reducing job growth
- Public "safety net" policies such as disability insurance and unemployment insurance reduce employment by causing people to become less willing to seek work

Labor-market recommendations derived from a classical point of view tend to focus on getting rid of regulations and social programs that are seen as obstructing proper market behavior.

Figure 7.3 **A Supply and Demand Model for Labor**

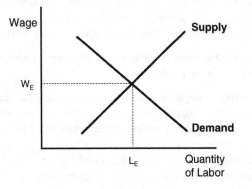

In a smoothly functioning market, the equilibrium wage and quantity of labor would be set by market forces.

Figure 7.4 **Classical Unemployment**

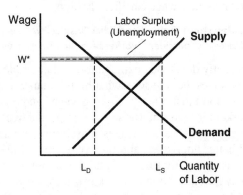

In a classical (idealized) market for labor, the only thing that can cause true unemployment is something that interferes with the adjustments of free markets, such as a legal minimum wage.

Like other classical proposals, such labor market proposals assume that the economy works best under the principle of laissez-faire—"leave it alone."

3.2 IMPERFECT LABOR MARKETS

The classical theory of labor markets depends on rapid market adjustment—in particular, the elimination of any labor surplus through falling wages and a resulting full-employment equilibrium at a lower wage rate. But is this realistic? John Maynard Keynes, reflecting on the experiences of the Great Depression, pointed out that certain aspects of real-world human psychology and institutions make it unlikely that wages will fall quickly in response to a labor surplus. No one likes to feel that they are losing something. (How would you feel if your boss told you she was *cutting* your wage?) Employers may be slow to reduce wages because they fear that workers will strongly resist such a move—perhaps with strikes, mass demonstrations, or even violence.

As the classical-Keynesian synthesis (introduced in Chapter 1) took form, many economists came to favor a more Keynesian explanation for cyclical unemployment. Given enough time, they argued, markets might be able to adjust as described in the classical model. But Keynesian-oriented economists also developed **"sticky wage" theories**, which hypothesize that wages may stay at a level above equilibrium for some time. Wages may eventually adjust in the way shown in the classical model, but too slowly to keep the labor market always in equilibrium.

> **"sticky wage" theories:** theories about why wages may stay at above-equilibrium levels, despite the existence of a labor surplus

In addition to psychological resistance to wage cuts, as mentioned above, a minimum wage might also make wages "sticky." Wages may also become set at particular levels by long-term contracts, such as many large employers negotiate with labor unions.

More recently, economists have also come up with other theories. One is that the efforts of "insiders" may contribute to keeping wages high. "Insiders" are people who already have jobs within an organization. Insiders may be able to keep their wages high by setting up various barriers that prevent their employer from dismissing them and hiring lower-priced "outsiders." Insiders may have contracts that specify a high wage and that make them difficult to fire. Or they may refuse to cooperate with new workers or harass them, reducing new workers' productivity. In the **insider-outsider theory**, employed workers use the power they derive from such labor turnover costs to keep their wages artificially high.

> **insider-outsider theory:** the theory that "insider" workers who are already employed may have the power to prevent "outsider" workers from competing with them and lowering their wages

Yet another recently developed explanation is that employers may find it to their advantage to pay employees wages that are somewhat higher than would be strictly necessary to get them to work. Managers don't just offer "the going wage" and then sit back. They must attract, train, and motivate workers if their enterprise is to be productive. **Efficiency wage theory** suggests that paying higher-than-necessary wages may improve employee productivity. Workers may be healthier and better nourished, and therefore more able to do quality work, when they are better paid. (This is especially true when talking about wage rates at the low end of the scale.) Also, workers may quit less often if they know they are getting "a really good deal" from their employer than if they are getting barely enough to motivate them to take the job, or just the same as they could get anywhere else. A lower likelihood of quitting makes employees more valuable to an employer because the employer saves on the costs of training new workers. Workers may also work more efficiently if being caught shirking means potentially losing their "really good deal." If the higher-than-necessary efficiency wages creates a pool of unemployed people, this only further reinforces employees' incentives to work hard because then they will be even more afraid of losing their good jobs.

> **efficiency wage theory:** the theory that an employer can motivate workers to put forth more effort by paying them somewhat more than what they could get elsewhere

In sum, in the classical-Keynesian synthesis, legally or contractually set wages, fear of worker unrest, the power of insiders, and efficiency wages are thought sometimes to cause wages to be "sticky." By making real-world labor markets work differently from the market pictured in the classical model, these phenomena mean that it is unrealistic to expect that labor markets can adjust rapidly to maintain full employment.

What sort of policies do "sticky wage" theories lead to? To the extent that unemployment is seen as a real problem in these theories, more government activity to relieve unemployment-related hardship may be proposed, such as the aggregate demand policies we will discuss in Part Three of this book, or programs of unemployment benefits or job creation. Some economists also argue that a moderate level of economy-wide price inflation tends to relieve some "sticky wage" unemployment. How could this be so? Suppose you are working for $12 per hour now, and your employer says he wants to cut your wage to $10 per hour. You would probably resist—especially if you see that other people are *not* suffering such wage cuts. But suppose, instead, that your wage stays at $12 per hour, and, over time, inflation reduces the purchasing power of your wage to $10 per hour (in terms of prices of the base year). Your *nominal* wage has stayed the same, but your *real* wage (and thus your real cost to your employer) has fallen. Since this has happened more subtlety—and is felt more economy-wide—than a cut in your personal nominal wage, you may not feel as compelled to resist. According to some theories, such a drop in the wage (in real terms) should cause employment to increase.

3.3 UNEMPLOYMENT AND AGGREGATE DEMAND

While Keynesian economics is often closely associated with "sticky wage" theories, Keynes' own critique of classical views (as explained in Chapter 19 of his 1936 book, *The General Theory*) actually went much farther. He questioned whether the theory of a smoothly functioning labor market, as portrayed in Figure 7.3, is really a good starting place for thinking about macroeconomics and unemployment. This view is carried forward today by a number of economists (who sometimes call themselves Keynesian, or also post-Keynesian or institutionalist).

Recall that the supply-and-demand diagram, as we introduced it in Chapter 4, was meant to be a way of thinking about a single spot market in which a single, completely standardized good is being traded. But "the economy" as a whole is not just one smoothly functioning market in which prices move to equate quantity supplied and quantity demanded. It is made up of markets for potatoes and markets for health care, markets for steelworkers and markets for schoolteachers, markets for real estate and markets for credit, markets for goods and services to be delivered now and for goods and services to be delivered months (or longer) in the future—as well as nonmarket institutions and transfers of all sorts. All these arenas of economic action have their own institutional peculiarities, and all are interwoven by a network of flows of incomes and payments. Hence, economists who are critical of classical theory see diagrams such as Figure 7.3 and 7.4, which portray only an idealized, abstract, detached, and institutionless labor market, as fundamentally misleading and beside the point.

In the real world, where issues of motivation, labor relations, and power are important, even the classical idea that minimum wages cause substantial unemployment may be called into question. In a well-known study, economists David Card and Alan Krueger found that a moderate increase in the minimum wage in New Jersey did not cause low-wage employment to decline, and may even have increased it. The study came under fire from economists who believed (given graphs such as Figure 7.4) that such a result simply could not be true. But the classical world assumes perfect competition, whereas real-world employers may have enough power in the labor market to be able to pay workers less than what they are worth. Labor markets seem to be more complicated than a simple supply-and-demand model suggests.

Keynes' own focus was on the level of aggregate demand in the economy, and on businesses expectations about future profitability (to be discussed more in Chapter 9). Keynes believed that even if wages *did* fall quickly in a number of labor markets, this might do more harm than good. To see why, examine Figure 7.5. Workers' incomes give them the ability to spend on goods and services, and this spending stimulates firms to produce. The cycle is completed when this production in turn generates incomes. But what happens when wages fall? Workers who have lower wages will have less to spend, reducing demand for goods being produced by businesses all over the economy. If businesses cannot sell their goods, they will tend to cut back on their

Figure 7.5   The Keynesian Model of Employment Determination

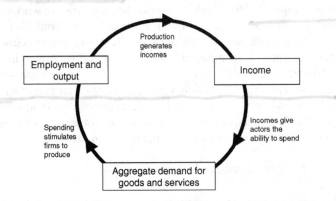

In the Keynesian model, aggregate employment depends on the level of aggregate demand in the economy as a whole. If total spending is low, then employers will not want to produce a great deal because they do not want to end up with unsold goods. If production is low, they will not need many workers. If few workers are hired, then aggregate income will be low—in what can become a vicious cycle.

investments and on their number of workers. Prices as well as wages may fall (as was observed during the Great Depression), keeping real wages constant and thus giving employers no incentive to hire more workers. Low aggregate demand for goods and services could lead to a vicious cycle of unemployment, low incomes, and low spending in the economy as a whole.

Rather than blaming unemployment on "the wage being too high," as illustrated in a graph of a hypothetical unified national labor market, Keynes identified the cause of cyclical unemployment as *insufficient labor demand* in many individual labor markets, economy-wide, leading to a glut of workers overall. Fixing the problem of unemployment in a recession or depression, then, to Keynes and his followers, is not just a matter of making labor markets work more smoothly. Rather, aggregate demand in the economy has to be increased in order to stimulate hiring. Questions of aggregate demand and Keynesian policy will be taken up in Part Three of this book.

3.4 IS THERE A "NATURAL" RATE OF UNEMPLOYMENT?

Because of macroeconomists' special interest in cyclical unemployment, many have adopted a somewhat unfortunate term—the **"natural" rate of unemployment**—to describe the rate of unemployment *that they hypothesize would occur in the absence of cyclical fluctuations.* Figure 7.6 shows what might happen in a highly stylized business cycle in which actual unemployment fluctuates around a "natural rate." Booms are said to reduce unemployment below a stable "natural rate," and recessions to make unemployment rise above it.

> **"natural" rate of unemployment:** the rate of unemployment that would prevail in the absence of business cycles, according to some theories

A related concept is that of the **non-accelerating inflation rate of unemployment (NAIRU)**. This is conceptualized as the lowest rate of unemployment that can be maintained without causing the economy to "overheat." The concept of the NAIRU can best be understood by looking back at the Phillips curve graph we created in Chapter 2, reproduced as Figure 7.7. In this graph, you can see that inflation rises steadily but not dramatically as unemployment is reduced toward 4 percent. But as the unemployment rate passes below about 4 percent, the Phillips curve distinctly

Figure 7.6 **The "Natural" Rate of Unemployment**

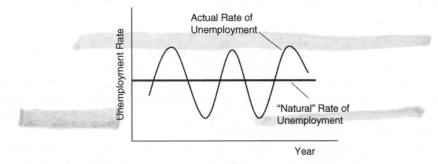

In this highly stylized graph, recessions cause unemployment to rise above its "natural" rate and booms cause unemployment to fall below it.

Figure 7.7 **The Non-Accelerating Inflation Rate of Unemployment (NAIRU)**

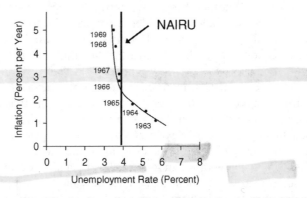

Very low rates of unemployment can be a sign of an "overheated" economy. During the 1963–69 period, it seems that an unemployment rate below about 4 percent was associated with accelerating inflation rates.

bends upward, with inflation rising more sharply from year to year. Since unemployment below about 4 percent seems to be associated with rapidly rising inflation, we could say that the NAIRU during 1963–69 appears to be about 4 percent, as represented in the graph by the vertical line.

> **non-accelerating inflation rate of unemployment (NAIRU):** the lowest rate of unemployment that can be sustained without causing rapidly rising inflation

If the world were as simple these two figures suggest, the "natural" rate and the NAIRU would mean essentially the same thing. Unemployment higher than the NAIRU, like unemployment higher than the "natural" rate, would be associated with low production and a sluggish economy. Unemployment lower than NAIRU or "natural" rate would be associated with higher production and inflation.

But the world is not so simple. If you refer back to Figure 2.4 in Chapter 2, you will see that after 1969 the relation between inflation and unemployment doesn't look a bit like the Phillips curve in Figure 7.7. Over longer periods of time, it is clear that if a NAIRU exists at all, it certainly moves around. Some economists argue that NAIRU is a useful concept, even if it can be difficult to say just what number should be associated with it. Other economists believe the concept is no longer useful.

The concept of a "natural" rate has even more significant problems. First, the word "natural" sometimes leads people to think that there is something *right* or *inevitable* about unemployment at the "natural" rate—no matter how much *non*cyclical unemployment (such as structural unemployment from shifts in international trade) people may be suffering. Second, the concept reflects one particular theory, that of the classical school of macroeconomics. The inventor of the "natural rate of unemployment" concept was economist Milton Friedman, who was a great believer in the efficiency of market forces.

Second, as with the NAIRU, the study of history shows that it is very difficult to match a particular number with the "natural" rate idea. Figure 7.8 reproduces data from the previous section. You can see that the actual pattern is not the flat line suggested in theory in Figure 7.6. If we were to suppose that unemployment was fluctuating around *some* specific rate, it might appear that this rate climbs during the 1970s and then gently falls after the early 1980s, as illustrated in Figure 7.8. (This is one of many possibilities. Others might picture the "natural" rate rising in steps like a staircase, or in other patterns.)

A "natural" rate that changes over time is a slippery concept, however. A current unemployment rate of 5 percent would be considered excessive due to cyclical considerations if you believe that the "natural" rate is 4 percent. But the same rate would be considered to be a sign of a vibrant macroeconomy if you believe that the "natural" rate is 6 percent. Because of this problem, a number of economists do not believe that the "natural" rate concept is very useful.

While economists from the classical school believe that the economy will tend to return to an equilibrium position whenever it is pushed away, and thus favor the concept of a "natural" rate, other economists question whether an economy is really a stable system at all. Some economists, including John Maynard Keynes and Joseph Schumpeter, envisioned economies as more dynamic and evolving. While Keynes is often associated with a rather pro-government political stance, and Schumpeter with the more libertarian, small-government views held by adherents of the Austrian school of economics, both Keynes and Schumpeter stressed the inherent *instability* of economic systems. To them, factors such as uncertainty, innovation, institutions, and technological advance made economies quite unpredictable.

To use a hiking analogy, classically minded economists believe that the path of an economy is like a walking trail already laid out through the woods. While a hiker (economy) sometimes steps off the trail (diverges from the "natural" path), he always returns to it. The path of an economy as envisioned by Keynes and Schumpeter and others, on the other hand, is more akin to the path taken by a hiker who ventures into the unknown wilderness, creating the trail as she goes. As society and institutions evolve, these economists and their followers believe the economy can move in any direction, often quite unpredictably.

Discussion Questions

1. Which arguments seem most convincing to you, those of classical labor market theorists, "sticky wage" theorists, or economists concerned with aggregate demand? What are some strengths and weaknesses of each argument? (Is one argument more elegant—that is, does it seem to explain a great deal with a minimum of fuss? Is one argument more realistic?)
2. Can you, looking at Figure 7.2 or 7.7, predict where the unemployment rate is headed next?

Figure 7.8   **Empirical Data and the "Natural" Rate**

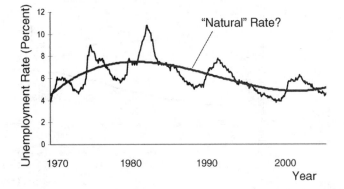

Looking at real-world data, there does not seem to be any one constant rate around which unemployment fluctuates. In recent decades the "natural" rate might be considered to be anywhere from about 4 percent to over 7 percent. (Source: U.S. BLS, Current Population Survey)

4. Employment, Unemployment, and Well-Being

Because the world we live in is constantly changing, macroeconomics also has to adapt to take into account changes in the labor force, the changing the nature of work, and the evolution of people's goals regarding employment. This section looks at some of the current challenges to how we think about employment and unemployment issues on a national scale.

4.1 The Changing Labor Force

The labor laws and labor-related social policies that were enacted during and after the Great Depression made certain assumptions about what a "good job" was. Most workers were men, and the assumption was that men who were employed full time—perhaps with options for overtime hours as well—could provide for their families, and form the base of a solid, reliable workforce and a stable society. These assumptions influenced macroeconomic thinking, as well. Full-time employment of the male "breadwinner" was the explicit or implicit goal of employment policies.

Over the second half of the twentieth century, however, the composition of the labor force changed considerably. Women's labor force participation (LFP) rate rose dramatically, while men's LFP dipped. The labor force participation rate is calculated as

$$labor\ force\ participation\ rate = \frac{number\ of\ people\ in\ the\ labor\ force}{number\ of\ people\ in\ the\ civilian,\ noninstitutionalized\ age\ 16\ and\ over\ population} \times 100$$

The LFP rate indicates the fraction of potential paid workers who are either in paid jobs, or who are seeking and available for paid work. Figure 7.9 shows the labor force participation (LFP) rates of men and women (age sixteen and older). In 1950, many women worked only until they were married, or after their children were grown, so that women's LFP was only 34 percent. During the next four decades, women increasingly entered the labor market, until women's LFP

Figure 7.9   **Labor Force Participation Rates by Sex, 1950–2007**

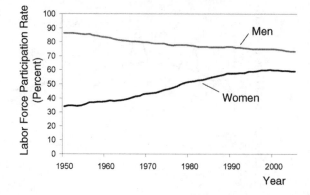

During the latter half of the twentieth century, women's rate of participation in paid labor market activities increased dramatically, while men's tapered off. (Source: U.S. BLS, Labor Force Statistics from the Current Population Survey, Historical Data)

rate flattened out at about 59–60 percent from the mid-1990s onward. The rise of the civil rights and women's movements during the 1960s and 1970s certainly contributed to this expansion in women's labor market activities. Some economists also point to expansion of the service sector (discussed in Chapter 8), reductions in the average number of children per family, and other factors to help explain this increase.

Men's LFP, meanwhile, dropped from 86 percent in 1950 to 73 percent in recent years. Tendencies such as increased time spent in schooling before beginning work, and earlier retirement from work, explain some of this change. In 1950, 70 percent of the people in the labor force were male; now, the figure is only 54 percent.

The labor force has changed in other ways as well. In 1975, Hispanics or Latinos made up only about 4 percent of the U.S. labor force. Currently, this statistic is 13 percent.

4.2 THE CHANGING NATURE OF WORK

For most of the twentieth century, people often thought of "a job" (or at least a *good* job) as something you typically did Monday through Friday, forty hours a week, for a wage or salary and benefits (such as health insurance and pension plans). People often expected to stay in the same job for years, or even decades. In recent years, it has become popular to talk about how employment is becoming more "flexible." The term "flexibility" has two very different meanings in the context of macroeconomics and labor economics, however.

One meaning of "flexible" work is work that is more suited to people's varying needs, especially given family constraints, desires to get an education, and so on. Some workers—especially professional and managerial workers—now enjoy "flextime" or the ability to set their starting and ending times. Job-sharing and part-time work allow employment to be more easily combined with family care, studying, or leisure pursuits. It is still the case, however, that many jobs are inflexible and not "family friendly." The United States is practically alone among industrial nations in not offering paid job-guaranteed leaves for new parents. A lack of flexibility creates problems for people who want "good jobs" with good pay and promotion opportunities, but who want to be able to pursue other life goals and make other important contributions as well. The term "flexibility" can also refer to people's ability to change jobs when they want to, or retrain for new careers.

But the term "flexibility" has also been used to refer to policies that make things easier for employers—and often make life more difficult from a worker's perspective. Many employers would like to be able to have complete discretion over setting their workers' hours and pay, to be able to terminate employees quickly and without fuss, and to offer little in the way of benefits. Increasingly, some firms have hired "independent contractors" or "consultants," or part-time workers, to avoid having to pay the benefits that they pay their regular full-time employees. More people now work non-standard workweeks, whether they want to or not, in an economy that is increasingly "24/7" (twenty-four hours a day, seven days a week). Given short hours and low pay, some workers find themselves working two or more part-time jobs to get by.

Since labor unions often try to block such "flexibilization" of work by bargaining for guaranteed hours, increased benefits, and assurances of job security, the reduction in union power is one component of this phenomenon. Union membership topped out at about one-third of the workforce in the mid-1950s, with significant membership from private industry. Currently, only about 13 percent of workers are union members, and many of these are public sector employees such as teachers, police, and firefighters.

To some extent, "flexibility" from the employee's perspective is also in the interest of employers. Workers who are better rested and less stressed about their families, because of accommodating schedules and expectations, can be more productive. And to some extent, "flexibility" from the employer's perspective is also in the workers' interest. An overly rigid labor market, in which workers are too expensive and difficult to fire, could cause employers to try to minimize the number of workers they must hire, thus reducing the number of jobs. From a well-being perspective, the question is how a good balance can be achieved.

Another aspect of work patterns that has changed substantially in the last few decades is the pattern of *hours* of work. While some observers claim that people in the United States are now working increased hours, and others claim that we are now benefiting from increased leisure, the *average* workweek has, in fact, changed little in the last thirty or so years. What has happened, however, is that some *groups* of people are increasingly working very long hours, and others very short hours, so that there are now more people at both extreme ends of the spectrum.

In 2000, 26.5 percent of employed men and 11.3 percent of employed women worked fifty or more hours per week, up from 21 percent and 5.2 percent, respectively, in 1970. Often people in this group are professionals or managers with heavy job responsibilities.[1] People in such job categories usually receive fringe benefits from their employers—but do not, by law, have to be paid extra when they work overtime. On the other hand, the number of people working *short* hours has also been increasing. In 2000, 8.6 percent of employed men and 19.6 percent of employed women worked thirty hours a week or less, up from 4.5 percent and 15.5 percent in 1970. Often these employees are in hourly wage jobs where overtime pay would be required by law (if the employers would offer the extra hours). Part time workers are less likely than full time workers to be offered fringe benefits.

Is the increasing divergence in the hours that people work evidence that they are now able to tailor their workweeks to their own convenience? Or that their employers are making them work too much, on the one hand, or offering so little work that they find it hard to get by financially, on the other? Survey evidence suggests that, in many cases, it is the latter. Jerry A. Jacobs and Kathleen Gerson, in their book *The Time Divide,* report that "Those who work few hours on average prefer to work more, while those who work many hours on average prefer to work less."[2] In one survey, 80 percent of men and 90 percent of women working over fifty hours per week stated that they would prefer to work less. Those who worked between fifty and sixty hours stated that, on an average, they would prefer thirteen fewer hours. On the other hand, many people working short hours wanted to work more. Most people tend to prefer workweeks between twenty-five and forty hours.

This is important when thinking about the macroeconomics of labor markets, since any given number of total employment hours can have very different well-being consequences depending on how the hours are spread across the population of workers. One case would be an economy in which some groups of people work very long hours, while other people are unemployed or underemployed. Another case would be where working hours are distributed more evenly, allowing workers to have time for family care while reducing the number of unemployed.

Several countries in Europe have moved toward shorter standard working hours, often for macroeconomic reasons of reducing unemployment, but also to encourage strong families and to reduce consumption for ecological reasons. Most European countries have legal limits on the number of hours per week an employee is allowed to work, and vacation time of at least one month per year is standard—even for workers who are just starting out. Because of these different patterns of employment, a typical full-time worker in Europe now works an average of about two hundred hours (the equivalent of five forty-hour weeks) less per year than a full-time worker in the United States.

4.3 Concluding Thoughts

Whether an economy is able to generate and sustain "good jobs" (and good families and communities) depends on the whole institutional structure and dynamics of the national economy. The actions of business, governmental units, nonprofits (including unions, industry associations, and universities) and households all work together to determine the numbers and types of jobs that are generated, the number of workers in the labor force, and the skills with which workers are equipped. The responses of a country's business leaders, policymakers, workers and consumers to natural resource constraints and to the challenges and opportunities offered by participation in global markets for goods, services, and finance further significantly impact the employment situation. Studying macroeconomics only begins to equip one for addressing these challenges.

Discussion Questions

1. What was the labor force experience of your grandparents (or others you know that are in that generation)? Of your parents (or their generation)? What do you expect your own labor force participation to be like? Do the patterns in your family reflect the national pattern of changes discussed in the text, or not?
2. What evidence have you seen—in your own family, or through the media—of increasing "flexibility" in labor markets? Do you think these changes have been beneficial, harmful, or both?

Review Questions

1. What population is included in the official household survey that measures employment and unemployment?
2. What questions are asked to determine if someone is "employed"?
3. What makes a person count as "unemployed"?
4. How is the unemployment rate calculated?
5. What groups tend to have particularly high unemployment rates? Particularly low rates?

6. List four ways a person may enter unemployment.
7. What are "discouraged workers," and why are they of concern?
8. List the three types of unemployment, and describe them.
9. What policies may be used to combat frictional and structural unemployment?
10. Describe the classical theory of unemployment.
11. What are some of the reasons an economy might offer less than the optimal number of jobs, according to classical theory?
12. Describe how "sticky wages" could lead to unemployment.
13. What are some reasons that wages might be "sticky"?
14. Explain the "insider-outsider" theory of sticky wages.
15. What are "efficiency wages," and why might payment of them lead to unemployment?
16. On what grounds do some economists criticize classical and "sticky wage" theories?
17. In the Keynesian model of employment determination, what is the key factor explaining the level of employment in an economy?
18. Compare and contrast the concepts of the "natural rate of unemployment" and the "non-accelerating inflation rate of unemployment."
19. What are some problems with the "natural" rate and NAIRU concepts?
20. How is the labor force participation rate calculated?
21. What have been some of the major changes in the characteristics of the labor force over the last several decades?
22. What sorts of "flexibility" are good for workers? For employers?
23. How has the number of hours worked by different groups changed over the last few decades?

EXERCISES

1. The small nation of Neverland counts its unemployed using the same methods as the United States. Of the population of 350 people, seventy are under age sixteen, 190 are employed in paid work, and eighty are adults who are not doing paid work or looking for work because they are doing full-time family care, are retired or disabled, or are in school. The rest are unemployed. (No one is institutionalized, and the country has no military.) Calculate the following:
   a. The number of unemployed.
   b. The size of the labor force
   c. The unemployment rate
   d. The labor force participation rate (overall, for both sexes)

2. The population of Tattoonia is very small. Luis works for pay, full-time. Robin works one shift a week as counter help at a fast-food restaurant. Sheila is retired. Shawna does not work for pay, but is thinking about getting a job and has been flipping through the want ads to see what is available. Bob has given up looking for work, after months of not finding anything. Ana, the only child in the country, is twelve years old.
   a. How would a household survey, following U.S. methods, classify each person?
   b. What is the labor force participation rate in Tatoonia?
   c. What is the unemployment rate in Tatoonia?

3. Suppose an economy is suffering unemployment due to "too high" wages, as theorized by classical economists.
   a. Draw and numerically label a graph illustrating this case, in which the going wage is $20, the equilibrium wage is $15, fifty million people want to work, but only thirty million are employed.
   b. Describe some of the assumptions about labor markets that underlie this graph.

4. A computer software company advertises for employees, saying "We offer the best-paid jobs in the industry!" But why would any company want to pay more than it absolutely *has to,* to get workers? Can this phenomenon help to explain the existence of unemployment? Explain in a paragraph.

5. Match each concept in Column A with a definition or example in Column B.

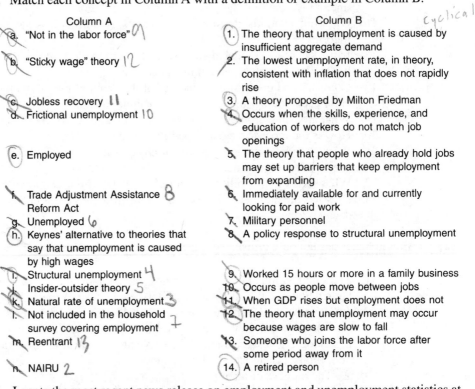

Column A	Column B
a. "Not in the labor force" 01	1. The theory that unemployment is caused by insufficient aggregate demand
b. "Sticky wage" theory 12	2. The lowest unemployment rate, in theory, consistent with inflation that does not rapidly rise
c. Jobless recovery 11	3. A theory proposed by Milton Friedman
d. Frictional unemployment 10	4. Occurs when the skills, experience, and education of workers do not match job openings
e. Employed	5. The theory that people who already hold jobs may set up barriers that keep employment from expanding
f. Trade Adjustment Assistance Reform Act 8	6. Immediately available for and currently looking for paid work
g. Unemployed 6	7. Military personnel
h. Keynes' alternative to theories that say that unemployment is caused by high wages	8. A policy response to structural unemployment
i. Structural unemployment 4	9. Worked 15 hours or more in a family business
j. Insider-outsider theory 5	10. Occurs as people move between jobs
k. Natural rate of unemployment 3	11. When GDP rises but employment does not
l. Not included in the household survey covering employment 7	12. The theory that unemployment may occur because wages are slow to fall
m. Reentrant 13	13. Someone who joins the labor force after some period away from it
n. NAIRU 2	14. A retired person

cyclical

6. Locate the most recent news release on employment and unemployment statistics at the Bureau of Labor Statistics website (*www.bls.gov*). In a paragraph, describe how the labor force, overall unemployment rate, and unemployment rates by race and ethnicity, age, and education differ from the numbers (for October 2007) given in the text.

NOTES

1. The data in this section are from Jerry A. Jacobs and Kathleen Gerson, *The Time Divide: Work, Family, and Gender Inequality* (Cambridge: Harvard University Press, 2004).

2. Jacobs and Gerson, *The Time Divide,* pp. 65–66.

8 The Structure of the United States Economy

The United States economy is the largest in the world. In 2006 it produced over $13 trillion in final goods and services—close to 30 percent of total global economic production as measured by traditional national accounting methods. While macroeconomics often considers "the economy" as a whole, such a large and complex national economy as the United States' cannot be viewed as a homogenous entity. Different parts of a national economy pursue different goals, respond to different incentives, and are affected by different circumstances. We've already considered some ways to classify a macroeconomy into slightly smaller units. We defined the three economic spheres in Chapter 3: the core, business, and public-purpose spheres. We saw in Chapter 5 that the U.S. national accounts classify the economy into four sectors: households and institutions, businesses, government, and the foreign sector.

In order to gain a deeper understanding of how a macroeconomy functions and changes over time, in this chapter we take a look at the U.S. economy—especially the business sphere—in slightly more detail. One implication of studying economics "in context" is that explanations for macroeconomic growth and fluctuation often require looking at history. The economy of the United States has not only *grown* over time, it has also *changed*. In this chapter we will consider how the economy has changed, delving into issues such as the relative decline (in certain terms) of farming and manufacturing, and the relative and absolute growth of services.

1. The Three Major Productive Sectors in an Economy

In the United States system of national accounts, the economy is divided into sectors based on *who* produces goods and services. We now turn to classifying the economy based on *what* is being produced. Economists still use the term "sectors" in this new classification scheme—but you'll need to remember that these sectors are not the same ones discussed back in Chapter 5.

Any national economy can be broadly classified into three productive economic sectors: primary, secondary, and tertiary. The **primary sector** involves the harvesting and extraction of natural resources and rudimentary processing of these raw materials. Industries in the primary sector include agriculture, commercial fishing, mining, and the timber industry. Generally, the products produced in the primary sector are not sold directly to households for final consumption but are sold to manufacturers as inputs. For example, the wheat grown, harvested, sorted, and dried in the primary sector would be sold to milling and baking companies in the secondary sector, which would then process the wheat into bread.

> **primary sector**: the sector of the economy that involves the harvesting and extraction of natural resources and simple processing of these raw materials into products which are generally sold to manufacturers as inputs

The **secondary sector** involves converting the outputs of the primary sector into products suitable for use or consumption. The secondary sector includes manufacturing industries such as aerospace, automobile production, the chemical industry, petroleum refining, the pharmaceutical industry, and electronics production. It also includes the construction of buildings and highways and utilities such as those that generate and distribute electricity.

> **secondary sector**: the sector of the economy that involves converting the outputs of the primary sector into products suitable for use or consumption. It includes manufacturing, construction, and utilities.

Finally we have the **tertiary sector**, also called the service sector. This sector involves the provision of services rather than tangible goods. The tertiary sector includes such services as the transportation, marketing, and retailing of physical goods. It also includes direct services without the distribution of any physical goods, such as consulting, education, technology, administration, and tourism.

> **tertiary sector**: the sector of the economy that involves the provision of services rather than of tangible goods

Firms in the business sphere of the economy are distributed among all of these sectors. Entities from the public-purpose and core spheres can also be classified into one or more of these three sectors. For example, a household growing food in a garden is contributing to the primary sector, even though this activity is not measured in traditional national income accounting. Most of the work of government and nonprofit organizations is accounted for in the tertiary sector.

Recognizing the limitations of national accounting presented in Chapter 5, such as the exclusion of household production and environmental services, we can nonetheless use National Income and Product Accounts (NIPA) data to gain some perspective on the relative size of the three sectors. The NIPA data published by the United States Bureau of Economic Analysis measure the contribution of different industries toward total gross domestic product. We can assign each of these industries to one of the three sectors presented in this chapter.

As we can see in Table 8.1 the U.S. economy is dominated by the private tertiary sector (64 percent of the total economy). Since the majority of government activities also involve the provisioning of services, this would imply that about three-quarters of the U.S. economy is comprised of services. Does this mean that the other sectors are relatively unimportant? No—clearly the tertiary sector relies heavily on outputs from the other two sectors. Consider, for example, that a restaurant would not be able to provide food services without meat and vegetable products from agriculture, a building produced by the construction industry, furniture made from wood products and manufactured as durable goods, etc.

The relative magnitude of the three sectors has changed over time in the United States. Figure 8.1 shows the share of the U.S. private economy (excluding government) attributed to each of the three sectors since the late nineteenth century. While the tertiary sector has been the dominant sector of the private economy for as long as reliable data are available, its share has risen steadily in the last several decades. The primary sector share was about 20 percent of the private economy in the late 1800s but declined during most of the twentieth century to its current share of only about 3 percent. Meanwhile, the share of the private economy attributable to the secondary sector generally rose after the Great Depression until peaking at about one-third of the economy in the 1950s and 1960s. However since the late 1960s the secondary sector's share has steadily declined, falling to only 22 percent in 2005.

In addition to assessing the relative importance of each sector based on GDP shares, we can also consider employment as a measure of significance. Employment is even more concentrated

Table 8.1   **Value Added by Sector, 2005, billions of dollars**

Industry	Value Added	Percent of GDP
Primary Sector		
Agriculture, forestry, and fishing	123	1.0
Mining	233	1.9
Primary Sector Total	356	2.9
Secondary Sector		
Utilities	248	2.0
Construction	611	4.9
Durable goods manufacturing	854	6.9
Nondurable goods manufacturing	658	5.3
Secondary Sector Total	2,371	19.0
Tertiary Sector		
Wholesale trade	743	6.0
Retail trade	824	6.6
Transportation and warehousing	345	2.8
Information	555	4.5
Finance and insurance	958	7.7
Real estate and rental and leasing[a]	1,578	12.7
Professional, scientific, and technical services	864	6.9
Management of companies and enterprises	256	2.1
Administrative and waste management	369	3.0
Educational services	116	0.9
Health care and social assistance	860	6.9
Arts, entertainment, and recreation	114	0.9
Accommodation and food services	331	2.7
Tertiary Sector Total	7,913	63.5
GDP Attributed to Government	1,564	12.6
Economy Total	12,456[b]	100.0[b]

Source: U.S. Bureau of Economic Analysis, *Survey of Current Business,* vol. 87(1), January 2007.

[a] The category of "real estate" included in the tertiary sector differs from "construction" (in the secondary sector), because it refers to the services of existing structures, as well as to the services provided by those who help people buy, sell, or lease properties. Real estate appears to be the largest single industry listed in Table 8.1, accounting for 12.7 percent of GDP. This is an artifact of the way GDP is calculated. As mentioned in the chapters on national accounts, GDP includes the non-marketed value of services that are provided by owner-occupied housing—the value of the housing services that owners "rent to themselves." The fact that this was about 9 percent of GDP in 2005 accounts for the high total value-added figure for the real estate industry.

[b] The total for GDP is greater than the sum of GDP for the three private sectors and government because the total includes additional industries not classified separately.

than GDP in the tertiary sector, with 83 percent of all workers. The primary sector, meanwhile, employs less than 1 percent of all workers in the United States.

> Eighty-three percent of all employed workers in the United States are engaged in production of services. Seventeen percent work in industries that produce tangible goods, with fewer than 1 percent of all U.S. workers engaged in the primary sector work of harvesting and processing natural resources.

Figure 8.1   **Share of U.S. Private Economy by Sector, 1869–2005**

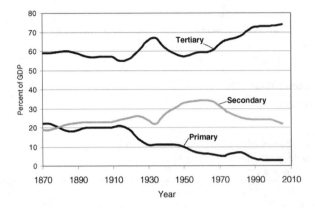

Note that this graph shows relative, not absolute, magnitudes. The relative size of the three sectors has changed over time, but throughout the history of the United States the tertiary sector has dominated. (Source: Various editions of the *Statistical Abstract of the United States*)

Using the data in Figure 8.1, we can now tell a simple story of how economic growth in the United States has proceeded since the late 1800s. During the first part of this period, up to about 1920, all sectors grew at approximately the same rate. Then, between about 1920 and the early years of the Depression, the relative share from the tertiary sector increased while the other two sectors declined. As the economy began to recover from the Depression, the secondary sector took off while the tertiary sector went into a relative decline. This trend continued as the demands of World War II fueled industrial growth. During the post-war period, industrial growth remained strong while the relative share of the primary sector declined. Finally, since the 1960s the secondary sector has declined while the tertiary sector has been the fastest-growing sector—a trend that is likely to continue in the twenty-first century.

Despite the dramatic data shown in Figure 8.1, with the associated employment figures, we should not conclude that the primary sector is unimportant in the U.S. economy. On the contrary, the primary sector remains the ultimate source for our food, fibers, and construction materials. In relatively simple economies the production chains for these things can be short, turning logs into homes, or wool or plant fibers into clothing, with far fewer people involved in intermediate steps than is normally the case today. At higher levels of industrialization the number and complexity of production steps increases, leading to an increase in the value added that is attributed to the secondary and tertiary sectors.

Although industrialization generally coincides with a declining share of national income going to the primary sector, this does not imply that a society's needs for the products of the primary sector have decreased. If anything, increasing levels of industrialization have tended to be associated with an increasing absolute demand for minerals, food, energy, and other primary sector products. But the technological improvements that come with industrialization mean that products from the primary sector can be obtained with fewer workers. Thus the share of national income going to the primary sector falls even as a society uses more and more natural resources.

The preceding paragraphs explain the primary sector's decline as a proportion of GDP and of national employment, relative to manufacturing. It is not so obvious how or why the tertiary sector has risen so markedly, to absorb over 70 percent of private sector GDP, not only in the United States, but in many other rich countries such as Australia, France, and Denmark. That part of the story will be discussed in the last section of this chapter.

Discussion Questions

1. Think about the businesses and industries in your community. Can you list several businesses that would be classified into each of the three sectors described above? Does your answer to this question concur with the notion that the majority of economic activity takes place in the tertiary sector?

2. Consider the following statement: "Global climate change will mainly impact primary sector industries such as agriculture, forestry, and fishing. Given that these industries only account for a couple of percent of U.S. GDP, the overall economic impact of climate change on the United States will therefore be very small." Do you agree with this statement? Can you present a counterargument?

2. NATURAL RESOURCES: THE PRIMARY SECTOR

For most of human history, people obtained food, tools, and other products directly from their natural environment. Today, most people in industrial countries have no direct connection with the complex chain of events that convert raw natural resources into the products we use and consume every day. Although modern technology can mask this process, one thing remains the same—every physical good ultimately can be traced back to component natural resources.

Although the United States and other industrial countries have become increasingly service-oriented, this has not shielded these nations from macroeconomic variability arising from disturbances to primary sector industries. This is most apparent with industrial nations' dependence on fossil fuels. Significant reductions in global oil supplies can quickly remind us that modern economies are still ultimately dependent on the natural world. We now take a more detailed look at the primary sector, beginning with agriculture.

2.1 THE FOOD SYSTEM

Throughout its early history, the United States was an agrarian economy. In the late 1700s approximately 90 percent of the labor force was composed of farmers. By 1880, farmers still made up about half the labor force. Now less than 1 percent of the U.S. workforce is directly employed in agriculture. During the twentieth century agriculture in the United States underwent dramatic changes. Major trends included a decline in the total farm population, a decrease in the total number of farms, an increase in average farm size, and increasing agricultural productivity (i.e., output per acre, as well as output per worker).

Agricultural productivity has increased as human labor has been replaced by mechanization and as the use of agricultural chemicals and other technologies has spread. For example, in the last hundred years average corn yields in the United States have risen from around twenty-five to 140 bushels per acre, and wheat yields are up from twelve to forty bushels per acre. One American farmer now provides enough food and clothing for about 130 people.

As discussed in Chapter 3, natural capital is an important source of economic productivity that can be depleted or degraded depending on a society's level of resource maintenance. The productivity of the primary sector is particularly dependent on natural capital. Degradation of natural capital, such as soil quality and supplies of water for irrigation, can reduce agricultural output per acre, although to some extent these problems can be offset with produced capital such as chemical fertilizers and bioengineered seeds.

A particularly serious threat to agricultural productivity in the United States is the depletion of groundwater supplies. Agriculture is responsible for about four-fifths of the water use in the

Figure 8.2   **Number of Farms, Average Farm Size, and Total Land in Farms, United States, 1850–2002**

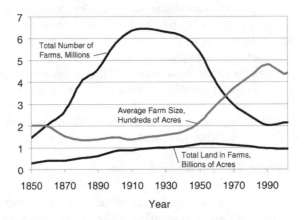

The decline in the total number of farms since the early 1900s has been offset by an increase in average farm size, leaving the total land in farms relatively constant. (Source: Various editions of the *Statistical Abstract of the United States*)

United States, primarily to irrigate crops in Western states. Over one-third of the irrigation water used in the country comes from groundwater aquifers, which are renewable resources that recharge very slowly and can become depleted when withdrawals exceed the rate of natural recharge. Currently, the United States is withdrawing groundwater approximately four times faster than it is being replenished. States particularly dependent on groundwater for irrigation include Texas, Kansas, and Nebraska, which rely on water from the Ogallala Aquifer, the world's largest known aquifer. The water table for the Ogallala Aquifer is declining up to two feet per year, and water supplies from the aquifer have already become exhausted in some areas. The declining water table in the aquifer has motivated increased use of efficient irrigation practices, but over time many more areas will lose access to this resource. Most likely these areas will either need to switch to different crops that require less water or be removed from agricultural production.

One aspect of American farming that has remained relatively constant is the total land area devoted to agriculture. As we see in Figure 8.2, the decline in the total number of farms during most of the twentieth century has been offset by an increase in average farm size. Since the early 1900s the total farmland in the United States has remained around one billion acres. Currently occupying 42 percent of the entire land area of the United States, agriculture continues to dominate the geographic landscape of the country. This is particularly evident in the Midwest, where about 90 percent of the land area of some states, such as Kansas and Iowa, is devoted to agriculture.

There are about two million farms in the United States, but a small number of very large farms produce most of the country's agricultural products. About 92 percent of the nation's farms are classified by the United States Department of Agriculture as "small family farms"—those with annual sales of $250,000 or less. However, these small farms produce less than one-third of the nation's agricultural output. Meanwhile, farms with annual sales of over $1 million (only about 1 percent of all farms) account for nearly half of the value of agricultural production. The largest farms in the country tend to be owned as corporate enterprises with annual sales in the millions of dollars.

Farm receipts in the United States are approximately evenly divided between livestock and crops. The most important crops in the country are, in order of sales: corn, soybeans, wheat,

Figure 8.3   **The Allocation of a Dollar Spent on Food in the United States, 2000**

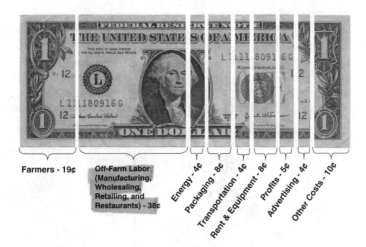

Farmers - 19¢   Off-Farm Labor (Manufacturing, Wholesaling, Retailing, and Restaurants) - 38¢   Energy - 4¢   Packaging - 8¢   Transportation - 4¢   Rent & Equipment - 8¢   Profits - 5¢   Advertising - 4¢   Other Costs - 10¢

Farmers receive only about 19 cents of every dollar spent on food. (Source: *Agriculture Factbook 2001-2002,* U.S. Department of Agriculture)

hay, and cotton. The majority of the grain produced in the United States (61 percent in 2003) is not directly used for human consumption but is fed instead to livestock.

Most of the agricultural products that people consume are not obtained directly from farmers but undergo significant processing prior to being sold to consumers. As we see in Figure 8.3, only about 19 cents of every dollar spent on food in the United States is paid to farmers. The remainder is spent for processing, marketing, and other costs. Thirty-eight cents out of each dollar pays off-farm workers in manufacturing, wholesaling, retailing, and eating establishments. About eight cents of every food dollar is spent on packaging, and four cents on advertising.

Figure 8.3 suggests that the impact of agriculture extends well into the secondary and tertiary sectors. Even though few people are directly employed in agriculture, nearly 20 percent of all American jobs can be considered dependent on agriculture. Most of these jobs are in wholesaling, retailing, or food services.

2.2 THE ENERGY SYSTEM

Modern production and consumption systems require energy—a lot of energy. The United States is by far the world's largest consumer of energy. While it has less than 5 percent of the world's population, it uses about one-quarter of the world's energy. This is currently more than twice the amount of energy used by China, the next-highest energy consumer (and a country whose population is about three times larger). The United States has one of the highest per capita energy usage rates in the world, exceeded only by a few nations such as the high-latitude countries of Canada, Norway, and Iceland.

We can also compare nations by looking at the amount of energy used per dollar of GDP. A low number is generally indicative of an economy that is energy efficient in its production processes. The United States is about average among all nations in the energy efficiency of production—more efficient than Finland or Canada, but less efficient than Switzerland, Ireland, or Japan.

Figure 8.4   **Energy Consumption in the United States, by Source and Use, 2006**

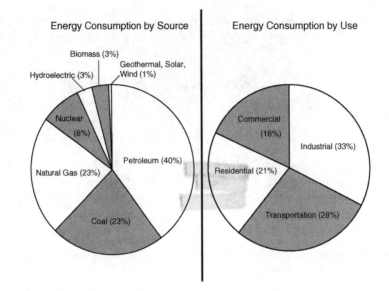

The United States obtains its largest share of energy from petroleum, and uses energy mostly for industry and transportation. (Source: Annual Energy Review 2006, U.S. Department of Energy, Energy Information Administration, Report No. DOE/EIA-0384 (2006))

Figure 8.4 presents two ways of classifying energy use in the United States. One approach considers the source of the energy. We can see that this country is heavily dependent on fossil fuels; petroleum is the single most important energy source, and carbon-based fossil fuels (petroleum, coal, and natural gas) provide 86 percent of all energy used in the country. Coal, often viewed as a fuel from an earlier industrial age, is still the primary fuel for electricity generation in the United States—the source of more than half of the nation's electricity in 2006. Meanwhile, petroleum provides nearly all the fuel for transportation. As no new nuclear power plants have been ordered in the United States since 1978, the current trend is for the national share of energy derived from nuclear power to decline in the future as aging plants are decommissioned. The United States currently obtains a small share of its energy from renewable resources, but a recent notable development is the rapid growth in the utilization of wind power. From 1998 to 2006 energy generated by wind power expanded by over 700 percent—the fastest-growing energy source in the country. However, as planners look on a global scale at future anticipated gaps between energy demand and supply, two points emerge. One is that many different sources and types of energy will emerge to replace carbon-based fuels. The other is that the largest of these potential sources is solar energy.

Another way to look at energy consumption is to consider how it is used. As shown in Figure 8.4 industry is the largest consumer of energy—about one-third of total usage. The share of energy used by industry has declined in recent decades. (It approached 50 percent in the mid-1950s.)

The United States is not only the world's major consumer of energy; it is also the largest producer. In 2005 the United States produced 15 percent of the world's energy, more than any other top producer, including China (14 percent), Russia (11 percent), Saudi Arabia (6 percent), and Canada (4 percent). The United States is the world's largest producer of energy from nuclear power, second behind China in producing power from coal, and behind only Saudi Arabia and Russia in producing energy from petroleum. Germany and Spain are larger producers of wind energy, while Japan has taken the lead in implementing the still relatively young solar technologies.

While energy *use* permeates every aspect of economic activity, the *production* of energy employs less than a million workers, or about 0.5 percent of the workforce, and directly contributes a similar small share to GDP. Yet fluctuations in energy supply and prices can have significant impacts on economy-wide variables such as GDP growth, inflation, and employment. Increases in energy prices lead to downstream increases in the price of many other products and higher inflation rates. Dramatic energy price increases in recent decades, particularly in the price of oil, have precipitated recessions both at the national and international levels.

In the 1950s the country was essentially energy-independent, obtaining only about 15 percent of its oil from imports. At the onset of the first energy crisis in 1973 the United States had come to rely on imports for about 35 percent of its oil. In 2006 this percentage had reached 60 percent, with the United States Department of Energy forecasting that imported oil will provide over 70 percent of supply by 2030.

A common fallacy is that the United States obtains most of its imported oil from the Middle East. In fact, only about one-quarter of the nation's oil imports come from the Middle East. The top two nations for oil imports in 2006 were Canada and Mexico, with Saudi Arabia being the third largest supplier. Other important sources of foreign oil include Venezuela and Nigeria. Still, U.S. oil imports from the Middle East are anticipated to increase in the future given that the majority of the world's oil reserves are found there.

2.3 OTHER PRIMARY INDUSTRIES

Other industries in the primary sector include mining, timber harvesting, and commercial fishing. These industries are relatively small in terms of their employment and contribution to GDP.

Non-fuel mining in the United States employed approximately a quarter of a million workers in 2006. Over half of these workers were employed in the mining of just two commodities: aluminum and crushed stone. The most important states for mining are California, Nevada, Arizona, and Texas.

Only about 60,000 workers in the United States were directly employed in forestry and logging industries in 2006. However, like other primary sector industries, forestry products provide the inputs for many secondary and tertiary industries. About 1.1 million workers are employed in the country in manufacturing industries based on forest products—about half in the production of wood products such as plywood and construction wood, and half in the production of paper and cardboard.

Currently about one-third of the United States is covered with forests. However, the country has lost the majority of its old-growth forests (defined as a forest containing trees of every maturity level). Only about 5 percent of the nation's old-growth forests remain, primarily located on public lands in the Pacific Northwest. The dwindling supply of highly-profitable old-growth trees available for harvesting in the Western states has resulted in a geographical shift of the timber industry. Timber harvesting in the Pacific Northwest declined by nearly 50 percent between 1976 and 2001, while harvesting in the Southeast increased by 50 percent during the same time period. The top timber harvesting states in the country in 2002 were (in order): Georgia, Alabama, Mississippi, Louisiana, and North Carolina.

The other major industry in the primary sector is commercial fishing. The United States National Marine Fisheries Service estimates that the fishing industry contributed $32 billion in value-added to the national economy in 2004 (about 0.3 percent of the total). The leading states for fishery products in 2004 were (in order by value of catch): Alaska, Massachusetts, Maine, Louisiana, and Washington. The most valuable species are shellfish, including shrimp, crabs, and clams, followed by salmon and halibut.

Total fishery catch in the United States was approximately constant at around five billion pounds annually from the 1950s to the mid-1970s. Then the annual harvest steadily rose, reaching more than ten billion pounds in the early 1990s and falling slightly since then to around 9.5 billion pounds in 2003. In a 1999 report the federal government estimated that 22 percent of the fishery stocks in the country were "overutilized"—meaning harvest levels are above the sustainable level. Another 39 percent were "fully utilized"—already being harvested at the maximum sustainable level.

Discussion Questions

1. What food did you eat for your most recent meal? Discuss the production steps that were required to get that food to you. Where do you think the food initially came from? What type of processing was required? How was the food transported? Who do you think profited the most from your food purchase?
2. We learned in this section that the United States is not only the world's largest consumer of energy—it also has one of the highest per capita rates of energy use. But we've also learned that the United States is supposedly a service-oriented country. How can this be? Do you think a country that becomes more service-oriented necessarily must use more energy? Can you describe how a country might become more service-oriented while using less energy?

3. The Production of Goods: The Secondary Sector

As we mentioned already in this chapter, the secondary sector in the United States has been declining as a percentage of GDP since the 1960s. But before we conclude that manufacturing has fled to other countries (an idea that we'll discuss in section 3.3), we should note that the United States remains the world's largest goods manufacturer. In 2004 American manufacturers produced about $1.5 trillion worth of goods (measured as value-added). This total is still 70 percent larger than the world's second-largest manufacturer (Japan) and over three times larger than the value of goods produced in China. In fact, the United States produces about one-quarter of the global value of goods manufactured each year. However the United States imports significantly more manufactured goods than it sells abroad, resulting in a trade deficit in goods of $838 billion in 2006.

The secondary sector is broadly classified into several sub-sectors: durable goods manufacturing, nondurable goods manufacturing, the construction and housing industry, and utilities. In this section we will only discuss construction and housing, and manufacturing. Then, focusing on the latter, we will address the questions that are often asked in contemporary news discussions: Why is the manufacturing sector losing jobs, and where are those jobs going?

3.1 Construction and Housing

The construction and housing industry includes the building of homes, highways, bridges, office buildings, power and communication lines, and public buildings. Of the approximately $1.1 trillion of new construction put in place in 2005, 56 percent was private residential construction, 22 percent was private non-residential construction (such as commercial buildings, office buildings,

Figure 8.5   **Annual Number of Private Housing Starts in the United States, 1965–2005**

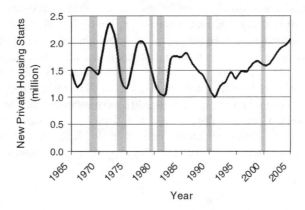

The number of private housing starts decline significantly during recessionary periods (indicated by the gray-shaded areas) and recover once a recession is over. (Source: Various editions of the *Statistical Abstract of the United States*)

and health-care buildings), and 21 percent was public construction. The latter primarily includes educational facilities and highways.

In 2006 there were over seven million individuals working in the construction industry. The majority of these—over half—were classified as contractors, including plumbers, electricians, roofers, and carpenters. Unlike most industries where the majority of workers are employees, most contractors are self-employed.

The primary factor affecting the construction and housing industry is the cyclical behavior of the domestic economy. During periods of recession, the construction industry can be particularly hard-hit. The number of private housing starts each year vividly illustrates the cyclical nature of the construction industry. Figure 8.5 shows that the number of housing starts can decline significantly during recessionary periods but recover once a recession is over. (The data follow housing *starts* since only the flow of newly constructed housing, not the level of the pre-existing stock of housing, count in measuring the production of the secondary sector.)

Despite cyclical variations in housing starts, a number of trends have continued in the housing industry. One is that the average size of new single-family homes has increased, doubling in size between 1970 and 2005. While houses are getting bigger, the average number of people living in them has decreased. In the 1950s there was an average of 3.4 people per household, while in 2004 this had fallen to 2.6 people.

In recent years housing prices have increased at a faster rate than prices in general. The median price of an existing single-family home in the United States in the fall of 2007 was about $221,000. This represents a doubling of home prices since 1995, even though the consumer price index only rose 37 percent during this period. Despite rising house prices, the percentage of Americans who own their own home, including those paying a mortgage, has gradually increased. In 2005, 69 percent of households owned their own home, up from 63 percent in 1965. Home ownership rates tend to be highest in the Midwest (where housing prices are the lowest) and lowest in the West (where housing prices are the highest). Home ownership rates also vary by the race of the householder. While about 72 percent of white householders owned their own homes in 2005, only 48 percent of black and 46 percent of Hispanic householders owned their own homes. Home ownership rates are also much higher for married couples and older householders than for younger, single people.

Issues in the housing industry can affect the entire economy. The boom in housing starts that began in 2002 was created in part by low interest rates, expectations of a continuing increase in the price of housing, and inadequate oversight of the sub-prime mortgage market. After the sub-prime mortgage market dramatically collapsed in late 2007, the impact spread to widespread problems in credit markets, and then to much of the rest of the economy.

As of late 2007, an alarming number of homeowners were unable to make their mortgage payments, and faced foreclosure (that is, loss of the ownership of their property). The highest foreclosure rates in the third quarter of 2007 were in Stockton, California, with one foreclosure filing for every 31 households, followed by Detroit, with one foreclosure filing for every 33 households. Other cities especially hard hit in this first wave of the gathering recession were Phoenix, Fort Lauderdale, Cleveland, Chicago, Miami, and Sacramento.

3.2 MANUFACTURING

In 2005 there were about 330,000 manufacturing enterprises in the United States. All together they employed about 13.7 million people, or about 10 percent of all workers. Table 8.2 presents a summary of the production and employment in major manufacturing industries in the country. No single manufacturing industry dominates, but the top industries include transportation equipment (mostly automobiles), computers and electronics, chemicals, and food. We will discuss just two: textiles and automobiles.

Textiles

In the 1800s the textile and apparel industry arose as this country's first large-scale manufacturing industry, with the majority of the mills located in the Northeast. The mills initially employed mostly women and girls, but increasingly switched to immigrant labor when the women organized unions and pushed to limit the work day to ten hours. The textile industry expanded rapidly, becoming the largest manufacturing employer in the country by the start of the twentieth century. In 1920 there were nearly two million workers in the industry. Then, faced with foreign competition, particularly from Japan, the industry stopped expanding. Employment in the American textile industry remained around two million workers for the next fifty years or so.

Since the 1970s the textile and apparel industry in the United States has been decimated—employment in the industry is down about 65 percent and the decline appears likely to continue into the future. The international textile industry has changed rapidly in just the last few years and further changes are anticipated. Imports from China are at the center of the debate on manufacturing job losses in the United States. In 2002 import quota restrictions were removed from twenty-nine categories of apparel. In just two years China more than doubled its exports of textiles and apparel to the United States. Chinese imports can be produced at lower cost than domestic goods primarily because of lower wages. The textile industry is China's largest manufacturing employer as well as its lowest-paying, with average wages below $1 per hour. Further reduction of quota restrictions under a World Trade Organization agreement suggests that American imports of textiles and apparel will continue to increase. American textile and apparel manufacturers are warning that their industry could be essentially eliminated by the end of the decade unless trade policy halts the growth of imports from China.

Textiles and clothing are outstanding examples of a category of manufactured items which (1) are labor intensive (i.e., their production requires a large number of labor hours in proportion to the cost of other inputs such as manufactured or natural capital), and (2) can be produced with

Table 8.2   **Manufacturing Industries in the United States, Production and Employment**

Industry	2005 Value Added (billions of dollars)	2005 Employment (thousands)
Durable Goods Industries		
Computers and electronics	135	1,486
Fabricated metals	131	1,520
Furniture	37	548
Machinery	111	1,107
Transportation equipment	167	1,636
Other durable goods	273	2,378
Durable Goods Total	854	8,675
Nondurable Goods Industries		
Chemical products	209	810
Food, beverages, and tobacco	176	1,623
Paper products	55	454
Petroleum and coal products	64	101
Textiles, apparel, and leather products	41	413
Other nondurable goods	113	1,346
Nondurable Goods Total	658	4,749

Sources: U.S. Census Bureau, *2005 County Business Patterns; Statistical Abstract of the United States,* 2006, United States Department of Commerce, Bureau of the Census, Table No. 980.

large numbers of unskilled laborers. These characteristics create conditions in which countries with large populations of poor people can compete on the international market.

Automobiles

In contrast to textiles, during the twentieth century the automobile industry in the United States benefited from a number of factors. One was the "first-mover advantage" gained by the leadership of Ford and others who innovated and created strong industries before most foreign competitors. Another was the transaction cost involved in shipping automobiles over long distances, creating a cost disadvantage for foreign producers. In addition, for a long time the technology of automobile production was such that the greater productivity of more skilled workers enabled them to compete against lower-wage workers who had less education, training, and skill (summarized in many economic discussions as "human capital").

The first challenge to the preeminence of the United States' auto companies for its enormous home market came with the oil crises of the 1970s. This motivated a surge in imports of high-quality, fuel-efficient vehicles from Japan. By 1980 the Japanese automobile industry, virtually non-existent twenty years earlier, had captured over 20 percent of the U.S. market. The impact of this first wave of foreign competition on the domestic motor vehicle industry was severe. Between 1977 and 1982 employment in the industry declined 30 percent. In the early 1980s Chrysler was on the verge of bankruptcy and was only saved by financial assistance from the federal government.

However, the domestic automobile industry recovered relatively quickly, for several reasons. First, United States automobile manufacturers improved the quality of their vehicles, often either emulating Japanese production methods or forming joint ventures with foreign producers. Another factor was the decline in gasoline prices after the 1970s oil crises, which shifted demand back toward larger domestic vehicles. Sales of pickup trucks and sport utility vehicles, initially produced almost exclusively by American companies, increased dramatically in the 1980s and 1990s.

Another important reason that employment in the American motor vehicle industry rebounded was that foreign companies began locating some of their production facilities in the United States. The number of vehicles manufactured in the United States by Japanese and European firms increased by a factor of sixteen between 1982 and 1990. Reasons for foreign firms producing vehicles in the United States include public relations, comparable labor costs, lower transportation costs, and avoidance of tariffs and quotas. While motor vehicle production for the domestic companies remains centered in Detroit, foreign companies have built factories throughout the country. As of 2006, Honda was producing vehicles in Ohio and Alabama; Toyota had factories in Kentucky, Indiana, and Texas; and Nissans were being manufactured in Tennessee. As a compelling example of the extent of globalization, BMW manufactures its Z4 and X5 vehicles exclusively at its factory in South Carolina for distribution not only in the United States but throughout the world. Current employment in the motor vehicle industry (around one million workers) is greater than it was before the onslaught of foreign competition. However, as noted in the News in Context box below, the quantity and quality of these jobs at U.S.-owned firms is declining.

3.3 WHERE HAVE ALL THE MANUFACTURING JOBS GONE?

In Figure 8.1 we saw that manufacturing generally increased, as a share of GDP, from the late 1800s until peaking at around one-third of the economy in the 1960s. Since then the share of GDP from manufacturing has declined to around 20 percent. However we would be wrong to conclude that the manufacturing sector has shrunk in absolute economic terms. In fact, the value added from manufacturing, when adjusted for inflation, is about the same magnitude now as it was in the 1960s. While the size of the manufacturing sector has not decreased, its share of GDP has declined because the size of the service sector has grown so much.

However, *employment in manufacturing* has declined, even while *the value of manufacturing output* has held fairly constant. As seen in Figure 8.6, while there were some ups and downs, total employment in manufacturing generally increased from 1950 until 1979. Since then there have been two periods of decline in manufacturing employment, first in the early 1980s, and more recently since the late 1990s. From a peak of over 20 million workers in 1979, the number of manufacturing jobs has declined by 30 percent.

Figure 8.6 shows that about 25 percent of all workers were employed in manufacturing during the 1950s and 1960s. By 2005, only 10 percent of all workers were employed in manufacturing. Between 2000 and 2005, over three million manufacturing jobs were lost in the United States.

Where have these jobs gone? Could it be that Americans are simply demanding fewer manufactured goods? Such an interpretation could emerge from Figure 8.1, which includes data only on domestic production; however American consumers can, of course, also purchase goods manufactured abroad. Up until the 1970s the United States ran a net trade surplus in manufactured goods, exporting more goods than it imported. Since then, however, the country has been running a trade deficit in manufactured goods that has grown substantially in recent years, reaching a level equivalent to 6.4 percent of GDP in 2006. When we combine the demand for both domestic and foreign goods, we find that the demand for goods as a percentage of total demand has remained remarkably constant over the past twenty years—even while services have increased both as a percentage of value added and in the percentage of employment generated by that sector.

This leads us to a second possible explanation for the loss of American manufacturing jobs— that they have essentially shifted overseas. In 1990 American manufacturers met 57 percent of

NEWS IN CONTEXT:
Auto Job Loss Put at 150,000; Analysis of Future of Big 3 Is Dour

With Chrysler's announcement last week of an additional 12,000 job cuts, the number of jobs to be eliminated from U.S. and Canadian automakers and their former parts divisions in the second half of this decade has grown to 150,000— and counting. With buyouts or early retirement offers expected at all three Detroit automakers after the new United Auto Workers union contracts that allow new hires to get less in pay or benefits, the number is sure to grow. And in the future, as the American automakers face competition from more and more rivals from low-cost countries, analysts say, more painful cuts will almost certainly follow.

Just days after hourly workers ratified a new labor contract, Chrysler said it plans to nearly double the 13,000 job cuts it announced in February, now targeting the elimination of more than 25,000 hourly and salaried workers, or nearly a third of its work force.

Add the Chrysler cuts to the expected job cuts—at least 137,400 of them—already in the works at General Motors Corp., Ford Motor Co. and its parts unit, and Delphi Corp. and the total American job reductions rise to about 150,000 between 2005 and 2009.

"We've been overbuilding for years and years, and now it's catching up to us because we're losing market share," said Kenyon Hall, a 31-year-old assembly worker at Chrysler's plant in Belvidere, Ill., where the automaker plans to eliminate a shift. "They waited too long to do something. Now it's going to be painful for a while."

Erich Merkle, analyst and chief forecaster at IRN Inc., an automotive consulting firm in Grand Rapids, Mich., agreed the domestic auto industry hasn't reached bottom yet. "In terms of pain, I don't have a solid number," Merkle said, "but in my opinion, they're still working around the edges."

Source: *Detroit Free Press*, November 6, 2007, Business 6D.

Does the action described in this news story continue a trend, or reverse a trend, discussed in the text?

the domestic demand for goods. In 2005, this percentage had fallen to only 26 percent. Thus, more of Americans' demand for goods is being met with imports rather than domestic production. The major sources of imports in goods are (in order of the 2006 value of imports): Canada, China, Mexico, Japan, and Germany. The U.S. trade deficit with all these countries has grown, especially with China—the value of imports from China (including both goods and services) increased 182 percent between 2001 and 2006 alone.

However, the decline in the absolute number of U.S. manufacturing jobs predates the dramatic increase of imports from China. In fact, this decline is not unique to the United States, but is a worldwide phenomenon. The absolute number of manufacturing jobs peaked years ago in virtually

Figure 8.6   **Total U.S. Manufacturing Employment and Manufacturing Employment as a Percentage of Total Employment, 1950–2005**

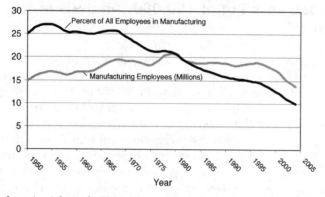

The number of manufacturing jobs in the United States has declined since 1979 while the number of manufacturing jobs as a percentage of all jobs has generally declined since the mid-1950s. (Source: Various editions of the *Statistical Abstract of the United States*)

all industrial countries. The same is true, or is rapidly becoming true, in emerging markets, where rapid productivity growth allows real wages and output to rise while manufacturing jobs decline and the service sector expands relative to manufacturing. China, the trading partner that has been perceived as the greatest threat to jobs in the United States, has been undergoing similar pain. Between 1995 and 2002 China lost 14.9 million manufacturing jobs, more than the entire current United States manufacturing workforce of less than 14 million. This is despite the fact that value-added manufacturing in China grew by 90 percent in real terms during this period.

What is the cause of this global phenomenon? It appears that recent decades have seen an acceleration in the process that began with the Industrial Revolution in the mid to late eighteenth century, in which technological change makes it possible for industries to substitute manufactured capital (i.e., machinery and automation) for human labor. Manufacturing productivity is commonly measured as an index of the value of the goods produced per hour of labor. Manufacturing productivity in the United States over the past few decades has been growing faster than overall business productivity and has particularly accelerated since 1990. During the 1980s manufacturing productivity increased by an average of 2.6 percent per year, but stepped up to over 3 percent per year in the early 1990s, and over 4 percent per year in the late 1990s.

This increase in productivity means that more goods can be produced with less human inputs. While global demand for manufactured goods continues to grow, it does not grow as fast as productivity: more things are produced and sold, but fewer people are required to produce them. Hence the worldwide availability of manufacturing jobs has been a "shrinking pie." Low wages or good education can make one or another country's workforce better able to compete for their share of the pie; but in this particular contest there are no long-range winners, only differences in how rapidly the loss occurs.

What does this mean for human well-being? An economist looking forward to this situation one or two hundred years ago might have said that this is exactly what progress is supposed to be about: People can get more of what they want with less work. However, people can only purchase the output of a market economy if they have income, and for most people income comes primarily through wages, which are attached to jobs.

As we have seen, the number of jobs in the tertiary sector has been growing steadily, taking up most or all of the slack left by the shrinking secondary sector. However, such transitions are

Figure 8.7   **Productivity and Wages in U.S. Manufacturing: 1978 to 2006**

In recent decades, the average real hourly wage in manufacturing has not increased as quickly as real output per hour. (Source: U.S. Bureau of Labor Statistics, http://www.bls.gov/fls/prodsupptabletoc.htm)

always painful: People who had developed valuable skills in one job may find that their labor commands a lower price in other types of work. Moreover, many manufacturing jobs have traditionally enjoyed institutional arrangements—including unionization and job characteristics negotiated with the help of unions—that increased the compensation and the quality of those jobs. Thus the distress and anxiety produced by the erosion of manufacturing jobs in the United States may be greater than that experienced in some other countries where such jobs never did include the extra institutional benefits some jobs in the sector enjoyed here.

Does all of this mean that we should be complacent about the large shifts going on in the economy? Should we shrug off individual complaints about job losses and down-shifting as merely temporary phenomena? To the individuals who have lost jobs, pensions, or homes it is no comfort that their losses are or will be made up for by someone else's gains. Beyond this, modern societies can be criticized for failing to turn dramatic economic success into equal increases in human well-being. As is shown in Figure 8.7, average worker salaries in the United States have not kept pace with increases in worker productivity. As we will see in Chapter 14, the achievement of greater openness in global markets has brought downward pressure on the prices of many goods, but at the same time global cost-cutting competition also pressures companies to cut back on worker benefits and working conditions, as well as on the cost of labor.

The secondary sector is probably not where these tensions will, or will not, be worked out. The arena where we can look for the next wave of attempts to turn economic progress into human progress is likely to be the growing tertiary sector. To that we now turn.

Discussion Questions

1. Section 3.1 seems to present a paradox. While house prices have been rising much faster than inflation (and wages) for many decades, the percentage of Americans that own their own homes has also been increasing. This seems to contradict the basic rules of supply and demand—how can this be? What other factors besides price and income might be relevant in explaining the rising rates of home ownership?

2. You've probably heard politicians in the United States talking about the need to prevent American jobs from being moved overseas. But the previous section suggests that manufacturing jobs are declining virtually all over the world. In light of this global reality, what policies make the most sense for the United States? Would the same policies be advisable for other countries? If all countries adopted the same policies, would they become less effective?

4. PRODUCTION OF SERVICES: THE TERTIARY SECTOR

Even more than the other sectors, the tertiary sector can't be defined as a homogenous economic category. As we saw in Table 8.1, the service sector includes a wide array of industries, including education, retail trade, waste management, and entertainment. Data on employment trends, wages, and other measures vary considerably across different service industries. For example, a common perception is that jobs in the service sector pay poorly. While this is true for such jobs as cashiers and childcare workers, it clearly isn't applicable to such service jobs as doctors and lawyers. With this caveat in mind, service jobs do pay less on average than manufacturing jobs. In 2006 the average hourly wage in goods-producing industries was $20.06, while the average pay in the service industries was $18.09 per hour.

While most international trade has traditionally involved the exchange of physical goods, trade in services is now expanding rapidly. While it is easy to picture a physical good moving between countries, it might be harder to imagine how *services* could be internationally traded. A service is "exported" if agents in the United States provide a service used by an individual or organization based abroad. For example, if someone from Argentina stays in a U.S. hotel, this is considered an "export" of U.S.-produced accommodation services. A service is "imported" if agents in the foreign sector provide a service used by individuals or organizations based in the United States. For example, if a U.S. manufacturer ships its goods using freighters registered in Liberia, it is said to "import" transportation services from Liberia. Between 1980 and 2004 global trade in services increased by a factor of 5.6, while trade in goods increased by a factor of 4.4. By 2004 about 20 percent of all international trade was in services. Improvements in information technology have made services such as customer call centers, software development, and data processing more transferable across national boundaries in recent years. The United Nations notes that cost savings of 20–40 percent are commonly reported by companies that offshore their service needs to low-wage nations. It is estimated that by 2015 3.4 million service jobs may shift from the United States to low-income countries.

In 2006 the United States exported more in services than it imported, but this trade surplus has been decreasing since 1997. The primary services exported by the United States are travel, financial, and educational services, while the main service imports are travel, telecommunications, and freight services.

As the tertiary sector includes so many industries, we don't have the space in this chapter to discuss them all. Instead, we'll look at just a few of the major service industries, considering some especially significant trends and issues.

4.1 HUMAN SERVICES

Human services include education, health care, social assistance, and child care. These services can be provided by private businesses, nonprofit organizations, or governments. A major difference between the United States and other developed economies is that human services in the

Figure 8.8   **Health Care Expenditures in the United States as a Percentage of GDP, 1960–2004**

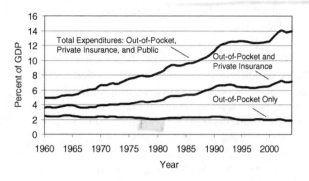

Health care expenditures in the United States have risen from about 5 percent of GDP in 1960 to 14 percent of GDP in 2004. (Source: Various editions of the Statistical Abstract of the United States)

United States are less likely to be provided by the public sphere. Perhaps the most vivid example of this difference is with respect to health care.

Health care

Health care is one of the fastest growing industries in the United States. In 2006, about 10 percent of the nation's workers were employed in the health care sector. As shown in Figure 8.8, national health-care expenditures have grown from about 5 percent of GDP in 1960 to 14 percent of GDP in 2004. Out-of-pocket costs (the amounts paid by individuals) have remained relatively constant over the years, but both private insurance and public costs have risen considerably. In 2004 annual per capita spending on health services and supplies in the United States was $5,900. The main categories of health-care expenditures include hospital care (32 percent of total health care costs in 2004), physician and clinical services (23 percent), prescription drugs (12 percent), and nursing home care (7 percent). Health care costs are expected to increase further, and become an even greater share of GDP, as the population ages and medical technology continues to become more sophisticated.

While the share of health expenditures made by the public sphere has increased in recent decades, public funding of health care in the United States is much smaller as a share of total health-care costs than in any other developed nation. In 2004 public funding paid for 45 percent of health-care costs in the United States, while the average among twenty-nine industrialized nations (including the United States) was 73 percent.

The dominance of private markets for heath care in the United States has not kept health-care spending or costs low. In fact, the United States spends a greater share of its GDP for health care than any other developed nation. While the United States spends about 14 percent of GDP for health care, Canada spends 10 percent, Sweden spends 9 percent, and the United Kingdom spends 8 percent. Also, health care prices in the United States are rising much faster than prices in general. Between 2000 and 2004 the consumer price index for medical care rose 19 percent while the overall price index only rose 10 percent. Health insurance premiums are rising at an even faster rate.

Given that these expenditures are so high in the United States, is the quality of health care better than in other developed nations? Using several common measures of national health, the

United States actually ranks lower than most other developed nations; this country has a relatively low number of physicians per capita and a lower-than-average rate of childhood immunization. Average life spans are less than in most other developed nations, and infant mortality rates are slightly above the norm.

These averages, however, fail to demonstrate the disparities in the American health-care system (see the News in Context box below). The United States offers some of the highest-quality medical care in the world; wealthy individuals from other nations often come to the United States to receive the best care possible. However, unlike all other developed nations, the United States does not have publicly funded universal health care coverage. About 16 percent of Americans were without any health insurance in 2006, and this percentage increased in recent years.

Thus the United States provides excellent health care for those who can afford it or have sufficient insurance, while those without insurance often go without cost-effective routine and preventative care. Many uninsured people resort to using emergency rooms as a source of primary care, which is partially responsible for the high health-care costs in the country. Comparisons between the United States health-care system and systems in other parts of the world raise the question of whether our costs would be lower, and health outcomes improved, under a system of universal coverage. In the past, medical and insurance industry lobbies have defeated efforts to shift responsibility for health insurance from employers to the government. Other industries are now beginning to argue the other side, pointing out that employer-based health insurance hurts the ability of American companies to compete with corporations in other countries who do not have this responsibility, and that this system will always leave too many people uncovered.

Education

The situation with education in the United States in many ways mirrors that of health care. The quality of education in American can be excellent, and many foreigners come to the United States for their higher education; about 20 percent of graduate students in the United States are foreign-born. Spending per student in the United States on elementary and secondary education is significantly higher than the OECD average (only Switzerland and Luxembourg spend more), and the United States spends more per student than any other nation on postsecondary education. However, the performance of American students is only mediocre. In a standardized test given in 2003 to fifteen-year-old students in forty nations with varying levels of economic development, U.S. students ranked twenty-eighth in math, eighteenth in reading, and twenty-second in science.

Education in the United States is provided by both public and private institutions. Education services employed about 9 percent of workers in 2006. There are about 73 million students enrolled in American schools; about 85 percent of these are in public schools. Among people twenty-five and older in the United States in 2005, 85 percent had graduated from high school and 28 percent had college degrees. Educational attainment differs by race and gender. For example, while 28 percent of whites had a college degree in 2005, only 18 percent of blacks and 12 percent of those of Hispanic origin had completed college. Although males are more likely than females to have a college degree (29 percent vs. 27 percent), more females are enrolled in college than males.

4.2 FINANCIAL AND INSURANCE SERVICES

Financial services include the management of stocks, mutual funds, money market accounts, and other investments, all of which are referred to as **financial assets**. About half of the nation's

NEWS IN CONTEXT:
Declare War on Diabetes

The neighborhoods where diabetes runs rampant are almost always short on parks for exercise and have schools that rarely conduct gym classes. Fast food restaurants abound; healthy food is often expensive or unavailable and bad diet choices—laden with sugar, fat and calories—are readily at hand. Diabetes is a disease defined by economic disparity. In heavily Hispanic East Harlem in Manhattan, the illness plagues 14 percent of the population; just to the south, across 96th Street on the more affluent Upper East Side, the rate is under 2 percent.

The sheer cost of caring for diabetics, who often do not get help until they are in catastrophic need, will keep going up. The financial burden of attending to diabetes' many uninsured victims eventually lands on state and local governments. In New York City—where one in eight adults has diabetes, almost 150 percent more than just 10 years ago—that cost is about $200 million annually and growing.

It should be no mystery that the United States, the only leading economic power without national health care, also leads the world in the per capita rate of diabetes. Care as basic as regular visits to a nutritionist is not typically covered by insurance. Reimbursement is easier when the disease is far along, and the patient needs dialysis or amputation of toes or limbs.

Source: *New York Times*, Feb. 6, 2006, Week in Review, p. 11

Health care provides an excellent example of the significance of all four of the basic economic activities. In this country a huge, and hugely important, industry trains medical personnel, supports research, and produces the other goods and services that are required in the production of health care. The distribution of health care differs widely between countries that provide over 90 percent of health care through public financing, and those that leave 90 percent of health care to be paid for privately. (The United States falls in between these extremes.) The consumption of health care—who gets how much care, of what quality—is tied closely to the distribution system. As the foregoing editorial indicates, the maintenance of health is strongly affected by the incentives built into the systems of consumption and distribution. As with many other major resources, maintenance is far less expensive than remediation—but will not receive adequate attention unless producers, distributors and consumers receive appropriate incentives.

financial assets are held by households, non-financial businesses, and governments. The rest are held by financial institutions (including banks, credit unions, pension funds, retirement funds, mutual funds, and security brokers) and insurance companies.

> **financial assets**: stocks (or shares in ownership of companies); bonds (or certificates indicating that the holder has loaned money to a government entity, which will repay the loan, with interest,

over time); money market accounts; and other holdings in which wealth can be invested with an expectation of future return

The financial and insurance sectors contributed about 8 percent of the value-added in the United States in 2005 and collectively employed about seven million people (about 5 percent of the workforce). The most common jobs in these industries are bank tellers, loan officers, and insurance agents.

Banks and credit unions, along with other institutions such as retail stores, phone companies, and oil companies, can issue credit cards to individuals and businesses. While using a debit card directly withdraws money from a checking or savings account, use of a credit card essentially amounts to a loan by the issuer. Generally, if the entire balance is paid off in a timely manner, no interest is charged to the credit card holder. If the entire balance is not paid, the issuer charges interest on the remaining balance. In general, credit card issuers charge higher rates of interest than are charged for other types of loans. For example, in 2005 the average interest rate charged for credit cards was 13 percent while the average rate on new car purchases was about 6 percent. With the deregulation of the credit card industry in the late 1970s, the maximum interest rate a credit card issuer can charge varies by state, and some states (such as South Dakota, Tennessee, and Delaware) have no legal limit on credit card interest rates.

There has been explosive growth in the use of credit cards in the United States. In 1980 credit card debt stood at $55 billion but by 2005 this had increased to $802 billion. The average American household carries a credit card debt of about $8,500 and pays $1,000 per year in credit card interest. A growing concern is the widespread use of credit cards by college students, with the average student carrying a credit card debt of over $2,000 in 2001. For more on the use, and abuse, of credit cards by college students, see the News in Context box below.

Insurances companies primarily provide life, automobile, and homeowners' policies. In 2004 there were over 1,000 life insurance companies in the United States holding over $4 trillion in assets. Americans hold about 400 million life insurance policies—an average of more than one policy per woman, man and child. The premiums charged for automobile and homeowners' insurance vary dramatically by state because of differences in state laws and regulations. For example, in 2005 the states with the highest automobile insurance premiums were New Jersey and New York at around $1,300 annually, while the lowest rates were in Iowa and Wisconsin at less than $700 per year.

4.3 RETAIL SERVICES

Few manufacturers sell their products directly to consumers. Instead, manufacturers typically sell their output to retailers, perhaps also using wholesalers as intermediaries. Retailers are categorized in the service sector because they normally do not manufacture any of the goods they sell. Prominent retailers such as Wal-Mart, Home Depot, and Borders purchase virtually all their products from suppliers.

Retail services as a whole are not becoming a larger share of the national economy, but there is a clear trend toward the dominance of a small number of very large retailers. We can use data on concentration ratios to illustrate the ascendancy of these firms. Figure 8.9 shows the change in the four-firm concentration ratios* for several types of retailers between 1992 and 2002. In

---

* A four-firm concentration ratio is calculated by dividing the domestic revenues of the four largest firms in an industry by the total domestic revenues in the industry.

NEWS IN CONTEXT:
Beyond Their Means

As college costs have increased, so has the cost of the college lifestyle, spurring millions of young adults ready to enter the professional world to take on an oppressive yoke of debt.

A 2000 survey by Nellie Mae, a leading provider of student loans, reports that 78 percent of undergraduate students [who apply for student loans] have credit cards, up from 67 percent in 1998. Of that 78 percent, nearly a third have four or more cards. For that same 78 percent, average credit card debt is $2,748. About 13 percent are $3,000-$7,000 in debt and about 9 percent have more than $7,000 in credit card debt.

That sucks," says Danette Tidwell of the Texas branch of the Jump$tart Coalition for Personal Financial Literacy, which pushes for financial literacy training in public school grades K-12. "It's deadly. It's one of the leading reasons second-year students drop out of college. They needed a second job to pay their bills."

It's a huge problem nationwide," said Dottie Bagwell, assistant professor of financial planning at Texas Tech University. "There are students living someone else's life, with somebody else's spending plan."

Students who haven't been exposed to revolving charge accounts before don't realize that the minimum payment on a credit bill is just that—a minimal payment. Soon, after several months of spending with minimal paybacks, the students are under an enormous amount of debt. "They don't realize they can't afford everything their parents can afford," said Dara Duguay, national director of Jump$tart. "They don't draw the connection that they can't afford it if they don't have the income for it."

Source: Roy Bragg, *San Antonio Express-News,* July 19, 2003.

What are some of the benefits of having credit cards while a college student? What are some of the dangers?

---

each case we can see the growing share of revenues captured by the largest four firms in the industry.

Large retailers have come to dominate their industries by offering consumers an array of choices and low prices. In the parlance of microeconomics, many of these retail industries are clearly oligopolistic, meaning that they are dominated by a small number of companies. However, the economic scale of the largest retailers has become so large that the behavior of individual firms has implications at the macroeconomic level. In 2006 Wal-Mart was the world's largest firm by revenues, with sales of $351 billion, and the world's largest employer with about two million employees.

Some researchers believe that a major reason productivity increased so much in the United States in the late 1990s is a result of Wal-Mart's pressure on suppliers to increase their efficiency.

Figure 8.9   **Four-Firm Concentration Ratios in Retail Industries, 1992–2002**

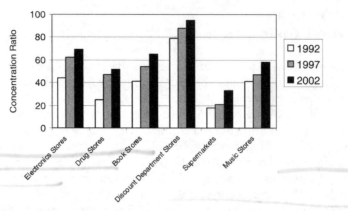

The four-firm concentration ratios in these retail industries have all increased since 1992. (Source: Economic Census publications, United States Census Bureau)

As another example of Wal-Mart's pervasive reach, the decline of the American textiles industry, described earlier in this chapter, can be partly attributed to Wal-Mart's search abroad for low-priced apparel. Consider that an estimated 10 percent of Chinese imports to the United States are for Wal-Mart. Economy-wide impacts such as these blur traditional distinctions between microeconomics and macroeconomics and call for new lines of research and analysis.

4.4 CONCLUDING THOUGHTS

The purpose of this chapter has been to provide a bird's-eye view of what the U.S. economy consists of. We have looked at primary sector activities that provide the raw materials on which everything else depends, noting that the importance of these activities is belied by the small percentage of GDP devoted to them. We have looked at secondary sector activities that process physical materials, turning them into goods for sale. And we have looked at the tertiary sector which accounts for about three-quarters of the economic activity in the United States.

This chapter has, we hope, given you a grasp of what goes on in the business sphere of the contemporary United States economy, as well as a little insight into the government part of the public-purpose sphere. But it should be evident that the relation between business sphere activity and well-being is by no means one-to-one. Measures of economic flows may be poor indicators of what matters most to people, or of how we spend most of our time. The statistics cited throughout this chapter have only covered the activities that go through the market. Goods, and especially services, that are not bought or sold do not show up in the national accounts. For example, the range of leisure activities includes things for which we pay, such as going to concerts, and being able to stay in hotels and motels when we travel. Other leisure activities enter the market through sales of music CDs, sports equipment, toys, materials for crafts and hobbies, etc. But our entertainments and relaxations also include many things for which we pay little or nothing: getting together with friends, walking or biking, reading, and so on. A sales-hungry economy finds ever more ways to sell equipment or fashionable gear that we can use in our leisure time; but still, much of what we do for fun is missed in the national accounts.

Also missing are the unpaid activities that may or may not be thought of as work but that are essential for maintaining the physical and social infrastructure of our lives—including preparing the food that is required for life itself. Again, seemingly inherent in our system is a drive to find ever more ways to replace what we do for ourselves with marketed services or products; the replacement of much home cooking with fast food, take-outs and rapid meal delivery is a prime example. Still, the services that people provide as friends, neighbors, family members, and citizens continue to be a large part of the economy, though unmeasured by flows of money, and therefore missing from GDP. Recall from Chapter 6 that even the most conservative estimates of the total value of household production come up with numbers equal to 25–35 percent of standard GDP in the United States.

In other words, the economy is bigger than it looks if we count only the economic activities that go through markets. In the larger, real economy, covering the core as well as the business and public-purpose spheres, the tertiary sector would still loom very large—much of the (non-monetized) economic activity in the core sphere is services—but its expansion would be largely in the areas of "private social services" and "entertainment."

Discussion Questions

1. Section 4.1 seems to present another surprising contradiction. Economic theory suggests that goods and services provided in competitive markets by private enterprises will result in lower prices compared to providing similar products through the public sector. But we've learned that the United States actually has the highest health-care costs in the world, although not better health outcomes than countries that provide public health care. Do you think the United States should provide health coverage to everyone through a public system? If so, do you think such a proposal could be politically feasible in the near future?

2. Try to estimate what share of your total expenditures is spent on products from the primary, secondary, and tertiary sectors. How do you think your expenditure patterns will change in the future? For example, assuming your income will rise when you graduate, do you see your share of expenditures on services increasing or decreasing?

REVIEW QUESTIONS

1. List and define the three major sectors of the United States economy, as discussed in this chapter.
2. Approximately what percentage of the United States GDP is produced in each of the three sectors? How has this allocation changed over time?
3. Summarize how agriculture in the United States has changed over the last century. About how much of each dollar spent on food currently goes to farmers?
4. Does the declining share of the primary sector imply that it is becoming less important?
5. What is the largest source of energy in the United States? What is the largest use of energy?
6. Why does the number of new housing starts in the United States show a cyclical pattern?
7. Contrast the recent history of the American textile and automobile industries.
8. Are some politicians correct when they say that American manufacturing jobs have been shifted overseas?
9. Is the service sector synonymous with low-paying jobs?

10. Summarize the state of health care in the United States.
11. What trend was emphasized in the chapter concerning retail services?

EXERCISES

1. Match each statement in Column A with a percentage in Column B.

Column A	Column B
13% a. The government percentage of U.S. GDP 3	1. 22%
83 b. The percentage of U.S. workers working in the tertiary 7 sector	2. 39%
39 c. The percentage of U.S. energy from petroleum 2	3. 13%
69 d. The percentage of Americans who own their own home 5	4. 3%
30 e. The percentage decline in U.S. manufacturing jobs since 1979 8	5. 69%
22 f. The secondary sector's share of the U.S. private economy 1	6. 45%
45 g. The percentage of U.S. health care costs paid for with public funding 6	7. 83%
3% h. The primary sector's share of the U.S. private economy 4	8. 30%

2. Search the Internet or other news sources for a recent article discussing the loss of U.S. jobs to other countries. Based on what you've learned in this chapter, present a critique of the article. Can you find any statements in the article that you think may be inaccurate?

3. The U.S. Bureau of Economic Analysis is the source of much of the data presented in this chapter. The BEA publishes "Annual Industry Account" on its website at http://www.bea.gov/industry. Find the table entitled "Value Added by Industry as a Percentage of Gross Domestic Product" and compare the data for the most recent year with Table 1.1 of this chapter. Has the percentage of U.S. GDP attributed to the primary, secondary, tertiary, and government sectors increased or decreased? Do these newer data continue the trends presented in Figure 8.1?

4. Match each statement in Column A with an answer in Column B.

Column A	Column B
a. The largest of the three economic sectors by value added 6	1. Cyclical
b. The smallest of the three economic sectors by value added 3	2. Ford Motor Company
c. An example of a business in the primary sector 7	3. Primary
d. An example of a business in the secondary sector 2	4. Wal-Mart
e. An example of a business in the tertiary sector 4	5. Declining
f. The current trend regarding the size of the secondary sector 5	6. Tertiary
g. The current trend regarding the size of the tertiary sector 8	7. A local farmer's market
h. The typical trend regarding the number of housing starts 1	8. Increasing

APPENDIX: THE TERTIARY SECTOR IN THE OVERALL MACRO CONTEXT

Early in this chapter we gave an intuitive explanation for why, even though people are just as dependent as they have always been on the materials extracted from nature, the primary sector has nevertheless shrunk in economic importance as societies have industrialized. It was not hard to explain how for a while manufacturing came to claim a larger part of every household budget, and therefore of the total economy, but we are still left with questions about how "services" (a broad term that covers much) have come to be so significant.

Figure 8.10   **Classification of GDP in the United States, 2005**

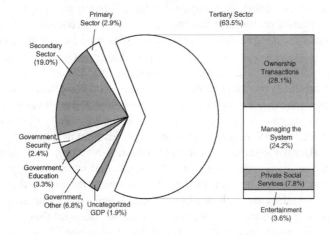

The production of services, accounting for nearly two-thirds of GDP in the United States, can be best understood if broken down into several additional categories.

Figure 8.10 is a depiction of the United States economy which we have assembled to take a closer look at the tertiary sector. It starts from the value-added approach to national accounting that was used for Table 8.1, earlier in this chapter. This approach, as you may remember from Chapter 5, includes intermediate inputs such as wholesale and retail trade, as well as management of companies and enterprises. The primary and secondary sectors of the economy are shown in Figure 8.10 in the same proportions as those given in Table 8.1. Government, shown as 12.6 percent of GDP in Table 8.1, is now divided into three portions. The two largest areas of government production are security (including national defense and public order and safety) and education. "Government-other" is compiled by adding up such categories as the salaries of elected officials, tax collection and financial management, transportation, natural resources, housing, and health.* It does not, however, include transfer payments such as welfare and disability.

Figure 8.10 then illustrates one potential way to further categorize the tertiary sector. These divisions are the authors' classification and do not represent any official government classification scheme. The four divisions presented in the figure are explained below.

- The largest category of activities that are reflected in GDP has been named, here, "OWN-ERSHIP TRANSACTIONS." Nearly 8 percentage points of this category represent the imputed value, to each homeowner, of the ongoing value of being able to live in that house. The remainder—a little over 20 percent of GDP—is essentially about buying and selling, covering activities that transfer ownership of goods and services from producers to buyers, or from previous owners to new owners. This includes transportation and

---

* Total government outlays are about 20 percent of GDP, but transfer payments do not represent an increase in output and are therefore not included in the government's contribution to GDP. Remember from Chapter 5 that, in the cases where "government production" cannot be evaluated by sale prices set in markets, its value is sometimes imputed as the cost of inputs, such as salaries paid to government employees. Note that some government salaries, housing costs, etc. could be allocated to government's production in the areas of defense and education; a more precise breakdown than that which can readily be extracted from BEA statistics would increase the amounts under these headings, while decreasing "government-other."

warehousing, wholesale and retail trade, and real-estate rental and leasing (aside from the already mentioned imputed value of homeownership).

Transportation and transportation-related activities that allow people in a modern society to acquire items that were not produced locally are an important part of "ownership transactions." They make it possible for you to enjoy fruits and vegetables when they are out of season for where you live, goods that are not produced in your area, and goods that you can purchase more cheaply because they were produced in other parts of the country—or, more often, of the world—where the cost is lower (leaving aside, for the moment, feelings you may have about the variety of reasons why production costs for certain goods are lower in some places than in others).

Another significant portion of the value-added in this category may be traced to "the middle man"—the person or organization that smoothes the transaction between the final buyer and the original producer, or between the previous owner and the next one (as is often the case with stocks and bonds, real estate, fine arts, and other things that tend to have a sequence of owners). It is sometimes said that a way to lower prices without hurting producers is to "get rid of the middle man," that is, to find a way to put the end user directly in contact with the producer. Perhaps more of this will happen over time, via the World Wide Web. In the meantime, in an advanced economy in which there is a huge amount of choice, for buyers, among objects that can come from anywhere in the world, it is not surprising that a significant portion of GDP should be devoted to making these connections.

• The next largest category, "MANAGING THE SYSTEM," covers the marketed services that keep the economic system going. These include information, finance and insurance, and professional, scientific, and technical services.* The category also includes the activities that the Bureau of the Census calls administrative and waste management, and management of companies and enterprises.

This category is about the organization and management of a hugely complex system—or, more accurately, a set of systems. Our society has come a long way from the relatively simple economies we described early in this chapter, when discussing how the secondary sector grew relative to the primary sector. Firms are more numerous; large (and enormous) firms are more numerous; and there is much organization and management to be done in negotiating the networks of relations inside these firms, and among them. Governments do some of this organization and management, and they in turn, along with the firms, need many kinds of support. Many individuals and families, too, have resources that they can use to purchase support for the complexities of operating in an industrialized world. The kinds of support that individuals and organizations want and can pay for include insurance and advice about insurance, as well as advice and assistance with the management and operation of hard-to-understand technologies, from automobile repair to cable company services.

• "PRIVATE SOCIAL SERVICES" (within the tertiary sector) covers only those portions of education, health care and social assistance that are not covered by government; they

---

* A major part of the finance industry is the buying and selling of paper or electronic claims to ownership of productive resources, such as stocks. The financial advisors, investment companies, and other money managers whose salaries, bonuses, etc., are represented as "finance" in "managing the system" are sometimes selling the right to own a piece of a new company; more often they are reselling previously owned stocks and bonds. If we could readily sort out these activities, it would perhaps be appropriate to move them to the category, "ownership transactions."

do not cover the cost of materials (such as medical supplies) that would show up as products of the secondary sector.

- The category "ENTERTAINMENT" is partially about "what we do for fun"; it covers services sold in relation to arts, entertainment and recreation, and accommodation and food services. Thus, for example, it comprises wages for musicians, but not the sale price of a new painting (accounted as a secondary sector product); it covers payments for movie tickets and wages for hotel and restaurant personnel as well as the people working in retail and wholesale who sell DVDs or food, but not the materials or manufacturing cost of DVDs or of food (whose value is divided between the primary and secondary sectors). A significant portion of this category is also work-related, including business lunches, accommodations for business trips, etc.

You may, after reading all of this, still have some questions about the relative emphasis given in our economy to different things. Yes, you may say, this is a complicated world, in which much effort is required just to make it all work—hence the large size of the tertiary sector. But surely education, social services, and entertainment are areas that are especially important for the quality of our lives, so why are these so relatively small? One answer may be found in the accounting approaches that were described in Chapter 5; for example, health care is easier to identify, and therefore looms much larger in the "spending approach" to national accounting than in the "product approach" we have used in this chapter. But another important point, as noted in the Concluding Thoughts section of this chapter (above), is that all of these accounts leave out non-marketed activities such as leisure and household production.

Part Three
Macroeconomic Theory and Policy

9 Aggregate Demand and Economic Fluctuations

What if, in a sophisticated contemporary economy such as that in the United States, many people were to suddenly decide to cut way back on buying things? You may have heard it said that it is people's *duty* to keep on spending, in order to keep the economy humming and employment high. National leaders have been known to exhort people to keep on buying things if it looks like the economy might be turning toward a recession. When environmentalists or people concerned about the harms of consumerism talk about cutting back on wasteful consumption, their opponents often respond that this would be "bad for the economy" because it would lead to a reduced level of economic activity and an increase in unemployment. How can we understand these various arguments?

1. THE BUSINESS CYCLE

Part Three of this textbook focuses in particular on the goal of economic stabilization—that is, keeping unemployment and inflation at acceptable levels over the business cycle. For the moment, we will set aside consideration of our two other goals—the goal of improvement in true living standards and the goal of maintaining the ecological, social, and financial sustainability of a national economy—in order to focus only on stabilization. As we will see, one crucial key to understanding macroeconomics is comprehending how the amount that people want to spend overall (or "aggregate demand," as we called it in Chapter 1) influences, and is influenced by, other macroeconomic variables. One of the key debates in macroeconomic policy is between Keynesians, who believe that aggregate demand needs active guidance if the economy is to be stable, and the classicals, who believe that aggregate demand can take care of itself.

In Chapter 1 we introduced the notion of the "business cycle," while in Chapter 7 we considered in detail how employment and unemployment vary over the cycle. Now we look in more detail at business cycles, or recurrent fluctuations in the level of national production, with alternating periods of recession and boom.

1.1 WHAT HAPPENS DURING THE BUSINESS CYCLE

Figure 9.1 shows the pattern of real GDP growth over the period 1985–2005. In most years, as you can see, GDP grew. But during two periods—during 1990–91 and during 2001—GDP "growth" went the other way. The level of real GDP actually went *down* from one calendar quarter to the next. As noted in Chapter 7, the National Bureau of Economic Research (NBER) declares a "recession" when economic activity declines, relying most heavily on GDP statistics to make this judgment. In other periods, you can see that GDP grows quite sharply. The positive GDP growth since 2001 shown in Figure 9.1 continued well into 2007, but as this textbook is

Figure 9.1   **U.S. Real GDP and Recessions**

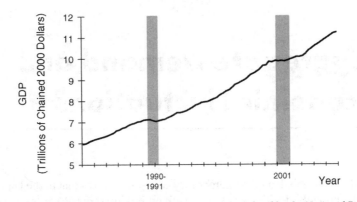

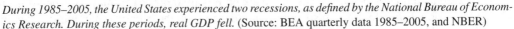

During 1985–2005, the United States experienced two recessions, as defined by the National Bureau of Economics Research. During these periods, real GDP fell. (Source: BEA quarterly data 1985–2005, and NBER)

being written in early 2008 there is speculation about whether the economy is again entering a recession. Macroeconomic stabilization policy attempts to smooth out such variations.

As we discuss the ins and outs of stabilization policy, there are two "stylized facts" that you need to keep in mind. Economists call these "stylized facts" because, while they form a very important base for the way we think about the economy, they are not always literally true.

Stylized Fact #1: During an economic downturn or contraction, unemployment rises, while in a recovery or expansion, unemployment falls. This is fairly easy to understand, since, when production in an economy is falling, it would seem natural to assume that producers need fewer workers—because they are producing fewer goods. Similarly, in an expansion, unemployment falls.* Some economists like to think of this relationship as being determined by an equation they call **Okun's law**. In the early 1960s economist Arthur M. Okun estimated that a 1 percent drop in the unemployment rate was associated with an approximately 3 percent boost to real GDP. The equation for Okun's "law" has been estimated many times since then, and in many different variations, and is best regarded as a rule of thumb rather than a "law."

> **Okun's "law":** an empirical inverse relationship between the unemployment rate and rapid (above-average) real GDP growth

We can see some strong evidence of this inverse relationship between output growth and employment by comparing Figure 9.1 with Figure 9.2, which shows the unemployment rate from 1985 to 2005, including the two recessions that occurred during this twenty-year period, as identified by the National Bureau of Economic Research. As output turns down in Figure 9.1, unemployment shoots up dramatically in Figure 9.2. The inverse relation, however, is not perfect. The unemployment rate continued to rise even after GDP started to rise again, after the last two recessions. These were the "jobless recoveries" discussed in Chapter 7. But, for most of Part Three of this book, we will assume that rising GDP is associated with increased employment.

---

* In a "jobless recovery," real GDP growth is slow (below average) so that it does not create jobs fast enough to counteract the normal increase in the labor force and decrease in labor demand due to increased output per worker.

Figure 9.2   **U.S. Unemployment Rate and Recessions**

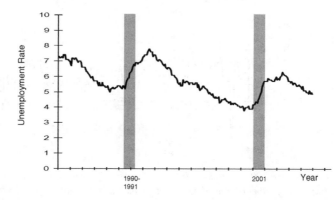

During the 1990–1991 and 2001 recessions, unemployment shot up sharply. (Source: BLS monthly data 1985–2005, and NBER)

Stylized Fact #2: An economic recovery or expansion, if it is very strong, tends to lead to an increase in the inflation rate. During a downturn or contraction, pressure on inflation eases off (and inflation may fall or even become negative). The reasoning behind this result is that, as an economy "heats up," producers come more and more into competition with each other for a limited supply of raw materials, labor, and so on. Prices and wages tend to be bid up, and inflation results or intensifies. In a slump, this upward pressure on prices slackens, or even reverses, so inflation may be lower or even, in some cases, negative (deflation). The picture most economists have in mind when they think of the link between booms and inflation is the Phillips curve that we explored in Chapter 2. That curve showed how, as output expanded and unemployment fell during the 1960s, the U.S. economy also experienced rising inflation. Figure 9.3 shows the inflation rate over the period 1985–2005, including the same two recessions highlighted in Figures 9.1 and 9.2.

Like the relation between booms and employment, the relation between booms and inflation is also only "stylized." You can see that, as expected, the two recessions shown in Figure 9.3 were accompanied by distinct downturns in the inflation rate. But wide fluctuations in the inflation rate also occurred during other periods, with both increases and downturns occurring during economic upswings. Business-cycle-led variations in the degree of competition for workers and resources is only *one* cause—and, in recent decades, not the most important cause—of variations in inflation. In Chapter 12 we will look at this issue more closely. But, for the discussion of business cycles in this and the following two chapters, we will assume that booms lead to at least a threat of rising inflation.

1.2 A STYLIZED BUSINESS CYCLE

When analyzing business cycles, it is often convenient to abstract away from the issue of economic growth. In Figure 9.1 the most striking pattern is the overall growth trend in GDP. For the analysis in Part Three of this book it will be more helpful to mentally remove the upward trend, and to think of business cycles in terms of the stylized picture shown in Figure 9.4. (We will return to the subjects of growth and development in Part Four.)

During a contraction, GDP falls until the economy hits the trough or lowest point. During an expansion, GDP rises from a trough until it reaches a peak. In Figure 9.4, the idea that there is a

Figure 9.3 **U.S. Inflation Rate and Recessions**

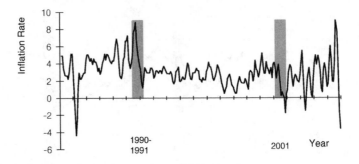

During the 1990–91 and 2001 recessions, inflation fell sharply. While inflation is thought to move countercyclically in general, other factors besides the stage of the business cycle also affect its behavior. (Source: *Economic Report of the President* 1985–2005; rate is calculated as a three-month moving average of the CPI; NBER)

Figure 9.4 **A Stylized Business Cycle**

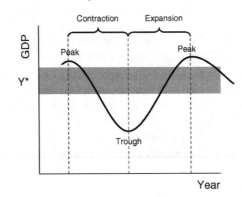

In this hypothetical economy, GDP contracts from peaks to troughs, and expands from troughs to peaks. The problem of macroeconomic instability can be characterized as a tendency of output to range outside its "full employment" band, indicated by Y*.

range of output levels that represent "full employment" is represented by the gray area labeled with the value *Y**. As we saw in Chapter 7, there is much controversy about what "full employment" means over the business cycle, so we have used a range rather than a specific level of GDP here to indicate **"full-employment output"** for modeling purposes. (Sometimes you may also see this referred to as "potential output.") At full-employment output the economy is, presumably, not suffering from an unemployment problem. But neither is the unemployment rate actually zero (as measured by the Bureau of Labor Statistics), due to the existence of at least some very short-term, transitory, unemployment.

> **"full-employment output" (Y*):** For modeling purposes, a level of output that is assumed to correspond to a case of no excessive or burdensome unemployment, but the likely existence of at least some transitory unemployment

What economists generally do agree on is that there have been—historically, at least—episodes when economies have "overheated" and output has gone above this range—giving rise

Table 9.1   **The Early Years of the Great Depression in the United States**

		1929	1933
(a)	Real Standard and Poor's Stock Index	100.0	45.7
(b)	Unemployment rate (official)	3.2%	24.9%
(c)	Price level (CPI)	100.0	75.4
(d)	Real gross domestic product	865.2 billion	635.5 billion
(e)	Real personal consumption expenditures	661.4 billion	541.0 billion
(f)	Real gross private domestic investment	91.3 billion	17 billion
(g)	Real private debt	88.9 billion	102.0 billion
(h)	Bankruptcy cases	56,867	67,031
(i)	Non-farm real estate foreclosures	134,900	252,400
(j)	Food energy *per capita* per day (calories)	3460	3280

Sources: (a) from *Historical Statistics of the United States,* p. 1004, series X495.; (b)-(c) from Dornbusch, Fischer, & Startz (2001);(d)-(f) from *http://www.bea.doc.gov/bea/dn/nipaweb/TableView.asp#Mid;* (g) from *Historical Statistics of the United States,* p. 989, series X399.; (h) from Bradley Hansen and Mary Eschenbach Hansen, *The Transformation of Bankruptcy in the United States* (http://academic2.american. edu/~mhansen/transform.pdf); (i) from *Historical Statistics of the United States,* p. 651, series N301; (j) from Ibid., p. 328, series 851; (d) and (e) are inflation-corrected using (b)

(by Stylized Fact #2) to inflationary pressures. And there have been episodes when economies have fallen into troughs, with (due to Stylized Fact #1) unacceptable levels of unemployment. In this stylized representation of the business cycle, the goal of stabilization policy is to keep an economy in the grey area, avoiding the threats of inflation and unemployment.

1.3 THE DOWNTURN SIDE OF THE STORY

It will take all of this chapter and the next three to build up a workable theory of the business cycle! Because this is a large and complex topic, we need to take things one step at a time. We will start by looking at the case of economic downturns.

The biggest downturn in U.S. history was, of course, the Great Depression. Production dropped dramatically from 1929 to 1930 and officially measured national unemployment soared, topping out at 25 percent. Some regions were especially hard-hit, with unemployment rates above the national average, and severe underemployment as well. Not only were times bad—they stayed bad. Unemployment stayed in the double-digits all through the 1930s. Nor was the Great Depression just a U.S. phenomenon. Most of this country's major trading partners were also hard-hit. Table 9.1 presents some additional descriptive data about the falloff in economic activity in the United States, and resulting hardships, during the Great Depression.

Notice that in our stylized business cycle in Figure 9.4 there is no scale on the "year" axis. The timing of the cycle is not regular or predictable, so that economists in the early years of the Depression differed on how to interpret it. Most economists in the 1930s, trained in the classical school, reassured public leaders that this sort of cycle was merely to be expected. They saw the economy as being in the "trough" stage, but it would soon start to expand again. In the long run, they assured officials, the economy would recover by itself, as it had recovered from other downturns in the past. In response, British economist John Maynard Keynes quipped that "in the long run, we are all dead." In 1936 he presented a theory for how economies can fall into recessions and stay there for a long time—and some ideas about how public policy might help economies get out of the trough more quickly. We start our detailed study of business cycle theory with models that illustrate classical and Keynesian theories concerning recession and depressions.

Discussion Questions

1. Do you know anyone who experienced the Great Depression of the 1930s? What do they say about the effects of that economic stagnation on their lives and those of their friends and neighbors?
2. Do you know what phase of the business cycle we were in two years ago? Is the U.S. economy currently in a recession or an expansion?

2. MACROECONOMIC MODELING AND AGGREGATE DEMAND

For economists, explanations often take the form of theoretical mathematical models. A theoretical model (as we saw in Chapter 2) is a "thought experiment" for helping us to see the world, which necessarily highlights some aspects of a situation. At the same time, due to simplifying assumptions, it neglects others. A mathematical model expresses the theory in terms of equations, graphs, or schedules. Models contain variables. These are abstract (simplified) representations of important macroeconomic measures—usually related to ones that we can observe empirically, such as GDP or the unemployment rate. Macroeconomists make simplifying assumptions about variables, for example assuming that all of the various interest rates that might coexist in the economy can be summarized as if they were a single one, referred to as "the interest rate." Mathematical models relate these variables together using algebraic formulas, graphs, and/or tables in such as way as to make clear how these variables affect each other, according to the theorist's understanding.

2.1 SIMPLIFYING ASSUMPTIONS

At the end of Chapter 5, you learned about the *traditional macroeconomic model* in which the economy is portrayed in a simplified form involving four sectors and a streamlined set of activities. Household expenditures on consumption, business expenditures on investment, government spending, and exchange with the foreign sector by way of net exports were said to add up to GDP. While the traditional model already abstracts away from many things—for example, from household and government investment—the models of aggregate demand we will now develop simplify even further:

- For all of the models in Part Three of this book, we will assume that the full-employment output level *does not grow*. In designing models, it is often useful to separate out different issues into different models. Chapters in Part Four of this text examine economic growth, and ignore business cycles. In Part Three, we take an opposite but complementary approach, concentrating on cycles and abstracting away from growth.
- For the remainder of the present chapter (only), we assume that the only actors in the economy are *households* and *businesses*. We also assume that all income in the economy goes to households, in return for the labor or capital services they provide. (In the real world, businesses often hold onto some of their profits as "retained earnings," rather than pay them all out to households, but we ignore that here.) We will reintroduce the government and foreign sectors in later chapters.
- For the remainder of the present chapter (only), we concentrate on the difference between the classical and Keynesian theories about the behavior of economies that face a threat of

Figure 9.5   **The Output-Income-Spending Flow of an Economy in Equilibrium**

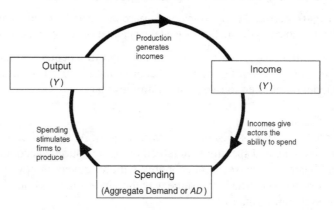

A macroeconomy is said to be in equilibrium when the incomes that arise from production give rise to a level of spending that, in turn, stimulates producers to produce the original level of output.

recession and rising unemployment due to (potentially) insufficient aggregate demand. Booms and inflationary pressures will be discussed in later chapters.

These simplifications will allow us to make some important points while still keeping the stories, with their accompanying math and graphs, reasonably simple.

2.2 OUTPUT, INCOME, AND AGGREGATE DEMAND

Recall from Chapter 5 that whether GDP is measured by the product approach or by the income approach, the number will be the same (in theory). So we defined the "*Y*" to mean "output" (or "product") or "income" interchangeably. The top arrow in Figure 9.5 illustrates that, in our simplified macroeconomy, production by firms generates labor and capital incomes to households.

But things get more interesting when we examine the flows from income into spending, and from spending (aggregate demand) to supporting a given level of output in the economy. A macroeconomy is in an *equilibrium* situation when output, income *and spending* are all in balance—when they are linked in an unbroken chain, each supported by each other at the equilibrium level, as illustrated in Figure 9.5.

But the Keynesian model turns on the idea that spending or aggregate demand, which we will denote by the symbol *AD*, may (at least temporarily) fall out of balance with the other flows. Aggregate demand in the economy depends on the spending behavior of the economic actors in the economy. Households make consumption spending decisions, and together the household sector generates an aggregate level of consumption, *C*. We assume that households always consume at the level they plan to, given their incomes—that what they end up spending is always exactly equal to what they *intended* to spend. But for firms, the situation can be more complicated, as we will see as this chapter progresses. Business firms invest, and we will call the amount they *plan* to invest over the course of a year *II* for *intended investment*. Since the only actors we are looking at right now are households and businesses, we begin our modeling of aggregate demand with the equation:

Aggregate Demand = Consumption + Intended Investment

$$AD = C + II$$

AD is the level of spending that would result if people are able to follow their plans.

> **aggregate demand (AD)** (traditional macro model with no government and a closed economy): what households and firms *intend* to spend on consumption and investment: AD = C + II

But, you might ask, didn't we say earlier (and in Chapter 5) that "output," "income," *and* "spending" are *all* just different ways of approaching GDP? The basic identity of the traditional macro model (simplified to two sectors) implies that

$$Y = C + I$$

This is true, too. $Y = C + I$ is an *accounting identity.* At the end of any year, when *actual* flows of output, income, and spending are tallied up in the national accounts, the spending by households and businesses *must* (in an economy with no government or foreign sector) be equal to GDP. This equation is true in the same way that, in business accounting, net worth is *defined as* equal to assets minus liabilities.

The equation $AD = C + II$, in contrast, represents something different. It is what is called a **behavioral equation**. It is made up by economists for modeling purposes—we do not have a national agency that looks into business leaders' minds and measures their *intentions*! You will work with *both* of the equations above later in this chapter. The accounting identity involves the *actual* level of investment, while the behavioral equation involves the level of *planned, desired, or intended* investment. While households always *actually* spend what they have *intended* to spend (so we do not need a separate symbol for "intended consumption"), *Y* and *AD* will only be the same if actual investment (*I*) is equal to intended investment (*II*).

> **behavioral equation:** in contrast to an accounting identity, a behavioral equation reflects a theory about the behavior of one or more economic agents or sectors. The variables in the equation may or may not be observable.
>
> Note that $Y = C + I$ is an *accounting identity,* which represents the actual level of aggregate spending that in fact occurs. $AD = C + II$ is a *behavioral equation,* which describes the levels of spending that economic actors *plan,* whether or not this planned level of spending matches what is actually achieved

The link from income (*Y*) to spending (*AD*) is the potential weak link in the chain illustrated in Figure 9.4. This is because the people who get the income do not just automatically go out and spend it all. This creates the problem of *leakages.*

2.3 The Problem of Leakages

The household sector, we have assumed, receives all the income in the economy. Households spend some of this income on consumption goods, and save the rest, according to the equation:

$$S = Y - C$$

where *S* is the aggregate level of saving. Saving is considered a "leakage" from the output-income-spending cycle, because it represents income that is *not* spent on currently produced goods and services. This is illustrated in Figure 9.6, which shows that some funds are *diverted* from the income-spending part of the cycle.

The other side of the coin, however, is that businesses need funds if they are going to be able to buy investment goods. (Remember, we have assumed that they do not hold onto any of the income they receive, but pass it all along to households as wages, profits, interest, or rents.) In our simple model we assume that firms must borrow from the savings put away by households

Figure 9.6   **The Output-Income-Spending Flow with Leakages and Injections**

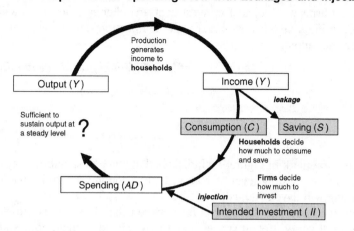

When households save rather than spend part of their incomes, funds are diverted from the income-spending flow. When firms spend on investment goods, this creates a flow into the spending stream.

in order to be able to finance investment projects. You can think of households depositing their savings in banks, with firms taking out loans from the banks to buy structures or equipment. In this way, firms can shoot funds back into the spending stream in the form of investment. This "injection" of spending through investment is also illustrated in Figure 9.6.

If the amount that households want to save is equal to the amount that firms want to invest, then these two flows will balance each other out:

In equilibrium:

leakages = injections

S = II

If the flows are in balance, then Figure 9.6 is just a more complicated version of the equilibrium situation portrayed in Figure 9.5. The income-spending flow is more complex, but all income still ends up feeding into *AD,* thus (you can mentally fill in the missing part of the circle) supporting the initial level of output. This is the kind of equilibrium you might encounter while pumping air into an inner tube that has a leak: the inner tube stays the same size because you put in more air just as fast as it is leaking out.

This can be seen mathematically as well. If we add *C* to each side of the equilibrium condition above, we get $C + S = C + II$. But from the equation defining saving (*S*) above, we know that the left side is equal to *Y,* while from the definition of aggregate demand above we know that the right side is equal to *AD.* Therefore, when leakages equal injections:

In equilibrium:

$Y = AD$

This equation says that spending is exactly sufficient to buy the output produced—the economy is in a macroeconomic equilibrium. But households and firms are two different sectors—what happens if their plans *don't* mesh?

Suppose that businesses suddenly lose confidence about the future and cut back on their plans for expansion (that is, reduce *II*). Or suppose that intended investment is unchanged, but households suddenly decide to consume less and save more, so that the flow into savings is larger than what firms want to use for investment. In either case, leakages will exceed injections. The leakage in Figure 9.6 is now larger than the injection. This means that *AD* will be smaller than income and output:

In the case of insufficient aggregate demand:

leakages > injections

$$S > II$$

$$Y > AD$$

The question mark in Figure 9.6 indicates that planned spending may or may not be sufficient to support the existing level of output. If the economy is not in macroeconomic equilibrium, something will have to adjust.

Here we reach the dividing point between the classicals and the Keynesians. These two theories tell very different stories about how this adjustment comes about. We will start with the classical story.

2.4 THE CLASSICAL SOLUTION TO LEAKAGES

In the classical model, we are essentially always in a perfectly balanced world, where output is always at its full-employment level. We saw in Chapter 7, looking at business cycles from an employment perspective, that classical economists believed that falling wages in flexible labor markets would bring the economy back to full employment. For the moment we will put this labor market story into the background, and ask our business cycle question in another way: How does an economy (which we assume to be running along at a full-employment level of production) keep leakages into saving *exactly equal to* injections coming from investment spending? Or, expressing this another way, how can the economy respond to a sudden shift in saving or intended investment that might cause insufficient aggregate demand? The classical argument is again, not surprisingly, that flexible markets will keep the economy at a full-employment level of spending and output.

In this case the relevant market is what economists call the market for *loanable funds*. In our very simple model, households save out of income from current production. Since they can earn interest on any savings they deposit in a bank rather than stuff under a mattress, they will prefer the bank. In this market, households are the *suppliers* of loanable funds and firms are the *demanders* of loanable funds. The classical theory about the market for loanable funds is illustrated in Figure 9.7. The vertical axis is the interest rate being paid from firms to households, which acts as the "price" of loanable funds.

The classicals assume that households make their decisions about how much to save by looking at the going rate of interest in this market. The higher the interest rate, the more worthwhile it is to save, because their savings earn more. The lower the interest rate, the less appealing it is to save. So the supply of loanable funds (saving) curve in Figure 9.7 is upward sloping.

To firms, on the other hand, the payment of interest is a cost. So when interest rates are low, this model assumes, firms will want to borrow more for investment projects because borrowing is inexpensive. High interest rates, in contrast, will discourage firms from borrowing. The demand curve in Figure 9.7 thus slopes downward. Where the curves cross determines the equilibrium "price" of funds—here, the interest rate of 5 percent—and the equilibrium quantity of funds borrowed and lent. In Figure 9.7, the amount saved by households and loaned out is 140—which is

Figure 9.7   **The Classical Model of the Market for Loanable Funds**

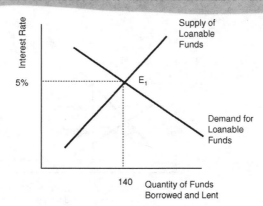

In the classical version of the macroeconomic model, household saving creates the supply of loanable funds and firms' borrowing for investment creates the demand for loanable funds. At the equilibrium interest rate, the amount households save and the amount businesses invest are equated.

also the amount borrowed and invested by firms.* (All numbers in our simple models are made up, and set to be easy numbers to handle. You could think of the unit for our numbers for Y, AD, C, I and S as billions of real dollars in some fictional economy.)

In Figure 9.8 we illustrate what happens in the classical model if, after starting from a position at point E_0 (which we will assume corresponds to a full-employment balance of S and I), firms suddenly change their plans, deciding to spend less on investment. The demand for loanable funds curve shifts leftward. If the interest rate remained at 5 percent, we would see a big drop in investment. But because the interest rate falls to 3 percent, part of the drop in investment will be reversed as firms take advantage of the cheaper loans. And because the interest rate is now lower, some households will choose to save less and consume more (indicated by the movement down along the supply curve). In the end, saving and (both intended and actual) investment will still be equal to each other, though at a lower level—in Figure 9.8, the level had dropped to 60. Aggregate demand will still be equal to the full-employment level—though now it is made up of somewhat less investment, and somewhat more consumption, than before the shift in investment plans. In short, the fall in intended investment was balanced by an increase in consumer spending (a decrease in saving).

In the classical model, both households' saving activity and firms' investment spending are assumed to be quite sensitive to changes in the interest rate, which serves as the "price of loanable funds." An adjustment in the interest rate, they theorize, can be trusted to quickly correct any threat of imbalances between the leakage of savings and the injection of investment. The interest rate is assumed to adjust quickly in a free-market economy. With saving and intended investment always in balance, there is no reason to think that the economy would ever diverge from full employment. The economy is thus self-sustaining at full employment due to the smooth working of the market for loanable funds (see Figure 9.9). We will assume (for now) that the level of output that corresponds to full employment is clearly known. As earlier in this chapter, we use the symbol Y^* to denote this level (or range of levels) of output and income.

---

* In the real world, households and institutions, firms, governments and the foreign sector all borrow and lend for various reasons, and much of the supply and demand for loanable funds reflects transactions in existing assets that have little to do with current flows of production and income. This model abstracts from these complications.

Figure 9.8   **Adjustment to a Reduction in Intended Investment in the Classical Model**

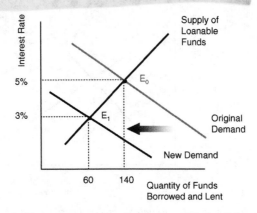

In the classical model, smooth adjustments in the market for loanable funds keep saving equal to investment, even if firms or households change their behavior.

Figure 9.9   **Macroeconomic Equilibrium at Full Employment in the Classical Model**

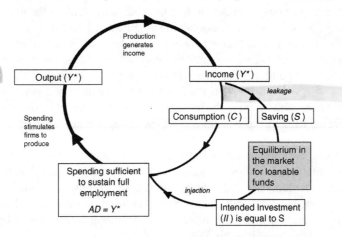

Leakages always equal injections in the classical model, because of smooth adjustments in the market for loanable funds. The economy is always in equilibrium at a full employment level of output (Y*).

During the Great Depression, however, the economy clearly did fall into a situation of severe and prolonged unemployment. People came to be dissatisfied with the classical theory. Could there be something wrong with this story? Could another theory do a better job of explaining the Depression—and even better, point toward how the economy might get out of it?

Discussion Questions

1. Who are the actors in this simple economic model? What is the role of each in determining the flow of currently produced goods and services? What is the role of each in the classical market for loanable funds?

2. Explain verbally why, in the classical model, the demand for loanable funds curve slopes downward. Explain verbally why the supply of loanable funds curve slopes upward.

3. THE KEYNESIAN MODEL

Keynes' major contribution was to develop a theory to explain why aggregate demand could stay persistently low. He called it *The General Theory,* because he believed that the case of full employment (Y^*) represents only a special case, one that is not always achieved. We will present the basics of his theory using (for the moment) the very simple closed-economy, no-government, no-growth model introduced above.

3.1 CONSUMPTION

Many things may affect the level of aggregate consumption in an economy, but one thing that very clearly affects it is the level of current aggregate income. Households are able to spend more on consumption goods and services when the economy is generating a lot of income than when it is not. So Keynes used in his model a very simple *consumption function* that expresses aggregate consumption as the sum of two components: an "autonomous" part and a part that depends on the level of aggregate income. In algebraic form, the Keynesian consumption function is expressed as:

$$C = \bar{C} + mpc\ Y$$

where $\bar{C}$ is "autonomous" consumption and *mpc* is the "marginal propensity to consume." We'll discuss the economic significance of these two parts of the function first, and then put the function to work.

Autonomous consumption can be thought of as the part of consumption that is not related to income. While in mathematical terms it represents the level of consumption when Y is equal to zero, this is not a very helpful interpretation for our purposes. While *individuals* may have zero income (say, if they become unemployed), it would be highly unusual for a *whole country* to produce no GDP at all. For purposes of economic analysis, it is more helpful to think about it as something that, when it changes, shifts the consumption schedule up or down (as we will see below). Some like to think of it as a minimum level of income that people feel required to spend for survival. Others see it as reflecting the amount of consumption spending people will undertake no matter what their current incomes are, reflecting their long-term plans, their commitments and habits, and their place in the community.

But of course, much of consumption does reflect current income and its changes. The name "*mpc*" comes from the fact that this term reflects the number of additional dollars of consumption spending that occur for every additional dollar of aggregate income. Using the notation "Δ" (which is read as the Greek letter delta) to mean "change in," the marginal propensity to consume can be expressed as:

$$mpc = \Delta C\ /\Delta Y$$

= (the change of C resulting from a change in Y) ÷ (the change in Y)

In the following example, we will use an *mpc* of 8/10 or 0.8. This means that for every additional $10 of aggregate income in the economy, the household sector spends an additional $8 on consumption. Logically the *mpc* should be no greater than one: An *mpc* greater than one would mean that people increase their consumption by *more* than the addition to their incomes. An *mpc* of about 0.8 has been the standard, historically, in Keynesian modeling exercises—though such a value may not correspond well to actual data on consumption in every time period. (See News in Context, below.)

Recall that any income not spent by the household sector is saved. Parallel to the consumption function, a savings function can be derived using the equation for savings and substituting in the equation for consumption:

$$S = Y - C = Y - (\bar{C} + mpc\ Y) = -\bar{C} + (1 - mpc)\ Y$$

The term multiplying Y is called the "marginal propensity to save" :

$$mps = 1 - mpc = \Delta S / \Delta Y$$

For example, if households spend 80 percent of additional income, or $8 out of an additional $10 in income, then they must save 20 percent (= 1–80 percent), or $2 out of $10. That is, if the *mpc* is 0.8, the *mps* must be 0.2.

If we assign number values to the parameters $\bar{C}$ and *mpc,* we can express the relation between income and consumption stated in the consumption function by a schedule, as in Table 9.2. Various income levels are shown in Column (1). We will, for now, set autonomous consumption equal to 20 (as shown in Column [2]). With an *mpc* set equal to 0.8, Column (3) shows how to calculate the second component of the consumption function. Adding together the autonomous and income-related components yields total consumption, shown in Column (4). We also show in Column (5), for later reference, the implied level of saving. For example, the shaded row indicates that when income is 400, $C = 20 + 0.8 (400) = 20 + 320 = 340$. Saving is calculated as $400 - 340 = 60$. Consumption and saving both steadily rise as income rises.

We can also see the relationships among consumption, income, and saving in this model in the graph in Figure 9.10. (For a review of graphing techniques, see the Math Review box.) The horizontal axis measures income (Y) while the vertical axis measures consumption (C). The consumption function crosses the vertical axis at the level of autonomous consumption ($\bar{C}$) of 20. The line has a slope equal to the marginal propensity to consume (*mpc*) of 0.8. Figure 9.9 also includes a 45° degree line, which tells us what consumption would be if people consumed all their income instead of saving part of it. So the vertical distance between the 45 degree "consumption = income" line and the consumption function tells us how much people save. We can see, for example, that at an income of 100, households, in this model, consume all their income. At levels of income lower than 100, consumption is higher than income, and they "dissave."* At an income of 400, how much do people save? Check for yourself that the information given in Table 9.2 and Figure 9.10 for income levels of 0, 100, and 400 are in agreement.

A number of factors can cause the consumption schedule for a macroeconomy to shift. Among the significant ones are:

- Wealth. When many people in a country feel wealthier—perhaps because the stock market or housing prices are high—the household sector as a whole may tend to spend more, even if households' actual annual incomes do not change.

---

* When the household sector "dissaves" it runs *down* assets (or increases debts) in order to pay for consumption. In this case, consumption exceeds income and savings are *negative*. This has happened, at a national level, in only two periods in U.S. history: first during the Great Depression, and then again in 2005 when people were feeling wealthy because of large increases in the value of homes. In 1984 U.S. households saved 10.8 percent of their after-tax income; in 2005 the figure was –0.5 percent; in 2007 the figure was positive but less than 1 percent.

Table 9.2   **The Consumption Schedule (and Saving)**

(1) Income (Y)	(2) Autonomous Consumption ($\bar{C}$)	(3) The part of consumption that depends on income, with mpc = 0.8 =0.8 × column(1)	(4) Consumption $C = 20 + 0.8\ Y$ = column(2) + column(3)	(5) Saving $S = Y{-}C$ = column(1) − column(4)
0	20	0	20	-20
100	20	80	100	0
200	20	160	180	20
300	20	240	260	40
400	20	320	340	60
500	20	400	420	80
600	20	480	500	100
700	20	560	580	120
800	20	640	660	140

Figure 9.10   **The Keynesian Consumption Function**

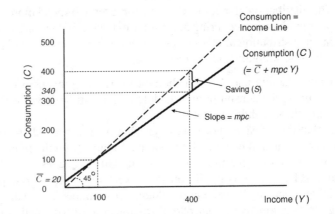

In the Keynesian model, consumption rises with income according to the equation $C = \bar{C} + mpc\ Y$

- Consumer confidence. When people feel less confident about the future—perhaps due to political turmoil or the fear of a coming recession—they may tend to hunker down and spend less on consumption goods. (See News in Context, below.)
- Attitudes toward spending and saving. If many people were to decide to consume less for reasons of health or the environment, that would also depress consumption.
- Consumption-related government policies. High levels of saving can be a source of capital for economic growth. Sometimes a country's leaders will exhort people to lower their consumption levels and raise their saving levels, in order to provide funds for investing for the future. (An exercise at the end of this chapter asks you to look at some implications of such a policy.)

Math Review Box: Graphing with a Slope-Intercept Equation

Linear equations are of the form $Y = a + bX$. On a graph the variable Y is measured on the vertical axis and the variable X is measured on the horizontal axis. X and Y are called "variables" and a and b are called "parameters." The parameter a is called "the intercept" and shows where the line representing the linear relationship between X and Y crosses the vertical axis. The parameter b is "the slope," and determines the steepness of the line. It reflects "rise over run": that is, starting from any point on the line and moving to any other point off to the right on the same line, the slope is the ratio of the number of units the line moves *upwards (rises)* to the number of units the line moves *sideways (runs)*.

The consumption function, $C = \bar{C} + mpc\, Y$, is of this same form, only with different variable and parameter names. The consumption function relates the variable C to the variable Y. It has an intercept of $\bar{C}$ and a slope of mpc.

- The distribution of income. Poorer people tend to spend more of their income than richer people, since just covering necessities may take all their income (and more). So a change in the distribution of income away from richer people toward poorer people may tend to raise consumption and depress saving.

Some of these factors may be best thought of as changing $\bar{C}$ in the Keynesian consumption function, causing the consumption schedule to shift up or down, while others may change the *mpc*, causing the schedule to rotate.

Notice that the classical model assumed that people made their decisions about how much income to consume and how much to save based largely on the interest rate, but the Keynesian model doesn't mention the interest rate at all. This is because the effects of interest rates on saving are, in fact, ambiguous. If you saw a very high interest rate prevailing in the loanable funds market—maybe 100 percent or "double your money in a year"—you might want to take advantage of it and increase your rate of saving, at least for a while. In this case you would be acting as the classicals assumed: A higher interest rate causes you to save more and consume less. But what if you are primarily saving to finance your college education, or your retirement, so you have a certain target level of accumulated wealth in mind? A higher interest rate also means that you can reach this target *faster* (and so revert to higher consumption sooner), or that you can reach the target in the same amount of time while saving *less*.

In fact, the more significant impact of changes in interest rates on household behavior comes from their effect on what households may *pay* in interest, rather than on what households may *earn*. While the simple classical model assumes that household are only on the saving and lending side of the market, in reality households frequently borrow in order to spend on capital goods for household production. When interest rates are high, households may postpone buying houses, cars, major appliances, and other consumer durables.

In any case, the simple Keynesian function we will be working with leaves the interest rate out entirely. The most important thing to remember about the Keynesian consumption function is that some amount of income generally "leaks" into saving (and so does not create aggregate

NEWS IN CONTEXT:
Spending Increases Less Than Forecast

Consumer spending and incomes in the U.S. rose less than forecast in October [2007], reinforcing Federal Reserve Chairman Ben S. Bernanke's warning of "headwinds" for the economy in coming months. The housing slump and climbing fuel bills are wearing down consumers, whose spending has helped sustain the six-year expansion. Bernanke acknowledged late yesterday that market "turbulence" tied to the collapse of the subprime mortgage market may have harmed the economy.

The 0.2 percent increase in purchases followed a 0.3 percent gain in September, the Commerce Department said today in Washington. Incomes also rose 0.2 percent. Purchases were little changed after adjusting for inflation, which are the figures used in calculating economic growth, the Commerce figures showed today. The inflation-adjusted change in spending was the smallest since March.

The savings rate fell to 0.5 percent from 0.7 percent in September.

Reports on retail spending "were downbeat in general," according to the report known as the Beige Book. Most Fed banks reported that retailers expect sales growth "to be modest at best in the upcoming holiday season," the central bank said.

Source: Joe Richter, Bloomberg.com, 11/30/2007

Why do economists worry about consumer spending slacking off?

---

demand), and that, unlike in the classical model, the interest rate is *not* considered to be an important factor in determining the size of this leakage.

3.2 INVESTMENT

In the real world, firms may take a number of things into account in thinking about how much to invest. The cost of borrowing (the interest rate) is certainly one factor, as are other things such as the prices of investment goods, their own accumulated assets and debt, and the willingness of people to lend to them. (Not everyone can qualify for a loan.) Keynes thought that, in general, interest rates were somewhat important in explaining the level of investment. But he thought that, in the case of a drastic slowdown of economic activity such as the Great Depression, a low interest rate would not be enough to motivate business firms to invest in building up new capacity. The most important factor in explaining aggregate investment spending, Keynes thought, is the general level of optimism or pessimism that investors feel about the future, or what he called "animal spirits." If firms' managers feel that they will be able to sell more of the goods or services they produce in the future, and at a good price, they will want to invest in equipment and structures to maintain and expand their capacity. If they don't see such a rosy future ahead, then how could even a low interest rate persuade them to invest? The borrowed funds will have

Figure 9.11   **The Keynesian Investment Function**

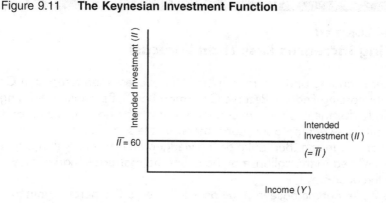

In the simplest Keynesian model, intended investment is a constant, no matter what the level of national income, being determined instead by long-term profit expectations.

to be repaid; the major question for the borrower is "are my prospects for success good enough to allow me to repay this loan?" The interest rate will change the amount to be repaid at the margin, but is not the major determinant of the answer to this question.

Because Keynes saw investment as future-directed, rather than related to any current, observable economic variables, the "function" for intended investment in the simple Keynesian model just says that investors intend to invest whatever investors intend to invest. All of intended investment is considered "autonomous" in this model. We can denote this as:

$$II = \bar{\bar{II}}$$

where $\bar{\bar{II}}$ is "autonomous intended investment." Don't worry too much about whether to put a bar over the symbol—we've introduced it here just to show you that it is similar in concept to the $\bar{C}$ in the consumption function. Just as $\bar{C}$ can go up or down depending on consumer confidence, $\bar{\bar{II}}$ can go up or down depending on investor confidence.

Figure 9.11 graphs investment against income, for the case where $\bar{\bar{II}} = 60$. Since investment does not depend on income, the graph is horizontal. The lack of attention to interest rates is a limitation of the simple Keynesian model. In later chapters we will depart from this simplification.

3.3 The Aggregate Demand Schedule

Earlier we defined *AD* as the sum of consumption and intended investment. We can now add intended investment to the consumption schedule and curve to get a schedule and graph for aggregate demand. In Table 9.3, Columns (1) and (2) just repeat Table 9.2. In Column (3) we have set intended investment equal to 60, for any level of income, in line with the notion that it is all "autonomous." Column (4) calculates the level of aggregate intended spending in the economy. We can see that when, for example, $Y = 400$, households and businesses together plan to spend 400 on consumption and investment.

Figure 9.12 shows the relationship between income and aggregate demand. The *AD* line lies exactly 60 units vertically above the *C* line, at every level of income. Its intercept is the sum of autonomous consumption and intended investment. Its slope is the same as that of the consumption function. We can see that when, for example, $Y = 400$, then $C = 340$ and $AD = 400$.

The *AD* shifts up or down as autonomous consumption or autonomous investment changes. Suppose that intended investment were 140, instead of the 60 we have been using in our example

Table 9.3   **Deriving Aggregate Demand from the Consumption Function and Investment**

(1) Income (Y)	(2) Consumption (C)	(3) Intended Investment (II)	(4) Aggregate Demand $AD = C + II$ = column (2) + column (3)
0	20	60	**80**
300	260	60	**320**
400	340	60	**400**
500	420	60	**480**
600	500	60	**560**
700	580	60	**640**
800	660	60	**720**

Figure 9.12   **Aggregate Demand**

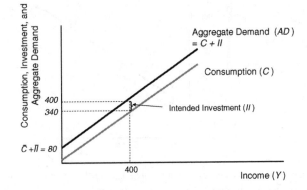

The AD curve is derived by adding the autonomous intended investment to consumption, at each income level. So at each level of Y, AD is the vertical sum of C and II.

up until now. Table 9.4 calculates *AD* for selected levels of income like those that we have used before, but with this higher level of *II*. Because neither $\bar{C}$ or the *mpc* has changed, Column (2) is the same as in earlier tables.

This aggregate demand schedule is graphed in Figure 9.13. The intercept is now 160, which is equal to $\bar{C}$ of 20 plus $\bar{II}$ of 140, while the slope is still equal to the *mpc*. Notice that now, at an income level of 400, aggregate demand is 480 instead of 400. With investment increased by 80, aggregate demand at any income level increases by 80 as well.

Figure 9.13 could also be used to illustrate an increase in $\bar{C}$ from 20 to 100 (an increase of 80) while intended investment remains at 60. Any combination of $\bar{C}$ and $\bar{II}$ that sums to 160 would yield this graph. In economic terms, any increase in consumer and investor desired spending (that is unrelated to changes in income) increases aggregate demand.

3.4 The Possibility of Unintended Investment

The key to the Keynesian model is understanding why and how *unintended* investment can occur, and how firms respond when they see it happening. Unintended investment occurs when aggregate demand is insufficient, because firms will not be able to sell all the goods they produce.

Table 9.4   **Aggregate Demand with Higher Intended Investment**

(1) Income (Y)	(2) Consumption (C)	(3) Intended Investment (II)	(4) Aggregate Demand (AD)
0	20	140	160
300	260	140	400
400	340	140	480
500	420	140	560
600	500	140	640
700	580	140	720
800	660	140	800

Figure 9.13   **Aggregate Demand with a Higher Level of Intended Investment**

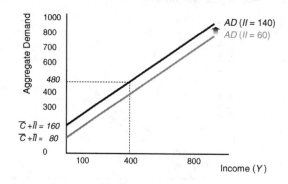

If intended investment increases (or autonomous consumption increases), the aggregate demand curve shifts upward. More output is demanded at each level of income.

Recall (from Chapter 5) that a nation's manufactured capital stock includes structures, equipment, *and inventories*. Many firms normally plan to keep as inventory some level of supplies they expect to use soon and products that they have not yet shipped out. *Unintended* inventory investment occurs when these inventories build up unexpectedly. A manufacturing firm, for example, experiences *excess inventory accumulation* when it can't sell its goods as quickly as expected and the goods pile up in warehouses. Conversely, a firm that sells its goods faster than expected experiences *excess inventory depletion,* as the goods "fly off the shelves" and the warehouse empties out.

Actual investment (*I*, as measured in the national accounts) is the sum of what businesses plan to invest, plus what they inadvertently end up investing if *AD* and *Y* don't exactly match up:

$$I = intended\ investment + excess\ inventory\ accumulation\ or\ depletion$$

In Table 9.5, columns (1) and (2) repeat information from Table 9.3, for intended investment of 60 and selected levels of income. Column (3) calculates levels of *un*intended investment. If, for example, income and output are 600 but aggregate demand is only 560, excess inventory accumulation of 40 will occur. Or, if income and output are 300 but firms and households want to buy 320, inventories will be depleted by 20 to meet the demand. Only at an income level of 400 is there a balance between income and spending.

Table 9.5   **The Possibility of Excess Inventory Accumulation or Depletion**

(1) Income (Y)	(2) Aggregate Demand (AD)	(3) Excess Inventory Accumulation (+) or Depletion (-) = column(1)- column(2)	(4) Intended Investment (II)	(5) Investment (I) = column(3) + column(4)	(6) Check that the macroeconomic identity still holds: Y = C+I
300	320	-20	60	40	300
400	400	0	60	60	400
500	480	20	60	80	500
600	560	40	60	100	600
700	640	60	60	120	700
800	720	80	60	140	800

Figure 9.14   **Unintended Investment in the Keynesian Model**

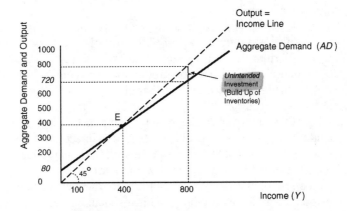

If income and output in an economy are above the level of aggregate demand, excessive inventories accumulate. This is illustrated for the income level of 800.

Columns (4) to (6) are included in Table 9.5 to show that both the equation $AD=C+II$ and the identity $Y=C+I$ hold at all times in this model. Column (5) of Table 9.5 calculates actual investment (I) as the sum of intended and unintended investment. Notice that the figures in Column (6) match those in Column (1)—when we include *unintended,* excess inventory accumulation or depletion, the basic macroeconomic identity $Y = C + I$ is still true.

Figure 9.14—often called the "Keynesian cross" diagram—illustrates this case for two income levels. The AD curve, as we know, represents the sum of consumption and investment at any income level. The dashed line is a 45-degree line that (just as in our earlier diagram about consumption, income, and saving) illustrates equality between the values on the two axes. With income on the horizontal axis and output on the vertical axis, all points on this line represent situations where output equals income. At an income level of 800, the AD curve indicates that aggregate demand is 720. But the "output = income" line indicates that output is 800, and so exceeds spending. There is unintended inventories build-up of 80, as indicated by the vertical distance between the AD curve and the 45-degree line, at this income level. (Check to see that this is consistent with Table 9.5.)

On the other hand, at an income level of 400 there is full macroeconomic equilibrium, since output, income, and spending are all at the same level. Unintended investment is zero.

At levels of income and output above 400 in Table 9.5 and Figure 9.14, business firms' managers are unhappy because more and more of their goods are gathering dust. For levels of income and output below 400, their inventories are getting too low for comfort. These are *not* equilibrium levels of income, and the economy will not stay at any of those income levels—things will change.

3.5 MOVEMENT TO EQUILIBRIUM IN THE KEYNESIAN MODEL

If firms are unhappy about unsold goods, they will do something to correct the situation. If inventories are building up more than intended, they will cut back on production. Their cutbacks in production will continue until they are no longer seeing inventories build up excessively—that is, until the level of what is actually produced matches what they can sell. Reductions in Y will continue until $Y = AD$. This is a little more complicated than it may at first seem, though, since any reduction in output leads to reduced income, which leads to reduced consumption, so that AD is a moving target. We will look at this complication below in Section 3.7, but for now we will stay with the main story.

In Figure 9.14, above, suppose that the economy were (for reasons to be explored later) initially at an income and output level of 800. From the figure and Table 9.5, we can see that this is not an equilibrium—producers are seeing excess inventory accumulation of 80 since AD is only 720. Producers will cut back on production. The equilibrium point E is obtained when aggregate output has fallen to 400 and AD has also fallen to 400.

So, what has happened here? If you look back at Table 9.2, you can see that at the initial income level of 800 there was a "leakage" into saving of 140. But firms, we have assumed, only want to spend 60 on investment. Leakages exceeded injections by 80, aggregate demand was insufficient, and inventories of 80 built up. Firms cut back on production. They continued to cut back until inventories are back where they want them.

Yet when the economy arrives at an equilibrium, the balance between saving and investing has been restored! Why is this so? Intended investment has not changed—it has been at 60 all along. But now that income has dropped, households have less income to use for consumption and saving, and so saving has dropped from its initial level of 140 to only 60. (See Table 9.2 to check that this is the level of saving at an income level of 400.) *It is changes in aggregate income, and the changes that these cause in consumption and saving, that have caused leakages and injections to become equal again!*

We can also see in the schedules and graphs what would happen if AD were for some reason to be *above* the current level of output. If output were to start out at 300, for example, desired spending of 320 (see Table 9.5) would cause produced goods to "fly off the shelves." According to this model, this would motivate firms to increase production. As production rises, income, consumption, and saving would also all rise. Again, equilibrium would be reached when Y and AD are both equal to 400, and S and I are both equal to 60.

3.6 THE PROBLEM OF PERSISTENT UNEMPLOYMENT

Now that the pieces of the model have been explained, the model can be put together to illustrate what Keynes taught about the Great Depression. Assume that 800 represents the full-employment level of output for this economy, as illustrated by the vertical "full-employment range" in Figure 9.15. With intended investment of 140, the economy is at an initial full-employment equilibrium at E_0. (Refer back to Table 9.4 and Figure 9.13 to confirm that at this level of income $Y=AD$.)

Figure 9.15   **Full Employment Equilibrium with High Intended Investment**

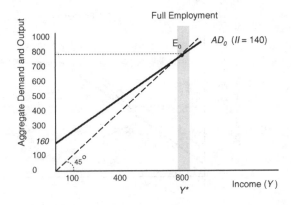

Supposing that Y = 800 represents full employment, an intended investment level of 140 generates spending sufficient to maintain this as an equilibrium.

But at the start of the Great Depression, the 1929 stock market crash and other events caused business and investor confidence to plummet. (Consumer confidence and financial wealth also plummeted, but we will simplify the story by concentrating on firms.) Producers became very uncertain about whether they would be able to sell what they produced, so they cut back radically on their investment spending. This is modeled in Figure 9.16 as a drop in aggregate demand caused by a drop in intended investment from 140 down to 60. (Note that 60 is the number used in Table 9.3, so that AD_1 in Figure 9.16 is identical to the AD curve in Figure 9.12.) With the drop in AD, income of 800 is no longer an equilibrium. Consistent with the adjustments toward equilibrium we just discussed, output, income, and spending contract until a new equilibrium is reached at a level of 400.

An income and output level of 400, however, is far below the level of production required to provide full employment for workers. Massive unemployment results. And, in the Keynesian model, there is no automatic mechanism (as there was in the classical model) that rescues the economy from this situation. The economy experiences a contraction, settling down at a new, persistent, self-reinforcing, low-income and high-unemployment equilibrium, as shown in Figure 9.17.

> To say a macroeconomy is "in equilibrium" just means that output, income, and spending are *in balance*. The important point about an equilibrium is that there tend to be forces (such as, in this model, firms' desire to avoid unintended inventories) that are likely to push an economy toward one, and that tend to keep it there once achieved. But achievement of an equilibrium *is not necessarily a good thing*—the level at which output, income, and spending balance may *or may not* be desirable.

In Keynes' view, there was nothing that would "naturally" or "automatically" happen to pull an economy out of such a low-employment situation. He believed that action needed to be taken to stimulate aggregate demand. Such policies are the topics of Chapters 10 and 11.

3.7 THE MULTIPLIER

In the example above, intended investment dropped from 140 down to 60 due to a fall in investor confidence—a decline of 80 units. But output dropped from 800 all the way down to 400—a

Figure 9.16   **A Keynesian Unemployment Equilibrium**

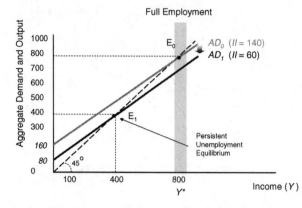

A fall in investor confidence causes the equilibrium level of output to fall. The initial excess of leakages over injections caused by low investment spending is corrected by a contraction in output, income, and saving. At E_1, leakages and injections are again equal.

Figure 9.17   **Movement to an Unemployment Equilibrium**

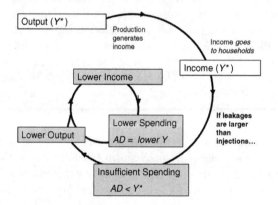

An excess of leakages over injections causes aggregate demand to be insufficient to support a full employment level of output. Output and income fall until equilibrium is restored.

decline of *400* units. Why is the decline in output so much bigger than the decline in investment spending that caused it?

The intuition behind this result is that, while the drop in investment spending leads to a drop in aggregate demand, which leads directly to a contraction in output, there are also feedback effects through consumption. Since consumption depends on income, and income depends on *AD* which depends on consumption, there are additional effects which "echo" back and forth. For example, reducing production in a factory does not merely involve laying off assembly-line workers (and buying less raw material and the like). The laid-off factory workers now have less income to spend at stores. This means that the stores will need to lay off some of their employees, who then also have less income. And so on. This process is illustrated in more detail in Table 9.6.

Table 9.6   **The Multiplier at Work**

(1)	(2)	(3)
Change in Intended Investment	Change in Aggregate Demand (as *C* or *II* change) and in Output and Income (as firms respond to changes in *AD*)	Change in Consumption $\Delta C = mpc \, \Delta Y$ = .8 × Column (2)
1. Investors lose confidence. $\Delta II = -80$	2. Reduced investment spending leads directly to $\Delta AD = -80$. Producers respond to reduced demand for their goods by cutting back on production. $\Delta Y = -80$	3. Less production means less income. With income reduced by 80, households cut consumption by $mpc \, \Delta Y = .8 \times -80$ $\Delta C = -64$
	4. Lowered consumption spending means lowered AD $\Delta AD = -64$ Producers respond. $\Delta Y = -64$	5. Households cut consumption by $mpc \, \Delta Y = .8 \times -64$ $\Delta C = -51.2$
	6. $\Delta Y = -51.2$	7. $mpc \, \Delta Y = .8 \times -51.2$ $\Delta C = -40.96$
	8. $\Delta Y = -40.96$	9. $\Delta C = -32.77$
	10. $\Delta Y = -32.77$	11. $\Delta C = -26.21$
	etc.	etc.
	Sum of changes in Y **= −80 + −64 + −51.2 + −40.96 + −32.77 + ...** **= −400**	

In the first row, for example, the drop in intended investment (step 1) leads to an immediate drop in *AD* of 80 (step 2). Firms see inventories piling up, and cut back production by 80. But this decreases the amount of income going to households, since firms are now paying less in wages, interest, dividends, and rents. Consumers react (in step 3) to a change in income according the relationship $\Delta C = mpc \, \Delta Y$. With 80 less in income, they reduce their spending by 64. (How do they manage to keep their budget in line, when they have only reduced their spending by 64 but their income went down by 80? See if you can think of the answer before you check the footnote.*)

The second and later rows show how decreases in consumption decrease aggregate demand, output, and income, and thus depress consumption even further. Notice that in each round, the decrease in *Y* gets a little smaller. Fortunately, a convenient result from mathematics means that we don't need to calculate the sum of all these changes in *Y* by continuing to extend the table, row after row (in theory, forever—although the numbers get very tiny after a while).** A result

---

* They economize by reducing both consumption *and saving*. They reduce their saving by 16 (which corresponds to the remaining 20 percent of the income change).

** Column 2 of the table can be summarized as:

$$\Delta Y = 1 + mpc \, \Delta \overline{II} + mpc \, (mpc \, \Delta \overline{II}) + mpc \, (mpc \, (mpc \, \Delta \overline{II})) + ...$$

$$= (1 + mpc + mpc^2 + mpc^3 + ...) \, \Delta \overline{II}$$

But the infinite series $(1 + x + x^2 + x^3 + \ldots + x^\infty)$ where x < 1 can be simplified to $1/(1-x)$.

from the mathematics of infinite series implies that, in the end, the total change in Y is related in the following way to the original change in II:

$$\Delta Y = \frac{1}{1-mpc} \Delta \overline{II}$$

which means, in this case,

$$\Delta Y = \frac{1}{1-.8}(-80) = \frac{1}{0.2}(-80) = 5(-80) = -400$$

The expression $1/(1-mpc)$ is called "the income/spending multiplier"—or, for short, the multiplier—and is abbreviated *mult:*

$$mult = \frac{1}{1-mpc}$$

In this case, with $mpc = 0.8$, the multiplier is 5. The initial decrease in intended investment causes, in the end, a decrease in income that is five times its size.

The value of the multiplier would be the same if it had been a decrease in consumer confidence, acting through a change in $\overline{C}$ that started this cascade in incomes, instead of a decrease in investor confidence. That is, $\Delta Y = mult\ \Delta \overline{C}$ as well. In the next chapter, we will add consideration of other factors that change aggregate demand, besides investor and consumer confidence.

Discussion Questions

1. If you receive a raise of $100 per month, how would you increase your spending per month? How much would you change your saving? What is your *mpc*? What is your *mps?*
2. Describe verbally how, in the Keynesian model, an economy can end up in a persistent unemployment equilibrium.

4. CONCLUDING THOUGHTS

In the classical economic theory, an economy should never go into a slump—or at least it should not stay in one very long. Any deficiency in aggregate demand would be quickly counteracted by smooth adjustments in the market for loanable funds. Keynes, on the other hand, theorized that deficiencies in aggregate demand, due to drops in investor (or consumer) confidence could explain the long-term, deep slumps many countries experienced during the Great Depression (as well as some of the other economic depressions that various economies have experienced over history). Any excess of "leakages" over "injections" into the aggregate demand stream would, he theorized, lead to progressive rounds of declines in consumption and income, until savings are so low that a new, lower-output-level equilibrium is established. In the next chapter, we will explore how the U.S. economy did, in fact, get out of the Great Depression.

But take a moment to consider the implications of this model as it relates to contemporary controversies over consumerism and the environment. In the Keynesian model it does, indeed, appear that keeping consumption and spending at high levels *is* necessary to keep the economy humming. The idea that cutting back on consumption spending would be "bad for the economy" is based on the Keynesian notion that reductions in aggregate spending lead to recessions or depressions, and that these could potentially be deep and persistent. This inference is, however, based on the idea that a cut in *wasteful* spending is the same thing as a cut in *aggregate* spending. We will revisit this assumption in Chapter 12 to see if it really is the case that what is good for the environment (and for future generations) has to be "bad for the economy."

Discussion Questions

1. Which theory—classical or Keynesian—seems to you more realistic in describing today's economy? Explain why.
2. Have you ever read articles or editorials that claim that high consumption is essential for a healthy economy? Does the Keynesian model seem to confirm or challenge this idea? What are some arguments for the opposite point of view?

REVIEW QUESTIONS

1. During a business cycle recession, which of the following typically rises: the level of output, the unemployment rate, and/or the inflation rate?
2. During the 1930s, how did economists' opinions about the Great Depression differ?
3. In the model laid out in this chapter, who receives income? Who spends? Who saves?
4. What is the definition of aggregate demand? How does it differ from measured GDP?
5. What conditions describe equilibrium in a macroeconomy?
6. Saving is described as a "leakage" from the circular flow. How is it a leakage?
7. How is it that an increase in saving (if not balanced by an increase in intended investment) might cause a shrinkage of the output-income-spending flow?
8. Describe the classical market for loanable funds. Who are the actors, and what do they each do?
9. Describe how the problem of leakages is solved in the classical model.
10. How did Keynes model consumption behavior? Draw and label a graph.
11. List five factors, aside from the level of income, that may affect the level of consumption in a macroeconomy.
12. Why isn't the interest rate included in the Keynesian consumption function?
13. What did Keynes think was the most important factor in determining investment behavior?
14. What determines aggregate demand in the Keynesian model? Draw and label a graph.
15. Do firms always end up investing the amount they intend? Why or why not?
16. Draw a "Keynesian cross" diagram, carefully labeling the curves and the equilibrium point.
17. Describe how adjustment to equilibrium occurs in the Keynesian model.
18. Does a macroeconomy being "in equilibrium" always mean it is in a good state? Why or why not?
19. What is "the income/spending multiplier"? Explain why a drop in autonomous intended investment, or in autonomous consumption, leads to a much larger drop in equilibrium income.

1. Carefully draw and label a supply-and-demand diagram for the classical loanable funds market. Assuming that the market starts and ends in equilibrium, indicate what happens if there is a sudden drop in households' desire to consume.
   a. Which curve shifts and in what direction?
   b. What happens to the equilibrium amount of loanable funds borrowed and lent? (You do not need to put numbers on the graph—just point out the direction of the change.)
   c. What happens to the equilibrium interest rate?
   d. What happens to the equilibrium amount of investment?

2. Suppose you see a toy store increasing its inventories in early December, right before the Christmas/Chanukah/Kwanzaa season. Is this a case of excess inventory accumulation? Why or why not?

3. Suppose that the relation between consumption and income is $C = 90 + 0.75 Y$.
   a. For each additional dollar that households receive, how much do they save? How much do they spend?
   b. What is the level of consumption when income is equal to 0? 360? 500? 600? (You may want to make a table similar to Table 9.2 in the text.)
   c. What is the level of saving when income is equal to 0? 360? 500? 600?
   d. As income rises from 500 to 600, by how much does consumption rise? What formula would you use to derive the *mpc* from your answer to this question, if you did not know the *mpc* already?
   e. Graph this consumption function, along with a 45-degree "consumption=income" line. Label the slope and intercept, and show how the level of savings when income is equal to 600 can be found on this graph.

4. Draw a Keynesian cross graph and assume that the macroeconomy starts and ends in equilibrium. Label the initial aggregate demand line AD_0. Then show what happens in the diagram when a rise in consumer wealth raises $\bar{C}$ (autonomous consumption) in your diagram. (This event might happen if the stock market or the housing market enjoys large price increases. You do not need to put numbers on the graph—just point out the direction of the change.)
   a. How does the *AD* line shift? Label the new line AD_1.
   b. What is the *initial* effect of this change on inventories? How will firms change production in response to this change in inventories?
   c. What happens to the equilibrium level of production, income, and spending? Does each rise, fall, or stay the same?

5. What happens in the Keynesian model if households decide to be "thriftier"—that is, spend less and save more? Do the following several-step exercise to find out.
   a. Suppose the economy starts out in a situation we already developed in the text: $C = 20 + .8Y$ and $II = 60$ (see Table 9.3). Carefully graph the resulting *AD* curve, labeling the levels of aggregate demand that result when income is equal to 0, 300, 400, and 500. Label the curve AD_0, add the 45-degree line, and label the equilibrium point E_0.

b. What is the equilibrium level of income, in this initial case? What is the equilibrium level of saving?

c. Now suppose that people decide they want to save more of their income, and spend less of it. In fact, their new level of autonomous consumption is zero, so the new consumption function is just $C = .8\,Y$. Calculate the levels of consumption and aggregate demand that would result from incomes of 0, 300, 400, and 500. (You might want to set up a table similar to Table 9.3, but using this new equation for consumption. Intended investment is still 60.)

d. *If income stayed at the equilibrium level determined in part (b) of this question, would people now be saving more? How much more? Show your work.*

e. Add the *AD* curve that arises from your calculations in part (c) on the graph you drew earlier. Label this curve AD_1 and the new equilibrium point E_1.

f. What is the new equilibrium level of income? What is the new equilibrium level of saving? Compare your answers to your answers to part (b).

g. Explain why this phenomenon arising from the Keynesian model is called "the paradox of thrift." Can you explain why this "paradox" arises?

6. Suppose that the behavior of households and firms in an economy is determined by the following equations:

$$C = 90 + 0.75\,Y$$

$$II = 35$$

a. Show in a table what the levels of C and AD would be at income levels of 0, 500, and 600.

b. If, for some reason, income were equal to 600, would there be unintended inventory investment? If so, would inventories be excessive or depleted, and by how much?

c. If, for some reason, income were equal to 500, would there be unintended inventory investment? If so, would inventories be excessive or depleted, and by how much?

d. What is the equilibrium level of income and output?

e. What is the income/spending multiplier equal to, in this model?

f. If intended investment were to rise by 25, by how much would equilibrium income increase? Use the income/spending multiplier.

7. (Appendix) Suppose that the behavior of households and firms in an economy is determined by the following equations:

$$C = 50 + 0.9\,Y$$

$$II = 50$$

Answer the following questions, using algebraic manipulations *only*.

a. What is the equation for the AD curve?

b. What is the level of equilibrium income?

c. If intended investment increases by 10 units to 60 units, by how much will equilibrium income rise?

8. Match each concept in Column A with a definition or example in Column B.

<table>
<tr><td colspan="2" align="center">Column A</td><td colspan="2" align="center">Column B</td></tr>
<tr><td>a.</td><td>*mult* $\Delta \overline{II}$</td><td>1.</td><td>Peak</td></tr>
<tr><td>b.</td><td>An injection</td><td>2.</td><td>An inverse relationship between unemployment and rapid GDP growth</td></tr>
<tr><td>c.</td><td>An assumption evident in the equation $AD = C + II$</td><td>3.</td><td>Households save more when income rises</td></tr>
<tr><td>d.</td><td>Okun's "law" 2</td><td>4.</td><td>$I - II$</td></tr>
<tr><td>e.</td><td>Classical assumption about saving 8</td><td>5.</td><td>The proportion of an additional dollar that households spend on consumption</td></tr>
<tr><td>f.</td><td>Unintended investment</td><td>6.</td><td>$\overline{C} + \overline{II}$</td></tr>
<tr><td>g.</td><td>The turning point from a business cycle expansion to contraction</td><td>7.</td><td>The amount that equilibrium GDP rises when autonomous investment rises</td></tr>
<tr><td>h.</td><td>*mpc* 5</td><td>8.</td><td>Households save more when the interest rate rises</td></tr>
<tr><td>i.</td><td>The intercept of the AD curve</td><td>9.</td><td>No government sector</td></tr>
<tr><td>j.</td><td>A Keynesian assumption about saving 9</td><td>10.</td><td>Intended investment</td></tr>
</table>

APPENDIX: AN ALGEBRAIC APPROACH TO THE MULTIPLIER

The formula for the multiplier in the simplest Keynesian model can also be derived using tools of basic algebra, starting with rearranging the equation for *AD:*

$$AD = C + II$$

we can substitute in for consumption, $C = \overline{C} + mpc\ Y$, and use the fact that in this model all investment is autonomous, to get

$$AD = (\overline{C} + mpc\ Y) + \overline{II}$$
$$= (\overline{C} + \overline{II}) + mpc\ Y$$

The last rearrangement shows that the AD curve has an intercept equal to the sum of the autonomous terms and a slope equal to the marginal propensity to consume. Changes in either of the variable in parentheses, by changing the intercept, shift the curve up or down in a parallel manner.

By substituting this into the equation for the equilibrium condition, $Y = AD$, we can derive an expression for equilibrium income in terms of all the other variables in the model:

$$Y = (\overline{C} + \overline{II}) + mpc\ Y$$
$$Y - mpc\ Y = \overline{C} + \overline{II}$$
$$(1 - mpc)Y = \overline{C} + \overline{II}$$
$$Y = \frac{1}{1 - mpc}(\overline{C} + \overline{II})$$

If autonomous consumption or intended investment, these each increase equilibrium income by $mult = 1/(1 - mpc)$ times.

To see this explicitly, consider the changes that would come about in Y if there is a change in $\overline{II}$ from $\overline{II}_0$ to a new level, $\overline{II}_1$, if autonomous consumption (and the *mpc*) stays the same. We can solve for the change in Y by subtracting the old equation from the new one:

$$Y_1 = \frac{1}{1 - mpc}(\bar{C} + \bar{\bar{II}}_1)$$

$$-[Y_0 = \frac{1}{1 - mpc}(\bar{C} + \bar{\bar{II}}_0)]$$

$$Y_1 - Y_0 = \frac{1}{1 - mpc}(\bar{C} - \bar{C} + \bar{\bar{II}}_1 - \bar{\bar{II}}_0)$$

But $\bar{C}$ (and the *mpc*) is unchanged, so the first subtraction in parentheses comes out to be zero. We are left with:

$$Y_1 - Y_0 = \frac{1}{1 - mpc}(\bar{\bar{II}}_1 - \bar{\bar{II}}_0)$$

or

$$\Delta Y = \text{mult } \Delta \bar{\bar{II}}$$

where *mult=1/(1−mpc)*. Similar analysis of $\Delta \bar{C}$ (holding intended investment constant) would show that the multiplier for that change is also *mult*.

10 Fiscal Policy

What happens when economic conditions are not good—when the economy enters a slowdown or recession? We often hear of the need to "stimulate" the economy. Sometimes political leaders advocate tax cuts or a variety of specific government spending programs. The common-sense idea behind this is that more spending, either by individuals and families who receive tax cuts, or by government, will create demand for goods and thereby expand employment and output. In terms of the macroeconomic theory sketched out in Chapter 9, these policies are intended to *increase aggregate demand,* generating positive *multiplier effects.* That sounds good. But critics sometimes argue that such policies will create other problems, such as large government deficits or inflation. The analysis of such issues is the subject of this and the next two chapters.

1. THE ROLE OF GOVERNMENT SPENDING AND TAXES

Economists often disagree about what tax and spending policies are best in different economic situations. These debates are about **fiscal policy**—what government spends, how it gets the money it spends, and the effects of these activities on GDP levels. To understand these issues, we need to extend the simple macroeconomic model of Chapter 9 to include the role of government.

> **fiscal policy:** government spending and tax policy

In Section 3 of this chapter, we will also introduce another step toward realism in our model of the economy by adding the international sector—exports and imports.

Bringing in the role of the government, the equation for aggregate demand used in previous chapters becomes:

$$AD = C + II + G$$

Government spending by federal, state, and local governments (G) is added to aggregate demand since it represents additional goods and services purchased. Taxes do not appear directly in this equation, but, as we will see, they have an impact through their effect on consumption spending.

We will examine the effects of these changes to our model one at a time, starting with the impact of a change in government spending.

1.1 A CHANGE IN GOVERNMENT SPENDING

Government spending (G) has a direct impact on the level of GDP. When the government purchases goods and services, this adds to aggregate demand, boosting equilibrium output. In Chapter 9 we showed how a decline in intended investment lowered the AD line, leading to equilibrium at a lower level of income. This suggests that government spending might be used as an antidote to low investment spending.

Suppose we start with the macroeconomic equilibrium that we showed in Chapter 9, Table 9.5 and Figure 9.14. Remember that this was an unemployment equilibrium. If we start at an unemployment equilibrium, additional aggregate demand will be needed to get back to full employment. Our first model assumed no government role; hence initial government spending (G) is equal to zero. Thus a simple policy would be to increase government spending on goods and services from 0 to 80. As you can see in Table 10.1 and Figure 10.1, the addition of 80 units of government spending causes the equilibrium to shift up by 400, to the full employment Y^* of 800. Why does this happen?

Let's look at a simple example—a new building construction program. Government money is spent to purchase goods such as concrete and steel, as well as to pay workers. This directly creates new aggregate demand. In addition, there are multiplier effects—construction workers will spend their paychecks to buy all kinds of consumer goods and services. The multiplier effects add to the original economic stimulus resulting from the government spending.

The effect is exactly the same as the multiplier for intended investment that we discussed in Chapter 9. The initial change in government spending ΔG becomes income to individuals (ΔY), which leads to a round of consumer spending ΔC equal to $mpc\ \Delta Y$, which in turn becomes income to other in individuals, leading to another round of consumer spending, and so forth. The whole process can be summarized using the same formula as in Chapter 9, but now applied to government spending rather than intended investment:

$$\Delta Y = \frac{1}{1 - mpc} \Delta G$$

or:

$$\Delta Y = mult\ \Delta G$$

Using the same mpc and multiplier as before (we had chosen the example where $mpc = 0.8$, resulting in $mult = 5$), this allows us to predict the impact of government spending on economic equilibrium. The multiplier applies to government spending in exactly the same way that it does to changes in intended investment. Therefore an increase in government spending of 80 leads to an equilibrium shift of $80 \times 5 = 400$. Looking at it the other way, if we start with the goal of an increase of 400 in Y, we can divide 400 by 5 to find the needed quantity of ΔG: $400/5 = 80$.

Note that at the original AD level, there is an equilibrium at 400, where $AD = Y$, and there is significant unemployment. After the addition of 80 in government spending (G), the new equilibrium is at the full-employment level of 800, where $AD_1 = Y$. (You can check other levels in the table to make sure that this is the only level at which $AD_1 = Y$.) Figure 10.1 shows the same thing graphically. The aggregate demand schedule moves up by 80 at each level of income, so that the horizontal intercept of the AD line moves up from 80 to 160. The slope of the AD line remains the same, since there has been no change in the mpc. The change in equilibrium income is equal to the change in government spending times the multiplier.

Using the multiplier, we can easily calculate the effect of further changes in government spending. For example, suppose government spending were reduced from 80 to 60. This negative change of 20 in G would lead to a change of $5 \times (-20) = -100$ in equilibrium Y. Income would fall from 800 to 700.

So we can see that an increase in government spending will raise the level of economic equilibrium, while a decrease in government spending will lower it. The multiplier effect, which is the same size in both directions, gives the policy extra "bang for the buck"—in this case, a

Table 10.1   **An Increase in Government Spending**

(1) Income (Y)	(2) Consumption (C)	(3) Intended Investment (II)	(4) Original Aggregate Demand (AD = C + II)	(5) Government Spending (G)	(6) New Aggregate Demand ($AD_1 = C + II + G$)
300	260	60	320	80	400
400	340	60	400	80	480
500	420	60	480	80	560
600	500	60	560	80	640
700	580	60	640	80	720
800	660	60	720	80	800

Figure 10.1   **Increased Government Spending**

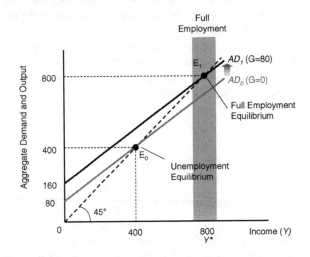

An increase in government spending has a similar effect to an increase in private fixed investment. It shifts the AD line upward, as government spending rises. This increases the equilibrium levels of income and output.

change in government spending leads to five times as great a change in national income. In real life the multiplier is rarely this large (see Appendices A2 and A3 for an algebraic treatment of some reasons why real-world multipliers tend to be lower), but there will usually be some multiplier effects from a change in government spending. Econometric studies of the U.S. economy generally indicate a multiplier effect of 2.0 or less.

1.2 TAXES AND TRANSFER PAYMENTS

To complete the picture of fiscal policies, we need to include the role of taxes and transfer payments. If voters and government officials do not want to raise government spending, they have another option. To raise GDP, the government could cut taxes and/or increase **transfer payments**. Transfer payments are government grants, subsidies, or gifts to individuals or firms.

Examples of transfer payments include Social Security payments and payments of interest to holders of government bonds.

> **transfer payments:** payments by government to individuals or firms, including Social Security payments, unemployment compensation, and interest payments

In recent decades the fiscal tool most often chosen by policymakers has been tax reductions. (Tax reductions, of course, tend to be politically popular in addition to providing economic stimulus.) Increases in transfer payments would have the same general positive effect on aggregate demand. The opposite policies—increasing taxes or decreasing transfer payments—would have a negative effect on economic equilibrium, similar to a reduction in government spending.

Changes in taxes and transfer payments, however, are not exactly similar to changes in government spending. The mechanism by which tax and transfer changes affect output differs from the process discussed above for government spending. While government spending *directly* affects aggregate demand and GDP, the effect of taxes and transfer payments is *indirect,* based on their effect on consumption or investment. There are many kinds of taxes and transfers, including corporate taxes, tariffs, and inheritance taxes, but we will focus here on the effects of changes in personal income taxes and transfers to individuals.

For example, let's say consumers receive a tax cut of 50. If they spent it all, that would add 50 to aggregate demand. But according to the "marginal propensity to consume" (*mpc*) principle, consumers are likely to use some portion of the tax cut to increase saving or reduce debt. With the *mpc* of 0.8 that we used for our basic model in Chapter 9, the portion saved will be $0.2 \times 50 = 10$, leaving 40 for increased consumption. Thus the effect on aggregate demand would be only 40, not 50 (since saving is not part of aggregate demand).

The same logic would hold if consumers received extra transfer income of 50. They would spend only 40, and save 10. The reverse would be true for a tax increase or a cut in transfer payments. With a tax increase or benefit cut of 50, individuals and families would have less to spend, and would reduce their consumption by 40.

Economists define **disposable income** (Y_d) as the income available to consumers after paying taxes and receiving transfers:

$$Y_d = Y - T + TR$$

where T is the total of taxes paid in the economy and *TR* is the total of transfer payments from governments to individuals.

> **disposable income:** income remaining for consumption or saving after subtracting taxes and adding transfer payments

Changes in taxes (T) or transfer payments directly affect disposable income, but only indirectly affect consumption and aggregate demand. Hence their impact on economic equilibrium is less than that of government spending, which affects aggregate demand directly.

For this reason, the multiplier effects of changes in taxes and transfer payments are less than the multiplier impacts of government spending. If taxes are "lump sum"—that is, set at a fixed level that does not change with income, then we can write $T = \bar{T}$. The **tax multiplier** for a lump sum tax works in two stages. In the first stage, consumption is reduced by *mpc* ($\Delta\bar{T}$), which can be expressed as:

$$\Delta C = -(mpc)\,\Delta\bar{T}$$

In the second stage, this reduction in consumption has the regular multiplier effect on equilibrium income. The combined effect can be expressed as:

$$\Delta Y = (mult) \Delta C = -(mult)(mpc)\Delta \overline{T}$$

The tax multiplier is equal to $\Delta Y/\Delta \overline{T} = -(mult)(mpc)$. Mathematically, $(mult)(mpc)$ always works out to exactly 1.0 less than the regular multiplier. (You can use the multiplier formula from Chapter 9 to work out why this is true.) Using the figures from our previous example, where $mpc = 0.8$ and $mult = 5$, the tax multiplier would be $-(0.8)(5) = -4$. (For a more detailed algebraic account of the tax multiplier for a lump sum tax, see Appendix A1.)

tax multiplier: the impact of a change in a lump sum tax on economic equilibrium, expressed mathematically as $\Delta Y/\Delta \overline{T} = -(mult)(mpc)$

Just as a tax increase has a contractionary effect, a tax cut will have an expansionary effect. Historically, tax cuts played an important role in U.S. economic policy in the 1960s, 1980s, and 2000s. In all cases, the effect on GDP was expansionary (though there is debate about the exact mechanism through which this occurred—not all economists accept the simple tax multiplier process that we have discussed).

Transfer payments, which as we noted are a kind of "negative tax," affect the level of output through a similar logic. An increase in transfer payments, like a tax cut, will give people more money that they can spend. But the expansionary effect only occurs when they actually do spend—so, according to the mpc logic, the impact of an increase in transfer payments is reduced by whatever portion of the extra income people decide to save. The multiplier impact of a change in transfer payments is therefore the same as that of a change in taxes, except in the opposite direction. A cut in transfer payments, like an increase in taxes, will be contractionary, tending to lower economic equilibrium.

In the real economy, income taxes are generally proportional or progressive—that is, they increase with income levels (as discussed in Chapter 3). In our model, the effect of a proportional tax would be to *flatten* the aggregate demand curve, since it has a larger effect at higher income levels. (See Appendix A2 for a more detailed treatment of the impact of a proportional tax—we omit analysis of progressive taxes, which is a bit more complex.) This in turn will affect the multiplier, reducing it somewhat.

How can we explain the effect of a proportional tax on the multiplier? Taxes that rise with income will tend to lower the proportion consumed out of each dollar increase in income. For example, with a 15 percent tax each extra dollar of income will be reduced to 85 cents of disposable income. Applying our original mpc of 0.80 to the remaining 85 cents, we get $0.8 \times 0.85 = 0.68$, indicating that 68 cents will be devoted to consumption (and 17 cents to saving). The result is similar to having a lower mpc, which also means a lower multiplier. This will damp down the effect of income changes on aggregate demand and economic equilibrium.

You might wonder what would be the effect of an increase in government spending that is exactly balanced by an increase in taxes (a balanced budget)? Since we have shown that the multiplier effect of taxes goes in the opposite direction from that of government spending, it might appear that the effects would cancel out. But this is not the case. Because the tax multiplier is less than the government spending multiplier, there is a net positive effect on aggregate demand and equilibrium. The difference between the two multipliers is equal to one, so the net multiplier effect will also be equal to one. In the example we have used, the government policy multiplier is 5, and the tax multiplier is 4, so the **balanced budget multiplier** $= 5 - 4 = 1$. Thus the impact on economic equilibrium is exactly equal to the original change in government spending (and taxes). So we can say that $\Delta Y = \Delta G$.

For example, an increase of $50 billion in government spending, balanced by an equal increase of $50 billion in taxes, would be expected to lead to a net increase in equilibrium output of $50 billion. One way of thinking about this is to consider that the original government spending boosts GDP, but its multiplier effects are cancelled out by the negative multiplier effects generated by the tax increase. This results in a weaker net effect than government spending of $50 billion alone, which would lead to $\Delta Y = (mult)\Delta G = 5 \Delta G$, or $250 billion in this example.

> **balanced budget multiplier:** the impact on equilibrium output of simultaneous increases of equal size in government spending and taxes. The multiplier is equal to positive 1, showing that the effect on GDP is equal in size to the original change in government spending and taxes.

1.3 EXPANSIONARY AND CONTRACTIONARY FISCAL POLICY

These three fiscal policy tools—changes in government spending, changes in tax levels, and changes in transfer payments—will affect income and employment levels, as well as inflation rates. They will also, of course, affect the government's budgetary position. The budget could be balanced, in surplus, or in deficit, depending on the combinations of spending and tax policies that are employed.

Increasing government spending is an example of what economists refer to as **expansionary fiscal policy**. Another expansionary fiscal policy would be to increase transfer payments or to lower taxes. Whether through a direct impact on aggregate demand, or through giving consumers more money to spend, these policies will increase aggregate demand and equilibrium.

> **expansionary fiscal policy:** the use of government spending, transfer payments, or tax cuts to stimulate a higher level of economic activity

If that was the whole story, macroeconomic policy would be simple—just use sufficient government spending or tax cuts to maintain the economy at full employment. But there are complications. One problem is that in order to spend more, the government either has to raise taxes, borrow, or "print money." (Issues of how government finances its expenditures will be discussed later in this chapter and in Chapter 11.) Raising taxes would tend to counteract the expansionary effects of increased spending. Borrowing money creates deficits and raises long-term government debt, which may or may not be a problem—we'll discuss this in Section 2 of this chapter.

Another problem is that too much government spending may lead to inflation. The goal of expansionary fiscal policy is to bring the economic activity up to its full-employment level. But what if fiscal policy overshoots this level? It's easy to see how this might occur. Government spending on popular programs is easy for politicians, and raising taxes to pay for them is hard. This can lead to budget deficits (discussed in Section 2 below), but it can also cause excessive aggregate demand in the economy. Excessive demand could also, in theory, arise from high consumer or business spending, but usually government spending, alone or in combination with high consumer and business expenditures, is partially to blame when the economy "overheats." The result is likely to be inflation.

According to our basic analysis, the cure for inflation should be fairly straightforward. If the problem is too much aggregate demand, the solution is to reduce aggregate demand. This could be done by reversing the process discussed in the previous section, and lowering government spending on goods and services. A similar effect can be obtained by reducing transfer payments or by increasing taxes. With lower transfer payments and/or higher taxes, businesses and consumers will have less spending power. Lower spending by government, businesses, and consumers will result in a lower equilibrium output level, and there will no longer be excess demand pressures creating inflation.

Thus we have identified another important economic policy tool—**contractionary fiscal policy**. This is a weapon that can be used against inflation, though it would generally be unwise to use it at times of high unemployment. (The problem of what to do if unemployment and inflation occur at the same time—something that isn't shown in our simple model—will be discussed in Chapter 12.) Of course, too large a spending reduction could overshoot in a downward direction, leading to excessive unemployment and possibly a recession.

> **contractionary fiscal policy:** reductions in government spending or transfer payments, or increases in taxes, leading to a lower level of economic activity

Although the effects of contractionary fiscal policy can be painful, it would be wrong to assume that expansionary fiscal policy is always beneficial, and contractionary policy always harmful. Contractionary policy can be essential when previous policies have "overshot" the goal, or when the economy is suffering from inflation. We'll discuss this issue of policy choice a lot more in this and the following chapters.

Discussion Questions

1. What recent changes in government spending or tax policy have been in the news? How would you expect these to affect GDP and employment levels?
2. Tax increases are generally politically unpopular. Would you ever be likely to favor a tax increase? Under what circumstances, if any, might a tax increase be beneficial to the economy?

2. BUDGETS, DEFICITS, AND POLICY ISSUES

The federal government budget includes spending on goods and services, transfer payments and taxes. (This is also true of state and local government budgets, but our focus for purposes of fiscal policy analysis is mainly on the federal budget.) Thus we can break down total government expenditures, or **government outlays**, into two categories. Total government outlays include not only government spending on goods and services (G) but also government transfer payments:

$$Government\ Outlays = G + TR$$

> **government outlays:** total government expenditures including spending on goods and services and transfer payments.

On the revenue side, government income comes from taxes (T). When revenues are not sufficient to cover outlays, the government borrows to cover the difference. The actual financing of a deficit is accomplished through the sale by the United States Treasury of **government bonds**—interest-bearing securities that can be bought by firms, individuals, or foreign governments. In effect, a government bond is a promise to pay back, with interest, the amount borrowed at a specific time in the future.

> **government bond:** an interest-bearing security constituting a promise to pay at a specified future time

Current federal sources of revenue and outlays are shown in Figure 10.2. The major sources of federal revenue are personal income and Social Security taxes. In fiscal 2006, the federal government also borrowed an amount equal to 9 percent of the total budget. Government borrowing varies from year to year, but deficits are more common than surpluses. The major categories of

Figure 10.2 **U.S. Federal Government Source of Funds and Outlays, Fiscal 2006**

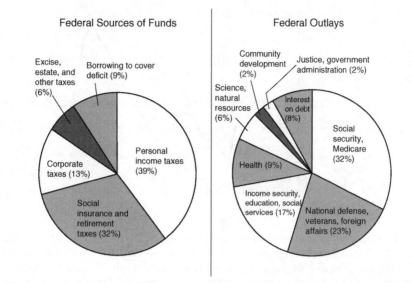

Federal Sources of Funds | Federal Outlays

The largest sources of federal revenues are personal income and Social Security taxes. Part of the budget—in 2006, 9 percent—is covered by borrowing (issuing government bonds). Net interest on the debt represented 8 percent of federal outlays. (Source: *Economic Report of the President*, 2007, Table B-81)

government spending are Social Security, defense spending, and social programs. Interest payments on the debt amounted to 8 percent of federal spending in fiscal 2006.

Clearly, government borrowing and interest payments on the debt will have economic impacts. What is the nature of these impacts? To answer this question, we need to look more carefully at the nature of government deficits.

2.1 THE GOVERNMENT BUDGET: SURPLUS AND DEFICIT

First, we need to define what we mean by the *government budget surplus or deficit*. This can be calculated by subtracting total government outlays from total government tax revenues. A positive result indicates a surplus; a negative one, a deficit.

$$Budget\ Surplus\ (+)\ or\ Deficit\ (-) = T - Government\ Outlays$$
$$= T - (G + TR)$$

Showing the government's deficit as a percentage of nominal GDP is a simple way to correct the numbers for the effects of both inflation and the ability of the economy to handle the deficit. The larger the economy—as measured by GDP—the easier it is to manage a given deficit, since both the fiscal and budgetary impacts of the deficit will be smaller relative to the size of the economy. A bigger economy means that people will have higher incomes, and are likely to be willing to purchase more government bonds, making it easier for the government to borrow.

State and local governments are generally required to separate their current spending and capital budgets. Current spending must be paid for out of current taxes, but money can be borrowed for

Figure 10.3   **Federal Surplus or Deficit as a Percentage of GDP**

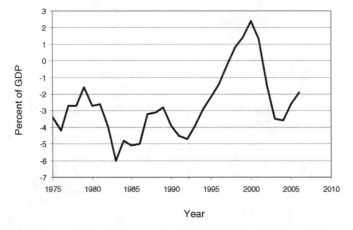

Year

The federal deficit—as measured by its borrowing—reached 6 percent of GDP in 1983, a year of deep recession. The deficit was reduced as a percent of GDP from the early 1990s until 1998, when the budget went into surplus. From 1998 to 2001, the government actually had a surplus in its budget (so that it retired some of its debt). After 2000, a recession combined with the Bush administration tax cuts put the budget back into deficit. (Source: *Economic Report of the President*, 2007, Table B-79)

investment ("capital") projects such as new schools, bridges, and transit systems. The federal budget, however, makes no such distinction between current and capital spending.

During the period 1992–2001, the U.S. federal government budget went from a large deficit to a surplus (Figure 10.3). Then in 2002 the government budget went back into deficit. Since 2004 the deficit has moderated a bit, but it is projected to continue in future years. This has led to an extensive debate about the impact of deficits on the economy. In this section, we examine this question and other issues related to the government budget and fiscal policy. As we will see, there is much continuing controversy, both among economists and the general public, about the significance of budgetary policy and deficits, and many different ideas about the best way to handle issues of government spending, taxes, and transfer payments.

Perhaps because the two terms sound so much alike, many people confuse the government's deficit with the *government debt*. But these two "D words" are very different. The deficit totaled about $248 billion during 2006, while federal debt owed to the public equaled about $8 *trillion* at the end of 2006. The reason why the second number is more than thirty times as large as the first is that the debt represents deficits accumulated over many years. In economists' terms, we can say that the government deficit is a *flow variable* while its debt is a *stock variable*. (See Chapter 3 for this distinction.)

The government's debt *rises* when the government runs a deficit and *falls* when it runs a surplus. Figure 10.4 shows some recent data on the government's debt, again measured as a percentage of GDP. This percentage was fairly steady during the period 1993-1996. After 1996, growth in GDP, combined with a government budget that moved from deficit into surplus, reduced debt as a percent of GDP from nearly 50 percent down to about 33 percent. The government debt started rising again as GDP growth slowed and as deficits became positive in the 2000s.

What is the impact of government debt on the economy? One commonly expressed view of the government's debt is that it represents a burden on future generations of citizens. There is some truth to this assertion, but it is also somewhat misleading. It implicitly compares the

Figure 10.4 **Government Debt Held by the Public as a Percentage of GDP**

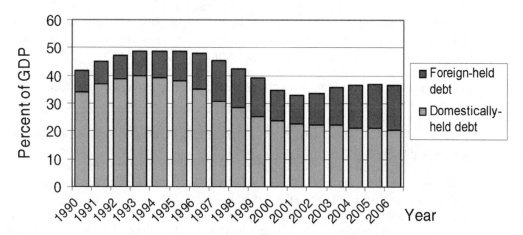

In the second half of the 1990s government debt (the tall line) fell as a percentage of GDP, as a result of government budget surpluses and strong GDP growth during that period. In 2002, it began to rise, as a result of the rising deficits of that period along with slower growth of GDP. Throughout, the fraction of the government debt that was owed to foreign citizens and governments (the shorter segment of each tall line) has increased significantly as a proportion of total debt in recent years, amounting to 44 percent of all federal debt in 2006. (Source: Analytical Perspectives, Budget of the United States Government, Fiscal Year 2008, Table 16-6)

government debt to the debt of a private citizen. Certainly, if you personally ran up a huge debt, this would not be a good thing for your financial future. But government debt is different in some important ways.

First, most of the government debt is owed to U.S. citizens. When people own Treasury bills (T-bills), Treasury notes, or Treasury bonds, they own government IOUs. From their point of view, the government debt is an asset, a form of wealth. If your grandmother gives you a U.S. Savings Bond, she is giving you a benefit, not a burden. These assets are some of the safest ones you can own.

Second, the government debt does not have to be paid off. Old debt can be "rolled over," i.e., replaced by new debt. Provided that the size of the debt does not grow too much, the government's credit is good—there will always be people interested in buying and holding government bonds. Most economists use the rule of thumb that as long as the government's debt does not rise significantly faster than GDP for several years in a row, it does not represent a severe problem for the economy. The government debt is currently a smaller percentage of GDP (less than 40 percent) than it was immediately after World War II (when it was more than 100 percent). The fact that this debt was not a severe burden is indicated by the relative economic prosperity of the 1950s and 1960s.

Third, the U.S. government pays interest in U.S. dollars. A country such as Argentina that owes money to other countries and must pay interest in a foreign currency (the U.S. dollar) can get into big trouble and go bankrupt. But it is much easier to manage a debt that is denominated in your own currency. Even if some of the debt is owed to foreigners we do not have to obtain foreign currency to pay it. And so long as foreigners are willing to continue holding U.S. government bonds, it will not be necessary to pay it at all—instead, the debt can be rolled over as new bonds replace old ones.

But this should not encourage us to believe that government debt is never a concern. Rising debt creates several significant problems. First, interest must be paid on the debt. This means that a larger share of future budgets must be devoted to paying interest, leaving less for other needs. It is true that most of this interest goes to U.S. citizens who hold government bonds. But it is also true that the largest holders of government bonds tend to be wealthier people, so that most of the interest paid by the government goes to better-off individuals. If this payment is not counteracted by changes in the tax system, it encourages growing income inequality. It also creates a problem of generational equity—future taxpayers will have to pay more interest because of government borrowing today.

A second problem is that in recent years an increasing proportion of the debt has been borrowed from foreign governments, corporations, and individuals (Figure 10.4). The interest payments on this portion of the debt must be made to those outside the country. That means that the United States must earn enough income from exports and other sources to pay not only for imports, but also for interest payments to the rest of the world. Alternatively, the country could borrow more, but it is best to avoid this solution in the long run. It also poses another problem—what if those foreign debt holders decided to sell the U.S. bonds they hold? In that case the government might have trouble finding enough people who are willing to hold government bonds (that is, lend money to the government). As we will see in Chapter 13, this could cause interest rates to rise sharply, which in turn would push the government budget further into deficit. Some painful belt-tightening would be needed as a result.

The question "is government debt worth it?" can only be answered if we consider what that debt was used to finance. In this respect, an analogy to personal or business debt is appropriate. Most people—including economists—do not reject consumer and corporate debt—rather, our judgment about debt depends on the benefits received.

For example, if debt is accumulated for gambling, it is a bad idea. If the bet doesn't pay off, then it is very difficult to pay the interest on the debt (not to mention the principal). But if borrowing is done to pay for intelligently planned investment, it can be very beneficial. If the investment leads to economic growth, this raises the ability of the government to collect tax revenue, so this kind of borrowing can pay for itself, as long as the investment is not for wasteful "pork barrel" spending, poorly planned or unnecessary projects, etc. Even if the debt finances current spending, it can be justifiable if it is seen as necessary to maintain or protect valuable aspects of life. Most people would not be opposed to borrowing to pay for clean up after a natural disaster or to contain a deadly pandemic. How about for military spending? Opinions will differ about whether particular defense expenditures are necessary to maintain or protect valuable aspects of life. But wasteful spending, or spending on unwise defense policies, would constitute a drag on more productive economic activity (as suggested by the production-possibilities curve "guns-versus-butter" analysis introduced in Chapter 2).

The management of debt involves standard principles of wise stewardship of finances. When we apply them to government deficits and debt, we will need to weigh the economic benefits of different spending and tax policies. In the following sections, we will look at some of the issues involved in the evaluation of fiscal policy.

2.2 AUTOMATIC STABILIZERS

Since the 1950s, government spending has been a major part of the U.S. economy. As we have seen, this was partly a result of the Keynesian idea that government spending was needed to prevent recession. In recent decades, the use of expansionary fiscal policy has been controversial, partly as a result of issues such as deficits and inflation. During this period, however, total

Figure 10.5   **Federal Government Outlays, Receipts, and Surplus/Deficit as a Percentage of GDP**

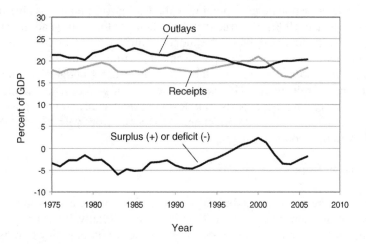

Federal government outlays as a percent of GDP have not changed much over the last thirty years. Tax receipts tend to rise during economic expansions and fall during recessions, leading to higher federal deficits in recession years such as 1975–76, 1982–83, 1991–92, and 2001–2. The Reagan tax cuts in the 1980s and the Bush tax cuts in the 2000s further lowered tax receipts and increased deficits. (Source: Economic Report of the President, 2007, Table B-79)

government outlays (including transfers and spending on goods and services) have not gone down, either in money terms or as a percent of GDP.

As Figure 10.5 shows, government receipts and outlays tend to fluctuate over time. For example, during the period from 1992 to 2000, when the economy was generally expanding, government receipts rose and outlays fell. Economists refer to this as the **automatic stabilization** effect of government spending and taxes. This refers to the way in which the government budget moderates fluctuations of aggregate demand even without any active decision-making or legislating by the government.

 automatic stabilizers: tax and spending institutions that tend to increase government revenues and lower government spending during economic expansions, but lower revenues and raise government spending during economic recessions

Even if no specific budgetary action is taken, the government's budget will vary over the business cycle. Suppose the economy is entering a recession. As aggregate demand falls, the government deficit generally rises. Tax revenues fall as falling GDP reduces people's incomes. In addition, more people receive unemployment insurance and "welfare" payments. If the agricultural sector declines, more farmers receive farm-support payments. This limits the fall in personal disposable income—and thus the fall in consumer spending.

If the federal government does not actively move to balance its budget, these automatic changes in spending and taxes tend to moderate the recession. In effect, the recession creates an automatic response of expansionary fiscal impacts—increased spending and lower taxes. It will also, of course, tend to increase the government deficit (or reduce any surplus).

Similarly, if aggregate demand is rising during an economic expansion, tax revenues rise. Fewer people receive unemployment or "welfare" payments, and farmers receive fewer subsidies if demand for agricultural products increases. This means that personal disposable income does not rise as quickly as national income. This in turn puts a damper on increases in consumer spending—and limits the inflationary over-heating that can arise from increased aggregate demand.

This phenomenon helps explain why the U.S. government was able to enjoy budgetary surpluses in the late 1990s. It is true that the policies of the Clinton administration, which included raising tax rates to try to balance the budget, contributed. But as private investment and consumer demand soared, this allowed the government's coffers to fill.

In addition to the automatic stabilizers, the federal budget has another aspect that levels the fluctuations of output. This is the steadiness of government spending. Unlike investment, consumer spending, net exports, and to some extent state and local government spending, most areas of federal spending do not change drastically from year to year. This adds an element of stability to the economy's aggregate demand.

2.3 Discretionary Policy

Sometimes the automatic stabilization effect of government spending and taxes cannot smooth economic ups and downs as much as is desired. Relatively severe problems of recession or inflation often give rise to proposals to use an active fiscal policy to remedy the situation. This issue is one that arouses more controversy among economists. Some economists, as we will see, believe that the government should *never* use activist fiscal policy—that it is likely to do more harm than good. Others believe that it should be used, but with caution. Regardless of economists' advice, the fact is that governments are making fiscal policy all the time, whether in a planned or unplanned manner. Each year the government revises its budget, including levels of spending and taxation. These spending and tax levels have effects on the economy, and it is important to try to understand them.

Historically, the first major experience with expansionary fiscal policy was during World War II. Prior to the war, President Franklin D. Roosevelt's New Deal had initiated some government spending programs intended to put the unemployed to work during the Great Depression. But these programs were dwarfed by the size of war spending in the 1940s. As a result, unemployment, which had been as high as 25 percent in 1933 and 19 percent in 1938, fell to about 2 percent by 1943.* The fall in unemployment was a beneficial side-effect of the onset of World War II and the war-induced spending.

After World War II, government spending never returned to pre-war levels, and it seemed that the beneficial effects of the expanded government role—steady economic growth with relatively low unemployment levels—justified this. In the 1960s, economists became even more optimistic about the benefits of fiscal policy. At that time, it was suggested that it would be possible for the government to "fine-tune" the economic system using fiscal policy, to ratchet aggregate demand up or down in response to changes in the business climate.

"Fine-tuning" was largely discredited in the 1970s and 1980s, as the economy struggled with inflationary problems that were partly a result of sharp increases in oil prices, but were also seen as having been worsened by excessive government spending (we'll look at this in more detail in Chapter 12). In addition, many economists argued that problems of **time lags** made fiscal policy unwieldy and often counterproductive.

> **time lags:** the time elapsing between the formulation of an economic policy and its actual effects on the economy

---

* Employment figures for that era covered a labor force in which a much lower proportion of women were seeking jobs than is the case today. During World War II, an unusually large number of women were employed, filling jobs left vacant by men who were serving in the armed forces.

To understand the problems with fine-tuning and time lags, we can use a common-sense example. Imagine that your apartment is too cold, so that you turn up the temperature on the thermostat. It might take so much time for the apartment to warm up that you do not get the benefits before you leave for work. You then might become impatient, raising the temperature again. In that case, it could easily happen that the apartment gets too hot, so when you return home you have to turn the thermostat down again. Thus delayed responses make your management of the apartment's temperature less effective. The best strategy is to set the thermostat at a single temperature and then to resist fiddling with it.

Similarly, time lags can make active fiscal policy less effective as a way to stabilize the economy. There are two types of lags: *inside* and *outside* lags. Inside lags refer to delays that occur within the government, while outside lags refer to the delayed effects of government policies. There are four major types of inside lags:

1. *A data lag:* It may take some time for the government to collect information about economic problems such as unemployment.

2. *A recognition lag:* Government decision-makers may not see an event as a problem right away.

3. *A legislative lag:* Discretionary fiscal policy must be instituted in the form of legal changes in the government's budget. The government's economists may want to increase spending or decrease taxes, but they have to convince both the president and Congress to act to solve the problem.

4. *A transmission lag:* These legal changes take time to show up in actual tax forms and government spending budgets. One solution is that changes can be made retroactive to speed up their implementation—for instance, a tax cut legislated now may apply to income received during the last year. However, this is not always done.

In addition, even if all these lags have been overcome, it takes time for the new policies actually to affect the economy (the "outside lag"). Suppose, for example, that the government responds to a rise in unemployment with increased government spending or a tax cut. By the time these policies are in place and create an economic stimulus, the economy may have recovered on its own. In that case, the extra aggregate demand will not be needed, and is likely to create inflationary pressures.

Despite these problems with discretionary fiscal policy, governments have continued to use it, with mixed results. Government fiscal stimulus, with or without a formal economic justification, was applied during the periods 1964–68, 1975–77, 1980–87, and in the early 2000s. An especially popular form of expansionary policy has been tax cuts, implemented under Presidents Kennedy, Reagan, and George W. Bush. In recent years overt policies of increased government spending have not been viewed favorably, but as Figure 10.5 shows, even conservative presidents have tended to maintain or increase the level of government spending. So while increasing spending is less often advocated as a desirable expansionary policy, it has frequently been practiced.

Proponents of tax cuts sometimes appeal to **supply-side economics** (first introduced during the Reagan administration) to support their policies. The supply-side argument for tax cuts is essentially that lower tax rates encourage more work, saving, and investment, thereby creating a more dynamic economy. According to the most enthusiastic advocates of supply-side economics, output will grow so rapidly in response to a cut in tax rates that total tax revenues will actually increase, not decrease. This is different from the logic of increased aggregate demand that we have discussed, which implies that tax cuts will create an economic stimulus, but are likely to raise the government deficit. The economic record seems to show that tax cuts do indeed create an economic stimulus—but debate continues among economists as to whether this effect

Economics in the Real World:
Fiscal Policy and the 2001–2007 Expansion

It is well known that, starting in 2001, federal policies in the United States have emphasized tax cuts. What is less well known is that during the same period federal spending has risen significantly. Between 2001 and 2006, total federal outlays rose from $1,863 billion to $2,655 billion, an increase of 43 percent. As a proportion of GDP, federal outlays rose from 18.5 percent to 20.3 percent during these years, while total federal revenues fell from 19.8 percent to 18.4 percent of GDP (see Figure 10.5). These combined changes in outlays and revenues led to a significant increase in the federal deficit (Figure 10.3).

Both tax cuts and spending increases are expansionary policies. Since the economy entered a recession in March 2001, it is reasonable to suggest that these expansionary policies contributed to the recovery that started in 2002 (see Figure 9.1 in the previous chapter). Real GDP grew at annual rates of between 2.5 percent and 3.6 percent per year from 2003 through 2006, and continued strong through the third quarter of 2007 (the last period for which data are available as of this writing).

Was this expansion partly a result of fiscal policy? Certainly government spending played an important role in increasing employment. Between 2001 and November 2007, total employment in the United States rose 4.5 percent, gaining about six million jobs. Of these new jobs, about 1.5 million jobs were created in the government sector—about 25 percent of the total gain in employment. Thus increased government spending directly accounted for a large proportion of the net gain in jobs over this four-year period.

According to the analysis of fiscal policy developed in this chapter, we would expect that both increased government spending and lower tax levels would have positive multiplier effects on GDP. The pattern of recovery and expansion in the economy during 2001–7 is consistent with this analysis. Classical economists would generally reject the idea that increased government spending can be beneficial to the economy, arguing that the incentive effects of lower taxes were the key factor in promoting recovery. Keynesian economists would suggest that both increased spending and tax cuts contributed to the recovery, but that tax cuts would have been more effective if targeted to middle- and lower-income families, who tend to have a higher marginal propensity to consume.

Whether the impact of government policies is felt more on the "demand side" (as Keynesian economists would suggest) or on the "supply side" (consistent with classical views), it seems that fiscal policies of increased spending and reduced taxes under the Bush administration had an expansionary effect on the economy—whether or not that was the deliberate intent.

Sources: *Economic Report of the President, 2007*; U.S. Department of Labor, Bureau of Labor Statistics; and the U.S. Bureau of Economic Analysis

is demand-led (as implied by our fiscal policy model) or based on supply-side effects. And in general, tax cuts have usually led to lower revenues and higher deficits (this was true both of the Reagan tax cuts in the 1980s and the Bush tax cuts in the 2000s).

> **supply-side economics:** an economic theory that emphasizes policies to stimulate production, such as lower taxes. The theory predicts that such incentives stimulate greater economic effort, saving, and investment, thereby increasing overall economic output and tax revenues.

2.4 BALANCED BUDGETS AND DEFICIT SPENDING

The long history of federal deficits has led some critics to call for legislation requiring a federal balanced budget. Under this proposal, the U.S. government would be subject to a "balanced budget amendment," compelling it to keep spending equal to tax revenues. Thus the U.S. government's budget would be like the current expenditure budgets of most state and local governments, which are generally required to be balanced.

To many people, a balanced budget amendment sounds good. It would prevent deficit spending and the accumulation of more federal debt. But our discussion of fiscal policy and automatic stabilizers suggests that there are three major problems with this idea:

1. A rule requiring a balanced budget at all times would make it difficult to respond to emergencies such as natural disasters and wars.

2. Every time the economy went into a recession, the automatic increase in the deficit would have to be counteracted by an increase in taxes, a cut in transfer payments, or decreased government spending. This would make the recession worse, since each of these policies decreases aggregate demand. In other words, this kind of rule would destroy the role of the automatic stabilizers.

3. The federal government would not be able to respond to severe recessions such as the Great Depression. Discretionary fiscal policy would be ruled out. Monetary policy (discussed in the next chapter) would still be possible, but many economists argue that monetary policy alone would be insufficient in the case of severe recession.

The theory of fiscal policy presented in this chapter suggests that deficit spending is sometimes necessary, and indeed can be beneficial to the economy. As we have noted, problems may arise when deficits are too large and continue for too long, pushing the government debt up significantly as a proportion of GDP. For this reason, economic judgment is required concerning what level of deficit is "too high." Economists often differ in their opinions on this issue. It is unlikely, however, that the problem can be solved with a single, inflexible rule.

Before we move on to other elements of economic analysis that are relevant to this debate—in particular a consideration of money, monetary policies, and inflation—we need to add one more element to our macroeconomic model—the international sector. In today's economy, it is impossible to get a complete picture of issues of fiscal policy, unemployment, and inflation, without considering the role of international trade and investment flows. We will go into these in greater detail in Chapter 14. But first, we can take some simple steps to add international trade to our basic model, which we will do in the next section.

Discussion Questions

1. "The national debt is a huge burden on our economy." How would you evaluate this statement?
2. Would you favor a federal balanced budget amendment? Why or why not?

3. The International Sector

How does trade affect the economy? It is certainly an important factor. Consumers who go to any U.S. shopping mall can't help but notice that a large proportion of the goods are imported. Many U.S. jobs are in industries that depend on export markets. We often hear concern expressed about the **trade deficit**. In 2006, as in many previous years, the U.S. trade deficit equaled about 5.5 percent of gross domestic product. This meant that people in the United States were spending much more on foreign goods and services (importing) than the United States was selling to foreign buyers (exporting). In other words, U.S. net exports (exports minus imports) were negative. In other countries, such as China, the situation is reversed—they are large net exporters. Clearly, it is important to examine how trade, trade deficits, and trade surpluses are related to macroeconomic issues of income, unemployment, and inflation. Here we will look at the relationship of trade to employment and equilibrium income levels; in Chapter 12 we will deal with the question of inflation.

> **trade deficit:** an excess of imports over exports, causing net exports to be negative

3.1 Exports and Imports

We can introduce trade into our macroeconomic model by adding Net Exports (NX) into the equation for aggregate demand:

$$AD = C + II + G + NX$$

As discussed in Chapter 5, Net Exports (NX) equals Exports minus Imports ($X - IM$). Exports, like intended investment and government spending, represent a positive contribution to aggregate demand. More exports mean more demand for domestically produced goods and services. Imports, on the other hand, are a negative in the equation. That means they represent a *leakage* from U.S. aggregate demand—a portion of income that is not spent on U.S. goods and services.

Negative net exports (when $X < IM$) therefore represent a net subtraction from demand for the output of U.S. businesses, and a net leakage from the circular flow. A decrease in exports (or increase in imports) tends to reduce the circular flow of domestic income, spending, and output—unless injections such as intended investment and government spending counteract this contraction. On the other hand, an increase in net exports encourages a rise in GDP and employment. For example, if Americans increase their purchases of foreign cars while buying fewer domestic cars, this will lower aggregate demand in the United States (and raise it in other car-exporting countries). On the other hand, if the U.S. computer software industry increases foreign sales, this will raise U.S. aggregate demand and employment.

The multiplier effect for an increase in exports is essentially the same as that for an increase in II or G. In our model (with a multiplier of 5), an increase of exports of 40, for example, would lead to an increase of 200 in economic equilibrium.

$$\Delta Y = mult \, \Delta X$$

We can use exactly the same logic for a lump-sum increase in imports—the effect on equilibrium income just goes in the opposite direction. An increase in imports of 40 would lower the equilibrium level of income by 200, and a decrease in imports of 40 would raise the equilibrium by 200.

The multiplier logic becomes a little more complicated, however, when we consider how import levels are determined. In general, when people receive more income in an economy that is open to trade, they spend some of it on domestically produced goods and some on imports. The proportion spent on imports, as we noted above, is a "leakage" that does not add to domestic demand. If we want to account for this fully, we need to modify our multiplier logic. The effect is similar to that of a proportional tax on consumption: It will tend to flatten the aggregate demand curve, and for the same reason. When people receive extra income, some portion of it "leaks" away into imports. This portion does not stimulate the domestic economy, so multiplier effects are smaller and the economic response a bit less dynamic. (For a full treatment of this effect, see Appendix A3.)

In effect, a portion of any aggregate demand increase goes to stimulate *someone else's economy* via imports. Thus American consumers who buy imported goods from Canada are creating jobs and income in Canada, not the United States. Does this mean that imports are bad for the United States? Not necessarily. Two other factors are important to consider. One is that U.S. consumers and U.S. industry benefit from cheaper imported goods and services, raw materials, and other industrial inputs. Another is that at least some of the money spent on imports is likely to return to the United States as demand for exports, which as we have seen stimulates an increase in GDP and employment. Problems can arise, however, when trade deficits (negative net exports) are too large for too long. We will explore this issue further in Chapter 13.

3.2 A COMPLETE MACROECONOMIC MODEL WITH TRADE

We have now completed our basic macroeconomic model. We started with a very simple economy, with just consumers and businesses, then added government spending, taxes, and the international sector. We can sum things up by referring back to the macroeconomic circular flow diagram shown in Chapter 9, Figure 9.6. In that simple model, there was one "leakage" from the macroeconomic circular flow (saving), and one "injection" back into the flow (intended investment). As we discussed, the process of macroeconomic equilibrium essentially concerns balancing these leakages and injections.

Now we have a more complex model, with three leakages (saving, taxes, and imports) and three injections (intended investment, government spending, and exports). Taxes and imports are considered leakages because, like saving, they draw funds away from the domestic income-spending flow. Government spending and exports add funds to the flow. We can modify our original circular flow diagram to show all these flows (Figure 10.6).

Macroeconomic equilibrium involves balancing the three types of leakage with the three types of injection. A change in any one will alter the equilibrium level of output. The model we have constructed allows us to understand how all these factors are related to levels of income and employment.

Does this complete our study of macroeconomic theory? No, for two major reasons. One reason is that, as we noted in Chapter 9, economists differ about how the economy works at the macro level. Economists in the classical school tend to believe that the leakages and injections will balance themselves automatically at the full-employment level of output, provided that government does not adversely affect the situation with excessive government spending. Economists of the Keynesian school believe that government policy is essential to achieve acceptable levels of income and employment. We will have a lot more to say about these economic policy debates in the next chapters.

The other reason is that we have yet to consider a very important aspect of the economy: the money supply and monetary policy. The supply of money in the economy is a very important

Figure 10.6   **Leakages and Injections in a Complete Macroeconomic Model**

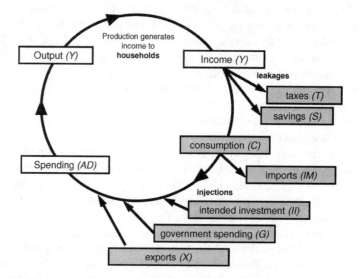

Leakages from the circular flow include taxes, saving, and imports. Injections include intended investment, government spending, and exports. The level of macroeconomic equilibrium will depend on the balance of all these flows as well as consumption levels.

factor affecting, among other things, interest rates and inflation. We need to understand how the money supply is created and regulated, and how this relates to other macroeconomic factors. This is the topic of Chapter 11. After we have covered the topics of money and monetary policy, we will return to a consideration of the issues of unemployment and inflation, and appropriate policies to respond to them, in Chapter 12.

Discussion Questions

1. What will be the likely effect of increased imports on U.S. GDP? Do imported goods undercut employment in the United States? What other developments in the economy might counteract this effect?
2. Savings, imports, and taxes are all considered to be "leakages" from aggregate demand. Are they bad for the economy? Or is there an important function for each? How are their levels related to equilibrium GDP, income, and employment?

REVIEW QUESTIONS

1. What is the impact of a change in government spending on aggregate demand and economic equilibrium?
2. What is the impact of a lump-sum change in taxes on aggregate demand and economic equilibrium? How does it differ from a change in government spending?
3. Give some examples of expansionary and contractionary fiscal policy.
4. How is the federal budget surplus or deficit defined? How has the federal budget position varied in recent years?

5. How is the federal debt different from the deficit? How has the federal debt varied in recent years?
6. What is meant by an automatic stabilizer? Give some examples of economic institutions that function as automatic stabilizers.
7. What are some of the advantages and disadvantages of discretionary fiscal policy? Give some examples of the use of discretionary fiscal policy.
8. How would a balanced budget amendment work? What are some of the arguments for and against it?
9. How does an increase in exports affect economic equilibrium?
10. How would an increase in the trade deficit affect economic equilibrium?
11. What are the three leakages and three injections in a complete macroeconomic model? How do they affect the level of economic equilibrium?

EXERCISES

1. Using the figures given in Table 10.1, determine the economic equilibrium for a government spending level of 60.
2. Using Table 10.1 and the formulas and figures given in the text for the multiplier and tax multiplier, calculate the effect on equilibrium GDP of a government spending level of 100 combined with a tax level of 100. What does this imply about the impact of a balanced government budget on GDP, as compared to government spending alone?
3. Go to the *Economic Report of the President* at http://www.gpoaccess.gov/eop/. Consult the most recent *Report*'s table on "Gross Domestic Product." For the last year, with final rather than preliminary figures, find the values of gross domestic product personal consumption expenditures, and gross private domestic investment. Now find the value for fixed investment (which is the same thing as what we have called intended investment). You will notice that the column on the right titled "Change in Private Inventories" is equal to the difference between total and fixed investment (just as we have noted that total investment equals intended investment plus change in inventories). Calculate personal consumption expenditures (*C*) and fixed investment (*II*) as percentages of gross domestic product (*Y*). Calculate a simple measure of aggregate demand (*C + II*) without government spending.
4. Continuing from the question above, go to the table "Government Consumption Expenditures and Gross Investment." Find the total for the same year. This is what we have referred to as *G* (government spending on goods and services). Approximately what percentage is *G* of gross domestic product? Calculate aggregate demand including government spending (*C + II + G*). Now go to the table "U.S. International Transactions" and look at the column entitled "Balance on Goods and Services" for the same year. This is what we have identified as *(X – IM)*. Finally, calculate aggregate demand (*C + II + G + X – IM*). This final figure for aggregate demand should be very close to the gross domestic product (*Y*)—the difference will be change in inventories and a statistical discrepancy.
5. Which of the following are examples of automatic stabilizers, and which are examples of discretionary policy? Could some be both? Explain.
   a. Tax revenues rise during an economic expansion
   b. Personal tax rates are reduced
   c. Government spending on highways is increased

  d. Farm support payments increase

  e. Unemployment payments rise during a recession

6. Suppose exports (*X*) rise by 120 billion and imports (*IM*) rise by 200 billion, resulting in an increase of 80 billion in the trade deficit. In an economy with an *mpc* of 0.75, what will be the effect of these changes on economic equilibrium? (Calculate the multiplier for this economy using the formula given in Chapter 9, Section 3.7 and repeated on page 235 of this chapter. Then apply this multiplier to the changes in *X* and *IM*.)

7. Match each concept in Column A with a definition or example in Column B.

Column A	Column B
a. Tax multiplier 9	1. Reduction in income tax rates
b. Disposable income 3	2. Unemployment compensation
c. Expansionary fiscal policy 1	3. *Y* – *T* + *TR*
d. Contractionary fiscal policy 6	4. Imports
e. Government outlays 5	5. *G* + *TR*
f. Automatic stabilizer 2	6. Reduction in government spending
g. Trade deficit 4	7. *X* < *IM* exports & imports
h. Leakage from circular flow 7	8. Intended investment
i. Injection into circular flow 8	9. – (*mult*) (*mpc*)

8. (Appendix) Using the formula given in Appendix A3 for a multiplier in an economy with proportional taxes and imports dependent on income, calculate the effect of an increase in government spending (*G*) of 150 billion on economic equilibrium. Assume that *mpc* = 0.75, *t* = 0.2 and *mpim* = 0.1. How does this more sophisticated multiplier differ from the basic multiplier? What effect will this have on the aggregate demand curve and on the economy's response to a fiscal stimulus?

APPENDIX: MORE ALGEBRAIC APPROACHES TO THE MULTIPLIER

A1. AN ALGEBRAIC APPROACH TO THE MULTIPLIER, WITH A LUMP-SUM TAX

A lump-sum tax is a tax that is simply levied on an economy as a flat amount. This amount does not change with the level of income. Suppose a lump-sum tax is levied in an economy with a government (but no foreign sector). Since consumption in this economy is $C = \bar{C} + mpc\, Y_d$ while disposable income is $Y_d = Y - \bar{T} + TR$, we can write the consumption function as:

$$C = \bar{C} + mpc\,(Y - \bar{T} + TR)$$

Thus aggregate demand in this economy can be expressed as:

$$AD = C + II + G$$
$$= \bar{C} + mpc\,(Y - \bar{T} + TR) + II + G$$
$$= (\bar{C} - mpc\,\bar{T} + mpc\,TR + II + G) + mpc\,Y$$

The last rearrangement shows that the AD curve has an intercept equal to the term in parentheses and a slope equal to the marginal propensity to consume. Changes in any of the variable in parentheses, by changing the intercept, shift the curve up or down in a parallel manner.

By substituting this into the equation for the equilibrium condition, $Y = AD$, we can derive an expression for equilibrium income in terms of all the other variables in the model:

$$Y = (\bar{C} - mpc\ \bar{T} + mpc\ TR + II + G) + mpc\ Y$$

$$Y - mpc\ Y = \bar{C} - mpc\ \bar{T} + mpc\ TR + II + G$$

$$(1 - mpc)Y = \bar{C} - mpc\ \bar{T} + mpc\ TR + II + G$$

$$Y = \frac{1}{1 - mpc}(\bar{C} - mpc\ \bar{T} + mpc\ TR + II + G)$$

If autonomous consumption, intended investment, or government spending change, these each increase equilibrium income by $mult = 1/(1-mpc)$ times the amount of the original change. If the level of lump-sum taxes or transfers changes, these change Y by either negative or positive $(mult)(mpc)$ times the amount of the original change.

To see this explicitly, consider the changes that would come about in Y if there is a change in the level of the lump sum tax from T_0 to a new level, T_1, if everything else stays the same. We can solve for the change in Y by subtracting the old equation from the new one:

$$Y_1 = \frac{1}{1 - mpc}(\bar{C} + II + G - mpc\ \bar{T}_1 + mpc\ TR)$$

$$- [Y_0 = \frac{1}{1 - mpc}(\bar{C} + II + G - mpc\ \bar{T}_0 + mpc\ TR)]$$

$$Y_1 - Y_0 = \frac{1}{1 - mpc}(\bar{C} - \bar{C} + II - II + G - G - mpc\ \bar{T}_1 + mpc\ \bar{T}_0 + mpc\ TR - mpc\ TR)$$

But $\bar{C}$, II, G, TR (and the mpc) are all unchanged, so most of the subtractions in parentheses come out to be zero. We are left with (taking the negative sign out in front):

$$Y_1 - Y_0 = -\frac{1}{1 - mpc}\ mpc(\bar{T}_1 - T_0)$$

or

$$\Delta Y = -(mult)(mpc)\Delta \bar{T}$$

As explained in the text, the multiplier for a change in taxes is smaller than the multiplier for a change in government spending, because taxation affects aggregate demand only to the extent that people *spend* their tax cut, or pay their increased taxes by reducing *consumption*. Since people may also *save* part of their tax cut or pay part of their increased taxes out of their *savings*, not all of the changes in taxes will carry through to changes in aggregate demand. The tax multiplier has a negative sign, since a *decrease* in taxes *increases* consumption, aggregate demand, and income, while a tax increase decreases them.

A2. AN ALGEBRAIC APPROACH TO THE MULTIPLIER, WITH A PROPORTIONAL TAX

With a proportional tax, total tax revenues are not set at a fixed level of revenues, as was the case with a lump sum tax, but rather are a fixed *proportion* of total income. That is, $T = tY$ where t is the tax rate. The equation for AD becomes

$$AD = \bar{C} + mpc(Y - tY + TR) + II + G$$

$$= (\bar{C} + mpc\ TR + II + G) + mpc(Y - tY)$$

$$= (\bar{C} + mpc\ TR + II + G) + mpc(1 - t)Y$$

Figure 10.7   **A Cut in the Proportional Tax Rate**

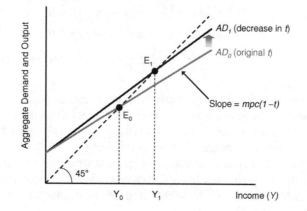

A tax cut increases the slope of the AD curve and raises equilibrium income, when the tax is proportional.

With the addition of proportional taxes, the AD curve now has a new slope: $mpc\,(1-t)$. Since t is a fraction greater than zero but less than one, this slope is generally flatter than the slope we've worked with before. A *cut* in the tax rate rotates the curve *up*ward, as shown in Figure 10.7.

Substituting in the equilibrium condition, $Y = AD$, and solving yields:

$$Y = (\bar{C} + mpc\ TR + II + G) + mpc(1-t)Y$$

$$Y - mpc(1-t)Y = \bar{C} + mpc\ TR + II + G$$

$$(1 - mpc(1-t))Y = \bar{C} + mpc\ TR + II + G$$

$$Y = \left[\frac{1}{1 - mpc(1-t)}\right](\bar{C} + mpc\ TR + II + G)$$

The term in brackets is a new multiplier, for the case of a proportional tax. It is smaller than the basic (no proportional taxation) multiplier, reflecting the fact than now any change in spending has smaller feedback effects through consumption. (Some of the change in income "leaks" into taxes.) For example, if $mpc = .8$ and $t = .2$, then the new multiplier is $1/(1 - .64)$, or approximately 2.8, as compared to the simple model multiplier $1/(1 - .8)$ which is 5. Changes in autonomous consumption or investment (or government spending or transfers) now have less of an effect on equilibrium income—the "automatic stabilizer" effect mentioned in the text.

Is there a multiplier for the tax *rate*, t? That is, could we derive from the model a formula for how much equilibrium income should change with a change in the rate (rather than level) of taxes? For example, if the tax rate were to decrease from .2 to .15, could we calculate the size of the change from Y_0 to Y_1 illustrated in Figure 10.7? Yes, but deriving a general formula for a multiplier relating the change in Y to the change in the tax rate requires the use of calculus, so it will not be pursued here.

A3. An Algebraic Approach to the Multiplier, in a Model with Trade

Suppose, in addition to consumption depending on income, imports depend on income according to the equation $IM = mpim\ Y$ where $mpim$ is the marginal propensity to import (the proportion of extra income spent on imports). The *mpim* is a fraction. In an economy including trade, the equation for aggregate demand is:

$$AD = C + II + G + X - IM$$
$$= \bar{C} + mpc(Y - tY + TR) + II + G + X - mpim\ Y$$
$$= (\bar{C} + mpc\ TR + II + G + X) + [mpc(1-t) - mpim]Y$$

The AD curve now has the intercept given by the first term in parentheses. Changes in exports shift the curve up or down. The new slope is given by the term in brackets. The slope is flatter, due to the subtraction of *mpim*.

Solving for Y (using the same method as above—but we will now leave out some of the intermediate steps) yields:

$$Y - mpc(1-t)Y + mpim\ Y = \bar{C} + mpc\ TR + II + G + X$$

$$Y = \left[\frac{1}{1 - mpc(1-t) + mpim} \right] (\bar{C} + mpc\ TR + II + G + X)$$

The term in brackets is a new multiplier that includes both proportional taxes and imports that depend on domestic income. This multiplier is even smaller than the previous two. For example, if *mpc* = .8, *t* = .2, and *mpim* = .1, the new multiplier is $1/(1-.64+.1)$ or approximately 2.2. This is because now any increase in Y "leaks" not only into saving and taxes, but also into increases in imports (which takes away from demand for domestic products).

11 Money and Monetary Policy

Everybody would like to have more money, right? Well, maybe not. In 2004 it was pretty easy to be a millionaire in Turkey—many times over. With a million Turkish lira being worth about $.75 in United States dollars, a 20,000,000-lira bill was worth about US $15. People routinely just put their thumb over the last six digits when looking at a value expressed in liras. The Turkish lira was named by *Guinness World Records* as the world's least valuable currency. But you could have lots of it!

1. Why Money?

So far, this book has said very little about money, finance, or interest rates. Yet many people consider these to be the quintessential economic issues. What is the relation of money and finance to macroeconomic behavior? Before we get into the details of how money and credit work in a sophisticated contemporary economy, let's get a few simpler—and dramatically different—pictures in our minds. These scenarios, drawn from real-world situations and events, inform how economists have come to think about money and the macroeconomy.

1.1 Money and Aggregate Demand

Let's start with a case of an economy in which inflation is running at only a low to moderate rate. Suppose further that this economy has a banking system that is sophisticated and in reasonably good shape. You are a businessperson who has a great idea about how to expand your business. Or, in your role as a household member, you are interested in buying a home for your family. But you don't have the cash. You go to a bank and ask for a loan. The bank will evaluate your trustworthiness as a borrower, see how much it currently has available to lend, and then either deny you a loan or offer you a loan on particular terms. If you receive a loan offer and accept the terms, you will take out the loan and go out and spend. If you are denied the loan, or if you think the terms are too harsh, you will forgo expanding your business or buying the house.

To the extent the government of a country can affect the volume and terms of loans made by banks, it can thus affect the level of spending in the economy. We've seen in the last two chapters how the level of spending (or aggregate demand) in an economy is related to levels of employment and output. Monetary policy that affects the behavior of banks, then, may also be a significant factor in achieving the goals of macroeconomic stabilization and low unemployment.

But not all economies enjoy low inflation rates and stable banking systems. Our next two touchstone cases illustrate these issues.

1.2 "RUNNING THE PRINTING PRESS"

Consider a country with a very simple government and banking system. The country's government is housed in a single building and pays its employees and its bills in cash. In the basement of the building is a printing press that prints paper money. The government finds it very difficult to collect enough taxes to pay its operating expenses, so it just runs the printing press every time an employee needs to be paid or a bill comes due.

What would be the effect of this on the economy? If the national economy is very large and growing, relative to the size of government expenditures, the fresh bills may just be absorbed into circulation without much effect. But if the economy is stagnant or staggering, and expenditures are large, there will soon be a classic situation of inflation caused by "too much money chasing too few goods."

If this goes on for long, a situation of hyperinflation can result. Germany after World War I, Hungary after World War II, Bolivia in the mid-1980s, Argentina during various periods, and the Ukraine in the early 1990s experienced famous hyperinflations. In Germany, for example, the economy was in tatters after the war and the government found it impossible to collect taxes in order to support its operations, let alone pay the reparations demanded by the victors. So it resorted to running the printing presses. Inflation reached a high of 41 percent—per *day!* Stories were told of people taking stacks and stacks of Deutschmarks to town in a wheelbarrow in order to make a modest purchase, and—after leaving it for a moment—returning to find the wheelbarrow stolen and the bills stacked on the ground. Or of people in a bar ordering their beers two at a time, because the price of beer was rising faster than the beer would get warm. In 1920 a German postage stamp cost 4 marks; in 1923 the same stamp cost *50 billion* marks.

In such a situation, it obviously becomes very difficult to keep a sophisticated economy going. People tend to resort to **barter**—exchanging goods directly for other goods—to try to avoid having to deal with a rapidly inflating currency. It becomes impossible to think about making a deposit in a bank, or to work out reasonable terms for a loan, and so normal patterns of saving and lending are disrupted. If they can, people may try to get a hold of—or at least keep their accounts in—a "hard," non-inflating currency issued by foreign country. Hyperinflation is obviously not a good situation, and production tends to be lowered and unemployment raised by the chaos that hyperinflation causes in an economy.

> **barter:** exchange of goods, services, or assets directly for other goods, services, or assets, without the use of money

Usually, what eventually ends a hyperinflation is that the nearly valueless currency is abandoned, and people exchange very large denominations of the old currency for small denominations of a new currency. If this is accompanied by a credible government promise to stop "running the printing press," it draws the episode of hyperinflation to a close.

Even if inflation does not reach astronomically high hyperinflation levels, high inflation can be disruptive to an economy. Ongoing high inflation tends to wipe out the value of people's savings, and hurts people who are on fixed incomes (such as non-indexed pensions). It redistributes wealth from creditors to debtors, since people now repay debts in money that is worth less than the money they originally borrowed. It creates "menu costs"—literally, the cost of time and effort made to update printed menus and other sorts of price lists. Rising and/or variable inflation rates create a great deal of uncertainty, which can make it very difficult for households and businesses to make sensible plans regarding savings, retirement, investment, etc. For these reasons, stabilization of a country's price level is among the important goals of macroeconomic policy.

1.3 DEFLATION AND FINANCIAL CRISES

Finally, consider an economy in the opposite situation, in which there is too *little* money in circulation. In this case, prices must be bid *down*. This is the case of **deflation**. Why would deflation be a problem? While deflation makes people's savings *more* valuable and *helps* people on fixed incomes, it is still disruptive. In this case, wealth is redistributed from debtors to creditors. You borrow "cheap" money, but later have to pay back with money that is "dear." It creates menu costs. It creates uncertainty. When people come to expect deflation, it may also cause them to cut back on spending. Why buy a big item such as a car or computer now, if you believe you will be able to get the same item cheaper next year?

> **deflation:** when the aggregate price level falls

Deflation is often touched off by a financial crisis in which many people lose access to the opportunity to obtain loans, and perhaps access to their own deposits at banks as well. If you can't withdraw money from your account at a bank, and you can't get a loan, then you can't pay for things. If many people are in this situation, the economy grinds to a halt—or at least slows down considerably. With less money being spent, prices fall. The Great Depression in the United States was accompanied by just such a collapse in the banking system. The "bank runs" or "banking panics" of 1930–33, in which people all rushed to try to withdraw their deposits all at once, caused many banks to fail. Since deposit insurance didn't exist yet back in those days, people's accounts at those banks were wiped out. The price level dropped 25 percent over the span of a few years.

But deflation isn't just "ancient history." Japan has also recently experienced deflation touched off by a financial crisis. In late 1989 a speculative bubble in real estate and stocks came to a sudden end. Japanese banks had, it turned out, racked up huge amounts of bad loans—loans they would never be able to collect. Some banks were ordered to shut down, while others teetered. People became justifiably leery of depositing funds—or of spending, with the future so uncertain. With deposits shrinking, banks were unable to lend as much, and with spending shrinking, the Japanese economy slid into recession. Over the next several years, prices gently but steadily fell at a rate of about 1 percent per year.

These situations can be very frustrating, when looked at from the perspective of the real potential productivity of an economy. People may want to work and spend, and businesses might have great ideas for expansion, but they are constrained by the lack of spendable assets to grease the wheels of the economy. For this reason, stability of the financial system is an important policy goal for governments, and closely related to both the goal of price stability and the goal of raising living standards.

Discussion Questions

1. Which of the three states just described—low inflation, high inflation, or deflation—best characterizes the U.S. economy right now? Do you know of any country currently in one of the other states?
2. Unemployment and inflation are usually considered to be the "bads" that come with business cycles. Compare the costs to society of unemployment to the costs to society of inflation.

2. What Is Money?

You have no doubt that the bills and coins you have in your wallet are "money." Economists would agree with you on that. But in other ways, the way economists use the term is very different from the way it is used in popular speech. Money, to an economist, is something that plays three specific roles in an economy, and the cash in your pocket is only one form.

2.1 The Roles of Money

One way money can be understood is by the roles it plays in an economy. It is a very special kind of financial asset (form of financial capital) that has three important functions.

First, it is a *medium of exchange.* That is, when you sell something, you accept money in return. When you buy something, you give over money to get the good or service you want. Without a decent medium of exchange, an economy would have to run as a barter system, as mentioned earlier. You would have to directly trade a tangible object or service in order to get a good or service in exchange. This could be quite inconvenient—there would have to be what is called a "double coincidence of wants." For example, if you want pizza and can offer Web design services, you would need to hunt around for pizza makers in need of Web design. Such merchants may or may not exist, and even if they do, you would certainly have to spend some considerable time finding them. With money, on the other hand, you can sell your services to anyone who wants them, and use the money you get to buy pizza from anyone who supplies it.

Second, money is also *a store of value.* That means that, even if you hold onto it for a while, it will still be good for transactions when you are ready to use it. This is obviously a necessary property, since the pizza makers are unlikely to accept your money in exchange unless they know that, a month from now, their landlord will also accept the same money in exchange. In serving as a store of value, money serves as a way of holding wealth—just like any other form of financial or real capital that is held because it is worth something. The thing that makes money distinct from other assets is its **liquidity**, that is, the ease with which it can be used in exchange. Money is highly liquid—you can take it to the store and use it immediately. If you own a car, shares in a business, or a valuable piece of jewelry, these are also ways of storing your wealth, but they are not liquid. You would need to convert the value you've stored in them to money before you could buy something else.

> **liquidity:** the ease of use of an asset as a medium of exchange

The third role of money is that it is *a unit of account.* Sometimes things are assigned money values even if they are not actually being bought and sold. When a firm values unsold inventories in its warehouses in order to calculate its profits or losses, for example, or a town assesses the dollar value of a house even though there are no plans for it to be sold, they are using money as a unit of account.

> Money has three roles: as a medium of exchange, a store of value, and a unit of account

Some things that are commonly called "money" are not money in the way that economists use this term. For example, we might commonly say that someone "makes a lot of money" because he has a high annual *income.* Income, however, is a *flow* variable, measured (as described in Chapter 3) over a period of time. Money is a *stock* variable—a particular kind of asset. A person who makes a lot of income over a year may acquire a large stock of money—or he may not. If he quickly spends his income on goods and services he may have high *income* (over the year) but accumulate little *money* (measured at a point in time). We also may say that someone "has a lot of money" if she has accumulated a lot of *wealth*. But this is also not technically correct. A wealthy person may hold a lot of her assets in the form of corporate shares, real estate, or Renaissance paintings, rather than as spendable, liquid money. Middle-class families are sometimes described as "house rich, cash poor" exactly for this reason. If they attempt to hold a high proportion of their assets as home equity, they may end up with very little in the way of funds they can actually spend—that is, *money*.

| Money is *not* the same thing as *wealth* or *income*

2.2 TYPES OF MONEY

Throughout much of history, **commodity money** was the most common type of money. Commodity money is made up of something that is valuable in itself, and also used in exchange. Coins made of gold or silver are probably the most familiar example. Decorative beads, shells, fish hooks, and cattle have served the purpose in some cultures. In prisons and prisoner of war camps, cigarettes have often developed into a medium of exchange. "Prices" for chocolate or other goods and services are then quoted in terms of numbers of cigarettes required in exchange.

| **commodity money:** a good used as money that is also valuable in itself

To be used as money, a commodity must be *generally acceptable, standardized, durable, portable, scarce,* and, preferably, easily *divisible.* Cigarettes have been used as money even by non-smokers, for example, because they know that because cigarettes are generally accepted in trade, they can use them to get what they actually want. Standardization is important, so that disputes don't arise about the quality and value of the money. Coins stamped by the government are a popular sort of money because the stamp is a sign that they are of equal weight and purity of mineral content. Gold and silver have historically been popular because coins made from them are durable. The scarcity of gold and silver was also an important factor. Coins made of, say, wood, in an area with many forests would rapidly lose value as everyone could just make their own. Divisibility is also important. Heavy gold ingots might be useful for buying expensive real estate, but are not very useful for buying pasta for dinner. Smaller coins, and coins made of less valuable minerals, were historically minted to provide a medium of exchange for smaller purchases.

Gold and silver coins, while fairly portable, can still be pretty inconvenient to carry around in large quantities. Individual banks, state governments, and national governments have at various times issued paper monies that represent claims on actual commodities, usually gold or silver. For many years, starting in the late 1880s, government-issued silver certificates were the main form of domestic paper money in the United States. International transactions were, for many years, based on gold reserves. When people carried such a piece of paper, they could think of it as a certificate showing that they owned a bit of an ingot in Fort Knox.

In the 1960s, however, due to an increase in the price of silver, the government eliminated silver certificates and replaced them with what you probably have in your pocket today. What is commonly called a "dollar bill" is, if you look at it, officially called a Federal Reserve Note. About the same time, the United States government also removed silver coins from circulation, replacing them with look-alike coins made from cheaper nickel-clad copper. In 1971, President Richard Nixon took the U.S. economy off the international gold standard.

So what is the basis of value of the coins and dollar bills we use today? The basis of value is—precisely and no more than—the expectation that the dollar bill will be acceptable in exchange. The currency and coins we use now are what are called **fiat money**. "Fiat" in Latin means "let it be done," and a legal authority does something "by fiat" when it just declares something to be so. *A dollar bill is money because the government declares it to be money.* Fiat money is what some people call a "social construction"—something that works in society because of how people think and act toward it, not because of something it intrinsically "is." Fiat money works fine as long as people are generally in agreement that it has value. Later in this chapter, we will examine some cases in which people have stopped agreeing—when people have lost confidence in the value of their money.

> **fiat money:** a medium of exchange used as money because a government says it has value, and people accept it

As economies get more and more sophisticated, however, even carrying around paper money gets inconvenient. These days, you are likely to take care of many of your transactions by other means, such as making electronic funds transfers from your bank. Understanding what types of transactions are said to involve "money" requires understanding how various assets differ in their liquidity and also understanding the distinction between money and credit.

2.3 MEASURES OF MONEY

Because different assets have different degrees of liquidity, it can be difficult to draw distinct lines between which assets are "money," which are ambiguous "near money," and which are "not money." As a result, economists have devised various ways to define and measure the volume of money that is circulating in a given economy.

Coins and bills are obviously "money." In the United States today, coins are manufactured by the U.S. Mint at four locations around the country, while bills are created by the Bureau of Engraving and Printing. When economists measure a country's "money supply," only currency that is *in circulation* is included—not currency that is for example, sitting in a vault at the Mint or at a bank. In November 2007, for example, currency in circulation in the United States totaled $764 billion.

But checking accounts are also extremely liquid. People can pay for many things using paper checks and, increasingly, debit cards and electronic transfers that take funds directly from their checking accounts. The most commonly used measure of the amount of money in an economy at a given point in time, then, includes not only currency in circulation but also the value of checkable deposits, as well as the value of traveler's checks. It is called **M1**. In November 2007, checkable deposits totaled $594 billion, and travelers checks were $6.4 billion, so that total M1 was measured at $1.36 trillion.

> **M1:** a measure of the money supply equal to currency, checkable deposits, and traveler's checks

But many people can now move funds from their savings accounts to their checking accounts with the click of a mouse, or make electronic payments directly from their savings accounts. So shouldn't savings accounts also be considered "money"? A measure called M2 includes everything in M1, plus savings deposits and some other funds such as small certificates of deposit and retail money market funds. M2 is now over five times the size of M1. When economists talk about "the money supply" they usually mean either M1 or M2.

What about if you use a credit card to make a purchase? From the user's point of view, using a credit card often seems to be very much like using a debit card or cash from one's pocket. In economists' terms, however, one does *not* use "money" when one uses a credit card. This is because when you use a credit card, you are, technically speaking, taking out a temporary loan from the credit card company. Only one day a month, when you send a check or electronic transfer to your credit card company from your checking account, do you make a "money" transaction.

Discussion Questions

1. Suppose you asked someone who has not taken an economics class what makes a dollar bill have value. What do you think he or she would say? Would he or she be correct?
2. What do you commonly use to make payments? Cash? Credit cards? Online payments? In which of these cases are you using "money"?

3. THE BANKING SYSTEM

It is pretty easy to understand how the United States Mint and the Bureau of Engraving and Printing create currency, and how they could create more or less of it. But how does currency make its way into people's wallets? How are bank deposits such as checking accounts created? How can the volume of currency and deposits be increased or decreased over time, as a matter of macroeconomic policy? To understand the answer to these questions, we need to know more about how a contemporary banking system works.

In the United States, the Federal Reserve System (or "Fed," for short) determines how much currency should be produced, and puts it into circulation. In addition, the actions of the Federal Reserve together with actions of private banks create the economy's volume of checkable deposits. For much of Europe, now that many countries have joined together using the Euro as their currency, the equivalent institution to the Fed is the European Central Bank (ECB). Most countries have combined systems of private and central banking, which work at least roughly like the system described here. We will start by looking at private banks.

3.1 PRIVATE BANKS

In the discussion of the classical market for loanable funds in Chapter 9, we assumed that some agents lend and others borrow, but we paid no attention to how borrowers and lenders would find each other. An individual might go to a relative for a loan. When the borrower is operating in a more impersonal way—perhaps because it is a business, not an individual, or because the would-be borrower does not have personal contacts with individuals who can make the needed loan—then there is need for an intermediary that can put together would-be lenders with would-be borrowers. A private bank is a type of institution called a **financial intermediary**. Individuals and organizations deposit funds with financial intermediaries, for safekeeping, or to provide the convenience of writing checks, or to earn interest. The financial intermediaries use the funds deposited with them to make loans to individuals and organizations that seek to borrow funds. Besides banks, financial intermediaries include savings and loan associations, credit unions, and life insurance companies.

> **financial intermediary:** an institution such as a bank, savings and loan association, or life insurance company that accepts funds from savers and makes loans to borrowers

A private bank is a for-profit business, meaning that it seeks to make earnings on its activities. It does this by charging interest (and perhaps other fees) on the loans it makes. One of its functions is to screen the parties seeking loans, in order to determine their credit-worthiness. Loaning is a risky business—not all loans made will be paid back in full. Some of the risk can be

Table 11.1 **A Simplified Balance Sheet of a Private Bank**

Assets		Liabilities	
Loans	$ 70 million	Deposits	$ 100 million
Government bonds	$ 20 million		
Reserves	$ 10 million		

alleviated by demanding physical assets as collateral. For example, mortgages and home-equity loans are collateralized by the value of a house, which the bank may take possession of if the owner defaults on the loan. Many educational loans are backed up by government guarantees. Other loans are made on the basis of an evaluation of, say, the strength of a business plan and a business's record in paying back past loans. Banks may charge different interest rates depending on the riskiness of a loan, or deny a loan request entirely.

To understand what happens in a banking system, we will start with a private bank's simplified balance sheet, shown in Table 11.1. A balance sheet is a standard double-entry accounting representation of a private bank's assets and liabilities. It must "balance" in that assets and liabilities must add up the same amount. The right side of a balance sheet, as shown in Table 11.1, lists an organization's liabilities. An economic liability is anything that one economic actor owes to another. The funds you deposit in a bank are listed among the bank's liabilities, because it has an obligation to repay these funds to you.

Except in the case of banking panics, depositors are not likely all to show up at the same time, demanding their funds in cash. Although the bank needs to keep some funds around to meet depositors' withdrawal needs, it normally can use most of the deposits it holds to obtain earnings.

Assets of an organization are listed on the left side of a balance sheet, as shown in Table 11.1. **Bank reserves**, shown as an asset in Table 11.1, include vault cash that the bank keeps around to meet likely short-term calls, such as depositors' withdrawals. Reserves also include deposits that the private bank has in an account at the Federal Reserve (which will be discussed further below). These are things that the bank owns. Reserves do not earn interest.

> **bank reserves:** funds not loaned out by a private bank, but kept as vault cash or on deposit at the Federal Reserve

One quite safe way the bank can earn some interest is to loan money to the federal government. Recall from Chapter 10 that the United States Treasury borrows from the public when it needs to finance a government deficit or refinance part of the debt. It does this by issuing government bonds, which give the buyer the right to specific payments in the future. Depending on the duration of the loan, these securities may be called "bills" (you may have read about "T-bills" in the financial pages of the newspaper), "bonds," or "notes." We will continue to use the term "government bonds" to represent any federal government security. Very active markets exist for trading federal bonds, and a particular bond may change hands many times before it is paid off. Banks tend to keep some of their assets—about one-quarter, on average—in government bonds, because bonds earn interest but are also relatively liquid. If it looks like depositors will want more cash back than a bank has in its vault, the private bank can quickly sell some of its Treasury bonds on the open bond market.

The major asset of a private bank—and the major way it makes its earnings—is its portfolio of (other) loans. These are funds that are owed to the bank by businesses, households, nonprofits, or non-federal levels of government. Unlike T-bills, which can be liquidated quickly if necessary, some of these loans may be business loans, home mortgages, or consumer loans that won't be repaid for years. These assets are generally far less liquid than vault cash or T-bills. The health of a private banking system depends on depositors remaining confident in the safety of the funds they have entrusted to the banking system, and not trying to withdraw their funds faster than such loans are repaid.

3.2 The Federal Reserve System

In 1907, the U.S. economy experienced a banking panic, in which depositors lost trust in banks, tried to withdraw their deposits all at once, and as a result caused many banks to fail. In response, Congress enacted legislation creating the Federal Reserve system in 1913. The Fed is a rather odd organization in that is not exactly part of the government, yet not entirely separate from it, either. It is overseen by a board of governors whose seven members are nominated by the president and approved by the Senate, and who serve fourteen-year terms. One member of the board is named as chair, and serves in that capacity for a four-year term (though many have served consecutive terms). The long terms of service are intended to help insulate the Fed from short-term political pressures.

The Fed performs a number of important functions. As we have already noted, it serves as a "banker's bank" by holding deposits made by private banks. One of the Fed's important day-to-day functions involves using these deposits to clear checks drawn on one bank and deposited in another. When a check is drawn on a bank, the piece of paper goes to a Fed clearinghouse. The bank's account at the Fed is debited by the amount of the check. When a check is deposited, that bank's account at the Fed is credited with the funds. If a bank is in need of vault cash, it can also buy currency from the Fed, using the funds in its Fed account as payment. The Fed orders banks to keep a certain percentage of their deposits as **required reserves**, in the form of either vault cash or in such deposit as the Fed. Currently, banks are required to keep an amount equal to 10 percent of their checkable deposits as reserves. If it wishes, a bank may keep reserves in excess of the required amount, although if it does it may forgo profitable earnings opportunities.

> **required reserves:** reserves that banks are required to hold by the Fed

Another of the Fed's important tasks is to attempt to stabilize the rate of exchange between domestic and foreign currencies. And the Fed, along with other organizations such as the Federal Deposit Insurance Corporation (FDIC), regulates banks, attempting to make sure that banks operate as much as possible without error or fraud. Because the FDIC guarantees the value of many accounts, and the Fed is willing to make emergency loans to banks that get into a liquidity crunch, the sorts of crises in depositor confidence that led to bank runs in the past are now far less likely.

In terms of structure, the Federal Reserve system consists of the board of governors based in Washington, D.C., and twelve regional Federal Reserve Banks based in cities including New York, San Francisco, St. Louis, and Chicago. The structure of the European Central Bank is somewhat similar, in that while it has headquarters in Frankfurt, Germany, each of the fifteen member countries also retains its own national central bank.*

The Fed keeps close track of the economy, and tries to sense whether some adjustment in the money supply might be necessary in order to support aggregate demand (as discussed in

---

* The European Central Bank operates in the 15 European Union countries (as of March 2008) that have adopted the euro as their currency. The remaining EU countries have yet to meet the criteria for adopting the euro.

Table 11.2   **A Simplified Balance Sheet of the Federal Reserve**

Assets		Liabilities	
Government Bonds	$ 750 billion	Currency in Circulation	$ 700 billion
		Bank reserves	$ 50 billion

Section 1.1 above) or counteract undesirable changes in the inflation rate (as were discussed in Sections 1.2 and 1.3). We will examine the macroeconomic consequences of Fed actions later in this chapter, but for right now we will concentrate on the mechanics of *how* the Fed influences the money supply.

3.3 THE CREATION OF MONEY AND CREDIT

The Fed has various means of changing the volume of money and credit in the economy, all of which involve changing the level of bank reserves. The most commonly used tool is **open market operations**. In open market operations, the Federal Reserve Bank of New York changes the level of bank reserves by buying or selling government bonds. Such operations are directed by the Federal Open Market Committee (FOMC). Let's see what happens when the FOMC undertakes a purchase of government bonds on the open market.

open market operations: sales or purchases of government bonds by the Fed

A simplified balance sheet for the Federal Reserve is shown in Table 11.2. Because currency is issued by the Fed, currency in circulation is the Fed's major liability. Its other major liability is the reserves held by private banks. Recall that these consist of vault cash and deposits the banks have at the Fed. Just as deposits made by individuals at banks are the liabilities of the banks, deposits made by banks at the Fed are liabilities of the Fed. The Fed holds various assets, but the most important one for our story is its stock of government bonds.

When the Fed makes an open market purchase of bonds, its holdings of bonds increase. It generally makes such purchases from a commercial bank, so it pays for the purchase by crediting the bank's account with the Federal Reserve System by the amount of the purchase. What does it pay *with*? Unlike any other actor in the economy, the Fed can create funds with the proverbial "stroke of a pen," or, these days, alteration of a computer database at the New York office. It simply declares that the bank's reserves are now higher. Remember how we explained above that dollar bills are "fiat" money, whose value depends on a government declaration that they are money? Bank reserves are similar: Odd as it may seem, the Fed can create reserves by simply declaring that the balance in a bank's account is now higher.

When the Fed makes an open market purchase, it increases something called the **monetary base** (or **high-powered money**). This is defined as the sum of currency in circulation and bank reserves. The monetary base is the sort of "money" that the Fed directly controls.

monetary base (or **high-powered money**): currency plus bank reserves (directly controlled by the Fed)

Suppose the Fed buys $10 million worth of government bonds from ABCBank. The changes in the Fed's balance sheet and the balance sheet of a ABCBank are shown in Table 11.3. The Fed increases its holdings of bonds, an asset, and bank reserves, a liability. ABCBank changes the mix of assets it holds, now holding less in bonds and more in reserves. Notice that both balance

Table 11.3   **An Open Market Purchase of Government Bonds by the Fed**

(a) Change in the Fed Balance Sheet

Assets		Liabilities	
Government bonds	+$ 10 million	Bank reserves	+$ 10 million

(b) Change in ABCBank's Balance Sheet

Assets		Liabilities	
Government bonds	−$ 10 million		
Reserves	+$ 10 million		

Table 11.4   **A Loan by ABCBank Becomes a Deposit in XYZBank**

(a) Next Change in the ABCBank's Balance Sheet

Assets		Liabilities	
Loans	+$ 10 million		
Reserves	−$ 10 million		

(b) Change in XYZBank's Balance Sheet

Assets		Liabilities	
Reserves	+$ 10 million	Deposits	+$ 10 million

sheets still balance—if total assets equaled total liabilities before the change, they will still be equal after the open market purchase.

So far in our story, reserves have risen by $10 million, but the supply of money in circulation (as measured by M1 or other measures) has not changed. But if ABCBank sees opportunities to make profitable loans, it will not let its new $10 million in reserves just sit at the Fed. If it just met its reserve requirement before the bond purchase, then all of this new $10 million is *excess* reserves. It can use this $10 million to make $10 million of new loans. This movement of $10 million from reserves to new loans is shown in Table 11.4(a).

Suppose it makes a $10 million loan to Jane's Construction, and that, after obtaining the loan in the form of a check, Jane's Construction deposits the entire amount of the funds at XYZBank. (We assume a different bank, so we can keep track of changes in balance sheets more easily.) The changes in the balance sheets of XYZBank are shown in Table 11.4(b). Since the way that the Fed clears checks is by increasing or decreasing the deposits it holds for banks, the initial impact on XYZBank of the deposit of the check by Jane's Construction is a $10 million increase in both its checkable deposits and its reserves at the Fed.

Note, first of all, that the money supply has now increased. Checkable deposits are part of M1, and there are now $10 million more of checkable deposits in the economy than there were before. Through an open market purchase of bonds paid for by a "stroke of the pen," the Fed has brought new money into being.

Second, note that XYZBank now has excess reserves, so this is not the end of the story. If required reserves are 10 percent of deposits, it can loan out much of the $10 million of new funds it has received—$9 million—while keeping only 10 percent ($1 million) as reserves. These new loans will, in turn, become new deposits in one of these banks or elsewhere. Then M1 will have increased by the initial 10 million, plus the second-round $9 million—already an increase totaling $19 million, which is quite a bit larger than the initial $10 million increase in high-powered money. Of course, the bank that receives the $9 million in deposits resulting from XYZBank's loans will find that it has excess reserves, and will also be able to make new loans, and the process will continue. Where will it all end?

The story is actually somewhat more complicated than this, because sometimes banks hold excess reserves and often people who take out loans want to hold some of the funds in cash or in types of deposits that are not part of M1. So not all high-powered money creation will translate directly into new deposits and loans, and monetary expansion will not be quite as dramatic as in the example above. Economists define the **money multiplier** as the ratio of the money supply to the monetary base,

$$money \ multiplier = \frac{money \ supply}{monetary \ base}$$

Using M1 as the measure of money, empirical studies have shown the money multiplier in the United States to be currently very close to two. That is, if the Fed acts to increase reserves and currency by $10 million, the total increase in the money supply would be expected to be around double that:

$$\Delta \ money \ supply = money \ multiplier \times \Delta \ monetary \ base$$

$$\$20 \ million = 2 \times 10 \ million$$

With "the stroke of a pen," the Fed open market purchase of government bonds increases the money supply by about twice the value of the initial bond purchase.

> **money multiplier:** defined as the ratio of the money supply to the monetary base, it tells by how much the money supply will change for a given change in high-powered money.

Notice that, looking at the same story in a slightly different way, the action of the Fed can also be seen as increasing the amount of *credit* extended to private actors in the economy. The Fed, in making an open market purchase of government bonds, in essence takes that portion of the public debt out of circulation. (Recall from Chapter 10 that government bonds are issued by the Treasury to finance federal budget deficits.) The new bank reserves created by the purchase of government bonds allow banks to extend more credit—new loans—to private actors in the economy. Traditionally macroeconomists have tended to look at the assets side of the banks' balance sheets and perceive the story outlined above as a matter of increasing deposits and hence increasing the money supply. More recently, some macroeconomists have focused more on the liabilities side of the banks' balance sheets, and see this as a story of an expansion of credit. While in some sense, the two views are just "two sides of the same coin," looking at the money face of monetary policy tends to draw more attention to people's need for liquidity, while looking at the credit face draws more attention to issues of how financial capital is created and distributed within the economy.

3.4 OTHER MONETARY POLICY TOOLS

So, if the Fed wants to increase the volume of money and private credit circulating in an economy, it can use open market operations. Open market purchases of government bonds increase reserves. Banks will generally then increase their loans, which increases deposits and hence the money supply.

While this is, in fact, what the Fed usually does when it wants to expand the money supply, it also has other tools at its disposal. Another thing it can do is lower the required reserve ratio. This would expand the money supply by allowing banks to make more loans on a smaller base of reserves. It uses this tool rather rarely, however.

If a bank falls short of having the required amount of reserves on hand, it can borrow funds from the Fed at what is called the "discount window" at a rate of interest traditionally called the **discount rate**. In theory, a reduction in the discount rate should increase the money supply, because this would lower the cost to a bank of being found to be below its required level of reserves. A bank could then be somewhat more aggressive about making loans. In fact, however, since the Fed frowns on (and penalizes) banks who are found to be low on reserves too often, banks tend to prefer to borrow from each other if they look like they will come up short.

> **discount rate:** the interest rate at which banks can borrow reserves from the Fed discount window

The Fed can cause the money supply (and credit) to contract, as well. If instead of making an open market purchase of government bonds, it makes an open market *sale,* everything in the story we've just told happens in reverse. Private banks will now hold *more* in government bonds and *less* in reserves. If they hold less in reserves, then they have to tighten up on loans. If they tighten up on loans, then there will be fewer deposits. The money multiplier also works in reverse.

> The Fed can increase the money supply by making an open market purchase of bonds, lowering the required reserve ratio, or lowering the discount rate. It can decrease the money supply by making an open market sale of bonds, raising the required reserve ratio, or raising the discount rate.

In a growing economy, however, a central bank would rarely want to shrink the money supply in absolute terms. A growing economy, as measured by GDP, means ever more transactions need to be facilitated by a readily available liquid asset, and a generally growing demand by private economic actors for loans. "Loose" monetary policy, in the case of a real-world growing economy, then, usually means making the money supply grow *faster* than it has been growing. "Tight" policy means making the money supply grow *slower,* rather than actually making M1 fall. While we assume a no-growth economy for simplicity in many of our models, this reality should be kept in mind.

In this section, we've discussed the technical question of *how* the Fed or another economy's central bank can change the volume of money and credit in an economy. Now we can move on to the more interesting questions of *why* it may—or may not—want to do so. We will introduce these issues by taking two extreme cases first.

- The first case is where inflation can be assumed to be fairly stable, and the main thing policymakers are worried about is output.
- The second case is where policymakers are primarily worried about inflation.

These important base cases are useful for analyzing the situation of certain economies at particular times. The last section of this chapter looks at the more complicated case where nothing is assumed to be stable, and delves into controversies about monetary policies.

Discussion Questions

1. From the description of the Fed and the earlier discussion of money, can you name some things that private banks had to do for themselves before the Federal Reserve System was created? What were some of problems that resulted?
2. Describe in words how a Fed open market operation can increase the volume of money in the economy.

4. THE THEORY OF MONEY, INTEREST RATES, AND AGGREGATE DEMAND

Our discussion up to this point has focused on the volume of money and credit in the economy. Up through the 1960s, the Fed generally formulated its goals in terms of raising, lowering, or keeping steady the growth rate of measures of money such as M1 or M2. Economists still, conventionally, talk about monetary policy in terms of expanding or contracting the money supply. The Appendix to this chapter develops a model of money supply and money demand that can be helpful in understanding how academic economists commonly address these issues.

In an economy that is experiencing fairly low inflation, and that has a healthy banking system, however, most of the concern with the money supply is really a concern about interest rates, the availability of credit, and the consequences of these for aggregate demand. In contemporary discussions of the Fed's monetary policy, the focus is almost always on interest rates. How does the Fed affect interest rates, and how do changing interest rates affect the macroeconomy? The following explanation will help you understand how monetary policy is commonly discussed in the media.

4.1 THE FEDERAL FUNDS RATE AND OTHER INTEREST RATES

In recent years, when changes in monetary policy are announced by leaders of the Fed or discussed in the financial pages of the newspaper, attention usually focuses on what is called the **federal funds rate**. This is the going rate of interest determined on a private market of bank-to-bank loans. If a bank finds it has more reserves than it needs to meet its reserve requirements, it offers funds on the "federal funds" market, usually just overnight. If another bank is short on reserves, it borrows on that market, and pays back the next day. Although a quick reading of reports in the media often make it sound as though the Fed directly controls the federal funds rate (for example, headlines may read, "Fed Announces Cut in Federal Funds Rate of 0.25 Percent"), this in not, in fact, the case. The Fed announces desired *target* or *benchmark levels* for the federal funds rate, and then acts on bank reserves in order to try to achieve that target. Because the Fed is generally quite effective at this, the difference between the (official) *target* federal funds rate and the (market-determined) *actual* federal funds rate often seems blurred.

> **federal funds rate:** the interest rate determined in the private market for overnight loans of reserves among banks

A simplified model of the federal funds market is portrayed in Figure 11.1(a). The quantity of funds is on the horizontal axis, and the federal funds rate—the price of borrowing on this market—is on the vertical axis. (Note that this is just a specific variant of the sort of "market for loanable funds" discussed in Chapter 9.) The actors on both sides of this market are banks. The supply curve for federal funds is upward sloping, since higher returns on this market will mean that banks with excess reserves will be more likely to lend them here, rather than finding other ways to lend them out. The demand curve for federal funds is downward sloping, since

Figure 11.1   **The Market for Federal Funds and an Open Market Purchase**

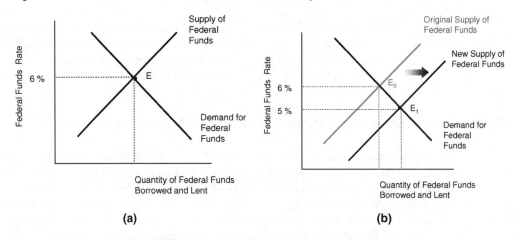

When the Federal Reserve makes an open market purchase of government bonds, it increases the supply of reserves that can be lent on the federal funds market, lowering the federal funds rate.

the lower the interest rate, the more willing banks are to borrow. In Figure 11.1(a), the federal funds rate at which the market clears is 6 percent. (Interest rates are generally stated in annualized terms—what the borrower would pay if they held the loan for a year—no matter how long the loan is actually held.)

The Fed undertakes open market operations with the goal of pushing the going rate for loans in that market to the level it chooses. Recall that when the Fed makes an open market purchase, it increases the quantity of reserves that banks hold. All else being equal, this increases the amount of reserves available for private lending in the federal funds market. In Figure 11.1(b), this is shown as the supply curve for federal funds shifting to the right. The federal funds rate falls.

Since 1995, the Fed has explicitly announced its targets for the federal funds rate, and then taken the necessary steps to keep the actual rate as close to the target rate as possible. Figure 11.2 shows how the Fed reacts to a shift in the demand for federal funds. A rise in demand for federal funds is shown by shift A. If the Fed took no action in response to this shift, the increase in demand would cause the interest rate to rise. The Fed counteracts this upward pressure by putting more reserves into the system via open market purchases, shifting the supply curve outward (shift B). The effect is to virtually fix this important interest rate. Conversely, the Fed would meet a decrease in the demand for federal funds with open market sales.

Because financial markets in a sophisticated economy tend to be very interlinked, a drop in the interest rate in one major market will tend to carry over into other markets. When banks have to pay more to borrow reserves, they will tend to charge more to their own customers. Figure 11.3 shows how the **prime bank rate**—the rate banks charge their most creditworthy commercial customers—closely follows the federal funds rate. Banks have generally kept their prime rate at the federal funds rate plus 3 percentage points. The rate you, as an individual, will be charged by a bank on a loan will generally be higher than the prime rate, and the interest rate you receive on your deposits will always be lower than the prime rate (so the bank can make a profit). But you may notice that consumer rates also often go up or down with changes in the federal funds rate.

prime bank rate: the interest rate that banks charge their most trusted commercial borrowers

Figure 11.2   **Maintaining the Federal Funds Target Rate**

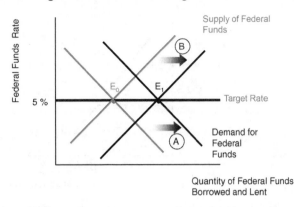

If the Federal Reserve sees the demand for reserves rising (shift A), it supplies more reserves to banks and thus to the federal funds market (shift B). It does the opposite if it sees demand falling. The result is a rate that is virtually fixed at the level targeted by the Federal Reserve.

Figure 11.3   **The Federal Fund and Prime Rates, 1994–2007**

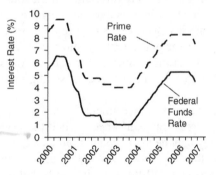

A number of other interest rates in the economy, including the prime rate charged by banks to commercial borrowers, tend to follow the Federal Funds Rate. (Source: Federal Reserve Board, monthly data)

As a stylized fact, then, economists tend to say that an expansionary monetary policy expands credit and lowers interest rates economy-wide. Conversely, contractionary monetary policy tends to shrink the volume of credit and raise interest rates, economy-wide.*

4.2 INTEREST RATES AND INVESTMENT

Economists are particularly interested in interest rates because of their effect on investment. To the extent that agents make investments using borrowed funds, higher interest rates make investing more expensive, and, hence, less attractive. Residential investment, in particular, has

---

* Things get more complicated when we consider the duration of loans, and the willingness of banks to lend in various parts of the business cycle. We address these issues in the Appendix.

Figure 11.4   **The Intended Investment Schedule**

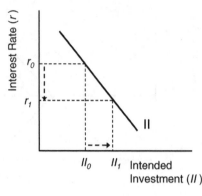

All else equal, if the interest rate falls (from r_0 to r_1), intended investment should rise (from II_0 to II_1).

historically been especially sensitive to variations in interest rates. Traditionally, investment in homes has been financed by fifteen- or thirty-year mortgages. A small change in the interest rate can add up, over time, to a very big difference in the total cost of buying a house.

The case for interest rate effects on intended business investment on *nonresidential* structures, equipment, and inventories, however, is a bit more mixed. We saw in Chapter 9 that Keynes did not think that changes in the interest rate would be sufficient to get the economy out of the Great Depression. Investor pessimism, during that period, was very deep. Trying to encourage businesses to invest when they see no prospect of selling more of their goods is like the proverbial problem of pushing on a string.

The idea that business fixed investment primarily responds to changes in sales, much more than to changes in interest rates, has been called the **accelerator principle**. If businesses see their sales rising, they may need to expand their capacity—that is, invest in new equipment and structures—in order to keep up with demand for their product. Since the best overall indicator of expanded sales is a rising GDP, this principle says that the best predictor of investment growth is GDP growth. Conversely, a small decline—or even just slowing down—of demand, may lead to a disproportionate drying up of intended investment, as firms come to fear being caught with too much capacity. To the extent the accelerator principle is in force, changes in the interest rate may have only a relatively minor effect on levels of investment.

accelerator principle: the idea that high GDP growth leads to high investment growth

Given a particular level of optimism or pessimism, however, firms can be expected to pay at least some attention to interest rates in deciding how much to invest. Combining this logical assumption with the empirically observed sensitivity of residential investment to interest rates, our simple model of macroeconomic stabilization says that, *all else being equal,* lower interest rates will lead to higher intended investment spending (and vice versa for higher interest rates). Intended investment will be inversely related to the interest rate, *r,* as shown in Figure 11.4.

Changes in investor confidence, related to actual (via the accelerator principle) or expected levels of spending, can be portrayed as shifting this intended investment curve. An increase in investor confidence, for example, shifts the curve to the right as shown in Figure 11.5. At any given interest rate, firms now want to invest more. A decrease in investor confidence would shift the curve to the left.

Figure 11.5   **An Increase in Investor Confidence**

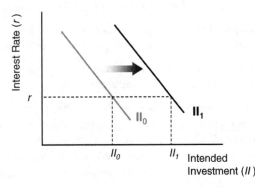

If firms become more confident about future sales, and want to increase their capacity, the intended investment schedule shifts to the right.

Figure 11.6   **Expansionary Monetary Policy and the AD Curve**

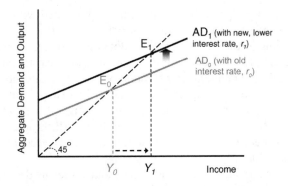

In this model, expansionary monetary policy lowers interest rates, raises investment spending, and raises aggregate demand, income and output.

4.3 MONETARY POLICY AND AGGREGATE DEMAND

Our basic model of aggregate demand, developed in Chapters 9 and 10, can now be expanded to include the effect of monetary policy. In an economy with low inflation and a stable banking system, expansionary monetary policy should tend to lower interest rates (Figures 11.1(b) and 11.3) and raise intended investment (Figure 11.4). Since intended investment spending, *II,* is part of $AD = C + II + G + NX$, this should shift the AD schedule upward, and raise the equilibrium levels of aggregate demand, income, and output, as shown in Figure 11.6.

The chain of causation can be summarized as:

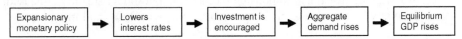

If the economy is headed toward a recession, then, monetary policy that is relatively loose, increasing the money supply in order to help maintain output, can have a desirable stabilizing effect. Sometimes such an **expansionary monetary policy** is called an **accommodating monetary**

policy, especially (though, these days, not exclusively) when the Fed is reacting to a specific economic event that might otherwise tend to send the economy toward a recession.

> **expansionary monetary policy:** the use of monetary policy tools to increase the money sup-ply, lower interest rates, and stimulate a higher level of economic activity

> **accommodating monetary policy:** loose or expansionary monetary policy intended to coun-teract recessionary tendencies in the economy

Contractionary monetary policy, on the other hand, would be prescribed if the economy seems to be heading toward a boom and possible inflation. In that case, the Fed seeks to slow growth and "cool down" the economy. In the aggregate demand model, a decrease in the money supply will raise interest rates, lower intended investment, shift the AD schedule downward, and lower the equilibrium levels of aggregate demand, income, and output.*

> **contractionary monetary policy:** the use of monetary policy tools to limit the money supply, raise interest rates, and encourage a leveling-off or reduction in economic activity

4.4 THE FED AND INVESTMENT, 2000–2007

The effect of Fed policy on investment can be illustrated with a recent historical example. In late 2000, the federal funds rate stood at 6.5 percent. But there were signs that the economy might be heading toward recession: The "dot com" stock market bubble had burst, and policy-makers were worried that the pattern of enthusiastic investment and consumer spending that had fueled GDP growth in the 1990s might be coming to an end. Orders for goods had slowed down. Inventories had built up. In January 2001 the Fed, publicly expressing concern about the weakness of the economy, took the dramatic action of lowering the federal funds rate by 0.5 percent. Then, the next month, it lowered it again. All through the period 2001–3, it steadily pushed interest rates down, as shown in Figure 11.7. The federal funds rate reached a low of 1 percent in early 2004.

What was the consequence for investment and aggregate demand? The bottom half of Figure 11.7 shows the data for residential and nonresidential private fixed (that is, noninventory) invest-ment. Nonresidential fixed investment—business investment in equipment and structures—might seem to move in the direction *opposite* to that predicted by the theory of investment presented earlier (Figure 11.4). As interest rates steadily fell through 2001 and most of 2002, this kind of investment *fell*. But recall that the theory said that "all else being equal" a lower interest rate should lead to higher intended investment—and all else was *not* equal during this period. Busi-nesses had too much capacity and inventory, and were pessimistic about sales. In terms of the model, Figure 11.8 shows this pessimism shifting the intended investment schedule to the left. The lowered interest rates due to Fed action may have kept investors from cutting back even more, but the lower rates were not enough to entirely prevent the downturn in nonresidential (and overall) investment.

Residential investment, on the other hand, shows what many consider to be a success story for monetary policy during this period. While fixed business investment fell markedly, Figure 11.7 shows that investment in housing did not fall, but in fact steadily increased. Even though the economy in general was in a recession for much of 2001, and investment overall was in a

---

* In Chapter 13, we will look at how monetary policy may also change *AD* by affecting international capital flows, the relative values of national currencies, and net exports. If exchange rates are flexible, the effects of a loose monetary policy on *NX* should be in the same direction as the effect on *II*, making the change in *AD* larger.

Figure 11.7 **Monetary Policy and Investment, 2000–2007**

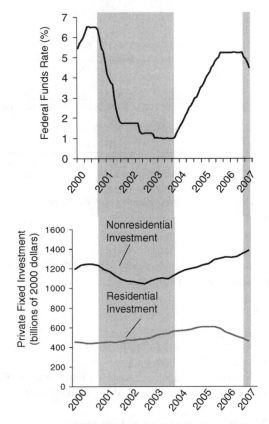

The grey areas show periods of expansionary monetary policy. The interest rate cuts of 2001–3 helped spur residential investment. The later slump in housing markets, along with the subprime credit crisis, spurred the Federal Reserve to expansionary action again in late 2007. (Source: Federal Reserve and BEA)

slump, housing investment grew steadily. By November of 2002, nonresidential investment had started growing again.

By May 2004, the Fed felt that the recovery was well underway and self-sustaining. It returned to focusing on its other main macroeconomic goal: the control of inflation. For the next three years, the Fed steadily increased the federal funds rate in an attempt to keep the economy from "overheating."

But in late 2007, the Fed again switched to an expansionary stance, largely due to problems that had developed in the housing market. As you can see in the lower graph, residential investment went into a slump in 2006. Many believe that overbuilding in the earlier period contributed to this. Problems in the financing of home mortgages also created a crisis in the credit markets. As was mentioned in Chapter 4, banks had aggressively moved into the marketing of "sub-prime" mortgages (loans given to people whose incomes or credit histories are not good enough to qualify them for regular mortgages) during the 2004–7 period. When borrowers found it impossible to pay back these loans, the borrowers lost their homes, and banks took a financial hit as

Figure 11.8   **Expansionary Monetary Policy in an Environment of Pessimism**

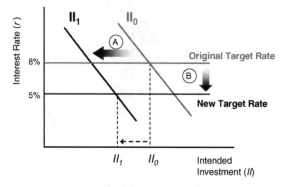

If investors become pessimistic (shift A), the level of intended investment can still fall, even though Fed actions lower the interest rate (shift B).

the securities they held rapidly lost value. Fearing recession, the Fed took steps to make more money available. (See News in Context.)

Discussion Questions

1. What sorts of interest rates do you deal with in your own life? Do you think Fed policies affect their levels?
2. Is it always true that an increase in the money supply leads to an increase in investment and aggregate demand? Why, or why not?

5. THE THEORY OF MONEY, PRICES, AND INFLATION

Throughout the preceding section, we have largely assumed that we are in an economy in which inflation is low and steady, the banking system is stable, and the main thing the Fed has to worry about is helping to stabilize the levels of investment, aggregate demand, and output. Now let's switch to the opposite extreme. Suppose the central bank's main worry is controlling inflation. For understanding this case, a different approach will be helpful.

5.1 THE QUANTITY EQUATION

Some very different theories of money from that which we've discussed up to now are based on the **quantity equation**:

$$M \times V = P \times Y$$

In this equation, Y is, as usual, real output or GDP. P indicates the price level as measured by, for example, the GDP deflator. The multiplication of these two variables means that the right hand side of the equation represents *nominal output*. On the left-hand side, M measures the level of money balances, such as the M1 measure discussed above. V, the only really new variable here, represents the velocity of money.

> **quantity equation:** $M \times V = P \times Y$, where M is the money supply, V is the velocity of money, P is the price level and Y is real output

NEWS IN CONTEXT:
Fearing Broader Slump, Fed Cuts Key Interest Rate

The Federal Reserve cut its benchmark short-term interest rate yesterday [Dec. 11, 2007] by a quarter of a percentage point, to 4.25 percent, and suggested that it would lower rates again if the credit crisis continued to damage not just housing, but the rest of the economy as well. In an unusual move, which followed a sharp drop in the stock market after the midafternoon announcement, Fed officials put out word that they might take other steps before year-end to inject money into the banking system.

Since the credit crisis erupted in August, the Fed has shaved a full percentage point from the federal funds rate, which is what banks pay to borrow from each other overnight. Rates on car loans, mortgages, and consumer credit often rise and fall with that rate, and the hope is that with lower borrowing costs, lending will pick up again and spending will rise, preventing the economy from sliding into a recession. The bottleneck is the credit squeeze—the reluctance of banks and other financial institutions to lend because of fear that they will not be re-paid, given the defaults and foreclosures spreading in the mortgage market.

In their statement after the meeting, Ben S. Bernanke, the Fed chairman, and his colleagues sidestepped a trap they had fallen into the last time they gathered, on Oct. 31, when they left the impression they were done with their rate cuts. But the economy weakened during November, various indicators suggested, and big financial institutions disclosed new multibillion-dollar write-downs on their portfolios of subprime mortgages. Bernanke finally signaled, in a speech on Nov. 29, that the Fed would cut rates again, after all, at yesterday's meeting.

Source: Louis Uchitelle, *New York Times* News Service, December 12, 2007

What did the Fed hope to prevent, by taking the action described above? What term would an economist use to describe this type of policy?

The **velocity of money** is the number of times a dollar has to change hands in a year, in order to support the level of output and exchange represented by nominal GDP. Since nominal GDP and M1 are observable, velocity can be calculated as the ratio of the two,

$$V = \frac{P \times Y}{M}$$

For the quantity equation to become the basis for a *theory*, rather than merely represent definitions of variables, an assumption needs to be made about velocity. Two theories we will discuss below—classical and monetarist—assume that velocity is constant—changing very little, if at all, with changing conditions in the economy. If this is true, then the level of the money supply and the level of nominal GDP should be tightly related. We will denote this assumption that velocity is constant by putting a bar over the top of *V*. The **quantity theory of money**, then, is characterized by the relation,

$$M \times \bar{V} = P \times Y$$

where $\bar{V}$ is read "V-bar." More Keynesian-oriented theories, on the other hand, while they may make use of the quantity *equation,* do not assume that velocity is constant. They are not based on the quantity *theory.*

> **velocity of money:** the number of times a dollar would have to change hands during a year to support nominal GDP, calculated as $V = (P \times Y)/M$

> **quantity theory of money:** the theory that money supply is directly related to nominal GDP, according to the equation $M \times \bar{V} = P \times Y$

5.2 Classical Monetary Theory

Classical monetary theory is based on the quantity theory of money, plus the assumption that output is always constant at its full-employment level. That is,

$$M \times \bar{V} = P \times Y^* \quad \text{—full employment output}$$

where Y^*, as usual, denotes full-employment output. In this case—in contrast to the aggregate demand model described in the previous section—changes in the money supply can have *no* effect on the level of output. The inability of changes in the money supply to affect real output is called **monetary neutrality**. The only variable on the left side that is not constant is the money supply, while the only variable on the right side that is not constant is the price level. Thus, all that a change in the money supply can do is change prices. Rather than an increase in the money supply increasing output, in this model the only thing an increase in the money supply does is cause inflation.

> **monetary neutrality:** the idea that changes in the money supply may affect only prices, while leaving output unchanged

Classical economists, then, tend to see no need for discretionary monetary policy. In the case of a non-growing economy classical theory would prescribe a stable money supply level in order to avoid unnecessary changes in the price level. In a growing economy, classical theory says that the money supply should grow at the same rate as real GDP in order to keep prices stable.* If we assume that the rate of real GDP growth is fairly constant, then money supply should just grow at a fixed percentage rate per year. A central bank that does this is said to be following a **money supply rule**.

> **money supply rule:** committing to letting the money supply grow at a fixed percentage rate per year

5.3 Monetarism

Another famous theory based on the quantity equation is **monetarism**, propounded by Milton Friedman and Anna Jacobson Schwartz in their book, *A Monetary History of the United States, 1867–1960,* published in 1963. While Keynes had argued that insufficient investment and aggregate demand caused the Great Depression, Friedman and Schwartz argued that it was caused by a drastic contraction in the money supply.

---

* In keeping with the general no-growth assumption of Part Three of this book, we concentrate on the quantity theory written in terms of levels of money supply, prices, and GDP. In growth terms, it can be written as $m = \pi + y$ where m is the growth rate of money, π is the inflation rate, and y is the growth rate of GDP.

monetarism: a theory associated with Milton Friedman, which claims that macroeconomic objectives are best met by having the money supply grow at a steady rate

Friedman had earlier propounded the quantity theory of money, and has become known for his saying that "inflation is always and everywhere a monetary phenomenon." But unlike the pure classical theorists, he thought that *bad* monetary policy could have, at least temporarily, *bad* effects on the real economy. During the early years of the Great Depression, he and Schwartz pointed out, both the money supply and the level of nominal GDP fell sharply. This empirical observation can be seen as consistent with the quantity theory of money:

$$\underset{\downarrow}{M} \times \underset{\substack{\downarrow \\ no \\ change}}{\bar{V}} = \underset{\downarrow}{P} \times \underset{\downarrow}{Y}$$

They argued that the contraction in the money supply *caused* the reductions in both the price level and real GDP—an assertion that remains controversial. Because of his belief in the potential for bad monetary policy to cause harm, Friedman was one of the most vocal proponents of the idea that central banks should simply follow a money supply rule.

5.4 MONEY AND HYPERINFLATION

The quantity equation can also be used to shed light on the problem of very high inflation, described early in this chapter. Suppose that the level of output in an economy is stagnant or staggering. Suppose that the central bank is causing the money supply to grow very quickly. If people come to expect high inflation, money may tend to become a "hot potato"—people want to hold it for as short a time as possible, since it loses value so quickly. They will try to turn money into non-inflating assets—real estate, hard currency, jewelry, or barterable goods—as quickly as they can. This means that the velocity of money also rises. A situation of hyperinflation in a stagnant economy can be illustrated as:

$$\underset{\uparrow}{M} \times \underset{\uparrow}{V} = \underset{\uparrow}{P} \times \underset{\substack{no \\ change}}{\bar{Y}}$$

where the bar over Y indicates that output is stuck at a level below full employment. With output stagnant, and both money supply and velocity rising, inflation must result.

While we imagined a printing press in the government's basement in our earlier story about hyperinflation, a sophisticated economy can also essentially "run the printing presses" if the agency that issues government debt and the central bank work together. For example, suppose the United States Treasury issues new debt, and the Fed immediately buys the same amount of new debt and injects new money into the economy. The effect is the same as if the Fed had just printed new currency, except that the increase in bank reserves is in the form of "a stroke of the pen" instead of freshly printed paper. This is called **monetizing the deficit**. In the United States, however, the Fed does not automatically buy new government debt. It may, as an accommodating move, monetize some deficit spending by the government in order to help the economy out of a recession, but it is not obliged to do so.

monetizing the deficit: when a central bank buys government debt as it is issued (equivalent to "running the printing presses")

Even in less extreme cases, loose money can lead to inflation. For example, suppose the economy is functioning relatively normally but output has reached its full-employment level

(Y^*). If monetary policy continues to be expansionary, inflation is likely to result. (This will be discussed more in Chapter 12.)

5.5 IMPORTING INFLATION

Inflation can also be triggered by international economic developments. An increase in the price of imports can lead to upward pressure on prices. This might occur because of a devaluation or depreciation of the domestic currency (as will be discussed further in Chapter 13). In that case, more dollars are required to buy foreign currency, making foreign goods more expensive in general. Or it may be that only the price of some particular imported goods rise—as in the important case of the oil price shocks of the 1970s. This can be portrayed in the quantity equation as:

$$M \times V = \underset{\uparrow}{P} \times Y$$

What happens to the other variables in the quantity equation depends on the reactions of actors in the economy. Changes in the relative prices of goods can generally be expected to cause some disruptions in production. If the Fed takes a strictly anti-inflationary stance, it could make such adjustments especially difficult. Keeping the *average* price level steady in the presence of imported inflation would mean that the prices of non-imported goods and services would have to go *down*. Since wages and prices tend to be "sticky" downward (as discussed in Chapter 7), a strict anti-inflationary stance may contribute to a deeper recession. On the other hand, monetary policy that is accommodating—that is, that tends to be relatively loose, increasing the money supply in order to facilitate relative price adjustments—may lead to somewhat increased upward pressure on prices, but less downward pressure on output.

   If the dollar increases in value, or the prices of important imports fall, of course, then this chain of causality works in the opposite direction. Downward pressure on prices, as well as upward pressure, can originate in the foreign sector.

Discussion Questions

1. What is the difference between the quantity *theory* of money and the quantity *equation*?
2. Have there been any reports in the news lately about inflation and its causes? If so, can you tell from news reports whether the cause is a quickly growing money supply, a peak in the business cycle, "imported" inflation, or some combination (or yet some other phenomenon)?

6. COMPLICATIONS AND POLICY CONTROVERSIES

In the real world, central banks generally have to be concerned both about output and inflation, as well as banking regulation and stability, all at the same time. When the goals include *both* stabilization of prices and of output, how does this complicate the analysis, and what does this mean for policy?

6.1 THE FED'S DILEMMA

The Fed can use expansionary monetary policy—policies that increase the money supply, lower interest rates, stimulate investment, and thus increase aggregate demand—to try to get the economy out of a recession (as we saw in Section 4). But if it goes about increasing the money supply too vigorously, or at the wrong time (such as when the economy is already nearing full employment), then it can cause inflation to rise (as we saw in Section 5). If inflation is "heating up," then the Fed should use contractionary monetary policy—reining in the money supply, raising interest rates, and discouraging investment in the interest of "cooling off" aggregate demand and economic activity.

This may seem very straightforward, but there are actually many complications in policymaking. For one thing, there is the controversial question of what exactly the "full-employment" level of employment is, at any given time. Suppose, for example, that the Fed starts to get nervous about inflation too early in an economic upswing. Perhaps the unemployment rate could have fallen to, say, 4 percent, with little increase in inflation, if the recovery had been allowed to continue, but the Fed switches into inflation-fighting mode at an unemployment rate of, say, 6 percent. By halting the recovery too early, the Fed may end up being blamed for causing unnecessary suffering. But if conditions in the economy are such that letting unemployment fall to 4 percent would cause a large rise in inflation, then if the Fed lets the recovery keep running it will end up being blamed for inflation, instead.

There is also considerable controversy about what rates of inflation can be considered acceptable. Some economists find only inflation rates from 0 percent to 2 percent to be acceptable; others do not see an urgent need for monetary control unless inflation is 5 percent, 10 percent, or even higher. Debate among economists and policymakers about the proper weight to give to GDP stabilization goals versus price stabilization goals is intense.

Another practical problem is that monetary authorities have to pay attention to issues of timing. Remember from Chapter 10 that, in the case of fiscal policy, the "inside lags" of decision making and implementation tend to be rather long, but the "outside lag" of an enacted policy having an effect on aggregate demand is rather short. For monetary policy, the case tends to be reversed. The Federal Open Market Committee is scheduled to meet eight times a year, and may schedule extra meetings. A monetary policy decision only requires discussion and agreement among the FOMC's twelve members, unlike the much longer and larger discussions required to get a tax or spending change through Congress. Hence decisions about monetary policy can generally be made more quickly than decisions about fiscal policy. On the other hand, monetary policy only has an effect on aggregate demand as people change their plans—often their very long-term plans—about spending. So the "outside lag" is generally thought to be longer. There is a danger that the effects of a policy intended to counteract a recession may not be felt until during the next boom, or the effects of policies intended to counteract a boom might not be felt until the next recession, exacerbating the business cycle instead of flattening it out.

Lastly, it is not always the case that an economy suffers from *either* recession *or* high inflation. Sometimes it suffers from both at the same time. Since one problem would seem to require expansionary policies while the other calls for contractionary ones, in this case the dilemma facing the Fed is especially sharp. We will take up this topic in Chapter 12.

6.2 RULES VERSUS ACTIVISM

Given all these caveats about monetary policy, you might think that the Fed would do better to just follow a money supply growth rule as suggested by the quantity theory of money. Indeed, a number of classically oriented macroeconomists make just this argument.

But the quantity theory has its problems. For one thing, the velocity of money is not as constant as the theory assumes. Because financial markets have many interlinkages, people's desire to hold some of their assets as money, as opposed to in some other asset, can cause velocity to make wide swings. For example, when interest-bearing checking accounts became very popular in the 1980s, M1 grew quickly as people shifted assets from other forms into this new, highly liquid *and* interest-bearing form. Since *V* is the ratio of nominal GDP to money balances, the sudden rise in the denominator of this ratio caused the velocity of M1 to fall sharply. Likewise, when the stock market takes a dive, it is common for many people to seek the relative security of money and near-money assets, hence also driving M1 up and velocity down.

Other changes in velocity are harder to explain. Partly this is because people need liquidity not only to facilitate transactions related to GDP—that is, domestic newly produced goods and services—but also to facilitate transactions related to used goods, purchases and sales of assets, and foreign dealings. Financial market innovations, shocks to asset markets, and many other developments in the economy can affect velocity. The more unpredictable velocity is, the harder it is to make policy based on the assumption of a stable relationship between money supply and nominal GDP.

Nor is it the case that output is always at its full-employment level, as we saw looking at unemployment rates in Chapter 7 and at business cycles in Chapter 9. Nor is it the case that changes in the prices are only caused by changes in monetary policy. We discussed one example of this under the heading "importing inflation" above.

As a result, many macroeconomists argue for a more flexible and activist monetary policy stance. Rather than the Fed locking onto a particular rule, they suggest that the Fed keep an eye on inflation but also remain flexible, so it can respond to new developments including financial market changes, price shocks, and threats of recession.

In the next chapter, we will bring together monetary policy, fiscal policy, and the twin goals of output and price stabilization. What effects have world events, and policy responses to them, had on the United States economy over the last several decades?

Discussion Questions

1. What are some arguments in favor of the Fed following a money supply rule? What are some arguments against it?
2. Does fiscal policy or monetary policy have a longer "lag"?

REVIEW QUESTIONS

1. Describe three scenarios that could describe economies in very different situations, in regard to their banking systems and price (in)stability.
2. Describe the three roles of money.
3. Describe at least three very different types of money.
4. Describe at least two measures of money.
5. Draw up and explain the components of a balance sheet for a private bank.
6. Draw up and explain the components of the balance sheet of the Federal Reserve.
7. Show what happens to the Fed's balance sheet and the balance sheet of a bank, when the bank sells bonds to the Fed.
8. Describe how a Fed open market purchase leads to a sequence of loans and deposits, and thus a multiplier effect.
9. Describe two tools the Fed can use to affect the money supply, other than open market operations.
10. Describe how a Fed open market purchase changes the federal funds rate.

11. What are two important factors affecting investment? Show how they work using graphs.
12. Show the effects of an expansionary monetary policy in a Keynesian cross diagram.
13. Describe how Fed policy operated during the 2000–2007 period.
14. What is the quantity equation?
15. What is the quantity theory of money?
16. Describe classical monetary theory.
17. What is monetarism?
18. Discuss how monetary expansion can lead to high inflation, using the quantity equation.
19. Describe how inflation can be "imported."
20. What are some of the problems the Fed faces in trying to enact good policies?
21. What are some of the problems with using a monetary rule?

EXERCISES

1. Suppose the Fed makes an open market purchase of $200,000 in bonds from QRSBank.
   a. Show how this affects the Fed balance sheet.
   b. Show how this affects the balance sheet of the QRSBank.
   c. Assume that the required reserve ratio is 10 percent and that QRSBank loans out as much as it can, based on this changed situation. What does its balance sheet look like after it makes the loans?
   d. Assume that all the proceeds from those loans are deposited in TUVBank. What is the effect on TUVBank's balance sheet?
   e. What new opportunity does TUVBank now face? What is it likely to do?

2. Suppose the Fed makes an open market *sale* of $15 million in bonds to HIJBank.
   a. What is the effect on the Fed's balance sheet?
   b. What is the initial effect on HIJBank's balance sheet?
   c. Show in a graph the effect on the market for federal funds. (No numbers are necessary, for this or later sections of this exercise.)
   d. Assuming the level of business confidence remains unchanged, show on a graph how this open market sale will change the level of intended investment.
   e. What is the effect on aggregate demand and output? Show on a carefully labeled graph.
   f. What is the effect on equilibrium consumption and saving? (You may need to refer back to Chapter 9 to answer this.)

3. Suppose that investor confidence falls, and the Fed is alert to this fact. Using the model presented in this chapter, show (a)–(c) below graphically:
   a. How a fall in investor confidence affects the schedule for intended investment.
   b. What the Fed could do, influencing the federal funds market, to try to counteract this fall in investor confidence.
   c. The effect on *AD* and output if the Fed is able to *perfectly* counteract the fall in business confidence.
   d. Is the Fed likely to be as accurate as assumed in part (c)? Why, or why not?

4. Suppose the level of nominal GDP in Estilvania is $30 billion, and the level of the money supply is $10 billion.
   a. What is the velocity of money in Estilvania?
   b. Suppose that the money supply increases to $15 billion and nominal GDP rises to $45 billion. Which theory is supported?
   c. Suppose that the money supply increases to $15 billion and nominal GDP rises to $40 billion. Which theory is supported?
   d. Suppose that the money supply decreases to $5 billion, and as a result both the price level and real GDP fall, so that nominal GDP falls to $15 billion. Which theory is supported?
   e. Suppose that the money supply increases to $15 billion. Real GDP stays the same, at its full-employment level, but the price level rises so that nominal GDP becomes $45 billion. Which theory is supported?

5. Match each concept in Column A with the best definition or example in Column B.

Column A	Column B
a. Expansionary monetary policy	1. The idea that changes in the money supply only affect prices, not output
b. Fiat money	2. Residential investment
c. Accelerator principle	3. Standardization
d. Monetary neutrality	4. A dollar coin made of minerals worth $.10
e. Velocity	5. The ease with which an asset can be used in trade
f. Liquidity	6. Federal Reserve open market sale of bonds
g. Commodity money	7. A silver coin
h. A good property for money to have	8. A silver certificate
i. A piece of paper representing a claim on something of value	9. Vault cash and bank deposits at the Federal Reserve
j. Bank reserves	10. Currency in circulation, checkable deposits, and traveler's checks
k. M1	11. The number of times a unit of money changes hands in a year
l. Very sensitive to interest rates	12. Relates investment to GDP growth
m. Contractionary monetary policy	13. The Federal Reserve lowers the discount rate

6. The chair of the Federal Reserve semiannually gives testimony before Congress about the state of monetary policy. Find the most recent such testimony at http://www.federalreserve.gov/newsevents.htm. What does the Fed chair identify as the most significant issues facing the economy? How is the Fed proposing to deal with them?

7. (Appendix) Suppose you have a bond with a face value of $200 and coupon amount of $10 that matures one year from now.
   a. If the going interest rate is 3 percent, how much can you sell it for today?
   b. If the going interest rate is 8 percent, how much can you sell it for today?
   c. What does this illustrate about bond prices and interest rates?

8. (Appendix) Show, on a money supply and money demand graph, the effect on the interest rate of a decrease in the money supply.

9. (Appendix) Suppose the nominal prime interest rate for a one-year loan in an economy is currently 6 percent.

a. If inflation is running at 1 percent per year, what is the current real interest rate?

b. Suppose many people believe that the inflation rate is going to rise in the future—probably up to 2 percent to 3 percent or more within a few years. You want to borrow a sum of money for ten years, and are faced with deciding between

1. a series of short-term, one-year loans. The interest rate on this year's loan would be 6 percent, while future nominal interest rates are unknown. Or

2. a ten-year fixed-rate loan on which you would pay a constant 6.25 percent per year.

If you agree with most people and expect inflation to rise, which borrowing strategy do you expect might give you the better deal? Why? Explain your reasoning.

c. Could your reasoning in part (b) help explain the pattern of interest rates shown in Figure 11.12? Explain.

Appendix: More Models and Issues of Monetary Policy

Some economists prefer to think about monetary policy in terms of markets for bonds or money, rather than in terms of the federal funds rate. Also, in trying to keep the chapter relatively brief and comprehensible, we have glossed over issues of real versus nominal interest rates and special topics such as credit rationing and liquidity traps. These appendices remedy these omissions.

A1. Bond Prices and Interest Rates

The process by which monetary policy influences interest rates can be explained by examining the market for federal funds, as was seen in the body of this chapter. Alternatively, it can also be explained by looking at the market for government bonds.

A bond represents debt, but, as a particular kind of financial instrument, bonds have some characteristics worth mentioning. When the government (or a business) borrows by selling a **bond**, it makes promises. It promises to pay the bondholder a fixed amount of money each year for a period of time, and then, at the end of this time, to repay the principal of the loan. The fixed amount paid per year is called the **coupon amount**. The date that the principal will be repaid is called the maturity date. The amount of principal that will be repaid is called the **face value** of the bond.

> A **bond** is a financial instrument that, in return for the loan of funds, commits its seller to pay a fixed amount every year (called the **coupon amount**), as well as to repay the amount of principal (called the bond's **face value**) on a particular date in the future (called the **maturity date**).

So far it seems simple enough—a bond may specify, for example, that its issuer will pay you $5 a year for ten years, and then pay you $100 at the end of ten years. What makes bond markets more complicated, though, is that bonds are often sold and resold, changing hands many times before they mature. During the period to maturity, many factors affecting the value of the bond may change, and so the **bond price**—the price at which bondholders are willing to buy and sell existing bonds—may change.

> **bond price**: the price at which trades are made

For example, suppose you bought the bond just described at its face value of $100. The **bond yield to maturity**, or annual rate of return if you hold a bond until it matures, would obviously be

5 percent ($5 annually is 5 percent of the $100 bond price). Suppose that after a couple years you want to sell your bond (perhaps you need the cash), but meanwhile the rate of return on alternative (and equally safe) investments has risen to 10 percent. No one will be interested in buying your bond at a price of $100, because they would get only a 5 percent return on it, whereas they could get a 10 percent return by investing their $100 elsewhere. To sell your bond you will need to drop the price you demand, until your bond looks as attractive as other investments—that is, until the $5 per year represents a 10 percent yield to maturity.*

> **bond yield to maturity:** the amount a bond returns during a year, if held to maturity, expressed in percentage terms. The yield is determined by the coupon amount, the bond price, and the time to maturity.

Conversely, if the return on alternative investments has fallen, say to 2 percent, the $5 per year on your bond looks pretty good, and you will be able to sell it for *more than* $100.** The higher the bond yield, the lower the bond price, and vice versa.

> Bond price and bond yield have an inverse relationship.

The United States Treasury actually issues a variety of different kinds of bonds. Treasury "bills" have a zero coupon amount, and mature in one year or less. Because the holder receives no coupons, they are sold at a discount from their face value. Other Treasury bonds pay a coupon amount every six months, and have maturities that range from two to thirty years. In the real economy, then, there are a variety of "government bond" prices—and of interest rates. It is only for the sake of simplicity of modeling that we assume only one type of bond and one interest rate.

While many, many people and organizations buy and sell government bonds on what is called the "secondary market" (the "primary market" being the Treasury's initial offering of the bonds), the Fed is a major player. Its actions on the market for government bonds are large enough to have discernable effects on the whole market.

A simplified (secondary) bond market is shown in Figure 11.9(a). The price of bonds (and the corresponding nominal interest rate) is on the vertical axis, and the quantity on the horizontal. The supply curve, in this case, is determined by the willingness of people to sell bonds—that is, to *stop* lending to the government, exchanging their government debt for cash. The demand curve is determined by people's willingness to buy bonds—that is, to lend to the government. The effect of a Fed open market purchase of bonds is illustrated in Figure 11.9(b). A sizable Fed *purchase* shifts the demand curve for government bonds to the right. As a result, the price of bonds rises. Because bond prices and interest rates are inversely related, the rise in the price of bonds means that the going interest rate on them falls.

While this explanation focuses on the market for government bonds, it is actually parallel to the earlier discussion of the Fed and the market for federal funds. The interest rate for three-month Treasury bills and the federal funds rate are graphed together in Figure 11.10 and they track each other closely. The bottom line of this story is the same as that given by the model of federal funds used in this chapter: A Fed open market purchase drives down interest rates.

---

* If the bond has one year left to maturity, for example, its value one year from now is $105. We can use the formula [Value next year] / (1 + interest rate) = [Value now] to find out what you could get by selling the bond today. If the interest rate on alternative investments is 10 percent, then $105/(1 + .10) ≈ $95.45.

** Continuing from the previous footnote, if the interest rate is 2 percent, then $105/(1+ .02) ≈ $102.94.

Figure 11.9 **The Market for Government Bonds**

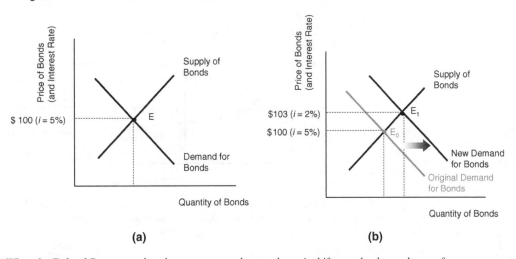

(a)   (b)

When the Federal Reserve undertakes an open market purchase, it shifts out the demand curve for government bonds. This raises the price of bonds, lowering their interest rate.

Figure 11.10 **The Federal Funds and Three-Month Treasury Bill Rates, 2000–2007**

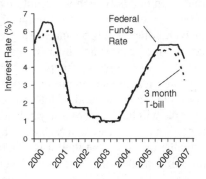

The market for federal funds and the market for short-term Treasury bills are closely related. (Source: Federal Reserve Board, monthly data)

A2. MONEY SUPPLY AND MONEY DEMAND

The process by which monetary policy influences interest rates can be explained by examining the market for federal funds, as was seen in the body of this chapter, or by examining the market for government bonds (Appendix A1). A third alternative is to examine the market for money.

Assume that money is the only asset that can be used in exchange, and pays no interest. Assume that other assets cannot be used in transactions, but *do* pay interest. The **transactions demand model** for money assumes that people need money balances for transactions, but forgo earnings on the money balances they hold. For simplicity, we will call the alternative, interest-bearing asset "bonds."

Figure 11.11 **The Demand and Supply of Money, with an Increase in Supply**

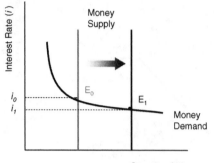

The demand for money curve slopes downward, since a higher interest rate increases the opportunity cost of holding money. The money supply curve is set by the Federal Reserve. If the Federal Reserve increases the money supply, it drives down the interest rate.

> **transactions demand model:** a model of the money market in which money is assumed to be liquid and pay no interest, while an alternative asset is assumed to be illiquid and pay interest

Money demand is shown as a curved, downward sloping line in Figure 11.11. The higher the (nominal) interest rate is on bonds (which we denote by i), the higher is the opportunity cost of holding money in terms of earnings forgone. So the higher the interest rate, the more people will try to economize on holding money balances. They may, for example, make transfers from interest bearing accounts into cash or non-interest bearing checking accounts several times a week. The money demand curve slopes up steeply as it approaches the vertical axis, since even with very high interest rates this model assumes that people need at least a minimal amount of money for transactions. On the other hand, if interest rates are low, there is not much cost to holding money, and people will hold larger money balances. When interest rates are low, people will keep a larger proportion of their assets in cash, or as balances in non–interest bearing checking accounts, and a smaller proportion of their assets in bonds.

This model assumes that the Fed directly sets the level of the money supply, largely through open market purchases and sales. The Fed can drive down interest rates by increasing the money supply through open market purchases of government bonds, as shown in Figure 11.11. If after the Fed shifts the money supply curve out, the interest rate were to remain at i_0, an excess supply of money would occur. People would want to get rid of more of their money in exchange for bonds. In the process of trying to get more bonds, they would drive the price of bonds up, which would in turn (as explained in the previous section) drive the interest rate down. Conversely, if the Fed wanted to increase interest rates, it could reduce the money supply.

Notice that the bottom line of this story is the same as that given by the model of federal funds: A Fed open market purchase drives down interest rates. This model, while widely taught, has fallen out of favor among some macroeconomists as financial innovations (such as interest-bearing checking accounts) have blurred the distinction between money and interest-bearing assets.

A3. Real Versus Nominal Interest Rates

In the model of interest rates and aggregate demand discussed in Section 4 of the text, we assumed that the Fed, through open market operations, could change the interest rate that influences investment spending. In Figure 11.8 we used the symbol r to denote a generalized interest rate. In real life, however, there are a number of different interest rates that have to be taken into account. We will lay out some basic facts about short-run vs. long-run, and real vs. nominal interest rates. We will note the difference between the Fed's focus on the short term, nominal interest rate, and the interest rate that investors often consider the most relevant: that is, the long-term, real interest rate.

In Section 4.1 we discussed the federal funds rate, as the principal interest rate targeted by the Fed. This is a short-term, nominal interest rate. It is short term, because while this rate is quoted in annualized terms (that is, what a borrower would pay if they kept the loan for a year), the loans are actually made one day and paid back the next. The Fed uses a portfolio of government securities with various maturity dates in its open market operations, but many of these have maturity dates of three years or less. The federal funds rate—like any interest rate you normally see quoted—is a *nominal* interest rate, not adjusted for inflation. The interest rates determined in markets for loanable funds are always nominal rates.

But if you are considering undertaking a substantial business investment project or buying a house, the interest rate you should be taking into account, if you are a rational decision maker, is the *real* interest rate over the life of the business loan or mortgage. The **real interest rate** is:

$$r = i - \pi$$

where r is the real interest rate, i is the nominal interest rate, and π is the rate of inflation. For example, suppose you borrow $100 for one year at a nominal rate of 6 percent. You will pay back $106 at the end of the year. If the inflation rate is zero, then the purchasing power of the amount you pay back at the end of the year is actually $6 more than the amount you borrowed. On the other hand, if inflation runs at 4 percent during the year, the $106 you pay back is in "cheaper" dollars (dollars that can buy less) than the dollars that you borrowed. The real interest rate on your borrowing will be only 2 percent. The higher the inflation rate, the better the deal is for a borrower at any given nominal rate (and the worse it is for the lender).

> **real interest rate:** nominal interest rate minus inflation, $r = i - \pi$

If inflation is fairly low and steady—as we assumed in the aggregate demand model—then this difference between real and nominal interest rates is not of crucial importance. If inflation is steady at, say, 2 percent, then both lenders and borrowers just mentally subtract 2 percent to calculate the real rate that corresponds to any nominal rate. If the Fed lowers the prime rate from 8 percent to 5 percent, for example, then it correspondingly lowers the real rate from 6 percent to 3 percent. Through much of the 1990s and into the first few years of the twenty-first century, for example, this wasn't such a bad assumption to make. Inflation varied only from about 1 percent to about 2.5 percent over those years.

But inflation is not always so predictable. When inflation is high and/or variable, it is very important to realize that investors' decisions are in reality influenced by the **expected real interest rate**, r^e:

$$r^e = i - \pi^e$$

where i is the nominal rate the borrower agrees to pay and π^e is the *expected* inflation rate. The actual real interest rate (r) can only be known with hindsight. That is, *after* information on inflation has come for last month or last year, you can calculate what the real interest rate *was* in that period. But you never know with certainly what the real interest rate is right now, or what it will be next year. The more changeable inflation is, the harder it is to form reliable expectations about real interest rates. During the 1970s, unexpected bouts of high inflation meant that

Figure 11.12   **Federal Funds, Nominal and Real Thirty-Year Fixed Mortgage Rates, 1995–2007**

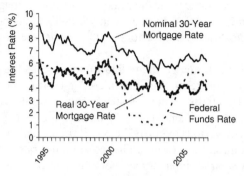

Long term interest rates and real interest rates do not always move in tandem with the Federal Funds rate. (Source: Federal Reserve Board monthly data, Bureau of Labor Statistics, and authors' calculations. Inflation is measured by twelve-month changes in the CPI, excluding food and energy)

some real interest rates temporarily became *negative.* One of the authors of this book received government student loans carrying a 3 percent nominal interest rate during that period, while inflation was running at 6 percent per year or more. In real terms, it was as though for every $100 she borrowed for college she had to pay back only about $97!

> **expected real interest rate:** the nominal interest rate minus expected inflation, $r^e = i - \pi^e$

Many loans are made for a number of years—even decades—into the future. In this case, an investor has to form expectations not only about real interest rates in the short term, but where real interest rates will be likely to be going. Expectations, or guesses, enter in when investors want to speed up their projects to take advantage of low rates that they think will disappear in the future, or postpone projects if they think the real rate will be coming down.

When considering issues of inflation and expectations about the future, economics has to turn from mechanical exercises in equations and curve-shifting into something more like social psychology. How do people form their expectations about a truly unknowable future? What sorts of information do they gather, about the economy and about policymaking, in forming their decisions? What effect do these expectations, and variations in these expectations from person to person, have on economic behavior?

We can see some evidence about the importance of long-term expectations by comparing the behavior of the federal funds rate with an important long term interest rate, the average rate on thirty-year fixed-rate mortgages. As shown in Figure 11.12, from 1995 until mid-2000, the real long-term mortgage rate tracked the federal funds rate fairly closely, while the nominal mortgage rate was a few points higher. But while the long-term rate dropped somewhat in both real and nominal terms during the loose monetary policy period between 2001 and early 2004, it did not drop nearly as much as the federal funds rate. Nor did it rise as much when the Fed later tightened up. Moreover, it sometimes went up when the federal funds rate was dropping, and vice versa. The interest rate on thirty-year mortgages is determined in a market in which people are paying attention to many things, including expectations of future inflation, business trends, and Fed policy actions.

We saw earlier that the loose Fed policy in the early 2000s *did* seem to encourage a continued expansion in residential investment, even during a recession. In Chapter 12 we will continue to use the aggregate demand model, assuming—as seems generally reasonable—that Fed policies can *influence* some important real interest rates in the macroeconomy, even if they cannot determine them precisely. As a student of economics, however, you should also be aware that this relationship is not quite as unambiguous as the simple model assumes.

A4. LIMITATIONS OF POLICY: THE LIQUIDITY TRAP AND CREDIT RATIONING

In early 2004, the federal funds rate was down to only 1 percent. If the Fed had wanted to continue loosening up monetary policy, could it have done so? The case where it is impossible for a central bank to drive interest rates down any lower was called a **liquidity trap** by Keynes. The Fed was approaching something like this in early 2004. The only way the federal funds rate could get substantially lower would be for it to turn negative. Japan hit this monetary policy wall in 1999, when the Bank of Japan reduced interest rates to virtually zero. Monetary policy had reached its limit.

> **liquidity trap:** when interest rates are so low that the central bank finds it impossible to reduce them further

The name "liquidity trap" refers to the fact that in such a situation the general public has a strong preference for holding the most liquid asset—that is, money. When the central bank increases the money supply by buying government bonds, people are so eager to make this swap that no change in bond prices (as discussed in Appendix A1) or interest rates occurs. The "liquidity trap" can be illustrated in terms of Figure 11.11 in Appendix A2: If the money demand curve becomes perfectly horizontal at a low or zero rate of interest, then increases in money supply have no effect on the interest rate.

The institutions and interests represented in the private banking system also put limitations on the effectiveness of Fed policy. Recall that for expansionary monetary policy to work in the predicted way, banks have to respond to increases in their reserves by making new loans. But what if banks do not feel that very many of their customers are creditworthy, or their usual customers are not very interested in taking out new loans? Low interest rates may not translate into new credit and new investment, if bankers don't make new loans.

On the other hand, when money is tightened up and interest rates rise, a simple loanable funds model predicts that those borrowers willing to pay the highest rates will get the loans. But bankers know that the people willing to agree to the highest rates also tend to be the people with the riskiest, most speculative projects. Banks may tend to engage in **credit rationing** in order to assure their own profitability. Rather than let the forces of supply and demand raise interest rates and then lend to all comers at the equilibrium rate, they may put a ceiling on interest rates and then lend to the customers they deem most creditworthy. If this happens, some firms will get the funds they need, while others—and particularly smaller firms and firms with less established reputations—may be frozen out. Hence monetary policy may have significant distributional effects.

> **credit rationing:** when banks keep their interest rates below "what the market would bear" and deny loans to some potential borrowers, in the interest of maintaining their own profitability

The possibility of a liquidity trap, or of a reluctance on the part of bankers and investors to lend and borrow, means that the Fed faces limitations in its ability to stimulate a sluggish economy. The possibility of credit rationing means that Fed actions can have repercussions on the economy that go beyond the intended macroeconomic stabilization effects.

12 Aggregate Supply, Aggregate Demand, and Inflation: Putting It All Together

If you read the financial pages in any newspaper (or sometimes the front pages if economic issues are pressing), you will see discussion about government budgets and deficits, interest rate changes, and how these affect unemployment and inflation. You may also see news about changes in the availability of certain crucial resources—particularly energy resources—and about how the impact of such changes in resource supplies spread throughout the nation's economy. How can a person make sense of it all?

In Chapter 9, we started to build a model of business cycles, focusing at first on the downturn side of the cycle and the problem of unemployment. In Chapters 10 and 11 we explained economic theories concerning fiscal and monetary policy. So far our models have all been "demand side," illustrated by shifts of the Aggregate Demand curve. In this chapter, we complete the demand-side story so that it includes explicit attention to the upturn side of the story and the potential problem of inflation. Then we move on to the issue of the actual productive capacity of the economy, or "supply-side" issues. Finally, we will arrive at a model that we can use to "put it all together." First we present a general form of the model, closely relating it to the macroeconomic performance of the United States in recent decades, as measured by government statistics. Then we discuss controversies about the implications of this model from Keynesian and classical points of view, and from the point of view of environmental sustainability.

1. INFLATION AND AGGREGATE DEMAND EQUILIBRIUM

The AD curve in the Keynesian model used in the previous three chapters was graphed with income on the horizontal axis and output on the vertical axis. We mentioned that if output is above its full-employment level there may be a threat of rising inflation, but nothing in the figures incorporated this idea. It is time now to remedy that omission.

How does aggregate demand in the economy change as the rate of inflation changes? Economists have modeled this with a simple relationship that we will call the Aggregate Demand Equilibrium (ADE) curve.* This curve represents the various equilibrium points (points where our Keynesian AD curve crosses the 45-degree line) that are consistent with various levels of inflation.

---

* If you have friends taking a macroeconomics class using a different book, you may find they are using a different graph with different labels to study inflation and aggregate demand equilibrium (and aggregate supply, to be discussed in Section 2 below). This is because economists have not converged on a completely standard treatment of these issues. We have included here a model that we believe represents the best of contemporary macroeconomic research, as it can be presented in an introductory-level textbook.

Figure 12.1 **The Federal Reserve Reaction Rule**

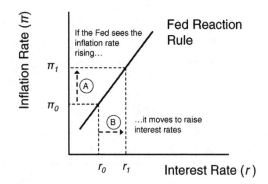

The Federal Reserve, on a month-to-month basis, would like to help stabilize output. If it sees inflation rising, it will usually take this as a sign that the economy is "overheating." It will try to raise interest rates in order to "cool off" the economy.

The ADE relationship builds on the Keynesian AD relationship discussed in the last three chapters. In addition, it incorporates two assumptions about the behavior of the Federal Reserve: Goal #1: The Federal Reserve generally sees its major month-to-month responsibility as aiding in the stabilization of *output,* helping to keep the economy from either overheating or going into a slump; and Goal #2: Over the long haul, the Federal Reserve would also like to stabilize *prices*—that is, get the inflation rate to be fairly low.

If the ongoing inflation rate is already low, there is little contradiction between the two goals. But if the inflation rate is high, these two goals may be in conflict. In our model, we will incorporate the first goal in deriving the *slope* of the ADE curve, and the second goal in deriving its *position*. In later sections of the chapter, this curve will be used to examine actual Fed actions and macroeconomic performance in recent decades.

1.1 DERIVING THE AGGREGATE DEMAND EQUILIBRIUM CURVE

Before we get to the ADE curve itself, we need to model the Fed's behavior with respect to the goal of output stability (Goal #1). Figure 12.1 graphs the Fed reaction rule. Inflation, denoted by the Greek letter π ("pi") is on the vertical axis, and the interest rate is on the horizontal axis. Suppose the Fed observes that inflation is on the rise, as noted by arrow A in Figure 12.1. This is often taken as a sign that the economy is "overheating"—that output is being pushed up too high. (Recall Stylized Fact #2 from Chapter 9, which said that increases in inflation may be caused by strong economic expansions.) The Fed reaction rule shows that the Fed will use contractionary monetary policy (as described in Chapter 11) to try to "cool down" the economy by raising interest rates, as shown by arrow B.

We know from the last chapter that, according to standard theories about the effect of monetary policy, an increase in the interest rate should tend to reduce the level of investment. Figure 12.2 shows the effect of contractionary monetary policy on investment and aggregate demand. According to the Fed reaction rule, higher inflation will cause the Fed to raise interest rates (as shown in Figure 12.1). This Fed action discourages investment, shifting the aggregate demand schedule down (as shown by arrow A in Figure 12.2), thus reducing equilibrium income and

Figure 12.2   **Changing AD Equilibrium due to the Federal Reserve Reaction**

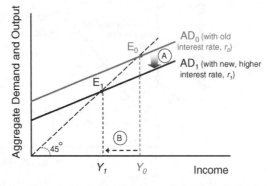

If the Federal Reserve succeeds in raising interest rates and discouraging investment spending, aggregate demand, income, and output will fall.

output (as shown by arrow B.) Higher interest rates thus lead to lower aggregate demand and a lower level of equilibrium GDP.

Thus, overall, there is an inverse relationship between inflation and output, as shown in Figure 12.3. The economy before the rise in inflation is characterized by relatively high output, but if the Fed observes inflation rising it will (according to this model) seek to "cool off" the economy through contractionary policy.

We can summarize the chain of events just described with the following diagram:

The negative slope of the ADE curve, moving from a low inflation rate to a higher one, shows how the Fed attempts to "cool off" an inflationary economy by raising interest rates.

The story about the inverse relation between inflation and output would also hold if we had started with the inflation rate *falling*. A falling inflation rate is often a sign that an economy is going into a slump (as also discussed in Stylized Fact #2 in Chapter 9). In this case, stabilization goals require that the Fed undertake *expansionary* monetary policies, *lowering* the interest rate, and seeking to *raise* aggregate demand and output as described here:

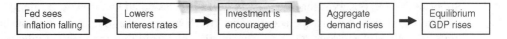

So the negative slope of the ADE relationship also says—this time, moving from a high inflation rate to a lower one—that the Fed will use relaxed monetary policy to help the economy avoid a recession. This is a sensible strategy for the Fed to the extent that it is concerned about employment and output in the economy in the near term (or what economists call the "short run").

> The aggregate demand model (of Chapters 9, 10, and 11) illustrates how equilibrium real income, output, and spending might be determined in an economy in which changes in the price level are not an issue. The two curves in that model are the AD curve and the 45° line. The ADE curve (introduced here) expands on that model, illustrating how, given reactions of the Fed to variations in prices, levels of aggregate demand and equilibrium output may vary with the rate of inflation.

Figure 12.3   **The Aggregate Demand Equilibrium Curve**

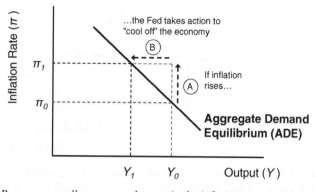

Because the Federal Reserve normally reacts to changes in the inflation rate, "cooling down" the economy if inflation is rising (and stimulating the economy if inflation is falling), the inflation rate and level of aggregate spending in the economy are inversely related.*

1.2 SHIFTS OF THE ADE CURVE: SPENDING

The downward-slope of the ADE curve shown in Figure 12.3 is based on the short-run Fed reaction rule, but, because the position of the curve relies on the Keynesian AD relation, the position of the ADE also reflects specific levels of government spending, taxation, autonomous consumption, autonomous investment, and net exports. Changes in these variables cause the curve to shift.

For example, if the government were to undertake expansionary fiscal policy, this would shift the ADE curve to the right, as illustrated in Figure 12.4. At any level of inflation, there would now be aggregate demand sufficient to support a higher level of output.

An increase in autonomous consumption or investment would have a similar effect, as would an increase in net exports. Recall that autonomous consumption is the part of household spending that does not depend on income, and autonomous investment is the part of business spending that does not depend on the interest rate. These are often taken to represent consumer and business "confidence." Thus an increase in consumer or investor confidence could also cause the rightward shift in Figure 12.4. Conversely, of course, contractionary fiscal policy, drops in consumer or investment confidence, or drops in net exports would shift the ADE curve to the left.

1.3 SHIFTS OF THE ADE CURVE: FED INTEREST RATE TARGETS

The sorts of monetary policy the Fed executes when, on a month-to-month basis, it tries to keep inflation near some initial level is a rather passive sort of monetary policy. Such policy reacts to immediate issues concerning the economy overheating or slowing down, and is reflected in the inverse slope of the ADE curve. A more active form of Fed policy occurs when the Fed's leaders decide that the economy should move to a lower inflation rate target over the long run (Goal #2). A change in the target inflation rate signals a major shift in monetary policy.

---

* If you have taken a lot of math you might be tempted to try to read Figure 12.3 as showing that "a change in output leads to a change in inflation" since in math class you measure x on the horizontal axis and y (which is a function of x) on the vertical axis. This, however, is *not* the appropriate interpretation here. Economists use the AD curve to illustrate how, due to Fed policy targets, *output* might be seen to respond to (that is, be a function of) *inflation*. The causal relationship between the variables on the two axes is the reverse of the usual.

Figure 12.4   **The Effect of Expansionary Fiscal Policy or Increased Confidence**

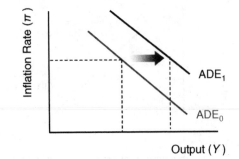

If government spending increases, taxes decrease, consumers or investors become more confident, or net exports increase (at the existing levels of inflation and the interest rates), demand for goods in the economy rises.

Figure 12.5   **The Effect of a Lower Target Inflation Rate**

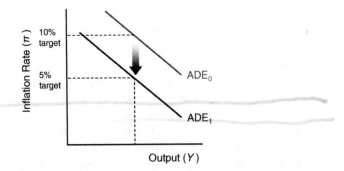

If the Federal Reserve sets a lower target rate of inflation, the ADE curve shifts downward.

Suppose the economy is experiencing, say, steady 10 percent inflation. If the Fed's target rate for inflation is also 10 percent, then, according to this model, it will undertake the sort of month-to-month passive policy we discussed earlier in order to support this target. The Fed would apply some contractionary pressure when it sees inflation rising above 10 percent, or some expansionary encouragement when the rate drops below 10 percent.

Contrast this to the case where the Fed decides on a new target inflation rate. Figure 12.5 shows what would happen in this model if, instead of trying to keep the inflation rate at 10 percent, the Fed chooses a lower inflation rate target of 5 percent. The ADE curve would shift *down*, showing that the Fed now believes that a lower inflation rate would be better for the economy and will use "tight money" policies as necessary to achieve this. Conversely, of course, if the Fed decided to aim for a higher target inflation rate, this would shift the ADE curve up—but this is unlikely.

To summarize:

- The ADE curve indicates levels of equilibrium GDP at different possible rates of inflation, assuming that the Fed responds to increases in inflation by tightening monetary policy and to decreases in inflation by loosening monetary policy.
- The ADE curve can be shifted by changes in levels of autonomous consumer spending, autonomous investment, fiscal policy, net exports, or by changes in the Fed's target inflation rate.

Discussion Questions

1. "The negative slope of the ADE curve says that higher levels of output will lead to lower levels of inflation." Is this statement correct or not? Discuss.
2. Does the Fed always want the inflation rate to be as low as possible? Why or why not?

2. CAPACITY AND THE AGGREGATE SUPPLY RESPONSE

As we've noted, increases in AD can push output up towards the full employment level. But what happens when output reaches—or maybe even exceeds—the full employment level? In a graph such as Figure 12.2, for example, there is nothing in the model that would seem to prevent expansionary policies from just shifting the AD curve, and output, up and up and up.

Obviously, this can't be true in the real world. At any given time, there are only certain quantities of labor, capital, energy, and other material resources available for use. The U.S. labor force, for example, comprises about 150 million people. The United States simply can't, then, produce an output level that would require the work of 200 million people. This is a *hard capacity constraint:* What happens as an economy approaches maximum capacity can be modeled using the aggregate supply response (ASR) curve. The ASR curve shows combinations of output and inflation that can, in fact, occur within an economy, given the reality of capacity constraints.

2.1 THE AGGREGATE SUPPLY RESPONSE CURVE

Figure 12.6 shows the theoretical aggregate supply response relationship between inflation and output. Starting from the right, at high output levels, we can identify four important, distinct regions of the diagram.

First, the vertical **maximum capacity output** line indicates the hard limit on a macroeconomy's output. Even if every last resource in the economy were put into use, with everybody working flat out to produce the most they could, the economy could not produce to the right of the maximum capacity line.

> **maximum capacity output:** the level of output an economy would produce if every resource in the economy were fully utilized

Just below the maximum capacity level of output, the ASR curve has a very steep, positive slope. This indicates that, as an economy closely approaches its maximum capacity, it is likely to experience a substantial increase in inflation. If lots of employers are all trying to hire lots of workers and buy lots of machinery, energy, and materials all at once, workers' wages and resource prices will tend to be bid upward. But then, to cover their labor and other costs, producers will need to raise the prices they charge for their own goods. Then, in turn, if workers see the purchasing power of their wages being eroded by rising inflation, they will demand higher wages . . . which lead to higher prices, and so on. The result is a phenomenon called a **wage-price spiral**, in which pressure to produce very high levels of output leads to a steep rise in self-reinforcing inflation.

> **wage-price spiral:** when high demand for labor and other resources creates upward pressure on wages, which in turn leads to upward pressure on prices and, as a result, further upward pressure on wages

Figure 12.6   **The Aggregate Supply Response (ASR) Curve**

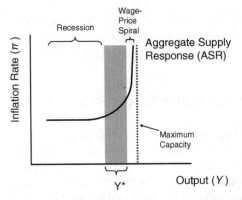

The ASR curve shows the relationship between inflation and an economy's physical capacity to produce. As production levels approach maximum capacity, inflation rises due to bottlenecks and wage-price spirals.

In the real world, such steep increases in inflation are usually the result of dramatic pressures on producers, such as often occur during a national mobilization for war. During World War II, for example, the United States government pushed the economy very close to its maximum capacity—placing big orders for munitions and other supplies for the front, mobilizing the necessary resources by encouraging women to enter the paid labor force, encouraging the recycling of materials on an unprecedented scale, encouraging the planting of backyard gardens to increase food production, and in general pushing people's productive efforts far beyond their usual peacetime levels. Measured unemployment plummeted. The government, knowing that such pressures could lead to sharply rising inflation (as shown in the wage-price spiral region of Figure 12.6), kept inflation from getting out of hand by instituting **wage and price controls**—direct regulations telling firms what they could, and could not, do in the way of price or wage increases.

> **wage and price controls:** government regulations setting limits on wages and prices, or on the rates at which they are permitted to increase

The shaded area to the left of the wage-price spiral region in Figure 12.6 indicates, as it has in past chapters, a range of full-employment levels of output. While it is controversial to say just exactly where that level may be, it is thought of as being an output level high enough that unemployment is not considered to be a national problem. And because it must be low enough to allow for at least some small measurable level of transitory unemployment, the *full-employment* level of output is distinct from, and lower than, the *maximum capacity* level of output. (Sometimes you will also hear economists refer to "potential output," meaning either full employment or maximum capacity output.)

Within the full-employment range, Figure 12.6 shows a gently rising ASR relationship. This is because, even well before an economy approaches the absolute maximum capacity given *all* of its resources, producers may tend to run into "bottlenecks" in the supply of *some* resources. Agricultural workers may be plentiful, for example, but professional and technical workers may be in short supply. Or fuel oil may be plentiful, but there may be a shortage of natural gas. Shortages in the markets for particular kinds of labor and other inputs may lead to speed-ups in inflation in some sectors of the economy. Since the measured inflation rate looks at the average over the economy as a whole, some aggregate increase in inflation may be observed. This sort of increase in inflation that comes along with high (but not extremely high) production is what economists expect to happen when the economy nears a business cycle "peak." Notice, however, that the ASR curve has been drawn as nearly flat in part of the Y^* range, indicating that combinations of full employment and stable inflation may also be possible.

When output is below its full-employment level the economy is, of course, in a recession. The flat ASR line shown in Figure 12.6 for this region indicates that, in this model, there is assumed to be no tendency for inflation to rise or fall. Since a considerable amount of labor and other resources are unemployed, there is no pressure for inflation to rise. Since wages and prices tend to be slow in adjusting downward, inflation won't fall either—at least not right away.

2.2 SHIFTS OF THE ASR CURVE: INFLATIONARY EXPECTATIONS

When people have experienced inflation, they tend to come to expect it. They then tend to build the level of inflation they expect into the various contracts they enter. If a business expects 5 percent inflation over the coming year, for example, it will add 5 percent to the selling price it quotes for a product to be delivered a year into the future, just to stay even. If workers also expect 5 percent inflation, they will try to get a 5 percent cost of living allowance (or COLA), just to stay even. A depositor who expects 5 percent inflation and wants a 4 percent real rate of return will only be satisfied with a 9 percent nominal rate of return. In this way, an expected rate of inflation can start to become institutionally "built in" to an economy. As a first approximation, it is reasonable to assume that people expect something like the level of inflation they have recently experienced (an assumption economists call "adaptive expectations").

Since different contracts come up for renegotiation at different times of the year, the process of building in particular inflationary expectations will only take place over time. Because of the time it takes for prices and wages to adjust, we need to make a distinction between short-run and medium-run aggregate supply responses.

The ASR curve in figure 12.6 was drawn for a particular level of expected inflation in the *short run*. Before people have caught on to the fact that the inflation rate might be changing, their expectations of inflation will continue to reflect their recent experience. The rate of inflation at which the ASR curve becomes horizontal is the expected inflation rate. In this model, an economy in recession, or in the flattish part of the ASR curve in the full-employment range, will tend in the short run to roll along at pretty much the same inflation rate it has experienced in the past. Only tight labor and resource markets caused by a boom will tend to increase inflation, which will come as a surprise to people, and will not immediately translate into a change in expectations. For the purposes of this model, you might think of the short run as a period of some weeks or months.

Over a longer period of time—the *medium run*—however, a rise in inflation due to tight markets will tend to increase people's expectations of inflation. If they expect 5 percent inflation, but experience 7 percent inflation, the next time they renegotiate contracts they may build in a 7 percent rate. Figure 12.7 shows how the ASR curve shifts up as people's expectations of inflation rise. Note that the maximum capacity of the economy has not changed—nothing has happened that would affect the physical capacity of the economy to produce. All that has happened is that now, at any output level, people's expectations of inflation are higher.

Similarly, if people experience very loose markets for their labor or products, over the medium run the expected inflation rate may start to come down. Employers may find they can still get workers even if they offer lower COLAs in the new contracts. Producers may raise their prices less this year than last year, because they are having trouble selling in a slow market. When people start to observe wage and price inflation tapering off in some sectors of the economy, they may change their expectations about inflation. As people react to the sluggish aggregate demand that occurs during a recession, they will tend, over time, to lessen their expectations about wage and price increases. The graph for this would be like Figure 12.7, but would show the ASR curve shifting downward instead of upward.

Figure 12.7 **An Increase in Inflationary Expectations**

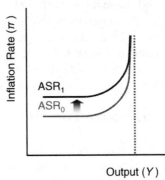

If people come to expect a higher level of inflation and build this into their contracts, a higher inflation rate could accompany any level of output.

Figure 12.8 **A Beneficial Supply Shock**

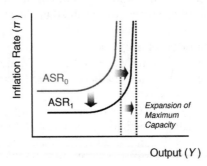

A beneficial supply shock, such as unusually high agricultural production or an improvement in technology, increases the economy's capacity to produce and generally lowers inflation.

2.3 SHIFTS OF THE ASR CURVE: SUPPLY SHOCKS

The aggregate supply response relation in the macroeconomy also changes when the capacity of the economy changes. A **supply shock** is something that changes the ability of an economy to produce goods and services. Supply shocks can be beneficial, as when there is a bumper crop in agriculture or a new invention allows more goods or services to be made using a smaller quantity of resources. Increases in labor productivity also allow an economy to produce more goods and services.

| **supply shock:** a change in the productive capacity of an economy

In such cases, the real capacity of the economy expands, as shown in Figure 12.8. The line indicating maximum capacity shifts to the right, showing that the economy can produce more than before. We model the beneficial supply shock as moving the ASR curve both to the right and downward. It moves to the right because capacity has increased. It moves downward because beneficial supply shocks are often accompanied by decreases in prices. As computer technology has improved, for example, the price of any given amount of computing power has dropped rapidly. To the extent that computers play a significant role in the economy, this tends to undermine inflation.

Supply shocks can also be adverse. In fact, economists were first forced to start theorizing about supply shocks when the oil embargo during the early 1970s resulted in steeply rising oil prices. Oil prices rose even more dramatically toward the end of the 1970s. Natural occurrences such as hurricanes or droughts, and human-made situations such as wars that destroy capital goods and lives, are other examples of adverse supply shocks. These reduce the economy's capacity to produce, and, by concentrating demand on the limited supplies of resources that remain, tend to lead to higher inflation. These would be illustrated in a graph such as Figure 12.8, but with the direction of all the movements reversed.

Discussion Questions

1. Describe in words how the ASR curve differs from the ADE curve. What does each represent? What explains their slopes?
2. Do you get "cost of living" raises at your job, or know people who do? Why does this practice have important macroeconomic consequences?

NEWS IN CONTEXT:
Crude Oil Price Closes Above $80

HOUSTON—Crude oil closed above $80 a barrel for the first time on Thursday, breaking a longstanding psychological barrier. . . . The record close capped a recent run-up that had sent oil nearly 10 percent higher in nine business days, potentially a fresh drag on the economy at a time when it appears to be weakening because of problems in the housing market . . .

Oil prices have soared nearly fourfold since 2000 because of several factors: increased demand from China and India, declining production in Venezuela and Mexico and supply disruptions resulting from political crises in the Middle East and Africa. Gasoline prices have periodically spiked in recent years because of high crude prices and disruptions and tight capacity at American refineries. . . .

"Once the latest storm threat passes, we may see pump prices drop with the autumn leaves," said Tom Kloza, an analyst with the Oil Price Information Service. But traders said all bets were off if a serious hurricane hit the gulf, as Rita and Katrina did two years ago, crippling production and sending prices soaring. . . .

As high as oil prices appear to many consumers, experts noted that they are nowhere near the levels reached during the supply crisis in early 1980. Adjusted for today's dollars, a barrel of oil then sold for the equivalent of almost $102.

Source: Clifford Krauss, *New York Times* 9/14/2007

After this article appeared, oil prices continued to rise, surpassing $130 per barrel in May 2008 (when this book went to press). Why do higher oil prices create a "drag on the economy"? How would macroeconomists illustrate this in a model?

3. PUTTING THE **ASR/ADE** MODEL TO WORK

Economists invented the ASR/ADE model to illustrate three points about the macroeconomy:

1. Fiscal and monetary policies affect output and inflation:

    *   *Contractionary fiscal and monetary policies* tend to push the economy toward lower output. Inflation is unlikely to fall quickly, but a persistent recession will tend to lower inflation over the long term.
    *   *Expansionary fiscal and monetary policies* tend to push the economy toward higher output. If the economy is approaching its maximum capacity, they will also cause inflation to rise.

2. *Supply shocks* may also have significant effects:

    *   Adverse supply shocks lower output and raise inflation.
    *   Beneficial supply shocks raise output and lower inflation.

3. *Investor and consumer confidence* and expectations also have important effects on output and inflation.

We will see how this model has helped economists explain some of the major macroeconomic events of the last several decades.

Figure 12.9   **An Economy in Recession**

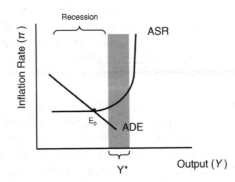

At point E_0, the inflation rate is stable, but the economy is in a recession with output below full employment.

3.1 AN ECONOMY IN RECESSION

In Figure 12.9, we bring together the ASR and ADE curves for the first time. The (short-run) equilibrium of the economy is shown as point E_0, at the intersection of the two curves. Depending on how we place the curves in the figure, we could illustrate an economy that is in a recession, at full employment, or in a wage-price spiral.

In this specific case, the fact that E_0 is to the left of the full-employment range of output indicates that the economy is in a recession. Private spending, as determined in part by investor and consumer confidence, along with government and foreign sector spending, are not enough to keep the economy at full employment. The fact that the curves intersect on the flat part of the ASR curve indicates that inflation (in the short run) is stable. So in this situation unemployment is a problem. What can be done?

Figure 12.10 **Unemployment and Inflation in the United States, 1963–65**

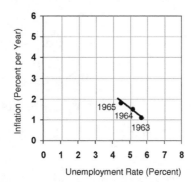

In 1963, the rate of inflation was very low, but the economy was in a recession, with unemployment above 5 percent. The Kennedy tax cuts stimulated the economy in 1964–65, reducing unemployment but also causing a small increase in inflation. (Source: *Economic Report of the President.* The measure of inflation used is the Implicit Price Deflator)

Figure 12.9 models the real-world situation of the United States economy in the early 1960s (as well as during other periods). In 1963 inflation was quite low but unemployment was above 5 percent, as shown in Figure 12.10. Policymakers at the time felt that this unemployment rate was excessive.

The administration of President John F. Kennedy undertook to get the economy out of the recession. It pushed for expansionary tax cuts, which were enacted in 1964. The result, in terms of the empirical data, is shown in Figure 12.10. During the period shown, the unemployment rate dropped by over one percentage point while inflation rose by less than one percentage point.

This historical sequence can be understood using the ASR/ADE model as shown in Figure 12.11. Expansionary fiscal policy shifts the ADE curve to the right. Now that we also have the supply side of the story in place, we can see the effects of such a shift on equilibrium output and inflation. According to this model, a shift of the size shown could put the economy well into the full-employment range, while—because the new equilibrium is on the gently sloping part of the ASR curve—leading to only a small rise in inflation.

The path traced out by the equilibrium points on the theoretical graph can be regarded as essentially a mirror image of the empirical graph. It is a *mirror* image because while unemployment rises as we go to the left in Figure 12.11, it rises as we go to the right in Figure 12.10.

Although we will return to other issues concerning this policy later, the success of the Kennedy tax cuts in creating an economic expansion led to great optimism at the time about macroeconomists' ability to "fine tune" the economy using appropriate policies.

3.2 AN OVERHEATED ECONOMY

The tax cuts were not the only thing going on in the 1960s, however. High government spending, and particularly spending for the Vietnam War, meant that fiscal policy continued to be expansionary well after the 1964 tax cuts. Monetary policy during this period tended to accommodate the fiscal expansion. The effects of these continued expansionary policies on inflation and unemployment are traced in Figure 12.12. Unemployment continued to fall by about one percentage point after 1965, to under 4 percent. But inflation rose steeply over the second half of the decade, reaching 5 percent in 1969. This curve may look familiar to you—it is the Phillips curve you derived from the underlying data back in Chapter 2.

Figure 12.11   **Expansionary Fiscal Policy When the Economy Starts in a Recession**

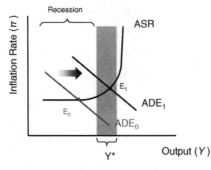

Expansionary fiscal policy shifts the ADE curve to the right, restoring full employment with only a small rise in inflation.

Figure 12.12   **Unemployment and Inflation in the United States, 1963–69**

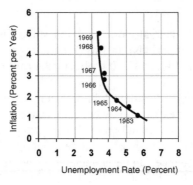

Continued high government spending, particularly for military purposes, drove unemployment down but led to steeply rising inflation in the latter years of the 1960s.

This period of history is modeled in Figure 12.13. The ADE curve shifts out further due to the increases in government spending. It shifts from ADE_0, which corresponds to a full-employment equilibrium, to ADE_1, which crosses the ASR curve in the wage-price spiral range. The economy became overheated, moving beyond full employment to a point such as (the new) E_1.

As you can see, the equilibrium points in the theoretical graph trace out a mirror image of the Phillips curve. This is no coincidence. The models that economists developed during the 1960s grew out of observing such a pattern of unemployment and inflation rates, and trying to explain why it occurred. The Phillips curve relationship seemed to suggest that policymakers could "trade off" inflation and unemployment—that they could, by use of policies, choose to settle the economy at any point along the curve. Policymakers could push up inflation in order to keep unemployment low, or perhaps sacrifice some employment in order to push down inflation—or so it was thought for a while.

3.3 Stagflation

The occurrences of the early 1970s came as a shock to Phillips-curve-minded economists and policymakers. Figure 12.14 shows the pattern of unemployment and inflation movements during these years. From 1969 to 1970 unemployment and inflation *both* rose, and both stayed fairly

Figure 12.13 **Expansionary Fiscal Policy When the Economy Is at Full Employment**

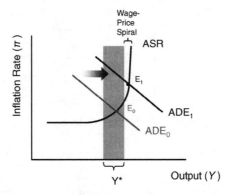

Expansionary policy causes the economy to "heat up." In the short run, people respond by increasing output, but tight markets for labor and other resources cause inflation to rise as well.

Figure 12.14 **Unemployment and Inflation in the United States, 1963–73**

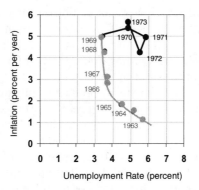

In the early 1970s, the economy entered a period of stagflation, with inflation and unemployment both high.

high through the 1970–73 period. This combination of economic stagnation (recession) and high inflation came to be known as **stagflation**.

> **stagflation:** a combination of rising inflation and economic stagnation

What happened? In 1968, worried by rising inflation, President Lyndon Johnson got Congress to enact an income tax surcharge. In our model, we show this contractionary fiscal policy as a leftward shift of the ADE curve in Figure 12.15.

This policy move is widely considered to have been "too little, too late" to curb consumer and investor spending. By the time the economy started to cool off, inflationary expectations had become firmly implanted. Having recently experienced a wage-price spiral, people had built expectations of higher inflation into their wage and price contracts. As one economist commented, inflation is like toothpaste—once you squeeze it out of the tube, you can't get it back in. Although the fiscal cutbacks contributed to falling GDP and rising unemployment, they didn't bring down inflation due to this institutional "ratcheting up" of inflationary expectations.

The combination of the contractionary fiscal policy and the rise in expectations is shown as moving the economy from a boom point of E_0 in Figure 12.15 (such as the United States economy in 1969) to a recessionary, high inflation point of E_1 (such as 1970–71).

Figure 12.15 **Contractionary Fiscal Policy and Rising Inflationary Expectations**

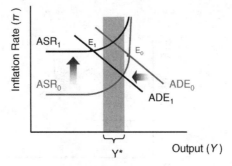

A tax surcharge should cool off the economy, as shown by the ADE shift. However, the policy action won't bring down inflation if inflationary expectations have risen, as shown by the ASR shift.

3.4 THE OIL PRICE SHOCK

Economists in the early 1970s were just getting used to the idea that inflation and unemployment could not necessarily be "traded off" over the long run when the worldwide economy got hit by another big surprise. As mentioned in Chapter 1, in 1973–74 the countries belonging to the Organization of Petroleum Exporting Countries (OPEC) cut production, drastically increased the price at which they sold their oil, and even temporarily stopped shipping oil to certain countries. The price of oil, a key input into many production processes, suddenly quadrupled. What effect did this have on the macroeconomy? Figure 12.16 shows that both inflation and unemployment rose dramatically from 1973 to 1975. (Note that we have changed the scale on this graph—the top value for inflation is now 10 percent instead of the 6 percent used in earlier graphs, and the top value for unemployment is now 10 percent instead of 8 percent.) Later, in 1976, the inflation rate came back down to its 1973 level, while employment recovered slightly.

We can explain the immediate effect of the adverse oil supply shock of the early 1970s in terms of the ASR/ADE model shown in Figure 12.17. The economy starts off in a recession at point E_0, which is substantially to the left of the initial maximum capacity line. The cut in foreign oil production meant that the United States (and many other oil-importing countries) now suffered from a reduced capacity to produce goods, as shown by the maximum capacity line and ASR curves shifting to the left. Even if labor resources were fully employed, an economy with reduced access to other inputs would not be able to produce as much.* At the same time, the rise in oil prices had an immediate and direct effect on inflation, shifting the ASR curve up as well, as also shown in Figure 12.17.

Now that the economy is in recession, what will happen? After the initial dramatic hike in oil prices in 1974, the price of oil remained fairly steady through 1978. So there was no impetus for increasing inflation coming from further oil price hikes during this period. Because of this, and the fact that economy was suffering from unemployment, we can think of Figure 12.18 as modeling the macroeconomy during the years 1975–76, when actual and expected inflation came down.

---

* Remember that throughout the chapters in this part of the textbook, we are not including longer-term GDP *growth*. In a growing economy, an adverse supply shock deals the economy a setback, but output can eventually return to—and then surpass—its original level if growth is strong.

Figure 12.16 **Unemployment and Inflation in the United States, 1963–76**

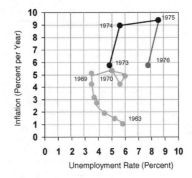

A sharp rise in petroleum prices sent both inflation and unemployment skyrocketing from 1973 to 1975. Inflation eased off in 1976.

Figure 12.17 **The Immediate Effect of the Oil Price Shock**

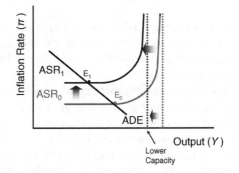

With a vital input now harder to get, the economy cannot produce as much, shifting the maximum capacity line and ASR curve to the left. The rise in the price of oil also has an immediate and direct effect on the inflation rate, shown by the upward shift in the ASR curve. The economy moves deeper into recession, with higher inflation.

Figure 12.18 **Medium-Run Adjustment to the Oil Price Shock**

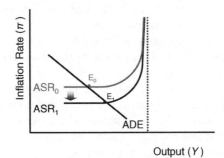

The fact that oil prices have stopped rising, and that the economy is in a deeper recession, causes inflation to ease over the medium run.

Figure 12.19   **Unemployment and Inflation in the United States, 1963–83**

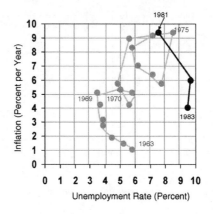

The Federal Reserve's tight monetary policies in the early 1980s brought the inflation rate down, but at the cost of increasing unemployment.

3.5 A Hard Line Against Inflation

However this was still not the end of the story. Oil prices jumped again in 1979 and 1980. In 1979 the price of oil was *ten* times higher than it had been in 1973. The overall inflation rate in the United States was over 9 percent for the year 1979—and up into the double digits (measured at an annual rate) during some months.

A number of economists thought that the high rates of inflation experienced in the late 1970s—even if they would become predictable, after a while—were unhealthy for the economy. Even though the economy was already in a recession, with an unemployment rate above 7 percent, Paul Volcker, who became chair of the Fed in 1979, took deliberate—and many would say drastic—action to bring the long-term inflation rate down. The effects of Volcker's "tight money" policies during the early 1980s can be seen empirically in Figure 12.19.

As discussed earlier, in the ASR/ADE model a reduction in the target inflation rate shifts the ADE curve down. This is shown in Figure 12.20. This model predicts that the immediate effect of this policy will be to send the economy even deeper into a recession, with output falling even farther below its full-employment level.

This contractionary policy was accompanied by many stories in the media about how Volcker was really committed to bringing down inflation, no matter what the cost. Because people found this commitment to be credible, their expectations of inflation also came down. The effect of this decrease in inflationary expectations is shown in Figure 12.21. Such a recession with falling inflation is, in fact, what happened during the Volker contraction. By 1983, the inflation rate had been reduced to 4 percent, but at a significant human and economic cost. Unemployment during 1982 and 1983 had risen to nearly 10 percent.

This is a point about macroeconomic social behavior that can be quite puzzling and frustrating. The vast majority of individual people and organizations don't *want* a recession and unemployment. Yet, as we saw earlier, the major reason why a given rate of inflation persists in an economy is that people get used to it and build it into their contracts and ways of doing business. Wouldn't it be much easier if we could just get everyone to *agree* to use a new, lower level of inflation when making their plans? Something like this had been tried earlier, during the administration of President Gerald Ford. He attempted to change people's attitudes with his 1974 "Whip Inflation Now" speech. "WIN" buttons appeared on the lapels of public leaders. This attempt at moral

Figure 12.20 **The Immediate Effect of a Lowered Inflation Target**

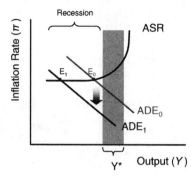

When the Federal Reserve chooses a lower target inflation rate, the ADE curve shifts down. The economy goes deeper into recession.

Figure 12.21 **The Medium-Run Effect of a Lowered Inflation Target**

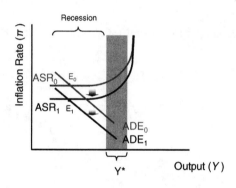

As inflationary expectations fall, the ASR curve shifts down. As the Federal Reserve continues to take a hard line on inflation, ADE continues to fall. Inflation falls, and output says low.

suasion, however, is generally agreed to have been a dismal failure. So debates persist about whether the costs in jobs and livelihood of a deliberate policy to bring down inflation by causing (or deepening) a recession are worth the benefits of a lower inflation rate.

Fed chair Ben Bernanke, appointed in 2005, is known as a strong supporter of using target rates for inflation. He has sometimes been quoted as saying that a 2 percent target rate would be appropriate. Two years into his term, however, the Fed was dealing with the 2007 subprime mortgage crises and the effects of rising oil prices. Fed actions at the time seemed to be directed toward attempting to maintain financial system stability and a non-recessionary level of aggregate demand. Although the Fed tried not to increase the inflation rate in the process of addressing these issues, lowering inflation was not the primary concern at that time.

3.6 TECHNOLOGY AND GLOBALIZATION

Following the substantial recession and disinflation of the early 1980s, output began to recover again. Figure 12.22 shows how inflation and unemployment have fluctuated until recently. Such fluctuations continued, though within narrower bands than during the earlier years. From 1984

Figure 12.22   **Unemployment and Inflation in the United States, 1983–2007**

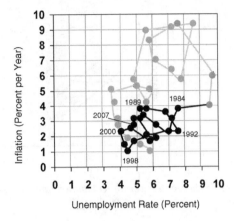

Unemployment and inflation have continued to fluctuate in recent decades, although (at least through 2007) within narrower bands than in the previous years.

Figure 12.23   **Unemployment and Inflation in the United States, 1992–99**

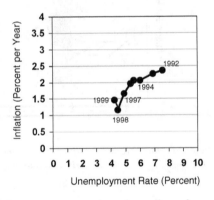

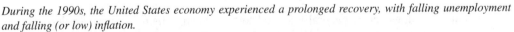

During the 1990s, the United States economy experienced a prolonged recovery, with falling unemployment and falling (or low) inflation.

to 2004, unemployment varied from 4 percent to about 8 percent, and inflation from 1 percent to about 4 percent.

We will choose one last period to focus on in detail—the expansion of the 1990s. From 1992 through 1998, unemployment rates and inflation rates steadily fell, as shown in Figure 12.23. (Note that the scale of the graph has been changed again.) In 1998, unemployment was 4.5 percent, the lowest it had been since 1965. Inflation was running at 1.1 percent, as low as it had been way back in 1963. This was clearly the best macroeconomic performance that had been seen in decades. Unemployment continued to fall on into 1999.

What caused this sustained recovery? Alan Greenspan, then chair of the Federal Reserve, commented in January 2000 that:

> When we look back at the 1990s, from the perspective of say 2010 . . . [w]e may conceivably conclude from that vantage point that, at the turn of the millennium, the American

Figure 12.24   **The Effects of Technological Innovation**

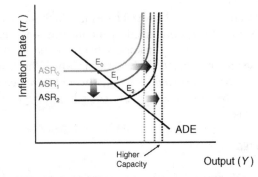

During the 1990s, innovations—particularly in information technology—increased the productivity of the economy, creating a series of beneficial supply shocks.

economy was experiencing a once-in-a-century acceleration of innovation, which propelled forward productivity, output, corporate profits, and stock prices at a pace not seen in generations, if ever.[1]

Most economists agree with Greenspan that innovation—particularly enormous leaps in information technology, including the advent of widespread use of the Internet and information systems for business supplies, deliveries, and product design—is important in explaining this period of superior macroeconomic performance. This can be modeled as a period of beneficial supply shocks, as shown in Figure 12.24.

Many economists also point to increasing global competitiveness as a factor in the rising productivity of this period. Competition from foreign firms, they argue, made U.S. firms work harder to become efficient. Meanwhile, competition from foreign workers and anti-union government policies weakened the power of domestic unions. This helped keep wage and price inflation low (though it also had consequences for the U.S. distribution of income, as described in Chapter 3).

The strong performance of the macroeconomy in the 1990s made optimism run high. A number of commentators wondered if we might be entering a "New Economy" in which business cycles would become a thing of the past. However, as Greenspan also noted in the same speech quoted above:

> Alternatively, that 2010 retrospective might well conclude that a good deal of what we are currently experiencing was just one of the many euphoric speculative bubbles that have dotted human history. And, of course, we cannot rule out that we may look back and conclude that elements from both scenarios have been in play in recent years.

Greenspan's last remark, in retrospect, seems to have been the most prescient. Just two months after he spoke, the stock market crashed as the "dot-com" speculative bubble burst. About a year later, the economy slid into recession. Similarly, after recovering from that recession for several years, the economy again showed signs of heading toward a possible recession in late 2007, after the collapse of the subprime mortgage market. We have not, apparently, entered some new, business-cycle-free, "recession-proof" state of history. On the other hand, the real productivity gains made during the 1990s did not go away, and the effects of that part of the expansion persist to this day.

Discussion Questions

1. This section mentions several cases in which the real-world macroeconomy seemed to develop in ways predicted by the macroeconomists of the time, and in the directions desired by policymakers. What were these cases?
2. This section mentions several cases in which the real-world macroeconomy seemed to develop in ways *counter* to what would have been predicted by the macroeconomists of the time, and/or were not what policymakers had hoped for. What were these cases?

4. COMPETING THEORIES

So far, the ASR/ADE model has given us a way to gain insight into some of the major macroeconomic fluctuations of the last several decades. But there remains much room for controversy. Was it *necessary* to enact expansionary fiscal policy in order to get the economy out of the slump of the early 1960s? Was it a *good idea* for the Federal Reserve to move so vigorously to fight inflation in the early 1980s? Economists differ greatly in their views on these issues, and their theoretical backgrounds tend to inform their answers to these and other more contemporary questions. We will review two of the major theories, one that calls for a minimum of government activity, and another that calls for more active government involvement in macroeconomic stabilization. Additional theories—some of which take positions between these two poles—are reviewed in the appendix to this chapter.

4.1 CLASSICAL ECONOMICS

As discussed in previous chapters, economists with ties to the classical school tend to believe in the self-adjusting properties of a free-market system. Classical labor markets clear at an equilibrium wage (Chapter 7). Classical markets for loanable funds cause savings and investment to be equal at an equilibrium interest rate (Chapter 9). In theory, then, a smoothly functioning economy should never be at anything other than full employment.

In terms of the ASR/ADE model, the classical theory implies an aggregate supply response curve that is quite different from the one we have been working with, as shown in Figure 12.25. In such an economy, output would always be at its full-employment level (now shown as a distinct value, rather than a range). The level of aggregate demand would determine the inflation rate, but nothing else. The rationale for this vertical ASR curve is as follows. At the full-employment level, people are making their optimizing choices about how much to work, consume, and so on. If for some reason the economy were to produce at less than the full-employment level, the unemployed workers would bid down wages and full employment would be restored. If the economy were to produce at more than its full-employment level, wages would be bid up, and employment would drop back to its full-employment level. Such processes are assumed to work so quickly and smoothly that the economy is virtually always right at full employment.

What, in the classical model, is the effect of aggregate demand management policies? As we can see in Figure 12.25, expansionary fiscal or monetary policy can have no effect on the output level. Classical economists believe that increased government spending just "crowds out" private spending, particularly spending on investment. With a "fixed pie" of Y^*, more spending by government just means less spending by other actors. Monetary expansions are believed to lead only to increased inflation. The central bank should just choose a certain growth rate of the money supply or level of the interest rate to support and stick to it, they say, and not concern

Figure 12.25 **The Classical Aggregate Supply Curve**

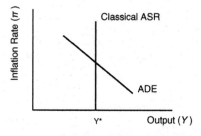

Classical economists assume the economy will virtually always be at a full employment level of output. The level of aggregate demand only influences the inflation rate.

itself about unemployment and output. Classical theory tends to support politically conservative policies emphasizing small government and strict rules on monetary policy. Classical economists would tend to say that the fiscal expansionary policies of the early 1960s were unnecessary for the purposes of macroeconomic stabilization, but that the Volcker contraction of the early 1980s was a good idea.

4.2 KEYNESIAN MACROECONOMICS

The original Keynesian belief was that market economies are inherently unstable. The Keynesian notion of the influence of "animal spirits" on investment refers to the tendency of private decision-makers to get over-optimistic and create booms in investing and production. Many business cycle theorists believe that this is due to something intrinsic to human nature. And the higher the boom, the deeper the crash. Firms that have overextended and overproduced during an upswing need time to regroup, sell off inventory, and so on, before they will be ready to go on the upswing again. Households that have overextended and overspent during a boom also need to regroup, and perhaps pay down debt, before they will be willing to restart an optimistic spending bandwagon.

In Chapter 9 we started the discussion of macroeconomic stabilization policy with a stylized graph of the business cycle, showing fluctuations in GDP over time. That figure is repeated here as Figure 12.26(a). Now we can see what this looks like in terms of the model we've developed. We can see business cycles as fundamentally caused by an ADE curve that is perpetually on the move, swinging outward and back as investor and consumer confidence wax and wane, as shown in Figure 12.26(b). Peaks are indicated by point A in both graphs, and troughs by point B. In between, the level of GDP swings through—but does not stop at—the full-employment range. If the world works this way, then government action to tone down the peaks and raise aggregate demand in the troughs—to try to keep the ADE curve more stable by counteracting the swings in private autonomous demand—makes sense.

This view of perpetual business cycles is, we cannot stress too strongly, a fundamentally different worldview from those which presume a "settling down" of the economy at a full-employment equilibrium. Keynes did *not* believe that macroeconomic phenomena could be explained by assuming rational, optimizing behavior by individuals and then extrapolating from models of individual markets to the macroeconomy. He believed that important macroeconomic factors, such as large scale waves of optimism and pessimism, or the way that occurrences in one market might carry over into other markets, could only be explained on a societal rather than an

Figure 12.26 **Business Cycles**

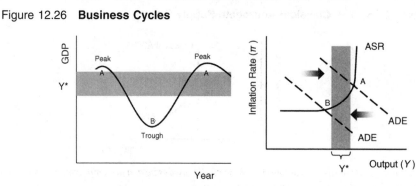

(a)   **(b)**

If firms and households are prone to alternating bouts of confidence and caution, the economy will have a fundamental tendency to swing between peaks (point A) and troughs (point B).

individual level.* His theory of "animal spirits" also suggests that we might need to be somewhat skeptical about the assumption that people always act rationally, if we want to understand real-world macroeconomic phenomena.

The traditional model of Keynesian business cycles must be modified to deal with new events such as supply shocks and sustainability issues. These require models that are flexible enough to address new issues as they arise. Such models are best built on the understanding that economies are subject to a variety of forces, many of which, much of the time, swamp those particular forces that would be expected to lead to a classical situation of full employment equilibrium.

Discussion Questions

1. It has become popular in some circles to think of Keynesian macroeconomics as simply equivalent to classical macroeconomics, with the added assumption that downward wage and price adjustments tend to be slow ("sticky wages"). (See "The Classical-Keynesian Synthesis" in the Appendix.) From the description of Keynesian theory above, would you say this characterization is accurate?
2. Which do you think gives a better description of economic realities, classical or Keynesian macroeconomic theory? Explain.

5. ARE STABILIZATION AND SUSTAINABILITY IN CONFLICT?

These past four chapters have emphasized how a high level of aggregate demand is necessary to support a high output level, keeping income levels up and unemployment down. But there

---

* Some suggest that the links between microeconomic and macroeconomic phenomena involve a fundamental "phase shift," as the concept is used in the physical science. For example, if you cool water, the water behaves one way until it reaches a certain temperature, and then behaves in a very different way as it begins to turn into ice. You cannot explain the properties of ice by studying liquid water. Similarly, economic behavior may create one sort of pattern at the level of individual agents and markets, but new behavior may emerge as we look at behavior economy-wide.

are three goals that a macroeconomic system should aim for, and maintaining living standards and stabilization are only the first two. As outlined in Chapter 1, achieving financial, social, and ecological *sustainability* is also important.

5.1 EXAMINING GOALS AND ASSUMPTIONS

Taking the models we have built at face value, it would seem that stabilization goals (particularly the goal of low unemployment) and ecological sustainability goals are in direct conflict. Stabilization would seem to require maintaining a rapid rate of "throughput"—that is, of conversion of material and energy resources into goods and services for consumption, as measured by GDP. Consumption, investment, government spending, and net exports need to stay high, according to these models, in order to generate the level of aggregate demand that supports full employment.

Ecological sustainability, on the other hand, is threatened by high rates of throughput that deplete nonrenewable (or only slowly renewable) resources and lead to other problems such as global climate change and species extinction. It is becoming increasingly clear that any serious movement toward ecological sustainability will require consuming *less* of some things we are used to, particularly fossil fuel energy resources. The oil supply shocks of the 1970s might just have been the proverbial "shot over the bow" regarding capacity constraints—an early warning sign that societies would do well to pay attention to. But would aiming for a sustainable economy therefore mean having to accept large-scale recession, income loss, and unemployment?

Some of this apparent conflict is due to the simplifying assumptions we have made in developing our macroeconomic model. To the extent that these assumptions may not be true, the conflict may not be as large as it seems. For example, in the models developed starting in Chapter 9, we have assumed:

- More employment is always better, because it gives people money incomes and unemployment is stressful and demoralizing. High levels of overall production are needed to keep employment high.
- Only the levels of consumption, investment, government spending, and net exports are important. The composition of this spending in terms of the types of goods and services produced, or the production methods used in generating GDP, are not important.

Let us examine these assumptions more closely.

5.2 WHAT DO WE REALLY WANT FROM EMPLOYMENT?

There is no doubt that needing a job and not being able to find one can be very tough on the unemployed. Besides the lack of income—which can throw a worker and his or her family into real hardship and poverty—unemployment can also have severe psychological repercussions. People often feel demoralized and depressed when they find they aren't wanted. Studies of the effects of business cycle swings on health and mortality show, unambiguously, that suicide rates rise during economic downturns. Clearly, a humane society should want to keep such suffering at a minimum, to the extent possible.

Beyond alleviating such situations, however, what we want from high national employment is a little less clear. Is more always better, when it comes to work at paid jobs? More work does tend to give people higher incomes. In Chapter 13, we will examine the long-term relationship between people's incomes and their health and well-being—and see that the relationship is not as strongly positive as is often supposed. What might be even more surprising, however, is that employment and measures of well-being do not always seem to be positively associated with each other over the business cycle. Although, as mentioned above, suicides tend to rise during downturns, in general mortality rates tend to *fall* when the economy slows down and *rise* during economic upswings, in industrialized countries.[2]

It may seem counterintuitive that death rates rise when the economy is "doing well," but several facts about the population in general (not just the unemployed population) can help to explain this. For example, during an upswing, construction jobs, which tend to be some of the most dangerous in the economy, are especially likely to increase. During upswings, many new and inexperienced people are put to work in industries such as logging and manufacturing, and inexperienced people are especially likely to be injured or killed on the job. Thus mortality from on-the-job accidents tends to rise during an upswing (and fall during a downturn). During an upswing, people also tend to drive more miles. Since traffic accidents are a major cause of injury and death, this also contributes to a higher mortality rate. Higher deaths from cardiovascular disease during booms may be related to longer hours and a faster pace of work. There also is some evidence that people tend to exercise more, maintain a better body weight, and drink less heavily when the economy is in a downturn—perhaps because reduced incomes and reduced hours encourage a wider variety of activities.

Rather than just thinking about "employment" and "unemployment," then, perhaps macroeconomists should be thinking more about the *quality, types,* and *intensity* of employment an economy offers, and what these mean for people's well-being. Being entirely pushed out of the wage-earning system is clearly injurious to the involuntarily unemployed, and being deprived of sufficient income is very tough on the working poor. But the solution need not mean that everyone should always work forty or more hours a week in order to produce the most they can, using up large amounts of energy and materials in the process. As discussed in Chapter 7, people also benefit from hours they spend away from paid employment: This time gives them greater opportunities to do unpaid work, including family care, and to pursue leisure activities. It may be possible to keep *employment* levels high while reducing material and energy throughput, if we, as a society, think creatively enough about *what sorts* of employment we really want.

In France, for example, the standard workweek was cut back from thirty-nine hours to thirty-five hours for many employees beginning in 2000. Partly, this was due to the government's wish to cut unemployment levels by spreading work more broadly. A number of unions lobbied for the cut in hours, arguing that it would improve workers' quality of life. The French Green (ecological) party supported the legislation as well. While the law has undergone some modifications since it was enacted, and the question of how well it worked in achieving its goals is debated, this is one example of innovative macroeconomic policy that takes into account both stabilization and sustainability concerns.

5.3 WHAT DO WE REALLY WANT FROM PRODUCTION?

The model we have developed works only with the *level* of output, *Y,* and says nothing about the *composition* of output. From a sustainability perspective, however, the composition of output makes a very big difference. Some things we benefit from and enjoy require relatively little use of material and energy inputs. Eating locally grown produce, taking a bike ride with friends, or downloading a new tune from the Internet, for example, puts little stress on the natural environment. Other activities, such as heating and furnishing a very large house, driving an SUV, or chemically maintaining a perfect lawn have more negative impacts. Shifting away from producing those goods and services that are most damaging to ecological systems, and shifting toward producing goods and services that are less destructive—or even environmentally beneficial—could allow an economy to maintain consumption, investment, and employment in a less environmentally damaging way.

For example, one thing that has to happen for the world's economies to become ecologically sustainable is that the global population must cease to grow. But a stabilizing population is necessarily, at least for a considerable period of transition, also a graying population. The United States and many countries in Europe are already experiencing a growing ratio of older people to active workers. Many elderly people need extra medical care and personal care. This suggests that while an economy may need to release some workers from high-throughput jobs for sustainability reasons, there will also be a shrinking supply of workers, and an increased demand for workers in medical and social services. These demographic shifts suggest that excessive unemployment may not be the result of changes made to pursue sustainability goals, if these are well managed.

Similarly, while some opportunities for investment would die out in a more sustainable economy, many more would open up. Investments in energy-saving infrastructure for transportation, in wetland restoration, and in conversion of residential and commercial buildings to more environmentally friendly patterns of energy and chemical use, for example, would create jobs, not destroy them.

The way in which products are produced and distributed—that is, the composition of *inputs* into production—is also important. When music recordings first became popular, a record was a substantial piece of petroleum-derived vinyl. These days, a recording is a stream of electrons that may be downloaded onto a device that fits in your pocket, and the need for vinyl in the music industry has been correspondingly reduced. Sometimes producers and consumers have a hard time thinking beyond their usual ways of doing things, simply because we tend to be creatures of habit. Thinking seriously about environmental macroeconomics should encourage people to look at production methods in new ways. In a study of dangerous chemicals such as industrial solvents in the waste stream, for example, it was found that manufacturers could sometimes cut their emissions *and save on expenses* by instituting fairly simple changes in their procedures. Simply being aware of the issues can be a substantial first step.

The problems of transitioning to a more sustainable macroeconomy should not be minimized. People who build SUVs today, for example, cannot just start building solar panels tomorrow—changes in human and manufactured capital must take place first. But neither should these problems be enlarged out of all proportion. Scientific evidence suggests that a conversion to a less resource-greedy economy is not a matter of *if*, but rather a matter of *when* and *how*. And the longer the conversion is put off, the more difficult it is likely to be.

5.4 POLICIES FOR STABILIZATION AND SUSTAINABILITY

In Chapter 10, we saw how government spending and taxing policies can contribute to stabilization, and in Chapter 11 we looked at issues of money and credit. A society committed to both stabilization and sustainability could find ways to use these standard macroeconomic tools work toward both goals. For example, many economists recognize that fossil fuel products are currently priced at less than their full social cost, and advocate putting extra taxes, sometimes called carbon taxes, on them in order to encourage a more socially efficient pattern of use. In 1997, over 2500 economists including eight Nobel Laureates signed the "Economists' Statement on Climate Change," which suggested, among other things, the institution of carbon taxes. Revenues from such a tax could be used, for example, to fund government investments in projects to preserve and enrich natural capital, or to stimulate similar private investments by offering investment tax credits or subsidized interest rates. Other proposed policies to address climate change are described in Chapter 15. While such policies would shift the economy toward new paths, evidence from other national mobilizations in the past—such as for wars, or for developing the science for space exploration—suggest that such redirection need not be damaging to the macroeconomy. Many such policies could, in fact, stimulate increased innovation and productivity gains.

The failure, up to this point, of economists and government decision makers to fully incorporate sustainability goals in their discussions of macroeconomic policy is disturbing to those who take a long-term, multi-generational view of social well-being. But it is *not* the case, as you may sometimes hear it argued, that the basic principles of macroeconomics require that environmental concerns be dismissed. On the contrary, adequate macroeconomic policy *requires* considering long-term goals, including environmental ones, as well as short-term stabilization goals. In the next chapter, we switch from a focus on relatively short-term business cycles to a focus on long-term growth and development.

Discussion Questions

1. Cutting the length of the standard full-time workweek could be one way to keep people employed while cutting down on the "throughput" of materials and energy. Can you think of other policies that might also have this effect?
2. Suppose you work thirty hours a week and rely on a bicycle or public transportation, but everyone you know works forty hours a week and drives a car or truck. Compare this to a situation in which everyone has work and transportation patterns that are similar to yours. Which situation do you think you would find more comfortable? What does this suggest about the relationship between individual action and public policy?

REVIEW QUESTIONS

1. What is the "Fed reaction rule"? Explain in words and show in a graph.
2. What does the ADE curve represent, and why is it downward sloping?
3. What shifts the ADE curve?
4. What does the ASR curve represent, and why does it have the shape it has?
5. What shifts the ASR curve?
6. Describe, using the ASR/ADE model, the consequences of President Kennedy's 1964 tax cuts.
7. Describe, using the ASR/ADE model, the consequences of continued fiscal expansion during the high-employment late 1960s.
8. Describe, using the ASR/ADE model, a combination of events that might cause an economy to suffer from "stagflation."
9. Describe, using the ASR/ADE model, the immediate impact of an adverse supply shock.
10. Describe, using the ASR/ADE model, what happens over time after a one-time adverse supply shock has thrown an economy into a recession.
11. Describe, using the ASR/ADE model, how a committed Fed policy might bring down inflation over time.
12. Describe, using the ASR/ADE model, the effects of a series of positive supply shocks.
13. What does the ASR curve look like in the classical model, and why?

14. What underlying dynamic did Keynes believe is behind the business cycle? Illustrate in graphs.

15. Is it necessary to have continual high spending and "throughput" to have an economy with healthy, employed people? Why, or why not?

16. Are there some types of production an economy would need more of, or different techniques of production that could be used, if economies move toward ecological sustainability?

EXERCISES

1. For each of the following, indicate which curve in the ASR/ADE model shifts, and in which direction(s):
   a. A beneficial supply shock
   b. An increase in government spending
   c. A monetary contraction designed to lower the long-run inflation rate
   d. An increase in taxes
   e. An adverse supply shock
   f. A fall in people's expectations of inflation
   g. A decrease in consumer confidence

2. Suppose the inflation rate in an economy is observed to be falling. Sketching an ASR/ADE model for each case, determine which of the following phenomena could be the cause. (There may be more than one.)
   a. The federal government gives households a substantial tax cut
   b. Agricultural harvests are particularly good this year
   c. Businesses are confident about the future and are buying more equipment
   d. The Fed is trying to move the economy toward a lower long-run inflation rate

3. Suppose an economy is currently experiencing full employment, and inflation is only slightly higher than had been expected.
   a. Draw and carefully label an ASR/ADE diagram that illustrates this case. Label the point representing the state of this economy $E_{(a)}$.
   b. Suppose that investors' confidence is actually only in the middle of an upswing. As investor confidence continues to rise, what happens to inflation and output? Add a new curve to your graph to illustrate this, as well as explaining in words. Label the point illustrating the new situation of the economy $E_{(b)}$.
   c. What sort of tax policy might a government enact to try to counteract an excessive upswing in investor confidence? Assuming this policy is effective, illustrate on your graph the effect of this policy, labeling the result $E_{(c)}$.

4. Suppose an economy is in a deep recession.
   a. Draw and carefully label an ASR/ADE diagram that illustrates this case. Label the point representing the state of this economy E_0.
   b. If no policy action is taken, what will happen to the economy over time? Show on your graph, labeling some new possible equilibrium points E_1, E_2 and E_3. (Think about which curve shifts over time, and why, when the economy stagnates. Assume that no changes occur in investor or consumer confidence or in the economy's maximum capacity output level.)

    c. Suppose the changes you outlined in (b) were to occur very rapidly and dramatically. Would it seem, then, that government policy is necessary to get the economy out of the recession?

    d. Write a few sentences relating the above analysis to the dispute between classical and Keynesian macroeconomists.

5. Many environmental scientists warn that inadequate attention to the genetic diversity of agricultural crops (and thus their resistance to pests and disease), as well as the depletion of midwestern underground aquifers, could reduce the agricultural and food-processing capacity of the United States in years to come. According to the ASR/ADE model, how would this be expected to affect the economy's maximum capacity, future output, and inflation? Draw a graph.

6. The data for the empirical graphs in this chapter were taken from the *Economic Report of the President.* Go to http://www.gpoaccess.gov/eop/ and download statistical tables for the "civilian unemployment rate" and "price indexes for gross domestic product." Jot down data on the *seasonally adjusted* unemployment rate and the *percent change in the GDP implicit price deflator* for recent periods. Plot a few points on an empirical graph, such as those in this chapter, to show how the economy has performed recently. (Sometimes data may be presented for months or calendar quarters, rather than for years. For the purposes of this exercise, you may simply average the numbers within a year to get a number for the year.)

7. Match each concept in Column A with a definition or example in Column B.

Column A	Column B
a. Relates inflation rates to the economy's physical capacity	1. COLAs
b. Relates inflation rates and interest rates	2. Output approaching its maximum capacity level
c. A completely vertical ASR curve	3. Stagflation
d. Characterized the U.S. economy during the 1960s	4. Carbon tax
e. A way that inflationary expectations get institutionalized	5. Suicide rates
f. Increase during economic booms	6. A classical assumption
g. A cause of rising inflation	7. ASR curve
h. Characterized the U.S. economy during most of the 1990s	8. Fed reaction rule
i. A cause of falling inflation	9. Rising inflation and falling unemployment
j. Relates inflation rates to economy-wide spending levels	10. Keynes' theory
k. Increase during recessions	11. A prolonged recession
l. A policy to encourage more efficient resource use	12. Falling inflation and falling unemployment
m. Characterized the U.S. economy in 1974–75	13. Mortality rates
n. A shifting and unstable ADE curve, due to changes in confidence	14. ADE curve

8. (Appendix) Suppose that rational expectations theory is correct. If the Fed decides to set a lower target inflation rate, and announces and carries through on this in a credible fashion, how would inflation and output be affected? Draw a graph. Compare and contrast this outcome to the actual response to the Volcker contraction, described in the body of the chapter.

Appendix: More Schools of Macroeconomics

A1. New Classical Economics

Faced with the empirical evidence of widely fluctuating output and unemployment rates, modern day classical economists—often called "new classical" economists—have come up with a number of theories that seek to explain how classical theory can be consistent with the observed fluctuations.

At the most classical extreme, some economists have sought to redefine full employment to mean pretty much whatever level of employment currently exists. Assuming that people make optimizing choices and markets work smoothly, one might observe employment levels rise and fall if, for example, technological capacities or people's preferences for work versus leisure shift over time. Some new classical economists, who have worked on what is called **real business cycle theory**, have suggested that "intertemporal substitution of leisure" (that is, essentially, people voluntarily taking more time off during recessions) could be at the root of the lower employment levels observed during some historical periods.

> **real business cycle theory:** the theory that changes in employment levels are caused by change in technological capacities or people's preferences concerning work

Economists of the **rational expectations school** (influential during the 1970s and '80s) proposed a theory as to why monetary policy should only affect the inflation rate, and not output. This model can be explained by using the ASR/ADE model developed in this chapter to illustrate changes due to policies and expectations, while also adding the classical ASR from Figure 12.25 to show that the economy remains at full employment. Suppose that the full-employment level of output really corresponds to that shown in Figure 12.27, and the economy starts at point E_0. But suppose that the central bankers believe that full employment will not be achieved unless output is higher. (Recall that the level of "full employment" unemployment is controversial.) The model we have been using predicts that the Fed will use expansionary policy to try to shift the ADE curve to the right, as shown.

> **rational expectations school:** a group of macroeconomists who theorized that people's expectations about Fed policy would cause predictable monetary policies to be ineffective in changing output levels

But the rational expectations school economists said that people use all economically available information in making their decisions and plans, including available information about economic models (such as the one we've been studying) and reports about attitudes of and actions taken by leaders of the Fed. Therefore, if they think those leaders feel that current output is too low, they will know from their economic model that the Fed will undertake expansionary policy. Correctly anticipating the Fed's move, they will immediately incorporate higher inflation into their inflationary expectations. This immediate rise in expected inflation, shown by the shift up in the curved ASR curve, will cancel out the expansionary effects of the policy. Output won't change, and the economy stays on the classical ASR curve.

Other new classical economists accept that unemployment is real, and very painful to those it affects. However, they see aggregate demand policies as useless for addressing it. Rather, they claim that unemployment is caused by imperfections in labor markets (the "Classical Unemployment" described in Chapter 7). To reduce unemployment, new classical economists may prescribe getting rid of government regulations (such as rigorous safety standards or minimum wages) that limit how firms can do business, restricting union activity, and/or cutting back on

Figure 12.27   **Expansionary Monetary Policy with Rational Expectations**

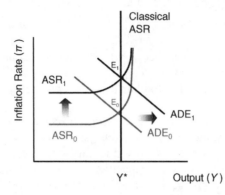

In the rational expectations model, people see right away what sort of inflation central bank policy will lead to, and adjust accordingly. Deliberate monetary policy changes thus have no effect on output.

government social welfare policies that make it attractive (according to the new classicals) to stay out of work. Market pressures, they believe, will be enough on their own to support full employment—if given free rein.

A2. THE CLASSICAL-KEYNESIAN SYNTHESIS AND NEW KEYNESIAN MACROECONOMICS

Somewhere in the middle ground is what has been called the classical-Keynesian synthesis. In this way of looking at the world, Keynesian theory, which allows for output to vary from its full-employment level, is considered to be a reasonably good description of how things work in the short run and medium run. However, this view holds that the classical world prevails in the long run.

You may have noticed that in the exposition of the ASR/ADE model above, we talked about the short run and the medium run, but did not mention the long run. This is because in more decidedly Keynesian thought (to be discussed below), the economy is really a succession of short and medium runs. Shocks to the economy are so frequent and so pronounced, and price and wage adjustments (especially downward ones) so slow, that the economy never has a chance to "settle down." In the classical-Keynesian synthesis, on the other hand, it is assumed that the economy, if left to its own devices for long enough, would settle back at full employment, due to the (eventual) success of classical wage and price adjustments. Models built on this basis would use an analysis much like that presented in the ADE/ASR model used in the body of this chapter, but add a vertical ASR curve such as that shown in Figure 12.27, labeling it the "long run aggregate supply response."

To the extent that classicals and many Keynesians agree on this model, then, debates come down to a question of how long it takes *to get to* the long run. New classical economists tend to emphasize that excessive unemployment is merely temporary, and believe that (at least if government regulations would get out of the way) the long run comes fairly soon. Some Keynesian economists, often called **New Keynesians**, have accepted the challenge from classically minded economists to present all their analysis in terms of individual optimizing behavior, micro-level markets, and possible "imperfections." They have built up theories (such as efficiency wage theory and insider-outsider theory, discussed in Chapter 7) to explain why wages don't just fall during a recession. They tend to work within the classical-Keynesian synthesis, but claim that due to institutional factors the long run may be a long, long way away. They believe that government action, then, is often justified.

> **New Keynesian macroeconomics:** a school which bases its analysis on micro-level market behavior, but which justifies activist macroeconomic policies by assuming that markets have "imperfections"

A3. POST-KEYNESIAN MACROECONOMICS

Post-Keynesian economists believe that modern economies are basically unstable, and do not accept the idea of a long-run equilibrium at full employment. They tend to stress the view that history matters in determining where the economy is today. They also believe that the future, although it will depend to some extent on the actions we take now, is fundamentally unpredictable, due to the often surprising nature of economic evolution and world events.

> **post-Keynesian macroeconomics:** a school that stresses the importance of history and uncertainty in determining macroeconomic outcomes

For example, one argument that some make is that high unemployment, like high inflation, may also be "toothpaste" that is very difficult to get back into the tube. When people are unemployed for a long time, they tend to lose work skills, lose work habits, and may get demoralized. If this is true, then government action to counter unemployment is even more needed, since high unemployment now may tend to lead to high unemployment in the future, even if the demand situation recovers. (Economists tend to refer to this idea that future levels of unemployment—or any other economic variable—may depend on past levels as "hysteresis" or "path dependence.") Post-Keynesian economists would tend to say that the fiscal expansionary policies of the early 1960s were a good idea, because they do *not* believe that an economy left to its own devices will naturally return to full employment, even "in the long run." On the other hand, they would tend to see the Volcker contraction of the early 1980s as unnecessarily harsh, because of their emphasis on the detrimental and persistent effects of high unemployment.

NOTES

1. Remarks by Chairman Alan Greenspan, January 13, 2000, available at http://www.federalreserve.gov.
2. See the symposium in the December 2005 issue of the *International Journal of Epidemiology.*

Part Four
Macroeconomic Issues and Applications

13 The Global Economy

Do you know how many Philippine pesos, South African rand, or Peruvian nuevos soles you can get for a United States dollar? No? You might be surprised, if you traveled to one of these countries, to find out that the average person on the street in any city can often easily quote you the going rate between their currency and the United States dollar. People in smaller economies have always been very vulnerable to international economic conditions and hence make it a habit to keep on top of them.

In contrast, because the United States is a large economy and its currency currently dominates the world financial system, people living in the United States historically tended to be relatively unaware of global economic conditions. In recent years that has changed. Now international trade and global borrowing and lending have significantly increased in importance, for the United States as well as globally. A large proportion of consumer goods at Wal-Mart or other discount stores come from abroad. The person who responds to your phone inquiry about computer services may be based in a foreign country. International flows of financial capital are less evident to the average person, but are very important in affecting U.S. interest rates and financial markets. Employment patterns have been impacted by foreign trade, and it is hard to miss discussions about the merits and demerits of "globalization."

1. MACROECONOMICS IN A GLOBAL CONTEXT

In earlier chapters, we have seen that nations tally up imports and exports in their national accounts (Chapter 5), and that an increase in domestic incomes tends to increase our demand for imports from other countries (Chapter 10). But it is time to get more specific about how national economies are linked together, and the opportunities and problems this creates.

1.1 GLOBAL CONNECTIONS

As discussed in Chapter 5, an economy that has no international linkages is called a *closed economy*, while one that participates in the global economy is called an *open economy*. The economic linkages among countries can take many forms, including:

- International *trade flows,* when goods and services that have been created in one country are sold in another
- International *income flows,* when capital incomes (profit, rent, and interest), labor incomes, or transfer payments go from one country to another

- International *transactions in assets,* when people trade in financial assets such as foreign bonds or currencies, or make investments in real foreign assets such as businesses or real estate
- International *flows of people,* as people migrate from one country to another, either temporarily or permanently
- International flows of *technological knowledge, cultural products,* and other intangibles, which can profoundly influence patterns of production and consumption, as well as tastes and lifestyles
- International sharing of *common environmental resources,* such as deep-sea fisheries and global climate patterns
- The institutional environment created by international monetary institutions, international trade agreements, international military and aid arrangements, and banks, corporations, and other private entities that operate at an international scale

Any one of these forms of interaction may be crucially important for understanding the macroeconomic experience of specific countries at specific times. Mexico and Turkey, for example, receive significant flows of income from remittances sent home by citizens working abroad. Biological hazards, such as diseases or insects that threaten human health or agriculture, can travel along with people and goods. Trade in "intellectual property" such as technology patents and music copyrights is currently an issue of hot dispute.

Thoroughly describing the international economic system is much too grand a project for one textbook. This chapter will lay out some basics of international trade and international finance, looking briefly at selected international institutions and the question of how global linkages can affect living standards and macroeconomic stabilization. Later chapters will look in more detail at issues of growth and sustainability.

1.2 Major Policy Tools

Governments can try to control the degree of "openness" or "closedness" of their economies through a variety of policy tools. The most drastic way to "close" an economy is to institute a **trade ban**. In theory a country could prohibit all international trade, but this hardly ever happens. More often countries make trade in selected goods illegal, or ban trade with particular countries (such as the United States' ban on trade with Cuba). Inspections at the country's borders, or at hubs of transportation such as airports, are used to enforce a ban.

> **trade ban:** a law preventing the import or export of goods or services

A less drastic measure is a **trade quota**, which does not eliminate trade, but sets limits on the quantity of a good that can be imported or exported. A quota on imports, by restricting supply, generally raises the price that can be charged for the good within the country. An import quota helps domestic producers by shielding them from lower-price competition. It hurts foreign producers because it limits what they can sell in the domestic market. Foreign producers may, however, get some benefit in the form of extra revenues from the artificially higher price.

> **trade quota:** a restriction on the quantity of a good that can be imported or exported

A third sort of policy—which has been used very often throughout history—is a **tariff** (or "duty"). Tariffs are taxes charged on imports or exports. Tariffs, like quotas, may serve to reduce trade since they make internationally traded goods more costly to buy or sell. Like quotas, import tariffs benefit domestic producers while raising prices to consumers. Unlike quotas, however, import tariffs provide monetary benefit to the government. Also unlike quotas, tariffs do not give foreign producers an opportunity to increase prices—in fact, foreign producers may be forced to lower prices in order to remain competitive with domestic producers who do not pay the tariff.

| **tariffs:** taxes put on imports or exports

The last important major category of trade-related policies—**trade-related subsidies**—may be used to either expand or contract trade. Export subsidies, paid to domestic producers when they market their products abroad, are motivated by a desire to *increase* the flow of exports. Countries can also use subsidies to promote a policy of **import substitution**, by giving domestic producers extra payments to encourage the production of certain goods for domestic markets, with a goal of *reducing* the quantity of imports.

| **trade-related subsidies:** payments given to producers to encourage more production, either
| for export or as a substitute for imports

| **import substitution:** the policy of encouraging domestic producers to make products that can
| be used in place of imported goods

Government policies can also influence international capital transactions. Central banks often participate in foreign exchange markets with policy goals in mind (as will be discussed below). Countries sometimes institute **capital controls**, which are restrictions or taxes on transactions in financial assets such as currency, stocks, or bonds, and/or on foreign ownership of domestic assets such as businesses or land. Restrictions on how much currency a person can take out of a country, for example, are one type of capital control. Such controls are usually instituted to try to prevent sudden, destabilizing swings in the movement of financial capital.

| **capital controls:** the regulation or taxation of international transactions involving assets

Countries may also regulate the form that foreign business investments can take. Some have required that all business ventures be at least partially owned by domestic investors. Some have required that all traded manufactured goods include at least a given percentage of parts produced by domestically owned companies. Sometimes such controls are related to a development strategy (see Chapter 14), while in other cases they simply reflect a desire to avoid excessive foreign control of domestic economic affairs.

Some trade polices are enacted to try to attract foreign investment, for example by giving foreign companies tax breaks and other incentives. A popular form of this is the **foreign trade zone**, a designated area of the country within which many tax, tariff, and perhaps regulatory policies that usually apply to manufacturing are not enforced. By attracting foreign investment, countries may hope to increase employment or gain access to important technologies. A well-known example is the *maquiladora* policy in Mexico under which manufacturing plants can import components and produce goods for export free of tariffs.

| **foreign trade zone:** a designated area of a country within which foreign-owned manufacturers
| can operate free of many taxes, tariffs, and regulations

Migration controls are another important aspect of policy. Countries generally impose restrictions on people visiting or moving into their territory, and a few also impose tight regulations on people leaving the country. While beliefs about race, national culture, and population size are often the most obvious influences behind the shaping of these controls, economic concerns also play a role. For example, policies may be affected by concerns about the skill composition of the domestic labor force or the desire to get remittances from out-migrants.

| **migration controls:** restrictions on the flows of people into and out of a country

Countries do not necessarily choose sets of policies that consistently lead toward "openness" or consistently toward "closedness." Often there is a mix—policies are chosen for a wide variety of reasons, and can even run at cross-purposes. Nor do countries choose their policies in a vacuum. Policymakers need to take account of the reactions of foreign governments to their policies. Increasingly they also need to pay attention to whether their policies are in compliance with international agreements.

1.3 PATTERNS OF TRADE AND FINANCE

International trade has grown immensely in recent years. Sometimes the sum of a country's imports and exports of goods and services, measured as a percent of GDP, is used as a measure of an economy's "openness." Growth in trade according to this measure is shown in Figure 13.1, for the years 1965-2004.* While trade still remains relatively less important in the United States than in other countries, its importance has been increasing here as well.

Why has trade grown over time? One reason is improvements in transportation technology. The costs and time lags involved in shipping products by air, for example, are far reduced now from what they were in 1950. Fruit from Chile and flowers from Colombia are now flown into the United States every day—and are still fresh when they arrive. A second reason for increased trade is advances in telecommunications. The infrastructure for communication by phone, fax, and computer has improved dramatically, making it much easier for businesses to communicate with potential overseas suppliers and customers. Apparel companies in New York, for example, can communicate details about styles and sizes to their foreign suppliers almost instantaneously. Better telecommunications even make it possible for some kinds of services such as customer support to be directly imported from, for example, call centers in India. Thirdly, many governments have, over time, lowered their tariffs and other barriers to trade.

Figure 13.2 shows the volume of exports that the United States sells to the top eight buyers of its goods, and the volume of its imports that come from the top eight countries that sell to it. Historically, the near neighbors of the United States—Canada and Mexico—have been very important trading partners. Various Western European economies, and Japan after it industrialized have also, not surprisingly, played a strong role. For political reasons the U.S. government has historically encouraged trade with certain strategic allies, including South Korea and Taiwan, explaining their presence among the major trading partners.

The biggest development in recent years has been the emergence of China as a major source of U.S. imports. Until about 1980, U.S. trade with China was negligible. Since then, U.S. importation of Chinese products—especially electronics (including computers and televisions), clothing, toys, and furniture—has boomed. Although China buys some U.S. goods, including agricultural products and aircraft, the value of U.S. imports from China far exceeds the value of U.S. exports to China.

The volume of global financial transactions has also exploded in recent years. For example, foreign exchange flows in mid-2007 were averaging about $3.2 trillion—*per day!* This daily

---

* While it might be tempting to interpret this measure as "the part of GDP that is traded," that is not correct. Recall that only *net* exports (that is, exports *minus* imports) is a component of GDP. This measure of "openness" (exports *plus* imports, divided by GDP), on the other hand, can even exceed 100 percent for countries very active in trade. The purpose of expressing the volume of total trade as a percent of GDP is simply to control for the overall growth of production over time.

Figure 13.1 **Trade Expressed as a Percentage of Production, World and United States, 1965–2004**

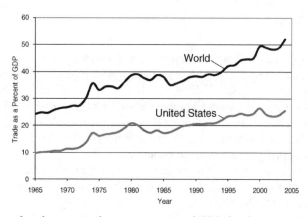

The worldwide volume of trade, expressed as a percentage of GDP, has been increasing over the past four decades. While the United States remains less "open" than many economies, trade has become more important here as well. (Source: World Development Indicators, World Bank, 2007)

Figure 13.2 **Top Purchasers of Goods from the United States and Suppliers of Goods to the United States, 2006**

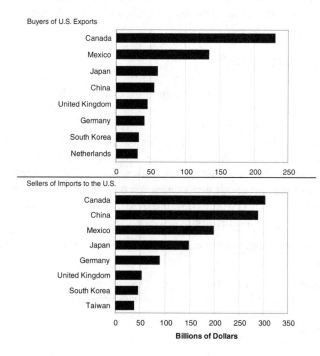

The United States' neighbors, Canada and Mexico, have long been among its major trading partners. But China has been an increasingly important source of merchandise imports. (Source: U.S. Census Bureau, Foreign Trade Statistics, Top Trading Partners, 2006)

figure equates to over $500 per person on earth. The volume in mid-2007 was over 50 percent higher than it had been only three years earlier.

1.4 CONTROVERSIES ABOUT TRADE AND FINANCE

Is greater openness to international trade and finance a good thing, or a bad thing? You have probably heard arguments in the media about how globalization can "destroy" jobs by causing industries to move overseas. Many people feel that when capital moves too freely, interests of local communities and the environment can suffer. On the other hand, many commentators—with a number of economists often among them—argue that globalization is a good thing. Although a few people may end up having to suffer temporary losses, they say, a more integrated global economy will bring greater overall benefits.

In the next section, we will describe the basic logic behind the story that free trade, by creating efficiencies in production and allocation that countries could not achieve on their own, leads to better living standards. Then we will examine the many other issues that may cause countries to *maintain* trade barriers, at least in regards to some goods and services.

Discussion Questions

1. How do international linkages affect your own life? Can you give examples of the sorts of linkages listed in Section 1.1 that have had direct effects on you or your family?
2. Production of apparel has been widely globalized in recent years. Before going to class, check the labels on a number of items of clothing you own. What countries are represented?

2. THE CASE FOR "FREE TRADE"

Economists and policymakers have argued for centuries about whether it is better for a country to engage in free trade with other countries, or to limit trade using the policy tools discussed earlier. Many economic theorists argue for a "**free-trade**" position, using the **Ricardian model of trade** to argue that a country that engages in trade can reap significant welfare gains. David Ricardo, in *On the Principles of Political Economy and Taxation* (1817), presented a simple model that showed how national specialization in the production of one of two goods, followed by exchange of the two goods across national boundaries, could allow two countries to achieve levels of consumption that would be impossible on their own. In this section, we present Ricardo's basic model, along with other arguments for free trade.

> **free trade:** exchange in international markets that is not regulated or restricted by government actions
>
> **Ricardian model of trade:** a two-good, two-country model, created by David Ricardo in 1817, that shows both countries gaining from specialization and trade

2.1 THE RICARDIAN MODEL

Ricardo used the example of two goods—wine and cloth—and two countries, Portugal and England. England has a relatively cool and cloudy climate that makes it ill-suited for grape-growing. Portugal, meanwhile, has a relatively warm and sunny climate, good for grapes.

Figure 13.3   **Portugal's Production-Possibilities Frontier**

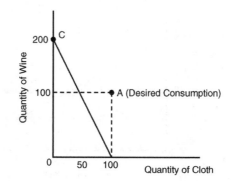

Portugal can produce 200 units of wine if it specializes in wine, or 100 units of cloth, if it specializes in cloth. Or it can produce any combination on the line between these two points. It would like to consume, however, a larger bundle—represented by point A.

Suppose that, given its resources, Portugal can produce a maximum of 200 units of wine, if it devotes all its resources to wine, or 100 units of cloth, if it devotes all of its resources to cloth. (A "unit" is just a specified amount, for example 1,000 bottles of wine, or 1,000 bolts of cloth—we use this terminology to keep the example numerically simple.) This is illustrated in Figure 13.3, using a production-possibilities frontier (as introduced in Chapter 2), along with the simplifying assumption that production has constant returns (so the frontier is just a straight line). Meanwhile, England can produce a maximum of 200 units of wine or 400 units of cloth, as illustrated in Figure 13.4.

But suppose that the Portuguese would like to be able to consume 100 units of wine and 100 units of cloth, as represented by point A in Figure 13.3, and the English would like to be able to consume 100 units of wine and 300 units of cloth, represented by point B in Figure 13.4. As we can see, if each relies only on its own production possibilities, points A and B are unachievable.

But suppose that Portugal *specialized* in producing wine, while England specialized in cloth production. This production combination is illustrated in the Production section of Table 13.1 and by points C and D in Figures 13.3 and 13.4. Total production would be 200 units of wine, and 400 units of cloth.

Further, suppose that Portugal and England were to agree to *trade* 100 units of Portuguese wine for 100 units of English cloth, as listed in the Exchange section of Table 13.1. The costs of imports relative to exports are called the **terms of trade**. In this example, when England and Portugal exchange 100 units of wine for 100 units of cloth, the terms of trade are 1:1.

terms of trade: the price of imports relative to exports

Now Portugal and England could each *consume* the quantities listed in the Consumption section of Table 13.1. Note that their total consumption does *not* exceed the total amount produced of each good, but Portugal can now consume at point A, and England at point B—the desired points that they could not each reach on their own!

The "magic" behind this result is that Portugal and England differ in their *opportunity costs of production.* For every unit of cloth Portugal produces, it must give up the production of two units of wine. For every unit of cloth England produces, it needs to give up production of only half a unit of wine. England has a comparative advantage in *cloth* production, since cloth costs

Figure 13.4   **England's Production-Possibilities Frontier**

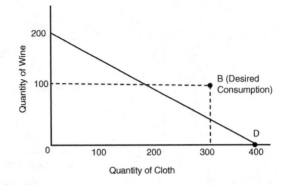

England can produce 200 units of wine if it specializes in wine, or 400 units of cloth, if it specializes in cloth. Or it can produce any combination on the line between these two points. It would like to consume, however, a larger bundle—represented by point B.

Table 13.1   **Production, Exchange, and Consumption of Wine and Cloth**

Production	Wine	Cloth
Portugal	200	0
England	0	400
Total	200	400
Exchange		
Portugal	sell 100	buy 100
England	buy 100	sell 100
Consumption		
Portugal	100	100
England	100	300
Total	200	400

less in terms of the other good (wine) in England than in Portugal. Portugal, likewise, has a comparative advantage in production of *wine*. An additional unit of wine comes at the cost of half a unit of cloth when produced in Portugal, but requires giving up two units of cloth when produced in England, as noted in Table 13.2.

The **principle of comparative advantage** says that you should *specialize* in what you do (relatively) best. Even if it turns out that one of the countries is more efficient at producing *both* goods, it still pays to specialize.* Only if both countries have the same opportunity costs will there be no possible gains from trade.

---

* When a country can produce a good at a lower absolute cost than another country—for example, by producing it using fewer labor hours along with the same (or lesser) quantities of other inputs—the country is said to have an *absolute* advantage. But absolute advantage is not necessary for trade, nor will having an absolute advantage in a particular good necessarily prevent a country from importing that good. If a country exists that has low absolute production costs in *all* goods, it should still buy the goods that it is *relatively* less efficient at producing from higher-cost countries, allowing it to specialize in the goods in which it is *relatively* most efficient.

Table 13.2 **Opportunity Cost and Comparative Advantage**

Country	Opportunity Cost of 1 Unit of Cloth	Opportunity Cost of 1 Unit of Wine
Portugal	2 units of wine	**½ unit of cloth**
England	**½ unit of wine**	2 units of cloth

> **comparative advantage (principle of):** gains from trade occur when producers specialize in making goods for which their opportunity costs are relatively low

In the case of Ricardo's story, the source of comparative advantage was climate and other resource endowments that differed between England and Portugal. It's not hard, by extension, to understand why bananas are currently exported by Ecuador, while Sweden finds it advantageous to import bananas rather than grow them in greenhouses.

But comparative advantage can also be created by human action. Countries can become more efficient in producing particular goods by investing in the physical capital needed to produce them. Sometimes technological advances or changes in the social organization of work can change the pattern of comparative advantage, and the evolution of comparative advantage over time may thus be unpredictable.

Economists often like to make a distinction between countries that are thought to be more suited for **labor-intensive production** processes, such as stitching clothing or making handicrafts, and others that specialize in relatively **capital-intensive production**, such as the manufacture of airplanes or automobiles. The fact that the United States has more manufactured capital per worker than does Bangladesh, for example, is considered to be an explanation for why Bangladesh exports clothing. Bangladesh presumably has a comparative advantage in relatively labor-intensive industries. Clothing production, meanwhile, has nearly disappeared from the United States (see Chapter 8).

> **labor-intensive production:** production using methods that involve a high ratio of labor to capital

> **capital-intensive production:** production using methods that involve a high ratio of capital to labor

The economic theory of **factor-price equalization** predicts that free trade should tend to equalize the returns to capital and labor across countries. For example, to the extent that the United States is rich in capital, and relatively lacking in labor power, returns to capital are theorized to be relatively low and returns to labor relatively high, in the absence of trade. (The logic of this is that a scarce factor will command a higher return—higher demand for a factor, relative to available supplies, increases the price that must be paid for it.) Since factor endowments in Bangladesh are the opposite, capital investments there would be expected to receive high returns in the absence of trade, while workers receive low wages compared to those in the United States.

Once the two countries start to trade, however, the demand for capital in the United States should rise (because the country now has a larger market for selling its capital-intensive goods), increasing the return on investments there. The demand for labor, however, will fall, since the United States now imports labor-intensive goods from Bangladesh. Meanwhile, the demand for labor in Bangladesh should rise (because it now exports labor-intensive goods), putting upward pressure on wages in that country, while returns to capital there fall. According to this theory, in a (hypothetical) world of perfectly free trade, we would expect wages to eventually converge, so that workers in the United States and Bangladesh would be paid about the same. Returns to capital investments would also be equalized.

> **factor-price equalization:** the theory that trade should eventually lead to returns to factors of production being equal across countries

These simple categories of "labor intensity" and "capital intensity" and the theory of factor-price equalization can be misleading, however. One reason is that investments in *human* capital—health, skills, and education—blur the distinction between "labor" and "capital." Some studies suggest that the United States' comparative advantage is now tilted toward goods that require production by an *educated and skilled* workforce, and away from production that involves merely heavy machinery (as well as away from lower-skilled work). When production is intensive in *human* capital, the earlier two-way classification is harder to apply. Meanwhile studies of factor prices are mixed in their support of the theory of factor-price equalization. Ongoing changes in technology, skills, and the composition of production, as well as deliberate government policies that limit and shift patterns of trade, make it difficult to test the theory.

2.2 OTHER ARGUMENTS FOR FREE TRADE

Specialization and trade can lead to improvements in economic efficiency, as the "gains from trade" story points out. Trade allowed Portugal and England, in Ricardo's story, to more efficiently organize the use of their resources to produce wine and cloth. The result was a more highly valued level and combination of outputs than the countries could have achieved without trade. Ricardo's result is the main justification behind some economists' advocacy of free trade—international trade that is not regulated or restricted by governments in any way. Many commentators have also pointed to additional advantages international trade could have, in theory.

One of these desirable outcomes is technical. A production process is characterized by **economies of scale** if the cost per unit of production falls as the volume of production rises. With trade, the volume of a country's production of a good can be substantially higher than what its internal (domestic) market can use, increasing the opportunity for economies of scale to be realized. A larger market means that goods can be produced more cheaply.

> **economies of scale:** reductions in the average cost of production resulting from a higher output level

Other advantages are related to what some economists see as positive attributes of free opportunities for trade or exchange, in general. Free trade gives countries the incentive to produce goods that have high value on the world market. This may encourage competition and innovation, to the ultimate benefit of all. In addition, some argue, countries with thriving trade relations are more likely to remain at peace, since war would eliminate all the benefits of trade.

2.3 INTERNATIONAL TRADE AGREEMENTS

Up through the early decades of the twentieth century, many countries remained quite closed to trade, charging high tariffs or imposing strict quotas on imported goods. After World War II this began to change. Countries rarely reduce their barriers to trade unilaterally, since a country that lets in more foreign imports usually also wants its products likewise to be welcomed abroad. But, starting in the 1940s, many countries became more interested in negotiating mutual reductions in tariffs and quotas.

Some trade agreements are "bilateral," meaning that two countries negotiate directly with each other. Other agreements are "multilateral," involving a group of countries. In 1948, twenty-three countries joined the General Agreement on Tariffs and Trade (GATT), which sought to set out rules for trade and enhance negotiations. Eight subsequent negotiation "trade rounds," some of which led to significant reductions in average tariff rates among participating countries, were sponsored by GATT. In 1995, the Uruguay Round of GATT trade negotiations led to the creation of a new forum for multilateral negotiations, the **World Trade Organization (WTO)**. Currently, the WTO includes 149 member countries. Besides being a forum for trade negotiations, the WTO attempts to set out rules about trade and is charged with investigating and making judgments when countries have trade disputes.

> **World Trade Organization (WTO):** an international organization that provides a forum for trade negotiations, creates rules to govern trade, and investigates and makes judgment on trade disputes

Meanwhile, some countries have entered into regional trade agreements with their neighbors. Leading examples of such attempts to integrate trade within a regional area include the European Union (EU), formed in 1992, which now counts 27 countries as members; the North American Free Trade Agreement (NAFTA) entered into in 1994 by the United States, Canada, and Mexico; and Mercosur in Latin America. There is some debate about whether such regional agreements promote "free trade" or retard it. Regional integration promotes both trade *expansion* (within the region) and trade *diversion* (away from trade with other regions). It is not clear whether the benefits of trade expansion always outweigh the losses from trade diversion.

Discussion Questions

1. Suppose that in a one-hour time period, you can buy six bags of groceries *or* clean three rooms. Your housemate, on the other hand, is slower-moving and can buy only three bags of groceries, or clean only one room, in an hour. You clearly have an absolute advantage in production of both these services. Does this mean you should do all the work?

2. Ricardo's model discusses benefits to countries at an aggregate level. But what if you were a Portuguese cloth maker or an English winemaker? Might you have a different view about the benefits of trade? What sorts of factors might influence how you feel about your country's trade policies?

3. Why Nations Often Resist "Free Trade"

The Ricardian arguments for "free trade" emphasize efficiency, increased production and consumption, and the possible benefits of an integrated global economy. This leads some economists to argue that free trade is always best. But the "free trade" arguments may also neglect issues of institutional, political, social, and environmental context that can drastically reduce the possible "gains from trade"—or even make free trade work *against* national or global well-being. An examination of contemporary real-world issues and policies shows how complex the picture is.

3.1 The Health of Nations, Regions, Industries, and Jobs

One very important reason that many policymakers have, historically, restricted trade is that they feel this is necessary to "protect" domestic industries and jobs from foreign competition.

Countries have frequently engaged in **protectionist policies** to discourage imports and/or encourage exports of specific goods. The United States, for example, still engages in protection of a variety of industries including Southern cotton, Northwestern timber, and Midwestern sugar beets. Without government protection, these industries would lose market share to lower-cost foreign producers. Such adjustment to global competition can be very painful. When United States automakers began to lose out to foreign competition, for example, a swath of the Midwest became so economically depressed that it became known as the "rust belt."

> **protectionist policies:** the use of trade policies such as tariffs, quotas, and subsidies to protect domestic industries from foreign competition

Sometimes protectionism is called a "beggar-thy-neighbor" approach, since each country is, in effect, trying to gain at the expense of other countries. Each country wants to *raise* its own production levels while simultaneously *reducing* the access of foreign producers to its market. If protection is successful, does it actually make a country better off? Since the Ricardian model demonstrates the benefits of trade, you might think that anything other than *mutual free trade* must yield lower benefits. But, in fact, other theories in economics demonstrate that an *individual* country may be able to do better than "free trade" if, while engaging in some amount of trade, it can use tariffs to turn the terms of trade in its own favor. A country that can force another country to be open to its exports, while selectively putting some level of duty on imports from that country, may be able to gain relative to the "free trade" case. The other country loses out. Yes, trade can yield benefits—but the selective use of protectionist policies can be used to distribute these benefits to the advantage of the more powerful parties. (See Economics in the Real World box and end-of-chapter Exercise 4.)

"Beggar-thy-neighbor" policies can only work if other countries do not retaliate with their own protective policies. But this is often not the case. During the Great Depression, for example, the United States enacted the Smoot-Hawley tariff in an attempt to support domestic agriculture and industry. This tariff bumped up average tariff rates to a high of nearly 60 percent. Other countries responded with retaliatory tariffs, creating what is sometimes called a "trade war." As a result, the volume of global trade declined by two-thirds between 1929 and 1934. The Smoot-Hawley tariff decreased imports, as it was intended to—but it also ended up dramatically decreasing the ability of U.S. producers to sell their goods abroad. While the trade war did not, itself, cause the Great Depression, the contraction of international trade that it created certainly did not help the major countries involved escape it, either.

Even after decades of trade negotiations—and encouragement by economists to "liberalize" their trade regimes—many countries continue to have protectionist policies, at least of a modest, piecemeal sort. While simple economic theory ignores issues of power differentials between countries, and assumes that labor and capital resources can immediately and smoothly adjust to new patterns of commerce, in real life things can be quite different. Trade relations continue to be an arena where countries try to exert dominance over each other. Policymakers continue to be concerned about the job losses and industrial dislocations that global competition can cause. Policies to ease structural unemployment (see Chapter 7) may help, but there is no sign that—at least in democratic countries—policymakers will completely abandon protectionist tendencies anytime soon.

3.2 REVENUE

Another historically important reason for tariffs is that they may be an important source of government revenue. Until 1913, for example, the United States had no income tax, and the federal

Economics in the Real World:
England, Portugal, and the Treaty of Methuen

When Ricardo wrote about trade between England and Portugal in 1817, it was indeed true that England exported cloth to Portugal in return for wine. But this was not pure "free trade," and it had not come about simply due to the impersonal forces of economic efficiency and comparative advantage.

Prior to the Treaty of Metheun in 1703, Portugal had severely restricted the importation of cloth from abroad, and England had imported wine primarily from France. But England lost much of its access to French wine during the War of Spanish Succession. Portugal, meanwhile, was pressured to join a military alliance with England by displays of England's superior naval power. The 1703 treaty cementing their alliance also contained economic terms: Portugal would admit English cloth without charging any tariffs at all, while England would reduce its tariffs on Portuguese wine to two-thirds of what it collected on French wine. Some commentators argue that this was a crucial—and negative—turning point for the development of Portuguese manufacturing.

government relied heavily on tariffs to run its operations. In many poorer countries today, it is still very difficult to collect taxes on incomes and property. People may be spread over wide geographical areas and much of the economy may not be monetized. In contrast, taxes on monetized transactions at harbor facilities or airports may be relatively easy to collect. Thus tariffs can be an important source of revenue for health, education, defense, and other governmental activities.

3.3 INDUSTRIAL POLICY AS A STRATEGY FOR GROWTH

Ricardo's two-country, two-good model is a "static" model that doesn't take into account the passage of time. But patterns of comparative advantage can change. Should a country simply follow whatever comparative advantage it happens to have at a given time, or should it explore policies that might *change* its comparative advantage? If the country could end up better off in the long run by deliberately changing its mix of productive capabilities, it might achieve "dynamic efficiency" overall—that is, efficiency-based welfare gains over a sustained period of years—even if "static efficiency" is sacrificed over the short run.

> Issues of *dynamic* comparative advantage may justify using trade barriers as a way to improve the mix of productive capacities in an economy, bringing higher benefits over the long run.

In fact, many countries that have achieved high rates of industrialization—including the United States, the United Kingdom, Japan, South Korea and others—did so behind substantial tariff barriers. If these countries had stayed with their natural comparative advantages as they existed in the past, the United States might still be known mostly for its production of wheat and raw cotton and the U.K. for its wool, while South Korea and Japan would still import all their cars. Policies that excluded foreign imports of manufactured textiles or automotive parts helped these countries to shift their economies away from less-processed goods toward a more industrial economic base. Now they all compete in global markets for sophisticated manufactured goods.

The **infant industry** argument asserts that sometimes industries can take a while to get established in a country, and that "learning by doing" helps industries get more efficient over time. Governments adopt an infant industry approach when they use trade policies to protect selected domestic industries from foreign competition until the industries become able to compete on world markets. The main drawback to an infant industry approach is that, for these policies to work well, governments also have to stop protecting or subsidizing industries that do not achieve sufficient levels of efficiency. This can be politically difficult if these industries have in the meantime become entrenched and powerful. If inefficient industries get government help for too long—as some believe has happened in India and parts of Latin America—the policy can encourage dependence on government subsidies and protection, rather than encourage innovation and competitiveness.

infant industry: an industry which is relatively new to its region or country

Although poorly designed support of specific industries can be harmful, the historical record suggests that the deliberate manipulation of trade in order to encourage particular industries has played an important role in the economic development of many countries. Countries that have *not* engaged in the encouragement of specific industries have often remained "locked in" to patterns of trade in which they specialize in only raw materials (such as minerals or crops) or labor-intensive manufactures. Concerns about global inequality might suggest that poor countries should be allowed to practice more protection, while countries that have already achieved a high standard of living should be especially encouraged to open their markets to imports from poorer countries.

3.4 MILITARY AND FOOD SECURITY

Countries often limit trade for security reasons. In the United States, for example, some of the same people who argue for "free trade" in most goods also argue for increased development of domestic petroleum (or other energy) resources, on the grounds that excessive reliance on imports decreases economic self-sufficiency and military preparedness. The United States also bans the export of weapons, certain strategic materials, and technology to countries thought of as potential enemies.

Food security is also an issue for many countries. Japan, for example, is heavily dependent on food imports, and some worry that this could make the country very vulnerable in the case of a war or other disruption in trade. Japan has long used quotas and tariffs to limit rice imports, providing protection for its domestic rice producers.

One of the arguments for free trade mentioned above was that trade should encourage cooperative behavior and peace. However, to the extent a country becomes dependent on other countries for vital resources such as oil, water, or food, this may also become a *cause* for war. Some commentators interpret United States military actions in the Middle East, for example, as primarily motivated by a desire to assure a steady supply of imported petroleum.

3.5 DIVERSIFICATION IN AN UNPREDICTABLE WORLD

While specialization for trade has clear advantages, it may also have a significant downside. A country that has specialized becomes more vulnerable to certain kinds of problems. Two of these have already been mentioned: "lock-in" to a dynamically disadvantageous mix of production capabilities, and security problems related to military and strategic goods. Because the future is uncertain, it is hard to know whether a current choice to specialize will be wise in the long run.

Another especially important source of uncertainty is variation in the terms of trade. Changes in terms of trade can occur as a result of changes in international supply and demand. When a bumper crop occurs, or a new country starts to export a good, or people's tastes change, the terms of trade may fluctuate in unforeseen ways. The structure of international prices can also be subject to deliberate manipulation through the exertion of political and military power. Lastly, terms of trade may also be manipulated by large corporate international traders, some of whom have gained substantial market power in their field of commerce.

Variations in the terms of trade have created serious problems in many countries. In Ethiopia, for example, producing coffee for export currently provides the means for life for about one-quarter of the population. When the price of an important export is high in international markets, economies that rely on one or a few exports for a good deal of their income do well. But when prices weaken—or plummet, as coffee prices did in 1989—economies dependent on specialized exports are subjected to major crises that are outside of their control. Countries that specialize in a particular crop also become very vulnerable to ecological events such as droughts or plant diseases. While the "gains from trade" story emphasizes the benefits of specialization, these kinds of considerations suggest that some degree of *diversification* may be wise. Countries may use trade policies such as tariffs, quotas, and subsides to try to encourage more variety in the range of goods and services they produce.

3.6 LABOR, ENVIRONMENTAL, AND SAFETY STANDARDS

Traditionally, democratic governments have been able to enact policies perceived to be in the public interest, even though they are not always in the perceived self-interest of business actors. Minimum standards for pay and safety on the job, for example, as well as reasonable environmental standards and safety standards for consumer products are widely considered necessary for a healthy, just society. Yet such policies are often resisted by some in the business community because they may increase costs and decrease profits.

With capital increasingly mobile, multinational corporations are able to move their operations to countries with lower labor and environmental standards. Countries that want to hold on to their business base may therefore find themselves drawn into a **race to the bottom**, in which they compete to attract businesses based on their country's *lack* of attention to social and environmental concerns. Such competition has the potential to create quite a different relationship between states and businesses than has been assumed in the past: Rather than governments shaping business and macroeconomic conditions, large corporations are now playing an increasing role.

> **race to the bottom:** a situation in which countries or regions compete in providing low-cost business environments, resulting in deterioration in labor, environmental, or safety standards

One way in which countries can try to avoid such a "race to the bottom" is to ban both the domestic manufacture and importation of goods that are considered hazardous to consumers, or have been made under labor standards that are considered inhumane, or made using production processes that cause serious damage to the environment. In this way, at least the *domestic* market is reserved for producers who follow higher standards. The setting of standards may also encourage potential trading partners to raise their environmental, labor, or safety standards, so that their goods can be admitted.

3.7 When Is Limiting Trade "Unfair"?

When should a limitation of trade be considered legitimate, and when should it not be? This is a complicated question that is a topic of vigorous, ongoing debate. Most countries will staunchly defend their right to restrict trade for purposes such as military security or consumer safety, so international trade agreements tend to stop short of banning all restrictions.

But beyond agreement on a few principles, debates become heated. Consider three examples:

GMO products. The European Union has banned the importation of GMO (genetically-modified organism) products, on the grounds that they present threats to public health and the environment. The United States and other grain-producing countries have contested this at the WTO, arguing that GMO products are safe and the real reason for the ban is that the EU simply wants to protect its farmers. (The WTO recently ruled that the ban was illegal—but the ruling is unlikely to end the debate.)

Dumping. The United States has accused China of subsidizing the production of many of its products and **dumping** them on United States markets. "Dumping" is the selling of products on foreign markets at prices that are unfairly low (that is, below the cost of production), and is forbidden in international agreements. The United States argues that it has the right to retaliate by putting quotas and tariffs on Chinese goods. But China, of course, can argue that it simply is blessed with a low-cost production environment, and that the United States is engaging in protectionism.

> **dumping:** selling products at prices that are below the cost of production

Labor standards. In some extreme cases, such as the use of slave labor, restrictions on trade are usually considered permissible. But should countries be allowed to use trade restrictions to punish unfair labor practices? Some poorer countries have accused richer countries of imposing unreasonably high labor standards. Under the pretext of trying to protect global workers, they say, the richer countries are just trying to protect their workers from fair competition.

Questions of what will be ruled "fair" or "unfair" by the WTO—and whether such rulings can be enforced (see the News in Context box)—often come down to questions of political economy. Large, powerful countries and corporations use the WTO negotiations and dispute resolution mechanisms as ways to advance their own interests. Smaller and less powerful groups have a more difficult time getting their voices heard. Many labor, environmental, and social justice groups, for example, charge that the WTO primarily serves the interests of powerful multinational corporations. They worry that WTO negotiations have served to speed up the "race to the bottom" and have reduced national sovereignty. Observers concerned about economic development believe that WTO rules disadvantage countries that are still relatively poor, by forbidding the use of the sorts of industrial policies that helped other countries achieve economic growth at an earlier time.

In 2001, the WTO officially launched the Doha Round of negotiations, which was, in its official statements, intended to take special account of the needs and interests of poorer countries. At the time of this writing, however, the Round is at a stalemate. Many poorer countries pushed for richer countries to reduce their tariffs and subsidies, particularly on agricultural goods. On the other hand, top priorities for richer countries included getting poorer countries to open their service industries (such as banking and airline transportation) to foreign companies and to abide by stricter rules on intellectual property (for example, to stop making less expensive versions of patented drugs). With the wealthier nations showing little willingness to reduce protection of their domestic agricultural industries, Doha Round talks were suspended in July 2006.

NEWS IN CONTEXT:
WTO Launches Probe into U.S. Cotton Subsidies

The World Trade Organization (WTO) launched a probe on Thursday into whether the United States has dismantled huge subsidies to its cotton farmers that have been ruled illegal. The move was sought by Brazil, which says Washington has not complied fully with a landmark 2004 verdict in which the Geneva-based trade referee decreed part of the multi-billion dollar U.S. cotton support program broke global trade rules and demanded sweeping changes. The investigation will take at least 90 days. If it wins, Brazil could be entitled to levy billions of dollars of retaliatory sanctions against U.S. goods.

According to Oxfam, U.S. subsidies to the country's 25,000 cotton farmers totaled $5 billion in 2005 for a crop that was worth less than $4 billion.

Sources: ABC News and Reuters, Sept. 28, 2006.

Some people might say this news story illustrates how the WTO interferes with national sovereignty—the right of a country to make its own laws and policies. Others might say that it shows how difficult it is to make powerful countries follow fair trading rules. What do you think?

Discussion Questions

1. What international trade issues have you seen in the news recently? What views are presented by different interest groups in trade debates? Are there any issues that particularly affect your community?
2. Which reasons for limiting trade seem to you to be the most legitimate? Which ones seem more questionable to you? What could you do to find out more about the issues?

4. INTERNATIONAL FINANCE

In addition to trade in goods, countries are also linked through exchange of currencies, flows of income, and by purchases and sales of real and financial assets across national borders. As we move into considering how international finance is related to trade and to domestic macroeconomic policies, the realization that "everything is linked to everything else" can get overwhelming. Most topics we've discussed earlier in this book—such as supply and demand, interest rates, inflation, aggregate demand, and the Fed—will come back into play. In order to ease into the topic, we will focus on relatively simple concepts and models, starting with the market for currency exchange.

4.1 PURCHASING POWER PARITY

Purchasing power parity (PPP) refers to the notion that, under certain idealized conditions, the **exchange rate** between the currencies of two countries should be such that the purchasing power of currencies is equalized. Consider, for example, the exchange rate between United States dollars ($) and European euros (€). At the time of this writing, one dollar is worth about .64 euros. When we say "the exchange rate" for the dollar, what we mean is the number of unit of the foreign currency you can get for a dollar.*

> **purchasing power parity (PPP):** the theory that exchange rates should reflect differences in purchasing power among countries

> **exchange rate:** the number of units of one currency that can be exchanged for a unit of another currency

If currencies can be traded freely against each other, goods are freely traded and totally identical across countries, and transportation costs are not important, then there is a certain logic to this theory. Suppose a gold chain costs $200 in New York. If you live in the United States and change $200 into euros, the theory of PPP says that the number of euros you get for your dollars should be exactly enough for you to buy the identical gold chain in Paris. If, indeed, the chain costs €128 (= 200 dollars × .64 euros per dollar) in Paris, PPP holds. You might notice that this theory is similar to that of "factor-price equalization" discussed earlier, and the logic behind the two theories is the same. If economies really were as smoothly integrated as we are assuming in our idealized world, an item (whether a gold chain or an hour of labor services) should cost the same, no matter where you are.

If this *isn't* true, there should be pressures leading toward change. For example, suppose the gold chain costs $200 in New York and €128 in Paris, but the exchange rate is higher, at 1 euro per dollar. Why would anyone buy a chain in New York, if by changing their money into euros they could order the chain from Paris and save €72? For chains to be sold in both locations—in this idealized world—the price in New York would have to be bid down, the price in Paris would have to be bid up, or the exchange rate would have to fall.

Of course, in the real world, national economies are not nearly as integrated as this theory assumes. Transportation costs do matter; there are many varieties of goods; markets for goods and services do not work as quickly, smoothly, and rationally as was assumed; and exchange rates are often "managed" (see Section 4.5 below). Any of these factors can mean that converting monetary figures from one country to another using the prevailing exchange rates may be misleading. If the price of a gold chain in New York is higher than in Paris, this might, for example, reflect the fact that the general cost of living in New York is higher.

Sometimes you will see comparisons of international income levels expressed "in PPP terms." Rather than simply using going exchange rates to convert all the various income levels into a common currency, **purchasing power parity adjustments** try to take into account the fact that the cost of living varies among countries. The "Big Mac Index" published each year by *The Economist* magazine is a somewhat lighthearted attempt to determine how much goods prices and exchange rates vary from PPP predictions, by comparing the prices (converted into dollars using market exchange rates) of a MacDonald's hamburger across various countries. More sophisticated analysis uses a larger "basket" of goods to make such comparisons and estimate appropriate PPP adjustments.

---

* Exchange rates can be (confusingly) quoted either as units of foreign currency per unit of domestic currency (as above, considering the home country to be the United States) or as units of domestic currency per unit of foreign currency. The two rates are inverses of each other. For example, when the number of euros per dollar is .64, the number of dollars per euro is $1/.64 = 1.56$.

Figure 13.5　**A Foreign Exchange Market**

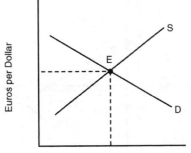

When currencies are traded against each other on a market, the "price" is the exchange rate, that is, the number of units of the other currency that are required to buy a unit of the currency in question.

> **purchasing power parity (PPP) adjustments:** adjustments to international income statistics to take account of differences in the cost of living across countries

4.2 FOREIGN EXCHANGE MARKETS

What makes exchange rates go up and down? Currencies are traded off against each other all over the world, as people offer to sell and buy. The supply-and-demand model explained in Chapter 4 can be helpful here, once we realize that an exchange rate is really just another kind of price.

Figure 13.5 shows an idealized foreign exchange market in which United States dollars are traded for European euros. The quantity of dollars traded is given on the horizontal axis, and the "price" of a dollar is given on the vertical axis, in terms of the number of euros it takes to buy one.

In a well-behaved foreign exchange market, the supply curve of dollars is largely determined by domestic residents, who decide how many dollars they are willing to offer. While the actual trading is usually done by professional currency traders and banks, underlying the supply of dollars on the international foreign exchange market reflects the desire of domestic residents for foreign-produced goods and services and for foreign assets. Since these must be paid for in the currency of the country from which they will be purchased, dollars must be traded in the foreign exchange market. The more euros United States residents can get for their dollars, the cheaper European items are to them, and the more they will want to buy from Europe rather than from domestic producers. Thus, the higher the exchange rate, the more dollars they will offer on the market. The supply curve slopes upward.

The demand curve for dollars is largely determined by foreign residents, who may want to buy goods and services from the United States, or to invest in United States bonds or businesses. To make these purchases, they must acquire dollars. The more euros they have to *pay* to get a dollar, the more likely they are to go elsewhere than the United States for what they want, and the lower will be the quantity of dollars they demand. So the demand curve slopes downward. Market equilibrium is established at point E.

Even in this simple representation, however, we must mention another reason that many traders buy and sell currency, and that is speculation. As discussed in Chapter 4, sometimes people buy something not because they need it (for example, in this case, for facilitating a trade in real items), but because they are betting that its price will go up or down in the future. Speculative buying and selling of currencies often plays a large role in foreign exchange markets.

Figure 13.6   **A Supply Shift in a Foreign Exchange Market**

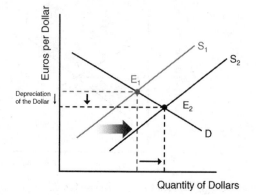

Quantity of Dollars

When people become more eager to sell a currency, this causes it to lose value, that is, to depreciate.

When the exchange rate falls, we say a currency has depreciated. Suppose, for example, a European technology firm comes out with a new music-listening device that everyone wants to buy. In their desire to get euros to buy the good, people in the United States will offer more dollars on the foreign exchange market, shifting the supply curve to the right. Excess supply will, as in any other market, cause the price to fall, as shown in Figure 13.6. Commentators may say that the dollar is now "weaker" against the euro. (Conversely, of course, the euro is now "stronger" against the dollar.)

On the other hand, if demand for United States products or assets rises, this will lead to an appreciation of the dollar. For example, if investors become eager to buy United States real estate, the demand curve for dollars will shift outward and the dollar will appreciate, that is, gain in value.

> When a currency *depreciates,* it become less valuable. This might occur if, for example, peoples' desire for imports causes them to offer more of their own currency on the foreign exchange market. When a currency *appreciates,* it becomes more valuable. This might occur if, for example, increased demand for a country's exports causes an increase in demand, abroad, for its currency.

The story is a bit more complicated when different levels of inflation in different countries are taken into account. What matters to people is the **real exchange rate** between currencies. A country with high inflation, for example, will generally experience a steady depreciation of its nominal exchange rate against the currencies of lower-inflation countries, even without any changes in demand for its items. Foreigners will only be willing to purchase the country's products at the higher prices resulting from inflation if they can also get more currency units per unit of foreign exchange they offer, so that the real price remains the same.

> **real exchange rate:** the exchange rate between two currencies, adjusted for inflation in both countries

4.3 FINANCIAL FLOWS AND THE BALANCE OF PAYMENTS

The flows of payments into and out of a country are summed up in its **balance of payments (BOP) account**, as shown in Table 13.3 for the United States in 2006. The top part of the table

Table 13.3   **United States Balance of Payments Account (2006, Billions of Dollars)**

Current Account			
Inflows:			
Payments for Exports of Goods	1,023		
Payments for Exports of Services	423		
Income Receipts	650		
Total		2,096	
Outflows:			
Payments for Imports of Goods	−1,861		
Payments for Imports of Services	−343		
Income Payments	−614		
Net transfers	−90		
Total		−2,908	
Balance on Current Account			
(= Inflows − Outflows)			−811
Financial Account			
Outflows (e.g., U.S. lending abroad, or FDI abroad)		−1,055	
Inflows (e.g., U.S. borrowing from abroad, or FDI			
in the United States)[a]		1,889	
Balance on Financial Account			
(= Inflows − Outflows)			833
Statistical discrepancy (and "capital account")[b]			−22
Balance of Payments			0

Source: U.S. BEA, U.S. International Transactions Accounts Data, Table 1, with rearrangements and simplifications by authors.

[a] Also includes the net value of financial derivatives (financial instruments whose values are linked to an underlying asset, interest rate, or index, such as futures or options).

[b] The financial account used to be called "the capital account," and you may still hear that term in use. In contemporary BOP accounts, there is a quite small item called "the capital account" that has been absorbed into the statistical discrepancy for simplicity.

tallies the **current account**, which tracks flows arising from trade in goods and services, earnings, and transfers.

Various kinds of transactions lead to payments flowing into this country (and to a demand for dollars in the foreign exchange market). Obviously, when we export goods, we get payments in return. So the first entry under current account inflows is the $1,023 billion the United States earned from exports. Exports of services (such as travel, financial, or intellectual property) also bring in inflows, as do incomes earned abroad (as profits, wages, or interest) by U.S. residents. All told, inflows into the United States from exports and incomes totaled about $2.1 trillion in 2006.

> **balance of payments (BOP) account:** the national account that tracks inflows and outflows arising from international trade, earnings, transfers, and transactions in assets
>
> **current account (in the BOP account):** the national account that tracks inflows and outflows arising from international trade, earnings, and transfers

Other transactions lead to payments going abroad (and to a supply of dollars to the foreign exchange market). When we import goods and services, we need to make payments to foreign residents. Foreign residents can take home incomes earned in the United States. The BOP account

Figure 13.7   **U.S. Imports and Exports of Goods and Services, 1950–2006**

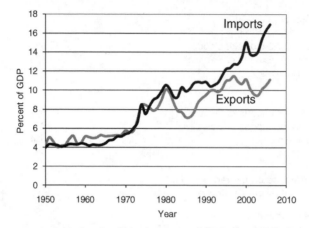

In 1950 imports and exports were each only about 4 percent of GDP. Since then, however, trade—and trade deficits—have increased. In 2006 the United States imported goods and services with a value equal to about 17 percent of GDP, while exports were equivalent to about 11 percent of GDP. (Source: BEA NIPA Tables 4.1 and 1.1.5)

also includes a line for net transfers abroad, such as monies paid out in government foreign aid programs. All told, outflows of payments from the United States due to these transactions totaled about $2.9 trillion in 2006.

The balance on the current account is measured as inflows minus outflows. Since outflows exceeded inflows on the current account in 2006, the United States ran a current account deficit. When a country imports more than it exports of goods and services, it runs a trade deficit (as was discussed in Chapter 10). As you can see in Table 13.3, imports of goods exceeded exports by a very large amount. Since income flows and transfers were relatively balanced, it was the trade deficit that largely accounts for the current account deficit of $811 billion. In fact, as you can see in Figure 13.7, the United States has had trade deficits fairly steadily since about 1980, with the gap between imports and exports widening to about 6 percent of GDP in recent years.

How can a country steadily import more than it exports? If you, personally, want to buy something that costs more than you have the income to pay for, you might take out a loan or perhaps sell something you own such as your bicycle or your car. Likewise, countries can finance a trade deficit by borrowing, or by selling assets. These are the sorts of transactions listed in the **financial account**.

> **financial account (in the BOP account):** the account that tracks flows arising from international transactions in assets

To the extent the United States *lends* abroad (for example, when the government extends loans to other countries, foreigners borrow from U.S. banks, or people in the United States buy foreign bonds), financial capital *outflows* are generated. This terminology may be confusing. Think about financial flows as going *in the direction of* the country that ends up with "the cash" or the power to purchase goods, and *away from* the country that "buys something." In the case of a loan, the borrower gets "the cash," while the creditor "buys" a bond or other security representing a promise to repay; thus a loan is an outflow to the lender. Similarly, if a U.S. firm buys all or part of a business in another country—what is called **foreign direct investment (FDI)**—it is the people abroad who end up with "the cash," while the U.S. company gets the interest in the business. This is also counted as an *outflow.* From Table 13.3, we can see that the United States had $1,055 billion in financial outflows during 2006.

> **foreign direct investment (FDI):** investment in a business in a foreign country

A country gets financial *inflows* when it borrows from foreigners, or when foreigners purchase assets here. In the case of the United States, a great many people abroad buy United States government bonds, since they are considered a very secure investment. For similar reasons, many also put funds into bank accounts here. These are both capital *inflows*—the sellers of the U.S. securities and the U.S. banks get "the cash." Likewise, if a foreign multinational buys an interest in a United States publishing company, that is a capital *inflow.* In 2006, the United States received over $1.8 trillion in capital inflows.

The balance on the financial account is measured as inflows minus outflows. The United States, hence, ran an $833 billion financial account surplus in 2006. It was this willingness of foreigners to buy United States securities (and other assets) that financed the deficit in the current account. Many commentators worry that the United States is putting itself in a vulnerable position by relying on borrowing to "spend beyond its means" on imports. Notice that *present-day financial inflows* create the obligation to pay *future income outflows:* The interest due in the future on U.S. government bonds sold abroad this year, and future profits made by firms located in the United States that were bought by foreign parties this year, will become part of "income payments" in the outflows section of the current account, in years to come.

The statistical discrepancy in Table 13.3 represents an inability of the BEA to make the accounts exactly balance, given problems in the quality of the data, and some small items we will not get into here. Allowing for this discrepancy, the balance in the current account and the balance in the financial account *have to* add to zero (the "balance of payments"). A surplus in one account has to be matched by a deficit in the other.

4.4 MONETARY POLICY IN AN OPEN ECONOMY

In Chapter 11 we discussed monetary policy in a closed economy. In an open economy, it turns out, monetary policy is more effective in changing aggregate demand, because it works through two channels rather than only one.

Suppose the Fed believes the United States economy needs a boost, and lowers interest rates in an attempt to stimulate aggregate demand. As we saw in Chapter 11, the decrease in interest rates should tend to encourage investment spending. But in an open economy, the fall in interest rates should also increase net exports, another component of aggregate demand. Recall from Chapter 10 that $AD = C + II + G + NX$, where $NX = X - IM$.

This is because the fall in United States interest rates should tend to drive away some foreign financial capital. If interest rates here fall, people abroad will be less inclined to buy U.S. government bonds or put their money in United States bank accounts. As they choose to send their financial capital elsewhere, this decreases the demand for United States dollars. This would be portrayed as a leftward shift of the demand curve in a market such as pictured in Figure 13.5. A decrease in the demand for dollars will cause the dollar to depreciate.

A depreciation in the dollar means that a dollar now buys fewer units of foreign exchange, which will discourage spending on imports. Meanwhile, the fact that a dollar can be purchased for fewer units of foreign exchange means that U.S. exports become "cheap" to foreign buyers. Exports should increase. Because it is demand for U.S-produced goods and services, less imports, that enters into aggregate demand, aggregate demand rises. Thus both an increase in exports and a decrease in imports will tend to raise aggregate demand.

The openness of the economy can be thought of as adding an extra loop to the chain of causation discussed in Chapter 12, as illustrated below:

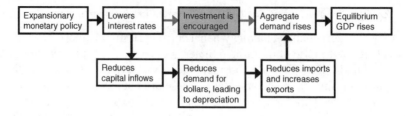

4.5 MANAGED VERSUS FLEXIBLE FOREIGN EXCHANGE

So far, we have assumed that exchange rates are determined by market forces, as modeled in Figure 13.6. In a **flexible** or **floating exchange rate system**, countries let their exchange rates be directed by the forces of supply and demand. But this is not always the case.

> **flexible (floating) exchange rate system:** a system in which exchange rates are determined by the forces of supply and demand

Flexible exchange rates can create significant uncertainties in an economy. A manufacturer may negotiate the future delivery of an imported component, for example, only to find that exchange rate changes make it much more expensive than expected to complete the deal. Foreign exchange markets are also very susceptible to wild swings from speculation. A mere rumor of political upheaval in a country, for example, can sometimes create a rush of capital outflows as people try to move their financial assets into foreign banks, causing a precipitous drop in the exchange rate. Or an inability to obtain short-term foreign loans may put an economy into crisis—and send its exchange rate swinging—even if over a longer period the economy would be considered financially sound. It can be hard to maintain normal economic activities when exchange rates fluctuate wildly.

So creating a more rational and predictable environment for foreign trade is one reason why many countries have tried to control the value of their currencies. The strictest kind of control is a **fixed exchange rate system**. In this case, a group of countries commits to keeping their currencies trading at fixed ratios over time. Starting in 1944, many countries, including the United States, had fixed exchange rates under what was known as the Bretton Woods system.

> **fixed exchange rate system:** a system in which currencies are traded at fixed ratios

The exchange rates in such a system do not, however, all usually stay firmly fixed over the long term. In a fixed-rate system, governments retain the power to alter their exchange rates from time to time. When a government lowers the level at which it fixes its exchange rate, this is called a **devaluation**, and when it raises it, that is called a **revaluation**. But too many changes undermine the system, and when key currencies such as the dollar come under too much selling pressure a fixed exchange rate system can break up. This is what happened to the Bretton Woods system in 1972.

> **devaluation:** lowering an exchange rate within a fixed exchange rate system
>
> **revaluation:** raising an exchange rate within a fixed exchange rate system

Since the break-up of the Bretton Woods system, some countries have moved to "floating" while others have tried to exert some management over their currencies by trying to maintain

Figure 13.8   **Foreign Exchange Intervention**

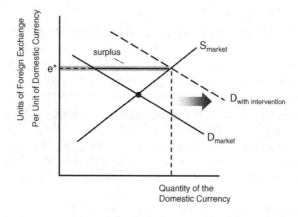

In order to keep the exchange rate at the target level e*, the central bank has to buy up the surplus of domestic currency, using in payment its reserves of foreign exchange.

certain target exchange rates, by "pegging" their currency to some particular foreign currency, or by letting it "float" but only within certain bounds.

How does a country keep its exchange rate fixed, or at least within bounds? There are two main tools a government can use. One way is to impose capital controls. For example, a country that wants to limit foreign exchange trading may require that importers apply for licenses to deal in foreign exchange, or impose quotas on how much they can get. By only allowing highly regulated transactions, it can control the prices at which exchange transactions are made. The other technique is **foreign exchange market intervention**.

> **foreign exchange market intervention:** an action by central banks to buy or sell foreign exchange reserves in order to keep exchange rates at desired levels

To see how intervention works, consider Figure 13.8. Suppose the government would like to keep the exchange rate of its domestic currency at (or above) the level *e**, but market pressures are represented by the curves S$_{market}$ and D$_{market}$. At the exchange rate *e**, there is an excess supply of domestic currency, and so there is pressure on the exchange rate to fall. The central bank must artificially create more demand for the domestic currency, as shown by demand curve D$_{with intervention}$. It does this by going into the market and exchanging foreign currency for domestic currency—essentially "soaking up" the surplus domestic currency. The problem is that the central bank can only do this as long as it has sufficient reserves on hand of foreign exchange. If it runs out of foreign exchange, it will be unable to support the currency and be forced to devalue.

Is devaluation a bad thing? The answer to this question is complex. Devaluation is generally thought to be good for exporters, since it makes the country's goods cheaper abroad. But it also means that people in the country will find that imports are now more expensive. And sometimes devaluation is taken as a sign of instability or poor policy in a country, or leads to international runs of speculation or competitive devaluation. Many economists have become cautious about too-easily recommending devaluation as a cure for international imbalances.

On the other hand, a country can keep its exchange rate *lower* than market forces would dictate by supplying lots of its domestic currency on the market and amassing large amounts of foreign reserves. Recently, China has used this tactic, keeping the value of its yuan artificially low in order to stimulate exports. China has, in the process, become a large holder of United

NEWS IN CONTEXT:
China's Trade Surplus Sets Another Record

China's trade surplus with the world ballooned last month to $18.8 billion as exports soared, setting a fourth consecutive monthly record, according to preliminary customs figures released on Monday.

The surplus gives fresh ammunition to requests by American and European officials that China intervene less in currency trading to hold down the value of its currency, the yuan. Letting market forces set the yuan's value could lead to faster appreciation of the currency, making Chinese exports less competitive and making imported foreign goods more competitive in China.

Source: Keith Bradsher, *New York Times* September 12, 2006.

Draw a graph illustrating Chinese intervention in the market for yuan. What would happen if the government stops intervening?

States dollars, as well as other currencies. China has been under pressure from many countries to revalue the yuan (see News in Context).

One complication with fixed exchange rates is that they make it impossible for a country to conduct independent monetary policy. The reason is that if the central bank is intervening on money markets to buy and sell its currency for foreign exchange reasons, this will necessarily affect its domestic money supply, and vice versa. A country can choose to set its exchange rate *or* its interest rate, but not both. If it chooses to keep its exchange rate fixed relative to some other currency, the interest rates in the two countries will tend to move together.

The adoption of the euro by a number of countries of the European Union is a dramatic recent example of fixed exchange rates—taken a step further. In 1999 eleven member countries established fixed exchange rates between their national currencies and the euro—although, at that time, the euro was just an accounting notation. Then, in 2002, euro banknotes and coins were put into circulation and national currencies were withdrawn. The countries that have adopted the euro have given up having separate monetary policies, putting the European Central Bank in control of monetary policymaking for the group as a whole.

4.6 INTERNATIONAL FINANCIAL INSTITUTIONS

The Bretton Woods system of fixed exchange rates was only one of the international financial institutions established in the 1940s. Also established during this period were the **World Bank**, established to promote economic development through loans and programs aimed at poorer countries, and the **International Monetary Fund (IMF),** established to oversee international financial arrangements. Although fixed exchange rates have been abandoned, the World Bank and the IMF continue—with considerable controversy—to play significant roles in international affairs.

> **World Bank:** an international agency charged with promoting economic development, through loans and other programs

| **International Monetary Fund (IMF):** an international agency charged with overseeing international finance, including exchange rates, international payments, and balance of payments issues

The IMF was charged with overseeing exchange rates, international payments, and balance of payments issues, and with giving advice to countries about their financial affairs. IMF has a complicated governance structure based on voting shares allocated to member countries, but in fact its policymaking has historically been dominated by the United States and Europe. The appointed members of its executive board represent the United States, the United Kingdom, Germany, France, and Japan. The IMF recently restructured its voting system to give China, South Korea, Turkey, and Mexico slightly larger shares. Both the World Bank and IMF have their central offices in Washington, D.C.

When a country is in financial trouble—for example, when it is unable to pay the interest it owes on its foreign debts, or is experiencing wild swings in its exchange rate—the IMF (in conjunction with the World Bank, if the country is poor) often advises the government on how to remedy the problem. The IMF has tended to encourage poor and medium-income countries with debt problems to remove their barriers to trade and capital flows, arguing that such liberalization promotes economic growth. The countries are also advised to minimize the size of their government and its expenditures, as a way to reduce the need for borrowing. They are told to keep their inflation rates down, and are often advised about their exchange rate policies as well. The policy prescriptions of trade liberalization, privatization, deregulation, and small government became known as the "Washington Consensus" during the 1980s and 1990s. The policies have also become the source of much controversy, as many economists have come to believe that rigid, "one-size-fits-all" application of such policies often works against, rather than for, human welfare and international stability (see Economics in the Real World box).

While the lending power of the IMF gives it considerable say in the affairs of many countries—for better or worse—the powers of any international organization are limited, especially with regard to the countries that are larger and more powerful. The international financial scene would probably be much more stable—for example, the Japanese crisis and deflation discussed in Chapter 11 would not have occurred, nor the sub-prime mortgage crisis in the United States in 2007–08—if all countries had well-designed, transparent, and responsible financial systems. But these cannot be forced on a country from the outside. Many commentators worry about the undervalued Chinese yuan, but there is currently no international institution with the power to force China to change its policies. The volume of foreign debt being taken on by the United States likewise has many commentators worried. If foreigners become less willing to lend to the United States, a deep international and domestic crisis could result.

Currently, many are calling for reforms in the international financial system, and perhaps for new international institutions. Dissatisfaction over the IMF prescriptions for liberalization have caused some changes within the organization itself. But some argue that these changes are not enough, and more radical changes are necessary. Increased regulation of international banking, substantial reforms and increased transparency in multinational corporate governance, restrictions on short-term capital flows, a "Tobin tax" on speculative transactions in foreign exchange (see Chapter 4), and establishment of an international bankruptcy court are among the suggestions for new international institutions.

Discussion Questions

1. To check your understanding of international linkages, consider the following hypothetical scenario. Suppose that people overseas become less interested in buying

Economics in the Real World:
The IMF and the Argentine Default

In December of 2001 the Argentina government announced a moratorium on payments on its $155 billion of public foreign debt. This default—the largest by a sovereign nation in history—rocked the international financial world. Was there more that the IMF could have done to prevent this? Or might IMF advice have been part of the reason the default occurred?

In 1991 Argentina had pegged its currency to the United States dollar, as a way of bringing hyperinflation to a halt. The IMF, believing that this would lead to more discipline in Argentine policy-making, approved the peg. But with the dollar strong against the currencies of Europe and Brazil, Argentina's major trading partners, the peg made Argentina's exports expensive. This discouraged Argentine industry and encouraged the purchase of imports. Trade deficits resulted, financed by borrowing from abroad. Unemployment rose.

The IMF advised the Argentine government to address its financial issues by cutting back on government expenditures and privatizing its social security program. The nation's leaders compiled, even though the country's economy was in a downturn. The IMF encouraged Argentina to institute free trade policies, though major markets in the United States and Europe remained closed to its exports. Meanwhile, financial crises in Asia, Mexico, and Brazil made investors more nervous about lending to middle-income countries. The fact that the Argentine economy was visibly struggling caused foreign lenders to demand higher interest rates to compensate them for the risk of default. This in turn made the debt even harder to bear, in a vicious circle.

In December 2001, the situation reached a crisis. With official unemployment nearing 20 percent, people demonstrated in the street and the government was brought down. Unable to make its debt payments, the interim government announced the default. The Argentine economy continued in a downward slide well into 2002.

Some commentators have blamed the default on corruption and mismanagement by the Argentine government, and suggested that the crisis might have been avoided if the government had cut its expenditures even *more*. By IMF logic, small governments and open capital markets should attract a steady supply of foreign lending at attractive interest rates. Others, observing that the government budget deficit was actually of a quite reasonable size (less than three percent of GDP), believe that the inappropriate IMF advice is at least as much to blame. Basic principles of macroeconomics say that a government should raise—not lower—spending during a recession, but the IMF policies went in the opposite direction, pushing the economy into a downward spiral. According to this view, given IMF advice, default was only a matter of time.

Based on Joseph E. Stiglitz, "Argentina, Shortchanged: Why the Nation That Followed the Rules Fell to Pieces" *Washington Post,* May 12, 2002 and other news sources.

How does this story illustrate the ways in which international openness and international institutions complicate the making of macroeconomic fiscal and monetary policy? Do you think the IMF gave the correct advice?

United States government bonds (perhaps because they start to think of them as less secure). What would be the effect on:
   a. The BOP financial account?
   b. The supply and/or demand for United States dollars?
   c. The value of the United States dollar?
   d. The BOP current account?

2. Have international trade or financial imbalances, or actions of the IMF, been in the news lately? What is the nature of current controversies?

REVIEW QUESTIONS

1. What are seven ways in which economies are connected internationally?
2. List four policies related to international trade.
3. List two policies related to international capital transactions.
4. Briefly describe the recent history of U.S. and world trade, and list the United States' major trading partners.
5. Describe the Ricardian model of trade.
6. What is meant by the "principle of comparative advantage"?
7. What is the theory of "factor-price equalization"?
8. What are some international organizations and agreements dealing with trade relations?
9. List six reasons why nations often limit trade.
10. What is "protectionism," and why do countries often engage in it?
11. How does the notion of "dynamic comparative advantage" explain some countries' adoption of "infant industry" policies?
12. What are three things that can cause shifts in the terms of trade?
13. How can international openness cause a "race to the bottom"?
14. Give some examples of recent controversies in trade policy.
15. What is the theory of "purchasing power parity"?
16. Who creates the supply of a currency on the foreign exchange market? Who creates the demand?
17. Draw a carefully labeled graph illustrating a depreciation of the dollar against the euro.
18. What are the two accounts in the Balance of Payment Account, and what do they reflect?
19. What has happened to the United States trade deficit in recent years?
20. How and why is an imbalance (surplus or deficit) in the current account related to an imbalance in the capital account?
21. Does having an open economy make monetary policy stronger or weaker? Why?
22. Distinguish between floating and fixed exchange rate systems.
23. How and why might a central bank "intervene" on a foreign exchange market?
24. What three international institutions dealing with finance were created in the 1940s? Which two remain?
25. What is the "Washington Consensus"?
26. What are some changes that have been suggested for the international financial system?

Exercises

1. Singapore is a natural-resource-poor country that has built its economy on the basis of massive imports of commodities and raw materials, and similarly massive exports of refined and manufactured goods and services. In Singapore, exports are 178 percent of GDP! But how can a country export *more* than its GDP? (Hint: Review the definition of GDP and the conventions of national income accounting from Chapter 5, if necessary.)

2. Classify each of the following as a *trade flow, income flow,* or *asset transaction:*
   a. A U.S. software company sells its products to European consumers
   b. A Saudi investor buys European real estate
   c. A U.S. retailer imports Chinese-made appliances
   d. A worker in the U.K. sends some of her wages back to her family in India
   e. A Mexican manufacturer pays interest on a loan taken from a Canadian bank

3. Hereland and Thereland are two small countries. Each currently produces both milk and corn, and they do not trade. If Hereland puts all its resources toward milk, it can produce two tanker truckloads, while if it puts all its resources toward corn production, it can produce eight tons. Thereland can produce either two loads of milk or two tons of corn. (Both can also produce any combination on a straight line in between.)
   a. Draw and label production-possibilities frontiers for Hereland and Thereland.
   b. Suppose Hereland's citizens would like one truckload of milk and six tons of corn. Can Hereland produce this?
   c. Suppose Thereland's citizens would like one load of milk and two tons of corn. Can Thereland produce this?
   d. What is the slope of Hereland's production-possibilities frontier? Fill in the blank: "For each truckload of milk Hereland makes, it must give up making ___ tons of corn."
   e. What is the slope of Thereland's production possibilities frontier? Fill in the blank: "For each truckload of milk Thereland makes, it must give up making ___ tons of corn."
   f. Which country has a comparative advantage in producing milk?
   g. Create a table similar to Table 13.1, showing how Hereland and Thereland could enter into a trading relationship in order to meet their citizens' consumption desires as described in (b) and (c).
   h. Suppose you are an analyst working for the government of Hereland. Write a few sentences, based on the above analysis, advising your boss about whether to undertake trade negotiations with Thereland.
   i. Would your advice change if you know that unemployment in Hereland is high, and that retraining corn farmers to be diary farmers, or vice versa, is very difficult to do?
   j. Would your advice change if Thereland insists in trade negotiations that one truckload of milk be exchanged for exactly four tons of corn?

4. Continuing the Ricardian story from Section 3.1 of this chapter, suppose that England were, after a while, to put a tariff on imports of Portuguese wine. Since we only have wine and cloth in this story, we will have to (somewhat unrealistically) express this tax in terms of units of goods rather than units of currencies. Say that England demands that Portugal "pay a tariff of 40 units of cloth" if it wants to sell 100 units

of wine. Or, in other words, England now says that it will give Portugal only *60 units of cloth* instead of 100, in exchange for 100 units of wine.

   a. With production unchanged, what would exchange and consumption be like under these modified terms of trade? (Create a table like Table 13.1.)

   b. Does England benefit from instituting this tariff?

   c. Would Portugal voluntarily agree to continue trading, with these changed terms of trade? (Assume Portugal has no power to change the terms of trade—it can only accept England's deal or go back to consuming within its own production-possibilities frontier.)

   d. Because trade is voluntary, does that mean it is *fair?* Discuss.

5. Suppose that, due to rising interest rates in the United States, the Japanese increase their purchases of United States securities.

   a. Illustrate in a carefully labeled supply-and-demand diagram how this would affect the foreign exchange market and the exchange rate expressed in terms of yen per dollar.

   b. Is this an appreciation or depreciation of the dollar?

   c. Would we say that *the yen* is now "stronger"? Or "weaker"?

   d. If the rise in interest rates was due to a deliberate Fed policy, does this international connection make such policy more, or less, effective? Explain in a few sentences.

6. Determine, for each of the following, whether it would appear in the *current account* or *financial account* section of the United States Balance of Payments Accounts, and whether it would represent an *inflow* or an *outflow.*

   a. Payments are received for U.S.-made airplanes sold to Thailand

   b. A resident of Nigeria buys a U.S. government savings bond

   c. A U.S. company invests in a branch in Australia

   d. A Japanese company takes home its profits earned in the United States

   e. The U.S. government pays interest to a bondholder in Canada

7. Match each concept in Column A with a definition or example in Column B.

Column A	Column B
a. Tariff	1. Makes international incomes comparable, by accounting for differences in the cost of living
b. Current account	2. A rise in the value of a currency, caused by market pressures
c. Appreciation	3. An organization charged with facilitating international trade
d. Purchasing power parity adjustment	4. Investing in a foreign business
e. Dumping	5. Tracks flows arising from trade, earnings, and transfers
f. Quota	6. A tax put on an internationally traded item
g. Dynamic comparative advantage	7. Changes in the opportunity cost of production over time
h. WTO	8. A rise in the value of a currency, under a fixed exchange rate system
i. IMF	9. An organization charged with overseeing international finance
j. Comparative advantage	10. An industry that needs protection until it is able to compete

k. Revaluation

l. FDI

m. Infant industry

n. Protectionism

11. Selling goods abroad at below the cost of production
12. Putting a quantity limit on imports or exports
13. Putting a tariff on orange juice imports to help Florida orange growers
14. A country is relatively more efficient in the production of some good(s)

14 How Economies Grow and Develop

How do economies develop? How does the economic status of countries and the well-being of their peoples change over time? Most of the macroeconomic theory we have presented so far has assumed that we are talking about an advanced economy similar to the United States. But if we think back a hundred years, the United States was a very different place from what it is today. Most transportation was still horse-drawn, with only a few cars operating on a poor-quality road system. Most rural areas did not have electricity or telephone service. In 1900, real per capita income in the United States was about $5,000 (measured in 2000 dollars). During the twentieth century, real per capita income in the United States rose about sevenfold, to over $35,000.

The median income in the world today is about equal to that of the United States in the early 1900s. Although billions of people still live in severe poverty, many formerly poor nations are rapidly developing. Others have experienced little progress. It is both interesting and important to evaluate how economies grow, how the growth process differs in different cases, and why some countries are very successful at promoting rapid growth, while others seem to be "stuck" at a low level of income.

"Economic growth" refers to increases in aggregate levels of production and income, and is usually measured as the percentage change in GDP or GDP per capita from year to year. "Economic development" is a somewhat more complex concept, referring to the process of moving people from a situation of poverty to material plenty through investments in productive capacity and changes in the organization of work. This chapter evaluates how economies grow, how the economic growth process differs across countries, and why some nations have been very successful at promoting development, while others have not. In the next chapter we'll consider the (sometimes problematic) relationship of economic growth and development to broader goals, including the goal of environmental sustainability and richer conceptions of human well-being.

1. The Standard Theory of Economic Growth

As we noted in Chapter 6, there are many criticisms of the use of GDP as a measure of economic progress. Economists' traditional models of economic growth, however, are all based on this measure, and it is these models we review in this section.

1.1 Defining Economic Growth

The simplest definition of economic growth is an increase in real GDP (that is, GDP adjusted for inflation). The growth rate of real GDP is the percentage change in real GDP from one year to the next. Using what we learned in Chapter 5, we can express the rate of growth in, for example, the period 2005–6, as follows:

$$growth\ rate\ of\ real\ GDP = \frac{RealGDP_{2006} - RealGDP_{2005}}{RealGDP_{2005}} \times 100$$

U.S. real GDP in 2005 (in chained 2000 dollars) was 11.00 trillion and in 2006 it was 11.32 trillion. Thus the growth rate of real U.S. GDP from 2005 to 2006 was

$$= \frac{11.32 - 11.00}{11.00} \times 100 = .32 / 11.00 \times 100 = 2.9\%$$

For purposes of evaluating how economic growth can feed into economic development it is often helpful to focus on the growth rate of GDP *per capita*—that is, output *per person*—rather than simply on overall output. Mathematically, GDP per capita is expressed as:

GDP per capita = GDP / Population

The growth rates of GDP, population, and GDP per capita are related in the following way:

Growth Rate of GDP = Growth Rate of Population + Growth Rate of GDP per capita

or:

Growth Rate of GDP per capita = Growth Rate of GDP – Growth Rate of Population

Thus, for example, an economy that has a GDP growth rate of 4 percent and a population growth rate of 2 percent would have a per capita GDP growth rate of 2 percent. The per capita GDP growth rate is especially important because it indicates the actual increase in average income being experienced by the people of the country. If a country had a 2 percent GDP growth rate, but a 3 percent population growth rate, its per capita GDP growth rate would actually be negative, at –1 percent. The people would on average be getting poorer each year, even though the overall economy is growing. A more positive way of putting it is that, for people's incomes on average to increase over time, the GDP growth rate must exceed the rate of population growth.

In terms of the aggregate supply and demand (ASR/ADE) graphs we used in Chapter 12, economic growth can be shown as a rightward shift of the ASR, increasing the economy's maximum capacity (Figure 14.1). If this kind of increase in aggregate supply took place without any shift in ADE, its effects would include growth in output and a declining rate of inflation. In practice, however, economic growth is usually accompanied by, and at least in part is often caused by, an increase in aggregate demand. Thus a more typical pattern for economic growth would be for *both* the ADE and ASR curves to shift to the right. In this case output clearly rises, but the effect on inflation is ambiguous.

1.2 MODELING ECONOMIC GROWTH

What causes economic output to increase? One way that output can increase is if there is an expansion in the inputs used to produce it. In Chapter 3 we outlined *five kinds of capital.* Human-produced capital is called *manufactured capital* to distinguish it from the other kinds of capital. Land and natural resources are *natural capital,* and all the skills and knowledge possessed by humans are also a kind of capital—*human capital.* In addition we noted the importance of *social* and *financial* capital, which both refer to institutional arrangements that make production possible.

Economists sometimes think about output as being generated according to a "production function," which is a mathematical relation between various inputs and the level of output. In the most general sense we might say that the output of an economy should be expressed as a func-

Figure 14.1   **Economic Growth in the ADE/ASR model**

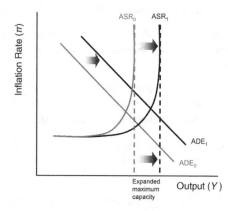

Economic growth increases the maximum capacity of the economy. It involves both supply-side and demand-side expansions, and does not necessarily involve a change in the rate of inflation.

tion of flows from *all* the different types of capital that make production possible. The inputs to the production function are commonly referred to as **factors of production**. In the production functions most commonly used by economists, the factors that are emphasized are manufactured capital and labor. Sometimes, but not always, natural resources also are included.

> **factors of production:** the essential inputs for economic activity, including labor, capital, and natural resources

One very influential, and more specific, model of economic growth was developed by economist Robert Solow in 1957. In his model, he assumed that an economy-wide production function can be written in the simple form:

$$Y = A \, K^{0.3} L^{0.7}$$

where *Y* is aggregate output; A is a number based on the current state of technology, as described below; *K* is a quantitative measure of the size of the stock of manufactured capital; and *L* the quantity of labor used during the period of time, measured as the number of workers. *K* and *L* are the only factors of production explicitly included in the model. Both capital and labor are needed for the production of output, with the exponents in the equation reflecting their relative contributions.*

A is called **total factor productivity**, and includes all contributions to total production not already reflected in levels of *K* and *L*. Often, "total factor productivity" has been interpreted as reflecting the way in which technological innovation allows capital and labor to be used in more effective and valuable ways. For example, the development of computer word-processing greatly increased efficiency compared to the use of typewriters. Typewriters, which seem antique to us today, were themselves a huge productive advance over clerical work using pen

---

* The exponents "0.3" and "0.7" are derived from a combination of facts and assumptions. The facts include information from national data on capital and labor incomes (which historically in the United States have run at about 30 percent and 70 percent of total income). The principal assumption is the neoclassical assumption that factors of production are paid in proportion to their contribution to production.

and paper. This process of improved technological methods has resulted in an increase in labor productivity—more output can now be produced with fewer labor-hours.

> **total factor productivity** (Solow growth model): a measure of the productivity of all factors of production. It represents contributions to output from sources other than quantities of manufactured capital and labor.

After some mathematical manipulations, the production function above can be converted to an equation for the growth rate of output per worker as a function of "total factor productivity" and the growth rate of manufactured capital per worker:

$$\begin{pmatrix} growth\ rate \\ of\ output \\ per\ worker \end{pmatrix} = \begin{pmatrix} growth\ rate \\ of\ total\ factor \\ productivity \end{pmatrix} + 0.3\begin{pmatrix} growth\ rate\ of \\ manufactured \\ capital\ per\ worker \end{pmatrix}$$

For example, if "total factor productivity" grows at 1 percent per year and capital per worker grows at 2 percent per year, this equation says that output per worker will grow at 1.6 percent per year (1 percent + (0.3)2 percent = 1.6 percent). This became known as the "growth accounting" equation.

Note that output per worker is what is commonly referred to as "labor productivity." While labor productivity and GDP per capita are not quite equivalent (some people in the population do not work, for example), they are obviously closely related. Thus, this model implies that the way to raise income per capita—to achieve economic growth—is to increase the amount of capital that each person works with (the second term) and improve technology (the first term).

> According to the Solow model, growth in per capita income is caused by (1) growth in the amount of manufactured capital per worker and (2) growth in "total factor productivity," which is often associated with technological innovation.

The use of the Solow growth model served to highlight some important factors in economic growth. In particular, the model led to much discussion of the role of savings in providing the basis for growing levels of manufactured capital per worker. Technological change also received attention, since this was thought to be the main driver behind growth in the value of "A." For many years, economists tended to treat growth as primarily a matter of encouraging savings, investment, and the creation and dissemination of technology.

In more recent years, other economists have suggested that perhaps this model has directed *too much* attention to savings and technology. Some have argued that other factors such as good institutions that support markets, innovations in the organization of work, or access to global markets should be thought of as equally important in promoting economic growth. It is not helpful, they suggest, to fold all issues of social, human, financial, and natural capital into just one, rather vague, "A" term. These and other qualifications to the model will be discussed when we look at development policy later in this chapter.

Discussion Questions

1. Locate recent news stories about economic growth in your country or region. Can you find current estimates of GDP growth? What factors are discussed in these stories as fostering (or hampering) economic growth? Are these the same factors included in the Solow growth model?
2. In the context of the Solow growth model, discuss ways in which the government can affect the levels of the three explanatory variables (A, K, and L). Which of these three factors do you think public policy can have the most influence upon?

2. PATTERNS OF GROWTH AND DEVELOPMENT

To understand present circumstances, and what is possible in the future, it is helpful to look at the past. Events and concepts dating back to the onset of industrialization, beginning about 250 years ago, remain relevant in explaining modern development patterns. Using that history to set the stage, we will then look at more recent records of growth and development around the world.

2.1 THE INDUSTRIAL REVOLUTION

The **Industrial Revolution**, which began in the British Isles and Western Europe, dramatically changed the nature of economic production. It is important not just as a historical episode, but because the pattern of economic development that it established has become in many ways a model for development worldwide. Although, as we will discuss later, there are criticisms of the applicability of this model to current development issues, its strong influence on standard views of economic growth makes it an important starting point for understanding development.

> **Industrial Revolution:** a process of social and economic change, beginning in eighteenth-century England, that developed and applied new methods of production and work organization which resulted in a great increase in output per worker

Several elements were critical in creating the Industrial Revolution. First, new agricultural techniques, along with new kinds of tools and machines, made agriculture more productive. That meant that more agricultural output could be produced per worker and per acre of land. These productivity increases, continuing and eventually spreading across the globe, meant that human populations could grow dramatically—as, indeed they have done, first reaching a billion around 1810, and continuing to increase to the present global numbers of well over six billion. Because of the great increase in agricultural labor productivity, the number of workers needed to produce food for the rest of the population was shrinking even while the population as a whole was growing.

A second outstanding characteristic of the Industrial Revolution was the invention and application of technologies using inanimate sources of power (increasingly, fossil fuels) and machinery for production of goods. Mechanization created jobs in factories, largely replacing the previous patterns of producing goods at home. Railroads and other advances in transportation, as well as the new kinds of work organization, made it possible to assemble large numbers of workers in factories, resulting in huge urban agglomerations.

Another important factor in England's increasing industrialization was its ability to rely on other countries, including its extensive network of colonies, for supplies of raw materials and as markets for its goods. England imported cotton fiber from India, for example. It discouraged the further development of cotton manufacturing within India by putting high import tariffs on Indian-made cloth, while requiring that India let in British-made cloth tariff-free.

An ever-increasing variety of things were produced in the emerging industrial sector. Some of these were items never seen before, such as bicycles, flushing toilets, communication by telegraph, early cameras, and steamships. Other products of industry were household goods, such as china dishes and cotton cloth, which had previously been used only by a small, rich elite. Others were, of course, the various kinds of machinery that were used to produce consumer items. These included the cotton gin, steam-powered textile machines, a steam-powered printing press that could turn out tens of thousands of copies of a page per day, and rotary mixers to make bread in commercial bakeries.

While the Industrial Revolution began in England, by the nineteenth and early twentieth centuries it was well along in much of Western Europe and other "early industrializing" countries such as the United States, Canada, and Australia. It is important not just as a historical episode, but because the pattern of economic development that it established has become, in many people's minds, the model for how development should proceed worldwide. The vocabulary of referring to rich countries as "developed" and poorer countries as "developing," for example, involves an implicit assumption that poorer countries are on a path of industrialization, on the road to perhaps eventually "catching up" to rich countries' lifestyles and levels of wealth.

2.2 Global Economic Growth in the Twentieth Century

During the twentieth century, real income in the United States rose about sevenfold, and world per capita economic output grew about fivefold. Most of this growth came in the second half of the twentieth century. Figure 14.2 shows the record of global growth since 1960. Gross world product went up by a factor of five during this period (in inflation-adjusted terms). This was accompanied by more than a tripling in the use of energy, primarily fossil fuels. Even though world population approximately doubled over the period 1960–2004, food production and living standards grew more rapidly than population, leading to a steady increase in per capita incomes.

This economic growth, though rapid, has been very unevenly distributed among countries (as well as among people within countries). Table 14.1 shows the per capita national incomes and rates of economic growth for selected countries and income categories during the period 1990–2005. The table gives national income in purchasing power parity (PPP) terms, comparing nations based on the relative buying power of incomes.

As you can see from Table 14.1, the record is very variable, with some countries achieving less than 1 percent annual per capita economic growth, and others achieving over 4 percent, with China in the lead at a sizzling 8.7 percent. Some already poor countries, such as Haiti and the Congo, are growing even poorer. While the table indicates that the low- and middle-income countries are growing slightly faster than high-income countries, this is largely a result of high growth rates in China and India, as we'll discuss later in the chapter.

What accounts for the striking differences in economic fortunes across countries? And can we expect these differences to increase or decrease?

2.3 Growth in Industrialized Countries

Economies such as those of the United States, Europe, and Japan have benefited from many decades of economic growth. This growth has not been uniform; periods of expansion have alternated with periods of slowdown or recession. But overall, GDP in these countries has increased due to a combination of factors including growth in aggregate demand and labor productivity, technological innovation, and investment in manufactured capital. In addition, successful economic growth has often resulted from taking advantage of trade opportunities. Although industrialized countries have generally benefited from openness to trade, they have also typically used protectionism to foster the development of important domestic industries.

These same factors have contributed to growth in all currently industrialized economies, but the patterns of growth have varied in many ways. Japan's extremely rapid growth in the period 1950–80 was often referred to as an "economic miracle." More recently, the so-called "East Asian Tigers" of South Korea (see Economics in the Real World box), Singapore, Taiwan, and Hong Kong, have experienced similar "miracle" growth rates (at least until the Asian financial crisis of 1997).

Figure 14.2   **World Economic Growth, 1960–2004**

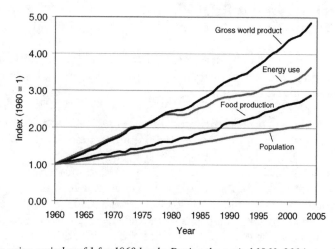

All series are shown using an index of 1 for 1960 levels. During the period 1960–2004, population doubled, food supply nearly tripled, energy use more than tripled, and gross world product went up by nearly a factor of five. (Source: World Bank, *World Development Indicators Database 2007*)

Table 14.1   **Income, Growth, and Population Comparisons, Selected Countries and Country Groups**

Country or Category	GDP per Capita, 2005 (PPP, 2000 US $)	Percent Growth in GDP Per Capita (PPP, Annual Average, 1990-2005)	Percent of World Population (2005)
High Income	*29,041*	*1.8*	15.7
United States	37,437	1.8	4.6
Hong Kong	28,643	2.6	0.1
Japan	27,568	1.3	2.0
France	26,941	1.4	0.9
South Korea	19,560	5.0	0.8
Middle Income	*6,535*	*3.1*	47.7
Argentina	12,899	1.9	0.6
Mexico	9,132	1.3	1.6
Russia	9,747	-0.2	2.2
Brazil	7,808	0.8	2.9
China	5,878	8.7	20.3
Low Income	*2,253*	*3.1*	36.6
India	3,118	4.1	17.0
Bangladesh	1,786	2.7	2.2
Haiti	1,642	-2.4	0.1
Nigeria	1,058	1.7	2.0
Ethiopia	896	1.1	1.1
Congo, Dem. Rep.	679	-5.4	0.9

Source: World Bank, World Development Indicators Database 2006

Economics in the Real World:
The South Korea "Miracle"

South Korea is one of the "East Asian Tigers" (along with Singapore, Hong Kong, and Taiwan) that maintained consistently high rates of economic growth from the early 1960s until the 1997 Asian financial crisis. As shown in Table 14.1, South Korea now has a GDP per capita approaching that of major developed nations such as France and Japan.

Economists agree on several factors that helped produce South Korea's "miracle." First, South Korea invested heavily in human capital. By 1960 South Korea had achieved universal primary education, and incentives were created to promote investment in higher education. Second, investment in physical capital was also encouraged through policies that increased household savings and private domestic investment. The gross domestic savings rate in South Korea has been approximately one-third of GDP since the mid-1980s, among the highest rates in the world. Third, South Korean growth has been "export-led," with exports rising from less than 10 percent of GDP in the early 1960s to about 40 percent by the mid-1980s.

Some economists point to South Korea to illustrate that an open economy is an important ingredient for economic growth, especially for countries with relatively small domestic markets. But the country clearly did not follow a purely free-market approach to development. Instead, the government targeted specific industries for growth, such as petrochemicals in the 1960s and consumer durables in the 1970s, and protected these industries with high import tariffs and other trade barriers. Exporters could also benefit from tax reductions and preferential interest rates. As the country has developed it has gradually reduced its tariffs (from an average of about 40 percent in the 1960s to around 10 percent now) but its average tariff levels are still relatively high.

Another notable feature of South Korea's economic growth is that it occurred in conjunction with an egalitarian distribution of income. In 1960 the country had one of the most equal distributions of income in the world and inequality generally fell even further as economic growth accelerated. Relative equality may have facilitated economic growth because the government could institute policies without pressure from entrenched powerful elites.

South Korea's economic growth faltered in 1997 with the onset of the Asian financial crisis. Unable to pay its foreign debt obligations as a result of its currency devaluation, South Korea accepted a loan from the IMF in exchange for implementing structural reforms to increase foreign investment, reduce the links between business and government, and dismantle monopolies. The South Korean economy has rebounded in recent years but growth has been significantly less than before the crisis (GDP growth averaged 4.2 percent over 1998–2004, compared to 7.1 percent during 1993–97).

A major cause of Japan's extraordinary growth was its high savings rate, which peaked at more than 20 percent of household income in the mid-1970s. High savings were encouraged through low tax rates and a relatively modest social security system. The government played an active role in directing the national savings toward investments in particular industries targeted for expansion through subsidized loans.

Japan and the other "Asian Tigers" have demonstrated a pattern of **virtuous cycles** in which high savings and investment lead to greater productivity, a competitive export industry, and growth of domestic industries. The financial capital that results can be invested in machines, tools, factories, and other equipment that can further enhance productivity—and the cycle begins again. In addition, as the economy grows, more resources are available to invest in the development of health and educational systems. This sounds simple and obvious—yet many nations have had great trouble in achieving such virtuous cycles.

> **virtuous cycles (in development):** self-reinforcing patterns of high savings, investment, productivity growth, and economic expansion

As is often the case when studying economic development, an approach that appears to drive growth in one case does not necessarily apply elsewhere. A counter-example to the importance of savings in the Asian experience is U.S. economic growth, which in recent decades cannot be attributed to high savings rates. Net national savings (gross savings by individuals, corporations, and governments, minus the consumption of fixed capital) has fallen from around 10 percent of GDP in the 1970s to nearly zero in 2005, and about 2 percent in 2006, still one of the lowest rates in the industrial world.

However, a factor that appears to be essential in almost every case for promoting growth and development is human capital. While U.S. savings are low, American investment in human capital is relatively high. For example, only Sweden, Korea, and Finland have college enrollments beyond high school that are higher than that of the United States. The Asian Tigers have also benefited from generally excellent educational systems, along with industrial structure that (especially in Japan) motivated workers with good employment benefits linked to company profitability.

Another critical factor in Japan's growth was the way in which it encouraged the production of specific goods for export. Investment in technology-intensive industries, along with export-favorable policies, allowed Japan to quickly become a world leader in technology goods. While domestic aggregate demand in Japan was initially low, Japan was able to take advantage of growing world demand for its rapidly expanding output. But Japan also used tariffs and other barriers to promote their businesses, as well as channeling investment capital to government-favored industries.

Early theories of development assumed that the lessons from industrialized economies simply needed to be applied to nations at lower levels of income, so that they could follow a similar path of economic growth. But the global record of uneven development and inequality, as well as some recently recognized resource and environmental problems, makes the picture significantly more complex. In the rest of this chapter we will explore issues of global growth, inequality, and differing strategies for economic development; in the next chapter, we will deal with environmental and social issues related to development.

2.4 GLOBAL GROWTH AND INEQUALITY

The global distribution of per capita GDP across countries is shown in Figure 14.3, where each country's per capita GDP in 2004 has been translated into real 2000 U.S. dollars and adjusted for purchasing power for comparability. The United States, along with Canada, most of Europe,

Figure 14.3   **GDP per Capita in 2004 (in constant 2000 PPP $ per person)**

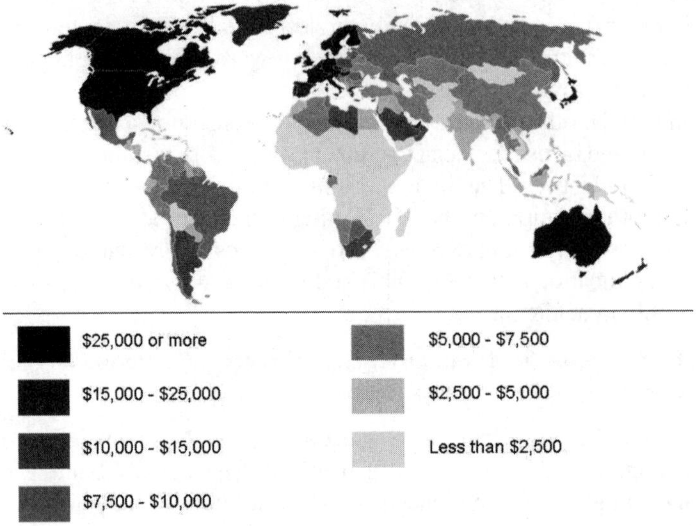

$25,000 or more	$5,000 - $7,500
$15,000 - $25,000	$2,500 - $5,000
$10,000 - $15,000	Less than $2,500
$7,500 - $10,000	

Income per person is highest in the industrialized countries of North America and Europe, along with Japan, Australia, and New Zealand. Income per person is lowest in many African and Asian countries. (Source: World Bank, *World Development Indicators Database 2006*)

Australia, New Zealand, Japan, and a few other countries, enjoys a per capita GDP of more than $25,000. The poorest countries on earth tend to be in Africa and Asia, where income per capita can be below—sometimes *much* below—$2,500.

Figure 14.4 gives us more information about how income is distributed across *households* (using per capita GDP as our indicator). In this figure, the world's population is organized into successive income quintiles, each representing 20 percent of the world's population. Thus the bottom quintile represents the poorest 20 percent of humanity, the next quintile represents the second-poorest 20 percent, and so on. The dark area associated with each quintile is in proportion to how much of the world's income they receive. As we can see in the figure, nearly three-quarters of the world's income goes to the richest 20 percent. Meanwhile, the poorest 40 percent only receive 5 percent of the world's income.

Traditionally, many economists have taken an optimistic view concerning the future of global income inequality. A pattern of faster growth in poorer countries is predicted by the traditional Solow growth model. According to elaborations of that theory, a given increase in the manufactured capital stock should lead to a greater increase in output in a country that is capital-poor than in a country that is already capital-rich. Therefore, some economists have reasoned, it is just a matter of time until "less developed" countries catch up with the countries that have already "developed." The idea that poorer countries or regions are on a path to "catch up" is often referred to as **convergence**. Describing low-income countries as "developing" assumes that they are on a one-way path toward greater industrialization, labor productivity, and integration into the global economy.

> **convergence:** (in reference to economic growth) the idea that underlying economic forces will cause poorer countries and regions to "catch up" with richer ones

Figure 14.4   **The Unequal Distribution of the World's Income, 2000**

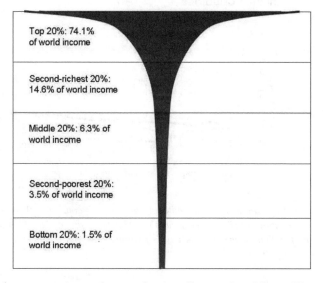

Top 20%: 74.1%
of world income

Second-richest 20%:
14.6% of world income

Middle 20%: 6.3% of
world income

Second-poorest 20%:
3.5% of world income

Bottom 20%: 1.5% of
world income

The uneven pattern of past economic growth means that a small proportion of the world's population now benefits disproportionately from global production. (Source: Data from "Trends in Global Income Distribution, 1970–2000, and Scenarios for 2015," Yuri Dikhanov, U.N.D.P. Human Development Occasional Paper 2005/8)

Is it true that "developing" countries are, in general, catching up with the "developed" countries? A number of studies of GDP per capita growth rates have concluded that lower-income countries are catching up to higher-income countries (as shown by the data for country groups in Table 14.1). However, this has largely been due to the strong growth rates experienced by the very populous countries of China (categorized as a middle-income nation) and India (a low-income nation). Because these two countries have such large populations, they have a disproportionate influence on the average growth rates for low- and middle-income nations shown in Table 14.1. If, on the other hand, we count each country equally, the results suggest that convergence is not occurring in the majority of developing countries. In fact, if we count each country equally the average annual growth rate of real GDP per capita (PPP) over 1990–2005 was 0.8 percent in the low-income nations, 2.0 percent in the middle-income nations, and 2.1 percent in the high-income nations—suggesting further divergence rather than convergence.

We can see what has happened to some "developing" countries' incomes relative to high-income countries better in Figure 14.5. Here, GDP per capita is expressed as a proportion of average GDP per capita in the high-income countries. While India's per capita income rose in absolute dollar terms, India made only slow gains in comparison to the high-income countries (though its growth has accelerated recently). Other countries fared worse. Nigeria, along with many other countries in sub-Saharan Africa, actually lost ground. Income per capita went from about 6 percent of the rich country level to an even lower level—around 4 percent of the rich country average in 2005. In China, on the other hand, the movement has clearly been toward "convergence," with PPP-adjusted per capita income rising from 4 percent to 20 percent of the rich country average during this period.

Figure 14.5   **Per Capita GDP Expressed as a Percentage of per Capita GDP in High-Income Countries**

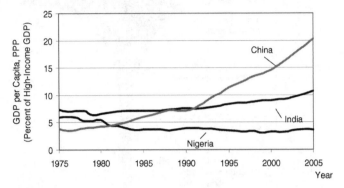

If poor countries are "converging" or "catching up" to rich countries, their incomes should be rising when expressed as a percentage of rich country incomes. This has happened for China, but is happening only slowly for India, while for Nigeria the income gap is actually growing. (Source: World Bank, *World Development Indicators Database 2006*)

Figure 14.6   **Growth and Income Relationship with Area Proportional to Population**

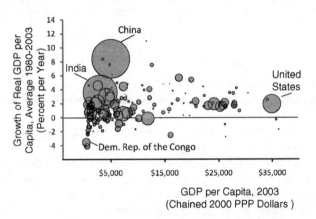

Each circle represents a country. The size of the circle corresponds to the size of the country's population. The location of the circle shows GDP and GDP growth rate. (Source: Alan Heston, Robert Summers and Bettina Aten, *Penn World Table Version 6.2*, Center for International Comparisons of Production, Income and Prices at the University of Pennsylvania, September 2006)

2.5 CURRENT PATTERNS OF GROWTH

Figure 14.6 summarizes a wealth of information about economic growth across countries since 1980. The horizontal axis measures GDP per capita in 2003, in constant chained 2000, PPP-adjusted dollars. The United States and other industrialized countries are represented by spheres off to the right, and poorer countries are represented by spheres off to the left.

The vertical axis measures average annual real GDP per-capita growth rates from 1980 to 2003. Thus faster-growing countries, including China and India, are high on the graph, while slower-growing countries are represented by dots closer to the horizontal axis. Some countries have experienced negative growth—that is, their levels of income per person have actually fallen in recent years after adjusting for inflation. High-income countries have generally experienced moderate, positive average growth rates (on the order of 1 percent to 2 percent), while growth rates diverge much more as one moves down the income scale. At very low incomes, average growth rates diverge dramatically (ranging down to −4 percent).

The size of the spheres are proportional to the population of the country represented, so that the United States shows up as a medium-sized sphere, while China and India—together, home to nearly 40 percent of the world's population—are represented by very large spheres. China and India represent the "good news" side of the development story. While many people in these countries remain desperately poor, at least the trend is going in the right direction. Because of strong growth in these two very populous countries, a large number of people have been lifted out of poverty in recent decades.

The countries of sub-Saharan Africa, which have been particularly hard-hit by AIDS and war, account for a substantial proportion of the very low and negative growth rates. This is the very "bad news" side of the contemporary development story (see the Economics in the Real World box). Far from "developing," such countries have actually become poorer in recent decades.

Discussion Questions

1. Do you have any firsthand experience with economic circumstances in a developing country? What seem to be the living conditions of the average citizen in the country (or countries) you are familiar with? If you are familiar with discussions about the development process there, what are the issues that concern people?
2. Many economists believe that economic development can be promoted in poor countries without reducing economic growth rates in wealthy countries—or even that development in poor countries depends on economic growth in wealthy countries. Do you agree with this perspective? On the other hand, do you think that wealthy countries should be willing to forego some amount of economic growth in order to promote economic development and reduce global inequities?

3. WHAT EXPLAINS THE VARIETY IN GROWTH EXPERIENCES?

What accounts for the striking differences in economic fortunes across countries? If there were just one, simple story about how economic growth occurs, economic analysis would be much easier. In fact, however, one can point to a great variety of factors, all of which may play a role in development. But their significance—and even the direction of their effect, positive or negative—may vary greatly from country to country.

3.1 SAVINGS AND INVESTMENT

Investment in manufactured capital requires savings—or financial capital: Some of a country's current output might not be immediately consumed, but rather set aside and spent on assets that will increase productivity in the future. So one reason why a country may do well is if it has high levels of savings and investment.

Investment in industrial manufactured capital, however, is not the only important kind of investment. Investments in agriculture, through improvement of seeds, irrigation, and the like, have also often contributed to growth. Nations can also invest in human capital by improving

Economics in the Real World: Sub-Saharan Africa

Sub-Saharan Africa (SSA) is the poorest region of the world. Twenty-three of the twenty-five poorest nations in the world are found there, including Ethiopia, Niger, Kenya, and Rwanda. According to the economic theory of convergence, poorer regions will grow faster than richer regions, as globalization promotes the spread of technology, and nations with low input costs (especially labor) increase exports. However, in the case of sub-Saharan Africa, not only has convergence failed to occur, but the last few decades show a period of divergence instead—where sub-Saharan Africa has fallen further behind developed nations.

Since the early 1980s, real GDP per capita and life expectancy in SSA have fallen, while the rates of poverty and undernourishment have remained about the same or increased. The World Bank estimates that the total number of people living in extreme poverty (below $1 per day) in SSA increased from 217 million to 291 million between 1987 and 1998. Meanwhile, the spread of HIV/AIDS and the ongoing civil strife in countries such as Sudan and Somalia have made a bad situation even worse.

Why has economic development failed in most of sub-Saharan Africa? It seemed evident that since SSA was too poor to save and invest, this investment shortfall could be filled by international aid. But while aid to Africa did increase during the 1970s and 1980s, the evidence suggests that this money was used for consumption purposes, often by elites and corrupt bureaucrats, rather than for investment in produced or human capital. Economists agree that SSA remains in need of either foreign investment or international aid. Few economic sectors are currently capable of attracting foreign investment so it appears that further aid is needed, but it must be accompanied with an increase in the efficiency of investment. Sub-Saharan Africa's difficulties are compounded by trade policies implemented by richer nations that discriminate against Africa's exports. Rich countries often protect their own agricultural sectors, such as cotton production, to the detriment of African growers.

One way to increase the efficiency of investment is to improve a nation's financial system. Statistical analysis has shown that those SSA nations that improved their financial systems also tended to grow the fastest. Additional impediments to growth in many SSA countries are their external debts. The United Nations advocates a moratorium on debt payments along with no further accumulation of interest.

Economic development and poverty alleviation in SSA will likely require both standard development policies and new policies that improve income equity and delivery of basic services. Changes in industrialized nations' trade policies could help promote export growth—but rich nations, though often preaching free trade, have generally been slow to open their own markets to products from the developing world.

their country's systems of education and health care. Workers who are skilled and healthy are more able to be productive. Many economists stress that education in science and technology, in particular, is likely to have significant effects on growth.

However, additions to capital do not automatically lead to growth. Unwise development projects have sometimes led to waste or even harm. Inappropriate factories have sometimes been left to rust, while misguided irrigation projects have sometimes destroyed fields through salinization. Investment must be well directed in order to have long-term benefits. Governments have often been the culprits when major investment schemes have gone awry; in other cases, however, governments have also designed very successful, countrywide investment policies.

3.2 TECHNOLOGICAL INNOVATION AND ENTREPRENEURSHIP

Countries often enhance productivity by adopting technology that was originally developed elsewhere. They may obtain this technology by buying machinery, by having their workers or engineers trained in foreign countries, or by welcoming foreign-owned businesses that will introduce more advanced technologies. Other countries have jumped ahead in economic growth by nurturing strong domestic programs of research and development, often supported by government funds.

Advances in technology in China and India have been particularly interesting. According to conventional economic wisdom, such labor-rich developing countries should follow their natural comparative advantage and export relatively low-tech, labor-intensive goods. Yet these countries have deliberately broken into international markets in sophisticated products such as high-tech electronic equipment and computer software, exporting goods and services that embody a far higher level of technology than one might expect from them. This pattern may be a crucial factor in explaining their strong economic growth.

Along with investment in capital, change in the social organization of production is one of the hallmarks of development. For a country to experience change someone, somewhere, must be willing to "do something different." This has often been an advantage of private entrepreneurship. The prospect of earning profits can be a strong motivation for an innovator to gather together the necessary resources and inputs to start a new production process, even while knowing that he or she also faces a substantial risk of failure.

Sometimes development can be assisted by ensuring that financial capital gets to the people who have "good ideas." Recently, some development projects have focused on distributing "micro-credit" to very small-scale entrepreneurs, often women, so that they can build up their businesses. In other cases, foreign companies are welcomed to a country because it is believed that their experience in organizing production, marketing, and the like (as well as the capital and technology they may bring) will cause domestic resources to be put to fuller use. It is hoped that their risk-taking example and their management knowledge will have positive "spillover" effects on domestic businesses.

Advances in management and organization can, however, be short-circuited by bad policies, whether active or passive. In some cases, business innovation has been discouraged by government imposition of very high tax rates or excessively burdensome regulations. Governments may also discourage entrepreneurship by failing to create good infrastructure such as roads and communication facilities, or to invest in the health and education of their citizens, or when they have tolerated traditions of bribery or other corrupt practices.

At the same time, some governments have played crucial roles in *encouraging* organizational innovation. Many currently high-income countries used industrial policies to boost development, by selecting certain industries to receive special governmental support. A massive industrial push, on the scale seen, for example, during Japan's industrialization, or currently in China and India, is generally both too large and too risky to be accomplished solely by private, decentralized businesses.

3.3 MACROECONOMIC POLICY AND TRADE

Since there would be little point in increasing production if what is made cannot find a market, the level of aggregate demand in an economy is also important for growth. Macroeconomic policies to stabilize aggregate demand—and particularly, to prevent or aid recovery from recessions—are thus also crucial. Many nations, however, have suffered from bad macroeconomic policies that, though often intended to promote growth, have actually damaged the economy. A common policy error is to use excessive government spending to stimulate demand. Large budget deficits can offer short-term stimulation, but if continued almost always lead to severe inflation, which undermines stability and growth. On the other hand, strict budget-balancing policies, often forced on developing countries by international lending agencies, can undercut essential investment in human capital and infrastructure. Striking a good macroeconomic balance is often difficult for countries struggling to cope with the many difficulties involved in development.

Access to international markets for inputs, and for places in which to sell products, has also been an important factor in increasing production and aggregate demand. As mentioned earlier, England built up its manufacturing industry in part by relying on its colonies for cheap inputs, and selling its manufactured goods to them. Countries such as Japan and South Korea broke into the ranks of more advanced economies by developing powerful export industries. China is now following this same path. A growing export market provides steadily increased demand for production, boosting GDP. It also provides foreign exchange to purchase investment goods and gain access to new technologies.

Export dependence, however, can also be a trap that stifles economic development when countries depend on exporting products for which world demand is limited. Producers of agricultural exports, in particular, often suffer when world terms of trade turn against them, so that the value of what they can sell on the world market drops relative to the value of what they want to import. Successful industrializers have also tended to make use of strategies of infant industry protection and import substitution (discussed in Chapter 13)—limiting the penetration of trade in some parts of their economies—to build and diversify their industrial base. Once again, the issue is not just what a government chooses to do, but how it does it. The strategies just mentioned have worked when applied well, and not worked otherwise.

3.4 NATURAL RESOURCES

Natural resources are an important asset for development, but the overexploitation of natural resources can lead both to environmental degradation and to economic distortion. Large expanses of arable land, rich mineral and energy resources, good natural port facilities, and a healthy climate may make it easier for a country to prosper, while a poor natural endowment, such as a climate that makes a country prone to malaria or drought, can be a serious drag on development.

But here again, the historical record includes some surprises. Hong Kong and Singapore have prosperous trade-based economies, even though they have very scant domestic resources, with little land or energy of their own. Countries such as Nigeria have found that oil reserves, seemingly a source of wealth, can easily be misused with very damaging effects on development. Uncontrolled oil revenues can lead to massive corruption and waste. Other sectors of the economy are starved of investment and resources, as available resources go primarily toward oil production. And since oil is a depletable resource, the country can eventually run out of oil and find itself worse off than before.

3.5 FOREIGN CAPITAL

What happens if a country is not able to finance the investments it needs for development out of its own domestic savings? In this case, grants, loans, or investments from abroad might finance investments in manufactured or human capital. The sources of foreign capital for development can be either public or private.

Public aid for development can take the form of either bilateral assistance or multilateral assistance. **Bilateral development assistance** consists of grants or loans made by a rich country's government to a poorer nation. Many developing nations also receive **multilateral development assistance** from institutions such as the World Bank and regional development banks such as the Inter-American Development Bank. Countries may also borrow from the IMF, particularly during times of crisis.

> **bilateral development assistance:** aid (or loans) given by one country to another to promote development
>
> **multilateral development assistance:** aid or loans provided with the announced intention of promoting development by the World Bank, regional development banks, or United Nations agencies such as the United Nations Development Program (UNDP)

Private foreign investment is carried out by private companies or individuals. Foreign direct investment (FDI) occurs when a company or individual acquires or creates assets for its own business operations (for example, a German company building a factory to produce televisions in Mexico). FDI may or may not actually increase the capital stock in the recipient nation, since it can include acquisitions of existing capital. Private flows also include loans from private banks.

In recent years, private capital flows have become increasingly important in supplying financial capital to developing countries, as shown in Figure 14.7. Net private flows to developing countries, including both FDI and loans, have risen as investors have sought high returns in "emerging markets." Figure 14.7 also includes a line for workers' remittances, since funds sent home by emigrant workers are an important source of income and foreign exchange for many countries. Studies have shown that these remittances are often spent on household investments in education, health, and small-scale entrepreneurship. Their importance has also been increasing. Meanwhile bilateral aid grants have risen only slightly, while multilateral flows turned negative in 2005. This was largely due to multi-billion dollar repayments sent by middle-income developing countries (including Argentina and Brazil) to the IMF. This analysis should not be taken to overstate the importance of foreign investment, however. For most countries, the volume of investment financed by domestic funds is still considerably higher than FDI—on the order of ten times as much, on average.

The empirical evidence concerning the contribution of public and private foreign capital economic growth is, however, very mixed. Some of the countries that are still among the poorest have also been the heaviest recipients of concessional aid. In some cases, aid went to corrupt leaders who spent it on their own luxurious lifestyles rather than on benefits for their people. Many poor countries are now highly indebted, and spend more on debt service than on health care for their own populations.

Welcoming foreign businesses also can have a downside. When a large, powerful transnational corporation moves into a developing country, not all of the effects are necessarily positive. Foreign enterprises may "crowd out" local initiatives, by competing with them for finance, inputs,

Figure 14.7   **Net Capital Flows to Developing Countries, 1997–2005**

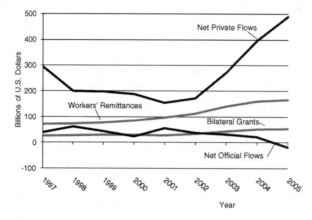

In recent years, official flows have diminished, and in 2005 flowed toward the industrialized world. Meanwhile private loans and investments have risen dramatically. Official flows and bilateral aid grants together are less than one fifth of private flows. (Source: World Bank, 2006, *Global Development Finance: The Development Potential of Surging Capital Flows,* Table 1, p. 3)

or markets. They may also be disruptive politically or culturally. Some of the most oppressive actions in development history (such as peasants being forcibly turned off their land, or union organizers repressed with violence) have come about through alliances between large transnational corporations and corrupt governments.

3.6 Financial, Legal, and Regulatory Institutions

Recently, policymakers have come to a greater appreciation of the role played by financial, legal, and regulatory institutions (which fit into the category of social capital) in encouraging—or discouraging—growth. Very poor countries sometimes have banking and legal systems that do not reach very far into rural areas, and provide credit only for the well-connected, making financing difficult for small businesses and entrepreneurs. The Japanese banking crisis of 1989, which sent the country into recession, brought renewed attention to issues of banking regulation and corporate governance. The case of Russia, which experienced a fall in GDP of over 40 percent during its emergence from communism in the 1990s, highlighted the need for markets to be based in a good institutional framework.

Countries that have been successful in maintaining growth generally have effective systems of property rights and contract enforcement, which allow entrepreneurs to benefit from their investments, as well as effective corporate and bank regulation. Even in the case of property rights, however, the conventional wisdom does not always hold. China and Vietnam, for example, have been able to attract significant amounts of investment, even though, being at least nominally still communist countries, they do not have systems of private property rights. Nevertheless they are able to assure firms that they will benefit from their investments by other means.

Some developing nations suffer from severe corruption, internal conflict, and other factors that make it difficult for effective institutions to take root. Political instability leads to economic inefficiency, difficulty in attracting foreign investment, and slow or no growth. This in turn means that less savings are available for future investment, reinforcing the problems. Breaking this vicious cycle is essential for development, but can be very difficult in practice.

1. In Chapter 9 ("Aggregate Demand and Economic Fluctuations"), saving was labeled as a "leakage" from the income-spending-production cycle, and it was pointed out that an increase in saving could cause an economy to go into a recession. Section 3.1 above, however, claims that savings are necessary for growth. So is a high savings rate good or bad? Can a high savings rate ever be compatible with high aggregate demand?

2. If you were the representative of a transnational corporation seeking to do business in a poor country, what arguments might you use to try to convince the country's government to allow you to operate freely there? If, on the other hand, you were a government official in that country, what concerns would you raise about having the corporation in your country?

4. DEVELOPMENT POLICIES

Development policies have evolved as a combination of domestic policy and foreign interventions, including aid, loans, and trade agreements. International institutions such as the World Bank have played a major role, both as sources of capital and policy advice. In fact, the World Bank and other international agencies have often gone beyond advice, putting great pressure on developing nations to adopt particular policies as a condition of receiving loans. This has led to considerable controversy as to which policies are best—and indeed whether some policies promoted by international agencies may do more harm than good. In this section, we review some of the elements of these controversies.

4.1 INTERNATIONAL AID

During much of the twentieth century, the dominant view among most economists and policymakers was that the key bottleneck to development in poorer countries was a lack of adequate financial capital. Development theorists believed that if countries were provided with more financial capital—mostly as loans, though sometimes as outright grants—the countries would then be able to buy the goods and services need to build up their stocks of human and manufactured capital. This would make their economies more productive, and they would then be able to pay back the loans out of their increased GDP. This was the guiding principle behind the founding of the World Bank after World War II—to provide capital to help less developed countries "catch up."

Many people—especially in the United States—are under the impression that rich countries give a great deal of money in "foreign aid." The amounts, however, are generally quite small as a percent of the GDP of the donor countries—generally only a fraction of 1 percent (see Table 14.2). The uses of international aid vary both in intention, and in the kind of impact they have. Some bilateral aid is motivated by the donor's wish to increase its own exports and is "tied" to requirements that the money be spent to make purchases from the donor country. Some has political motives, such as buying friends in countries that are important to the donor, because of their natural resources (such as oil), or for other reasons of geopolitical advantage. While the category "development aid" is not supposed to include military aid, it may sometimes be used directly or indirectly to acquire weapons.

Some bilateral aid is credited with achieving more clearly development-related objectives, such as increased school attendance, better health, and increased agricultural productivity. In

Table 14.2   **Net Official Development Assistance, 2005, Selected Countries**

Donor	Amount Given in 2005, Billions US $	Amount Given in 2005 as a Percentage of GDP
United States	27.5	0.22%
Japan	13.1	0.29%
United Kingdom	10.8	0.49%
France	10.1	0.48%
Germany	9.9	0.36%
Italy	5.1	0.30%
Canada	3.7	0.33%

Source: World Bank, 2006, *Global Development Finance: The Development Potential of Surging Capital Flows,* Table 3.1, and *World Development Indicators Database, 2006.*

other cases, aid serves primarily to promote the strategic interests of the donor nations, and may even create greater dependence, rather than economic progress, in the recipient nations.

Most multilateral support comes in the form of loans that must be repaid with interest. In fiscal 2005, the World Bank provided $22 billion in loans, of which $8.7 billion went to the poorest nations as "concessional" loans (loans on easy terms) or outright grants. Even in the cases when the projects promoted by multinational institutions have not been beneficial to the countries involved, the loans must still be repaid.

Developing countries as a group currently have over $2 trillion in debt, on which they must pay over $300 billion in interest and principal repayment (debt service) each year. Of course, they can also receive new loans, but even taking this into account, the net flows associated with the debt burden mean that developing nations are currently paying out more than they take in each year (as shown by the recently negative official flows in Figure 14.7). Although more successfully developing countries can afford some debt service, it can be a crippling burden for the poorest nations. In 2005, Latin America, South Asia, and sub-Saharan Africa, including some of the world's poorest nations, together owed over a trillion dollars in outstanding debt.

In addition to bilateral and multilateral aid, funds from non-government organizations (NGOs), including church-related charities and independent medical groups, play an important role. These sources are usually smaller in volume than government funds, but they often finance "pilot" projects that demonstrate to potentially larger donors—rich nations and multilateral institutions—a variety of models of how development assistance can be applied in better ways.

Some loans and grants have truly supplied just the missing factor that was needed, at the right time, and have achieved significant success. In other cases, however, such interventions are made without sufficient attention to the many complex factors that go into development, and are often far less effective than intended.

4.2 STRUCTURAL REFORMS

The failure of aid to stimulate sustained growth in many countries caused a great deal of frustration among policymakers. By the 1980s, the idea that countries should engage in "structural reforms" as a precondition for being granted aid gained ground. Multilateral institutions began to insist that *all* recipient governments undertake a broad swath of policy changes in order to qualify for further loans.

The set of favored policies came to be known as the "Washington Consensus" (as mentioned in Chapter 13). The main principles of the Washington Consensus were:

- *Fiscal discipline.* Developing countries were urged to end fiscal deficits and balance government budgets by developing reliable sources of tax revenue and limiting spending.
- *Market liberalization and privatization.* Abolition of government-controlled industries, price controls and other forms of intervention in domestic markets were seen as essential to promoting growth.
- *Trade liberalization and openness to foreign investment.* Countries were pressured to remove tariffs and other barriers to trade, as well as capital controls and other restrictions on foreign investment flows.

Loans from the World Bank, IMF, and other institutions were made conditional on moving toward making such "structural reforms" or "structural adjustments" in a country's economy. The slogan "stabilize, privatize, and liberalize" governed the thinking of development policymakers. The implicit promise was that if these policies were followed, the conditions for rapid growth would be created.

The results of structural adjustment policies during the 1980s and 1990s were not nearly as positive as was hoped. Some countries progressed, but the countries that most strictly followed the World Bank's market-oriented development path, including many of the formerly communist economies, suffered the most severe crises. In Africa, where investment in health and education is desperately needed, stringent financial policies often forced cutbacks in these areas of social investment. The idea of "fiscal discipline" made it impossible for countries to use fiscal policy for macroeconomic stabilization.

Meanwhile, countries such as China and India, which experienced high levels of economic growth during this period, generally did *not* follow the Washington Consensus policies. While these countries did increase their market-orientation, they combined this with high levels of trade protection, continued state control or guidance of important sectors of the economy, and divergent fiscal policies.

After two decades of Washington Consensus policies, overall rates of growth have generally been lower than in previous decades. The mixed results of the policies promoted by the World Bank and other international institutions have led to an ongoing debate between critics and defenders of the Washington Consensus.

4.3 Current Controversies

In 2005 the World Bank published a report, *Economic Growth in the 1990s: Learning from a Decade of Reform,* in which it accepted some of the arguments made by the critics of the Washington Consensus. Market reform, the report concluded, is not enough. Strengthening institutions, promoting greater social equity, and investing in human capital are also essential. Perhaps most importantly, the Bank acknowledged that there is no "one-size-fits-all" set of policies for economic growth. Different countries have different needs, and policymakers in these countries have sometimes been more aware of these specific needs than World Bank economists seeking to impose a particular set of reforms. According to the report's preface:

Unquestionably, macroeconomic stability, domestic liberalization, and openness lie at the heart of any sustained growth process. But the options for achieving these goals vary widely. . . . In dealing with the growth process, economists have no formula. They have broad principles and tools . . . the manner and sequence in which economic principles and tools are used will determine whether specific country growth strategies will succeed or not.

Meanwhile, the IMF has replaced its "structural adjustment" policies with an emphasis on "poverty-reduction" policies that are intended to give countries more voice in creating their own development plans.

For many critics, these reforms do not go far enough. They suggest that the policies of liberalization and openness advocated by the World Bank and IMF go in the wrong direction. For successful development, they say, countries need to engage in active industrial policy: promoting particular industries, using tariffs, subsidies, and other economic tools as needed, even when this implies active government modification of market outcomes. They point out that currently high-income economies *all* used such policies in earlier stages of growth; it is only now that they have grown wealthier that they preach free trade and fiscal reform to others. In addition, according to this alternative perspective, government policies aimed at improving the equity of income distribution should be an important element of development, balancing free-market forces that may tend to increase inequality.

Critics also point out that recent developments in the World Trade Organization may further threaten—rather than encourage—growth in poor economies. WTO agreements increasingly forbid the sorts of tariffs and subsidies used by developed countries during their own industrializing periods. In addition, the "trade-related aspects of intellectual property rights" (TRIPS) provisions of the WTO increase enforcement of patents and copyrights held by rich countries' corporations. This could make it more difficult for poor countries to access needed technology. Some analysts suggest that changes in trade regimes, such as reduced tariffs by rich countries on poor countries' products (and particularly, manufactured products), would go much further in increasing poor countries' incomes than most programs of aid.

The debate on development continues. Undoubtedly, a combination of market and government-led policies will be used as countries continue to strive to develop. The unsettled question is how to determine the combination that will work best for a particular country, and how best to promote a combination of economic development and social goals.

Discussion Questions

1. What sorts of "foreign aid" programs, either official or private, are you familiar with? Would you characterize current levels of aid from rich to poor countries as generous, moderate, or stingy? What responsibilities, if any, do you think wealthy people should have toward those in developing countries? What institutions would you recommend, if any, for assuring that these responsibilities are met?
2. What have you heard about current debates over the roles of the World Bank, WTO, and IMF? Do you think these organizations are sincere in their efforts to promote economic development, or do you think they serve other interests?

5. CONCLUSION: ECONOMIC DEVELOPMENT IN PERSPECTIVE

The world has seen dramatic economic growth over the past century, but the benefits of this growth have been unevenly distributed. Some developing nations, such as India and China, are now experiencing rapid growth rates. Others, such as much of sub-Saharan Africa and some countries in Latin America and Central Asia, are still struggling with low, or negative, growth rates. In terms of living standards and well-being, much of the world's population has been left out of the significant progress that appears in aggregate statistics. For the future, further development is clearly essential, but simple models of economic growth may fail to capture important elements of the development challenge.

In this chapter, we have focused on traditionally defined economic growth and economic development. But this perspective leaves out consideration of some broader goals. One of these is the goal of *ecologically sustainable* development. Another important question is whether economic growth, where it is achieved, will always bring greater well-being. Most of the economic analysis we have studied focuses on marketed goods, but once people have achieved a reasonable standard of living their happiness may depend more on other factors, such as healthy communities, social harmony, free time, and a clean environment, rather than more consumption.

Fundamental to any measure of economic success is the issue of social justice. If economic growth does indeed bring benefits, but these benefits are very unequally distributed, leaving billions in poverty, this can hardly be seen as a success. Great inequalities also feed social tensions and conflicts, often leading to violence that can undermine and reverse economic gains.

In the next chapter, we will consider some of these issues in an attempt to understand the meaning of development in the twenty-first century. The fundamental concepts of economic growth that we have outlined here will certainly remain relevant, but they will need to be balanced with broader concerns of environmental and social sustainability.

REVIEW QUESTIONS

1. What two variables can be added together to obtain the growth rate of GDP in a country?
2. How can economic growth be represented using the ASR/ADE graphs discussed in Chapter 12?
3. According to the Solow growth model, what does the output in an economy depend on?
4. What is the growth accounting equation?
5. What was the Industrial Revolution? What factors were essential to creating the Industrial Revolution?
6. How evenly has economic growth been distributed among different countries in recent decades?
7. What factors are generally considered to be responsible for GDP growth in developed nations? Have the factors responsible for growth been the same in all developed countries?
8. About how much of the world's income goes to the richest 20 percent? How much goes to the world's poorest 40 percent?
9. What is the concept of convergence in economic growth?
10. What is the evidence for and against economic convergence?
11. How can investment be used to promote economic development?
12. Is an abundance of natural capital a prerequisite for economic development?
13. How can export development both promote and threaten economic growth?
14. In what different methods can foreign capital be provided to promote economic development?
15. What has been the most significant source of foreign capital for economic development in recent years?
16. About how much foreign aid do rich countries give to poor countries?
17. What are the main principles of the Washington Consensus?
18. What is the evidence regarding the performance of the Washington Consensus recommendations?

19. What recent reforms have been instituted at the World Bank and IMF in recent years?

EXERCISES

1. Suppose the real GDP of Macroland is $1.367 trillion in Year 1 and $1.428 trillion in Year 2. Also, assume that population in Macroland also grew from 128 million in Year 1 to 131 million in Year 2.
    a. What is the growth rate of real GDP in Macroland during this period?
    b. What is the growth rate of real GDP per capita in Macroland?
    c. What is real GDP per capita in Macroland in Year 2?

2. Suppose we know that the growth rate of output per worker in Macroland is 1.7 percent per year and the growth rate of total factor productivity is 0.8 percent per year. Using the growth accounting equation, calculate the growth rate of manufactured capital per worker in Macroland.

3. Using the data for each country in Table 14.1, create a graph similar to Figure 14.6 showing real GDP per capita in 2005 on the horizontal axis and the rate of real GDP per capita growth for 1990–2005 on the vertical axis. (You don't need to include the three country income groups.) Draw each data point as a sphere approximately equal to the population of the country. Does your graph support economic convergence? Explain.

4. Match each concept in Column A with a definition or example in Column B

Column A	Column B
a. The percent of GDP that rich countries give to poor countries as aid	1. Nigeria
b. A country that has shown significant economic convergence in recent decades	2. Public aid from one country to another
c. Foreign direct investment	3. 5 percent
d. The percentage of global income going to the top 20 percent of households	4. Singapore
e. Fiscal discipline	5. A characteristic of the Industrial Revolution
f. An example of a country that has grown despite a low savings rate	6. 3 percent
g. Total factor productivity	7. The variable in the Solow growth model that reflects technology
h. The percentage of global income going to the bottom 40 percent of households	8. A structural reform under the Washington Consensus
i. Bilateral development assistance	9. Less than 1 percent
j. A country that has grown despite a lack of natural resources	10. China
k. High savings and investment rates	11. 74 percent
l. Growth in GDP per capita if population grows by 1 percent and GDP grows by 4 percent	12. A common factor in the economic development of the "East Asian Tigers"
m. A country that has not shown economic convergence in recent decades	13. United States
n. The use of inanimate sources of power	14. Over 400 percent
o. The percentage increase in world gross product from 1961–2004	15. A European company purchases a factory in an African country

15 Macroeconomic Challenges for the Twenty-First Century

What will the world be like in the year 2050, or 2100? Will the world situation be characterized as one of widespread material affluence and social peace? Or will the gap between the "haves" and the "have-nots" be even bigger, and the planet afflicted by widespread social conflict and environmental damage? What will the world be like for your children, when they get to be your age? What will it be like for your grandchildren? Of course, no one can foresee the future. But we can at least consider how some especially pressing social and environmental challenges will affect the macroeconomics of the future.

1. Macroeconomic Goals: Looking Forward

Macroeconomics is, at its base, concerned with human well-being. The goals of macroeconomic institutions and policies are (as described in Chapter 1) the achievement of good living standards; stability and security; and financial, social, and ecological sustainability. Much of traditional macroeconomics, as we have seen, tends to focus on the stability and growth rate of real GDP. To the extent that GDP growth leads to well-being growth, this is a sensible strategy. But as we saw in Chapter 6 on alternative national accounts, GDP does not take into consideration many important well-being issues such as environmental deterioration, unpaid home production, and inequality in the distribution of wealth and income. GDP rises when there is increased production of goods that are damaging to society or the environment, or that simply make up for damage already done. A narrow focus on stability and growth in GDP also ignores changes in the conditions of work, stresses imposed on families, and developments in the social and financial infrastructure of an economy.

Some people believe that continued GDP growth and technological innovation will solve the social and environmental problems of the present and future. Others, however, believe that many of the social problems of today—including environmental degradation, growing inequality, and gaps in health care and child care—can be traced to the fact that existing forms of economic growth and development have in some ways worked against "true" or sustainable well-being.

This final chapter examines two important challenges to macroeconomics in the twenty-first century. The first has to do with the nature of society and human experience. As economic development has progressed in many parts of the world, it has solved some problems, created others, and also revealed that economic development alone is not sufficient—though it is often necessary—for fostering and maintaining human well-being. The second challenge has to do with the impacts of economic growth and development on the environment.

To comprehend the broad sweep of issues that will be taken up here it is useful to recall the major types of economic activity that were defined in Chapter 3: resource maintenance, production, distribution, and consumption. In Section 3 of this chapter you will see strong reasons for emphasizing resource maintenance. You will also see the global relevance of the issue of distribution, which, otherwise, is often viewed as a microeconomic issue. First, however, in Section 2, we will compare the broader concept of "human development" to the narrower concept of "economic development." There we will concern ourselves with the well-being implications of the other two types of economic activity: consumption and production.

Discussion Questions

1. Review the problems with GDP as a measure of well-being outlined in Chapter 6, and the alternative measures of well-being—the Genuine Progress Indicator and the Human Development Index—described there. Do you think discussions of growth and development in Chapter 14 would have been different, if changes in GPI or HDI had been the focus, instead of GDP?
2. What do you think is the most pressing current macroeconomic problem? The most pressing problem for the next hundred years? Are the problems that occur to you national, or global, or both?

2. MACROECONOMICS AND HUMAN DEVELOPMENT

Scholars and commentators have used a variety of terms to talk about kinds of "development" that go beyond a focus on GDP, productivity, and industrialization. In Chapter 1 of this book we talked about "living standards growth." Others talk about "people-centered development," "development with a human face," or "socially sustainable development." In this section we will explore the concept of "human development" as proposed by the United Nations Development Program (UNDP). While a basic index generated by the UNDP—the Human Development Index (HDI)—was covered in Chapter 6, the concept of human development actually arises from a more sophisticated philosophical base, and has wide-ranging implications for policy.

2.1 HUMAN DEVELOPMENT DEFINED

How do we judge whether a particular kind of society, economic structure, or policy helps people or harms people? Nobel laureate economist Amartya Sen has argued that our evaluations should be based on the notion of **capabilities**, that is, on the opportunities that people have to be well-nourished, decently housed, and in many other ways live lives that they find worthwhile. The capability approach evaluates institutions, policies, and actions according to the opportunities (or freedoms) they give people for valuable ways of living. In a very broad way, the capability approach tries to answer the question "What do we really want from development?" The capabilities view shifts attention away from measures of income or wealth, and focuses instead on issues such as opportunities for health and participation in society. By focusing on the *opportunities* created, rather than how much health or participation people actually *achieve,* it preserves some space for individual freedom. For example, it is important that a society provide access to food and health care, even though some individuals may choose to fast or refuse medical treatment (perhaps for religious reasons).

> **capabilities:** the opportunities people have to pursue important aspects of well-being, such as being healthy and being able to participate in society

In 1990 the UNDP issued its first *Human Development Report,* influenced by the work of Sen and under the direction of economist Mahbub ul Haq. The UNDP defined **human development**

Economics in the Real World:
What Is Human Development?

The United Nations Development Program describes "human development" as follows:

Human development is about much more than the rise or fall of national incomes. It is about creating an environment in which people can develop their full potential and lead productive, creative lives in accord with their needs and interests. People are the real wealth of nations. Development is thus about expanding the choices people have to lead lives that they value. And it is thus about much more than economic growth, which is only a means—if a very important one—of enlarging people's choices. Fundamental to enlarging these choices is building human capabilities—the range of things that people can do or be in life. The most basic capabilities for human development are to lead long and healthy lives, to be knowledgeable, to have access to the resources needed for a decent standard of living and to be able to participate in the life of the community. Without these, many choices are simply not available, and many opportunities in life remain inaccessible.

This way of looking at development, often forgotten in the immediate concern with accumulating commodities and financial wealth, is not new. Philosophers, economists, and political leaders have long emphasized human well-being as the purpose, the end, of development. As Aristotle said in ancient Greece, "Wealth is evidently not the good we are seeking, for it is merely useful for the sake of something else."

In seeking that something else, human development shares a common vision with human rights. The goal is human freedom. And in pursuing capabilities and realizing rights, this freedom is vital. People must be free to exercise their choices and to participate in decision making that affects their lives. Human development and human rights are mutually reinforcing, helping to secure the well-being and dignity of all people, building self-respect and the respect of others.

Source: http://hdr.undp.org/hd

as being about expanding people's choices, so that they can develop their full potential and lead productive, creative lives (see Economics in the Real World box).

> **human development** (United Nations Development Program): the process of creating an environment that expands people's choices, allowing people to develop their full potential and lead productive, creative lives in accord with their needs and interests

Some have suggested that development should be primarily geared to meeting basic needs for food, shelter, and health care. The human development approach includes attention to such basic needs, but goes further to encompass other dimensions of a worthwhile life. Recent UNDP reports have, for example, examined how rampant domestic violence limits the human development of women in many regions, and how human development may be limited by political oppression along ethnic or other lines. Such issues affect countries with high material standards of living, as well as those still unable to supply basic goods.

2.2 THE RELATIONSHIP OF HUMAN DEVELOPMENT TO ECONOMIC DEVELOPMENT

The Human Development Index, as discussed in Chapter 6, combines measures of life expectancy and literacy with a measure of GDP. While very simple, a shift from looking at only well-being "input" measures (such as GDP per capita) to including even a single "outcome" measure (such as life expectancy) can be revealing.

As an example, Figure 15.1 plots average life expectancies for various countries against GDP per capita, with spheres proportional to the population of the country represented. A curve is drawn to fit the general pattern made by the data points. Looking at the far left side of the figure, it is clear that living in a very poor country such as Ethiopia dramatically increases the chance that one will die prematurely, as compared with living in a somewhat less poor country such as India or China. In nations with very low per capita incomes, many people do not have access to adequate food, clean water, or basic knowledge of health and sanitation. It is clear that substantial increases in the provision of at least some goods and services are necessary to increase human well-being in such countries.

In the middle section of the graph, moving from left to right, there appears to be some relationship between income and life expectancy, but the relationship is less clear than for the lowest-income countries. Countries such as Mexico have achieved average life expectancies that are fairly close to those of the richest countries, even though their average incomes per head are not even half as high.

The spheres for the Russian Federation and South Africa lie far below the line, reflecting cases in which economic transition and inequality have made it difficult to translate a moderate *average* level of income into well-being and longevity. The situation in these countries illustrates how factors other than GDP can have dramatic implications for human development.

Looking at the spheres representing Western Europe, Japan, and the United States at the right of the figure, yet another story emerges. The positive relationship between income and life expectancy essentially disappears. At high incomes, further increases in GDP per capita are associated with little or no gain in average life expectancy. In the industrialized countries, access to basic foodstuffs, clean water, and basic health and sanitation are not generally a problem (though they remain a problem within some poorer groups and regions). Although highly sophisticated medical care can extend the lives of some ill individuals, the effect on average life expectancy of these gains is quite small relative to the gains from more basic kinds of provisioning.

To summarize, "more"—at least more of key goods and services that make for a healthy life—is clearly needed in very poor countries, for human development to occur. Specifically health-related interventions are needed in some countries, particularly in Africa. At high incomes, as we will see below, more material wealth does not necessarily bring more of all the other things that constitute well-being.

2.3 HUMAN DEVELOPMENT WHEN THERE IS ALREADY "ENOUGH"

In rich countries it has become increasingly important to recognize that "too much" can be a problem as well as "too little." Increasing consumption can actually be worse for individuals who may suffer ill health from overeating, psychological disturbances from certain kinds of overstimulation, and (some say) spiritual malaise from exclusive or excessive attention to material things. For example, diets high in sugars and fats can lead to people becoming over-

Figure 15.1 **The Relation between Life Expectancy and Income, with Area Proportional to Population**

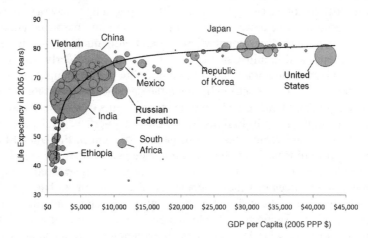

At very low levels of income per head, increases in per capita income are associated with steep increases in life expectancy. Once a middle-income level of GDP per capita is reached, however, increases in income are associated with much more modest increases in life expectancy, and at high incomes the relationship flattens out. (Source: World Bank, *World Development Indicators Database 2007*)

weight. Obesity, in turn, is a risk factor for all four leading causes of death in the industrialized world—stroke, heart disease, cancer, and diabetes. In the United States about 300,000 people a year die from health problems related to obesity. Obesity is a growing problem among the more affluent classes in less developed countries, as well, even while hunger remains a serious problem for the very poor.

Does having "more" make people feel that their lives are more satisfactory and valuable? Psychological research indicates that people's feelings of well-being adapt over time to their situation, and that they pay attention to how what they have compares to what people around them have. To the extent that a society emphasizes the consumption of material goods, this means that subjective feelings of happiness and satisfaction can be maintained only by continually ratcheting up consumption levels. A long line of distinguished economists has pointed out this ratcheting-up effect, and the great degree to which consumption in affluent societies tends to be less about staying alive and healthy than about achieving status or "keeping up with the Joneses."*

Over time, and on a society-wide scale, more income does *not* seem to be related to more happiness in already affluent societies. In 1957, for example, 35 percent of respondents to a U.S. survey indicated that they were "very happy." Between 1957 and 1998 the purchasing power of the average citizen of the United States roughly doubled. In 1998, the proportion saying they were "very happy" was a little lower, at 32 percent. The situation of rising consumption levels has been compared to one in which the front row of a crowd of spectators stands on tiptoe to see better. Everyone else has to stand on tiptoe also, just to see as well as before. All are more uncomfortable, but none except the front row is better off. There is probably no net gain.

---

* Thorstein Veblen (1857–1929) wrote about "conspicuous consumption." John Kenneth Galbraith's *The Affluent Society* (1958), Tibor Scitovsky's *The Joyless Economy* (1976), Juliet Schor's *The Overspent American* (1998), and Robert Frank's *Luxury Fever* (1999) and *Falling Behind* (2007), took up this theme.

At high income levels, other dimensions of human development, such as freedom from violence, closer and more peaceful families and communities, investments in the productive and creative capacities of the next generation, or the opportunity to have a satisfying work life (whether paid or unpaid) may be more important than having more marketed goods and services.

A large portion of every country's social and individual well-being depends on the maintenance of homes and families, including care of sick and elderly people, and other productive activities that go on in homes and communities but are not bought and sold in formal markets. Many adults today feel squeezed between the demands of conventional, forty hours (or more) per week paid employment, and the time requirements of their families. As we saw in Chapter 7, full-time employment in Europe, by contrast, requires the equivalent of five fewer weeks of work, annually, on average, than full-time employment in the United States. It is commonly believed that Europeans have chosen to translate part of their increased labor productivity into increased leisure, instead of using it all to increase earnings and consumption.

Economic practices that make people "rich" as consumers but "poor" as family and community members is not consistent with the human development goal of having the freedom to live a valuable life. Supporting people in their roles as parents, friends, community builders and citizens has often been overlooked in macroeconomics, with its emphasis on paid employment. But providing such a broader base for human development is an important challenge for the twenty-first century. Public support for essential tasks of caring can help both care receivers and caregivers "participate in the life of the community" (as outlined in the UNDP human development goals).

2.4 HUMAN DEVELOPMENT GOALS AND POLICIES

In September 2000 the member states of the United Nations unanimously declared their intention to try to reach a set of development objectives called the **Millennium Development Goals (MDGs)**. These goals focus on improvements in the life of the very poorest people in the world, emphasizing food security, education, gender equity, and health care (see Economics in the Real World box). The MDGs include mention of environmental sustainability (to be discussed in Section 3 of this chapter). Most of the goals set a deadline of 2015 for achievement.

> **Millennium Development Goals (MDGs):** A set of goals declared by the United Nations in 2000, emphasizing eradication of extreme poverty; promotion of education, gender equity, and heath; environmental sustainability, and partnership between rich and poor countries

Each of the eight main *goals,* such as "reduce child mortality," is accompanied by one or more specific *targets,* such as "reduce by two-thirds, between 1990 and 2015, the under-five mortality rate." These targets in turn may relate to a number of policy actions, such as increasing education for mothers, vaccinating against measles, and distributing malaria-fighting mosquito nets. The eighth goal, "develop a global partnership for development," points to some policies the richer countries should enact. These include eliminating tariff barriers to poor countries' products, canceling and/or restructuring debts, increasing foreign aid, easing the flow of essential drugs, and sharing technology.

The MDGs have been criticized by some who believe the goals do not go far enough in addressing inequalities and injustices between rich and poor countries. The 2005 *Human Development Report,* for example, points out that "The $7 billion needed annually over the next decade to provide 2.6 billion people with access to clean water is less than Europeans spend on perfume and less than Americans spend on elective corrective surgery. This is for an investment that would save an estimated 4,000 lives each day."[1] As a high-profile, specific commitment of

Economics in the Real World:
The Millennium Development Goals

1. **Eradicate extreme poverty and hunger**—Halve, between 1990 and 2015, the proportion of people whose income is less than $1 a day, or who suffer from hunger
2. **Achieve universal primary education**—Ensure that, by 2015, children everywhere, boys and girls alike, will be able to complete a full course of primary schooling
3. **Promote gender equality and empower women**—Eliminate gender disparity in all levels of education no later than 2015
4. **Reduce child mortality**—Reduce by two-thirds, between 1990 and 2015, the under-five mortality rate
5. **Improve maternal health**—Reduce by three-quarters, between 1990 and 2015, the maternal mortality ratio
6. **Combat HIV/AIDS, malaria, and other diseases**—By 2015 have halted and begun to reverse the spread of HIV/AIDS, malaria, and other major diseases
7. **Ensure environmental sustainability**—Integrate the principles of sustainable development into country policies and program and reverse the loss of environmental resources. Halve, by 2015, the proportion of people without sustainable access to safe drinking water and basic sanitation. Have achieved, by 2020, a significant improvement in the lives of at least one hundred million slum dwellers
8. **Develop a global partnership for development**—Including fair trade, debt relief, and access to health and information technology

United Nations members, however, the MDG declaration has served to increase the attention paid to the promotion of human development.

Regarding human development in richer countries, advocacy has largely been led by nonprofit organizations. In the United States, nonprofits such as Redefining Progress and the Center for a New American Dream are encouraging people to examine what they really want from their economic life. Throughout the United States and other industrialized countries, groups are experimenting with ways of getting off the consumer treadmill, both through personal changes in patterns of work and consumption, and community changes such as co-housing (community-oriented housing) and walking- and bicycle-friendly urban environments. In some cases, private companies and local governments are aiding experiments in new kinds of work-life patterns and community life.

2.5 WHITHER HUMAN DEVELOPMENT?

Although the Millennium Development Goals are a noble statement of intent, the follow-through on them since their declaration in 2000 has been disappointing. If current trends continue, the United Nations estimates that the goals regarding hunger, child and maternal health, sanitation, and gender equity will not be met. The United Nations currently projects that the MDG of halving the proportion of people in developing countries living on less than $1/day between 1990 and 2015 will be met by 2015, but primarily as a result of poverty reductions in China and India. In Africa, by contrast, the number of people living in extreme poverty *increased* by 140 million between 1990 and 2002.

New HIV/AIDS infections continue to increase, although the prices of drugs to treat it have been brought down. Debts are being cancelled for nineteen of the very poorest highly indebted countries, but debts remain a burden for many others. Only five countries (all European) have met the United Nations target for international aid of 0.7 percent of gross national income, and the Doha Round of WTO trade negotiations (see Chapter 13, Section 3.7) failed to make substantial progress in opening up rich countries' markets to the products of poorer countries. The spread of some kinds of technology (particularly cell phones), has been rapid in some areas, but a technological gulf between rich and poor countries persists. As stated in the 2005 *Human Development Report,* "the promise to the world's poor is being broken."

Real human development is still an unattained goal for many, in both rich and poor countries. Consideration of the environmental impact of growth makes this issue even more complicated, as we will see in the next section.

Discussion Questions

1. How important are your income goals to you, relative to your other goals? A recent survey, for example, asked respondents to say whether each of the following was absolutely necessary, very important, somewhat important, not very important, or not at all important "for you to consider your life as a success." How would you answer?

Earning a lot of money	Having an interesting job
Seeing a lot of the world	Helping other people who are in need
Becoming well-educated	Living a long time
Having a good marriage	Having good friends
Having a good relationship with your children	Having strong religious faith

2. Looking at the issue of human development, in what ways do the interests of people in rich countries and people in poor countries come into conflict? Are there also shared areas of concern that could justify and motivate cooperative action?

3. MACROECONOMICS AND ECOLOGICAL SUSTAINABILITY

In Chapter 14 we noted that world economic production has more than quadrupled since the early 1960s. Further economic growth is clearly desirable in developing nations in order to improve the well-being of over a billion people who are now living in desperate poverty. Continued economic growth has been a principal policy objective in developed countries. But as the twenty-first century goes on, we must consider whether it is possible, or even desirable, to continue along the economic growth trajectory of the twentieth century. Economic growth has been accompanied by an increasing demand for natural resources, as well as increases in waste, pollution, and ecosystem damages. Many ecologists warn us that the current scale of human impact on the natural world is already unsustainable. The ecological implications of a further doubling, quadrupling, or more, of human economic activity is an issue that, to date, has received little attention from macroeconomists.

In this section we consider the implications of current environmental issues for economic growth and development. First, we present an overview of some of the most pressing global environmental problems. Then we explore the relationship between economic growth and environmental quality, and discuss policies to promote ecologically sustainable development.

3.1 MAJOR ENVIRONMENTAL ISSUES

A number of environmental issues are closely related to economic growth. These include:

- **Global population.** Economic and technological growth since the Industrial Revolution has fostered a dramatic increase in the world's population. Global population was approximately one billion in 1800, increasing to two billion around 1930 and three billion in 1960. By 2000, it had increased to six billion. Human population growth contributes to increases in many environmental pressures, including those related to food production. While intensification of food production has so far kept pace with population growth, it has led to significant costs in terms of land degradation, pollution from fertilizers and pesticides, and overdraft of water supplies.

   Global population growth rates are currently declining and many projections indicate that the human population will peak sometime in the twenty-first century (see Appendix). A stable or declining global population would eventually ease environmental pressures, but a substantial population increase is still predicted in the coming decades. United Nations low and medium range projections show a global population of between 7.7 and 9.2 billion people in 2050, with almost all future population growth occurring in developing nations.

- **Resource Depletion.** Depletion of important renewable and non-renewable resources has accompanied economic growth. Many of the world's fisheries are in decline due to over-fishing. Tropical forests are being lost at a rapid rate. Nearly a billion people live in countries where water is in scarce supply. In almost all of these areas, water supplies continue to be overdrawn and polluted. Stocks of key mineral resources, such as aluminum and copper, are for the most part not close to exhaustion, but high-quality reserves are being depleted, and recovery of lower-quality reserves tends to involve higher energy and environmental costs.

   Probably no other natural resource has been more critical for modern economic growth than fossil fuels. These fuels (oil, coal, and natural gas) currently provide 86 percent of global energy supplies. The U.S. Department of Energy projects that global demand for fossil fuel energy will increase approximately 60 percent between 2006 and 2030. However, many estimates suggest that global production of oil, the most-used energy source, will peak within the next few decades. If this occurs—and global demand continues to climb—it will create a situation of increasing scarcity and rising prices. Given the current dependence on fossil fuels, this threatens both the potential for developed countries to maintain their living standards and for developing countries to reduce poverty.

- **Pollution and Wastes.** As discussed in Chapter 6, damages from pollution are not reflected in traditional national accounting measures, even though they clearly reduce welfare. Industrial countries generate the vast majority of the world's pollution and waste. While the rich countries have only about one-sixth of the world's population, they generate about two-thirds of global industrial wastes by volume. But pollution also jeopardizes economic development in poorer nations. For example, a "Green GDP" estimate for China's Shaanxi province indicated that costs attributed to pollution alone amounted to over 10 percent of the official GDP for 2002. In some cases, toxic wastes are exported from industrialized countries to low-income nations that are ill-equipped to receive them. Rapid future development will mean that such problems are likely to grow, despite efforts to control them with environmental regulations.

While all of these issues are important, global climate change has recently emerged as the primary environmental challenge of the twenty-first century. Research over the last several years has virtually eliminated any doubts that human activities are affecting the earth's climate. Emissions of various greenhouse gases, particularly carbon dioxide, trap heat near the earth's surface, leading not only to a general warming trend but to sea-level rise, ecological disruption, and an increase in severe weather events such as hurricanes, floods, and droughts.

Greenhouse gases persist for decades or more in the earth's atmosphere. In addition, there is a time lag between the time a gas is emitted and the time when its effects are fully realized. Thus, even if annual emissions of greenhouse gases were immediately stabilized at current levels, the concentration of these gases in the atmosphere would continue to rise for some time. Global emissions of greenhouse gases will eventually need to be reduced significantly—up to 80 or 90 percent lower than current levels by 2050—if we are to avoid the most dangerous effects of climate change. However, rather than declining, emissions of the major greenhouse gases are rising rapidly, primarily driven by fossil-fuel-based economic growth. According to the U.S. Department of Energy, global emissions of carbon dioxide rose by 13 percent between 2000 and 2004. The U.S. Department of Energy projects a further increase in global carbon dioxide emissions of over 60 percent by 2030.

Predicting the precise effects of climate change is subject to substantial uncertainty. In 2001 the Intergovernmental Panel on Climate Change (IPCC)* produced a report summarizing the predictions of various climate change models. They reported a range in which the average global temperature was expected to be between 1.4 and 5.8 degrees Celsius (2.7 and 10.8 degrees Fahrenheit) warmer in 2100 when compared to pre-industrial levels, as illustrated in Figure 15.2. The IPCC's median-range projection is for a temperature increase of about 2.8 degrees Celsius (5.0 degrees Fahrenheit). The likely effects of only a 2°C increase in global average temperature include:

- A 20–30 percent decrease in water supplies in already vulnerable regions such as Southern Africa and the Mediterranean;
- Significant declines in crop yields in tropical regions;
- 40–60 million more people exposed to malaria in Africa;
- Up to 10 million more people affected by coastal flooding each year, with major low-lying areas swamped and coastal cities endangered;
- 15–40 percent of species possibly facing extinction.

While these conclusions regarding the effects of a 2°C increase in global average temperature have gained additional scientific support, findings since the 2001 IPCC report have made use of new data and new analysis to conclude that climate change will likely occur more rapidly than was anticipated just a few years ago, and that the impacts will be more severe. A report sponsored by the British government in 2006 finds that under a "business-as-usual" scenario there is at least a 50 percent chance of an average temperature increase of more than 5°C (9° F) by the early twenty-second century. Climate change of this magnitude could lead to catastrophic effects such as the irreversible melting of the Greenland ice sheet, the collapse of the Amazon

---

* The IPCC was formed in 1988 by the World Meteorological Organization and the United Nations Environment Program to assess the scientific and socio-economic information relevant to understanding human-induced climate change.

Figure 15.2   **Range of Predictions of Global Average Temperature Increase over Pre-Industrial Levels, 2000–2100.**

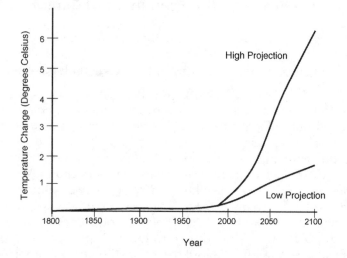

Global average temperature is predicted to be between 1.5 and 6 degrees Celsius warmer in 2100 compared to pre-industrial levels. (Source: IPCC, 2001)

forest, and flooding of major cities including London and New York. (See the Economics in the Real World box for more on this report.)

The 2006 British report estimates the costs of climate change in the twenty-first century as equivalent to 5–20 percent of global GDP, while the most severe effects of climate change could be avoided at a cost of around only 1 percent of global GDP. Thus it now appears that the benefits of current actions to minimize climate change significantly exceed the costs.

Two other climate change issues should also be mentioned. First, while the most dangerous impacts of climate change will not occur for several decades or more, the actions taken in the next few decades will have a profound effect on those ultimate impacts. Delaying action for a decade will lead to a much greater risk of catastrophic effects. Second, the impacts of climate change will fall disproportionately on the developing countries, including coastal flooding, agricultural yield reductions, spreading of tropical diseases, and water supply shortages. While the rich nations will, to some extent, be able to adapt to many of the effects of climate change, the poor countries lack the financial and technical resources to adapt. As the IPCC notes, climate change will likely exacerbate global inequalities and impede economic development in poorer nations.

3.2 THE RELATIONSHIP BETWEEN ECONOMIC GROWTH AND THE ENVIRONMENT

Some researchers have suggested that economic development eventually reduces environmental damages per capita when sufficient wealth and technology allow nations to adopt clean production methods and move toward a service-based economy. Further, environmental quality is generally considered a "normal good"—meaning that people will demand more of it as they become wealthier. The environmental Kuznets curve (EKC) hypothesis posits an inverted U-shaped relationship between economic development and environmental damages. According to this logic, environmental damage per capita increases in the early stages of economic development,

Economics in the Real World:
The Stern Review—The Economics of Climate Change

Published in October 2006, the British government report written by former World Bank chief economist Nicholas Stern presents an urgent case for strong and immediate action to respond to the threat of global climate change. Excerpts from the report:

The scientific evidence is now overwhelming: climate change presents very serious global risks, and it demands an urgent global response. . . . Under a BAU (business as usual) scenario, the stock of greenhouse gases could more than treble by the end of the century, giving at least a 50% risk of exceeding 5°C global average temperature change during the following decades. This would take humans into unknown territory. An illustration of the scale of such an increase is that we are now only around 5°C warmer than in the last ice age. Such changes would transform the physical geography of the world. A radical change in the physical geography of the world must have powerful implications for the human geography—where people live, and how they live their lives.

The evidence gathered by the Review leads to a simple conclusion: the benefits of strong, early action considerably outweigh the costs. The evidence shows that ignoring climate change will eventually damage economic growth. Our actions over the coming few decades could create risks of major disruption to economic and social activity, later in this century and in the next, on a scale similar to those associated with the great wars and the economic depression of the first half of the 20th century. And it will be difficult or impossible to reverse these changes. Tackling climate change is the pro-growth strategy for the longer term, and it can be done in a way that does not cap the aspirations for growth of rich or poor countries. The earlier effective action is taken, the less costly it will be.

In summary, analyses that take into account the full ranges of both impacts and possible outcomes—that is, that employ the basic economics of risk—suggest that BAU climate change will reduce welfare by an amount equivalent to a reduction in consumption per head of between 5 and 20%. Taking account of the increasing scientific evidence of greater risks, of aversion to the possibilities of catastrophe, and of a broader approach to the consequences than implied by narrow output measures, the appropriate estimate is likely to be in the upper part of this range. . . . It is still possible to avoid the worst impacts of climate change; but it requires strong and urgent collective action. Delay would be costly and dangerous.

Source: The Stern Review is online at www.sternreview.org.uk.

reaches a maximum, and then diminishes as a nation attains higher levels of income. If the evidence supported this hypothesis, then it would imply that economic development will eventually promote a cleaner environment.

Figure 15.3 **Environmental Kuznets Curve for Sulfur Dioxide Emissions**

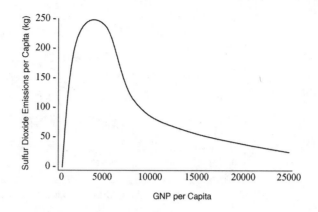

The empirical relationship between sulfur dioxide emissions and the level of economic development in a nation supports the EKC hypothesis. (Source: T. Panayotou, "Empirical Tests and Policy Analysis of Environmental Degradation at Different Levels of Development," International Labour Office Working Paper, 1993)

Does this principle really work? The EKC relationship does seem to hold for some pollutants. Figure 15.3 shows the findings of a study that estimated the relationship between per capita sulfur dioxide emissions (the primary cause of "acid rain") and the level of economic development in a nation. Sulfur dioxide emissions per capita peak at a GNP per capita of around $5,000 and decline as incomes rise further. Studies of some other pollutants, predominantly other air pollutants, also give limited support to the EKC hypothesis.

However, the EKC relationship does not appear to hold for many other environmental problems. Studies of municipal waste and energy use find that environmental impacts generally continue to rise as incomes rise. Perhaps most importantly, carbon dioxide emissions tend to show a positive relationship with average income, as shown by the upward-sloping trend line in Figure 15.4. This means that carbon emissions can be generally expected to increase as economies grow, unless current dependence on fossil fuel energy is drastically altered.

Thus economic development alone appears unlikely to provide a guaranteed path toward environmental sustainability. The relationship between economic development and the environment is, in reality, more complex. Not only is the level of economic development a relevant factor in determining environmental impacts, but the distribution of resources also plays a key role. Most definitions of sustainable development focus on the imperative of reducing economic inequalities along with preserving the environment.

Some environmental damages, such as soil erosion and deforestation, may occur because poor people undertake unsustainable practices simply to survive. Programs to eliminate poverty in developing nations can provide people with choices that are less destructive toward the environment. Meanwhile, environmental degradation typically hits the poorest people the hardest.

Policies that improve the environment can thus also serve to reduce poverty and economic inequality. So we see that the objectives of human development and environmental protection are actually interlinked goals. The promotion of human development in poor nations can improve environmental quality while policies to improve the environment can also reduce economic disparities. This suggests the need for a coordinated policy response that considers the linkages between human development and the environment.

Figure 15.4   **Carbon Dioxide Emissions vs. GDP per Capita, 2003**

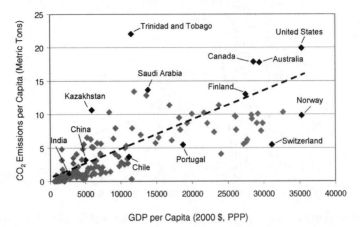

Carbon dioxide emissions per capita tend to increase with higher levels of economic development in a country. (Note: Four countries appear outside of the graph, Luxembourg, Bahrain, Kuwait, and United Arab Emirates. The last three are oil-producing nations with very high CO_2 emissions per capita.) (Source: World Bank, *World Development Indicators Database 2007*)

3.3 POLICIES FOR SUSTAINABLE DEVELOPMENT

Much of macroeconomic theory and policy is currently oriented toward promoting continuous economic growth. What kind of policies would be required to promote ecological sustainability? How can these policies be designed to also maintain well-being and promote human development, especially in developing countries?

Some ecologically oriented economists view "sustainable growth" as a contradiction in terms. They point out that no system can grow without limit. However, some kinds of economic growth seem essential. For the large number of people in the world who cannot satisfy their basic needs, an increase in consumption of food, housing, and other goods is clearly required. For those who have achieved a high level of material consumption, there are possibilities for improved well-being through expanded educational and cultural services that do not necessarily have a large negative environmental impact. But there is nothing in standard macroeconomics that guarantees that economic growth will be either equitable or environmentally benign. Specific policies for sustainable development are therefore needed.

What might such policies involve? Some possibilities include:

- "Green" taxes that make it more expensive to undertake activities that deplete important natural resources or contribute to the degradation of the environment. They discourage energy- and material-intensive economic activities, while favoring the provision of services and labor-intensive industries. An example of a green tax would be a tax on fuels such as gasoline and diesel in proportion to the carbon emissions of the fuel. All countries have implemented environmentally based taxes to some extent. As shown in Figure 15.5 environmental taxes in industrial countries can range from 3.5 percent to over 10 percent of total tax revenues.

    Green taxes are strongly supported by economic theory as a means to internalize negative externalities such as pollution. When there exists a negative externality such

Figure 15.5 **Environmentally-Based Taxes as a Share of Total Tax Revenue, Select Developed Countries, 2006**

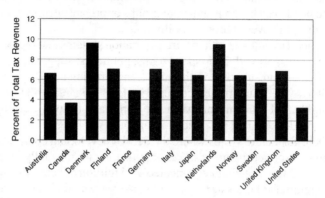

Environmentally-based taxes account for about 10 percent of total tax revenue in Denmark and the Netherlands, but only about 3 percent of total revenue in the United States. (Source: Organization for Economic Cooperation and Development, *OECD/EEA Instruments Database 2007*)

as pollution, an unregulated market will result in an inefficient allocation (see Chapter 2). Two common objections arise to green taxes. First, green taxes would likely fall disproportionately on lower-income households. A rebate or credit to these households could be implemented to avoid making a green tax regressive. The other criticism is that green taxes are politically unpopular—no one wants higher taxes. Increases in green taxes can be offset by decreases in other taxes, such as income taxes, so that the tax burden on a typical household remains unchanged. And unlike income-based taxes, households would have options to lower the amount of green taxes they pay by undertaking energy conservation measures and other environmentally friendly practices.

- Elimination of agricultural and energy subsidies that encourage the over-use of energy, fertilizer, pesticides, and irrigation water. Sustainable agricultural systems rely on the recycling of nutrients, crop diversification, and the use of natural pest controls, minimizing the use of artificial chemicals and fertilizer. These systems also tend to be more labor-intensive and thus could boost employment.

- Policies to promote greater recycling of materials and use of renewable energy. Through research and development grants, subsidies, and tax breaks, governments can support the expansion of energy from solar power, wind, and geothermal heat. Strategic public investment in new technologies such as fuel cells and high-efficiency industrial systems can eventually make these technologies cost-competitive.

- Tradable permit systems that set an overall limit on pollution by offering a limited number of permits that allow permit holders to emit specific quantities and types of pollution. These plans are based on the principle that a process of pollution reduction may be most efficiently achieved by allowing businesses to choose between finding economical ways to reduce their emissions or paying to buy permits. Once the permits are distributed to firms, they can then buy or sell them from or to other firms. Pollution reduction will occur first where it can be done most economically. This efficiency characteristic makes tradable permit systems popular among economists. While environmentalists have sometimes objected, on principle, to the idea of government issuing "permits to pollute," it is recognized that tradable permits have been used successfully in several instances, most notably to reduce sulfur dioxide emissions in the United States. Such permits can also be purchased by environmental groups or private citizens in order to retire them and thus reduce the overall level of pollution.

- Policies to promote efficient transportation systems that replace energy-intensive automotive transport with high-speed trains, public transit, greater use of bicycles, and redesign of cities and suburbs to minimize transportation needs. In countries such as the United States where automobile-centered systems are already extensively developed, the use of highly fuel-efficient cars would be important; in some developing countries automobile dependence might be avoided altogether.
- Debt-for-nature swaps where the debt of developing countries would be forgiven if they agree to protect nature reserves or pursue environmentally friendly policies. For example, in 2002 the United States canceled $5.5 million of debt owed by Peru to the United States in return for Peru's agreement to conserve ten rainforest areas covering more than 27.5 million acres. This innovative form of international fiscal policy was authorized by the Tropical Forest Conservation Act of 1998.

As many modern environmental problems are global in scope, they require a coordinated international response. The challenge of global climate change presents an illustration of how difficult this can be in practice. The Kyoto Protocol, drafted in 1997, committed developed nations to reduce their greenhouse gas emissions an average of 5 percent below their 1990 emissions by 2008–12. Enough nations ratified the treaty so that it entered into force in 2005. The United States, the world's largest emitter of greenhouse gases, has refused to ratify the treaty on the grounds that it would hurt the U.S. economy, and because it does not bind developing nations to any emissions targets. It also now appears that many of the nations that have ratified the treaty will not meet their emissions targets. In December 2007 representatives from 190 nations met in Bali and agreed upon a negotiation "roadmap" for drafting a treaty to succeed the Kyoto Protocol when it expires in 2012. Although the nations agreed that "deep cuts" in greenhouse gas emissions are necessary, they failed to agree on firm emissions targets or to decide how to allocate responsibility between developing and developed countries.

3.4 SUSTAINABILITY AND CONSUMPTION

As discussed earlier, global inequalities currently mean that many people in the world have too little to live on, while others consume at high levels. Some theorists have suggested replacing the goal of ever-increasing consumption with the goal of *sufficiency.* This idea is developed at two levels. On the individual level there is the question of what levels of consumption are sufficient to support human well-being. On the macro or global level there is the question of what kinds and amounts of consumption can be continued, by humanity as a whole, without destructive environmental consequences. Note that the second question includes two importantly different issues: the *kinds* of consumption, and the aggregate *quantities* consumed.

Alan Durning, author of *How Much Is Enough: The Consumer Society and the Future of the Earth,* has proposed dividing the global population into three groups classified according to their consumption levels and environmental impacts. Table 15.1 presents a similar classification using updated data. We see that energy use, carbon emissions, and vehicle use for those in the global lower-income class are all much lower than in the rest of the world. Although these households are often forced to undertake ecologically unsustainable actions simply to survive, their impact on global environmental problems is relatively minor. Durning identified "the global middle

Table 15.1 **Global Population Classification by Income and Environmental Impacts, 2005**

	Global Lower-Income Class	Global Middle-Income Class	Global Upper-Income Class
Population (millions)	2,343	3,018	1,004
Average income per capita (US dollars)	507	2,274	32,112
Energy use per capita (kg oil equivalent)	501	1,373	5,410
Electricity power consumption per capita (kWh)	358	1,720	9,503
Carbon dioxide emissions per capita (metric tons)	0.8	3.3	12.8
Passenger cars per 1,000 population	6	51	433

Source: *2006 Little Green Data Book,* World Bank. Classification based on Durning, *How Much Is Enough: The Consumer Society and the Future of the Earth.*

class" as the group that leads the most environmentally sustainable lifestyle. They rely primarily on bicycles and public transportation, eat a grain-based diet, and use a moderate amount of energy. Durning suggests that the entire world population could live at this level of affluence without overstepping the ecological carrying capacity of the planet. The global upper-income class relies on private vehicles and air transportation, eat a diet with daily meats, and use a significantly greater amount of energy than the other classes. Their lifestyle could not be emulated by the rest of the world without exceeding the capacity of the biosphere.

Each group must approach environmental sustainability with different objectives. For the lower-income group, the focus must be on improving material living standards and expanding options while taking advantage of environmentally friendly technologies. The challenge for the middle-income group is to keep overall environmental impacts per capita relatively stable by pursuing a development path that avoids a reliance on fossil fuels, disposable products, and ever-increasing levels of material consumption. Finally, the high-income group must find a way to reduce environmental impacts per capita through technological improvements, intelligently designed policies, and changes in lifestyle aspirations.

3.5 SUSTAINABILITY AND INVESTMENT

If an ecological perspective implies limits on consumption, what happens to investment? As we have seen earlier in this book, investment spending has often been crucially important for aggregate demand and employment. Yet additional investments in traditional sorts of plant and equipment, heavily reliant on fossil fuels, may work against environmental sustainability. This dilemma can only be resolved by forms of investment that improve well-being but do not increase "throughput" of natural resources and creation of wastes. Fortunately the social and environmental challenges that have been outlined in this chapter define the need for large investment expenditures, many of which are not directly related to increasing material consumption. Rather than being a burden or threat, the need for such investment expenditures may be the solution to maintaining employment with limited consumption.

As we saw in the preceding chapter, many countries in the past used industrial policies successfully, to push an economy from one phase to another. The United States could not have gone from a mostly agrarian economy to an industrial one without government assistance in developing transportation and communication systems. Japan's government carefully selected a sequence of industries to support, going from low-tech and labor-intensive to high-tech and information-intensive. All of the successful European, Asian and North American economies have depended on essential support from national investments in education and public health. Many such investments are "public goods" because, while they provide widespread benefits, it is hard to collect payment from the people who benefit from them; hence, if they are to occur, they need to be supported through national action. A similar set of strategic investments, focused on areas such as public transportation and alternative energy, could move nations toward a more environmentally sustainable economy. Such investments contribute to economically and environmentally positive development, but may not themselves pay the kind of return that would encourage private companies to undertake them. Yet with such strategic investments in place, the private sector can be relied on for much of the follow-through—much as, in the past, the United States government provided interstate highways, while the private sector supplied cars and trucks.

It is also important to remember that, as discussed in Chapter 6, "investments" should really refer to much more than just factories and equipment. Environmental policy is concerned with protecting, or avoiding *dis*investment in, the global commons—the oceans, the atmosphere, the world's store of living species, and other aspects of natural and social capital that greatly affect the possibilities and the quality of life for present and future human generations.

This kind of long-term investment requires a more future-oriented perspective than is used for most business investments. The use of market discount rates (see the Economics in the Real World box) tends to limit the planning horizons of most businesses and individuals to about twenty to thirty years. But long-term sustainability demands a generational perspective, since many of the most severe impacts of problems such as global climate change will take decades, or even centuries, to unfold.

Discussion Questions

1. Considering the environmental problems discussed in this section, in what ways do the interests of people in rich countries and people in poor countries come into conflict? Are there also shared areas of concern that could justify and motivate cooperative action on environmental problems?
2. How do you think your environmental impacts compare with those of the average person in the world? Would overall environmental impacts be greater or lesser if everyone had impacts similar to you?

4. Concluding Thoughts

Throughout the twentieth century the main objective of macroeconomics has been steady, strong economic growth. Looking to the challenges we face in the twenty-first century, it seems that macroeconomics itself is in need of further development. Employment, price stability, and GDP growth will continue to be issues of great importance—not as ends in themselves, however, but as means to the broader goals of human development and sustainability.

With the ultimate well-being goals in mind, macroeconomics needs to look beyond the experience of the past, and ask some bold questions.

Economics in the Real World: Discounting the Future

In economic theory, future costs and benefits are often evaluated with a technique called discounting. The theory behind discounting is that a dollar today is worth more than a dollar tomorrow—even after correcting for inflation. The discount rate, sometimes referred to as the "time discount rate," is the annual rate at which dollar values are considered to change over time (this is a different, broader use of the term than the Federal Reserve Bank discount rate offered to member banks, discussed in Chapter 11).

Thus, at an 8 percent discount rate, $1.00 today becomes worth $1.08 next year and $(\$1.00)(1.08^{10}) = \$2.16$ ten years from now. Similarly, $1.00 to be received ten years from now is worth only $(\$1.00) \div (1.08^{10}) = \$0.46$ today. For most commercial and financial calculations, the use of a discount rate makes sense. However, its application to social and environmental costs and benefits is more complicated.

For longer time periods, the impact of discounting becomes much more dramatic. The present value of $1,000 fifty years from now is only $87.20 at a 5 percent discount rate, and the value of $1,000 one hundred years from now is only $7.60. At a 10 percent discount rate, the value of $1,000 one hundred years from now is only 7 cents! This would mean that, applying a discount rate of 10 percent, it is not worth spending more than 7 cents today to avoid $1,000 worth of damages one hundred years from now. This has led to a serious criticism of the discounting approach. How can we justify a technique that may evaluate serious damages to future generations as less important than moderate costs today?

Discounting is essential if we are considering the economics of, for example, taking a mortgage to buy a house or a loan to finance a business investment. The benefits of being able to own and live in the house starting today may well outweigh the future costs of paying interest on the mortgage over the next twenty years. Similarly, the income generated by the business investment can be compared to the annual payments on the loan— if the rate of return on the investment exceeds the discount rate, it brings net benefits.

In such cases it makes sense to use the commercial discount rate, determined in current markets, to compare present and future costs and benefits. But can we say that a GDP gain today, or in the near future, outweighs major damage in the next generation? How should we evaluate broader environmental impacts that will continue over long periods of time?

We can try to resolve the problem by defining a **social discount rate**—a rate that attempts to reflect the appropriate social valuation of the future. Estimates of social discount rates vary, but are usually significantly lower than commercial discount rates, and include a rate of zero. But of course private market actors such as corporations will base their decisions on the current market rate of interest, not a social discount rate. Public investments, by contrast, can be based on a judgment that the appropriate social discount rate is lower—which means that the future should be weighed more heavily. This might justify, for example, more investments in energy efficiency and carbon-free energy sources today, to avoid damages from climate change that are likely to occur in future decades.

> **social discount rate:** a discount rate that reflects social rather than market valuation of future costs and benefits; usually lower than the market discount rate

A fundamental question confronting macroeconomics in the twenty-first century is how the majority of the world's population, currently at relatively low standards of living, can improve their well-being. The issues of "human development" involve a combination of traditional economic growth and new approaches more oriented to dealing with problems of poverty, inequity, and ecological sustainability.

Much work needs to be done in coming decades to develop technologies that can provide energy and materials for human consumption in ways that are far less destructive to the environment. Other work is needed for remediation of past damages. And there are some kinds of work that need to be prevented—such as fishing for species that are near extinction, or fishing in ways that are destructive to ocean ecosystems, destructive mining practices, and so on.

Another set of essential questions have to do with how macroeconomics can be reformed to take account of the distant future. A first step in this direction must be to recognize that there are important areas where it is inappropriate to discount the future. When our great-great-grandchildren are living, their lives and well-being will be as important to them as ours are to us. (This perspective, though often neglected in economics, is not new, and was emphasized by John Maynard Keynes in the 1930s—see the Economics in the Real World box.)

A macroeconomics that chooses not to discount the future when addressing serious, irreversible harms that may come out of present actions will make different calculations of risk and reward when making social investments. The very definition of externalities tells us that markets cannot be counted on to create the strategic, social investments necessary to deal with macro-level negative externalities; for these we must look to governments and other socially motivated actors. Many scholars and policymakers believe that irreparable damage will soon occur on a large scale, unless there is immediate and dramatic action. They believe that what is needed is a national—and international—mobilization, along the order of how countries respond to threatening military invasions.

The macroeconomics of the twenty-first century must be truly global. The social problems of poverty reduction, as well as major environmental problems such as global climate change, can be partly addressed at the national level, but the roles of international trade and global institutions are critical. Our earlier analyses of national income, fiscal and monetary policy, unemployment and inflation, etc., remain relevant, but need to be placed in the global context of developmental and environmental challenges.

With these sorts of questions in mind, you may look back over all that you have learned in this book, and consider a variety of questions through the lenses of well-being and sustainability. In addition to those posed above, some additional questions requiring answers are: What sorts of fiscal and monetary institutions and policies can best serve the goal of ecologically and socially sustainable development? What sorts of local, national, and international economic developments will be helpful?

These questions remain to be answered—and acted upon. With a grounding in the best knowledge of the past, and an eye to the problems faced in the present and future, perhaps you can contribute to achieving these goals.

Discussion Questions

1. Are you optimistic or pessimistic about the future when it comes to reducing global inequalities? Do you believe the world will be less or more unequal in fifty years' time? What about environmental problems—do you think they will get better or worse in your lifetime?

Economics in the Real World:
Economic Possibilities for Our Grandchildren

What can we reasonably expect the level of our economic life to be a hundred years hence? What are the economic possibilities for our grandchildren? John Maynard Keynes thought the following:

. . . a point may soon be reached, much sooner perhaps than we are all of us aware of, when these needs are satisfied in the sense that we prefer to devote our further energies to non-economic purposes. . . . I draw the conclusion that, assuming no important wars and no important increase in population, the economic problem may be solved, or be at least within sight of solution, within a hundred years. This means that the economic problem is not—if we look into the future—the permanent problem of the human race.

Thus for the first time since his creation man will be faced with his real, his permanent problem—how to use his freedom from pressing economic cares, how to occupy the leisure, which science and compound interest will have won for him, to live wisely and agreeably and well.

When the accumulation of wealth is no longer of high social importance, there will be great changes in the code of morals. . . . The love of money as a possession—as distinguished from the love of money as a means to the enjoyments and realities of life—will be recognized for what it is, a some-what disgusting morbidity, one of those semi-criminal, semi-pathological propensities which one hands over with a shudder to the specialists in mental disease. All kinds of social customs and economic practices, affecting the distribution of wealth and of economic rewards and penalties, which we now maintain at all costs, however distasteful and unjust they may be in themselves, because they are tremendously useful in promoting the accumulation of capital, we shall then be free, at last, to discard.

Of course there will still be many people with intense, unsatisfied purposiveness who will blindly pursue wealth—unless they can find some plausible substitute. But the rest of us will no longer be under any obligation to applaud and encourage them.

Source: Excerpts from the essay "Economic Possibilities for our Grandchildren," John Maynard Keynes, 1930.

2. Do you agree with Keynes's belief that developed nations will soon reach a point when needs will be "satisfied in the sense that we prefer to devote our further energies to non-economic purposes"? Do you think we are any closer to this point than when Keynes wrote his essay in 1930? Do you see any evidence that this is starting to occur?

REVIEW QUESTIONS

1. With whom did the concept of "human development" originate?
2. Describe the concept of "human development."
3. How does "human development" differ from "economic development"?
4. What are some of the major issues concerning human development in rich countries?
5. What are the eight Millennium Development Goals?
6. Describe the degree of progress being made on the MDGs.
7. What are some of the environmental issues related to economic growth?
8. What are some of the projected effects of future climate change?
9. What is the environmental Kuznets curve (EKC) hypothesis? What is the evidence regarding this hypothesis?
10. What are "green" taxes?
11. What are tradable permit systems?
12. What is a debt-for-nature swap?
13. What is the idea of sufficiency?
14. How do environmental impacts differ across the three global income classes?

EXERCISES

1. The UNDP's annual *Human Development Reports* are available online, at http://hdr. undp.org/. Each report begins with an Overview section. Answer the following questions, using the Overview section of the most recent issue:
   a. What special concern is highlighted in the most recent report?
   b. How is this concern related to the Millennium Development Goals?
   c. How does the report describe progress, or lack thereof, on this issue? If this issue is part of a MDG, is the MDG likely to be met?

2. Goal #8 of the Millennium Development Goals includes the following targets:

   Develop further an open, rule-based, predictable, nondiscriminatory trading and financial system (includes a commitment to good governance, development, and poverty reduction—both nationally and internationally); Address the special needs of the least developed countries (includes tariff- and quota-free access for exports, enhanced program of debt relief for Highly Indebted Poor Countries and cancellation of official bilateral debt, and more generous Overseas Development Assistance for countries committed to poverty reduction); Address the special needs of landlocked countries and small island developing states; Deal comprehensively with the debt problems of developing countries through national and international measures in order to make debt sustainable in the long term; In cooperation with developing countries, develop and implement strategies for decent and productive work for youth; In cooperation with pharmaceutical companies, provide access to affordable, essential drugs in developing countries; In cooperation with the private sector, make available the benefits of new technologies, especially information and communications.

   Declarations by international bodies, especially when they are based on wide consultation, must represent a variety of interests. Select four of the targets listed above, and see if you can identify some of the constituencies that are likely to have influenced them—perhaps by urging that the target be included, or by putting up resistance to making a stronger statement.

3. One of the objections the United States government has raised to the Kyoto Protocol is that it doesn't set emissions targets for developing nations such as China and India. Thus, while the treaty imposes emissions reductions on developed nations, developing nations are allowed to increase their emissions without restrictions. According to the United States, this gives developing countries an unfair competitive advantage in the global marketplace. Developing nations counter that any restrictions on them would limit economic development and that the developed nations should take action first, since they are responsible for the majority of global greenhouse gas emissions. Conduct some Internet research to locate articles supporting each of these positions. Then indicate whether you believe developing nations should be bound to emissions targets. Do you think an effective response to global climate change can be enacted without holding developing nations to emissions targets?

4. Match each concept in Column A with a definition or example in Column B.

Column A	Column B
a. An international organization concerned with human development	1. Opportunities people have to live worthwhile lives
b. Percent of tax revenue from green taxes in the United States	2. IPCC
c. Two variables with a positive relationship	3. 86 percent
d. Projected cost of climate change in the twenty-first century as a percentage of global GDP (according to 2006 British report)	4. Income and happiness in societies, measured over time
e. A hypothesis regarding the relationship between economic growth and the environment	5. 25–70 percent
f. Adopted by the United Nations in 2000	6. MDG
g. Capabilities	7. 3.5 percent
h. An international organization concerned with global climate change	8. UNDP
i. Percentage reduction in global greenhouse gas emissions necessary by 2050 if we are to avoid the most dangerous effects of climate change	9. Income and happiness measured among people at a point in time
j. Two variables with no relationship	10. 5–20 percent
k. Percent of global energy supplies from fossil fuels	11. EKC

APPENDIX: DEMOGRAPHIC CHALLENGES

One of the important issues in the area of human development and environmental sustainability is the question of *how many* humans we need to be concerned about. In 1700, the human population was about 600 million. By 1927, it was two billion. Currently, about 6.7 billion people share this planet. Will national and global populations continue to grow, level off, or even shrink? What are the macroeconomic challenges presented by likely demographic changes in the coming century?

The relations of demographic to economic issues are many and complex. On the one hand, growth in the size of economies is often associated with population growth, since more people means more workers, and hence more ability to produce. On the other hand, human well-being can be endangered when population growth outruns available resources, including environmental resources. If production of needed goods and services cannot keep pace with population, lower standards of living can result. In addition to the question of population size, issues about the composition of a population, when looked at according to characteristics such as age, can also be important in explaining economic change. This appendix, after introducing some basic concepts in demography (the study of populations), examines the macroeconomic challenges posed by continued growth in global populations and the dramatic aging of populations in many countries.

A.1 Basic Demographic Terms and History

While the terms "birth rate" and "fertility rate" may seem like they should mean the same thing, in the field of demography they have different meanings. The **birth rate** is the annual number of births per 1,000 *people* in a population. The **fertility rate**, on the other hand, refers to the average number of births *per woman of reproductive age* in a population. So you can see that the birth rate in any country will depend on two things: first, the proportion of people in the country who are women of reproductive age, and, second, the rate of fertility among these women. Similarly, the **death rate** is the annual number of deaths per 1,000 people, while a **mortality rate** refers to deaths within a specific group (such as among mothers or children).

> **birth rate:** the annual number of births per 1,000 population
>
> **fertility rate:** the average number of births per woman of reproductive age
>
> **death rate:** the annual number of deaths per 1,000 population
>
> **mortality rate:** the average number of deaths among a specific group (such as mothers or children)

If the fertility rate is equal to what is called the **replacement fertility rate**, then the next generation will be the same size as the current one—women will, on average, produce just enough children to replace themselves and one other adult. Currently, the replacement fertility rate for industrialized countries is about 2.1 children per woman. It is higher than 2 because slightly more males than females are born, and some females will not survive to reproduce. In countries with higher mortality rates or larger ratios of men to women, the replacement fertility rate is somewhat higher.

> **replacement fertility rate:** the fertility rate required in order for each generation to be replaced by a next generation of the same size. This requires an average fertility of 2.1 children per woman in industrialized countries.

It might seem that a country with fertility rates that are exactly equal to the replacement rate should have a stable population. However this is not necessarily so, due to a phenomenon called **population momentum**. Recall that the birth rate depends not only on the fertility rate, but also on the size of the childbearing population. Suppose a country contains relatively few older people and large numbers of people of childbearing age. Its population will continue to grow even with a replacement fertility rate because the birth rate will be high (reflecting the size of the childbearing group), while the death rate will be low (since only a small proportion of the population will be reaching the end of life). Only when birth rates and death rates are equal does a population stabilize.

Table 15.2   **Stages of Demographic Transition**

First Stage	Both birth and death rates are high. On average the number of children that survive in each family is just enough to keep the population stable or very slowly growing.
Second Stage	Death rates are reduced, while birth rates stay high, so that parents are typically survived by significantly more than the two children required to replace them. From the eighteenth through twentieth centuries this second stage developed in industrializing countries due to the nutritional advances that followed increased agricultural productivity, and also (especially after about 1850) better medical care and sanitation.
Third Stage	Birth rates start declining, but are still higher than death rates. The increased availability of contraception and improvements in female education contribute to this stage. In the third stage fertility rates are initially above replacement level, but will eventually drop to or possibly below replacement level. Population growth slows down, though it continues growing because of the number of childbearing-age women.
Fourth Stage	Birth rates and death rates equalize at a low rate. Population growth is zero—but the population is considerably larger than it was when the process began.
Fifth Stage	Birth rates are lower than death rates. When the demographic transition was first conceptualized, the process was expected to stop at the fourth stage. In fact, however, some nations may move fairly rapidly from above- to below-replacement birth rates, passing through the fourth stage of equal birth and death rates. Population actually declines.

population momentum: the trend in population size that results from its age profile, in particular the number of women who are of childbearing age or younger. For example, a population can continue to grow, in spite of having a fertility rate at or below replacement, if a large proportion of its members are of childbearing age.

Over the last two to three hundred years, the industrialized countries of the world have gone through a **demographic transition** from a combination of high birth rates and death rates to a combination of low birth rates and death rates. But this transition has not been smooth. Table 15.2 outlines the four—or perhaps five—stages of demographic transition.

demographic transition: the change over time from a combination of high birth and death rates to a combination of low birth and death rates

In the first stage, women expend much time and effort in childbearing and childrearing, at much risk to their own health, only to see many of their children die young. Thus moving away from the first stage is an important goal of human development. Populations in the third and fourth stage have moved past the highest birth and death rates, making a higher quality of life possible.

Although birth and death rates are crucially important for explaining population trends in any country, for some countries the net migration rate is also important. The **net migration rate** is the number of people gained by migration (calculated as the number of people moving into an area minus the number of people who moved out of the area) over a year, usually expressed per 1,000 people.

net migration rate: the net gain in population from migration, per 1,000 population

A.2 GLOBAL POPULATION PATTERNS AND POLICIES

The industrialized countries of the world are generally in the third or fourth stage of the demographic transition. The fertility rate in the United States is near 2.1, while most other industrialized nations have fertility rates well under 2.[2] Italy was one of the first countries to be recognized as having a below-replacement birth rate, entering the third stage in about 1960. Its population nevertheless continued to increase, from 50 to about 57 million now. Given current trends, Italy's fifth phase is about to begin; the population is predicted to sink to 54 million in 2025 and 38 million in 2050—a 33 percent decline from the peak. Germany and Japan are other nations where population decline has just begun. Government policies in such countries often now seek to increase births, especially among the ethnically dominant populations (see the News in Context box).

However, significant parts of the world still have growing populations. Many governments and international agencies working in poorer countries have tried to bring down fertility rates, in order to ease the stress that a quickly growing population puts on resources and productive capacities. These programs have often been successful, at least to a degree, and some population policies simultaneously serve other human development ends. Increasing women's access to health services and education has often played a crucial role, delivering not only knowledge about family planning but also often giving women the power to play a greater role in household decisions. However other policies, such as China's long-time policy of penalizing families that have more than one child, are more coercive, and have more ambiguous effects on human freedoms. Forced sterilizations, forced abortions, and infant abandonment (especially of infant girls, in cultures that prize boys) are the darker side of a strong emphasis on population control.

Population trends in China and India are especially noteworthy, since together they contain nearly 40 percent of the world's population. Even though China has put downward pressure on population with its one-child policy and had a fertility rate estimated at 1.73 in 2006, its population is still growing (due to population momentum). The United Nations projections suggest that its population will continue to grow until 2030, peaking at 1.45 billion. India currently has a smaller population than China, and its fertility rate has fallen by half since the 1960s. But with a current fertility rate of 2.9, India is expected to displace China as the world's most populous country within the next fifty years. Populations are also still growing in most middle-income countries, though their fertility rates vary, some being above and others below replacement.

Sub-Saharan Africa has had some of the world's highest fertility rates in modern times—up to seven children per woman, in some countries. Tragically, however, the HIV/AIDS pandemic has drastically increased mortality rates in many of these countries. South Africa, Lesotho and Swaziland are expected to have negative population growth by 2010 due to AIDS. Rather than moving through the demographic transition, these countries seem to have been thrown back to the first stage. The population story in the Russian Federation is also rather grim. Suffering from the special conditions of a poorly managed transition from socialism to a market economy, it has experienced both high death rates and low birth rates. Its population, at a high of 148 million in 1990, has fallen to 143 million today.

So what does this boil down to, as a global picture? It is impossible to see exactly what the future holds, but projections about population made by the United Nations Population Division forecast world population rising from its current level of 6.5 billion to between 7.7 billion and 10.6 billion by 2050. Most of the additional people will live in the less industrialized parts of the world. These projections assume that countries will converge toward a fertility rate that is at or below replacement, though the range in projections comes from variations in how rapidly

NEWS IN CONTEXT:
Shrinking Italy

While many environmentalists fret about overpopulation, Italians are fretting over the opposite. Despite the stereotype of its massive Catholic clans, Italy actually has one of the lowest birthrates in the world, a population set to shrink by a third by 2050, and the world's highest percentage of population aged 65 or older (18.6 percent in 2003). The country wants babies. Badly. Last year, the Italian government offered a $1,300 one-time payment to couples who had a second child. The rural village of Laviano, fearful of disappearing altogether, is offering $14,000 for every tyke produced. Studies show, however, that while cash payments may accelerate breeding schedules, they don't persuade tot-averse citizens to procreate. Some activists say what's really needed is more public-policy support for working mothers. If serious steps aren't taken, says Franca Biglio, mayor of Marsaglia (population 400), "Our bella Italia will become a deserted wilderness."

Source: Tracy Wilkinson, *Los Angeles Times,* February 9, 2005.

this is assumed to occur. The projections assume that life expectancy will increase except where affected by HIV/AIDS.

The United Nations projections, however, do not take into account the consequences of environmental degradation. Whether the resources of the world—including the sink function of the atmosphere in regards to carbon dioxide—will be able to continue to support such a growing population remains to be seen. If population should cease to grow in the coming century, will this be because of individual choices and human-development-oriented policies, such as increasing people's power to control their family size? Or because of coercive polices and/or high death rates due to flood, famine, and disease? Macroeconomic policies concerning resource use, development, and international economic relations hold part of the key to these important questions.

A.3 THE ISSUE OF AGING POPULATIONS

To those who have been concerned about the ecological, economic, and social impacts of rapid population growth or excessively high population density, shrinking populations are good news. It is probably for this reason—as well as the difficulty of comprehending a dramatic reversal of a trend we have become used to—that development thinkers have only recently begun to think about the threats and challenges inherent in the fourth and fifth stages of the demographic transition. The most obvious problems arise from the fact that rapidly falling birth rates lead to changes in the age structure of a population.

A convenient way to visualize the age structure of a population is to chart the numbers of men and women in different age categories, as shown in Figure 15.6 for the case of the United States. Such figures are called "population pyramids," because in populations with sizeable, steady birth rates and regular, steady death rates among older persons, they take on the triangular shape shown in Figure 15.6(a), representing the United States population in 1900.

Figure 15.6   **Population by Age and Sex, United States, 1900, 2000, and 2040 (projected)**

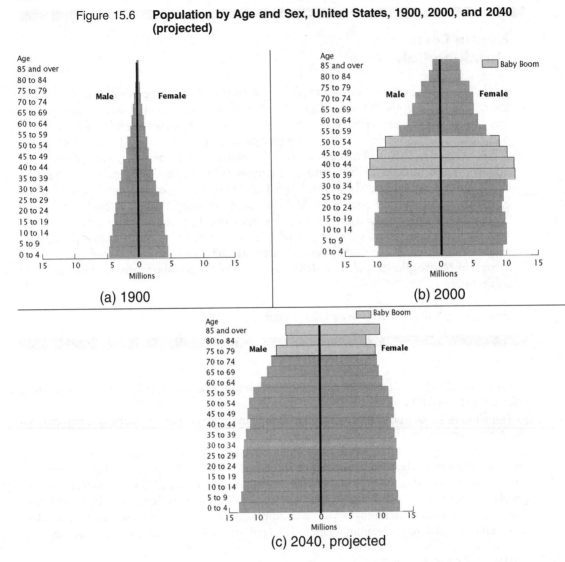

In 1900, the "population pyramid" shows a small elderly population, a larger middle-aged population, and an even larger population of children. By 2000, falling birth rates made the middle tiers of the "pyramid" bulge outward. The proportion of older people in the population is forecast to be unusually high in future decades. (Source: Wan He, Wan, Manisha Sengupta, Victoria A. Velkoff, and Kimberly A. DeBarros, U.S. Census Bureau, Current Population Reports, P23-209, *65+ in the United States: 2005,* U.S. Government Printing Office, Washington, DC, 2005)

Although fertility rates fell in the United States over the twentieth century, this fall was not steady. Fertility was particularly low during the Great Depression, and then partly sprang back during the post–World War II years. People born between 1946 and 1964 are thus said to belong to the "baby boom" generation. Then, after the "baby boom" came the "baby bust," and a transition to a substantially lower fertility rate. As a result, the "pyramid" by 2000 did not look

Figure 15.7   **Old-Age Dependency Ratios, 1950–2050**

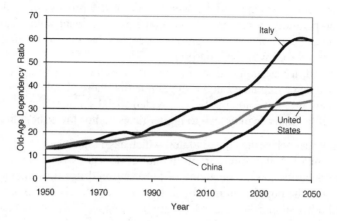

Nations with sharp declines in birth rates can expect to have a rising ratio of older people to working-age people over the next several decades. (Source: *World Population Prospects: The 2006 Revision*, Population Database, United Nations. Figure based on medium variant projections)

so triangular anymore. At the turn of the twenty-first century, an unusually high proportion of the population was in their prime working years, with relatively small numbers of the elderly and children, as shown in Figure 15.6 (b).

As the bulge created by middle-aged baby boomers moves farther up the pyramid over the coming decades, the proportion of the population who are in their retirement years will rise. (The first baby boomers turn 65 in 2011.) Government projections suggest that the age structure of the United States population is projected to look like Figure 15.6(c) in 2040—much more like a rectangle than a triangle.

Other countries that have experienced a "baby bust" will face similarly top-heavy age structures. This means that there will be fewer people of working age around to support people who have retired. The **old-age dependency ratio** is often defined as the number of people age 65 and over for each hundred people age 15–64. Figure 15.7 shows the projected rises in the old-age dependency ratio for three of the countries we have discussed: Italy, China, and the United States. In Italy, for example, the number of older people per one hundred working-age persons is projected to rise from about thirty now to nearly seventy in 2050.

> **old-age dependency ratio**: the number of people age 65 and over for each hundred people age 15–64

Such a changing age structure has a number of implications for national macroeconomic considerations:

- First, each future worker will have considerably more retired people dependent on his or her services. Even though people can save in a financial sense for their own retirements, the real food, housing services, and health care they need can only be provided or maintained by current workers. This suggests that there may be pressure in the future for people to start work earlier in life, retire later, or work more intensely than they have in the past. The need of the elderly for health and social services may also lead to a further sectoral shift toward service-sector employment. In some countries, the need for workers may be filled, in part, by increased immigration.

- Second, it has implications for savings rates. With more people drawing down their retirement savings, and fewer people in the process of building up their savings in preparation for retirement, one can expect national savings to be depressed. This may boost consumption and aggregate demand, but may also cause a lack of loanable funds needed for investment purposes.
- Third, it has implications for government budgets. An aging population means fewer people paying taxes, at the same time that more people become reliant on public retirement programs and publicly provided social services and medical care. Such strains on public finances may lead to higher taxes and/or lower benefits, or cuts in other areas.

In countries such as the United States, which has a long history of retirement support, the effect may be primarily felt through strains in public budgets—as current controversies over the future of Social Security and the financing of prescription drugs for the elderly already demonstrate. The aging of the population may be felt even more acutely in China, where pensions, medical care, and other support for the elderly are looming as possibly the leading social crisis.

A.4 DEMOGRAPHIC CHALLENGES AHEAD

The population pyramids shown in Figure 15.6 can be used, with a little assistance from your imagination, to illustrate another, very important point. Figure 15.6(a) showed the United States in 1900; it can also serve as a generalized picture of any nation that has a growing population impelled by fertility rates above replacement. More than half of the world's population—about 3.5 billion people—fit this picture. At the same time, Figure 15.6(c) is a reasonably good picture of the squared-off "pyramids" that will, in the foreseeable future, characterize nearly all the rich countries of the world: Western Europe, Japan, and a few other highly industrialized countries. Now you need to exercise your imagination to see how these relate to one another: The version of Figure 15.6(a) that would represent all of the poor, growing-population countries is just about three times as large (that is, it represents about three times as many people, at all the ages shown) as the version of Figure 15.6(c) that would represent the world's rich, declining-population countries.

These images illustrate a critical and growing aspect of global inequality. In the foreseeable future the rich countries will be concentrating their wealth among fewer people, while the poor in countries with expanding populations need to share the little they have with ever more people. This is an incendiary situation; the international strains and resentments that result are already evident in the statistics on border incidents, blocked migrations, and would-be migrants dying in the attempt to flee from severe poverty to the places that, as they have seen or heard in media, offer riches and opportunity.

These population images and the underlying realities, including growing inequalities of living standards, will be of great global significance for at least the next fifty years.

While there is no certainty that inequalities between rich and poor will diminish in the foreseeable future, by mid-century there will be some important additional factors to add to the picture just painted. China's population (as noted earlier) will have begun to decline by 2050. It also seems likely that India's declining fertility rate will not stop when it reaches 2.1, but will continue to fall, so that sometime in the second half of the twenty-first century India will join China in a new category of countries that, even if not yet rich, have nevertheless reversed the long growth trend of the second stage of the demographic transition.

With China and India, and a number of other countries as well, likely joining the list of nations with below-replacement fertility, it seems likely that within this century we will see a cessation of growth in the global human population. It is also possible that, beyond stabilization, the shrinking of populations will continue in the richer countries, and spread to others as well. In terms of Earth's ecological carrying capacity, this is desirable. However significant changes will be required in how people conceptualize and pursue their goals if a shift toward smaller populations is to be felt as positive rather than severely negative. Macroeconomic theory has a significant role to play in helping to understand and plan for these changes, including the need to revise expectations, behaviors, policies, and theories to assist shrinking populations in adapting to a changing age profile, including a growing proportion of elderly people. This has potentially large implications for medical care and other services, GDP, policy, and culture. One important challenge is to discover how the elderly population can be more of a resource than a drain; this is desirable from an economic point of view, and also in terms of the psychological well-being (sense of meaning and purpose in life) of the elderly.

Pulling back from that longer view, an overriding concern for the first half of the twenty-first century must be the need to provide food, energy, education, and productive work for a likely sizeable increase in the number of people on Earth—with virtually all of that increase occurring in areas where economic as well as social, cultural, and political systems are already hard-pressed to adapt to past and present population growth. Ecosystems everywhere in the world are showing signs of severe deterioration under the pressure of human populations that have multiplied since the early stages of the demographic transition.

The record of the last three hundred years is one of astonishing achievement, in which the total human population has multiplied over tenfold, with more than half of those now alive enjoying a level of material consumption that would have been considered great riches in any previous era. However the number still living in desperate poverty is also greater than the whole human population at the beginning of the demographic transition. And the natural capital on which humanity can draw is now much degraded compared to the riches with which our species was earlier endowed. The immediate moral of the demographic story is sobering: It is the need to find ways to provide better lives for more people, with diminishing natural resources.

NOTES

1. United Nations Development Program, *Human Development Report 2005,* Overview, p. 8.
2. The data in this section are largely taken from the World Bank's *World Development Indicators* database, the CIA *World Factbook* online, and the UN's *World Population Prospects: The 2004 Revision* online database.

Glossary

Note: The parenthetical number following the definition indicates the chapter in which the definition can be found.

abundance: resources are abundant to the extent that they exist in plentiful supply for meeting various goals (2)

accelerator principle: the idea that high GDP growth leads to high investment growth (11)

accommodating monetary policy: loose or expansionary monetary policy intended to counteract recessionary tendencies in the economy (11)

accounting identity: see identity

aggregate demand (AD) (traditional macro model, with no government and a closed economy): what households and firms *intend* to spend on consumption and investment: $AD = C + II$ (9)

aggregate demand: the total demand for all goods and services in a national economy (1)

automatic stabilizers: tax and spending institutions that tend to increase government revenues and lower government spending during economic expansions, but lower revenues and raise government spending during economic recessions (10)

balance of payments (BOP) account: the national account that tracks inflows and outflows arising from international trade, earnings, transfers, and transactions in assets (13)

balanced budget multiplier: the impact on equilibrium output of simultaneous increases of equal size in government spending and taxes. The multiplier is equal to positive 1, showing that the effect on GDP is equal in size to the original change in government spending and taxes (10)

bank reserves: funds not loaned out by a private bank, but kept as vault cash or on deposit at the Federal Reserve (11)

barter: exchange of goods, services, or assets directly for other goods, services, or assets, without the use of money (11)

base year: in the constant dollar method of estimating GDP, the year whose prices are chosen for evaluating production in all years. Real and nominal GDP are equal in the base year (5)

basic neoclassical model: a simple, mechanical model that portrays the economy as a collection of profit-maximizing firms and utility-maximizing households interacting through perfectly competitive markets (2)

behavioral equation: in contrast to an accounting identity, a behavioral equation reflects a theory about the behavior of one or more economic agents or sectors. The variables in the equation may or may not be observable (9)

bilateral development assistance: aid or loans given by one country to another to promote development (14)

birth rate: the annual number of births per 1,000 population (15, Appendix)

bond: a financial instrument that, in return for the loan of funds, commits its seller to pay a fixed amount every year (called the *coupon amount*), as well as to repay the amount of principal (called the bond's *face value*) on a particular date in the future (called the *maturity date*) (11, Appendix)

bond price: the price at which trades are made (11, Appendix)

bond yield to maturity: the amount a bond returns during a year, if held to maturity, expressed in percentage terms. The yield is determined by the coupon amount, the bond price, and the time to maturity. (11, Appendix)

Bureau of Economic Analysis (BEA): the agency in the United States in charge of compiling and publishing the national accounts (5)

Bureau of Labor Statistics (BLS): in the United States, the government agency that compiles and publishes employment and unemployment statistics (7)

business (trade) cycle: recurrent fluctuations in the level of national production, with alternating periods of recession and boom (1)

business sector (BEA definition): the sector including all entities concerned with producing goods and services for profitable sale. It also includes business-serving nonprofit organizations and government enterprises (5)

business sphere: firms that produce goods and services for profitable sale (3)

capabilities: the opportunities people have to pursue important aspects of well-being, such as being healthy and able to participate in society (15)

capital controls: the regulation or taxation of international transactions involving assets (13)

capital gain: an increase in the value of an asset over time (3)

capital income: rents, profits, and interest (3)

capital stock: a quantity of any resource that is valued for its potential economic contributions (3)

capital-intensive production: production using methods that involve a high ratio of capital to labor (13)

ceteris paribus: a Latin phrase meaning "other things equal" or "all else constant" (2)

chain-type quantity index: an index comparing real production in the current year to the reference year, calculated using a series of year-to-year Fisher quantity indexes (5)

change in demand: a shift of the demand curve in response to some determinant other than the item's price (4)

change in quantity demanded: movement along a demand curve in response to a price change (4)

change in quantity supplied: movement along a supply curve in response to a price change (4)

change in supply: a shift of the supply curve in response to some determinant other than the item's price (4)

classical economics: the school of economics, originating in the eighteenth century, that stressed issues of growth and distribution, based on an image of smoothly-functioning markets (1)

closed economy: an economy with no foreign sector (5)

commodity money: a good used as money that is also valuable in itself (11)

comparative advantage (principle of): gains from trade occur when producers specialize in making goods for which their opportunity costs are relatively low (13)

complementary good: a good that is used along with another good (4)

consumer durable goods: consumer purchases that are expected to last longer than three years. These are generally items of equipment, such as vehicles and appliances, used by households to produce goods and services for their own use. (5)

consumer price index (CPI): an index measuring changes in prices of goods and services bought by households (5)

consumption (*C*) (traditional macro model): the component of GDP that represents spending by households (5)

consumption: the final use of a good or service to satisfy current wants

contractionary fiscal policy: reductions in government spending or transfer payments, or increases in taxes, leading to a lower level of economic activity (10)

contractionary monetary policy: the use of monetary policy tools to limit the money supply, raise interest rates, and encourage a leveling-off or reduction in economic activity (11)

convergence: (in reference to economic growth) the idea that underlying economic forces will cause poorer countries and regions to "catch up" with richer ones (14)

core sphere: households, families, and communities (3)

countercyclical movement: when an indicator moves in the opposite direction from the business cycle. It moves up as the economy goes down (into recession), and down as the economy goes up (into recovery) (6)

coupon amount: the fixed amount paid by the seller of a bond every year (11)

credit rationing: when banks keep their interest rates below "what the market would bear" and deny loans to some potential borrowers, in the interest of maintaining their own profitability (11, Appendix)

current account: in the BOP account, the national account that tracks inflows and outflows arising from international trade, earnings, and transfers (13)

cyclical unemployment: unemployment caused by a drop in aggregate demand (7)

damage cost approach: assigning a monetary value to an environmental service that is equal to the actual damage done when the service is withdrawn (6)

death rate: the annual number of deaths per 1,000 population (15, Appendix)

defensive expenditures: expenditures necessary just to maintain a status quo situation (that is, necessary to keep well-being from going down in the face of negative developments) (6)

deflation: when the aggregate price level falls (11)

demand curve: a curve indicating the quantities that buyers are ready to purchase at various prices (4)

demographic transition: the change over time from a combination of high birth and death rates to a combination of low birth and death rates (15, Appendix)

dependency needs: the need to have others provide one with care, shelter, food, etc. when one is unable to provide these for oneself (3)

depreciation: decreases in the quantity or quality of a stock of capital (3)

devaluation: lowering an exchange rate within a fixed exchange rate system (13)

direct (or positive) relationship: the relationship between two variables when an increase in one is associated with an increase in the other (2)

discount rate: the interest rate at which banks can borrow reserves from the Fed discount window (11)

discouraged workers: people who desire and are available for a job, but give discouragement as the reason for no longer looking for work (7)

disposable income: income remaining for consumption or saving after subtracting taxes and adding transfer payments (10)

distribution: the allocation of products and resources among people (3)

division of labor: an approach to production in which a process is broken down into smaller tasks, with each worker assigned only one or a few tasks (1)

double-auction market: a market in which both buyers and sellers state prices at which they are willing to make transactions, and the item is sold to the highest bidder (4)

dumping: selling products at prices that are below the cost of production (13)

dynamic analysis: analysis that takes into account the passage of time (2)

economic actor (economic agent): an individual, group, or organization that is involved in economic activities (1)

economic development: the process of moving from a situation of poverty and deprivation to a situation of increased production and plenty, through investments and changes in the organization of work (1)

economic growth: increases in the level of production in a country or region (1)

economics: the study of the way people organize themselves to sustain life and enhance its quality (1)

economies of scale: reductions in the average cost of production resulting from a higher output level (13)

efficiency wage theory: the theory that an employer can motivate workers to put forth more effort by paying them somewhat more than what they could get elsewhere (7)

efficiency: the use of resources in a way that does not waste any inputs. Inputs are used in such a way that they yield the highest possible value of output, or a given output is produced using the lowest possible value of inputs (2)

empirical investigation: observation and recording of the specific phenomena of concern (2)

employed person (BLS household survey definition): a person who did any work for pay or profit during the week before they are surveyed by the BLS or who worked fifteen hours or more in a family business (7)

environmental service functions: the provision by the natural environment of the ecosystem services that support and enhance life (6)

environmentally adjusted net domestic product (eaNDP): suggested by the United Nations, this is equal to GDP less depreciation of both manufactured and natural capital (6)

equilibrium: a situation of rest, in which there are no forces that create change (4)

exchange rate: the number of units of one currency that can be exchanged for a unit of another currency (13)

exchange: trading one thing for another (3)

expansionary fiscal policy: the use of government spending, transfer payments, or tax cuts to stimulate a higher level of economic activity (10)

expansionary monetary policy: the use of monetary policy tools to increase the money supply, lower interest rates, and stimulate a higher level of economic activity (11)

expected real interest rate: the nominal interest rate minus expected inflation, $r^e = i - \pi^e$ (11, Appendix)

explicit contract: a formal, often written, agreement that states the terms of exchange and may be enforceable through a legal system (2)

externalities: side effects or unintended consequences, either positive or negative, that affect persons, or entities such as the environment, that are not among the economic actors directly involved in the economic activity that caused the effect (2)

face value: the amount of principle associated with a bond (11, Appendix)

factor-price equalization: the theory that trade should eventually lead to returns to factors of production being equal across countries (13)

factors of production: the essential inputs for economic activity, including labor, capital, and natural resources (14)

federal funds rate: the interest rate determined in the private market for overnight loans of reserves among banks (11)

fertility rate: the average number of births per woman of reproductive age (15, Appendix)

fiat money: a medium of exchange used as money because a government says it has value, and people accept it (11)

final good: a good that is ready for use, needing no further processing (5)

financial account: in the BOP account, the account that tracks flows arising from international transactions in assets (13)

financial assets: stocks (or shares in ownership of companies); bonds (or certificates indicating that the holder has loaned money to a government entity, which will repay the loan, with interest, over time); money market accounts; and other holdings in which wealth can be invested with an expectation of future return (8)

financial capital: funds of purchasing power available to facilitate economic activity (3)

financial intermediary: an institution such as a bank, savings and loan association, or life insurance company that accepts funds from savers and makes loans to borrowers (11)

fiscal policy: the manipulation of levels of government spending and taxation to raise or lower the level of aggregate demand (1, 10)

Fisher quantity index: an index that measures production in one year relative to an adjacent year by using an average of the ratios that would be found by using first one year, and then the other, as the source of prices at which production is valued (5)

fixed assets (BEA definition): equipment owned by businesses and governments; structures; residences; and software (5)

fixed exchange rate system: a system in which currencies are traded at fixed ratios (13)

flexible (floating) exchange rate system: a system in which exchange rates are determined by the forces of supply and demand (13)

flow: something whose quantity can be measured over a period of time (3)

foreign direct investment (FDI): investment in a business in a foreign country (13)

foreign exchange market intervention: an action by central banks to buy or sell foreign exchange reserves in order to keep exchange rates at desired levels (13)

foreign sector (BEA definition): the sector consisting of entities located outside the borders of the United States (5)

foreign trade zone: a designated area of a country within which foreign-owned manufacturers can operate free of many taxes, tariffs, and regulations (13)

free riders: people who seek to enjoy the benefit of a public good without paying for it (2)

free trade: exchange in international markets that is not regulated or restricted by government actions (13)

frictional unemployment: unemployment that arises as people are in transition between jobs (7)

"full-employment output" (Y^*): For modeling purposes, a level of output that is assumed to correspond to a case of no excessive or burdensome unemployment, but the likely existence of at least some transitory unemployment (9)

full employment: a situation in which everyone is working up to their potential and consistent with their desires. An economy may be considered to be at full employment even though some people may be temporarily in transition between jobs (2)

GDP deflator: *see* implicit price deflator

Genuine Progress Indicator (GPI): a measure of economic well-being that adds many benefits, and subtracts many costs, that are not included in GDP. This measure is calculated by the nonprofit group Redefining Progress (6)

genuine saving: proposed by the World Bank, this is equal to gross saving less depreciation of both manufactured and natural capital (6)

Gini ratio: a measure of inequality, based on the Lorenz curve, that goes from 0 (perfect equality) up to 1 (complete inequality) (3)

global economy: the system of economic rules, norms and interactions by which economic actors and actions in different parts of the world are connected to one another (1)

government bond: an interest-bearing security constituting a promise to pay at a specified future time (10)

government outlays: total government expenditures including spending on goods and services and transfer payments (10)

government sector (BEA definition): the sector that includes all federal, state and local government entities (except for government enterprises) (5)

government spending (G) (traditional macro model): the component of GDP that represents spending by federal, state and local governments (and that is assumed to be consumption-oriented) (5)

gross domestic product (GDP) (BEA definition): a measure of the total value of final goods and services newly produced in a country over a period of time (usually one year) (5)

gross investment: all flows into the capital stock over a period of time (3)

high-powered money: currency plus bank reserves directly controlled by the Fed (11)

historical investigation: study of past events (2)

households and institutions sector (BEA definition): the sector consisting of households and nonprofit institutions serving households (5)

human capital: people's capacity for labor and their individual knowledge and skills (3)

human development (United Nations Development Program): the process of creating an environment that expands people's choices, allowing people to develop their full potential and lead productive, creative lives in accord with their needs and interests (15)

Human Development Index (HDI): an index of well-being made by combining measures of health, education, and income. This index is calculated by the United Nations Development Program. (6)

identity (accounting identity): an equation where the two sides are equal by definition (5)

implicit contract: an informal agreement about the terms of exchange, based on verbal discussions and on common norms, traditions, and expectations (2)

implicit price deflator: a price index derived by dividing nominal GDP by real GDP (5)

import substitution: the policy of encouraging domestic producers to make products that can be used in place of imported goods (13)

imputation: a procedure in which values are assigned for some category of products, usually using values of related products or inputs (5)

index number: a figure that measures the change in size of a magnitude, such as a quantity or price, as compared to its magnitude in some other period (5)

Industrial Revolution: a process of social and economic change, beginning in eighteenth-century England, that developed and applied new methods of production and work organization that resulted in a great increase in output per worker (14)

infant industry: an industry that is relatively new to its region or country (13)

inflation: a rise in the general level of prices (1)

informal sphere: made up of businesses operating outside of government oversight and regulation. In less industrialized countries it may constitute the majority of economic activity. (3)

in-kind transfers: transfers of goods or services (3)

inputs: resources that go into production (3)

insider-outsider theory: the theory that "insider" workers who are already employed may have the power to prevent "outsider" workers from competing with them and lowering their wages (7)

institutions: ways of structuring the interactions between individuals and groups, including both formally constituted establishments and the generally recognized patterns of organization embodied in customs, habits, and laws (2)

intermediate good: a good that will undergo further processing (5)

International Monetary Fund (IMF): an international agency charged with overseeing international finance, including exchange rates, international payments, and balance of payments issues (13)

inventories: stocks of raw materials or manufactured goods being held until they can be used or sold (5)

inverse (or negative) relationship: the relationship between two variables if an increase in one is associated with a decrease in the other (2)

investment (*I*) (traditional macro model): the component of GDP that represents spending on structures, equipment and inventories by business firms (5)

investment: actions taken to increase the quantity or quality of a resource now, in order to make benefits possible in the future (3)

Keynesian economics: the school of thought, named after John Maynard Keynes, that argued for the active use of fiscal policy to keep aggregate demand high and employment rates up (1)

labor income: payments to workers, including wages, salaries, and fringe benefits (3)

labor force: defined by the BLS as people who are either employed or unemployed (7)

labor productivity: the level of output that can be produced per worker (1)

labor-intensive production: production using methods that involve a high ratio of labor to capital (13)

laissez-faire economy: an economy with little government regulation (1)

liquidity trap: when interest rates are so low that the central bank finds it impossible to reduce them further (11, Appendix)

liquidity: the ease of use of an asset as a medium of exchange (11)

living standards growth: improvements in people's diet, housing, medical attention, education, working conditions and access to care, transportation, communication, entertainment and the like, that can allow people to have long and enjoyable lives and have the opportunity to accomplish the things that give their lives meaning (1)

Lorenz curve: a line used to portray an income distribution, drawn on a graph with percentiles of households on the horizontal axis and the cumulative percentage of income on the vertical axis (3)

M1: a measure of the money supply equal to currency, checkable deposits, and traveler's checks (11)

macroeconomics: the study of how economic activities at all levels create a national (and global) economic environment (1)

macroeconomy: an economic system whose boundaries are normally understood to be the boundaries of a nation (1)

maintenance cost approach: assigning a monetary value to an environmental service that is equal to what it would cost to maintain the same standard of services using an alternative method (6)

manufactured capital: physical assets generated by applying human productive activities to natural capital (3)

market (first meaning): a physical place where there is a reasonable expectation of finding both buyers and sellers for the same product or service (2)

market (second meaning): an institution that brings buyers and sellers into communication with each other, structuring and coordinating their actions (2)

"market, the" (third meaning): a phrase that people often use to mean an abstract situation of pure exchange or a global system of exchange relationships (2)

market disequilibrium: a situation of either shortage or surplus (4)

market failure: a situation in which markets yield inefficient or inappropriate outcomes (2)

market power: the ability to control, or at least affect, the terms and conditions of the exchanges in which one participates (2)

market-clearing equilibrium: a situation in which the quantity supplied is equal to the quantity demanded (4)

maturity date: the date the principal of a bond will be repaid (11, Appendix)

maximum capacity output: the level of output an economy would produce if every resource in the economy were fully utilized (12)

means-tested programs: programs designed to transfer income to those most in need (3)

menu costs: the costs to a supplier of changing prices listed on order forms, brochures, menus and the like (4)

microeconomics: the study of the economic activities and interactions of individuals, households, businesses, and other groups at the sub-national level (1)

migration controls: restrictions on the flows of people into and out of a country (13)

Millennium Development Goals (MDGs): a set of goals declared by the United Nations in 2000, emphasizing eradication of extreme poverty; promotion of education, gender equity, and heath; environmental sustainability; and partnership between rich and poor countries (15)

model: an analytical tool that highlights some aspects of reality while ignoring others (2)

monetarism: a theory associated with Milton Friedman, which claims that macroeconomic objectives are best met by having the money supply grow at a steady rate (11)

monetarist economics: the school that focused on the effects of monetary policy, and argued that governments should aim for steadiness in the money supply rather than play an active role (1)

monetary base: *see* high-powered money (11)

monetary neutrality: the idea that changes in the money supply may affect only prices, while leaving output unchanged (11)

monetary policy: the use of tools controlled by the government, such as banking regulations and the issuance of currency, to try to affect the levels of money supply, interest rates, and credit (1)

monetizing the deficit: when a central bank buys government debt as it is issued (equivalent to "running the printing presses") (11)

money multiplier: defined as the ratio of the money supply to the monetary base, it tells by how much the money supply will change for a given change in high-powered money (11)

money supply rule: committing to letting the money supply grow at a fixed percentage rate per year (11)

mortality rate: the average number of deaths among a specific group (such as mothers or children) (15, Appendix)

multilateral development assistance: aid or loans provided with the announced intention of promoting development by the World Bank, regional development banks, or United Nations agencies such as the United Nations Development Program (UNDP) (14)

national income (NI): a measure of all domestic incomes earned in production (5)

National Income and Product Accounts (NIPA): a set of statistics compiled by the BEA concerning production, income, spending, prices and employment (5)

natural capital: physical assets provided by nature (3)

"natural" rate of unemployment: the rate of unemployment that would prevail in the absence of business cycles, according to some theories (7)

negative (or inverse) relationship: the relationship between two variables if an increase in one is associated with a decrease in the other (2)

net domestic product (NDP): a measure of national production above that needed to replace worn-out manufactured capital, found by subtracting depreciation from GDP (5)

net exports (*NX*) (traditional macro model): the component of GDP that represents the value of exports less the value of imports (5)

net investment: gross investment minus an adjustment for depreciation of the capital stock (3)

net migration rate: the net gain in population from migration, per 1,000 population (15, Appendix)

new Keynesian macroeconomics: a school which bases its analysis on micro-level market behavior, but which justifies activist macroeconomic policies by assuming that markets have "imperfections" (12)

nominal (current dollar) GDP: gross domestic product expressed in terms of current prices (5)

non-accelerating inflation rate of unemployment (NAIRU): the lowest rate of unemployment that can be sustained without causing rapidly rising inflation (7)

nonrenewable resource: a resource that cannot be reproduced on a human time-scale, so that its stock diminishes with use over time (3)

normative questions: questions about how things should be (1)

"not in the labor force" (BLS definition): people who are neither "employed" nor "unemployed" (7)

Okun's "law": an empirical inverse relationship between the unemployment rate and rapid (above-average) real GDP growth (9)

old-age dependency ratio: the number of people age 65 and over for each hundred people aged 15–64 (15, Appendix)

open economy: an economy with a foreign sector (5)

open market operations: sales or purchases of government bonds by the Fed (11)

opportunity cost method (for estimating the value of household production): valuing hours at the amount the unpaid worker could have earned at a paid job (6)

opportunity cost: the value of the best alternative to a particular economic choice (2)

outputs: the results of production (3)

perfectly competitive market: a market in which there are many buyers and sellers, all units of the good are identical, and there is free entry and exit and perfect information (4)

physical infrastructure: the equipment, buildings, physical communication lines, roads and other tangible structures that provide the foundation for economic activity (2)

population momentum: the trend in population size that results from its age profile, in particular the number of women who are of childbearing age or younger. For example, a population can continue to grow, in spite of having a fertility rate at or below replacement, if a large proportion of its members are of childbearing age. (15, Appendix)

positive (or direct) relationship: the relationship between two variables when an increase in one is associated with an increase in the other (2)

positive questions: questions are about how things are (1)

post-Keynesian macroeconomics: a school that stresses the importance of history and uncertainty in determining macroeconomic outcomes (12)

precautionary principle: the principle that we should err on the cautious side when dealing with natural systems, especially when major health or environmental damage could result (1)

price elasticity of demand: a measure of the responsiveness of quantity demanded to changes in price (4)

price elasticity of supply: a measure of the responsiveness of quantity supplied to changes in price (4)

primary sector: the sector of the economy that involves the harvesting and extraction of natural resources and simple processing of these raw materials into products which are generally sold to manufacturers as inputs (8)

prime bank rate: the interest rate that banks charge their most trusted commercial borrowers (11)

private property: ownership of assets by nongovernment economic actors (2)

production-possibilities frontier (PPF): a curve showing the maximum amounts of two outputs that society could produce from given resources, over a given time period (2)

production: the conversion of resources to goods and services (3)

progressive income tax: a tax which collects a larger share of the income from those most able to pay (3)

proportional income tax: a tax which collects the same share of income from households, no matter what their income level (3)

protectionist policies: the use of trade policies such as tariffs, quotas, and subsidies to protect domestic industries from foreign competition (13)

public goods: goods for which (1) use by one person does not diminish usefulness to others, and (2) it would be difficult to exclude anyone from benefiting (2)

public-purpose sphere: governments and other local, national, and international organizations established for some public purpose beyond individual or family self-interest, and not operating with the goal of making a profit (3)

purchasing power parity (PPP) adjustments: adjustments to international income statistics to take account of differences in the cost of living across countries (13)

purchasing power parity (PPP): the theory that exchange rates should reflect differences in purchasing power among countries (13)

quantity adjustments: a response by suppliers in which they react to unexpectedly low sales of their good primarily by reducing production levels rather than by reducing the price, and to unexpectedly high sales by increasing production rather than raising the price (4)

quantity equation: $M \times V = P \times Y$, where M is the money supply, V is the velocity of money, P is the price level and Y is real output (11)

quantity index: an index measuring changes in levels of quantities produced (5)

quantity theory of money: the theory that money supply is directly related to nominal GDP, according to the equation $M \times \bar{V} = P \times Y$ (11)

race to the bottom: a situation in which countries or regions compete in providing low-cost business environments, resulting in deterioration in labor, environmental or safety standards (13)

rational expectations school: a group of macroeconomists who theorized that people's expectations about Fed policy would cause predictable monetary policies to be ineffective in changing output levels (12)

real business cycle theory: the theory that changes in employment levels are caused by change in technological capacities or people's preferences concerning work (12)

real exchange rate: the exchange rate between two currencies, adjusted for inflation in both countries (13)

real GDP: a measure of gross domestic product that seeks to reflect the actual value of production goods and services produced, by removing the effect of changes in prices (5)

real interest rate: nominal interest rate minus inflation, $r = i - \pi$ (11, Appendix)

recession: traditionally defined as occurring when GDP falls for two consecutive calendar quarters, now "officially" marked by the National Bureau of Economic Research (7)

regressive income tax: a tax which collects a larger share of income from poorer households (3)

regulation: setting standards or laws to govern behavior (3)

renewable resource: a resource that regenerates itself through short-term processes (3)

replacement cost method (for estimating the value of household production): valuing hours at the amount it would be necessary to pay someone to do the work (6)

replacement fertility rate: the fertility rate required in order for each generation to be replaced by a next generation of the same size. This requires an average fertility of 2.1 children per woman in industrialized countries. (15, Appendix)

required reserves: reserves that banks are required to hold by the Fed (11)

resource functions: the provision by the natural environment of inputs into human production processes (6)

resource maintenance: the management of capital stocks so that their productivity is sustained (3)

revaluation: raising an exchange rate within a fixed exchange rate system (13)

Ricardian model of trade: A two-good, two-country model, created by David Ricardo in 1817, that shows both countries gaining from specialization and trade (13)

rule of 72: a shorthand calculation which states that dividing an annual growth rate into the number 72 yields approximately the number of years it will take for an amount to double (5)

satellite accounts: additional or parallel accounting systems that provide measures of social and environmental factors in physical terms, without necessarily including monetary valuation (6)

saving: refraining from consuming in the current period (3)

Say's law: the classical belief that "supply creates its own demand" (1)

scarcity: resources are scarce to the extent that they are not sufficient to allow all goals to be accomplished at once (2)

secondary sector: the sector of the economy that involves converting the outputs of the primary sector into products suitable for use or consumption. It includes manufacturing, construction, and utilities. (8)

shortage: a situation in which the quantity that buyers wish to buy at the stated price is greater than the quantity that sellers are willing to sell at that price (4)

sink functions: the provision by the natural environment of places to put waste materials (6)

social capital: the stock of trust, mutual understanding, shared values, and socially held knowledge that facilitates the social coordination of economic activity (3)

social discount rate: a discount rate that reflects social rather than market valuation of future costs and benefits; usually lower than the market discount rate (15)

social insurance programs: programs designed to transfer income to recipients if and when certain events (such as retirement or disability) occur (3)

specialization: in production, a system of organization in which each worker performs only one type of task (1)

speculation: buying and selling assets with the expectation of profiting from appreciation or depreciation in asset values (4)

speculative bubble: the situation that occurs when mutually reinforcing investor optimism raises the value of an asset far above what could be realistically justified (4)

spot market: a market for immediate delivery (4)

stagflation: a combination of rising inflation and economic stagnation (12)

static analysis: analysis that does not take into account the passage of time (2)

"sticky wage" theories: theories about why wages may stay at above-equilibrium levels, despite the existence of a labor surplus (7)

stock: something whose quantity can be measured at a point in time (3)

stock-flow diagram: an illustration of how stocks can be changed, over time, by flows (3)

structural unemployment: unemployment that arises because people's skills, experience, education, and/or location do not match what employers need (7)

substitutability: the possibility of using one resource instead of another (3)

substitute good: a good that can be used in place of another (4)

supply curve: a curve indicating the quantities that sellers are willing to supply at various prices (4)

supply shock: a change in the productive capacity of an economy (12)

supply-side economics: an economic theory that emphasizes policies to stimulate production, such as lower taxes. The theory predicts that such incentives stimulate greater economic effort, saving, and investment, thereby increasing overall economic output and tax revenues (10)

surplus: a situation in which the quantity that sellers wish to sell at the stated price is greater than the quantity that buyers will buy at that price (4)

sustainable socioeconomic system: a system in which the overall quality and quantity of the resource base required for sustaining life and well-being do not erode (3)

tariffs: taxes put on imports or exports (13)

tax multiplier: the impact of a change in a lump sum tax on economic equilibrium, expressed mathematically as $\Delta Y / \Delta \bar{T} = -(mult)\,(mpc)$ (10)

technological progress: the development of new products and new, more efficient, methods of production (2)

terms of trade: the price of imports relative to exports (13)

tertiary sector: the sector of the economy that involves the provision of services rather than of tangible goods (8)

theoretical investigation: analysis based in abstract thought (2)

theory of market adjustment: the theory that market forces will tend to make shortages and surpluses disappear (4)

third person criterion: the convention that says that an activity should be considered to be production (rather than leisure) if a person could buy a market replacement or pay someone to do the activity in his or her place (6)

time lags: the time elapsing between the formulation of an economic policy and its actual effects on the economy (10)

time-series data: observations of how a numerical variable changes over time (2)

total factor productivity (Solow growth model): a measure of the productivity of all factors of production. It represents contributions to output from sources other than quantities of manufactured capital and labor (14)

trade ban: a law preventing the import or export of goods or services (13)

trade deficit: an excess of imports over exports, causing net exports to be negative (10)

trade quota: a restriction on the quantity of a good that can be imported or exported (13)

trade-related subsidies: payments given to producers to encourage more production, either for export or as a substitute for imports (13)

traditional macroeconomic model: a simple, mechanical model that portrays the macroeconomy as being made up of businesses that produce and invest, and households and governments that (only) consume (5)

transaction costs: the costs of arranging economic activities (2)

transactions demand model: a model of the money market in which money is assumed to be liquid and pay no interest, while an alternative asset is assumed to be illiquid and pay interest (11, Appendix)

transfer payments: payments by government to individuals or firms, including Social Security payments, unemployment compensation, and interest payments (10)

transfer: the giving of something with nothing specific expected in return (3)

underemployment: working fewer hours than desired, and/or at a job that does not utilize one's skills (7)

unemployed person (BLS definition): a person who is not employed, but who is actively seeking a job and who is immediately available for work (7)

unemployment: seeking a paying job, but not being able to get one (1)

unemployment rate: the percentage of the labor force made up of people who do not have paid jobs, but who are immediately available and actively looking for paid jobs (7)

United Nations System of National Accounts (SNA): a set of guidelines for countries about how to construct systems of national accounts (5)

value-added: the value of what a producer sells less the value of the intermediate inputs it uses. This is equal to the incomes paid out by the producer. (5)

velocity of money: the number of times a dollar would have to change hands during a year to support nominal GDP, calculated as $V = (P \times Y)/M$ (11)

virtuous cycles (in development): self-reinforcing patterns of high savings, investment, productivity growth, and economic expansion (14)

wage and price controls: government regulations setting limits on wages and prices, or on the rates at which they are permitted to increase (12)

wage-price spiral: when high demand for labor and other resources creates upward pressure on wages, which in turn leads to upward pressure on prices and, as a result, further upward pressure on wages (12)

waste products: outputs that are not used either for consumption or in a further production process (3)

well-being: a shorthand term for the broad goal of promoting the sustenance and flourishing of life (1)

World Bank: an international agency charged with promoting economic development, through loans and other programs (13)

World Trade Organization (WTO): An international organization that provides a forum for trade negotiations, creates rules to govern trade, and investigates and makes judgment on trade disputes (13)

Index

About the Authors

Neva R. Goodwin (PhD, Boston University) is co-director of the Global Development and Environment Institute (GDAE) at Tufts University. Julie A. Nelson (PhD, University of Wisconsin, Madison) is a senior research associate at GDAE. Jonathan Harris (PhD, Boston University) is director of the Theory and Education Program at GDAE. Contributor Brian Roach (PhD, UC Davis) is a research associate at GDAE. James Devine (PhD, UC Berkeley) is a professor of economics at Loyola Marymount University, Los Angeles.